Encyclopedia of World

MILITARY AIRCRAFT

Volume 1: A to K

Edited by David Donald and Jon Lake

WORLD
AIR POWER
JOURNAL

Aerospace Publishing London
AIRtime Publishing USA

Published by
Aerospace Publishing Ltd
179 Dalling Road
London W6 0ES
England

Published under licence in USA and
Canada by
AIRtime Publishing Inc.
10 Bay Street
Westport, CT 06880
USA

Aerospace **ISBN: 1 874023 51 4**
AIRtime **ISBN: 1-880588-14-5**

Distributed in the UK,
Commonwealth and Europe by
Airlife Publishing Ltd
101 Longden Road
Shrewsbury SY3 9EB
England
Telephone: 0743 235651
Fax: 0743 232944

Distributed to retail bookstores in the
USA and Canada by
AIRtime Publishing Inc.
10 Bay Street
Westport, CT 06880
USA
Telephone: (203) 226-3580
Fax: (203) 221-0779

US readers wishing to order by mail,
please contact
AIRtime Publishing Inc. toll-free at
1 800 359-3003

Publisher: Stan Morse

Editors: David Donald
Jon Lake

Associate Editors:
Robert Hewson
Sophearith Moeng
Tim Senior
Gordon Swanborough

Production Editor:
Karen Leverington

Authors: David Donald
Robert F. Dorr
John Fricker
Bill Green
Bill Gunston
Robert Hewson
Paul Jackson
Jon Lake
Sophearith Moeng
Lindsay Peacock
Gordon Swanborough
Mike Verier

Artists: Chris Davey
Grant Race
Mark Styling
John Weal

**Origination by
Imago Publishing Ltd**

Printed in Singapore

WORLD AIR POWER JOURNAL
**is published quarterly and
provides an in-depth analysis
of contemporary military
aircraft and their worldwide
operators. Superbly produced
and filled with extensive color
photography, World Air Power
Journal is available by
subscription from:**

**UK, Europe and
Commonwealth:
Aerospace Publishing Ltd
FREEPOST
PO Box 2822
London, W6 0BR
UK
Telephone: 081-740 9554
Fax: 081-746 2556
(no stamp required if posted in
the UK)**

**USA and Canada:
AIRtime Publishing Inc.
Subscription Dept
10 Bay Street
Westport, CT 06880
USA
Telephone: (203) 226-3580
Toll-free number in USA:
1 800 359-3003**

Encyclopedia of World

MILITARY AIRCRAFT

Volume 1

Introduction

The *Encyclopedia of World Military Aircraft* covers all the aircraft that are in current service with the military air arms around the world, presenting detailed technical, service and operator information on each individual type.

The encyclopedia arranges the aircraft types in alphabetical order according to the current, or most recent, manufacturer. It is published in two volumes with consecutive page numbers. Volume 1 covers the entries from A to K (Aeritalia to Korean Government), with Volume 2 covering L to Z (Lake to Zlin). A complete index is provided at the end of Volume 2.

Further information on all current military aircraft, and regular updates as situations change, is provided in the quarterly publication *World Air Power Journal*, available from the addresses opposite.

Aeritalia (FIAT/Alenia) G91R/T

*Alenia
Via E. Petrolini 2
I-00197 Roma, Italy*

NATO's need for a light fighter and tactical support aircraft led to the formulation of a specification in December 1953. Circulated to West European industry in early 1954, it brought a number of proposals, that from the Italian manufacturer Fiat finally being selected. This came after the prototypes (the first of them flown on 9 August 1956) had taken part in technical evaluation trials at Brétigny, France, in 1957. There the **Fiat G91** demonstrated it could satisfy NATO requirements and also have the ability to operate, with or without stores, from semi-prepared airstrips.

The initial production version was the single-seat G91 ground-attack fighter with fixed armament of four 0.5-in (12.7-mm) Colt-Browning machine-guns (two mounted on each side of the cockpit). Four underwing pylons were provided for 500-lb (227-kg) bombs, tactical nuclear weapons, Nord 5103 AAMs, rocket pods and machine-gun pods. Operational evaluation of the G91 began with 103ª Squadriglia of the **Aeronautica Militare Italiana** during February 1959. During the development of the G91 the role of high-speed tactical reconnaissance was not ignored, resulting in the **G91R/1**, first flown during 1959. This was essentially a standard G91 with a shortened nose section mounting three 70-mm focal length Vinten cameras (forward-looking and oblique) suitable for high-speed low-level photography by day; vertical coverage from high altitude is also possible. The G91R/1 was adopted by the AMI and two examples were evaluated by the USAF. Subsequent versions included the similar **G91R/1A**, differing by installation of improved navigation aids as in the G91R/3;

the **G91R/1B**, similar to the G91R/1A but with a reinforced structure, landing gear and equipment changes; the similar **G91R/3**, built to **Luftwaffe** specifications with two 30-mm cannon, Doppler radar and a position and homing indicator; and, finally, the **G91R/4**, basically a G91R/3 but with R/1 armament and some equipment changes. Two G91R/3s and one G91T/1 trainer were evaluated by the US Army in 1961 as tactical support aircraft for operation from unprepared airstrips.

European service

The G91R and its corresponding trainer variant, the G91T, has served with three European air arms. The Federal German Luftwaffe received a total of 344 G91R/3s (74 built by Fiat and 270 licence-built in Germany), all of which were phased out of service in the mid-1980s. In addition, 24 ex-Luftwaffe G91Ts were operated at Husum by civilian contractor Condor Flugdienst to provide target facilities for the West German air force. These were supplanted in 1992 by the Pilatus PC-9. The **Portuguese air force** was allocated G91R/4s under the US MAP scheme and has used the type in its African wars. Forty ex-GAF G91R/3s and at least 10 G91T trainers were also acquired and were given a secondary air-defence capability with AIM-9L missiles. All Portuguese G91s were phased out in late 1993, following replacement by A-7Ps and F-16A/Bs. The sole surviving G91R/T operator is the AMI, which continues to operate 50 G91T trainers for the final stage of pilot training before conversion to an operational type. All AMI G91Rs were retired in April 1992.

SPECIFICATION

Aeritalia (Fiat/Alenia) G91T
Wing: span 8.60 m (28 ft 3 in); aspect ratio 4.46; area 16.42 m² (176.74 sq ft)
Fuselage and tail: length 11.67 m (38 ft 3.5 in); height 4.45 m (14 ft 7.25 in); wheel track 2.82 m (9 ft 3 in); wheel base 3.51 m (11 ft 6.25 in)
Powerplant: one Fiat-built Rolls-Royce (Bristol Siddeley) Orpheus Mk 803 rated at 5,000 lb st (22.24 kN) dry
Weights: operating empty 3865 kg (8,521 lb); normal take-off 5500 kg (12,125 lb); maximum take-off 6050 kg (13,338 lb)
Fuel and load: internal fuel 2100 litres (555 US gal); external fuel up to two 520- or 260-litre (137- or 69-US gal) drop tanks; maximum ordnance 680 kg (1,500 lb)
Speed: maximum level speed 'clean' at 5,000 ft (1525 m) 556 kt (640 mph; 1030 km/h); cruising speed at optimum altitude 350 kt (403 mph; 650 km/h)
Range: ferry range 1,000 nm (1,152 miles; 1854 km) with drop tanks; typical combat radius 173 nm (199 miles; 320 km) on a

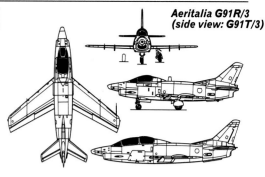

*Aeritalia G91R/3
(side view: G91T/3)*

hi-lo-hi attack mision
Performance: maximum rate of climb at sea level 6,000 ft (1830 m) per minute; climb to 13,125 ft (4000 m) in 4 minutes 30 seconds; service ceiling 40,000 ft (12190 m); take-off distance to 50 ft (15 m) 4,760 ft (1451 m) at maximum take-off weight; landing distance from 50 ft (15 m) 2,200 ft (671 m) at normal landing weight

A handful of G91Ts remain in service with the AMI. They are still used for advanced training purposes with 60ª Brigata at Amendola.

Aeritalia (FIAT/Alenia) G91Y

Whereas the original Fiat G91R was a single-engined fighter-bomber and tactical reconnaissance aircraft produced to a NATO specification, the **Aeritalia G91Y** (or 'Yankee' as it is unofficially known) was developed for the **Italian air force**. Compared with the G91R, which was retired in Italy during 1984, the 'Yankee' differs fundamentally in having two J85 afterburning turbojets side-by-side in a revised fuselage, these providing 60 per cent more thrust for only a small increase in weight. In order to increase combat radius, one engine can be shut down during the cruise phase of a mission. Fuel capacity of the fuselage and inner wing tanks is 3200 litres (704 Imp gal), but drop tanks may be carried on the four underwing pylons, giving a ferry range of 3500 km (2,175 miles). The G91Y retains the three-camera nose and two internal 30-mm DEFA cannon of later-model G91Rs, but is capable of carrying an increased warload. This includes provision for 1,000-lb (454-kg) bombs, 750-lb (340-kg) napalm tanks, four 7 x 2-in rocket packs, four 28 x 2-in rocket packs or four 5-in rocket containers. A more sophisticated avionics fit comprises position and homing indicator, twin axis gyro platform, Doppler radar ranger, air-data computer radar altimeter and electronic head-up display (HUD).

With the emphasis on STOL performance, the aircraft has provision for JATO rocket bottles which can halve the required take-off run, and an airfield arrester hook for use with SATS (Short Airfield for Tactical Support) installations. Operating from a semi-prepared surface, the aircraft will unstick in 914 m (3,000 ft) and land (unassisted) from 15 m (50 ft) in 600 m (1,970 ft). With the obvious exception of the engine compartment, the G91Y's airframe is based on the earlier G91T two-seat trainer, although accommodation is provided for a pilot only in an armoured, air-conditioned, pressurised cockpit fitted with a Martin-

Baker zero-zero ejection seat. The wing has 38° sweepback, full-span slats and electrically-actuated slotted flaps. Two airbrakes are hinged beneath the centre fuselage, and engine replacement entails removal of the rear fuselage, with the variable-incidence trimming tailplane. The first of two prototypes was flown on 27 December 1966. An order for 20 pre-series aircraft was followed by contracts for a further 53 production examples but, in the event, production ended at the 67th aircraft. A projected **G91YT** two-seat trainer was not developed, and the sole **G91YS** was demonstrated to the Swiss air arm without success.

Deliveries to the **AMI**'s 8° Stormo at Cervia began in May 1970 for a single over-sized squadron (101° Gruppo), while 32° Stormo (13° Gruppo) at Brindisi re-equipped from August 1973, assigning some of its aircraft an anti-shipping strike role and decorating them with sharksmouth markings. It was originally envisaged that the G91Y would be gradually replaced by the AMX from 1987. However, delays with the service introduction of the latter type have meant that the above units were still opera-

tional on the G91Y in early 1994. The G91Y will remain in service with the AMI until 1998, and from 1993 the fleet received the overall grey scheme worn by the AMX.

SPECIFICATION

Aeritalia (Fiat/Alenia) G91Y
Wing: span 9.01 m (29 ft 6.5 in); aspect ratio 4.475; area 18.13 m² (195.16 sq ft)
Fuselage and tail: length 11.67 m (38 ft 3.5 in); height 4.43 m (14 ft 6 in); tailplane span 4.00 m (13 ft 1.5 in); wheel track 2.04 m (9 ft 8 in); wheel base 3.56 m (11 ft 8 in)
Powerplant: two General Electric J85-GE-13A each rated at 2,720 lb st (12.10 kN) dry and 4,080 lb st (18.15 kN) with afterburning
Weights: empty equipped 3900 kg (8,598 lb); normal take-off 7800 kg (17,196 lb); maximum take-off 8700 kg (19,180 lb)
Fuel and load: internal fuel 3200 litres (845 US gal); external fuel up to two 520-litre (137-US gal) drop tanks; maximum ordnance 4,000 kg (1814 kg)
Speed: maximum level speed 'clean' at 30,000 ft (9145 m) 560 kt (645 mph; 1038 km/h) and at sea level 600 kt (691 mph; 1111 km/h); cruising speed at 35,000 ft (10670 m) 432 kt (497 mph; 800 km/h)
Range: ferry range 3500 km (1,889 nm; 2,175 miles) with drop tanks; typical combat radius 600 km (324 nm; 373 miles) on a lo-lo-lo attack mission with a

2,910-lb (1320-kg) warload
Performance: maximum rate of climb at sea level 17,000 ft (5180 m) per minute with afterburning or 7,000 ft (2135 m) per minute without afterburning; climb to 42,000 ft (12200 m) in 4 minutes 30 seconds with afterburning or 11 minutes 0 seconds without afterburning; service ceiling 41,000 ft (12500 m); take-off run 4,000 ft (1219 m) on a hard runway at 8700 kg (19,180 lb), or 3,000 ft (914 m) on a semi-prepared runway at 7000 kg (15,432 lb), or 1,500 ft (457 m) on a semi-prepared runway at maximum take-off weight with JATO boost; take-off distance to 50 ft (15 m) 6,000 ft (1829 m) on a hard runway at 8700 kg (19,180 lb), or 4,500 ft (1372 m) on a semi-prepared runway at 7000 kg (15,432 lb), or 2,500 ft (762 m) on a semi-prepared runway at maximum take-off weight with JATO boost; landing distance from 50 ft (15 m) 1,970 ft (600 m) at normal landing weight

The 'Yankee' was a considerable improvement over the original G91, on account of its twin engines. The type still serves the AMI in some numbers although it is slowly being replaced by the AMX. The aircraft is employed in the close support and reconnaissance roles, able to carry a variety of unguided air-to-ground weaponry and equipped with cameras in the nose.

Aermacchi (Lockheed) AL.60 Conestoga/Trojan

Aermacchi SpA
Via Sanvito Silvestro 80
CP 246, I-21100 Varese, Italy

All the design work on this aircraft was carried out in the United States by Lockheed, which first flew the prototype in 1959. Financial considerations persuaded the company to offer the type for licensed construction abroad. Lockheed-Azcarte in Mexico built 18 as the **LASA-60** in 1960, for the **Fuerza Aérea Mexicana**, but the chief licensee was Italy's Aermacchi. With room for six people in the cabin and good rough-field performance, the **AL.60** was also suitable for the casevac role. The original aircraft was improved to become the **AL.60C** by uprating the engine and adding a parachute door. It was this version, with its associated tail-wheel undercarriage, which was eventually sold, as the **AL.60C-5 Conestoga**, to the **Central African Republic** (these are probably the only

types left in service) and **Mauretania**. A second modified version, the **AL.60F-5 Trojan**, was sold to the **Rhodesian Air Force** but with the original tricycle undercarriage.

SPECIFICATION

Aermacchi (Lockheed) AL.60F-5 Conestoga
Wing: span 11.99 m (39 ft 4 in); aspect ratio 7.35; area 19.55 m² (210.44 sq ft)
Fuselage and tail: length 8.80 m (28 ft 10.5 in); height 3.30 m (10 ft 10 in); tailplane span 4.59 m (15 ft 0.5 in); wheel track 2.84 m (9 ft 4 in)
Powerplant: one Textron Lycoming IO-720-A1A rated at 400 hp (298 kW)

Weights: empty 2,394 lb (1086 kg); operating empty 2,731 lb (1239 kg); maximum take-off 4,500 lb (2041 kg)
Fuel and load: internal fuel 345 litres (91.1 US gal); external fuel none; maximum payload 1,440 lb (653 kg)
Speed: maximum level speed 'clean' at sea level 135 kt (156 mph; 251 km/h); maximum cruising speed at 10,000 ft (3050 m) 125 kt (144 mph; 232 km/h); economical cruising speed at 5,000 ft (1525 m) 94 kt (108 mph; 174 km/h)
Range: 560 nm (645 miles; 1037 km)
Performance: maximum rate of climb at sea level 1,085 ft (331 m) per minute; service ceiling 13,615 ft (4150 m); take-off run 645 ft (196 m) at maximum take-off weight; take-off distance to 50 ft (15 m) 1,100 ft (335 m) at maximum take-off weight; landing distance from 50 ft (15 m) 845 ft (258 m) at normal landing weight

A few AL.60C-5s were supplied to the Central African Republic for utility transport duties. These are still in service.

Aermacchi MB-326

Design of the **Aermacchi MB-326** two-seat basic trainer was started by Dr Ing. Ermanno Bazzocchi in 1954, and the first of two prototypes flew on 10 December 1957. This aircraft had a 7.78-kN (1,750-lb) thrust Bristol Siddeley (now Rolls-Royce) Viper 8 turbojet, but the second prototype, and 15 pre-production aircraft ordered for the Aeronautica Militare Italiana (AMI), used the 11.12-kN (2,500-lb) thrust Viper 11 engine as standard. The AMI received the first of 85 of these jet trainers (designated MB-326 in its initial form) in February 1962, in addition to the 15 pre-production aircraft. Intended for all stages of flying training, the basic airframe is simple, robust and has tandem two-seat accommodation in a pressurised cabin equipped with lightweight ejection seats.

The MB-326 has been built in many variants and clearly had potential for use in a light attack role. Such capability was offered by Aermacchi on the **MB-326A** with six underwing hardpoints for a variety of external stores, but the AMI at that time had no requirement for such an aircraft. However, orders for similar aircraft were received from **Ghana** (nine **MB-326F**) and Tunisia (eight **MB-326B**), and four unarmed **MB-326D** trainers were built as pilot trainers for Alitalia. The **MB-326H** with full armament provisions was assembled or licence-built in Australia by Commonwealth Aircraft Corporation as the **Commonwealth CA-30** for the Royal Australian Air Force (87) and Navy (10). Last of the early versions were 135 of a total of 151 aircraft known as the **Impala Mk 1 (MB-326M)** assembled or licence-built in the Transvaal by Atlas Aircraft Corporation for the South African air force. Sixteen complete aircraft (MB-326M) were delivered by Macchi from June 1966,

and 40 of the first Atlas-assembled aircraft contained Italian components. All Impala Mk 1s were powered by the uprated Viper Mk 540 engine of the MB-326G.

The more powerful Viper 20 engine was introduced in early 1967; combined with a strengthened airframe in the **MB-326G** prototype, the improved type had double the weapon load of earlier versions. It was built as the **MB-326GB** for the Argentine navy (eight) and the air forces of Zaïre (17) and Zambia (22); EMBRAER in Brazil licence-built 182 similar **MB-326GC** aircraft for the air forces of Brazil (167 **AT-26 Xavante**), Paraguay (nine) and Togo (six). Eleven ex-Brazilian EMB-326GBs were delivered to the Argentine navy air command in 1983. Aermacchi provided for the AMI six **MB-326E** aircraft with basically the MB-326GB airframe but the Viper 11 engine, and converted six earlier MB-326s to the same configuration. The final two-seat version was the **MB-326L** advanced trainer, based upon the single-seat MB-326K; two were supplied to Dubai and four to the Tunisian air force.

The delivery of the final EMB-326 in February 1983 completed MB-326 production, at the 761st aircraft.

SPECIFICATION

Aermacchi MB-326GB
Wing: span 10.854 m (35 ft 7.25 in) over tip tanks
Powerplant: one Rolls-Royce (Bristol Siddeley) Viper 20 Mk 540 rated at 15.17 kN (3,410 lb st)
Weights: basic operating 5,640 kg (2558 kg); normal take-off 9,805 lb (4447 kg); maximum take-off 11,500 lb (5216 kg)
Fuel and load: internal fuel 1392 litres (368 US gal); external fuel up to two 332-litre (88-US gal) drop tanks

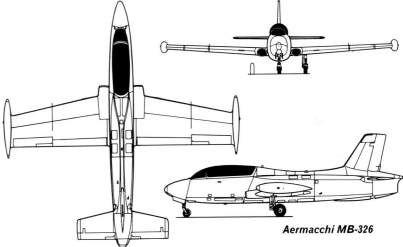

Aermacchi MB-326

Speed: maximum level speed 'clean' at optimum altitude 468 kt (539 mph; 867 km/h); cruising speed at optimum altitude 430 kt (495 mph; 797 km/h)
Range: ferry range 1,320 nm (1,520 miles; 2446 km) with drop tanks; combat radius 350 nm (403 miles; 648 km) on a hi-lo-hi attack mission with a 1,695-lb (769-kg) warload, or 70 nm (81 miles; 130 km) on a hi-lo-hi attack mission with a 4,000-lb (1814-kg) warload, or 50 nm (57 miles; 92 km) on a hi-lo-hi attack mission with 11-minute loiter with 1,700-lb (771-lb) warload
Performance: maximum rate of climb at sea level 3,550 ft (1082 m) per minute at 10,500 lb (4763 kg) or 3,100 ft (945 m) per minute at maximum take-off weight; climb to 10,000 ft (3050 m) in 3 minutes 10 seconds at 10,500 lb (4763 kg) or in 4 minutes at maximum take-off weight; service ceiling 39,000 ft (11890 m) at 10,500 lb (4763 kg); take-off run 2,100 ft (640 m) at 10,500 lb (4763 kg) or 2,770 ft (844 m) at

maximum take-off weight; take-off distance to 50 ft (15 m) 2,840 ft (866 m) at 10,500 lb (4763 kg) and 4,630 ft (1411 m) at maximum take-off weight; landing distance from 50 ft (15 m) 2,810 ft (856 m) at 9,250 lb (4195 kg)

OPERATORS

Two-seat trainer versions remain in service with the following air arms in 1994:
Argentine navy air command (16), Royal Australian Air Force (66), Brazil (50 – described separately under EMBRAER EMB-326 Xavante), Dubai (five), Ghana (five), Italy (44 MB-326, three MB-326D and six MB-326E), Paraguay (seven), South Africa (115 – described separately under Atlas Impala), Togo (four), Tunisia (12), Zaïre (nine) and Zambia (10).

Below: The MB-326 had some success on the export market, where Tunisia was one of the early customers, buying eight MB-326Bs for advanced training. Here five of them fly a training sortie over the desert.

Right: Having been replaced on advanced training units, Australia's remaining MB-326Hs are used for fighter support, including attack lead-in training. This aircraft is assigned to No. 76 Sqn.

Aermacchi MB-326K

Early use of the two-seat MB-326 had shown that the aircraft was an excellent and stable weapons platform, as evinced by the light attack variants. It seems surprising, therefore, that it was not until 22 August 1970 that the manufacturer flew the first **Aermacchi MB-326K** prototype, a single-seater for ground attack or close air support powered by the Viper 20 Mk 540 of the late-production MB-326 family.

From the outset, it had been intended to provide even more power for production aircraft, and the second prototype introduced the 17.79-kN (4,000-lb) thrust Viper 632-43 engine. This made it possible to add more potent armament, in the form of two electrically operated 30-mm DEFA cannon installed in the lower forward fuselage, with 125 rounds per gun. The increased fuselage volume gained by elimination of the second seat provided space for the ammunition drums for the cannon, additional fuel tankage, and the avionics formerly located in the nose. In most other respects the airframe was similar to that of the MB-326GB, but some additional localised structural reinforcement was introduced to cater for the increased stress of low-level manoeuvres, and for this latter reason hydraulically servo-powered ailerons were also provided. Six underwing pylons were provided for carriage of up to 4,000 lb (1814 kg) of external stores, comprising bombs, napalm containers, AS11 or AS12 ASMs, machine-gun and Minigun pods, MATRA 550 AAMs and launchers for 37-mm, 68-mm, 100-mm, 2.75-in or 5-in rockets. In addition, a four-camera tactical reconnaissance pod could be carried on the port inner station without affecting the weapons capability of the other five wing pylons.

Export orders

Although the test and development programme proceeded without major problems, there was a gap of almost two years before the first order was finalised for three MB-326Ks to provide Dubai with a counter-insurgency flight. Later deliveries included three more for Dubai, with others for the air forces of Ghana (six), Tunisia (eight) and Zaïre (six). In 1974 Aermacchi delivered to South Africa seven MB-326Ks in component form, followed by 15 more sets in the following year for assembly by Atlas Aircraft Corporation. Since that time Atlas has continued to build the type under licence as the **Impala Mk 2** (described separately), which retains the Viper 20 Mk 540 powerplant. The MB-326K currently serves with **Dubai** (three), **Ghana** (four), **Tunisia** (seven) and **Zaïre** (six).

SPECIFICATION

Aermacchi MB-326K

Wing: span 10.15 m (33 ft 3.6 in) without tip tanks and 10.85 m (35 ft 7 in) with tip tanks; aspect ratio 6.08; area 19.35 m² (208.29 sq ft)
Fuselage and tail: length 10.673 m (35 ft 0.25 in); height 3.72 m (12 ft 2 in); tailplane span 4.164 m (13 ft 8 in); wheel track 2.485 m (8 ft 2 in); wheel base 4.157 m (13 ft 7.5 in)
Powerplant: one Rolls-Royce (Bristol Siddeley) Viper Mk 632-43 rated at 18.79 kN (4,000 lb st) dry thrust
Weights: empty equipped 2964 kg (6,534 lb); normal take-off 4211 kg (9,285 lb); maximum take-off 5897 kg (13,000 lb)
Fuel and load: internal fuel 1660 litres (438.5 US gal); external fuel up to two 340-litre (90-US gal) drop tanks; maximum ordnance 4,000 lb (1814 kg)
Speed: maximum level speed 'clean' at 5,000 ft (1525 m) 480 kt (553 mph; 890 km/h) and at 30,000 ft (9145 m) with underwing weapons 370 kt (426 mph; 686 km/h)
Range: ferry range more than 2130 km (1,149 nm; 1,323 miles) with drop tanks; combat radius 145 nm (167 miles; 268 km) on a lo-lo-lo attack mission with a 2,822-lb (1280-kg) warload, or 70 nm (81 miles; 130 km) on a lo-lo-lo attack mission with a 4,000-lb (1814-kg) warload, or 400 nm (461 miles; 742 km) on a hi-lo-hi visual reconnaissance mission with two drop tanks, or 560 nm (645 miles; 1038 km) on a hi-lo-hi photo-reconnaissance mission with one camera pod and two drop tanks

Performance: maximum rate of climb at sea level 6,500 ft (1981 m) per minute; climb to 36,000 ft (10975 m) in 9 minutes 30 seconds; service ceiling 47,000 ft (14325 m); take-off run 2,200 ft (671 m) at 12,000 lb (5443 kg); take-off distance to 50 ft (15 m) 3,000 ft (914 m) at 12,000 lb (5443 kg)
g limits: -3.5 to +7.33

The attack version of Aermacchi's jet trainer did not prove as successful in export terms. Dubai led the way with an order for three MB-326Ks, a figure later doubled. Three of these are still in service, serving on counter-insurgency duties. For these they carry two 30-mm cannon and a variety of stores underwing.

Aermacchi MB-339

From experience gained by nearly 800 of its highly-successful MB-326 jet trainers in 12 air forces, including licensed production in Australia, Brazil and South Africa, Aermacchi developed a successor version with 13-in (33-cm) stepped rocket-boosted SICAMB/Martin-Baker Mk 1T-10F zero-zero ejection seats to improve the instructor's rear cockpit view, plus pressurisation in a new and deeper forward fuselage. After reviewing available powerplants, including new small turbofans and even twin-engine installations, Aermacchi decided to stay with the time-honoured Rolls-Royce Viper turbojet, despite its higher fuel consumption, because of its low first cost, good 'hot-and-high' performance and proven reliability. The uprated Viper 632-43 – developed and produced jointly by Rolls-Royce and Fiat Avi-

Serving as Italy's advanced trainer, the MB-339A offers good performance at low cost. The AMI fleet is being resprayed in light grey, with high-conspicuity panels.

azione – was selected for the **MB-339**, with 4,000 lb (17.8 kN) of take-off thrust and a better specific fuel consumption.

In April 1983, following earlier installation in the second prototype, flight trials also started in an MB-339 (MM54502/I-GROW) of the still more potent Viper 680-43, developing 450 lb (2 kN) more thrust from minor compressor modifications. This was intended for the projected **MB-339B** and single-seat **MB-339K** light ground-attack fighter.

With the same basic airframe aft of the rear cockpit as the MB-326, the MB-339 has a 25 per cent bigger fin, plus twin rear ventral strakes to balance the deeper forward fuselage, and a new wing leading-edge profile. Its also has hydraulic servo-operated ailerons for flight operations up to about Mach 0.86. For weapons training or light ground-attack roles, for which six Argentine navy **MB-339AA**s were used operationally in 1982 against British forces in the Falklands, up to 4,000 lb (1814 kg) of external stores may be carried on six underwing pylons, including two 30-mm (1.18-in) DEFA cannon. The MB-339 has also been cleared to operate with the AIM-9L/P Sidewinder AAMs.

Italian service

Two MB-339 prototypes preceded AMI orders for 100 production aircraft, the first (MM588/I-NOVE) initially flying on 12 August 1976 from the Venegono factory airfield. The MB-339 entered AMI service at the SVBIA flying school at Lecce in August 1989. Nineteen from the overall AMI purchase of 100, with tip-tanks removed and known as **MB-339PAN**s, also equipped from 1982 the 313° Gruppo Pattuglia Aerobatica Nazionale, better known as the 'Frecce Tricolori', the renowned Italian national aerobatic team. Between February 1981 and the late 1980s, eight specially-equipped **MB-339RM**s operated with the 8th Sqn of the 14th Radio Aids and Elec-

Malaysia purchased 12 MB-339As to replace its elderly Canadair CL-41s operating in the advanced training role with No. 3 Flying Training Centre at Kuantan. The MB-339s also undertake weapons training for the RMAF.

tronic Warfare Wing at Pratica di Mare.

In conjunction with Lockheed, Hughes and Rolls-Royce, Aermacchi is offering a version of the prototype Viper 680-powered MB-339B for the US JPATS joint basic trainer competition. This type, known as the **T-Bird II** (described separately), incorporates bigger wing-tip tanks and is fitted with an RB.582-01 Viper turbojet derated by some 1.8 kN (404 lb) to around 17.8 kN (4,000 lb) for reduced life-cycle costs. I-RAIB, a new prototype to this standard, made its initial flight on 8 April 1992 following abandonment of earlier JPATS plans for a twin P&WC JT15D-powered **MB-339D**.

SPECIFICATION

Aermacchi MB-339A
Wing: span 10.858 m (35 ft 7.5 in) over tip tanks; aspect ratio 6.1; area 19.30 m² (207.74 sq ft)
Fuselage and tail: length 10.972 m (36 ft 0 in); height 3.994 m (13 ft 1.25 in); elevator span 4.08 m (13 ft 4.75 in); wheel track 2.483 m (8 ft 1.75 in); wheel base 4.369 m (14 ft 4 in)
Powerplant: one Piaggio-built Rolls-Royce (Bristol Siddeley) Viper Mk 632-43 rated at 17.79 kN (4,000 lb st) dry
Weights: empty equipped 3125 kg (6,889 lb); operating empty 3136 kg (6,913 lb); normal take-off 4400 kg (9,700 lb); maximum take-off 5895 kg (12,996 lb)
Fuel and load: internal fuel 1100 kg (2,425 lb);

external fuel up to two 325-litre (86-US gal) drop tanks; maximum ordnance 2040 kg (4,497 lb)
Speed: never exceed speed 500 kt (575 mph; 926 km/h); maximum level speed 'clean' at 30,000 ft (9145 m) 441 kt (508 mph; 817 km/h) and at sea level 485 kt (558 mph; 898 km/h)
Range: ferry range 1,140 nm (1,311 miles; 2110 km) with drop tanks; range 950 nm (1,094 miles; 1760 km); combat radius 320 nm (368 miles; 593 km) on a hi-lo-hi attack mission with four Mk 82 bombs and two drop tanks, or 212 nm (244 miles; 393 km) on a hi-lo-hi attack mission with six Mk 82 bombs, or 275 nm (317 miles; 510 km) on a hi-lo-hi attack mission with two 30-mm cannon pods, two rocket launchers and two drop tanks, or 305 nm (351 miles; 565 km) on a hi-lo-hi attack mission with four rocket launchers and two drop tanks, or 165 nm (190 miles; 306 km) on a hi-lo-hi attack mission with six rocket launchers, or 200 nm (230 miles; 371 km) on a lo-lo-lo attack mission with four Mk 82 bombs and two drop tanks, or 146 nm (168 miles; 271 km) on a lo-lo-lo attack mission with six Mk 82 bombs, or 190 nm (219 miles; 352 km) on a lo-lo-lo attack mission with two 30-mm cannon pods, two rocket launchers and two drop tanks, or 193 nm (222 miles; 358 km) on a lo-lo-lo attack mission with four rocket launchers and two drop tanks, or 123 nm (142 miles; 228 km) on a lo-lo-lo attack mission with six rocket launchers; endurance 3 hours 45 minutes with drop tanks or 2 hours 50 minutes on internal fuel
Performance: maximum rate of climb at sea level 6,595 ft (2010 m) per minute; climb to 30,000 ft (9145 m) in 7 minutes 6 seconds; service ceiling 48,000 ft (14630 m); take-off run 1,525 ft (465 m) at

normal take-off weight or 3,000 ft (914 m) at maximum take-off weight; landing run 415 m (1,362 ft) at normal landing weight
g limits: -4 to +8

The MB-339 has sold well in many corners of the world. Nigeria bought a dozen to satisfy its advanced and weapons training requirements.

OPERATORS

Total MB-339A production stood at 161 in late 1993.

One hundred and one **AMI** MB-339As (including 19 PANs) were delivered between 1979-87 and operate mainly with the 212°/213° Gruppi of the 61ª Brigata Aerea at Lecce Galatina for all AMI basic training. Export customers have included the **Argentine navy** (10), **Dubai** air wing (seven), and the air forces of **Ghana** (two), **Malaysia** (13), **Nigeria** (12), and **Peru** (16).

Aermacchi MB-339A (side view: MB-339K)

Aermacchi **MB-339C**

Development of a relatively low-cost lead-in fighter trainer version of the MB-339 with advanced nav/attack systems and provision for ground and naval strike roles started in the mid-1980s, in collaboration with such companies as GEC Avionics in the UK and Kaiser Electronics in the US. Studies were initiated at the request of the AMI, which was interested in the possibility of supplementing its Tornado fleet with simpler aircraft to maintain combat proficiency for lower costs, for which Aermacchi proposed an MB-339 upgrade originally designated the **MB-340**.

For optimum cost effectiveness, equipment such as a Litton LR80 twin-gyro inertial platform, GEC Avionics 620K tactical area navigation system and a commercial ARINC 429 databus were selected in preference to more complex hardware, other items including a GEC AD-660 Doppler velocity sensor, Kaiser Sabre HUD/WAC, a stores management system by Logic of Italy, a FIAR/Ericsson P.0702 laser rangefinder, Aeritalia TV Maverick-compatible multi-function CRT display, Elettronica ELT-156 RWR and Honeywell radar altimeter.

The **MB-339C** was equipped to operate with such stand-off weapons as Maverick, Marte 2, AS34 Kormoran and laser-guided bombs. Powered by a Rolls-Royce Viper Mk 680-43 as used in the MB-339B prototype, developing some 14 per cent more thrust than the Viper 632-43 in the MB-339A, and with revised nose contours and bigger tip-tanks, the MB-339C prototype made its initial flight on 17 December 1985.

The AMI was originally reported in early 1989 to be the launch customer for the MB-339C with a requirement for 20 for operational and continuation training, the first production aircraft having made its initial flight on 8 November 1988. However, the sole customer to date for the MB-339C has been the **Royal New Zealand Air Force** from a NZ$266 million (US$157 million) order for 18 in May 1990, to replace the BAC Strikemasters of No. 14 Sqn at Ohakea. Despite defence economies in New Zealand, which at one time threatened the contract with cancellation before Aermacchi agreed to accept seven of the

RNZAF Strikemasters in part exchange, deliveries started with the airlifting of the first three aircraft to Christchurch on 9 March 1991, followed by the remainder in 1992-93, including some which flew in.

Following a 1986 Italian government contract to integrate the OTO Melara Marte 2A anti-ship missile with the MB-339 to give the AMI trainer fleet a secondary wartime role attacking fast patrol boats, detected by Atlantic ASW/MR aircraft transmitting target co-ordinates and launch data, Aermacchi started trials with this weapon on a prototype **MB-339AM** (MM54554) on 24 April 1991. These were largely concluded by late 1992, after successful launches of the Marte Mk 224 AShM from the MB-339AM at the Salto di Quirra NATO firing range in Sardinia, qualifying the MB-339C for an additional operational capability.

SPECIFICATION

Aermacchi MB-339C
generally similar to the Aermacchi MB-339A except in the following particulars:
Wing: span 11.22 m (36 ft 9.75 in) over tip tanks
Fuselage and tail: length 11.24 m (36 ft 10.5 in)
Powerplant: one Piaggio-built Rolls-Royce (Bristol Siddeley) Viper Mk 680-43 rated at 4,400 lb st (19.57 kN) dry thrust
Weights: empty equipped 3310 kg (7,297 lb); normal take-off 4635 kg (10,218 lb); maximum take-off 6350 kg (13,999 lb)
Fuel and load: internal fuel 1388 kg (3,060 lb)
Speed: maximum level speed 'clean' at sea level 487 kt (560 mph; 902 km/h)
Range: ferry range 1,187 nm (1,367 miles; 2200 km) with drop tanks; standard range 1,060 nm (1,221 miles; 1965 km);

combat radius 170 nm (196 miles; 315 km) on a lo-lo-lo attack mission with four Mk 82 bombs, or 270 nm (311 miles; 500 km) on a hi-lo-hi attack mission with four Mk 82 bombs
Performance: maximum rate of climb at sea level 7,300 ft (2225 m) per minute; climb to 30,000 ft (9145 m) in 6 minutes 42 seconds

Aermacchi MB-339C

WEAPON OPTIONS

Six underwing hardpoints can carry up to 1814 kg (4,000 lb) of stores. Four inboard pylons stressed for up to 454 kg (1,000 lb) each; two outboard pylons for 340 kg (750 lb) each. Stores can include various free-fall bombs and rocket pods, cluster bombs, flares or missile armament. RNZAF aircraft equipped for AGM-65 Maverick air-to-ground missiles and AIM-9 Sidewinder IR-homing air-to-air missiles. MATRA Magic optional for air-to-air role.

Two Macchi gun pods are offered, one housing a 30-mm DEFA 553 cannon with 120 rounds, the other accommodating a 12.7-mm AN/M-3 machine-gun with 350 rounds.
Reconnaissance pod with four 70-mm Vinten cameras optional.

New Zealand's 'Macchis' have replaced Strikemasters in the advanced and weapons training role. They could also be used in an emergency wartime offensive role.

Aermacchi MB-339K

The successful reception of the MB-339A trainer encouraged Aermacchi to adopt for this version a treatment similar to that for the two-seat MB-326/single-seat MB-326K. The company developed a single-seat **Aermacchi MB-339K** which it named **Veltro 2**, perpetuating the name given to Macchi's M.C.205V Veltro (greyhound), regarded as the best Italian fighter/fighter-bomber of World War II. However, this name was dropped in 1989.

The development process was characterised by the adoption of a new forward fuselage with single-seat accommodation. The increased fuselage volume provided room for avionics stowage, increased fuel and the installation of internally-mounted DEFA cannon. In other respects the MB-339K differs little from its two-seat counterpart, but for customers who might require more sophistication a wide range of optional avionics is available, including an ECM jammer pod, plus head-up and/or TV

display. The prototype (I-BITE), built as a private venture, had the standard licence-built Viper Mk 632-43 turbojet as its powerplant. This aircraft was flown for the first time on 30 May 1980 and subsequently displayed at the SBAC Farnborough air show in September of that year. No orders have been announced to date, and this may be because potential customers feel there is insufficient capability/performance improvement with respect to the MB-339A and MB-339C.

Aermacchi has subsequently developed an upgraded version incorporating changes to the powerplant, avionics system and equipment. In addition to its more powerful (19.79-kN/4,450-lb thrust) Viper 680-43 turbojet, the introduction of a nav/attack system (incorporating inertial navigation, a stores management system, a weapon-aiming computer and HUD) could make this aircraft more attractive for both training and combat use.

The MB-339K programme has resulted only in this prototype. The single-seat attack version has two internal 30-mm cannon.

Aermacchi/Lockheed MB-339 T-Bird II

Aermacchi was one of the first of the world's jet trainer manufacturers to answer the USAF and USN Statement of Operational Need for the Joint Primary Aircraft Training System (JPATS). In 1989 the company signed a co-operation agreement with Lockheed and Hughes to produce a version of the MB-339 modified to comply with the American service requirements. This includes an improved cockpit, new avionics and a strengthened canopy, together with some engine changes. Rolls-Royce, which joined the team in 1990, has offered the 17.79-kN (4,000-lb st) RB582 engine instead of the MB-339C's Viper 680

powerplant. In addition, the airframe will undergo some structural changes to enable it to meet the required service life of 14,400 hours with limits of +6*g*/-3*g*. The first production orders for more than 700 aircraft are expected in 1994 and, should the MB-339 emerge as the winner, the prime American airframe contractor will be Lockheed, which would also hold the manufacturing licence. Hughes would be responsible for the simulators and the overall training system.

Lockheed is Aermacchi's partner for the JPATS competition, offering a USAF-optimised MB-339.

Aero L-29 Delfin

Aero Vodochody Akciová CR-250 70 Odolena Vodo Czech Republic

Designed by a team under the leadership of Z. Rublic and K. Tomas to supersede the piston-engine trainers then in service with the Czech air force, the **Aero XL-29** prototype was flown for the first time on 5 April 1959. Following the flight of a second prototype in mid-1960, a small pre-production batch built for service evaluation was flown in competition with the P.Z.L. Mielec TS-11 Iskra and Yakovlev Yak-30 during 1961. The XL-29's excellent all-round performance resulted in the type being selected as the standard trainer for all Warsaw Pact air forces, with the exception of Poland, which opted to retain the nationally-designed and built TS-11. A mid-wing monoplane with retractable tricycle landing gear, the XL-29 prototype had flown initially under the power of a Bristol Siddeley Viper turbojet, but the second adopted the Czech-

designed Motorlet M 701 turbojet, and this latter powerplant was selected for production aircraft.

A straightforward design, simple to fly and easy to operate, the **L-29 Delfin** (dolphin) has docile handling characteristics and can be operated from grass, sand or waterlogged strips. Pupil and instructor are seated in tandem on synchronised ejection seats, and there is underwing provision for the carriage of light armament for training purposes. The first L-29s began to enter service in 1963, and when production ended in 1974 some 3,600 had been built. On the face of it, this large-scale manufacture may seem surprising, but this trainer was procured also for the Soviet air force (its L-29s gaining the NATO reporting name **'Maya'**), which accounted for over 2,000 of the production total. In addition to procurement for Bulgaria, Czechoslovakia, East Germany, Hungary, Romania and the USSR, L-29s were exported to several countries, including Afghanistan, Egypt, Guinea, Indonesia, Iraq, Nigeria, Syria and Uganda.

L-29s probably remain active in **Bulgaria, Czechoslovakia, Egypt, Iraq, Mali, Nigeria, Romania** and **Syria**. The L-29 has recently become available as a 'warbird' and has been sold in small numbers to private owners in the USA.

There have been just two variants of the type, the first being the single-seat **L-29A Delfin Akrobat**, built in only small numbers for aerobatic use, and a dedicated attack version designated **L-29R** which appeared only in prototype form.

Resplendent after overhaul at the Aero factory is an Egyptian air force L-29. The type serves in small numbers on basic training duties.

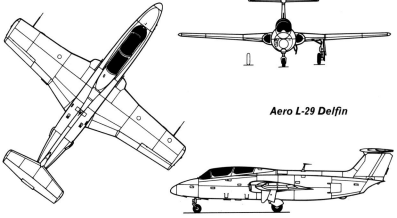

Aero L-29 Delfin

Aero L-39 Albatros

The evolution of a successor to the extensively built L-29 Delfin began about three years after that aircraft entered production. Designed by a team under the leadership of Dipl Ing. Jan Vlcek, the new type's development proceeded under close co-operation with the USSR which, subject to adequate performance, expected to adopt it to supersede the L-29 as its standard jet trainer. A key to much enhanced performance was adoption of the Ivchenko AI-25 turbofan engine, of practically double the power output of the Motorlet turbojet in the L-29; the achievement of full compatibility of this engine with an airframe of similar overall dimensions to the L-29 brought delays in design finalisation. The second of the first three prototypes (the first and third being used for structural test) was flown initially on 4 November 1968, and was joined later in the development programme by four other flying prototypes. It was not until late 1972 that a production go-ahead confirmed the **Aero L-39 Albatros** as a successor to the L-29 in the air forces of the USSR, Czechoslovakia and East Germany. Full service trials were conducted during 1973 and the L-39 began to enter service, initially with the Ceskoslovenské Letectvo, in early 1974.

A cantilever low-wing monoplane with retractable tricycle landing gear, the L-39 offers a significant improvement in performance over its predecessor (Mach 0.83 maximum speed, compared with the L-29's Mach 0.75). Tandem seating (on zero-height ejection seats in the L-39C) is retained, but naturally with the rear (instructor's) seat elevated to improve his view forward. Simultaneously, this enables the lower-placed front cockpit to slope downward towards a finely-pointed nose that reduces drag and contributes to enhanced performance.

Structure

Construction is modular, the airframe being broken down into only three major sub-assemblies (wing, fuselage and rear fuselage/tail unit) to facilitate major maintenance and overhaul. The entire wing, except for the moving surfaces, is in one piece, including the permanent tip tanks, and the swept fin is integral with the rear fuselage; the latter is removable to provide easy access to the engine for servicing. Including detachable items such as nosecone, control surfaces, landing gear and canopies, the entire L-39 airframe consists of little more than a couple of dozen basic components. This enables any unit to be replaced quickly and easily; plenty of access panels are provided for reaching individual systems or installations.

A first-class all-round view is available from both pressurised cockpits, and dual controls are, of course, standard. The rear seat is removed in the L-39ZO, presumably providing space, if required, for avionics or an additional fuel tank. A small auxiliary power unit (APU), in the form of a compressed-air turbine and generator, makes the aircraft independent of ground power sources for engine starting, fuel flow or other services.

More than 2,800 L-39s have been produced, including the **L-39C** basic and advanced trainer, **L-39V** target tug, **L-39ZO** weapons trainer with reinforced wings and four underwing weapon stations, and the **L-39ZA** for ground attack and reconnaissance, adding reinforced landing gear and an underfuselage gun pod to the L-39ZO. The **L-39ZE** is a version for Thailand with Elbit avionics.

SPECIFICATION

Aero L-39ZO Albatros
Wing: span 9.46 m (31 ft 0.5 in); aspect ratio 4.4 geometric or 5.2 including tip tanks; area 18.80 m² (202.37 sq ft)
Fuselage and tail: length 12.13 m (39 ft 9.5 in); height 4.77 m (15 ft 7.75 in); tailplane span 4.40 m (14 ft 5 in); wheel track 2.44 m (8 ft 0 in); wheel base 4.39 m (14 ft 4.75 in)
Powerplant: one ZMDB Progress (Ivchyenko) AI-25TL rated at 16.87 kN (3,792 lb st) dry
Weights: empty equipped 3540 kg; normal take-off 4525 kg (9,976 lb); maximum take-off 4700 kg (10,362 lb)
Fuel and load: internal fuel 824 kg (1,816 lb) plus provision for 156 kg (344 lb) in two 180-litre (48-US gal) non-jettisonable tip tanks; external fuel up to 544 kg (1,199 lb) in two 420-litre (110-US gal) drop tanks; maximum ordnance 1000 kg (2,200 lb)
Speed: never-exceed speed at 11000 m (36,090 ft) 850 km/h (459 kt; 528 mph); maximum level speed 'clean' at 5000 m (16,405 ft) 407 kt (755 km/h; 466 mph) and at sea level 388 kt (720 km/h; 447 mph)
Range: ferry range 1750 km (944 nm; 1,087 miles) with drop tanks; standard range 1100 km (593 nm; 683 miles) with internal fuel; endurance at 7000 m (22,975 ft) 3 hours 50 minutes with drop tanks or 2 hours 30 minutes with internal fuel
Performance: maximum rate of climb at sea level 1260 m (4,134 ft) per minute; climb to 5000 m (16,405 ft) in 5 minutes 0 seconds; service ceiling 11000 m (36,090 ft); take-off run 530 m (1,740 ft) at normal take-off weight; landing run 650 m (2,135 ft) at normal landing weight

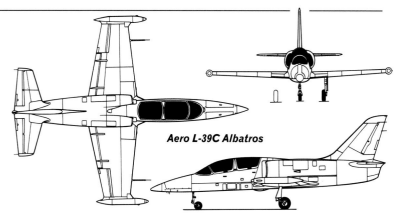

Aero L-39C Albatros

g limits: -4 to +8 operational and +12 ultimate at 4200 kg (9,259 lb)

OPERATORS

Large numbers of L-39s remain in service in Russia (L-39C) and other republics of the former USSR, and in Afghanistan (L-39C), Algeria (L-39ZA), Bulgaria (L-39ZA), Congo, Cuba (L-39C), Czechoslovakia (L-39C, V, ZA and ZO), Egypt (L-39ZO), Ethiopia (L-39C), Hungary (L-39ZO), Iraq (L-39ZO), Libya (L-39ZO), Nicaragua (L-39C and ZO), Nigeria (L-39ZA), North Korea, Romania (L-39 ZA), Syria (L-39ZA and ZO), Thailand (L-39ZE) and Vietnam (L-39C). The former East Germany's L-39ZOs and L-39Vs were retired on reunification and several have now been sold.

Above: One of the roles of the L-39 is target-towing. This East German L-39V has the KT-04 target towed from the centreline, with a winch in the rear cockpit.

Below: Twenty-four unarmed L-39C trainers were delivered to the Republic of Vietnam in 1980/81. They are based at Nha Trang with the 910th 'Julius Fucik' Training Regiment.

Aero L-39MS/L-59 Albatros

Development of the **L-39MS** began in the early 1980s and aimed to remedy the original aircraft's perceived lack of thrust. The first prototype (X-22, registered OK-184) made its maiden flight on 30 September 1986, and was followed by two further prototypes (X-24 and X-25). The designation changed to **L-59** for production.

Compared to the standard L-39, the L-59 is a much more capable aircraft with a strengthened airframe, new avionics (including a head-up display) and a new, more powerful engine, developed jointly by Lotarev in the USSR and ZVL in Czechoslovakia. The DV-2 is a 21.57-kN (4,850-lb) turbofan and fits into the existing L-39 engine bay, making retrofit to existing aircraft a real possibility. The L-59 also has new lightweight flaps, untabbed ailerons and fully powered elevators, and has a revised undercarriage with new brakes. Externally, the L-59 is identifiable by its more pointed nosecone and reshaped fin-tip. The first production L-59 flew on 1 October 1989. Six L-39MS aircraft serve with **Slovakia**.

Forty-eight L-59s, equipped with US avionics, have been ordered by **Egypt** for a reported $200 million, and deliveries began on 29 January 1993. Twelve similar aircraft have been ordered by **Tunisia**. Optimistically, a Garrett TFE731-4-powered development of the L-59, designated **L-139**, has been proposed as a contender to meet the USAF's JPATS requirement for a jet trainer. Also projected in 1994 is the **L-159**, a single-seat light fighter/attack derivative with a 2722-kg (6,000-lb) weapon load and Mach 0.85 capability using a Garrett F124, Rolls-Royce Adour or CDV-2 turbofan.

SPECIFICATION

Aero L-59 (originally L-39MS)
generally similar to the Aero L-39C except in the following particulars:
Wing: span 9.54 m (31 ft 3.5 in) including tip tanks
Fuselage and tail: length 12.20 m (40 ft 0.25 in)
Powerplant: one ZMDB Progress DV-2 rated at 21.57 kN (4,850 lb st) dry
Weights: empty equipped 4150 kg (9,149 lb); normal take-off 5510 kg (12,147 lb) as a trainer; maximum take-off 5700 kg (12,566 lb) with external stores from a grass strip
Fuel and load: internal fuel 1200 kg (2,645 lb) including two tip tanks; external fuel up to 544 kg (1,199 lb) in two 350-litre (92.5-US gal) drop tanks; maximum ordnance 1290 kg (2,844 lb)
Speed: maximum level speed 'clean' at 5000 m (16,405 ft) 876 km/h (473 kt; 544 mph)
Range: ferry range at 9000 m (29,530 ft) 1500 km (809 nm; 932 miles) with drop tanks
Performance: maximum rate of climb at sea level 1560 m (5,118 ft) per minute; service ceiling 11730 m (38,485 ft); take-off run 620 m (2,034 ft) at maximum take-off weight; landing run 650 m (2,135 ft) at normal landing weight

Above: The L-39MS/59 is an attempt to breathe life back into the Albatros design. A more powerful and economic turbofan is at the heart of the update, and can be retrospectively applied to L-39s.

Below: The first customer for the L-59 is Egypt, which has bought 48 for the Air Force Academy. These L-59Es are equipped with ventral gun pod and four wing pylons for the weapons training role.

Aérospatiale (Potez/Fouga) CM 170 Magister/CM 175 Zéphyr

Notable as the first jet trainer to enter service anywhere in the world, and for its use of a butterfly tail, the Magister was designed to meet a French air force specification. Three prototypes were built by the Fouga company, where Pierre Mauboussin had already pioneered the application of small jet engines to light aircraft and powered gliders. Following the first flight of the Fouga CM 170 Magister prototype on 23 July 1952, orders were placed in June 1953 for 10 pre-production aircraft and then in January 1954 for quantity production for the French air force.

In 1958, the Potez group took over responsibility for Fouga activities and continued CM 170 Magister production and development. This activity was, in turn, taken over by Sud-Aviation in April 1967, and production of the Magister continued into 1970, by which time the company had been absorbed into Aérospatiale. First flown on 7 July 1954, the pre-production Magister was to **CM 170-1** standard, as were the early production aircraft, the first of which flew on 29 February 1956.

Production of the CM 170 in France totalled 622 to meet orders from the French air force (400) and navy (32) and the air forces of Austria (18), Belgium (48), Brazil (seven), Cambodia (four), Congo Leopoldville (six), Finland (20), the Federal Republic of Germany (62), Israel (18) and Lebanon (four). In addition, Flugzeug Union Sud in Germany built 188, Valmet in Finland built 62 and IAI in Israel built 36, bringing overall production including prototypes to 921.

Improved variants

The initial production model, CM 170-1, had Marboré IIA engines, replaced in the **CM 170-2** by uprated Marboré VICs. Martin-Baker ejection seats under a modified canopy, and an increased fuel capacity, were features of the **CM 170-3**, first flown on 8 June 1964 and later redesignated **CM 173 Super Magister**. For the Aéronavale, the carrier-capable **CM 175 Zéphyr**, based on the CM 170-1, had an arrester hook among other changes. The first of two prototypes flew on 30 May 1959, and of 30 examples produced about 12 remain in service with 59 Escadrille at Hyères.

Some 150 Magisters remain with the Armée de l'Air, used by Division des Vols 5/312 at Salon de Provence for initial flight training of career officers, and for miscellaneous duties including communications/liaison in base flights and at squadron level. Similarly, about 12 remain with the Force

Six elderly Magisters still form the most potent equipment available to the Irish Air Corps. They are based at Baldonnel with the Light Strike Squadron, part of No. 1 Support Wing.

Left: The Magister still takes an important place in the Armée de l'Air training organisation. This example serves with the Ecole de l'Air.

Right: Initial carrier training for Aéronavale students is undertaken on the CM 175 Zéphyr, serving with Escadrille 59S at Hyères.

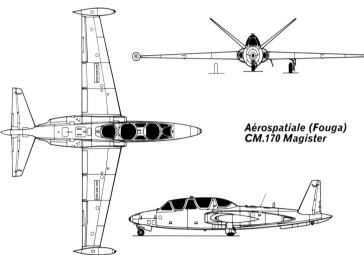

Aérospatiale (Fouga) CM.170 Magister

Aérienne Belge for communications and continuation flying.

Withdrawal from service of Magisters by the other original purchasers – except perhaps Lebanon, where two or three may remain flyable – led to acquisition of small quantities of CM 170s by several other air forces, for use as basic trainers and/or in the light attack role, for which gun and rocket pods or bombs could be carried. The Israeli Defence Force/Air Force remains a major Magister user, having added nine ex-Belgian and possibly other secondhand examples to its original purchase/production of 82. Between 1981 and 1986, some 80 in all were modernised by Bedek Division of IAI to have Marboré VI engines, new avionics and other upgrades, being then renamed **Tzukit** (Thrush) (described separately) in the Advanced Multi-mission Improved Trainer (AMIT) programme.

SPECIFICATION

Aérospatiale (Potez/Fouga) CM 170-1 Magister
Wing: span 11.40 m (37 ft 5 in) without tip tanks and 12.15 m (39 ft 10 in) with tip tanks; aspect ratio 7.51; area 17.30 m² (186.22 sq ft)
Fuselage and tail: length 10.06 m (33 ft 0 in); height 2.80 m (9 ft 2 in); tailplane span 4.38 m (14 ft 4.5 in); wheel track 3.80 m (12 ft 6.75 in); wheel base 4.49 m (14 ft 9 in)
Powerplant: two Turboméca Marboré IIA each rated at 3.92 kN (882 lb st) dry
Weights: empty equipped 2150 kg (4,740 lb); normal take-off 2850 kg (6,283 lb) without tip tanks and 3100 kg (6,834 lb) with tip tanks; maximum take-off 3200 kg (7,055 lb)
Fuel and load: internal fuel 730 litres (193 US gal) plus provision for 250 litres (66 US gal) in two non-jettisonable tip tanks, or for 460 litres (121.5 US gal) in two non-jettisonable ferry tip tanks; external fuel none; maximum ordnance 100 kg (220 lb)
Speed: maximum level speed 'clean' at 9000 m (29,525 ft) 715 km/h (386 kt; 444 mph) and at sea level 650 km/h (350 kt; 403 mph)
Range: ferry range 1200 km (648 nm; 746 miles) with auxiliary fuel; range 925 km (499 nm; 575 miles) with standard fuel; endurance 2 hours 40 minutes with tip tanks or 1 hour 55 minutes with standard fuel
Performance: maximum rate of climb at sea level 1020 m (3,346 ft) per minute; service ceiling 11000 m (36,090 ft); take-off run 655 m (2,149 ft) at 3100 kg (6,834 lb); take-off distance to 15 m (50 ft) 930 m (3,051 ft) at 3100 kg (6,834 lb)

OPERATORS

Current or recent users, sometimes as a result of deals that have involved French, German, Brazilian, Austrian and Israeli surplus aircraft, are Algeria (equipping two squadrons for light attack role), Bangladesh (for FTS at Jessore), Cameroon (counter-insurgency role), Gabon (used by Presidential Guard), Ireland (light strike, advanced training and aerobatic team), Libya (training), Morocco (light attack and training), El Salvador (light attack), Senegambia (basic training), and Togo (training). The major user remains France, aircraft serving with both air force and navy in the training and liaison roles.

Aérospatiale (Sud-Est/Sud) SE 310 Caravelle

Aérospatiale SNI
37 Boulevard Montmorency
F-75781 Paris Cedex 16, France

The Aérospatiale (Sud-Aviation) Caravelle was the world's first rear-engined airliner, making its maiden flight in May 1955. This 80-seat, short/medium-range, twin-engined passenger transport has been used by only a few military operators including Argentina (three **VIN**s), the Central African Republic (one **III**) and Yugoslavia (one VIN). Sweden's National Defence Research Institute operated two Series IIIs for ECM and Elint use. Serving until 1993, they were replaced by two Gulfstream IV SRAs to serve with F16M. Nine Caravelles were operated from 1962 by the **French air force** for VIP transport/liaison duties (two IIIs, one **VIR**, one **10R** and three **IIR**s), flight test research (one ex-VIP III), avionics research (one VIR) and as a SNECMA M53 engine testbed (one III). By early 1994, all French Caravelles had been retired, except for the sole Series 10R VIP/liaison transport operating from Orly, and two Caravelles operated by the CEV.

SPECIFICATION

Aérospatiale (Sud-Aviation) SE 310 Caravelle III
Wing: span 34.30 m (112 ft 6 in); aspect ratio 8.02; area 146.70 m² (1,579.12 sq ft)
Fuselage and tail: length 32.01 m (105 ft 0 in); height 8.72 m (28 ft 7 in); tailplane span 10.60 m (34 ft 9 in); wheel track 5.21 m (17 ft 0 in); wheel base 11.79 m (38 ft 7 in)
Powerplant: two Rolls-Royce Avon RA.29 Mk 527 each rated at 11,400 lb (50.71 kN) dry
Weights: manufacturer's empty 24185 kg (53,318 lb); operating empty 27210 kg (59,987 lb); maximum take-off 46000 kg (101,411 lb)
Fuel and load: internal fuel 19000 litres (5,019 US gal); external fuel none; maximum payload 8400 kg (18,519 lb)
Speed: maximum cruising speed at 7620 m (25,000 ft) 805 km/h (434 kt; 500 mph); economical cruising speed at 10675 m (35,000 ft) 725 km/h (391 kt; 450 mph)
Range: 1845 km (995 nm; 1,146 miles) with a 7620-kg

(16,799-lb) payload or 1700 km (917 nm; 1,056 miles) with maximum payload
Performance: take-off run 1830 m (6,004 ft) at maximum take-off weight; landing run 1800 m (5,906 ft) at normal landing weight

Believed to be the last military Caravelle, this aircraft serves with ET 3/60 at Paris-Orly. It works on ministerial transport duties.

Aérospatiale (Sud-Est/Sud) SA 313B/SA 318C Alouette II

The Alouette (lark) family of general-purpose helicopters originated with the three-seat SE 3120, which first flew on 31 July 1952. A product of the Société Nationale de Constructions Aéronautiques du Sud-Est (SNCASE), it was powered by a 149-kW (200-hp) Salmson 9NH radial piston engine and was aimed largely at the agricultural market. A complete redesign to utilise the 269-kW (360-shp) Turboméca Artouste I turboshaft resulted in the SE 3130 **Alouette II**, flown on 12 March 1955. French certification on 2 May 1956 cleared the way

The German army has been a staunch Alouette II operator, this example wearing a scheme to celebrate 25 years of service.

Aérospatiale (Sud-Est) SA 313B/SA 318C Alouette II

for production deliveries, and the designation changed to **SE 313B** soon after, when SNCASE merged into Sud-Aviation (which, in turn, was incorporated into Aérospatiale in 1970). Production aircraft used the Artouste IIC6 turboshaft.

Further evolution of the basic helicopter produced the SE 3140 with a 298-kW (400-shp) Turboméca Turmo II turboshaft, no production of which ensued, and then the SA 3180 with an Astazou IIA, flown on 31 January 1961. As the **Alouette II Astazou**, this was certificated in France in February 1964, production aircraft taking the designation **SA 318C** and deliveries commencing in 1965.

Large-scale production

Among the first production types to demonstrate the tremendous versatility of a small, multi-role helicopter in both civil and military spheres, the Alouette II achieved unprecedented levels of production for a European rotary-wing aircraft. Its 'bug-eye' glazed cabin seated up to five – pilot and passenger in front and three passengers abreast behind. An open fuselage structure carried the fuel tank immediately behind the cabin, the powerplant and, on the aft extension, the tail rotor. A skid-type landing gear was standard, with retractable wheels for ground manoeuvring, and high skids, wheels or pneumatic floats as options. A rescue hoist was available, with 120-kg (265-lb) capacity, and listed roles included flying crane, liaison, observation, training, agricultural work, photographic survey, and ambulance (with two stretchers). In the military role, rockets, guns or air-to-surface missiles could be carried.

Production ended in 1975 with a total of 1,305 built.

SPECIFICATION

Aérospatiale SA 318C Alouette II Astazou
Rotor system: main rotor diameter 10.20 m (33 ft 5.625 in); tail rotor diameter 1.91 m (6 ft 3 in); main rotor disc area 81.71 m² (879.58 sq ft); tail rotor disc area 2.87 m² (30.84 sq ft)
Fuselage and tail: length overall, rotors turning 12.10 m (39 ft 8.5 in) and fuselage 9.75 m (31 ft 11.75 in) with tail rotor turning; height overall 2.75 m (9 ft 0 in); skid track 2.22 m (7 ft 3 in)
Powerplant: one 530-shp (395-kW) Turboméca Astazou IIA derated to 360 shp (268 kW)
Weights: empty 890 kg (1,961 lb); maximum take-off 1650 kg (3,638 lb)
Fuel and load: internal fuel 580 litres (153.25 US gal); external fuel none; maximum payload 600 kg (1,323 lb)
Speed: maximum level speed at sea level 205 km/h (110 kt; 127 mph); maximum cruising speed at sea level 180 km/h (97 kt; 112 mph)
Range: 720 km (388 nm; 447 miles); endurance 5 hours 18 minutes
Performance: maximum rate of climb at sea level 396 m (1,300 ft) per minute; service ceiling 3300 m (10,825 ft); hovering ceiling 1550 m (5,085 ft) in ground effect and 900 m (2,955 ft) out of ground effect

OPERATORS

Among well over 120 users of the Alouette II (military and civil) in nearly 50 countries, Germany was the largest, with the Heeresfliegertruppen taking 226 SA 313Bs and 54 SA 318Cs from 1959. Some 50 remain in service with four Army Aviation Support Squadrons (HFS) at Celle, Rotenburg and Rheine, with a like number for training at the Army Aviation Weapons School, Bückenburg. Other military users of the Alouette II, mostly in small numbers, include Belgium, Benin, Cameroon, the Central African Republic, Congo Republic, Djibouti, Dominican Republic, France, Guinea-Bissau, Ivory Coast, Lebanon, Morocco, Portugal, Senegal, Sweden, Switzerland, Togo, Tunisia and Turkey.

The Alouette II is becoming quite rare in French army (ALAT) service, but a number are retained for regional defence force work and for training.

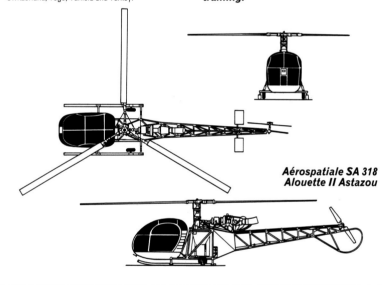

Aérospatiale SA 318 Alouette II Astazou

Aérospatiale (Sud) **SA 316/SA 319 Alouette III**

Aérospatiale helicopter division became Eurocopter France on 16 January 1992

The reliability and sales success of the Alouette II prompted Sud-Aviation to initiate development of an advanced version. The incorporation of a more powerful turboshaft engine and improved aerodynamics was considered essential to give greater payload capability and enhanced performance and, at the same time, the opportunity was taken to introduce new equipment. Initially designated **SE 3160**, the prototype **Alouette III** incorporated a larger and more enclosed cabin than that of its predecessor, able to carry a pilot and six passengers with baggage holds for luggage and parcels, or a pilot and six equipped troops. In a casevac role two stretchers and two sitting casualties or medical attendants could be accommodated behind the pilot or, alternatively, the six seats could easily be removed for the carriage of cargo; there was also provision for an external sling for loads of up to 750 kg (1,653 lb).

The prototype was flown for the first time on 28 February 1959 and early production examples followed in 1961. The initial production **SA 316A** helicopter, built for home and export markets, became the subject of a licence agreement with Hindustan Aeronautics Ltd in India. Subsequent development produced the main production **SA 316B**, first flown on 27 June 1968, which introduced the Turboméca Artouste IIIB turboshaft with uprated main and tail rotor transmissions, and was able to carry more payload. HAL-built versions are known as **Chetak** in Indian Air Force service. Last of the Artouste-powered Alouette IIIs was the **SA 316C**, built in only small numbers with an Artouste IIID engine. The SA 316B was also the subject of licence agreements with the Swiss Federal Aircraft Factory, and ICA-Brasov in Romania where the type was produced until 1989. The Romanian version, of which 230 examples were built, is desig-

Portugal was a major purchaser of the Alouette III, buying over 140. Around 30 are still in service, used mainly for utility transport but also for training.

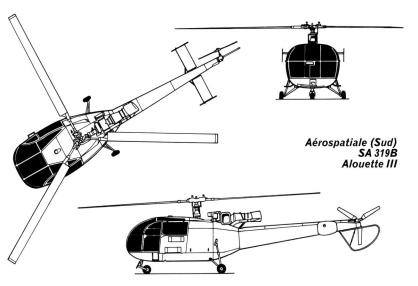

Aérospatiale (Sud)
SA 319B
Alouette III

nated **IAR 316B**. This formed the basis of the **IAR-317 Skyfox**, a dedicated gunship variant (both described separately).

The capability of the SA 316B soon led to two-seat military versions deployed in a variety of roles, with a range of weapon options that made them suitable for light attack and ASW. As with the Alouette II, a version was introduced with the Turboméca Astazou turboshaft, this being the **SA 319B** Alouette III with a 649-kW (870-shp) Astazou XIV derated to 447 kW (600 shp). A total of 1,453 Alouettes of all versions was built by Aérospatiale.

The Rhodesian air force operated two specialised versions of the Alouette III in support of quick-reaction units to intercept terrorist forces. The **G-Car** four-troop transport was armed with two side-mounted Browning machine-guns, whereas the **K-Car** was a dedicated gunship variant with a single 20-mm Mauser cannon mounted in the cabin and firing to port.

Limited production continues in India, where 322 examples of the Chetak had been produced by HAL by March 1991.

SPECIFICATION

Aérospatiale (Sud) SA 319B Alouette III Astazou
Rotor system: main rotor diameter 11.02 m (36 ft 1.75 in); tail rotor diameter 1.91 m (6 ft 3.25 in); main rotor disc area 95.38 m² (1,026.68 sq ft); tail rotor disc area 2.87 m² (30.84 sq ft)
Fuselage and tail: length overall, rotors turning 12.84 m (42 ft 1.5 in) and fuselage 10.03 m (32 ft 10.75 in); height to top of rotor head 3.00 m (9 ft 10 in); wheel track 2.60 m (8 ft 6.25 in)
Powerplant: one 870-shp (649-kW) Turboméca Astazou XIV derated to 600 shp (447 kW)
Weights: empty 1140 kg (2,513 lb); maximum take-off 2250 kg (4,960 lb)
Fuel and load: internal fuel 575 litres (152 US gal); external fuel none; maximum payload 750 kg (1,653 lb)
Speed: maximum level speed 'clean' at sea level

220 km/h (118 kt; 136 mph); maximum cruising speed at sea level 197 km/h (106 kt; 122 mph)
Range: 605 km (326 nm; 375 miles) with six passengers
Performance: maximum rate of climb at sea level 270 m (885 ft) per minute; hovering ceiling 3100 m (10,170 ft) in ground effect and 1700 m (5,575 ft) out of ground effect

OPERATORS

The Alouette III is currently operated by the air forces of Angola, Argentina (navy), Austria, Belgium (navy), Burkina Faso, Burundi, Cameroon, Chile (navy), Congo, Ecuador, El Salvador, Equatorial Guinea, France (all three air arms), Gabon, Ghana, Guinea, Guinea-Bissau, Indonesia, Iraq, Ireland, Lebanon, Libya (all three air arms), Mexico (all three air arms), Mozambique, Myanmar, Netherlands, Nicaragua, Pakistan (all three air arms), Peru (army and navy), Portugal, Romania, Rwanda, Serbia, South Africa, Spain, Suriname, Switzerland, Tunisia, United

With high installed power and a good-sized cabin, the Alouette III has proved popular in the search and rescue role. The Dutch aircraft were replaced in this role by Bell 412s in 1994.

Arab Emirates (Abu Dhabi), Venda, Venezuela, Zaïre and Zimbabwe.
HAL-built Chetaks are operated by Ethiopia, India (all three air arms), Nepal and the Seychelles.

In peacetime ALAT Alouette IIIs are used for training and general transport, but in wartime would be used to form offensive units.

Aérospatiale (Sud) **SA 315 Lama**

Following an Indian armed forces requirement, design of the **Aérospatiale Lama** was begun in late 1968. Externally resembling the Alouette II, the Lama is in effect a 'hot-and-high' variant of the SE 313B. The required performance is derived by combining features of the Alouette II and III; the Lama has the Alouette II's airframe (with some reinforcement) and dynamic components of the SA 316 Alouette III, including the rotor system and Artouste IIIB powerplant.

The SA 315B prototype flew on 17 March 1969 and production was launched simultaneously in France (where the name Lama was adopted) and India (with the name **Cheetah**). In Brazil, Helibras assembled the Lama, using French components, as the **HB 315B Gavião**. This version is operated by the **Bolivian air force** and the **Brazilian navy**.

French production of the SA 315B ended by 1991 with a total of 407 delivered. Production in India, where the first Cheetah flew on 6 October 1972, was initially for the **Indian Air Force**, equipping Nos 659-662 AOP/liaison squadrons. Since 1987, these units have been part of the **Indian Army Air Corps**. Current production of the Cheetah by HAL at Bangalore stands at 197 examples, including 20 assembled from French components. Lamas continue to fly with the air arms of **Angola**, **Argentina** (air force and army), **Cameroon**, **Chile** (air force and army), **Ecuador**, **El Salvador**, **Peru** (army) and **Togo**.

SPECIFICATION

Aérospatiale SA 315B Lama
Rotor system: main rotor diameter 11.02 m (36 ft

1.75 in); tail rotor diameter 1.91 m (6 ft 3.25 in); main rotor disc area 95.38 m² (1,026.69 sq ft); tail rotor disc area 2.87 m² (30.84 sq ft)
Fuselage and tail: length overall, rotors turning 12.91 m (42 ft 4.25 in) and fuselage 10.23 m (33 ft 6.25 in); height overall 3.09 m (10 ft 1.75 in); skid track 2.38 m (7 ft 9.75 in)
Powerplant: one 858-shp (640-kW) Turboméca Artouste IIIB derated to 542 shp (404 kW)
Weights: empty 1021 kg (2,251 lb); normal take-off 1950 kg (4,299 lb); maximum take-off 2300 kg (5,071 lb)
Fuel and load: internal fuel 575 litres (152 US gal); external fuel none; maximum payload 1135 kg (2,502 lb)
Speed: never-exceed speed at sea level 210 km/h (113 kt; 130 mph); maximum cruising speed at optimum altitude 192 km/h (103 kt; 119 mph)
Range: 515 km (278 nm; 320 miles)
Performance: maximum rate of climb at sea level

The Cheetah is a HAL-built Lama, used widely by India for mountain work. The type features raised skids for better ground clearance on rough terrain.

330 m (1,083 ft) per minute; service ceiling 5400 m (17,715 ft); hovering ceiling 5050 m (16,565 ft) in ground effect and 5600 m (15,090 ft) out of ground effect

---

Aérospatiale (Sud) **SA 321 Super Frelon**

To meet requirements of the French armed services for a medium transport helicopter, Sud-Aviation flew the prototype **SA 3200 Frelon** (hornet) on 10 June 1959. Powered by three Turboméca Turmo IIIB turboshaft engines, the SA 3200 had large external fuel tanks that left the interior clear for a maximum 28 troops, and a swing-tail fuselage to simplify loading cargo. Development was terminated in favour of a larger and more capable helicopter designed

in conjunction with Sikorsky in the USA, and with Fiat in Italy producing the main gearbox and transmission. What was to become Europe's largest production helicopter clearly shows Sikorsky influence, the rotor system being of Sikorsky design, and with its watertight hull suitable for amphibious operation. Two military prototypes of the Super Frelon were built, the SA 3210-01 troop transport flown on 7 December 1962, and the SA 3210-02 maritime version for

The Aéronavale Super Frelons were previously used for ASV and ASW work, but now they are used primarily for transport duties, including vertical replenishment of ships under way. The type serves with 32F at Lanvéoc, 33F at St Mandrier and 20S also at the latter base.

Aérospatiale (Sud) SA 321 Super Frelon

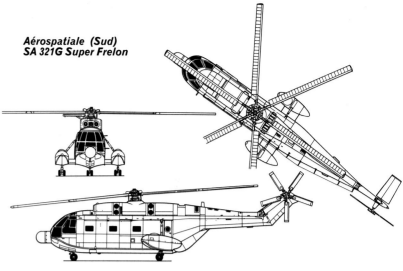

Aérospatiale (Sud)
SA 321G Super Frelon

Libya purchased both maritime and transport Frelon variants. This is one of the latter, distinguished by its sand and green camouflage.

the Aéronavale on 28 May 1963.

Four pre-production aircraft were built under the new designation **SA 321**. These were followed in October 1965 by an initial production series of 16 **SA 321G** ASW helicopters for the Aéronavale, which received a further 10 (including three pre-production models). This variant was identifiable by having a small stabilising float incorporating Sylphe surveillance radar mounted to the support structure of each main unit of the tricycle landing gear (later removed). Apart from ship-based ASW missions, the SA 321G also carried out sanitisation patrols in support of 'Rédoutable'-class ballistic missile submarines. Some were modified with nose-mounted targeting radar for AM39 Exocet missiles, giving an ASV capability. Five **SA 321Ga** cargo-carrying versions, originally used in support of the Pacific nuclear test centre, were transferred to assault support duties. The 20 surviving Aéronavale Super Frelons are currently assigned to transport duties including com-

mando transport, vertical replenishment of ships at sea and civilian support duties such as SAR. Six **SA 321GM**s fitted with Omera ORB-32WAS radar were delivered to Libya in 1980-81. The SA 321G was modified for air force and army service by removal of stabilising floats and external fairings on each side of the lower fuselage. Designated **SA 321H**, a total of 16 examples was delivered from 1977 to the Iraqi air force with Omera ORB-31D radar and AM39 Exocet ASMs. These aircraft were used in the Iran-Iraq conflict and the 1991 Gulf War, in which at least one example was destroyed.

The maritime variant was followed by the **SA 321F** commercial airliner for 34-37 passengers, and the commercial **SA 321J** intended for use as a 27-seat passenger transport, as a cargo carrier with a 4000-kg (8,818-lb) internal or 5000-kg (11,023-lb) external load, or for other utility purposes such as fire fighting. This version was later superseded by the **SA 321Ja** operating at a higher gross weight. The naval air arm of the **People's Republic of China** received 16 aircraft fitted with Omera ORB-31D targeting radar. Non-amphibious military export versions included 12 **SA 321K**

transports for Israel, 16 similar **SA 321L** transports for South Africa (retired in 1991) and eight **SA 321M** SAR/logistical support helicopters for Libya.

When French production ended in 1983 a total of 99 Super Frelons had been built. Production continues in China under licence-agreement as the **Changhe Z-8** (described separately). Eight survivors of the examples delivered to Israel were re-engined with GE T58 turboshafts (for performance improvement and commonality with Israel's CH-53 fleet) and later sold to Argentina.

SPECIFICATION

Aérospatiale (Sud) SA 321G Super Frelon
Rotor system: main rotor diameter 18.90 m (62 ft 0 in); tail rotor diameter 4.00 m (13 ft 1.5 in); main rotor disc area 280.55 m² (3,019.93 sq ft); tail rotor disc area 12.57 m² (135.27 sq ft)
Fuselage and tail: length overall, rotors turning 23.03 m (75 ft 6.625 in), fuselage 19.40 m (63 ft 7.8 in), and 17.07 m (56 ft 0 in) with main rotor blades and tail folded; height overall 6.76 m (22 ft 2.25 in), and 4.94 m (16 ft 2.5 in) with main rotor blades and tail folded; wheel track 4.30 m (14 ft 1 in); wheel base

6.56 m (21 ft 6.25 in)
Powerplant: three Turboméca Turmo IIIC3 each rated at 1100 kW (1,475 shp) or, in later helicopters, three Turboméca Turmo IIIC7 each rated at 1201 kW (1,610 shp)
Weights: empty 6863 kg (15,130 lb); maximum take-off 12500 kg (27,557 lb) in earlier helicopters or 13000 kg (28,660 lb) in later helicopters
Fuel and load: internal fuel 3975 litres (1,050 US gal) plus provision for 1000 litres (264 US gal) of auxiliary fuel in two cabin tanks; external fuel up to two 500-litre (132-US gal) auxiliary tanks; maximum payload 5000 kg (11,023 lb)
Speed: never-exceed speed at sea level 275 km/h (149 kt; 171 mph); maximum cruising speed at sea level 248 km/h (134 kt; 154 mph)
Range: 1020 km (550 nm; 633 miles) with a 3500-kg (7,716-lb) payload; endurance 4 hours
Performance: maximum rate of climb at sea level 300 m (984 ft) per minute; service ceiling 3100 m (10,170 ft); hovering ceiling 1950 m (6,400 ft) in ground effect

OPERATORS

Argentina (SA 321K), China (SA 321G and Z-8), France (Aéronavale SA 321G/SA 321 Ga), Iraq (SA 321H), Libya (SA 321GM/SA 321M).

Aérospatiale (Nord) N 262 Frégate

With its design origins in the piston-engined Max Holste MH-250 Super Broussard which flew on 20 May 1959, the definitive **Nord N 262 Frégate** differed in having a pressurised, circular-section fuselage. The powerplant comprised two Turboméca Bastan turboprops, as introduced by Max Holste in the MH-260 prototype (flown on 29 July 1960) and the 10 pre-production slab-sided MH-260s. After Nord had assumed responsibility for further development of the light transport for military and civil use, the N262 prototype first flew on 24 December 1962.

The first production aircraft flew on 8 June 1964 and Nord went on to build a total of 110 in several versions, production being completed after Nord was absorbed into Aérospatiale in 1970. Principal military users are the **French air force**, which bought five new-build **N 262A** and 24 **N 262D** Frégates plus other used aircraft, and the French navy, which acquired 25 new and secondhand. For the Armée de l'Air, five **N 262AEN**s fly in the training role to instruct navigators with GE 316 'Toulouse', for which purpose they are fitted with OMERA ORB-32 radar, Crouzet Oméga 600 navigation equipment and TACAN, with consoles for four students and three instructors. Other N 262s fly with several training and transport squadrons (ETE 41, 43, 44),

while most of the 24 original 262Ds serve in the light transport role with ET 1/65 'Vendôme' at Villacoublay.

The **Aéronavale** uses its Nord 262s as multi-engine trainers for co-pilots converting to the Atlantique, this being the responsibility of 55S, the Ecole de Perfectionnement sur Multimoteurs in Corsica. Navigation and flight engineer training is given by 56S at Nîmes/Garons, using **Nord 262E** conversions of the 262A with appropriate equipment. Three Nord 262Es also are used for inshore surveillance by 2S from Lann-Bihoué. Elsewhere, **Angola** continues to fly four ex-civil Nord 262As acquired in 1980, and the **Burkina-Faso** air force has two **N 262C** Frégates, but Gabon retired its three aircraft in 1990.

SPECIFICATION

Aérospatiale (Nord) N 262 Frégate Series D
Wing: span 22.60 m (74 ft 1.75 in); aspect ratio 9.10; area 55.79 m² (600.54 sq ft)
Fuselage and tail: length 19.28 m (63 ft 3 in); height 6.21 m (20 ft 4 in); tailplane span 8.80 m (28 ft 10.5 in); wheel track 3.13 m (10 ft 9 in); wheel base 7.23 m (23 ft 9 in)
Powerplant: two Turboméca Bastan VII each rated at 1,145 ehp (854 ekW)
Weights: basic empty 6200 kg (13,668 lb); operating

empty 7225 kg (15,928 lb); maximum take-off 10800 kg (23,810 lb)
Fuel and load: internal fuel 2000 litres (528 US gal) plus provision for 570 litres (151 US gal) of optional fuel; external fuel none; maximum payload 3075 kg (6,779 lb)
Speed: maximum level speed 'clean' at optimum altitude 418 km/h (226 kt; 260 mph); maximum and economical cruising speed at optimum altitude 408 km/h (221 kt; 254 mph)
Range: 2400 km (1,295 nm; 1,491 miles) with

maximum fuel or 1450 km (782 nm; 901 miles) with 26 passengers
Performance: maximum rate of climb at sea level 420 m (1,378 ft) per minute; service ceiling 8690 m (28,510 ft); take-off run 570 m (1,870 ft) at maximum take-off weight; take-off distance to 10.7 m (35 ft) 1070 m (3,510 ft) at maximum take-off weight; landing distance from 15 m (50 ft) 530 m (1,740 ft) at normal landing weight

Large numbers of Nord 262s remain in French service on both training and transport tasks. The Aéronavale uses this aircraft for communications work.

Aérospatiale (SOCATA) **TB 30B Epsilon**

Aérospatiale (SOCATA)
12 rue Pasteur
F-92150 Suresnes, France

SOCATA, Aérospatiale's light-aircraft subsidiary, began development in 1977 of a military basic trainer based on its TB 10 Tobago four/five-seat lightplane. Redesigned to meet a specification drawn up by the Armée de l'Air for a tandem trainer, the new design was proposed in **Aérospatiale TB 30A** and **TB 30B** versions with engines of 194 kW (260 hp) and 224 kW (300 hp), respectively. The TB 30B gained a development contract in 1979, and the first prototype was flown on 22 December 1979. The second prototype, flown on 12 July 1980, introduced the increased span, rounded wingtips, redesigned rear fuselage and tail which had been finalised for production **TB 30B Epsilon** aircraft. Following completion of the development programme, the first production aircraft was flown on 29 June 1983.

Of all-metal construction, the Epsilon has retractable tricycle landing gear, a large aft-sliding canopy and a cockpit layout and flying characteristics that are intended to prepare pupils for the Dassault-Breguet/Dornier Alpha Jet. Fully aerobatic and stressed for g limits of +6.7 and -3.35, the Epsilon has a Christen fuel system to permit up to two minutes of inverted flight. On 6 January 1982, before the development programme was completed, the **Armée de l'Air** ordered 150 for delivery at the rate of 30 per year. Two initial production batches were approved in 1982, each covering 30 aircraft. The Epsilon duly entered service with the Centre d' Expériences Aériennes Militaires (CEAM) at Mont-de-Marsan on 29 July 1983 to establish the training syllabus. Epsilons began to equip Groupement Ecole (GE) 315 at Cognac/Chateaubernard in June 1984, this unit eventually receiving 150 Epsilons by late 1989. GE 315 is the Basic

Flying School (Ecole de Formation Pilotage de Base) and receives direct-entry aircrew for a 23-week course involving 66½ hours. Four Flying Instruction Squadrons (EIV – Escadron d'Instruction en Vol) are partnered by the Instructors School (Ecole des Moniteurs) providing a 73-hour course.

Export orders for the Epsilon have been restricted to two customers. The **Portuguese air force** took delivery from 1989 of 18 Epsilons assembled locally by OGMA. These aircraft are operated by Esquadra 104 at Sintra. An armed version of the Epsilon was ordered by the **Togolese air force** in late 1984. This version is equipped with four underwing hardpoints, carrying a total of 300 kg (661 lb) of stores with pilot only, or 200 kg (441 lb) with two crew. Three aircraft were delivered in 1986 and were followed by a single attrition replacement in 1987.

SPECIFICATION

Aérospatiale TB 30B Epsilon
Wing: span 7.92 m (25 ft 11.75 in); aspect ratio 7.0; area 9.00 m² (96.88 sq ft)
Fuselage and tail: length 7.59 m (24 ft 10.75 in); height 2.66 m (8 ft 8.75 in); tailplane span 3.20 m (10 ft 6 in); wheel track 2.30 m (7 ft 6.5 in); wheel base 1.80 m (5 ft 10.75 in)
Powerplant: one Textron Lycoming AEIO-540-L1B5D rated at 300 hp (224 kW)
Weights: empty equipped 932 kg (2,055 lb); maximum take-off 1250 kg (2,755 lb)
Fuel and load: internal fuel 150 kg (331 lb); external fuel none; maximum ordnance 300 kg (661 lb)
Speed: never-exceed speed 520 km/h (281 kt; 323 mph); maximum level speed 'clean' at sea level 378 km/h (204 kt; 236 mph); cruising speed at 1830 m (6,005 ft) 358 km/h (193 kt; 222 mph)

Range: 1250 km (675 nm; 777 miles); endurance 3 hours 45 minutes
Performance: maximum rate of climb at sea level 564 m (1,850 ft) per minute; service ceiling 7010 m (23,000 ft); take-off run 410 m (1,345 ft) at maximum take-off weight; take-off distance to 15 m (50 ft) 640 m (2,100 ft) at maximum take-off weight; landing distance from 15 m (50 ft) 440 m (1,444 ft) at normal landing weight; landing run 250 m (820 ft) at normal landing weight

Epsilon of GE 315, used for basic training.

Portugal has 18 Epsilons for its basic training needs with Esq 104. The aircraft were assembled locally by OGMA.

Aérospatiale (SOCATA) **TB 31 Omega**

Aérospatiale's SOCATA light aircraft division developed as a private venture a turboprop version of its TB 30 Epsilon piston-engined basic trainer (of which 172 had been delivered to the French, Portuguese and Togo air forces from 1989), mainly to meet Armée de l'Air requirements for an eventual Fouga Magister replacement. The prototype Epsilon 01 was initially used as a flying testbed for the first 450-shp (335-kW) Turboméca TP319 turboprop, flat-rated to 350 shp (261 kW), to replace the original 300-hp (224-kW) Textron Lycoming AEIO-540-LIB5D flat-six piston-powerplant in an extensively-revised nose cowling with a chin intake. Initially fitted with a three-bladed Ratier-Figeac composite propeller, the **Turbo Epsilon** made its first flight in this form on 9 November 1985 but, after extensive engine development, underwent further modifications to emerge in 1989 as the **TB 31 Omega**.

Apart from installation of a developed 488-shp (364-kW) TP319-1A2 Arrius turboprop, derated to 360 shp (268 kW) and driving a Hartzell propeller, the Omega featured a new two-piece moulded canopy for improved cockpit visibility and room for stepped twin Martin-Baker 15FC lightweight zero-height/60-kt ejection seats if required, plus EFIS instrumentation and an additional dorsal fin. Despite a successful flight-test programme, which began on 30 April 1989 and confirmed the Omega's substantial increase in performance, French government preference for the much bigger and more powerful EMBRAER Tucano has so far inhibited SOCATA from launching production of the TB 31.

SPECIFICATION

Aérospatiale TB 31 Omega
Wing: span 7.92 m (25 ft 11.75 in); aspect ratio 6.97; area 9.00 m² (96.88 sq ft)
Fuselage and tail: length 7.81 m (25 ft 7.5 in); height 2.68 m (8 ft 9.5 in); wheel track 2.30 m (7 ft 6.5 in); wheel base 1.80 m (5 ft 10.75 in)
Powerplant: one 364-kW (488-shp) Turboméca TP 319 IA2 Arrius derated to 268 kW (360 shp)
Weights: empty equipped 860 kg (1,896 lb);

maximum take-off 1450 kg (3,197 lb)
Fuel and load: internal fuel 222 kg (489 lb); external fuel none; maximum ordnance 300 kg (661 lb)
Speed: never-exceed speed 595 km/h (321 kt; 370 mph); maximum level speed 'clean' at 4875 m (16,000 ft) 519 km/h (280 kt; 322 mph); maximum cruising speed at 3050 m (10,000 ft) 434 km/h (234 kt; 269 mph); economical cruising speed at optimum altitude 354 km/h (191 kt; 220 mph)
Range: 1308 km (706 nm; 813 miles)

The Omega remains in prototype form, having been developed from the piston-engined Epsilon.

Performance: maximum rate of climb at sea level 640 m (2,100 ft) per minute; service ceiling 9145 m (30,000 ft); take-off distance to 15 m (50 ft) 570 m (1,870 ft) at maximum take-off weight
g limits: -3.5 to +7

Aerostar (Yakovlev) **Yak-52**

Aerostar SA
9 Condorilor Street
R-5500 Bacau, Romania

Together with its single-seat Yak-50 counterpart, the two-seat **Yak-52** was developed by the Yakovlev OKB in Moscow to provide the Soviet air force with a successor for the Yak-18 primary trainer. First flown in 1976 (after the first Yak-50), the Yak-52 proved successful and its production was assigned to the IAv factory at Bacau in Romania. Production began there in 1979, the first Yak-52 flying at Bacau early in 1980. Deliveries to the **Soviet Union**

began later in 1980 and, by June 1992, IAv had completed 1,600 Yak-52s, virtually all for the former Soviet air force, with production continuing.

The fully-aerobatic Yak-52 features tandem seating. All three wheels of the tricycle undercarriage remain fully exposed when retracted, to give a measure of protection in the event of wheels-up landings. The Yak-52 is powered by the 268-kW (360-hp) Vedeneyev M-14P radial engine, but

Aerostar has also flown a developed prototype, known as the **Condor**, with a 300-hp (224-kW) Lycoming AEIO-540-L1B5D piston engine and redesigned tail unit.

The name of the company responsible for the factory has now changed to Aerostar SA, and the designation is rendered as **Iak-52**. In addition to the former Soviet air forces, the type is in widespread use with the **Romanian air force**. Twelve were purchased by **Hungary** in 1994.

SPECIFICATION

Aerostar (Yakovlev) Yak-52
Wing: span 9.30 m (30 ft 6.25 in); aspect ratio 5.77; area 15.00 m² (161.5 sq ft)
Fuselage and tail: length 7.75 m (25 ft 5 in); height 2.70 m (8 ft 10.25 in); wheel track 2.72 m (8 ft 10.75 in); wheel base 1.86 m (6ft 1.25 in)
Powerplant: one 268-kW (360-hp) VMKB (Vedeneyev) M-14P nine-cylinder air-cooled radial

Aerostar (Yakovlev) Yak-52

Weights: empty 1015 kg (2,238 lb); maximum take-off 1305 kg (2,877 lb)
Fuel and load: internal fuel 100 kg (220 lb); external fuel none
Speed: never-exceed speed 360 km/h (194 kt; 223 mph); maximum level speed at sea level 285 km/h (154 kt; 177 mph); maximum level speed at 1000 m (3,280 ft) 270 km/h (145 kt; 167 mph)
Range: 500 km (270 nm; 310 miles) at 500 m (1,640 ft), maximum fuel and 20 min. reserves
Performance: maximum climb rate at sea level

600 m (1,970 ft) per minute; service ceiling 4000 m (13,125 ft); take-off run 180-200 m (591-657 ft); landing run (flaps up) 285 m (935 m); landing run (flaps down) 260 m (853 ft)
g limits: -5 to +7

The Yak-52 is used in huge numbers by the air forces of the former Soviet Union, although production is undertaken in Romania.

Aérostructure (Fournier) RF-10

First flown on 6 March 1981, the **RF-10** was designed in France by René Fournier as a continuation of a series of motor-gliders and ultra-light aircraft based on classic sailplane design. Generally similar to the RF-9, the RF-10 introduced an all-composite structure with a carbon-fibre main spar and more powerful 59.5-kW (80-hp) Limbach L2000-LOI flat-four engine. After completing a second prototype, Fournier sold rights in the RF-10 to Aérostructure SARL, which put the type into production, with a T-tail replacing the low-mounted tailplane of the prototypes. The first production RF-10 flew on 10 May 1984 and about a dozen were built, of which four were purchased by the **Portuguese air force** to serve with No. 802 Squadron at the Air Force Academy, at Sintra, to allow career officers to go solo prior

to embarking on their flying training course. Rights in the RF-10 were subsequently acquired by AeroMot in Porto Alegre, Brazil, with a view to series assembly/manufacture as the **AMT-100 Ximango**.

SPECIFICATION

Aérostructure (Fournier) RF-10
Wing: span 17.47 m (57 ft 3.75 in); aspect ratio 16.3; area 18.70 m² (201.29 sq ft)
Fuselage and tail: length 7.89 m (25 ft 10.75 in); height 1.03 m (6 ft 4 in)
Powerplant: one Limbach L 2000 EOI rated at 80 hp (59.5 kW)
Weights: empty 600 kg (1,323 lb); maximum take-off 800 kg (1,764 lb)
Fuel and load: internal fuel 90 litres (23.8 US gal); external fuel none

Speed: maximum cruising speed at optimum altitude 200 km/h (108 kt; 124 mph); economical cruising speed at optimum altitude 180 km/h (97 kt; 112 mph); maximum gliding speed 245 km/h (133 kt; 153 mph) in smooth air and 180 km/h (97 kt; 112 mph) in rough air
Performance: maximum rate of climb at sea level 150 m (492 m) per minute; best glide ratio 30 at

Several air arms operate motor gliders for initial training. Portugal has four RF-10s.

100 km/h (54 kt; 62 mph); minimum sink rate 0.96 m (3.15 ft) per second at 90 km/h (49 kt; 56 mph)
g limits: -2.6 to +5.3

Aerotec T-23 Uirapuru

Designed as a private venture by two Brazilian engineers, the original **A-122 Uirapuru** was flown on 2 June 1965 with an 80.5-kW (108-hp) Lycoming O-235-C1 flat-four engine. The basic type was adopted by the **Brazilian air force** to replace its Fokker S.11 and S.12 primary trainers, with an order for 30, subsequently increased to 70. Designated **T-23**, the first of these flew on 23 January 1968, with a 119.5-kW (160-hp) Lycoming O-320-B2B engine. An update produced the **A-132 Uirapuru II** which flew on 26 February 1981 as the **T-23B**, later the **YT-17 Tangara**.

Planned production of 100 T-23Bs did not take place, but some features of the Uirapuru II were incorporated in 45 T-23s in 1979/80. Six Tangaras were completed in 1986 for sale to the **Bolivian air force**, which previously had procured 18 T-23 Uirapurus; a dozen of the latter, plus the A-132s, remain in service at the Military Aviation College at Santa Cruz. The only other

sale was to **Paraguay**, where eight (of about 20 procured, including a dozen ex-Brazilian air force) provide basic training at the Air Force Academy at Campo Grande. The T-23 was retired as a primary trainer by the Brazilian air force in 1980, a few remaining on strength for miscellaneous duties.

SPECIFICATION

Aerotec A-132 Uirapuru
Wing: span 8.50 m (27 ft 10.75 in); aspect ratio 5.33; area 13.50 m² (145.32 sq ft)
Fuselage and tail: length 6.60 m (21 ft 8 in); height 2.70 m (8 ft 10 in); tailplane span 2.80 m (9 ft 2.25 in); wheel track 2.40 m (7 ft 10.5 in); wheel base 1.53 m (5 ft 0.25 in)
Powerplant: one Textron Lycoming O-320-B2B rated at 160 hp (119.5 kW)
Weights: empty 515 kg (1,135 lb); operating empty 540 kg (1,190 lb); maximum take-off 840 kg (1,852 lb)
Fuel and load: internal fuel 140 litres (37 US gal)

plus provision for 100 litres (26.4 US gal) of auxiliary fuel in two tip tanks; external fuel none; maximum ordnance none
Speed: maximum level speed 'clean' at sea level 122 kt (140 mph; 225 km/h); maximum cruising speed at 5,000 ft (1525 m) 100 nm (115 miles; 185 km/h)
Range: 432 nm (497 miles; 800 km) with standard fuel; endurance 4 hours
Performance: maximum rate of climb at sea level 240 m (787 ft) per minute; service ceiling 4500 m

Its days as a primary trainer long over, the Aerotec T-23 nevertheless continues in Brazilian service as a hack. Bolivia and Paraguay do still use the type in its original role.

(14,765 ft); take-off run 200 m (656 ft) at maximum take-off weight; landing run 180 m (590 ft) at normal landing weight

Aerotek NGT

Although described by its manufacturer, Aerotek, a division of the South African CSIR (Council for Scientific and Industrial Research), as a composites technology demonstrator, the **NGT (New Genera-**

tion Trainer) was conceived primarily in response to an anticipated South African Air Force request for a successor to the veteran North American Harvard trainer.

Originally known as **Project Ovid**, the NGT was initiated in 1986 as an exercise in Kevlar/glass-fibre construction, and a prototype entered flight test on 29 April 1991. In the same performance category as the Pila-

tus PC-7, the NGT is claimed to be cheaper and easier to build and maintain owing to its all-composite construction. Of classic vertically-staggered tandem-seat configuration, the NGT has a one-piece, sideways-opening acrylic perspex framed canopy embodying a rollover bar. Powered by a 750-shp (559-kW) Pratt & Whitney Canada PT6A-25 turbo-prop, it is fully aerobatic. Evaluation against

the PC-7, P.Z.L. 130 Turbo Orlik, EMBRAER Tucano and Aérospatiale Omega resulted in a SAAF order for the PC-7 Mk II, which is essentially a PC-9 with a de-rated engine. Renamed the **Atlas/Denel Ace**, a second prototype became the subject of an international marketing campaign in 1993. Production aircraft will be lengthened to accept engines of up to 1,600 shp (1193 kW).

Agusta A 109

*Agusta SpA
Via Giovanni Agusta 520,
I-21017 Cascina Costa di Samarate, Italy*

Agusta, one of Italy's earliest aircraft manufacturers, became involved in helicopter construction in 1952, after acquiring a licence for the Bell Model 47, and still has licence agreements with Bell. Growing experience in helicopter design/construction led to the Agusta A 109, the company's first own-design helicopter to enter large-scale

production. The initial A 109 was powered by a single 515-kW (690-shp) Turboméca Astazou XII, but was revised in 1967 to use two 276-kW (370-shp) Allison 250-C14 turboshafts. The planned military utility A 109B was abandoned in 1969; instead, Agusta concentrated on the eight-seat civil A 109C Hirundo (swallow), the first of three proto-

types (NC7101) flying on 4 August 1970. However, it was 1976 before deliveries began of production aircraft, then redesignated A 109A. This model soon proved a commercial success, being used not only as a light passenger transport, but also as an air ambulance, for freight carriage and for search and rescue. Several air arms pro-

cured the type in small numbers for liaison and utility transport. Of four bought by Argentina, two were captured by the United Kingdom during the Falklands War and pressed into service with 7 Regiment, Army Air Corps, at Netheravon, later augmented by two more. These are used primarily to support SAS special operations with 8

Left: The Italian army adopted the A 109 to fulfil a variety of roles, including liaison, scouting and light attack.

Right: Wearing a civil-style scheme, this is one of the captured A 109s used by the British Army for support of Special Forces (SAS) operations.

Flight, flying mostly from Hereford.

From September 1981 the basic civil model was redesignated **A 109A Mk II** following modifications including uprated transmission, a new tail rotor driveshaft, a structurally redesigned tailboom and detailed cockpit improvements. In 1989, a 'wide body' **A 109C** version with uprated transmission was introduced, featuring a more roomy and comfortable cabin. One example was delivered to 31° Stormo of the **AMI** for the President of Italy.

Military development

The A 109 clearly had greater military potential, and was developed to fill a variety of military roles, including scout, aeromedical evacuation and attack. The **Aviazione Leggera dell'Esercito** (Italian army) procured 24 **A 109EOA** (Elicottero d'Osservazione Avanzata) helicopters powered by the Allison 250-C20R, delivered during 1988. These feature sliding cabin doors for rapid access, roof-mounted SFIM M334-25 daylight sight with boresighted CILAS laser rangefinder and a variety of armament options, the latter carried on two outrigger pylons either side of the main cabin. Further militarisation resulted in fixed landing gear, ECM equipment and crashworthy fuel system being fitted.

Agusta currently offers the **A 109CM** as its principal military model, similar to the A 109EOA but with a wider range of options, including different sights. The **Belgian army** is the only customer so far (designation **A 109BA**), having acquired 18 in scout configuration and 28 for the anti-armour role. The scouts feature a Saab Helios roof-mounted observation sight, while the anti-tank helicopters have a Saab/ESCO HeliTOW 2 sight and provision for eight Hughes TOW-2A anti-armour missiles. The A 109BAs are assembled in Belgium by SABCA, and feature cable-cutters.

With an eye on African and Middle East markets, more recent development has been concentrated on the multi-role 'hot-and-high' **A 109K**, with uprated transmission, a lengthened nose to house increased avionics and detail improvements. First flight of the A 109K took place in April 1983 and current orders stand at 15 **A 109K2**s for the Swiss mountain rescue service. Military versions are the **A 109KM** land-based version, with fixed landing gear and sliding cabin doors, and the similar **A 109KN** naval version, which adds shipborne capability and maritime weapons. More than 500 A 109s of all versions have been delivered to date.

WEAPON OPTIONS

Four hardpoints on lower fuselage sides allow the carriage of many different stores, including 7.62-mm or 12.7-mm machine-gun pods, 70-mm or 80-mm rocket launchers, up to eight TOW anti-tank missiles and Stinger air-to-air missiles. The A 109 can also carry light UAV (unmanned air vehicles), and in the maritime strike role can launch anti-ship missiles. Machine-guns can be pintle-mounted in the doors.

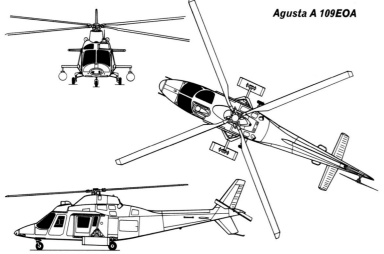

Agusta A 109EOA

Belgium has purchased 28 A 109BAs for the anti-armour role, complete with eight TOW launchers and roof-mounted sight. A further 18 aircraft are in scout configuration.

Agusta **A 129 Mangusta**

Conceived for an **Italian army** requirement in the mid-1970s as the first night/all-weather light attack helicopter to incorporate a fully computerised and redundant integrated management system for a minimum crew workload, the first of five prototype **A 129**s (MM.590/E.I.901), powered by two Piaggio-built Rolls-Royce Gem Mk 2-1004D turboshaft engines, made its initial flight on 11 September 1983. All five were flying by March 1986, and the first production A 129 of an initial batch of 15 from a requirement for 60 was scheduled for delivery to Italian army aviation (ALE) before the end of 1987. The first five **Mangusta**s were not delivered to the ALE centre at Viterbo, however, until July 1990, for operational trials and training, and although further deliveries of about 1.5 per month were reported to the 1° RALE 'Antares' Army Light Aviation Wing at the same base, only two operational squadrons appear to be planned within ALE's 49° Gruppo Squadroni 'Capricorno' in the 5° Army Aviation Region at Casarsa.

Deliveries were also delayed through funding problems for the full ALE requirement of 60 Hughes/Emerson/Saab HeliTOW systems, plus 20 more as spares. Normal armament comprises up to 2,645 lb (1200 kg) of external stores on four stub-wing pylons, including up to eight TOW-2A, HOT or six Hellfire ATMs, Stinger, Mistral or AIM-9 AAMs, 52 70-mm (2.75-in) or 81-mm (3.18-in) SNIA-BPD rockets, and 7.62-, 12.7- or 20-mm (0.3-, 0.5- or 0.787-in) gun pods, in conjunction with Honeywell IHADSS night-vision goggles, and eventually a helmet-mounted sight. Qualification trials have been completed with a Lucas chin turret mounting a 12.7-mm (0.5-in) machine-gun, although this is not currently planned for AMI use.

On 8 October 1986 preliminary agreement was reached in an MoU by the governments of Britain, Italy, the Netherlands and Spain to study an advanced version of the A 129 known as the Joint European

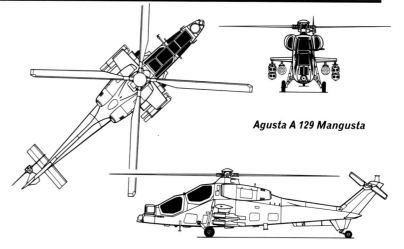

Agusta A 129 Mangusta

Helicopter **Tonal**, as a prospective European Light Attack Helicopter (LAH). The Tonal would feature more power, new high-speed rotor blades, an increase in take-off

outboard pylons, aimed with a Saab/ESCO HeliTOW sight system, with either gun pods or rocket launchers on the inboard. Gun pods can be of 7.62-mm, 12.7-mm or 20-mm calibre, while rockets are either 70-mm or 81-mm weapons. For a rocket attack mission, a 19-tube launcher is carried on the inboard pylon, and a seven-tube launcher on the outboard. Anti-armour missile options include up to six Hellfires or eight HOT. Air-to-air missiles (two) can be Stinger, Sidewinder, Mistral or Javelin. A mast-mounted sight is an option for the scout version, and anti-ship missiles could be carried.

SPECIFICATION

Agusta A 129 Mangusta
Rotor system: main rotor diameter 11.90 m (39 ft 0.5 in); tail rotor diameter 2.24 m (7 ft 4.25 in); wing span 3.20 m (10 ft 6 in); main rotor disc area 111.22 m2 (1,197.20 sq ft); tail rotor disc area 3.94 m2 (42.42 sq ft)
Fuselage and tail: length overall, rotors turning 14.29 m (46 ft 10.5 in) and fuselage 12.275 m (40 ft 3.25 in); height overall 3.35 m (11 ft 0 in) and to top of fin 2.65 m (8 ft 8.25 in); stabiliser span 3.00 m (9 ft 10 in); wheel track 2.20 m (7 ft 3.5 in); wheel base 6.955 m (22 ft 9.75 in)
Powerplant: two Rolls-Royce Gem 2 Mk 1004D each rated at 825 shp (615 kW)
Weights: empty equipped 2529 kg (5,575 lb); maximum take-off 4100 kg (9,039 lb)
Fuel and load: internal fuel 750 kg (1,653 lb); maximum ordnance 1200 kg (2,645 lb)
Speed: dash speed 170 kt (196 mph; 315 km/h); maximum level speed at sea level 140 kt (161 mph; 259 km/h); maximum cruising speed at optimum altitude 135 kt (155 mph; 250 km/h)
Range: combat radius 100 km (54 nm; 62 miles) for a 90-minute patrol; maximum endurance 3 hours
Performance: maximum rate of climb at sea level 2,150 ft (655 m) per minute; hovering ceiling 12,300 ft (3750 m) in ground effect

weight from 9,039 lb (4100 kg) to about 9,900 lb (4490 kg), a retractable landing gear contributing towards a 20 kt (23 mph; 37 km/h) level speed increase to about 160 kt (183 mph; 296 km/h), and IR-imaging TriGAT ATMs instead of Hughes TOW missiles. After protracted feasibility, cost and definition studies, rejection of Tonal full-scale development plans by the UK MoD's Equipment Policy Committee in June 1990, following UK and Dutch preference for the MDH AH-64, ended further European interest in this programme.

Tonal would have been similar in size and weight to the US Army's LHX scout/attack helicopter (now the T800-powered RAH-66 Comanche), for which competing submissions were made by Agusta of an A 129 Light Battlefield Helicopter powered by two 1,200-shp (894-kW) Allison/Garrett LHTEC T800 turboshaft engines for improved 'hot-and-high' performance. A Mangusta prototype started flying with these engines in October 1988, and was demonstrated to the United Arab Emirates shortly before the 1991 Gulf War. Agusta also proposed a 10-

12 passenger or 3,527-lb (1600-kg) payload, T800-powered, 11,000-lb (4990-kg) **A 139** utility version of the A 129, for which a collaborative programme had been discussed with Japan and Australia, and agreed in 1989 with TEA and Techint in Argentina, together with a naval attack development with anti-ship missiles. Neither of these projects, however, has so far materialised.

Scout version

At ALE's request, for possible third-batch procurement of another 30, Agusta produced plans for a scout/attack version (Elicottero da Esplorazione Scorta) of the A 129 for escort and anti-helicopter roles, fitted with a chin-mounted power turret for a 12.7-mm (0.5-in) or 15.5-mm (0.61-in) machine-gun and provision for air-to-air missiles and a mast-mounted sight. If the batch is not procured, 20 of the original aircraft will become convertible to the scout configuration. Interest has been expressed in acquiring A 129s by Iran, which in mid-1991, according to the Italian Foreign Minister, was prepared to sign a $154 million order

for an unspecified number, plus help from Italy with overhauling its fleet of Bell and Boeing Chinook helicopters.

WEAPON OPTIONS

On the stub wings are four hardpoints, each stressed for 300 kg (660 lb). Each pylon can be elevated 2° and depressed up to 10° to maximise missile envelope. Standard Italian army armament configuration consists of eight TOW 2A anti-tank missiles in four-round launchers on the

Above and right: The A 129 Mangusta is now taking its place as Italy's primary anti-armour weapon system. It has been deployed to Somalia as part of the UN peace-keeping force.

Agusta (Elicotteri-Meridionali/Boeing Vertol) CH-47C Chinook

A licence for production of the **CH-47C** in Italy was acquired from Boeing Vertol by Elicotteri Meridionali, and was subsequently continued by Agusta when EM became part of the latter group. Of a total of 95 Chinooks ordered by Iran, all but the first 22 were to have been from the Italian production line, but deliveries from the latter actually comprised 10 helicopters prior to the revolution, followed by six in 1979 and eight in 1981, all for the **Islamic Republic of Iran** army aviation. The **Italian army**

light aviation force has acquired a total of 30 CH-47Cs, including two flown on behalf of the SNPC. Italian production also provided Chinooks to **Egypt** (15), **Libya** (20) and **Morocco** (nine).

Agusta's licence for Chinook marketing covers the Mediterranean and Middle East region. Among the customers for the CH-47C was Egypt, which took 15 for army support.

Agusta (SIAI-Marchetti) S.211

D eveloped as a private-venture basic jet trainer, the **S.211** also has a light attack capability, bestowed by four underwing hardpoints for a total combined load of 660 kg (1,455 lb). First flown on 10 April 1981, it has been adopted by four air forces: **Singapore**, **Brunei**, **Haiti** and the **Philippines**, with aircraft for the last-mentioned assembled locally by PADC. Similarly, Singa-

pore Aerospace was responsible for assembly of 24 of an initial batch of 30 aircraft, which serve with Nos 131 and 132 Squadrons to provide advanced flying train-

The S.211 is one of the prime contenders for the JPATS competition, with Grumman acting as the US contractor.

Of the 18 S.211s for the Philippines, four were built in Italy and the remainder assembled locally from kits. They are split between these training aircraft and camouflaged aircraft for light attack.

ing at RAAF Pearce in Australia. The Royal Brunei armed forces, air wing, purchased four. The Haitian air corps ordered a similar number but has now disposed of its S.211s. A version of the S.211 with an improved nav/attack system has been planned, as has one with an uprated JT15D engine and increased fuel capacity.

SPECIFICATION

Agusta (SIAI-Marchetti) S.211
Wing: span 8.43 m (27 ft 8 in); aspect ratio 5.1; area 12.60 m² (135.63 sq ft)
Fuselage and tail: length 9.31 m (30 ft 6.5 in); height 3.80 m (12 ft 5.5 in); tailplane span 3.96 m (13 ft 0 in); wheel track 2.29 m (7 ft 6 in); wheel base 4.02 m (13 ft 2.25 in)
Powerplant: one Pratt & Whitney JT15D-4C rated at 2,500 lb st (11.12 kN) dry
Weights: empty equipped 1850 kg (4,078 lb); normal take-off 2750 kg (6,063 lb) as a trainer; maximum take-off 3150 kg (6,944 lb) as an attack warplane
Fuel and load: internal fuel 622 kg (1,371 lb); external fuel up to 390 kg (860 lb) in two 270-litre (71.3-US gal) drop tanks; maximum ordnance 660 kg (1,455 lb)

Speed: never-exceed speed 400 kt (460 mph; 740 km/h); maximum cruising speed at 25,000 ft (7620 m) 360 kt (414 mph; 667 km/h)
Range: ferry range 1,340 nm (1,543 miles; 2483 km) with drop tanks; combat radius 300 nm (345 miles; 556 km) on a hi-lo-hi attack mission with four rocket

launchers, or 125 nm (144 miles; 231 km) on a lo-lo-lo attack mission with four rocket launchers; endurance 3 hours 24 minutes
Performance: maximum rate of climb at sea level 4,200 ft (1280 m) per minute; service ceiling 40,000 ft (12190 m); take-off run 1,280 ft (390 m) at 2500 kg

(5,511 lb); take-off distance to 50 ft (15 m) 1,680 ft (512 m) at 2500 kg (5,511 lb); landing distance from 50 ft (15 m) 2,313 ft (705 m) at normal landing weight; landing run 1,185 ft (361 m) at normal landing weight
g limits: -3 to +6 at normal take-off weight or -2.5 to +5 at maximum take-off weight

Agusta-Bell **AB 204**

Having forged links with the Bell company through licence-production of the Bell 47 from 1954, Agusta in Italy went on to produce several hundred examples of the Bell 204B, equivalent to the US Army's UH-1B, starting in 1961. As the **AB 204**, Italian-built machines were supplied for military and civil use in the utility role, with up to 11 seats (including pilot) and provision for cargo-carrying, stretchers or slung loads. Optional powerplants were the 1,150-shp (858-kW) Lycoming T53-L-9, 1,200-shp (895.5-kW) Bristol Siddeley Gnome and 1,325-shp (989-kW) General Electric T58-GE-3 turboshaft. Pontoons could replace the skids for water/swamp operations.

Agusta also developed the **AB 204AS** for naval ASW operation, with radar, sonar, long-range tanks and provision to carry two Mk 44 torpedoes or air-to-surface missiles. About a dozen nations purchased military AB 204s; a few remain in service with 2 Staffel of Helicopter Wing III in the **Austrian army**, in the **Swedish army** medium helicopter squadron (using the local designation **Hkp 3C**), in the **Turkish gendarmerie**, and in the **Yemen Arab Republic**. The AB 204AS was purchased originally by the Italian and Spanish navies, now out of service, but a few remain in **Turkish naval aviation** service.

Austria flies eight AB 204Bs with HG III at Hörsching, these having received a refurbishment.

SPECIFICATION

Agusta-Bell AB 204AS
Rotor system: main rotor diameter 48 ft 0 in (14.63 m); tail rotor diameter 8 ft 6 in (2.59 m); main rotor disc area 1,809.56 sq ft (168.11 m²); tail rotor disc area 56.74 sq ft (5.27 m²)
Fuselage and tail: length overall, rotors turning 57 ft 0 in (17.37 m) and fuselage 41 ft 7 in (12.67 m); height overall 12 ft 7.25 in (3.84 m); stabiliser span 9 ft 4 in (2.84 m); skid track 8 ft 8 in (2.64 m)
Powerplant: one General Electric T58-GE-3 rated at

1,290 shp (962 kW)
Weights: empty equipped 6,480 lb (2939 kg); maximum take-off 9,500 lb (4309 kg)
Fuel and load: internal fuel 242 US gal (916 litres); external fuel none
Speed: maximum cruising speed at sea level 90 kt (104 mph; 167 km/h)
Range: operational radius 60 nm (69 miles; 111 km) for a 1.67-hour sonar search patrol

Agusta-Bell AB 204
generally similar to the Agusta-Bell AB 204AS except in the following particulars:
Rotor system: main rotor diameter 44 ft 0 in (13.41 m) or 48 ft 0 in (14.63 m); main rotor disc area 1,520.53 sq ft (141.26 m²) or 1,809.56 sq ft (168.11 m²)

Fuselage and tail: length overall, rotors turning 55 ft 0 in (16.76 m) or 57 ft 0 in (17.37 m)
Powerplant: one Textron Lycoming T53-L-11A rated at 1,100 shp (820 kW), or General Electric T58-GE-3 rated at 1,290 shp (962 kW), or Rolls-Royce Gnome H.1200 rated at 1,250 shp (932 kW)
Weights: empty equipped about 4,610 lb (2091 kg); normal take-off 8,510 lb (3860 kg)
Speed: maximum level speed 'clean' at sea level 104 kt (120 mph; 193 km/h); maximum cruising speed at sea level 96 kt (110 mph; 177 km/h)
Range: range 340 nm (392 miles; 630 km); endurance 4 hours
Performance: maximum rate of climb at sea level 1,400 ft (427 m) per minute; hovering ceiling 10,000 ft (3050 m) in ground effect and 4,500 ft (1370 m) out of ground effect

Agusta-Bell **AB 205**

Matching development by Bell of its Model 205 as an enlarged Model 204, Agusta put the **AB 205** into production in 1964 and went on to build several hundred for military and civil use. Like its US counterpart, the AB 205 differed from the AB 204 in having a longer cabin to accommodate up to 14 troops plus a pilot, and was powered by an uprated engine. Normally

unarmed, the AB 205 could have a pintle-mounted machine-gun in the cabin, firing through the door, or air-to-ground missiles mounted externally each side of the cabin. Also standard on the AB 205 was the 48-ft (14.63-m) main rotor, replacing the 44-ft (13.41-m) rotor used on the AB 204, although Agusta had also used the larger rotor on its AB 204AS. Later production in

Italy focused on the **AB 205A-I** version with a number of small improvements, and higher operating weights. Agusta also prototyped twin-engined versions of the type, as the **AB 205BG** with a pair of Gnome H 1200s and the **AB 205TA** with two Turboméca Astazous, but these did not achieve production.

Substantial use of the AB 205 continues, although production ended in 1988, the largest single operators being the **Turkish army**, which has some 130, in addition to about 50 used by the Turkish gendarmerie.

Turkey is one of the few users to have operated AB 205As in the gunship role, this helicopter serving elsewhere primarily as a transport, for SAR and for training. The Italian army flies more than 100 AB 205As (as **EM-2**s) and has provided detachments in support of the UN in Lebanon, Namibia and Kurdistan, and for the EC Monitor Mission in the former Yugoslavia. Both the **Greek army** and **Greek air force** are substantial users, the latter's No. 358 Mira providing flights for SAR and VIP flights at various bases. Others using AB 205As for transport/utility tasks are the **Iranian army** and **navy**, **Moroccan air force**, **Sultan of Oman air force** (No. 14 Sqn), **Royal Saudi AF** (Nos 12 and 14 Sqns), **Republic of Singapore AF** (Nos 120 and 123 Sqns), **Turkish army**, **Ugandan air force**, **Zambia**, and **Zimbabwe** (No. 7 Sqn), which operates the type as the **Cheetah**. Zimbabwe made extensive use of the Cheetah for anti-guerrilla operations. In **Spain**, the air force's Esc 783/Ala 78 has a few remaining in service for IFR training, designated **HE.10B**.

SPECIFICATION

Agusta-Bell AB 205
Rotor system: main rotor diameter 48 ft 3.5 in (14.72 m); tail rotor diameter 8 ft 6 in (2.59 m); main rotor disc area 1,831.61 sq ft (170.16 m2); tail rotor disc area 56.74 sq ft (5.27 m2)
Fuselage and tail: length overall, rotors turning 57 ft 2.75 in (17.98 m) and fuselage 41 ft 11 in (12.78 m); height overall 14 ft 8 in (4.48 m); stabiliser span 9 ft 4 in (2.84 m); skid track 8 ft 6.5 in (2.60 m)
Powerplant: one 1,400-shp (1044-kW) Textron Lycoming T53-L-13 derated to 1,250 shp (932 kW) for take-off and 1,100 shp (820 kW) for continuous running
Weights: empty 4,800 lb (2177 kg); normal take-off 8,510 lb (3860 kg); maximum take-off 9,500 lb (4309 kg)
Fuel and load: internal fuel 220 US gal (833 litres); external fuel none; maximum payload 3,000 lb (1361 kg)
Speed: maximum level speed at sea level 120 kt (138 mph; 222 km/h); maximum cruising speed at optimum altitude 110 kt (127 mph; 204 km/h)
Range: 313 nm (360 miles; 580 km); endurance 3 hours 48 minutes
Performance: maximum rate of climb at sea level 1,800 ft (549 m) per minute; service ceiling 15,000 ft (4575 m); hovering ceiling 17,000 ft (5180 m) in ground effect and 11,000 ft (3355 m) out of ground effect

The yellow band around this 358 Mira AB 205 marks it as one of the Greek air force's SAR helicopters. They have a secondary VIP role.

Agusta-Bell **AB 206 JetRanger**

Of the total of more than 7,000 JetRangers of all versions built, about 1,000 were contributed by Agusta, which began production of the **AB 206A** at the end of 1967 in continuation of its long-standing licence-agreement with Bell. The **AB 206B** was added in 1972, with uprated engine, and Agusta adopted the designations **AB 206A-1** and **B-1** for optimised military variants that incorporated features of the US Army OH-58A Kiowa, including the high-skid landing gear option, increased rotor diameter, local strengthening of the airframe, additional access doors and provision for armament.

The **Italian army** purchased 150 AB 206s, starting with 16 in a basically civil configuration for training, designated **ERI-2** by the army. The original 317-shp (236.5-kW) Allison 250-C18 engines were subsequently replaced by the more powerful 250-C20 model, helicopters with these engines continuing in service as **AB 206A-2s**. As **ERI-3s**, the remainder for the Italian army were AB 206A-Is, but these also have now been fitted with -C20 engines and features of the JetRanger III/OH-58C, taking the designation **AB 206C-1**. They serve the army's Aviazione Leggera in the Elicot-teri do Ricoynizione (reconnaissance helicopter) role, distributed in 16 of the ERI squadrons at bases throughout Italy.

Austria's Luftstreitkräfte bought 12 AB 206A-1s for training and SAR use, in 2 Staffel of Hubschraubergeschwader 1 at Tulln, and the **Royal Saudi Air Force** had 20 for training use by Nos 12 and 14 Squadrons at Taif. **Morocco** retains in service some 20 of the 25 JetRangers acquired, which included 20 of the AB 206B version to supplement five AB 205As bought in 1975. **Sweden** operates the AB 206A under the designation **Hkp 6A**. Nineteen JetRangers are on charge for liaison, observation and spotting duties, while seven Hkp 6As are used by the Swedish navy as part of the anti-submarine force with one torpedo, or three depth charges, as offensive capability. The **Iranian air force** continues to be a major operator of the JetRanger, with over 80 AB 206A/Bs used for liaison duties; further examples are used in a similar role by the navy (10) and air force (two).

Smaller quantities of the Italian-built JetRanger serve in **Greece** (two with No. 358 Mira Elikopteron for SAR and VIP flights, and over 15 with the army), **Libya** (five used by the army), **Malta** (one AB 206A for coastal duties and SAR), **Oman** (three AB 206B used by No. 14 Sqn at Seeb), the Amiri Guard air wing, **Sharjah** (three AB 206B), the **Spanish army** (four AB 206A-1, transferred from the air force, as **HR.12As** at the Centro de Ensenanza de las FAMET for training), **Tanzania** (two AB 206B), **Uganda** (four operated by the police), and **Yemen Arab Republic** (six).

SPECIFICATION

Agusta-Bell AB 206B JetRanger
Rotor system: main rotor diameter 33 ft 4 in (10.16 m); tail rotor diameter 5 ft 2 in (1.57 m); main rotor disc area 872.66 sq ft (81.07 m2); tail rotor disc area 20.97 sq ft (1.95 m2)
Fuselage and tail: length overall, rotors turning 39 ft 2 in (11.94 m) and fuselage 31 ft 2 in (9.50 m); height overall 9 ft 6.5 in (2.91 m); stabiliser span 6 ft 5.25 in (1.96 m); skid track 6 ft 3.5 in (1.92 m)
Powerplant: one 400-shp (298-kW) Allison 250-C20 derated to 317 shp (236 kW)
Weights: empty 1,504 lb (682 kg); normal take-off 3,200 lb (1452 kg) with an internal payload; maximum take-off 3,350 lb (1519 kg) with an external payload
Fuel and load: internal fuel 76 US gal (288 litres); external fuel none; maximum payload 1,200 lb (544 kg)
Speed: maximum level speed at sea level 122 kt (140 mph; 226 km/h); maximum cruising speed at optimum altitude 116 kt (133 mph; 214 km/h)
Range: 363 nm (418 miles; 673 km); endurance 4 hours
Performance: maximum rate of climb at sea level 1,360 ft (415 m) per minute; service ceiling more than 20,000 ft (6,095 m); hovering ceiling 11,325 ft (3450 m) in ground effect and 5,800 ft (1770 m) out of ground effect

Malta's small helicopter force includes this AB 206A, donated by the Libyan government.

Agusta-Bell **AB 212**

Production of the Bell 212 in Italy followed quickly upon development in the US of this twin-engined derivative of the Bell 205, undertaken in the first instance to meet USAF and Canadian Forces requirements. In essence, the Bell 212 (and AB 212) comprised the Model 205 airframe mated with the PT6T-3 Turbo Twin-Pac powerplant, comprising paired PT6 turboshafts. In its accommodation and equipment options, the **AB 212** closely resembled the AB 205A-I, with enhanced performance.

Following the precedent set with the AB 204AS, Agusta alone developed an anti-submarine warfare version of the AB 212, for which extensive modifications were made, particularly to the equipment. In the ASW role, Bendix AN/AQS-15B/F sonar is the basic sensor, whereas the ASV version has Ferranti Seaspray search radar; both are fully instrumented for all-weather operations by day and night from the decks of small ships. For SAR, a hydraulically-operated external hoist is fitted. The normal crew comprises three or four, with provision for up to seven passengers with two pilots, or four stretcher patients and an attendant.

Agusta built more than 100 **AB 212ASWs** for seven operators, of which the largest is the Italian navy, with 60. Of these, the first 12 had MEL ARI-5955 radar and the remainder MM/APS-705 matched to Aérospatiale AS12 ASMs. As the navy's standard shipboard helicopter aboard its destroyers and frigates, the AB 212ASW carries a pair of Mk 44, Mk 46 or MQ44 homing torpedoes, AS12s or Sea Killer 2 ASMs. Greece uses 14 of the ASWs, including three for ECM and the others from two 'Elli'-class frigates, while five with the Peruvian navy are used for reconnaissance. Spain's 10 AB 212ASWs, with AS12 and machine-gun armament, are used by Tercera Escuadrilla (Eslla 003) from the assault transport *Galicia* for close support duties. The Turkish navy bought 12, with Sea Spray radar and Sea Skua ASMs, to fly from 'Yavuz'-class frigates. Venezuela has six with OTO-Melara Sea Killer armament for its Esc Aero Antisubmarino 3, based at Puerto Cabello, to serve from 'Sucre'-class frigates.

A 1983 contract covered the sale of 10 AB 212ASWs to Iraq, but this was placed under embargo and discussions for their release were finally ended by the Iraqi invasion of Kuwait. Approximately 20 AB 212ASWs were ordered for the Iranian navy in early 1974 with provision for AS12 wire-guided missiles (these ASMs were used to attack Gulf shipping in 1985-86). The helicopters suffered from poor serviceability and are probably non-operational.

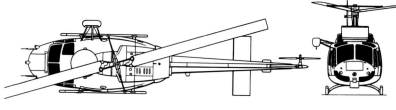

Agusta-Bell AB 212ASW

SPECIFICATION

Agusta-Bell AB 212ASW
Rotor system: main rotor diameter 48 ft 0 in (14.63 m); tail rotor diameter 8 ft 6 in (2.59 m); main rotor disc area 1,808.52 sq ft (168.10 m2); tail rotor disc area 56.74 sq ft (5.27 m2)
Fuselage and tail: length overall, rotors turning 57 ft 1in (17.40 m) and fuselage 42 ft 4.75 in (12.92 m); height overall 14 ft 10.25 in (4.53 m) and to top of rotor head 12 ft 10 in (3.91 m); stabiliser span 9 ft 4.5 in (2.86 m); skid track 8 ft 8 in (2.64 m)
Powerplant: one Pratt & Whitney Canada PT6T-6 Turbo Twin Pac rated at 1,875 shp (1398 kW)
Weights: empty equipped 3420 kg (7,540 lb); maximum take-off 5070 kg (11,177 lb) for the ASW mission with Mk 46 torpedoes, or 4973 kg (19,961 lb) for the ASV mission with AS12 missiles, or 4937 kg (10,883 lb) for the SAR mission
Fuel and load: internal fuel 1021 kg (2,250 lb) plus provision for auxiliary fuel in a cabin tank, plus provision for 356 kg (785 lb) of auxiliary fuel in one cabin and two external tanks; maximum ordnance 490 kg (1,080 lb)
Speed: never-exceed speed 130 kt (150 mph; 240 km/h); maximum level speed 'clean' at sea level

Distinguished by the large search radar above the cabin and large array of ESM antennas around the nose, the AB 212ASW is Italy's principal maritime helicopter. It can launch the Sea Killer missile in the anti-ship role.

106 kt (122 mph; 196 km/h); maximum cruising speed at optimum altitude 100 kt (115 mph; 185 km/h) with armament
Range: ferry range 360 nm (414 miles; 667 km) with auxiliary fuel; range 332 nm (382 miles; 615 km) on an ASV mission with AS12 missiles; maximum endurance 5 hours 0 minutes; typical endurance 4 hours 7 minutes on an ASV mission with AS12
Performance: maximum rate of climb at sea level 1,300 ft (396 m) per minute; hovering ceiling 10,500 ft (3200 m) in ground effect and 1,300 ft (396 m) out of ground effect

OPERATORS

Substantial numbers of AB 212s serve in military roles. In Austria, the air force has two squadrons of 12 each, serving in Hubschraubergeschwader I (Helicopter Wing) at Tulln and

Hubschraubergeschwader III at Hörsching, in the utility and transport role. The Italian air force has more than 30 divided between 208° Gruppo, 72° Stormo at Frosinone for training, and 85° Gruppo, 15° Stormo at Ciampino for SAR, and several of the 600-series squadrons that provide communications for the operational units at base level. Fifteen AB 212s in the Italian army serve (as EM-3s) in two squadrons (Nos 520 and 530) fulfilling the transport role at

Pontecagnano and Fontanarossa, respectively, with two on detachment to the Malta Helicopter Flight. For training and support missions, some 30 AB 212s obtained by Saudi Arabia serve in Nos 12 and 14 Squadrons at Taif. Other users include the Dubai police air wing (one), Lebanon (up to seven), Morocco (seven), Somalia (four, of which two for VIP), Spanish army (six), Sudan (11), the Yemen Arab Republic (six) and Zambia (two).

Agusta-Bell AB 412 Grifone

Collaborating closely with Bell, Agusta launched production of the **Model 412** in civil guise in 1981, after prototype testing in the US had begun with a first flight in August 1979. A further extrapolation of the design that had begun with the Model 204 (AB 204) in 1956, the Model 412 was, in effect, the Model 212 (AB 212) with a four-bladed rotor replacing the two-bladed rotor previously favoured for all Bell/Agusta-Bell production helicopters. Like the Model 212, the Model 412 depended for propulsion on the Pratt & Whitney Canada Turbo Twin Pac turboshafts.

Having put the civil **AB 412** into production, Agusta proceeded to evolve a military variant, which it named the **Grifone** (griffon) and flew for the first time in August 1982. With the needs of Italian military and quasi-military services particularly in view, the Grifone was designed to cope with a wide variety of roles that could include direct fire support and area suppression with one or two side-mounted cannon; scouting and reconnaissance with rocket pods and cable cutters; air defence with AAMs or other weapons; assault transport carrying up to 14 combat-equipped troops; and battlefield support. Subsequently, a maritime model was evolved for SAR, surveillance, mission monitoring, etc., for which it was provided with a 360° search radar on the roof, FLIR and TV sensors, four-axis autopilot and a special navigation system.

Special features of the Grifone include a strengthened undercarriage to absorb higher landing impacts, energy-absorbing armour-protected seats, armour for selected airframe areas, cabin floor fittings to provide for a wide variety of attachments for seats, stretchers, internal hoist or other special equipment, crash-attenuating seats for up to 14 troops in the personnel transport role, and an option for the installation of IR emission-reduction devices on the engine exhaust pipes.

In **Italy**, the AB 412 is now used by no fewer than six military and government agencies, including the national forest service and national fire service. A major user is the Carabinieri, with 20, while the SNPC (National Civilian Protection Service) agency has four or more.

Under Italian navy control, the coast guard has a growing fleet, with 24 in prospect ultimately. The largest single user in Italy is the army (Esercito Italiano), which has 30 to date – with more to come – under the designation **EM-4**, indicating the fourth type of Elicottero Multiruolo, or multi-role helicopter. Principal units flying the EM-4s are the 511 and 512 squadrons at Viterbo as part of 51° Gruppo Squadroni EM 'Leone' and one of the squadrons of 49° GSEM Capricornon at Casara.

Agusta also sold two Grifones to the **Uganda army air force**, which uses them in an armed anti-guerrilla role, and 12 to the **Air Force of Zimbabwe**, including

As one would expect, the largest operator of the AB 412 is the Italian army, which flies the type on assault transport/utility duties.

two equipped for VIP/ambulance missions. Other operators include the **Finnish coast guard** (two), the **Dubai air wing** (three), **Lesotho** (two) and the **Venezuelan army** (two).

SPECIFICATION

Agusta-Bell AB 412 Grifone
Rotor system: main rotor diameter 46 ft 0 in (14.02 m); tail rotor diameter 8 ft 6 in (2.59 m); main rotor disc area 1,661.90 sq ft (154.40 m²); tail rotor disc area 56.75 sq ft (5.27 m2)
Fuselage and tail: length overall, rotors turning 56 ft 0 in (17.07 m) and fuselage 42 ft 4.75 in (12.92 m); height overall 14 ft 2.25 in (4.32 m) with tail rotor

turning and to top of rotor head 1 ft 9.5 in (3.29 m); stabiliser span 9 ft 4.5 in (2.86 m); skid track 8 ft 6 in (2.59 m)
Powerplant: one 1,800-shp (1342-kW) Pratt & Whitney Canada PT6T-3B Turbo Twin Pac flat-rated at 1,400 shp (1044 kW) for take-off and 1,130 shp (843 kW) for continuous running
Weights: empty equipped 6,263 lb (2841 kg); maximum take-off 11,905 lb (5400 kg)
Fuel and load: internal fuel 330 US gal (1250 litres) plus provision for two 20- or 90-US gal (76- or 341-litre) auxiliary tanks; external fuel none; maximum payload 5,050 lb (2291 kg)
Speed: never-exceed speed at sea level 140 kt (161 mph; 259 km/h); maximum cruising speed at sea level 122 kt (140 mph; 226 km/h) and at 1500 m (4,920 ft) 125 kt (144 mph; 232 km/h); endurance at 4,920 ft (1500 m) 4 hours 12 minutes
Range: 434 nm (500 miles; 805 km) with standard fuel
Performance: maximum rate of climb at sea level 1,437 ft (438 m) per minute; service ceiling 17,000 ft (5180 m); hovering ceiling 4,100 ft (1250 m)

Agusta-Sikorsky AS-61

Under licence from Sikorsky, Agusta put the SH-3D Sea King into production in Italy in 1967, and began delivery in 1969 to the **Aviazione per la Marina Militare Italiana**. Production of up to 38 for the Italian navy included several variants with different equipment standards, the final batch matching US Navy SH-3H Sea Kings. They serve with the 1° and 3° Grupelicot. Also operating Agusta-built Sea Kings in the ASW role are the **Argentine navy** (four), **Brazilian navy** (nine) and **Peruvian navy** (five).

As the **AS-61A-4**, Agusta built a derivative of the SH-3D in the logistic and VIP transport role. This variant was sold to the

Italian air force (two), **Iraq** (six), **Iran** (two), **Egypt** (two), the **Royal Saudi air force** (one) and to the **Venezuelan army**, which bought four. Equivalent to the USAF's HH-3F SAR helicopter, the **AS-61R Pelican** was built by Agusta for the Italian air force, which initially acquired 20 and ordered 15 more in 1992. The AMI's AS-61Rs are being upgraded with new RWRs, chaff/flare dispensers and a dark green camouflage colour scheme. Two were deployed in 1993 to Somalia to aid the United Nations effort. Specifications for the Agusta-built S-61 variants are similar to those for their Sikorsky equivalents.

The armed AS-61R is used by the Italian air force for combat rescue duties. This is one of two aircraft deployed to Somalia.

SPECIFICATION

Agusta-Sikorsky AS-61R Pelican
Rotor system: main rotor diameter 62 ft 0 in (18.90 m); tail rotor diameter 10 ft 4 in (3.15 m); main rotor disc area 3,019.07 sq ft (280.47 m2); tail rotor disc area 83.86 sq ft (7.79 m2)
Fuselage and tail: length overall, rotors turning 73 ft 0 in (22.25 m) and fuselage 57 ft 3 in (17.45 m); height overall 18 ft 1in (5.51 m) and to top of rotor head 16 ft 1 in (4.90 m); wheel track 13 ft

4 in (4.06 m); wheel base 17 ft 1 in (5.21 m)
Powerplant: two General Electric T58-GE-100 each rated at 1,500 shp (1118 kW)

produced for the Italian navy's ASW force. This Exocet-armed example flies with Brazil. A derivative was produced without ASW equipment for the utility transport role.

Weights: empty 13,250 lb (6010 kg); normal take-off 21,240 lb (9634 kg); maximum take-off 22,050 lb (10002 kg)
Fuel and load: internal fuel 1,116 US gal (4225 litres); external fuel none; maximum payload 8,000 lb (3629 kg)

level 130 kt (150 mph; 241 km/h); economical cruising speed at sea level 75 kt (86 mph; 139 km/h) for maximum endurance
Range: range 770 nm (886 miles; 1427 km); radius 50 nm (57 miles; 92 km) on a SAR mission with a 5-hour loiter, or 240 nm (276 miles); 445 km) on a utility mission to collect 24 fully equipped troops; endurance 8 hours 0 minutes
Performance: maximum rate of climb at sea level 1,340 ft (408 m) per minute; service ceiling 11,100 ft (3385 m); hovering ceiling 7,200 ft (2195 m) in ground effect

AIDC **AT-3 Tsu Chiang**

Known to the Republic of China air force as the **Tsu Chiang,** the **AIDC AT-3** tandem two-seat basic trainer provides the initial 120-hour jet course at the service's academy at Kang Shan, Taiwan. The first military jet aircraft developed on Taiwan to achieve series production, the AT-3 was initiated in 1975 by the Aero Industry Development Centre (AIDC), and the first of two (**XAT-3**) prototypes entered flight test on 16 September 1980. Contracts were subsequently placed on behalf of the RoCAF for 60 production aircraft, the first of which was flown on 6 February 1984, with the last being delivered by early 1990.

The AT-3 is of conventional construction, the one-piece carry-through wing being a multi-spar light alloy structure with heavy-plate machined skinning and the fuselage being a light alloy semi-monocoque. The crew is accommodated in zero-zero ejection seats under individual manually-operated canopies, all fuel is carried in two rubber-impregnated nylon bladder fuselage tanks, and provision is made for an aerial target system to be carried on the fuselage centre-line and on outboard wing pylons.

In the late 1980s, Smiths Industries was appointed prime contractor for a programme to convert 20 AT-3 trainers for the close air support role, trials with two prototype conversions commencing in 1989. The basic training version was retrospectively designated **AT-3A,** and the converted close air support variant became the **AT-3B.** The conversion included installation

of a Westinghouse AN/APG-66 radar and fire control system, and the AT-3B has a manually-adjustable gunsight and a camera in the forward cockpit. A weapons bay beneath the rear cockpit can accommodate a variety of stores, including quick-change, semi-recessed machine-gun packs. A centreline pylon is stressed for a 2,000-lb (907-kg) ordnance load, two inboard wing pylons are each stressed for a 1,400-lb (635-kg) load, and the two outboard pylons are each stressed for 600 lb (272 kg). In addition, wingtip launch rails can be fitted for AAMs. The maximum external stores load of the AT-3B is 6,000 lb (2721 kg). This type equips one RoCAF unit, No. 71 Squadron of the 443rd TFW at Tainan.

An attack version designated **A-3 Lui Meng** was developed in the late 1980s, featuring similar armament to the AT-3B, but with a single-seat cockpit. Two prototypes were built, but development was probably halted in favour of the AT-3B.

SPECIFICATION

AIDC AT-3B Tsu Chiang
Wing: span 10.46 m (34 ft 3.75 in); aspect ratio 5.0; area 21.93 m² (236.06 sq ft)
Fuselage and tail: length 12.90 m (42 ft 4 in) including probe; height 4.36 m (14 ft 3.75 in); tailplane span 4.83 m (15 ft 10.25 in); wheel track 3.96 m (13 ft 0 in); wheel base 5.49 m (18 ft 0 in)
Powerplant: two Garrett TFE731-2-2L each rated at 3,500 lb st (15.57 kN) dry

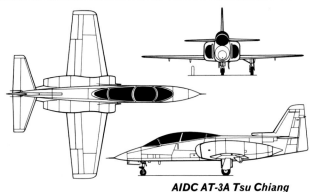

Above: The AT-3 represents a considerable achievement for the Taiwanese aerospace industry, developing its own advanced trainer. The standard AT-3A serves with the air force academy at Kangshan, also equipping the display team.

AIDC AT-3A Tsu Chiang

Weights: empty equipped 8,500 lb (3856 kg); normal take-off 11,500 lb (5216 kg); maximum take-off 17,500 lb (7938 kg)
Fuel and load: internal fuel 2,800 lb (1270 kg); external fuel up to 1,950 lb (884 kg) in two 150-US gal (568-litre) drop tanks; maximum ordnance 6,000 lb (2722 kg)
Speed: maximum level speed 'clean' at 36,000 ft (10975 m) 488 kt (462 mph; 904 km/h) and at sea level 485 kt (558 mph; 898 km/h); cruising speed at 36,000 ft (10975 m) 476 kt (548 mph; 882 km/h)
Range: 1,230 nm (1,416 miles; 2279 km) with standard fuel; endurance 3 hours 12 minutes
Performance: maximum rate of climb at sea level 10,100 ft (3078 m) per minute; service ceiling 48,000 ft (14625 m); take-off run 1,500 ft (458 m) at maximum take-off weight; take-off distance to 50 ft (15 m) 2,200 ft (671 m) at maximum take-off weight; landing distance from 50 ft (15 m) 3,100 ft (945 m) at normal landing weight; landing run 2,200 ft (671 m) at normal landing weight

Left: Camouflaged Tsu Chiangs undertake weapons training for the ROCAF. The similar AT-3B has a sophisticated weapons system for light strike duties, including internal weapons bay for the carriage of gun packs, underwing pylons and APG-66 radar. These potent aircraft serve with No. 71 Squadron.

AIDC T-CH-1 Chung Tsing

Possessing a close resemblance to the North American T-28, the **AIDC T-CH-1** tandem two-seat basic trainer was developed in the early 1970s by the AIDC at Taichung, Taiwan, to meet a Republic of China air force requirement. The first military aircraft of indigenous Taiwanese design to achieve production status, the T-CH-1 prototype was first flown on 23 November 1973. The production of 50 T-CH-1s was begun in 1976, with deliveries being concluded in 1981.

Powered by a 1,450-shp (1082-kW) Textron Lycoming T53-L-701 turboprop licence-manufactured in Taiwan, the T-CH-1 entered service at the RoCAF academy at Kang Shan in 1977, remaining standard basic training equipment until the introduction of a new flying training syllabus in which part of the spectrum covered by the T-CH-1 was taken over by the Beech T-34C and the remainder by the AT-3.

Progressively phased out of academy service from 1985, the T-CH-1 was adapted for the weapons training task, equipping No. 72 Squadron of the 1st Tactical Fighter Wing based at Tainan where some 20 examples now remain as **A-CH-1**s. Although the T-CH-1 was not fitted with armament during its service at the academy, all aircraft of this type had been built with wing hardpoints and their adaptation to A-CH-1 weapons trainer standard was thus facilitated. A few, designated **R-CH-1**, have a reconnaissance camera fitted in the lower fuselage.

SPECIFICATION

AIDC T-CH-1 Chung Tsing
Wing: span 12.19 m (40 ft 0 in); aspect ratio 6.0; area 25.18 m² (271.00 sq ft)

Fuselage and tail: length 10.26 m (33 ft 8 in); height 3.66 m (12 ft 0 in); tailplane span 5.56 m (18 ft 3 in); wheel track 3.86 m (12 ft 8 in); wheel base 2.39 m (7 ft 10 in)
Powerplant: one Textron Lycoming T53-L-701 rated at 1,450 ehp (1081 kW)
Weights: empty equipped 5,750 lb (2608 kg); normal take-off 7,500 lb (3402 kg); maximum take-off 11,150 lb (5057 kg)
Fuel and load: internal fuel 255 US gal (963 litres); external fuel none
Speed: never-exceed speed 370 kt (426 mph; 685 km/h); maximum level speed 'clean' at 15,000 ft (4570 m) 320 kt (368 mph; 592 km/h); maximum cruising speed at 15,000 ft (4570 m) 220 kt (253 mph; 407 km/h); economical cruising speed at 15,000 ft (4570 m) 170 kt (196 mph; 315 km/h)
Range: 1,085 nm (1,249 miles; 2010 km)
Performance: maximum rate of climb at sea level 3,400 ft (1036 m) per minute; service ceiling 32,000 ft (9755 m); take-off run 480 ft (146 m) at 7,600 lb (3477 kg); take-off distance to 50 ft (15 m) 800 ft (244 m) at 7,600 lb (3477 kg); landing distance from 50 ft (15 m) 1,250 ft (381 m) at normal landing weight; landing run 600 ft (183 m)

The T-CH-1 is notable as Taiwan's first indigenous military aircraft. Although replaced in the training role, a handful still fly coastal patrol work.

Wearing tactical camouflage, this is an R-CH-1, featuring a camera.

AIDC Ching-Kuo

Taiwan's ambitious programme to develop an advanced fighter to replace its fleet of F-5s and F-104s began in 1982, after the US government placed an embargo on the sale of the Northrop F-20 and any comparable fighter. The same restrictions were not placed on technical assistance, however, and US aerospace companies have collaborated closely with AIDC to develop an indigenous fighter and weapons system. The overall programme, codenamed An Hsiang (Safe Flight), has been managed through four subsidiary programmes for airframe, engines, avionics

and armament systems.

The airframe (which bears a passing resemblance to an F-16/F/A-18 hybrid) was developed with assistance from General Dynamics in the Ying Yang (Soaring Eagle) programme and has a design fatigue life of 8,000 flying hours. The prototypes and first 160 production aircraft were to be powered by two Allied-Signal/Garrett TFE-1042-70 (F125) turbofans. These are afterburning versions of the Garrett TFE73, developed under the Yun Han (Cloud Man) programme. These develop 4,820 lb st dry and 8,340 lb st with afterburning (21.44 and

37.09 kN). More powerful versions of the F125 or General Electric J101 were considered for later aircraft. Avionics have been developed by a team led by Smiths Industries under a programme codenamed Tien Lei (Sky Thunder), and the primary missile armament has been developed in the Tien Chien (Sky Sword) programme. The aircraft is equipped with a new Golden Dragon GD-53 multi-mode pulse-Doppler radar based on the GE AN/APG-67 (V) developed for the F-20 but incorporating some technology from the Westinghouse AN/APG-66 (used by the F-16A). The aircraft also has a Honeywell H423 inertial navigation system, and Bendix/King multi-function and head-up displays.

Of conventional all-metal construction

(although a progressively increasing proportion of composites will be introduced on production aircraft), the **Ching-Kuo** is of conventional configuration, albeit with wing/fuselage blending. Elliptical intakes are located below long LERXes for good high-Alpha performance. The pilot sits on a Martin-Baker Mk 12 ejection seat, under a blown canopy, and behind a single-piece windscreen. The pressurised cockpit is fitted with a sidestick controller, à la F-16, a wide-angle HUD, and three multi-function look-down displays. The aircraft has an internal 20-mm M61A1 cannon beneath the port LERX, and has two underfuselage and two underwing hardpoints, in addition to its wingtip missile launch rails. These will carry a variety of indigenous missiles, including the IR-homing Sky Sword I, the longer-range SARH Sky Sword II (two in tandem recesses under the fuselage only) or three Hsiung Feng II (Male Bee II) anti-ship missiles.

First flight

The first of three single-seat prototypes, 77-8001, made its maiden flight on 28 May 1989, but was seriously damaged in a take-off accident on 29 October. The second prototype (78-8002) flew on 27 September 1989 but was lost in a fatal crash caused by vibration during transonic acceleration on 12 July 1990. The third prototype (78-8003), with modified engine intakes, made its maiden flight on 10 January 1990, and was followed by the fourth prototype, the first two-seater (79-8004), on 10 July 1990.

There was originally a requirement for 256 aircraft, some of which would be two-

The fourth prototype Ching-Kuo was the first of the two-seaters, and was finished in the tactical camouflage adopted by operational aircraft. General Dynamics assisted with the design.

SKY SWORD II MISSILE
Although not carried on this aircraft, the Sky Sword II is a weapon developed for the Ching-Kuo. Carried in a tandem pair in recessed bays beneath the fuselage, the Sky Sword II is a semi-active radar homing missile similar to the AIM-7 Sparrow. However, the wing and fin planform is considerably different, with both sets of surfaces being heavily cropped, perhaps to fit the confines of the Ching-Kuo airframe. As with the Sky Sword I, the present status is unclear, as Taiwan has ordered both MICA and AIM-7 missiles from France and the United States.

SKY SWORD I MISSILE
Resembling an AIM-9 Sidewinder, the Tien Chien (Sky Sword) I missile is a closely-related infra-red-guided air-to-air missile carried on the wingtip launch rails of the Ching-Kuo, or from outboard wing pylons. Few details are available as to the differences between it and the AIM-9, and it is likely that the missile has all-aspect capability and active laser fusing. The first test firing was in April 1986 from an F-5, with production starting in 1989. The status of the programme is unclear, as Taiwan has ordered both Magic 2 and AIM-9s as part of its Mirage 2000-5 and F-16 buys.

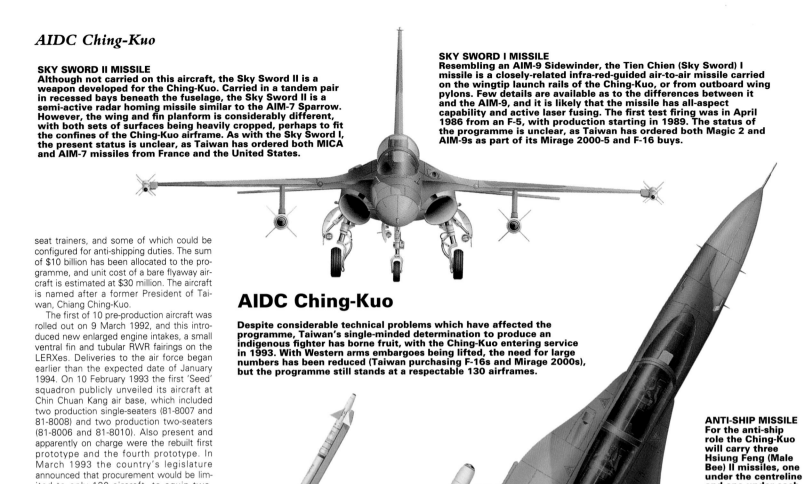

seat trainers, and some of which could be configured for anti-shipping duties. The sum of $10 billion has been allocated to the programme, and unit cost of a bare flyaway aircraft is estimated at $30 million. The aircraft is named after a former President of Taiwan, Chiang Ching-Kuo.

The first of 10 pre-production aircraft was rolled out on 9 March 1992, and this introduced new enlarged engine intakes, a small ventral fin and tubular RWR fairings on the LERXes. Deliveries to the air force began earlier than the expected date of January 1994. On 10 February 1993 the first 'Seed' squadron publicly unveiled its aircraft at Chin Chuan Kang air base, which included two production single-seaters (81-8007 and 81-8008) and two production two-seaters (81-8006 and 81-8010). Also present and apparently on charge were the rebuilt first prototype and the fourth prototype. In March 1993 the country's legislature announced that procurement would be limited to only 130 aircraft, to equip two, instead of the planned four, wings.

AIDC Ching-Kuo

Despite considerable technical problems which have affected the programme, Taiwan's single-minded determination to produce an indigenous fighter has borne fruit, with the Ching-Kuo entering service in 1993. With Western arms embargoes being lifted, the need for large numbers has been reduced (Taiwan purchasing F-16s and Mirage 2000s), but the programme still stands at a respectable 130 airframes.

WEAPON OPTIONS

In addition to the internal M61A1 20-mm Vulcan cannon, weapons identified with the Ching-Kuo include the GBU-12 227-kg (500-lb LGB), the CBU-87 Rockeye, the AGM-65B TV Maverick ASM, the AIM-9P Sidewinder IR-homing AAM and the indigenous Sky Sword I and Sky Sword II AAMs. The Sky Sword I closely resembles an AIM-9B or AIM-9D (though with wider span tailfins), while the Sky Sword II is similar to the AIM-7 Sparrow in appearance. For the anti-shipping role, the Ching-Kuo will be armed with three indigenous Hsiung Feng II sea-skimming anti-ship missiles. One of the two-seaters has been noted with an extra pair of underwing pylons accommodating a pair of F-5E-style 1040-litre (275-US gal) external fuel tanks.

SPECIFICATION

AIDC Ching-Kuo
Wing: (estimated) span over wingtip missile rails 8.53 m (28 ft 0 in)
Fuselage and tail: (estimated) length including probe 14.48 m (47 ft 6 in)
Powerplant: two ITEC (Garrett/AIDC) TFE1042-70 (F125) each rated at 6,025 lb st (26.80 kN) dry and 9,460 lb st (42.08 kN) with afterburning
Weights: normal take-off 9072 kg (20,000 lb)
Fuel and load: (estimated) internal fuel 1950 kg (4,300 lb)
Speed: maximum level speed 'clean' at 36,000 ft (10975 m) more than 688 kt (792 mph; 1275 km/h)
Performance: maximum rate of climb at sea level 50,000 ft (15240 m) per minute; service ceiling 55,000 ft (16760 m)
***g* limits:** +6.5

ANTI-SHIP MISSILE
For the anti-ship role the Ching-Kuo will carry three Hsiung Feng (Male Bee) II missiles, one under the centreline and one under each inboard wing pylon. The missile is reported to have been developed from the Israeli Gabriel, although the AGM-84 Harpoon may be the basis. It is similar in configuration to the AGM-84, with a small turbofan engine providing a range in the order of 50 miles (80 km).

SYSTEMS
Internal fuel capacity is 2517 litres (665 US gal). The undercarriage is by Menasco, and the ECS by AiResearch. Honeywell supplied the INS, and Bendix/King the two head-down and one head-up displays.

EJECTION SEAT
The Ching-Kuo crew sit on Martin-Baker Mk 12 zero-zero ejection seats.

ATTACK WEAPONRY
This two-seater is shown carrying the AGM-65 Maverick, used for precision attack of hardened targets. The main use of this missile is in the anti-armour role. A wide variety of bombs and cluster bombs can be carried.

CONTROLS
The Lear Astronics fly-by-wire system controls large all-moving tailerons, rudder and near full-span flaperons. Leading-edge slats are also tied to the system for maximum combat agility.

RADAR
The radar is a modified APG-67 known as the Golden Dragon 53. It has a range of 150 km (93 miles) and can operate in both air and sea search modes.

POWERPLANT
The Ching-Kuo features two ITEC (Garrett/AIDC) TFE1042-70 turbofans, equipped with full-authority digital controls. Plans for an improved performance engine were cancelled.

Airbus Industrie A310

Airbus Industrie
1 Rond Point Maurice Bellonte
F-31707 Blagnac Cedex, France

The **Airbus A310** short/medium-haul commercial transport was flown as a prototype for the first time on 3 April 1982. The first military order was placed early in 1990, comprising one aircraft for delivery to the **Royal Thai air force** in September 1991 for governmental transportation tasks. In the following year, the German **Luft-waffe** began to take delivery of three A310s originally flown by the defunct East German Interflug airline. Fitted with military communications equipment, these supplemented Boeing 707-320Cs operated by the special air missions squadron (FBS) at Köln/Bonn for VIP transportation and other support tasks. Similarly, the **Canadian Forces** adopted the A310 as a replacement for its five elderly Boeing 707s (CC-137s) used by No. 437 Sqn, with the purchase of three used A310s (designated **CC-150 Polaris**) from Canadian Airlines International in 1992/93 and an option on two more for 1993/94. One of the CC-150s was fitted with VIP interior, and was sold as part of a cost-cutting drive. The others may be subject to a tanker conversion. In 1992, France's **Armée de l'Air** became a customer for two used A310s, to replace DC-8s operated by ET 3/60 'Esterel'.

The Thais were the first to put the A310 into military colours, one being employed on VIP transport. France and Canada have followed since.

SPECIFICATION

Wing: span 144 ft 0 in (43.89 m); aspect ratio 8.8; area 2,357.30 sq ft (218.99 m²)
Fuselage and tail: length 153 ft 1 in (46.66 m); height 51 ft 10 in (15.80 m); tailplane span 53 ft 4.25 in (16.26 m); wheel track 31 ft 6 in (9.60 m); wheel base 49 ft 10.75 in (15.21 m)
Powerplant: two General Electric CF6-80C2A2 each rated at 53,500 lb (237.98 kN) dry thrust or Pratt & Whitney PW4152 each rated at 52,000 lb (231.31 kN) dry thrust

Weights: manufacturer's empty 158,380 lb (71840 kg) with CF6 engines or 158,250 lb (71781 kg) with PW4152 engines; operating empty 176,859 lb (80222 kg) with CF6 engines or 176,753 lb (80174 kg) with PW4152 engines; maximum take-off 337,305 lb (153000 kg) with options at 346,125 lb (157000 kg) and 361,560 lb (164,000 kg)
Fuel and load: internal fuel 108,112 lb (49039 lb); external fuel none; maximum payload 74,472 lb (33780 kg) with CF6 engines or 74,582 lb (33,830 kg) with PW4152 engines
Speed: maximum cruising speed between 31,000 and 41,000 ft (9450 and 12500 m) Mach 0.8
Range: range with 218 passengers 4,420 nm (5,090 miles; 8191 km) with CF6 engines or 4,400 nm (5,065 miles; 8155 km) with PW4152 engines
Performance: take-off field length 7,900 ft (2408 m) at maximum take-off weight with CF6 engines or 7,300 ft (2225 m) at maximum take-off weight with PW4152 engines; landing field length 4,850 ft (1479 m) at maximum landing weight with CF6 engines or 5,100 ft (1555 m) at maximum take-off weight with PW4152 engines

---

Airtech (CASA/IPTN) CN.235

Following on from the success of the Model 212 Aviocar, CASA joined forces with IPTN (Industri Pesawat Terbang Nusantara) on a 50/50 basis to begin development of a larger, more efficient transport for both civil and military use, under the joint company Airtech. Development work began on the **CN.235** in 1980, and prototypes were simultaneously constructed in both countries. Spain's ECT-100 flew first on 11 November 1983, followed by PK-XNC in Indonesia on 30 December. IPTN delivered its first aircraft on 15 December 1986, and CASA followed on 4 February 1987. A licence-assembly agreement has been reached with TAI of Turkey, which may lead to full Turkish production.

The standard military transport **CN.235M** is tailored to short-range cargo/trooping missions, exhibiting the accepted layout of high-set wing, circular-section pressurised fuselage, upswept rear fuselage with rear loading ramp, tall fin and main undercarriage in sponsons on the side of the fuselage. The wing incorporates powerful high-lift devices for STOL operation, and the undercarriage is designed for operation from semi-prepared surfaces. Power initially came from the General Electric CT7-7A turboprops fitted to the first 30 **CN.235 Series 10** aircraft, but is now provided by the CT7-9C engine in the current **Series 100** production machines; each powerplant being rated at 1,750 shp (1305 kW) for take-off with an emergency reserve.

Typically a crew consists of pilot, co-pilot and a loadmaster, and standard accommo-

Morocco operates six CN.235Ms on general transport duties, and a single example on VIP work. The type has achieved excellent military sales.

dation is provided for 48 troops or 46 paratroops. A roller cargo system can be installed and other options include electronic warfare equipment, 24 litters and four attendants in the medevac role or maritime patrol. For the latter role Airtech has developed the **CN.235MPA Persuader**, which features a lengthened nose housing search radar (APS-504), forward-looking infra-red and electronic surveillance equipment. Six underwing hardpoints are provided for the carriage of torpedoes or Exocet anti-ship missiles.

SPECIFICATION

Airtech (CASA/IPTN) CN.235M Series 100
Wing: span 25.81 m (84 ft 8 in); aspect ratio 11.3; area 59.10 m² (636.17 sq ft)
Fuselage and tail: length 21.353 m (70 ft 0.75 in); height 8.177 m (26 ft 10 in); tailplane span 11.00 m (36 ft 1 in); wheel track 3.90 m (12 ft 9.5 in); wheel base 6.919 m (22 ft 8.5 in)
Powerplant: two General Electric CT7-9C each flat-rated at 1,750 shp (1305 kW) without automatic power reserve or 1,870 shp (1394.5 kW) with automatic power reserve
Weights: operating empty 8800 kg (19,400 lb); maximum take-off 16500 kg (36,376 lb)
Fuel and load: internal fuel 4230 kg (9,325 lb); external fuel none; maximum payload 5000 kg

(11,023 lb) or maximum ordnance 3500 kg (7,716 lb)
Speed: maximum level speed 'clean' at sea level 240 kt (276 mph; 445 km/h); maximum cruising speed at 15,000 ft (4570 m) 248 kt (286 mph; 460 km/h)
Range: range 2,350 nm (2,706 miles; 4355 km) with a 3600-kg (7,936-lb) payload or 810 nm (932 miles; 1501 km) with maximum payload
Performance: maximum rate of climb at sea level 1,900 ft (579 m) per minute; service ceiling 26,600 ft (8110 m); take-off distance to 50 ft (15 m) 4,235 ft (1290 m) at maximum take-off weight; landing distance from 50 ft (15 m) 2,530 ft (772 m) at normal landing weight; landing run 1,306 ft (398 m) at normal landing weight

OPERATORS

Military sales have been brisk, to Botswana (two), Brunei (three MPAs), Chile (three for use on wheel/ski undercarriage), Ecuador (two), France (eight), Gabon (one), Indonesia (32 and six MPAs), Ireland (one M and two MPAs), Malaysia (32), Morocco (six transports and one VIP), Panama (one), Papua New Guinea (two), Saudi Arabia (two transports and two VIP), South Korea (12) Spain (18 transports, two VIP and six MPAs), Turkey (52, including 50 assembled by TAI) and United Arab Emirates (seven).

The CN.235 is useful for both passenger and cargo transport. This example wears French colours and the markings of EET 6/330, based at Mont-de-Marsan.

Alenia (Aeritalia/Lockheed) F-104ASA

Alenia
Via E. Petrolini 2
I-00197 Roma, Italy

Following the completion in March 1979 of the 246th and last of the GE J79-J1Q-engined **Lockheed F-104S Starfighter** interceptors developed and built under licence by Aeritalia, including 40 for the **Turkish air force**, an upgrade programme was launched in 1981 for 153 of 206 originally delivered to **Italy**'s AMI. These then equipped some six air defence squadrons (9°, 10°, 12°, 18°, 21°, 23° Gruppi), plus the OCU (20° Gruppo), and

one strike squadron (102° Gruppo). With Aeritalia (amalgamated with Selenia in late 1990 as the Alenia group) as prime contractor, the AMI's ASA (Aggiornamento Sistema d'Arma, or armament system modernisation) programme was planned to upgrade the low-level interception capabilities of the F-104S, as well as improving its air-to-ground performance.

Main changes, costing in all some $528 million, included replacement of the original

NASARR R21G/H fire-control radar by the FIAR R21G/M1 Setter non-coherent Doppler version with automatic frequency changing and improved detection and illumination capability over ranges of up to about 22 nm (25 miles; 40 km). The addition of a moving target indicator to the original R21G, in conjunction with a new processor and the introduction of the Selenia Aspide Mk 1A semi-active monopulse radar-guided development of its original AIM-7E Sparrow AAM, con-

fers look-down/shoot-down capability over a maximum range of around 19 nm (22 miles; 35 km).

Unlike the F-104S, the associated onboard guidance equipment for the Aspide was miniaturised so that the gun bay of the **F-104ASA** can again fulfil its function of housing the 20-mm T171E3 six-barrelled Vulcan rotary cannon of the F-104G. For ground-attack roles, the F-104ASA is equipped with AN/ALQ-70 or AN/ALQ-73

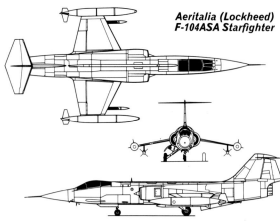

**Aeritalia (Lockheed)
F-104ASA Starfighter**

*Left: An operational F-104ASA in the markings of 36°
Stormo. The ASA has an internal cannon.*

ECM systems. New avionics also included more generator power, a four-digit NATO IFF, a new altitude reporting system and an improved weapons computer, plus provision for the all-aspect AIM-9L Sidewinder AAM in place of the original rear-attack only AIM-9B. The F-104ASA also features an

A development F-104ASA carries a Selenia Aspide air-to-air missile for a test launch. The Aspide is an Italian development of the AIM-7E Sparrow.

improved computer for the automatic low-speed pitch control system, which limits excessive angles of attack.

ASA enters service

After flight testing, which started in July 1983, the first 'production' F-104ASA was accepted on 19 November 1986 at Turin-Caselle by Cdte Canetto from the AMI's Reparto Sperimentale Volo (RSV, flight test centre) at Pratica di Mare. The 100th example had been completed by early 1990 and the 147th and last was redelivered in late

1991. Under economies planned for the AMI at that time as part of defence budget cuts following the collapse of Communism in the Eastern Bloc were disbandment of two of the remaining seven F-104ASA squadrons, leaving five in operation, plus the OCU, with 130 Starfighters on establishment (plus reserves), pending their eventual replacement by a similar number of European Fighter Aircraft early in the next century. Studies were made for further F-104S/ASA improvements through a proposed Operational Capacity Extension (ECO) programme, including a completely new radar, a head-up display and an air-refuelling probe, to extend Italian Starfighter service lives beyond the originally-planned 2005, in the event of delays to the EFA programme. The most basic service life extension, put forward by the Italian Defence Minister in late 1992, would necessitate fitting a new INS, a partial rewiring and the provision of new wings to 99 of the surviving 143 F-104ASAs to allow their continued operation until their planned replacement, for an overall cost, including operation, of some \$135 million. Considerable political opposition has been expressed to these proposals, although \$40 million was included in the 1993 defence budget for further F-104ASA upgrades. Such plans may now have been abandoned. RAF Tornados have been leased as interim air defence aircraft pending delivery of the Eurofighter EFA 2000,

SPECIFICATION

Alenia (Aeritalia) F-104ASA

Wing: span 21 ft 11 in (6.68 m) without tip tanks; aspect ratio 2.45; area 196.10 sq ft (18.22 m2)
Fuselage and tail: length 54 ft 9 in (16.69 m); height 13 ft 6 in (4.11 m); tailplane span 11 ft 11 in (3.63 m); wheel track 9 ft 8 in (2.74 m); wheel base 15 ft 0.5 in (4.59 m)
Powerplant: one General Electric J79-GE-19 rated at 11,870 lb st (52.80 kN) dry and 17.900 lb st (79.62 kN) with afterburning
Weights: empty 6760 kg (14,903 lb); normal take-off 9840 kg (21,693 lb); maximum take-off 14060 kg (30,996 lb)
Fuel and load: internal fuel 3392 litres (896 US gal); external fuel up to 2770 litres (732 US gal) in two 740-litre (195-US gal) drop tanks and two 645-litre (170-US gal) tip tanks; maximum ordnance 3400 kg (7,495 lb)
Speed: never-exceed and maximum level speed 'clean' at 36,000 ft (10975 m) 1,259 kt (1,450 mph; 2333 km/h), and at sea level 790 kt (910 mph; 1464 km/h); maximum cruising speed at 36,000 ft (10975 m) 530 kt (610 mph; 981 km/h)
Range: ferry range 2920 km (1,576 nm; 1,814 miles) with drop tanks; combat radius 1247 km (673 nm; 775 miles) with maximum fuel
Performance: maximum rate of climb at sea level 55,000 ft (16764 m) per minute; climb to 35,000 ft (10670 m) in 1 minute 20 seconds; service ceiling 58,000 ft (17680 m); take-off run 2,700 ft (823 m) at normal take-off weight with two AIM-7 Sparrow AAMs; landing run 2,500 ft (762 m)

Alenia (Aeritalia/Fiat) G222

The **Aeritalia Fiat G222** proposal was drawn up to meet the outlines of NATO's Basic Military Requirement Four (NBMR4) of 1962, which sought to develop a practical V/STOL transport for service with NATO air forces. Although a number of

advanced proposals came from several manufacturers, none was deemed sufficiently practical or attractive to gain even a prototype contract. However, the Aeronautica Militare Italiana believed that Fiat's proposal could prove a useful transport, if

finalised as a more conventional design in terms of powerplant and aerodynamics, and in 1968 signed a contract for two **G222TCM** prototypes and a static test airframe. Their manufacture was delayed by two successive total redesigns, and it was not until 18 July 1970 that the first prototype (MM582) was flown, the second (MM583) following on 22 July 1971. These began operational evaluation with the AMI on 21 December 1971, highly successful tests resulting in a contract for 44 production G222s, the first of them flown on 23 December 1975.

Italian production

From the outset other major Italian manufacturers were involved in the programme,

with Aermacchi responsible for the outer wings, CIRSEA for the landing gear, Piaggio for the wing centre-section, SIAI-Marchetti for the tail unit, and Aeritalia for the fuselage and for final assembly and testing. The G222 continues in production and has been built in several versions. These include the G222 standard military transport which serves with the armed forces of **Argentina**, **Dubai**, **Italy**, **Nigeria**, **Somalia** and **Venezuela**; the **G222R/M** (Radio Misure) for radio/radar calibration; the **G222SAA** (Sistema Aeronautico Antincendio) fire-fighter with equipment to disperse water or fire retardants; the **G222T** (Rolls-Royce Tyne-powered version) for the **Libyan Arab air force** which designates it **G222L**; and the electronic warfare

Chrysler/Alenia C-27A Spartan

A few of the AMI's G222s are assigned to special duties. This is a G222RM of the 8° Gruppo at Pratica di Mare, equipped for radio and navigation aid calibration. Other versions fly firefighting (G222SAA) and Elint missions.

G222VS (Versione Speciale). **Thailand** has six transports on order.

In August 1990, the **USAF** selected the Alenia (which took over Aeritalia) G222 as its RRITA (Rapid-Response Intra-Theater Airlifter) following extensive evaluation. The aircraft, designated **C-27A Spartan**, are procured from Alenia by Chrysler, the prime US contractor, and modified for USAF operations by installation of mission-specific communications, navigations and mission systems. An initial order for five aircraft led to a fleet of 10 C-27As, stationed at Howard AFB, Panama, to support US Southern Command operations in Latin America. Total deliveries of all versions, including the C-27A, stands at 100 in early 1994.

SPECIFICATION

Alenia (Aeritalia/Fiat) G222
Wing: span 28.70 m (94 ft 2 in); aspect ratio 10.05; area 82.00 m² (882.67 sq ft)
Fuselage and tail: length 22.70 m (74 ft 5.5 in); height 9.80 m (32 ft 1.75 in); tailplane span 12.40 m (40 ft 8.25 in); wheel track 3.668 m (12 ft 0.5 in); wheel base 6.23 m (20 ft 5.25 in)
Powerplant: two Fiat-built General Electric T64-GE-P4D each flat-rated at 3,400 shp (2535 kW)
Weights: empty equipped 15400 kg (33,951 lb); operating empty 15700 kg (34,612 lb); maximum take-off 28000 kg (61,728 lb)
Fuel and load: internal fuel 9400 kg (20,723 lb); external fuel none; maximum payload 9000 kg (19,841 lb)
Speed: maximum level speed 'clean' at 4575 m (15,010 ft) 292 kt (336 mph; 540 km/h); economical cruising speed at 6000 m (19,685 ft) 237 kt (273 mph; 439 km/h)

Range: ferry range 2,500 nm (2,879 miles; 4633 km); range 740 nm (852 miles; 1371 km) with maximum payload or 1,350 nm (1,555 miles; 2502 km) with 36 litters and four attendants
Performance: maximum rate of climb at sea level 520 m (1,706 ft) per minute; climb to 4500 m

(14,765 ft) in 8 minutes 35 seconds; service ceiling 7620 m (25,000 ft); take-off run 662 m (2,172 ft) at maximum take-off weight; take-off distance to 15 m (50 ft) 1000 m (3,281 ft) at maximum take-off weight; landing distance from 15 m (50 ft) 775 m (2,543 ft) at maximum landing weight; landing run 545 m (1,788 ft)

The Chrysler C-27 is a G222 fitted out in the US for service with the 24th Wing. It provides theatre transport for Southern Command, being able to land at most Central and South American airfields.

American Aircraft Corporation **Penetrator**

Late in 1991, AAC unveiled a prototype of its modified Bell UH-1D Iroquois, adapted for the assault and transport roles and named **Penetrator**. This prototype retains the 1,150-shp (858-kW) Avco Lycoming T53-L-13 turboshaft, transmission and rotor system of the UH-1. The Penetrator has a new all-composite fuselage with tandem

seating for the pilot (front) and gunner, the latter controlling a 20-mm cannon, two machine-guns, two forward-firing 37-mm rocket pods and up to eight missiles. Only the missiles and some rocket launchers are carried externally on stub wings, other weaponry being mounted internally. Two pintle-mounted machine-guns are carried in

the cabin, which accommodates up to 10 troops, and any production-model Penetrators will have retractable landing gear in place of the prototype's UH-1-style skids.

The Penetrator is based on the proven power/dynamic system of the Bell UH-1.

AMX International **AMX**

*AMX International
Alenia/Aermacchi/EMBRAER*

AMX development, started formally in April 1978 when Aeritalia and Aermacchi combined their resources to meet AMI requirements for an advanced multi-purpose strike/reconnaissance aircraft, received extra impetus in 1980 when Brazil joined the programme. A common specification, including good short-field performance, high subsonic operating speeds and advanced nav/attack systems, allowed initial agreement in July 1981 for the joint procurement of 266 aircraft. These comprised 79 AMXs for Brazil and 187 for Italy, plus six prototypes, from Aeritalia, Aermacchi and EMBRAER production lines (with relative

programme shares of 46.5, 23.8 and 29.7 per cent), as well as licensed-construction of the AMX's 11,030-lb (49.07-kN) thrust Rolls-Royce Spey Mk 807 turbofan. An extra development AMX (A11) later flew (from

The first Italian aircraft served with the RSV, the AMI's test and trials unit at Pratica di Mare.

April 1991) with a Spey 807A uprated to 13,500 lb (60.05 kN) for take-off, while Rolls-Royce has offered the new RB.168-821 Spey with a demonstrated 30 per cent bench-test thrust increase over the Mk 807.

AMX-A01 (MMX594) first flew at Aeritalia's Turin-Caselle factory flight-test centre in May 1984, the first of two Brazil-assembled prototypes (A04/YA-1-4200 and A06) following in October 1985 at São dos Cam-

AMX International AMX

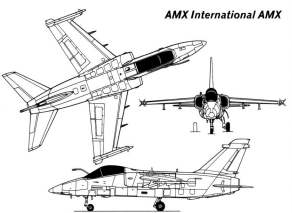

The AMX-T has few airframe changes compared to the single-seater. The second cockpit occupies the space vacated by the forward fuel tank, and combat capability remains the same, albeit with reduced range. The AMX-T is proposed as the basis for an electronic warfare/reconnaissance variant armed with anti-radiation missiles.

pos. Although the first Italian prototype crashed fatally on only its fifth take-off after an engine problem on 1 June 1984, development was concluded by four more prototypes in Italy and in Brazil.

Design features include HOTAS, Litton Italia INS, head-up and head-down digital data displays, digital databus, active and passive ECM, and provision for air refuelling. By mid-1989, programme totals had increased to 317 aircraft, with the addition of 51 two-seat **AMX-T**s to replace the Fiat G91Ts of the AMI's 201°/204° Gruppi of the advanced training wing at Amendola within the 60ª Brigata Aerea (redesignated the 32° Stormo at the same base in September 1992). Retaining the same dimensions and full combat capabilities as the single-seat AMX, the trainer version replaces a fuel bay behind the original cockpit with a second Martin-Baker Mk 10L ejection seat, with some reduction in range. The first of three AMX-T prototypes (MM55024) initially flew in Italy on 14 March 1990, although funding problems delayed first flight of the Brazilian two-seat prototype (TA-1 5650) until 14 August 1991. Radar-equipped versions of the AMX-T are also under development in Brazil and Italy for enhanced all-weather, ECR and maritime strike roles, with SMA/Tecnasa's SCP-01 Scipio installation favoured for all AMXs in the former country and FIAR's Grifo-F possibly replacing some of AMX's standard Elta/FIAR range-only radar in the latter. Trials have been completed in Italy for this version with Aérospatiale's AM39 Exocet radar-guided anti-ship missile by Aermacchi's Grifo-equipped AMX-T prototype. Other radars, notably the Westinghouse APG-66, are also envisaged for the AMX.

In the reconnaissance role the AMX can either carry external photo or IR pods, or can be equipped with any one of three pallets developed by Aeroelectronica for internal carriage in the forward fuselage.

By April 1992, Alenia, Aermacchi and EMBRAER had delivered 60 of 136 AMXs then funded by the AMI to equip five attack/reconnaissance squadrons, plus 37 of the required 51 AMX-Ts and 13 of 56 AMXs ordered by the FAB. First operational squadron to receive the AMX, in 1989, was the AMI's 103° Gruppo of the 51° Stormo CB (fighter-bomber wing) at Treviso/Istrana in north-eastern Italy. They were followed by the 132° Gruppo CR/3° Stormo (reconnaissance squadron) at Villafranca, and the 14° Gruppo/2° Stormo, also at Istrana. If funding permits, other AMI units to re-equip with 187 AMXs will comprise 102° Gruppo/5° Stormo at Rimini, 28° Gruppo/3° Stormo at Villafranca, 101° Gruppo/8°

Stormo at Cervia, and 13° Gruppo/32° Stormo at Brindisi.

In Brazil, the 1st Sqn of the 16th Aviation Group (1°/16° GAv) has been operating more than a dozen AMX (**A-1**) attack air-

craft from Santa Cruz, Rio de Janeiro since the first operational example was delivered on 17 October 1989. Total Brazilian AMX procurement currently remains at 79, including 14 two-seat AMX-T (**TA-1**) operational trainers, to equip four or five attack squadrons. With each of the three integrated production lines now producing about one aircraft per month, AMX International is actively pursuing possible export sales. The planned purchase in late 1990 by the Royal Thai air force, as the first overseas customer, of 26 AMXs and 12 AMX-Ts costing some $590 million, plus over $150 million for spares and technical support, was cancelled in February 1992 through funding problems for the 10-year budget commitment involved.

AMX International AMX

The '51' nosecode and cat-and-mouse fin badge identify this aircraft as one of those delivered to the first operational AMX unit, the 103° Gruppo, 51° Stormo at Istrana. This squadron was previously equipped with the Aeritalia G91R and had been based at Treviso. The aircraft wears an overall grey colour scheme – unusual for a dedicated ground attack aircraft – and new-style roundels with reduced-conspicuity white ring. The aircraft is depicted carrying four low-drag general-purpose bombs on the inboard pylons and two ballute-retarded bombs on the outboard pylons. The centreline mounts a reconnaissance pod, and wingtip AIM-9L Sidewinders complete the fit.

UNDERCARRIAGE
The hydraulically retracted undercarriage is designed by Messier-Hispano-Bugatti, but is built in Italy by ERAM (main gear) and Magnaghi (nose gear). The mainwheels rotate through 90° during the retraction cycle to lie flat in the undersides of the air intakes.

The AMX is designated A-1 by the Brazilian air force. This aircraft, the first Brazilian production TA-1 two-seater, wears the 'SC' code for Santa Cruz air base and serves with 1° Esquadrão of 16° Grupo de Aviação.

WORK-SHARE

The AMX originated from an AMI requirement for a G91/F-104G replacement issued in 1977. Aermacchi was already working with EMBRAER on the similar A-X requirement to replace Brazil's AT-26 Xavantes, and began working with Aeritalia (now Alenia) on the Italian air force requirement. Alenia is the programme leader, with 46.7 per cent of the share, and responsible for fuselage centre section, radome, fin, rudder, elevators, spoilers and flaps. Aermacchi has 23.6 per cent of the programme, and builds the forward fuselage, canopy and tailcone, and integrates the gun and avionics. EMBRAER accounts for the remaining 29.7 per cent, and constructs air intakes, wing, slats, pylons, external fuel tanks and reconnaissance pallets. The Brazilian factory is also responsible for the rear cockpit and systems integration on the AMX-T. The single-source component manufacture leads to assembly lines in both Italy and Brazil to satisfy local demands.

POWERPLANT

The Rolls-Royce Spey Mk 807 is built under licence by a consortium consisting of Fiat, Piaggio and Alfa Romeo Avia, in association with the Brazilian Companhia Eletro-Mecanica (CELMA). The engine develops 49.1 kN (11,030 lb) thrust, and is based on the Spey Mk 101 used in the Buccaneer. An option to uprate the powerplant to Mk 807A standard is possible with the use of Spey Mk 202 (RAF Phantom) components.

WEAPON OPTIONS

Internal armament comprises a 20-mm six-barrelled M61A1 Vulcan cannon with 350 rounds in Italian AMXs and two 30-mm cannon in the Brazilian aircraft. External stores of up to 3800 kg (8,377 lb) are carried on one fuselage, four underwing and two wingtip weapons pylons. The centreline and inboard wing pylons are each stressed to carry 907 kg (2,000 lb), while the outboard is stressed for 454 kg (1,000 lb). The wingtip rails are for infra-red guided air-to-air missiles (AIM-9 Sidewinder for Italy or MAA-1 Piranha for Brazil). Triple bomb carriers can be mounted on the inboard wing pylons and twin bomb carriers on the other stations. In addition to free-fall bombs, cluster munitions and unguided rockets,

A well-laden AMX displays the double bomb carrier on the centreline pylon. The wing has large slats on the leading edge, and large flaps. The small ailerons are augmented by overwing spoilers.

stores may include laser-guided munitions linked with such targeting pods as the GEC Ferranti TIALD or Thomson-CRT Defense ATLIS 2 or CLDP, electro-optical guided weapons and anti-ship missiles (trials with Exocet undertaken in 1991). Trials have also been completed with the CASMU Skyshark stand-off weapons dispenser, while recce equipment comprises either a visual-spectrum fuselage pack or Oude Delft Orpheus IR linescan pod. Two-seater also capable of being fitted for the electronic warfare role.

SPECIFICATION

AMX International AMX

Wing: span 8.874 m (29 ft 1.5 in) excluding wingtip missile rails and 10.00 m (32 ft 9.75 in) over wingtip AAMs; aspect ratio 3.75; area 21.00 m² (226.05 sq ft)

Fuselage and tail: length 13.575 m (44 ft 6.5 in); height 4.576 m (15 ft 0.25 in); tailplane span about 5.20 m (17 ft 0.75 in); wheel track 2.15 m (7 ft 0.75 in); wheel base 4.74 m (15 ft 6.5 in)

Powerplant: one Fiat/Piaggio/Alfa Romeo Avio/CELMA-built Rolls-Royce Spey RB.168 Mk 807 rated at 11,030 lb st (49.06 kN) dry

Weights: operating empty 6700 kg (14,771 lb); normal take-off 9600 kg (21,164 lb); maximum take-off 13000 kg (28,660 lb)

Fuel and load: internal fuel 2790 kg (6,151 lb); external fuel up to 1732 kg (3,818 lb) in two 1000-litre (264-US gal) or two 500-litre (132-US gal) drop tanks; maximum ordnance 3800 kg (8,377 lb)

Speed: maximum level speed 'clean' and maximum cruising speed at 36,000 ft (10975 m) 493 kt (568 mph; 914 km/h)

Range: ferry range 1,800 nm (2,073 miles; 3336 km) with two 1100-litre (290-US gal) drop tanks; combat radius 300 nm (345 miles; 556 km) on a lo-lo-lo attack mission with a 2,000-lb (907-kg) warload, or 480 nm (553 miles; 889 km) on a hi-lo-hi attack mission with a 2,000-lb (907-kg) warload, or 285 km (328 miles; 528 km) on a lo-lo-lo attack mission with a 6,000-lb (2722-kg) warload, or 500 nm (576 miles; 926 km) on a hi-lo-hi attack mission with a 6,000-lb (2722-kg) warload

Performance: maximum rate of climb at sea level 10,250 ft (3124 m) per minute; service ceiling 42,650 ft (13000 m); take-off run 2,070 ft (631 m) at 10750 kg (23,699 lb) increasing to 3,220 ft (982 ft) at maximum take-off weight; take-off distance to 50 ft (15 m) 4,730 ft (1442 m) at maximum take-off weight; landing distance from 50 ft (15 m) 2,470 ft (753 m) at maximum landing weight

g limits: -4 to +8

COCKPIT

The cockpit is covered by a one-piece sideways-hinging canopy, and one-piece wrap-around windshield which combine to give excellent visibility. The pilot sits on a Martin-Baker Mk 10L zero-zero ejection seat. The aircraft has an advanced cockpit to reduce pilot workload, with an OMI/Selenia head-up display. This is complemented by an Alenia head-down multi-function display which can present TV/IR and synthetic map images. The functions are controlled by HOTAS (hands on throttle and stick).

Antonov An-2 'Colt'

WSK-PZL Mielec
ul. Ludwego Wojska Polskiego 3
PL-39-300, Poland

One of the last biplanes in production, the An-2 remains in widespread military service, mainly as a utility transport and hack, although a handful may remain in use in the special forces insertion/support role, notably with North Korea. First flown on 31 August 1947 as the **SKh-1**, the An-2 proved popular with civil and military customers, and more than 5,000 were built at Kiev before production finally ceased in about 1965 (though a small number of An-2Ms were built until the early 1970s). Licensed production in China (which has now ceased) began in 1957, where approximately 1,500 were produced as **Harbin Y-5**s. PZL Mielec in Poland commenced licensed production in 1960, and has since produced almost 12,000 more. With a production run exceeding 18,000 aircraft, the unspectacular An-2 has been one of the great post-war success stories.

When the An-2 appeared in 1947, it was treated with some derision in the West and was regarded as an anachronistic and near-obsolete curio, destined for a very short lifespan. The unfashionable biplane configuration was chosen quite deliberately, however, with the new Antonov OKB willingly accepting drag penalties in order to exploit the configuration's many advantages – chiefly impeccable low-speed handling characteristics, agility and useful STOL performance. The aircraft's ruggedness and easy maintainability were also enhanced by a simple, straightforward engineering approach.

Despite its appearance, the An-2 did incorporate a host of modern features, including its full-span slats and electrically-actuated double-slotted trailing-edge flaps. Designed primarily for agricultural use, the An-2 has also seen service as a fire-bomber, light transport (**An-2-P**, **An-2T**, **An-2TP**) freighter, paratroop transport (**PZL An-2TD**), glider tug, air ambulance (**PZL An-2S**), survey platform, navigation trainer, meteorological research aircraft (**An-2ZA**) and even as a light bomber. Later improved agricultural versions include the **PZL An-2R**.

Acting as transports and make-shift bombers, An-2s were of crucial importance to the Croatian air force in the fighting that followed its secession from Yugoslavia in 1991.

and **An-2M**. A turbine-engined derivative, the **An-3**, did not reach production because of delays in availability of the selected engine. The type remains in large-scale service with a large number of air forces, with some on charge with most of Russia's Frontal Aviation regiments as hacks. The basic An-2 also serves as the basis for the proposed new **Delaero T-101 Gratch** utility monoplane, shown in mock-up form (in floatplane configuration) at the 1992 Moscow Aeroshow.

OPERATORS

Afghanistan
Albania (Harbin Y-5)
Angola
Azerbaijan
Byelorussia
Bulgaria
China (Harbin Y-5, Fong Shou 2 Harvester)
Croatia
Cuba
Czech Republic
Egypt
Georgia
Iraq
Laos
Latvia
Mali
Mongolia
Nicaragua
North Korea (Harbin Y-5)
Poland
Romania
Russia
Slovakia
Tadjikistan
Turkmenistan
Ukraine
Uzbekistan
Vietnam

SPECIFICATION

PZL Mielec (Antonov) An-2P
Wing: span, upper 18.18 m (59 ft 7¼ in); lower 14.24 m (46 ft 8½ in); aspect ratio, upper 7.6, lower 7.1
Fuselage and tail: length overall, tail up 12.74 m (41 ft 9¼ in); height, tail up 6.10 m (20 ft 0 in); wheel track 3.36 m (11 ft ¼ in)
Powerplant: one 1,000-hp (746-kW) PZL Kalisz ASz-621R (licence-built ASh-62)
Weights: empty 3450 kg (7,605 lb); maximum fuel 900 kg (1,984 lb); maximum take-off 5500 kg (12,125 lb)
Fuel and load: internal fuel 12,000 litres (317 US Gal, 264 Imp Gal)
Speed: maximum level speed at 1750 m (5,740 ft) 139 kt (258 km/h, 160 mph); economic cruising speed 100 kt (185 km/h, 115 mph)
Range: at 1000 m (3,280 ft) with payload of 500 kg (1,102 lb) 900 km (485 nm, 560 miles)
Performance: maximum rate of climb at sea level 210 m per min (689 ft per min); service ceiling 4400 m (14,425 ft)

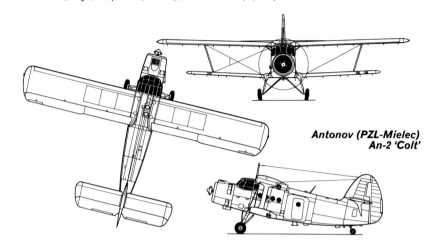

Antonov (PZL-Mielec) An-2 'Colt'

Antonov An-8 'Camp'

The twin-engined forerunner of the An-10, and of the Kiev-based bureau's better-known An-12 'Cub', remains in small-scale use with both Aeroflot and the **Russian air force** (and perhaps the air arms of some other former Soviet republics). Designed to meet a VVS requirement for a rear-loading tactical transport, and an Aeroflot requirement for a 42-48 seat passenger/freighter, the **An-8** first flew during late 1955, and Western sources usually indicate a production run of about 100. No new An-8s were ever delivered to Aeroflot, production being devoted to the military, which later passed examples on. Until recent years, the type was widely regarded as retired, but in the early 1990s small numbers have been discovered still active in support roles, around Moscow and in the hands of Aeroflot's former Far East Division. In the light of the efforts being made to dispose of remaining An-12s by the former Soviet Union, in favour of more modern types, serviceability of the An-8 must be extremely low.

Antonov An-10/An-12 'Cub'

Usually regarded as the 'Soviet C-130', the **An-12** is similar to the Hercules in many respects. Designed as a high-wing, four-engined, rear-loading military freighter, the Ukrainian-built aircraft has had considerable sales success in both civilian and military markets, and has been adapted to fulfil a variety of other roles. The prototype An-12 made its maiden flight during 1958. It is estimated that more than 900 were built at Kiev before production ceased during 1973, and more have been produced in China under the designation **Shaanxi Y-8**.

Developed from the passenger-carrying **An-10** (which was itself a stretched, four-engined derivative of the An-8, with a pressurised circular-section fuselage), the An-12 was designed from the start as a military transport and civilian freighter, with a rear-loading ramp like that of the An-8, and a partly-pressurised cabin forward of the main portion of the freight compartment. Unlike the C-130, the An-12 lacks an integral rear-loading ramp, with the upswept rear fuselage instead consisting of a pair of longitudinally-split inward-opening doors and a third upward-opening door aft.

Designated **'Cub'** by NATO's Air Standards Co-ordinating Committee, the An-12 has been produced in several versions. The **An-12BP** is the basic military freighter, although the very earliest versions, which had a smaller undernose radome and other detail differences, may have had a different designation. All basic freighter variants are known to NATO simply as 'Cubs'.

Large numbers of military An-12s have been converted to perform other roles (and some production 'special duties' An-12s may also have been manufactured). Factory

As a result of fatigue cracking in the main spar, the Indian An-12 fleet was reduced and finally withdrawn in 1993. Ten survivors were advertised for sale along with a stock of engines. Their replacement came, at first, in the shape of the Il-76, and more recently a C-130 Hercules buy has been proposed.

and air force designations for these shadowy aircraft remain unknown, and not all have separate NATO reporting names, although most remain in active front-line use with the successors to the Soviet air force. The first 'special duties' An-12 identified by NATO had blade antennas on the forward fuselage, plus other minor changes, and was a dedicated Elint platform. It is possible that this **'Cub-A'** was an interim type, since most Elint 'Cubs' encountered in recent years have had more extensive modifications. One such aircraft had prominent 'carrot' fairings on the fin and wingtips.

The **'Cub-B'**, which remained, until recently, in front-line service (even with the Russian air force in former East Germany), is a more obvious Elint conversion, with two prominent radomes under the belly and a host of other blade antennas. Some of these aircraft have been encountered in full Aeroflot livery and, during the 1970s, others may have worn Egyptian markings. **'Cub-C'** is understood to be a dedicated ECM platform, with palletised electrical generators and control equipment, and possibly chaff-cutters and dispensers in the cabin. Externally, the 'Cub-C' can be identified by the array of antennas on its underside, the cooling scoops and heat exchanger outlets fore and aft of the wing, and the bulged, ogival tailcone which replaces the normal gun turret. There have been suggestions that these 'stand-off' jamming platforms had a primary role of neutralising NATO air defence and surface-to-air missile radars.

The most recently identified version of the An-12, **'Cub-D'**, is a second ECM platform, with a different equipment fit and characterised by huge external pods on the lower 'corners' of the forward fuselage and on each side of the base of the tailfin. Unconfirmed reports suggest the existence of an airborne command post version of the An-12, which may have seen service during the Indo-Pakistan war, but details of its appearance are unavailable.

In addition to these aircraft, large numbers of An-12s have been converted as one-off test and research platforms, including a meteorological research aircraft, ejection seat test aircraft, avionics testbeds (SSSR-11417, -11700), icing rigs, and engine testbeds. In the latter category an Egyptian 'Cub' flew with its port inner engine replaced by a Helwan E-300 turbojet, developed for a stillborn indigenous fighter. A

Soviet An-12 (SSSR-11916) may have acted as a prototype for a proposed maritime reconnaissance and ASW variant.

OPERATORS

Although replacement, in the Soviet Union, by the jet-powered Ilyushin Il-76 began in 1974, sizeable numbers remain in service with the VTA and Aeroflot's fleet of 'Cubs' could also be commandeered. The An-12's main future role lies in the many 'special missions' conversions. Elsewhere, existing users are rapidly retiring their An-12s from use. In India, replacement by the Il-76 is underway and all surviving An-12s have been withdrawn and advertised for sale. Polish aircraft have also been retired. Surviving operators include the Czech Republic, Egypt, Ethiopia, Sri Lanka (Y-8), Ukraine and Yemen, while some aircraft may still be active in Iraq and Sudan.

SPECIFICATION

Antonov An-12BP 'Cub-A'
Wing: span 38.00 m (124 ft 8 in); aspect ratio 11.85; area 121.70 m² (1,310.01 sq ft)
Fuselage and tail: length 33.10 m (108 ft 7.25 in); height 10.53 m (34 ft 6.5 in); tailplane span 12.20 m (40 ft 0.25 in); wheel track 5.42 m (17 ft 9.5 in); wheel base 10.82 m (35 ft 6 in)
Powerplant: four ZMDB Progress (Ivchyenko) AI-20K each rated at 4,000 ehp (2983 kW)
Weights: empty 28000 kg (61,728 lb); normal take-off 55100 kg (121,473 lb); maximum take-off 61000 kg (134,480 lb)
Fuel and load: internal fuel 18100 litres (4,781 US gal); external fuel none; maximum payload 20000 kg (44,092 lb)
Speed: maximum level speed 'clean' at optimum altitude 777 km/h (419 kt; 482 mph); maximum cruising speed at opimum altitude 670 km/h (361 kt; 416 mph)

Above: This modified An-12 is an ejection seat testbed, firing seats from a modified tail housing. Note the camera pods under the wingtips.

The Sri Lankan air force's sole heavylift asset was a pair of Y-8s, provided as part of substantial Chinese assistance. One was lost in July 1992.

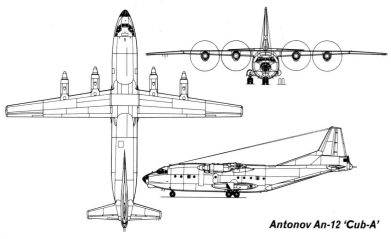

Range: 5700 km (3,075 nm; 3,542 miles) with maximum fuel or 3600 km (1,942 nm; 2,237 miles) with maximum payload
Performance: maximum rate of climb at sea level

600 m (1,969 ft) per minute; service ceiling 10200 m (33,465 ft); take-off run 700 m (2,297 ft) at maximum take-off weight; landing run 500 m (1,640 ft) at normal landing weight

Antonov An-12 'Cub-A'

Antonov **An-14 'Clod'**

Known as the **Pchelka** (Little Bee) to its manufacturers, the **An-14**, which first flew on 15 March 1958, was produced between 1965 and 1975 as a light twin-engined utility aircraft which could be flown by pilots of limited experience. While the launch of the An-14 was heralded with great fanfare, it then suffered eight years of redesign until true production could begin. The aircraft can accommodate a pilot and seven passengers, or a pilot, six stretchers

and an attendant. Access is via clamshell doors at the rear. About 300 were built and military customers included Bulgaria, East Germany, the Republic of Guinea, and the USSR.

Four An-14s may remain active in **Guinea**, but the type's main importance is that it formed the basis of the turboprop **An-14M** prototype of 1969, which eventually became the An-28 'Cash', built by PZL Mielec in Poland.

SPECIFICATION

Antonov An-14 Pchelka 'Clod'
Wing: span 21.99 m (72 ft 2 in); aspect ratio 12.15; area 39.72 m² (427.56 sq ft)
Fuselage and tail: length 11.36 m (37 ft 3 in); height 4.63 m (15 ft 2.5 in); tailplane span 5.00 m (16 ft 4.75 in); wheel track 3.60 m (11 ft 9.75 in); wheel base 3.71 m (12 ft 2 in)
Powerplant: two ZMDB Progress (Ivchyenko) AI-14RF each rated at 300 hp (224 kW)
Weights: empty 2600 kg (5,732 lb); maximum take-off 3270 kg (7,209 lb)
Fuel and load: internal fuel 385 litres (101 US gal);

external fuel none; maximum payload 720 kg (1,587 lb)
Speed: maximum level speed 'clean' at 1000 m (3,280 ft) 222 km/h (120 kt; 138 mph); normal cruising speed at 2000 m (6,560 ft) 180 km/h (97 kt; 112 mph)
Range: 800 km (353 nm; 407 miles) with maximum fuel, or 715 km (386 nm; 444 miles) with a 550-kg (1,212-lb) payload, or 650 km (351 nm; 404 miles) with maximum payload
Performance: maximum rate of climb at sea level 306 m (1,004 ft) per minute; service ceiling 4500 m (14,764 ft); take-off run 100 m (328 ft) at maximum take-off weight; take-off distance to 15 m (50 ft) 200 m (656 ft) at max take-off weight; landing distance from 15 m (50 ft), 300 m (984 ft) at normal landing weight; landing run 70 m (230 ft), at normal landing weight

Antonov Design Bureau
1 Tupolev Street
Kiev 252062, Ukraine

Antonov **An-22** 'Cock'

When the **An-22** prototype appeared at the 1965 Paris air show, only months after its 27 February 1965 maiden flight, it generated a storm of interest. Then the largest aircraft in the world, the An-22 weighed in at an astonishing 246-tonne maximum take-off weight and yet enjoyed relatively good take-off performance, despite a higher wing loading than any other military transport. This was achieved by the combination of powerful 11186-kW (15,000-shp) Kuznetsov NK-12MA turboprops whose prop wash was forced over highly effective double-slotted flaps which covered almost two thirds of the trailing edge.

In many respects, the An-22 is little more than a scaled-up An-12, with a new tail unit with twin endplate fins to give better control characteristics in asymmetric flight, and to avoid an excessive aircraft height. Like the An-12, it has a pressurised forward compartment (with the flight deck and 28 or 29 passengers) and an unpressurised main cargo hold. Unlike the An-12, though, it does have an integral rear loading ramp, plus four travelling gantries and two winches for loading heavy cargo. The undercarriage, which consists of twin nosewheels and three twin-wheel levered suspension units per side, is designed to allow off-runway operation. Three separate nose radars allow all-weather operation and accurate navigation over huge distances. Tyre pressures can be adjusted from the cockpit to optimise the undercarriage for landing weight and runway surface.

Until the introduction of the An-124, the An-22 was the only Soviet transport capable of carrying main battle tanks, and the 45 left in service (of perhaps 100 produced) are kept extremely busy. A handful of An-22s are used for externally carrying outsized cargoes (mainly An-124 wings). Most wear **Aeroflot** colours, but a handful seem to be

The bulk of Russian An-22s wear Aeroflot colours, though one aircraft has been seen wearing a three-tone green and brown camouflage scheme, with Soviet air force red stars. Twenty are based at Tver/Kalinin air base, 100 miles (160 km) north west of Moscow, alongside a number of An-12s.

permanently allocated to the **VTA** and at least one wears three-tone camouflage colours. Even the Aeroflot aircraft seem to undertake regular military tasking. Some reports suggest that the new **Ukrainian air force** may operate a small number of An-22s, but this cannot be confirmed.

SPECIFICATION

Antonov An-22 Antei 'Cock'
Wing: span 64.40 m (211 ft 4 in); aspect ratio 12.02; area 345.00 m2 (3,713.67 sq ft)
Fuselage and tail: length about 57.92 m (190 ft 0 in); height 12.53 m (41 ft 1.5 in)
Powerplant: four KKBM (Kuznetsov) NK-12MA each rated at 15,000 shp (11186 kW)
Weights: empty equipped 114000 kg (251,323 lb); maximum take-off 250000 kg (551,146 lb)
Fuel and load: internal fuel 43000 kg (94,797 lb); external fuel none; maximum payload 80000 kg (176,367 lb)
Speed: maximum level speed 'clean' at optimum altitude 740 km/h (399 kt; 460 mph); cruising speed at optimum altitude 520 km/h (281 kt; 323 mph)
Range: 10950 km (5,909 nm; 6,804 miles) with a 45000-kg (99,206-lb) payload and maximum fuel or 5000 km (2,776 nm; 3,197 miles) with maximum payload
Performance: service ceiling 7500 m (24,605 ft); take-off run 1300 m (4,260 ft) at maximum take-ff weight; landing run 800 m (2,620 ft) at normal landing weight

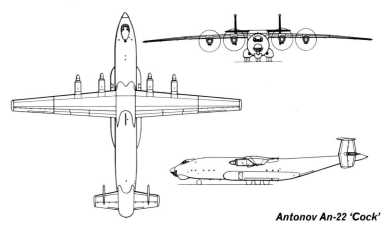

Antonov An-22 'Cock'

Antonov **An-24** 'Coke'

The **An-24** made its maiden flight on 20 December 1959, and was designed to meet an Aeroflot requirement for a turbine-engined replacement for the piston-engined Il-14s, Il-12s and even Li-2s (Soviet DC-3 copies) which operated on the airline's extensive network of local routes. Heavier, and with larger engines than the contemporary and largely equivalent Fokker F27, the export success of the An-24 was limited by its higher operating costs, although its robustness, strength and take-off performance widened its appeal to military customers. A total of 1,100 An-24s was built by the time production finished in 1978, but production continued in China, where the aircraft is designated **Xian Y-7** (described separately).

The basic **An-24V** seated 28-40 passengers, while the 1967 **An-24V Series II** seated 50. Substitution of a Tumanskii RU-19-300 turbojet for the gas turbine APU in the rear of the starboard engine nacelle resulted in the **An-24RV**, which enjoyed much improved take-off performance. Dedicated freighters, with the passenger door removed, and a freight access hatch in the underside of the rear fuselage, were the **An-24T** and **An-24RT** (with jet APU). The freight hatch hinged inwards from its rear edge, and small strakes on each side of the rear fuselage replaced the single centreline ventral fin of the standard An-24. An **An-24P** was evaluated for the firefighting role. Improved Chinese variants are designated **Y-7-100** and **Y-7-200A/B**. Most military An-24s are used for passenger and especially VIP transport duties, but overall the type has not enjoyed the sales success of the dedicated An-26 freighter and tactical transport.

OPERATORS

Afghanistan: 1 (VIP)
Angola: 3
Bulgaria: 8
China: 20 (An-24/Y-7)
Congo: 3/2 (An-24V/RV)
Cuba: 3
Czech Republic: 3 (An-24RV)
Hungary: 2 (An-24RV)
Iraq: 10
Mali: 2
Mongolia: 18 (An-24V/RV)
North Korea: 10
Romania: 10 (An-24RT/RV)
Slovakia: 3 (An-24RV)
Sudan: 5 (WFU)
Ukraine:
Vietnam: 12 (WFU)
Yemen: 3 (An-24V)

SPECIFICATION

Antonov An-24T 'Coke'
Wing: span 29.20 m (95 ft 9.5 in); aspect ratio 11.77; area 72.46 m2 (779.98 sq ft)
Fuselage and tail: length 23.53 m (77 ft 2.5 in); height 8.32 m (27 ft 3.5 in); tailplane span 9.08 m (29 ft 9.5 in); wheel track 7.90 m (25 ft 11 in); wheel base 7.89 m (25 ft 10.5 in)
Powerplant: two ZMDB Progress (Ivchyenko) AI-24A each rated at 2,550 ehp (1678 kW)
Weights: empty 14060 kg (30,996 lb); operating empty 14968 kg (32,998 lb); maximum take-off 19800 kg (43,651 lb)
Fuel and load: internal fuel 4760 kg (10,494 lb); external fuel none; maximum payload 4612 kg (10,168 lb)
Speed: normal cruising speed at 6000 m (19,685 ft)

The An-24, like this Hungarian An-24V, is a dedicated passenger aircraft with fixed seats. Freight and paradropping duties are exclusively the preserve of the An-26.

450 km/h (243 kt; 280 mph); economical cruising speed at 7000 m (22,965 ft) 450 km/h (243 kt; 280 mph)
Range: 3000 km (1,619 nm; 1,864 miles) with a 1612-kg (3,554-lb) payload, or 640 km (345 nm; 397 miles) with maximum payload

Performance: service ceiling 8400 m (18,520 ft); take-off run 640 m (2,100 ft) at maximum take-off weight; landing distance from 15 m (50 ft) 1590 m (5,217 ft) at normal landing weight; landing run 880 m (1.903 ft) at normal landing weight

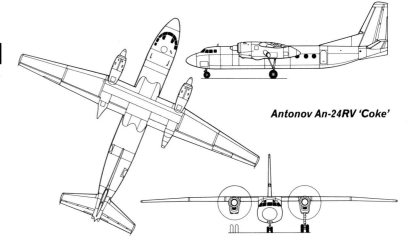

Antonov An-24RV 'Coke'

Antonov An-26 'Curl'

Although derived from the Antonov An-24, the **An-26** is a new design with a host of new features and improvements. The most obvious of these is a new rear loading ramp, which forms the underside of the upswept rear fuselage when closed, but which can be slid forward along tracks on each side of the fuselage to lie directly under the cabin, clear of the open hatch. This is especially useful when loading directly from a truck or for air-dropping. The actuators for the mechanism which slides the ramp forward are enclosed in prominent fibreglass fairings on each side of the rear fuselage, directly ahead of deep strakes which 'enclose' the more sharply swept rear fuselage. These improve airflow around the rear fuselage, which is particularly important when air-dropping loads. However, the nature of their construction (fibreglass) means they are easily damaged, a fact somewhat at odds with the An-26's role as a tactical transport.

All An-26s are fitted with a Tumanskii RU-19A-300 turbojet in the rear of the starboard engine nacelle. As well as acting as an APU, this can be used as a take-off booster and for increasing performance at other times. Many An-26s are also fitted with a large observation 'bubble' on the port side of the forward fuselage, replacing the normal navigator's window. This can be used in conjunction with an OPB-1R optical sight for accurately delivering air-dropped loads or paratroops. The Chinese-built **Xian Y7H** is described separately.

Less obvious is the fact that the An-26 has a fully-pressurised cargo hold (the first Soviet transport aircraft so equipped), or that on all but the earliest aircraft the belly has been toughened to withstand the erosion and abrasion which go hand-in-hand with rough field operation. A sheet of 'bimetal', with a titanium skin overlying aluminium alloy, protects the under-surfaces from debris. Other improvements adopted at the same time included more powerful AI-24T engines, and increased diameter (to 3.9 m/12.8 ft) AN-72T constant-speed, fully feathering four-bladed propellers. Since 1980, many An-26 engines have been upgraded to AI-24VT standard, giving a power output of 2103 ekW (2,820 ehp).

Internally, the An-26 features an electrically- or manually-operated conveyor flush with the cabin floor, while the later **An-26B** has roll gangs (panels fitted with rollers) which can be swung up against the cabin walls when not in use. These allow three standard freight pallets (weighing 1400 kg/ 4,041 lb and measuring 2.44 x 1.46 x 1.6 m/ 8 x 4.79 x 5.25 ft) to be unloaded, and another three loaded, by two men within 30 minutes. The hold can accommodate cargo up to 2.1 m (6.88 ft) wide and 1.5 m (4.92 ft) high, including a variety of commonly-used Warsaw Pact/Eastern Bloc vehicles. An electrically-powered mobile winch of 2000-kg (4,409-lb) capacity runs along rails on the cabin ceiling. In all An-26 versions, the interior can be reconfigured within 30 minutes

as a transport, with tip-up seats along the cabin sides to seat 38-40 passengers, or for casevac with 24 stretchers. Parachute static line points are fitted as standard.

The An-26 has mechanical controls, with electrical trim tabs on the servo-assisted ailerons and rudder. The flaps (single-slotted inboard, double-slotted outboard) are hydraulically actuated, as are the cargo ramp, emergency escape doors, forward-retracting undercarriage, nosewheel steering system and the brakes. The aircraft has two separate but interconnected fuel systems, with 5500 kg (12,125 lb) of fuel in integral tanks in the centre-section and five bag-type tanks in each wing. A single pressure refuelling point is located in the starboard engine nacelle, with gravity refuelling points above each tank area. An inert gas fire suppression system is incorporated.

A small number of An-26s have been converted as Elint/Sigint/EW platforms. These bear the NATO reporting name **'Curl-B'**, and have a profusion of swept blade antennas above and below the cabin. Painted as standard transports and often operating from the same bases, these aircraft remain in use with the Russian air force, including units based in former East Germany. Former East German special-duties An-26s were designated **An-26ST** (sometimes reported as **An-26SM** for calibration and **An-26M** for Elint). Similarly modified An-26s are in Czech service also.

An even more active combat role has been undertaken by Angolan and Mozambique An-26s, which have been fitted with bomb racks for use as makeshift COIN aircraft. These bomb racks are fitted on the fuselage, below the trailing edge of the wingroot. Some An-26s (most notably those used in Afghanistan) have had chaff/flare dispensers pylon-mounted in the same, or a very similar, position.

In line with other Antonov twins (most notably the An-32), a fire-bombing version of

Right: An An-26 formerly operated by the Soviet Northern Group of Forces at Legnica, Poland.

Below: Nominally on charge with the civil airline Hang Khong Vietnam, these An-26s flew from Tan Son Nhut airbase.

the An-26 has also been developed, utilising tanks along the fuselage, under the wing.

OPERATORS

Production ended after about 1,000 had been built, mostly for military operators who currently include Afghanistan, Angola, Bangladesh, Benin, Bulgaria, Cape Verde, China, Cuba, Congo, Czech Republic, Germany, Ethiopia, Guinea Bissau, Hungary, Iraq, Laos, Libya, Madagascar, Mali, Mongolia, Mozambique, Nicaragua, Poland, Romania, Russia, Serbia, Slovakia, Ukraine, Vietnam, Yemen and Zambia. Two hundred were built for Aeroflot and a handful more for other civilian users. The Y-7H-500 remains in production. The An-26 was replaced on the line by the An-32.

SPECIFICATION

Antonov An-26B 'Curl-A'
Wing: span 29.20 m (95 ft 9.5 in); aspect ratio 11.7; area 74.98 m² (807.10 sq ft)
Fuselage and tail: length 23.80 m (78 ft 1 in); height 8.575 m (28 ft 1.5 in); tailplane span 9.973 m (32 ft 8.75 in); wheel track 7.90 m (25 ft 11 in); wheel base 7.651 m (25 ft 1.25 in)
Powerplant: two ZMDB Progress (Ivchyenko)

AI-24VT each rated at 2,820 ehp (2103 kW) and one Soyuz (Tumanskii) RU-19A-300 rated at 7.85 kN (1,765 lb st) dry
Weights: empty 15400 kg (33,950 lb); normal take-off 23000 kg (50,705 lb); max take-off 24400 kg (53,790 lb)
Fuel and load: internal fuel 5500 kg (12,125 lb); external fuel none; maximum payload 5500 kg (12,125 lb)
Speed: maximum level speed at 5000 m (16,400 ft) 540 km/h (292 kts/336 mph); maximum level speed at sea level 510 km/h (275 kts/317 mph); cruising speed at 6000 m (19,685 ft) 440 km/h (237 kt; 273 mph)
Range: range 2550 km (1,376 nm; 1,585 miles) with maximum fuel or 1100 km (593 nm; 683 miles) with maximum payload
Performance: max rate of climb at sea level 480 m (1,575 ft) per minute; service ceiling 7500 m (24,605 ft); take-off run 780 m (2,559 ft) at max take-off weight; take-off distance to 15 m (50 ft) 1240 m (4,068 ft) at max take-off weight; landing distance from 15 m (50 ft) 1740 m (5,709 ft) at normal landing weight; landing run 730 m (2,395 ft) at normal landing weight

This Antonov An-26 'Curl-B' Elint aircraft was operational with the Group of Soviet Forces in Germany, flying from Sperenburg, near Berlin. Its antenna farm comprises 10 aerials, with an improved blade-aerial IFF above the nose.

Antonov An-30 'Clank'

Based on the airframe of the An-24RT freighter, and first flown in 1974, the **An-30** is a dedicated photographic and survey platform, with appropriate role equipment and a completely redesigned forward fuselage. It replaced a similarly modified version of the Ilyushin Il-14. A considerably raised cockpit gives access to the new glazed nose which accommodates the relocated navigator's compartment. There are few other structural changes (although some cabin windows are deleted) and the aircraft could theoretically be reconfigured for passenger or cargo duties by removing survey equipment and by fitting cover plates over the camera apertures, which are normally covered by remotely-controlled doors.

The An-30 is spacious, and a toilet, buffet and crew rest area with armchairs and couches is provided for the crew of seven (pilot, co-pilot, navigator, engineer, radio operator and two photographers), together with a darkroom and film storage area. The last two facilities account for the removal of the cabin windows.

The An-30 can carry a variety of mapping and survey equipment, including magnetometers (for mineral surveys) and microwave radiometers for surveying ice build-up, snow cover, flooding, soil type or seasonal changes of vegetation. More commonly, the An-30 can carry a variety of optical cameras (both vertical and oblique) in fixed or gyro-stabilised mountings. An extremely accurate navigation computer maintains the pre-programmed course, altitude and speed. A cloud-seeding version, the **An-30M 'Sky Cleaner'** has been

Romania was one of the few export customers for the specialised An-30 survey aircraft.

developed to disperse granular carbon dioxide to increase rain and snowfall, or fight fires.

Production of the An-30 has been very limited and only a handful serve in the air forces of **Russia**, **Bulgaria**, the **Czech Republic**, **Hungary**, **Romania** and, perhaps **Ukraine** and **Vietnam**.

SPECIFICATION

Antonov An-30 'Clank'
Wing: span 29.20 m (95 ft 9.5 in); aspect ratio 11.4; area 74.98 m2 (807.10 sq ft)
Fuselage and tail: length 24.26 m (79 ft 7 in); height 8.32 m (27 ft 3.5 in); tailplane span 9.09 m (29 ft 10 in); wheel track 7.90 m (25 ft 11 in); wheel base 7.65 m (25 ft 11.25 in)
Powerplant: two ZMDB Progress (Ivchyenko) AI-24VT each rated at 2,820 ehp (2103 kW) and one Soyuz (Tumanskii) RU-19A-300 rated at 7.85 kN (1,764 lb st)
Weights: operating empty 15590 kg (34,369 lb); maximum take-off 23000 kg (50,705 lb)
Fuel and load: internal fuel 6200 litres (1,638 US gal); external fuel none
Speed: maximum level speed 'clean' at optimum altitude 540 km/h (292 kt; 336 mph); cruising speed at 6000 m (19,685 ft) 430 km/h (232 kt; 267 mph)
Range: 2630 km (1,419 nm; 1,634 miles) with maximum fuel
Performance: service ceiling 7300 m (23,950 ft) without APU and 8300 m (27,230 ft) with APU; take-off run 710 m (2,330 ft) at maximum take-off weight; landing run 670 m (2,198 ft) at normal landing weight

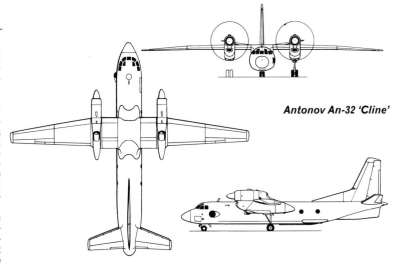

Antonov An-30 'Clank'

Antonov An-32 'Cline'

The **An-32** replaced the An-26 in production, and is designed to offer improved take-off performance, ceiling and payload, especially under 'hot-and-high' conditions. It retains the superb cargo ramp of the An-26, and has an increased capacity (3000 kg/ 6,615 lb) internal winch. Removable roller conveyors aid air-dropping or the extraction of loads by drag-parachute. The cabin can accommodate up to 50 passengers, 42 paratroops, or 24 stretcher loads and three attendants. The normal crew consists of pilot, co-pilot and navigator, with provision for a flight engineer.

Although the An-32 was originally offered with a choice of powerplant, all production aircraft are fitted with the 3812-ekW (5,112-ehp) Ivchenko AI-20D series 5, similar to (but more powerful than) the engine used by the An-12 and Il-18. These are mounted above the wing to give greater clearance for the increased-diameter propellers, reduce the danger of debris ingestion, and decrease noise levels in the cabin. The overwing position, however, results in very deep nacelles because the bulk of the An-26's original nacelle has been retained to accommodate the improved main undercarriage units when retracted. The overwing portion of the nacelle extended back only to about mid-chord on the An-32 prototype, but extends back almost to the trailing edge of

the original underwing nacelle on production aircraft. The 'turbojet APU' of the An-26 and some An-24 versions has been replaced by a simple TG-16M APU in the tip of the starboard landing gear fairing.

Besides these aerodynamic refinements, the undercarriage extension/retraction mechanism, and the de-icing, air conditioning, electrical and engine starting systems have all been improved. The improvements to the An-32 have been extremely successful, producing an aircraft which can operate from airfields with elevations of up to 4500 m (14,750 ft) above sea level, and which has set a host of world records for payload-to-height, and sustained altitude.

In 1993 the first **An-32B** was seen boasting uprated powerplants with approximately 200-shp (149-kW) extra power available per engine. At the Paris air show that same year, Antonov demonstrated the **An-32P** (Protivopozharny) water-bomber, named **Firekiller**. Like the similar An-26 conversion it features side-mounted tanks with a total capacity of 8000 kg (17,635 lb), though those of the An-32 are substantially larger and faired on. Flares are carried to induce artificial precipitation over fires. However, the tanks have to be refilled on the ground, necessitating specialised pumping equipment, and radius of action is quoted at a mere 150 km (93 miles).

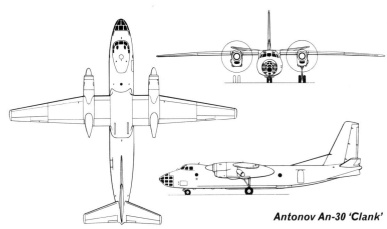

Antonov An-32 'Cline'

OPERATORS

The An-32 has already attracted a number of military customers, including the USSR (it is as yet unclear exactly which independent republics have taken over former Soviet An-32s), Afghanistan, Bangladesh, Cuba, India, Mongolia, Peru and Tanzania. It is unclear whether orders from Cape Verde, Nicaragua and São Tomé are from military or civilian customers. India's

order for 95 was to have been met by licence-production of the aircraft, which has the local name **Sutlej**, but this plan fell through and India's aircraft are Soviet built, albeit with a high content of indigenous equipment and avionics. In addition to the basic transport version of the An-32, fire-fighting, fisheries protection, air ambulance and agricultural versions have been offered for sale, while Peru's 15 An-32s have two bomb racks on each side of the fuselage, below the wings.

Left: Several 'tropical' operators, such as the Bangladesh (seen here) and the Peruvian air forces, have traded in their An-26s for more powerful An-32s.

Right: India too appreciates the An-32's good 'hot-and-high' performance, relying on six squadrons of the type for all of its tactical transport needs. The Antonov design was selected in 1979 in preference to the Aeritalia G222, DHC-5 Buffalo, and ex-RAF Andover C.Mk 1s.

SPECIFICATION

Antonov An-32 'Cline'
Wing: span 29.20 m (95 ft 9.5 in); aspect ratio 11.7; area 74.98 m² (807.10 sq ft)
Fuselage and tail: length 23.78 m (78 ft 0.25 in); height 8.75 m (28 ft 8.5 in); tailplane span 10.23 m (33 ft 6.75 in); wheel track 7.90 m (25 ft 11 in); wheel base 7.651 m (25 ft 1.25 in)
Powerplant: two ZMDB Progress (Ivchyenko) AI-20DM Series 5 each rated at 5,112 ehp (3812 kW)
Weights: empty 16800 kg (37,037 lb); maximum take-off 27000 kg (59,524 lb)
Fuel and load: internal fuel 5445 kg (12,004 lb); external fuel none; maximum payload 6700 kg (14,771 lb)
Speed: maximum cruising speed at 8000 m (26,245 ft)

530 km/h (286 kt; 329 mph); economical cruising speed at 8000 m (26,245 ft) 470 km/h (254 kt; 292 mph)
Range: 2500 km (1,349 nm; 1,553 miles) with a 3700-kg (8,157-lb) payload or 2000 km (1,070 nm; 1,243 miles) with maximum payload
Performance: service ceiling 9500 m (31,170 ft); take-off run 760 m (2,495 ft) at maximum take-off weight; take-off distance to 15 m (50 ft) 1200 m (3,940 ft) at maximum take-off weight; landing run 470 m (1,542 ft) at normal landing weight

An-32s, particularly Ukranian air force examples, are becoming increasingly involved in UN duties. This former-Soviet aircraft was engaged in relief flights in Africa.

Antonov **An-70T**

Development of the **An-70** began during the early 1980s, to enter production during 1988, but this was delayed by funding problems. Slightly larger than the proposed Euroflag, and considerably smaller than the C-17, the **An-70T** takes the An-12's place, but with modern technology (including a Mil-Std 1553B databus, SKI-77 HUD and Cat IIIB landing aids), powerful engines and advanced aerodynamics. The aircraft is equipped with a fly-by-wire control system with three digital and six analog channels. Antonov have also developed an innovative back-up hydraulic/electro-magnetic control system. Increased use of composites by Antonov is in evidence, as the An-70T features carbon fibre tail assemblies.

At a ceremony at its Kiev factory, Antonov rolled out the first An-70 on 20 January 1994. Present at the roll-out was VVS Commander-in-Chief Col Gen. Piotr Deinkin, reinforcing hopes for a substantial purchase by the Russian air force. Two thirds of all research and development funding was provided by the defence ministry of the former Soviet Union (project breakdown is 63 per cent Russian, 21 per cent Ukranian and 16

per cent among the other Republics). Ninety-five per cent of components are currently sourced in Russia, but Ukraine's share of these would rise to 13 per cent once production is underway. A prototype flew during June 1994 with series production undertaken both at Kiev, Ukraine, and Samara, Russia. Overall span is 44.06 m (114 ft 6¼ in), length is 40.25 m (132 ft ¼ in) and height is 16.120 m (52 ft 10 in). The cockpit is laid out for three, including a flight engineer. The cargo hold is pressurised and air-conditioned, but has no provision for any seating, barring two loadmasters in the forward fuselage. The crew door is positioned in the port forward fuselage, and there is no rear door, which excludes any future paradropping option. Maximum payload, using the ramp, is pegged at 30000 kg (66,135 lb), with maximum take-off weight an estimated 123000 kg (271,165 lb). The 10440-kW (14,000-hp) Zaporozhye Progress D-27 propfan is fitted with highly distinctive Stupino SV-27 contra-rotating propellers. Each engine drives eight 4.5-m (14-ft 7-in) blades in the first stage and six in the second, and all are of curved scimitar profile and

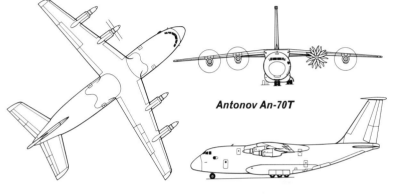

Antonov An-70T

feature electric de-icing. Estimated cruising speed will be 400 kt (740 km/h; 460 mph) at an altitude of 9500 m (31,000 ft). Operating from runways of 1800-2000 m (5,900-6,500 ft), the aircraft's maximum range will be 2,700 nm (5000 km/3107 miles). The An-70 will also be capable of rough field operations from strips as short as 600 m (1,970 ft).

The An-70T is intended for a life of 45,000 flying hours or 20,000 cycles, and is operable for 3,500 hours per year, with seven to eight man maintenance hours per

flight hour. Funding has passed to the Ukrainian government, and the Antonov OKB is actively courting interest in the aircraft, which could even be produced to fulfil the RAF's requirement for a C-130 replacement. An uninvited bid for the RAF's proposed Hercules replacement has been tendered under the designation **An-77**.

In March 1994 Antonov signed a joint venture with Daewoo, of South Korea, to build a new transport aircraft, based on the An-70T.

Antonov **An-72 'Coaler-A', 'Coaler-C'**

The **An-72** was developed as a turbofan-powered STOL transport to replace the turboprop An-26. The first of two prototypes made its maiden flight on 22 December 1977 and these, together with eight pre-series aircraft also built at Kiev, were given the reporting name **'Coaler-A'** by NATO's Air Standards Co-ordinating Committee. Series production at Kharkov was of a slightly modified aircraft with extended outer wing panels, a lengthened fuselage, no ventral fins and other detail changes. This initial production version was designated **An-72A**. This was codenamed **'Coaler-C'** because it appeared after the West had seen the long-span wing and lengthened fuselage on the An-74, which was allocated the 'Coaler-B' reporting name.

Because their aircraft flew for the first time only 17 months after the superficially similar Boeing YC-14, Antonov was unfairly accused of directly copying the US aircraft. There were certainly similarities, with a high wing, T-tail and high-mounted turbofan engines which discharged over the upper surface of the wing, using the Coanda effect in which jet exhaust is entrapped by

When the An-72 appeared at Farnborough in 1984, it was among the first Soviet aircraft to do so. When Antonov brought the An-72P to the 1992 show, it wore Ukrainian air force markings.

the extended flaps and thereby dramatically increases lift. The high-set wing, traditional on Soviet freighters, gives an unobstructed freight hold and eases production, while the high-set engines allow upper-surface blowing, as described above, but also minimise FOD ingestion problems.

The An-72's cargo ramp is little changed from that fitted to the An-32, and owes nothing to Western design practices. Telescopic struts fold down from the rear of each undercarriage fairing to support the rear fuselage when the ramp is swung forward under the belly for direct loading. The

undercarriage itself is similarly novel, and optimised for operation from semi-prepared strips, with low-pressure tyres, twin nose-wheels and main units which consist of two tandem trailing arms, each with a single mainwheel.

The An-72 has been built in several versions. The **An-72AT** is a dedicated freighter equipped to handle standard international containers. The **An-72S** is an executive transport with the cabin split into

Antonov An-72 'Coaler-A' and 'Coaler-C'

three compartments, the forward compartment housing the galley, toilets and wardrobe, with baggage, a three-seat sofa and a work table in the next compartment (or alternatively the sofa and three pairs of armchairs), and with 12 pairs of armchairs in the rear compartment. The An-72S can be reconfigured as a freighter, or as a 38-seat transport with tip-up seats along the cabin sides, or as an air ambulance with eight stretcher patients.

The latest version of the aircraft is the **An-72P**, a dedicated maritime surveillance platform and the most obviously military version of the aircraft to date. Operational aircraft wear a smart three-tone camouflage, and are armed with a GSh-23L 23-mm cannon in the starboard undercarriage fairing, and underwing rocket pods. A novel system of bombs carried on an internal hoist has been displayed, and the An-72P is currently being offered with a range of antiship missiles, torpedoes and depth charges. The aircraft features an advanced inertial navigation system, linked to on-board cameras which allow it to photograph target ships and record their exact position with great accuracy. Prominent bulged 'eyeball' windows aft of the flight deck give a better field of view. SFP-2A flares are carried for night photography. Linked to the autopilot, the navigation system can also automatically fly a wide variety of search patterns, and can be used to calculate the speed and course of its targets. The An-72P has an endurance in excess of five hours with a cruising speed of between 160 and 190 kt (295 and 350 km/h; 183 and 217 mph) at an altitude of 1000 m (3,300 ft). Antonov has now entered into a partnership with several Israeli firms, offering the An-72P with much improved systems. The deal, announced at

The An-72P appeared at the 1992 MosAero show, at Zhukhovskii, with a far more military air than on other occasions. The aircraft is in service with Russia's Border Guards.

the 1994 Asian Aerospace Show, at Singapore, has been struck with IAI and its subsidiaries. Elta have supplied an EL/M 2022A surveillance radar, and Elisra an improved ESM system. El-Op are responsible for a new stabilised, large-aperture, high-resolution all-weather sensor fit. The An-72P's current sensor fit includes A-86P lateral and oblique cameras for daytime use, and UA-47 vertical nightime cameras. A TV system is fitted beneath the port undercarriage fairing. The cameras are housed under the tail, alongside the photo-flash ejection system. The An-72P retains the pressurised fuselage of the transport version and can accommodate up to 40 folding passenger seats. Alternatively, 22 fully-equipped paratroops can be carried

A typical eight-hour maritime mission could survey an area of 120x140 km (10,440 sq mile), with the aircraft flying from the centre of the search area outwards. covering a swatch of 20 km. Three Antonov An-72Ps (of a total of eight ordered) entered

service with a **Russian Border Guards** unit based on the Pacific coast during July 1992, finding a Japanese fishing boat illegally operating in Russian territorial waters on their first operational mission.

SPECIFICATION

Antonov An-72A 'Coaler-C'

Wing: span 31.89 m (104 ft 7.5 in); aspect ratio 10.31; area 98.62 m² (1,061.57 sq ft)

Fuselage and tail: length 28.07 m (92 ft 1.25 in); height 8.65 m (28 ft 4.5 in); wheel track 4.15 m (13 ft 7.5 in); wheel base 8.12 m (26 ft 7.75 in)

Powerplant: two ZMDB Progress (Lotarev) D-36 each rated at 63.74 kN (14,330 lb st) dry, but to be replaced by two ZMDB Progress (Lotarev) D-436 each rated at 73.62 kN (16,550 lb st) dry

Weights: empty 19050 kg (41,997 lb); maximum take-off 34500 kg (76,058 lb) from a 1800-m (5,906-ft) runway, or 33000 kg (72,751 lb) from a 1500-m (4,921-ft) runway, or 27500 kg (60,626 lb) from a

1000-m (3,281-ft) runway

Fuel and load: internal fuel 12950 kg (28,549 lb); external fuel none; maximum normal payload 10000 kg (22,046 lb)

Speed: maximum level speed 'clean' at 10000 m (32,810 ft) 705 km/h (380 kt; 438 mph); cruising speed at 10000 m (32,810 ft) between 550 and 600 km/h (297 and 324 kt; 342 and 373 mph)

Range: range 4800 km (2,590 nm; 2,980 miles) with a 7500-kg (16,534-lb) payload or 800 km (430 nm; 497 miles) with maximum payload

Performance: service ceiling 11800 m (38,715 ft); take-off run 930 m (3,052 ft) at maximum take-ff weight; take-off distance to 10.7 m (35 ft) 1170 m (3,840 ft) at maximum take-off weight; landing run 465 m (1,525 ft) at normal landing weight

The An-72P's primary armament is a twin-barrelled GSh-23L 23-mm cannon and a pair of underwing UV-32M rocket pods. It can also carry four 100-kg (220-lb) bombs, which can be dropped through the rear ramp.

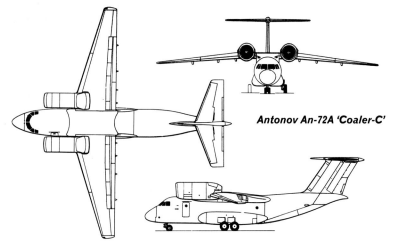

Antonov An-72A 'Coaler-C'

Antonov **An-74** 'Coaler-B' and 'Madcap'

The original **An-74** was a dedicated polar version, optimised for operation in the Arctic and Antarctic and designed to replace ageing Ilyushin Il-14s then in use for supporting Arctic scientific stations, Antarctic expeditions, and for observing and monitoring ice flows and ice build-up. Because it was the first version noted in the West after the original short-winged, short-fuselage prototypes and pre-series aircraft, it received the reporting name **'Coaler-B'**, whereas it was in fact a development of the series production An-72A which received the later reporting name 'Coaler-C'.

The An-74 had the same basic airframe as the production An-72, although there are two blister observation windows aft of the flight deck and at the front of the cabin on

the port side, and a larger radome whose underside does not follow the contours of the forward fuselage, giving a pronounced 'droop'. The aircraft carries a flight crew of five, with a pilot, co-pilot, flight engineer, radio operator and dedicated navigator, and is fitted with an advanced inertial navigation suite. Fuel capacity is significantly increased and provision is made for a wheel/ski landing gear to be fitted for operations from snow.

The An-74 'Coaler-B' made its Western debut at the Paris air show in 1987. Since then, despite the plethora of versions that have been announced, few examples have been noted.

The An-74 has spawned a family of variants, only some of which have the prominent nose radome of the basic aircraft, but most of which seem to have the observation blisters. The **An-74A** is a basic passenger/freighter, which is said to retain the larger nose of the basic aircraft. The **An-74T** (designated **An-74T-100** with navigator station) is a dedicated freighter with an internal winch, roller equipment and cargo mooring points, as well as provision for air-dropping cargo and static lines for paratroops. The **An-74TK** is a convertible cargo/passenger variant, with 52 folding passenger seats or a mix of passengers and freight, or all-cargo options. When a navigator station is provided the aircraft is designated **An-74TK-100**. The **An-74P-100** is a business aircraft or military VIP transport with a navigator's station (indicated by the -100 suffix) and a three-compartment interior similar to that of the **An-72S**. Telephone and fax facilities are included as standard, along with video entertainment and a refrigerator and bar. The forward compartment has four armchair seats in pairs, each pair separated by a work table, while the central compartment has a three-seat sofa to starboard, two more armchairs, and another table. The rear compartment has another three-seat sofa and two pairs of armchairs, bringing accommodation to 16.

At least one An-74 (SSSR-780151) was modified to serve as a prototype AEW platform. With a rotodome atop a new forward-swept fin and rudder, the aircraft may have been intended as a lower-cost AWACS system for the export market, or to augment the larger Ilyushin A-50 'Mainstay' in Soviet service or perhaps even as a shipborne AEW aircraft for the aircraft-carrier *Tbilisi* (now *Kuznetsov*). Development is understood to have been abandoned, perhaps in favour of the Yakovlev Yak-44, but not before NATO assigned the reporting name **'Madcap'**.

Production of the basic Antonov An-72, the An-72P and the An-74A, An-74TK, An-74TK-100 and An-74P-100 continues at the rate of about 20 per year (from the same assembly line) at their parent company's Kharkov plant. By early 1994 approximately 150 Antonov An-72 and An-74s had been completed. Further improved variants are likely to appear, and there are plans to re-engine the An-72 and An-74 with more powerful 73.53-kN (16,535-lb) ZMKB Progress (Lotarev) D-436K turbofans.

SPECIFICATION

Antonov An-74 'Coaler-B'
generally similar to the Antonov An-72A 'Coaler-C' except in the following particulars:
Range: 5300 km (2,860 nm; 3,293 miles) with a 1500-kg (3,307-lb) payload or 1,150 km (620 nm; 715 miles) with maximum payload

Above: The An-74 was intended for Arctic operations and many wore the high-visibility red scheme of Aeroflot's Polar Directorate.

Below: The only freely available picture of 'Madcap' (SSSR-780151), taken in 1987 during a visit by President Gorbachev to Antonov.

Antonov **An-124 Ruslan ('Condor')**

Only a handful of the (approximately) 40 **An-124**s delivered by early 1994 are assigned directly to the VTA, wearing full military markings, but other Aeroflot aircraft are frequently employed on military tasks. Named after Pushkin's legendary giant, the **Ruslan** is in many respects comparable to the slightly smaller Lockheed C-5 Galaxy, which has a very similar configuration. The An-124 remains the world's largest production aircraft (only the one-off An-225 is bigger), and has set a series of world records, most notably exceeding by 53 per cent the C-5's payload to 2000 m.

Designed to meet **Aeroflot** and **Soviet air force** (**VVS**) Long-Range Transport Aviation (VTA) requirements for an An-22 replacement, the An-124 has an upward-hinging 'visor-type' nose (with a folding nose ramp) and an enormous set of rear loading doors (with a three-part folding ramp) which allow simultaneous loading or unloading from both ends, or allow vehicles to be 'driven through'. The rear loading doors consist of the ramp, which can be locked in an intermediate position to allow direct loading from a truckbed, with an upward-hinging centre panel and downward-hinging clamshell doors behind.

The vast, constant-section cargo hold has a titanium floor with roll gangs and retractable cargo tiedown points, and is lightly pressurised, with a fully-pressurised upper passenger deck for up to 88 people. For ease of loading the aircraft can be made to 'kneel' in a nose-down position by retracting the nosewheels and supporting the nose of the aircraft on retractable feet. This gives the cargo hold a slope of 3°.

No simple, crude flying juggernaut, the An-124 has fly-by-wire controls and a super-critical wing, and makes extensive use of composite materials for weight saving. The aircraft is capable of carrying virtually any load, including all Soviet main battle tanks, helicopters and other military equipment. In an emergency, passengers can be carried in the partially pressurised main hold, and in 1990 an An-124 carried 451 Bangladeshi refugees (evacuated from Amman to Dacca during the Gulf crisis) using a foam rubber lining in the hold in lieu of seats.

SPECIFICATION

Antonov An-124 Ruslan ('Condor')
Wing: span 73.30 m (240 ft 5.75 in); aspect ratio 8.56; area 628.00 m² (6,759.96 sq ft)
Fuselage and tail: length 69.10 m (226 ft 8.5 in); height 20.78 m (68 ft 2.25 in)
Powerplant: four ZMDB Progress (Lotarev) D-18T each rated at 229.47 kN (51,587 lb st) dry
Weights: operating empty 175000 kg (385,802 lb); maximum take-off 405000 kg (892,857 lb)
Fuel and load: internal fuel 230000 kg (507,055 lb); external fuel none; maximum payload 150000 kg (330,688 lb)
Speed: maximum cruising speed at optimum altitude 865 km/h (467 kt; 537 mph); normal cruising speed at 10000 m (32,810 ft) between 800 and 850 km/h (432 and 459 kt; 497 and 528 mph)
Range: range 16500 km (9,140 nm; 10,523 miles) with maximum fuel and 4500 km (2,430 nm; 2,796 miles) with maximum payload
Performance: balanced take-off field length 3000 m (9,843 ft) at maximum take-off weight; landing run 800 m (2,625 ft) at maximum landing weight

The An-124's strategic importance lay in its ability to carry items such as main battle tanks, whole SAM systems and even the SS-20 mobile IRBM.

Antonov An-124 Ruslan ('Condor')

Antonov An-225 Mriya 'Cossack'

Despite high-profile appearances at a number of international air shows and a headline-grabbing series of 106 world records, the **An-225 Mriya** (**Dream**) remains something of an enigma. Reportedly developed to replace the pair of Myasishchev VM-T Atlants in use for carrying outsize loads, particularly those associated with the Soviet space programme's Energia rockets, the sole An-225 made its maiden flight on 21 December 1988, and flew with the Buran space shuttle on its back on 13 May 1989, visiting the Paris air show in the same year. Until recently, however, it apparently languished in storage, losing engines and other components to active An-124s. The VM-Ts remain active, and reports suggest that further VM-Ts may be produced through conversion of surplus 'Bisons'. Ambitious plans for the An-225, including a production run and leasing deal, as a launcher for Britain's (now defunct) HOTOL recoverable spacecraft seem to have fallen through, despite the huge potential.

The first aircraft to fly with a gross weight in excess of 1,000,000 lb (453600 kg), the An-225 is an ingenious derivative of the An-124 designed to offer a 50 per cent improvement in payload and maximum take-off weight. This was achieved by providing a stretched fuselage, six engines instead of four and seven pairs of wheels per side instead of five, plus redesigning the dihedral tailplane with endplate fins, deleting the rear loading ramp and increasing wingspan. The latter modification relieves airflow problems when carrying external loads. All controls are fly-by-wire. A second aircraft began to take shape on the line alongside standard An-124s in the early 1990s, but it remains unfinished and unwanted.

SPECIFICATION

Antonov An-225 Mriya 'Cossack'
Wing: span 88.40 m (290 ft 0 in); aspect ratio 8.63; area 905.00 m² (9,741.66 sq ft)
Fuselage and tail: length 84.00 m (275 ft 7 in); height 18.20 m (59 ft 8.5 in); tailplane span 32.65 m (107 ft 1.5 in); wheel track 8.84 m (29 ft 0 in); wheel base 29.10 m (95 ft 9.5 in)
Powerplant: six ZMDB Progress (Lotarev) D-18T each rated at 229.47 kN (51,587 lb st) dry
Weights: maximum take-off 600000 kg (1,322,275 lb)
Fuel and load: internal fuel 300000+ kg (661,376+ lb); external fuel none; maximum payload 250000 kg (551,146 lb)
Speed: maximum cruising speed at optimum altitude 850 km/h (458 kt; 528 mph); normal cruising speed at optimum altitude 700 km/h (378 kt; 435 mph)
Range: range 15400 km (8,310 nm; 9,570 miles) with maximum fuel or 4500 km (2,428 nm; 2,796 miles) with maximum payload
Performance: take-off balanced field length 3500 m (11,483 ft) at maximum take-off weight

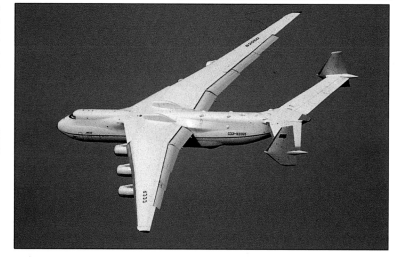

The An-225 has re-emerged from a period of storage and is once more being promoted by the Antonov bureau as a unique heavylift aircraft. Plans to build further examples remain in abeyance.

ASTA (GAF) Nomad/Searchmaster

ASTA Defence
Private Bag 4, Avalon Airport, Lara
Victoria 3212, Australia

The **ASTA** (Aerospace Technologies of Australia (PTY) Ltd, previously Government Aircraft Factory) **Nomad** was the product of a mid-1960s effort to provide Australia with an indigenous twin-engined STOL utility aircraft with military and civil potential. The aircraft was built in **N22** and **N24** versions with different fuselage lengths. The basic N22 (and **N22B** with increased weights) seated 12, whereas the N24 could accommodate 17. Military transport and maritime surveillance versions were marketed under the names **Missionmaster** and **Searchmaster**, respectively. The former has wing hardpoints and load-bearing drop-doors in the cabin floor; the latter carries search radar, either Bendix RDR-1400 in the nose (**Searchmaster B**) or Litton APS-504(V)2 in an undernose radome (**Searchmaster L**).

Production of the Nomad series ended in 1984 with 170 built, including 40 **N24A**s, which first flew on 23 July 1971. The **Australian Army Aviation Corps** uses 10 N22s, distributed equally between No. 173 (GS) Squadron and the School of Army Aviation, both based at Oakey. Two other N22s support the **RAAF**'s Aircraft Research and Development Unit, alongside one N24A. The **Philippine air force** is another user of the transport Nomad, having acquired 12 Missionmasters for the 223rd Tactical Squadron in the 220th Heavy Airlift Wing, later supplemented by four Searchmasters.

For the counter-insurgency role, the **Royal Thai air force** has a total of 22 N22B Missionmasters, shared between Nos 461 and 462 Squadrons in 46 Wing at Phitsanulok and No. 605 in 6 Wing at Don Muang. Acquired in 1982/83, some were immediately pressed into service as gunships (possibly with cabin-mounted machine-guns) to replace ageing AC-47s. Searchmasters are used by the **Indonesian navy**'s Skwadron Udara 800, which has received a total of 18, including 12 B and six L models. With Australian aid, the **Papua New Guinea** defence force has received up to seven assorted models and is operating both the Searchmaster `B and Searchmaster L for EEZ patrols.

SPECIFICATION

ASTA (GAF) N22B Searchmaster L
Wing: span 54 ft 2.3 in (16.52 m); aspect ratio 9.11; area 324.00 sq ft (30.10 m²)
Fuselage and tail: length 41 ft 2.4 in (12.56 m); height 18 ft 1.5 in (5.52 m); tailplane span 17 ft 8.4 in (5.39 m); wheel track 9 ft 6 in (2.90 m); wheel base 12 ft 3 in (3.73 m)
Powerplant: two Allison 250-B17C each rated at 420 shp (313 kW)
Weights: manufacturer's empty 4,613 lb (2092 kg); maximum take-off 9,100 lb (4127 kg)
Fuel and load: internal fuel 1,770 lb (803 kg) plus provision for 580 lb (263 kg) of auxiliary fuel; external fuel none; maximum ordnance 2,000 lb (907 kg)
Speed: normal cruising speed at optimum altitude 168 kt (193 mph; 311 km/h)
Range: 730 nm (841 miles; 1353 km)
Performance: maximum rate of climb at sea level 1,460 ft (445 m) per minute; service ceiling 21,000 ft (6400 m); take-off run 730 ft (223 m) at maximum take-off weight; take-off distance to 50 ft (15 m) 1,180 ft (360 m) at maximum take-off weight; landing distance from 50 ft (15 m) 1,340 ft (408 m) at normal landing weight; landing run 695 ft (212 m) at normal landing weight

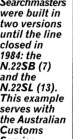

In 1976, 12 Nomads were delivered to the Philippines, and 10 are still in use. They operate from Mactan AFB alongside C-130s.

Searchmasters were built in two versions until the line closed in 1984: the N.22SB (7) and the N.22SL (13). This example serves with the Australian Customs Service.

Atlas XH-1 Alpha

Atlas Aviation (PTY) Ltd (a division of Denel)
PO Box 11, Kempton Park 1620, Transvaal
Republic of South Africa

The Atlas Alpha is a one-off systems demonstrator, developed to support South Africa's indigenous attack helicopter programme, and is based on the airframe, engine rotor and transmission system of the Alouette III. Atlas was awarded a contract to develop the aircraft in March 1981, and it made its first flight on 27 February 1986. A new narrow fuselage accommodated tandem cockpits for pilot and gunner, with a single-barrelled 20-mm cannon under the nose, aimed via the gunner's helmet-mounted sight. The aircraft was given a new tail unit and tailwheel undercarriage.

SPECIFICATION

Atlas Alpha XH-1
Rotor system: main rotor diameter 11.02 m (36 ft 1.75 in); tail rotor diameter 1.91 m (6 ft 3.25 in); main rotor disc area 95.38 m² (1,026.68 sq ft); tail rotor disc area 2.87 m² (30.84 sq ft)
Powerplant: one 649-kW (870-shp) Turboméca Artouste IIIB flat-rated at 425 kW (570 shp)
Weights: empty 1400 kg (3,086 lb); maximum take-off 2200 kg (4,850 lb)
Speed: maximum level speed 'clean' at optimum altitude 210 km/h (113 kt; 130 mph); maximum cruising speed at optimum altitude 185 km/h (100 kt; 115 mph)
Range: combat radius 275 km (148 nm; 171 miles)
Performance: maximum rate of climb at sea level 245 m (804 ft) per minute; service ceiling 3200 m (10,500 ft); hovering ceiling 2880 m (9,450 ft) in ground effect and 1520 m (4,985 ft) out of ground effect

Derived from the Alouette III, the XH-1 served as a weapons testbed for the Atlas Rooivalk. It led to the XTP-1 Beta (a converted Puma) and, ultimately, the XH-2 Rooivalk.

Atlas Oryx (Gemsbok) and XTP-1 Beta

South Africa was a major customer for the French-built Aérospatiale Puma, taking delivery of an estimated 70 SA 330F/J/L Pumas, eventually equipping or partly equipping Nos 15, 16, 18, 19, 22, 30 and 31 Squadrons. Attrition and defence economies reduced the force to three squadrons (15, 19 and 31) by early 1993, and substantial numbers of Pumas are now in storage. Improvements and upgrades to the aircraft began early in its career, Atlas soon building up considerable experience and expertise with the type, and in order to circumvent UN sanctions manufactured frequently required items such as tyres, transparencies, acrylic floor panels, gearboxes, engine hot sections, and rotor blades. It also manufactured newly-designed components optimised for SAAF requirements, including fuel tanks and armoured seats.

The first major upgrade programme resulted in the **XTP-1 Beta**, which featured extended engine intake filters, denoting installation of the Super Puma's Makila turboshafts, and with a tail unit similar to that fitted to the AS 532 Cougar. These modifications were later disclosed to be intended for retrofit across the Puma fleet, whereas the other modifications, which gave the aircraft its XTP- (Experimental Test Platform) designation, were not. These modifications included a long air data probe projecting from the port side of the cockpit, and stub wings mounted on the cabin sides, and apparently requiring the cabin doors to

be 'sealed shut'. The wings each carried two articulated pylons, capable of carrying 18-round 68-mm rocket pods. A 20-mm GA1 cannon was installed in a ventral turret (with a 1,000-round magazine) and was aimed by helmet-mounted sight.

Originally the XTP-1 was expected to form the basis of a gunship conversion of the Puma, but in fact it was a systems and weapons testbed, marking a further step towards the indigenous Rooivalk attack helicopter (described separately). The aircraft was later used as the basis of a low-cost alternative to the Rooivalk, and several stub-winged, cannon-armed Pumas entered operational evaluation during mid-1990. These had wingtip launch rails for the IR-homing Darter or Viper AAM, and a laser designator for the 'Swift' anti-tank missile. Atlas offered a range of four Puma gunships. Using detachable weapons pylons (so that aircraft could easily be reconfigured to a troop-carrying role, with 12 armoured seats), the most basic Option 1 saw the addition of a Kentron TC-20 ventral gun turret and helmet-mounted sights for the crew. Option 2 involved fitting four 68-mm rocket launchers. Aircraft modified to Option 3 standard added a nose-mounted Kentron HSOS (Helicopter Stabilised Optronic Sight) to the rocket armament. The 'full spec' Option 4 Oryx gunship will be equipped with ZT-3 Swift laser-guided anti-tank missiles. Option 3 and 4 aircraft are currently undergoing development.

The XTP-1's tail and (Makila) engine modifications, together with a new Super Puma style nose radome, formed the basis of the **Oryx**, originally known as **Gemsbok**, upgrade. The Oryx cockpit is also configured for single pilot operations. Pumas converted to this standard have replaced the SAAF's ageing Super Frelon, and entered service from 1988, with Nos 19 and 31 Squadrons.

SPECIFICATION

Atlas Oryx
Rotor system: main rotor diameter 15.00 m (49 ft 2.5 in); tail rotor diameter 3.04 m (9 ft 11.5 in); main rotor

The South African Air Force operates much-modified SA 330 Pumas in the shape of the re-engined, radar-equipped Atlas Oryx.

disc area 176.71 m² (1,902.20 sq ft); tail rotor disc area 7.26 m² (78.13 sq ft)
Fuselage and tail: length overall, rotors turning 18.15 m (59 ft 6.5 in) and fuselage 14.06 m (46 ft 1.5 in); height overall 5.14 m (16 ft 10.5 in) and to top of rotor head 4.38 m (14 ft 4.5 in); wheel track 2.38 m (7 ft 10.75 in); wheel base 4.045 m (13 ft 3 in)
Powerplant: two Turboméca Makila 1A1 each rated at 1400 kW (1,877 shp) for take-off and 1184 kW (1,588 shp) for continuous running
Fuel and load: external fuel up to two 350-litre (92.5-US gal) auxiliary tanks

Atlas XH-2/CSH-2 Rooivalk

The **Rooivalk** (Red Kestrel) programme continues despite defence cuts which once threatened the **SAAF** requirement for the aircraft. Development of an indigenous attack helicopter began in 1981 and involved the XH-1 Alpha and XTP-2 Beta as concept-proving and systems testbeds. The definitive Rooivalk prototype, originally designated **XH-2** (XH for Experimental Helicopter), made its maiden flight on 11 February 1990, and was later redesignated **CSH-2** (Combat Support Helicopter) and later still **XDM** (experimental development model). A second prototype, the **ADM** (advanced development model) flew soon afterwards, tasked with avionics and weapons development. Externally this differed from the first prototype in having a cropped 'tailfin', although the first prototype was later modified to a similar external configuration.

Although it looks like an entirely new aircraft, the Rooivalk is based on a degree of reverse engineering of the Aérospatiale Puma, using the same Turboméca Turmo IV engines (albeit slightly uprated), and the same rotor. The fuselage is entirely new, incorporating some composite structural components, with stepped tandem cockpits for pilot (rear) and co-pilot/gunner (front). Crew positions are reversed in the second prototype, which retains full dual controls and with the same three CRT displays and a HUD in each cockpit. The cockpits are covered by canopies formed from flat-plate or single curvature sheets to minimise glint. The engines are mounted on the sides of the fuselage, further aft than on the Puma, to give the pilot a better field of view, and this has dictated a redesign of the transmission system.

A nose-mounted, gyro-stabilised turret contains an automatic target detection and tracking system which incorporates a laser rangefinder, FLIR and TV camera, and the

two crewmen each have helmet-mounted sights. The cockpit is NVG-compatible, and night/all-weather capability is improved by twin redundant mission computers, twin weapon-aiming computers and a Doppler-based navigation system with moving map displays.

The Rooivalk is heavily armed, with an indigenous Armscor GA-1 Rattler 20-mm cannon turret mounted under the nose. An alternative XC-30 turret, containing a 30-mm DEFA 553 cannon, is also said to be a possibility. The cannon is backed up by weapons carried on the four underwing pylons. These can accommodate an 18-round 68-mm rocket launcher, or four-round launchers for the Atlas Swift laser-guided ATM. Air-to-air missiles can be carried on the wingtips. Rockets and missiles were test fired from a number of Puma testbeds before live firings from the Rooivalk were made during early 1994.

Provision is made for IR jammers and other ECM equipment, and the airframe is well protected by armour. If the aircraft

takes a catastrophic hit, the crewmen's energy-absorbing seats have a high degree of crashworthiness.

The full production standard Rooivalk will differ from the prototypes in a number of important respects. The pilot will be seated behind the WSO, unlike the arrangement in the ADM. Improved IR exhaust suppressers (pointing directly up into the rotor disc) will be fitted, together with enlarged sponson cheeks (similar to those on the AH-64C and AH-64D) housing avionics and ammunition. A pair of external seats can be fitted to these, allowing a Rooivalk to pick up the

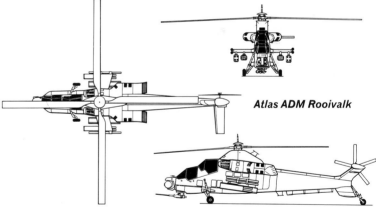

Atlas ADM Rooivalk

Visible on the ADM Rooivalk (to the rear) are its IR exhaust suppressors, weapons fit and revised rotor masthead.

Atlas XH-2/CSH-2 Rooivalk

crew of a downed helicopter, or to transport special forces soldiers.

The South African Minister of Defence has announced in Parliament that the Air Force will receive four aircraft for evaluation and indoctrinal/tactical development, and an order has since been placed for some 12 aircraft for at least one squadron. The aircraft's future can only really be secured by a major export order. With this in mind, Atlas have begun an intense marketing effort, which included displaying the demonstrator at the 1993 Dubai air show. The aircraft has been offered to Britain to fulfil the Army Air Corps requirement for a next-generation attack helicopter, and in April, Atlas were formally invited to tender for the requirement. The variant offered to Britain is known simply as the 'Kestrel', and differs from the intended SAAF production standard in having a new SWIM sight and a new weapons system, with provision for Short Starstreak missiles and NATO-type rockets. It will also have redesigned exhaust suppressors. This configuration will be adopted

The first aircraft, the XDH, is still a vital part of the Rooivalk programme, having amassed over 300 flying hours.

by the SAAF if finances and international sanctions permit. There have been some rumours that an export order, for a reported five aircraft, was placed during May 1991, and there have been discussions with a number of overseas partners regarding possible joint development and production.

SPECIFICATION

Atlas CSH-2 Rooivalk
Rotor system: main rotor diameter 15.08 m (49 ft 5.7 in)
Powerplant: two uprated Atlas-built Turboméca Turmo IV (Topaz) turboshafts
Weights: normal take-off 7200 kg (15,873 lb); maximum take-off 8000 kg (17,637 lb)
Speed: never exceed speed 170 kt (195 mph; 315 kt); maximum cruising speed at optimum altitude 145 kt (167 mph; 269 km/h)

Range: ferry range 720 nm (829 miles; 1335 km) with auxiliary fuel; range 507 nm (584 miles; 940 km) with standard fuel; endurance 7 hours 22 minutes with auxiliary fuel

Performance: maximum rate of climb at sea level 2,700 ft (823 m) per minute; service ceiling 20,500 ft (6250 m); hovering ceiling 13,800 ft (4205 m) in ground effect and 11,800 ft (3600 m) out of ground effect

Atlas Impala

In the mid-1960s **South Africa** finalised a contract with Aermacchi for a variant of the M.B.326GB which would be suitable for advanced training and the counter-insurgency (COIN) role. Designated **M.B.326M**, an initial 16 kits were supplied by Aermacchi, these being assembled by Atlas Aircraft at Kempton Park, Transvaal, the first of them being flown on 11 May 1966. The next 30 kits were less complete, requiring Atlas to fabricate a percentage before assembly, after which an additional 105 were built by Atlas, the last of these aircraft being completed in 1974. These duly entered service with the South African Air Force, which designated the type the **Atlas Impala Mk 1**, equipping first the Flying Training School at Langebaanweg. Impala Mk 1s are used by No. 83 Jet Flying School at Langebaanweg for streaming of jet- and transport-assigned pilots. The two-seat trainer is also the mount of the 'Silver Falcons', the five-ship aerobatic display team of the SAAF, which is co-located with No. 83 JFS. The SAAF currently operates 115

This Atlas Impala Mk 2, operated by the South African Air Force's No. 85 Air Combat School, was painted to resemble a gannet (the unit badge) for the school's 25th anniversary celebrations in September 1992.

Impala Mk 1s (of a total of 151 examples delivered).

Development by Aermacchi of the single-seat **M.B.326K** trainer/ground-attack aircraft was of considerable interest to South Africa, which acquired a licence for the type. Atlas production began (as with the M.B.326M two-seat trainer) by assembly of seven Italian-built kits, progressing to almost 90 per cent manufacture in South Africa. The first of the assembled aircraft entered service with the SAAF on 22 April 1974, being designated **Impala Mk 2**. These differ from the Aermacchi M.B.326K in minor details, primarily by retaining the same powerplant as the Impala Mk 1 instead of the more powerful version of the Rolls-Royce Viper of the M.B.326K.

A mixture of Impala Mks 1 and 2 equips Nos 5, 6, 7 and 8 Squadrons of the ACF (reserve) in the COIN/advanced training role. Impala Mk 2s are also used in the streaming

of future Cheetah pilots. The aircraft of No. 7 Squadron provide six-month single-seat conversion training as a prelude to transfer to No. 85 Combat Flying School at Pietersburg, where wingman and flight leader courses are undertaken. Selection for a squadron Cheetah (see entry below) posting is only considered after a minimum of 700 Impala hours.

It is believed that 100 Impala Mk 2s were eventually received by the SAAF, of which 75 are still in service. In addition to their current training roles, they have been exten-

sively used in South Africa's bush wars in Angola and Namibia, where the main tasks were ground-attack/close-support and aerial reconnaissance.

SPECIFICATION

Aermacchi M.B.326KM (Atlas Impala Mk 2)
generally similar to the Aermacchi M.B.326K except in the following particulars
Powerplant: one Rolls-Royce (Bristol Siddeley) Viper 20 Mk 540 rated at 3,410 lb st (15.17 kN) dry thrust

Atlas Cava

The indigenous Cava programme has now been abandoned, and is unlikely to be resurrected. The aircraft was an all-new design based on the airframe of the Mirage III, using the upgraded wing of the Cheetah, but with a fly-by-wire control system and powered by the SNECMA Atar 9K-50 engine. A twin-engined version, using the same powerplant, was also proposed. The aircraft were to have been newly built, not

conversions of existing Mirage IIIs or Cheetahs, and would therefore have enjoyed a long fatigue life, and the potential of a long production run, not restricted by airframe availability. The aircraft was primarily intended for air-to-ground operations as a replacement for the dwindling fleet of Buc-

caneers and Canberras and eventually for the Mirage F1s. A change of regime in South Africa, coupled with the reduction of tension in the area, have combined to put the future of the aircraft (and indeed of any indigenous fighter programme) in some doubt.

Atlas Cheetah

Since November 1977 **South Africa** has been prevented by arms embargoes from procuring advanced aircraft. The SAAF therefore attached a high priority to a mid-life update for survivors of the 74 Mirage IIIs received during 1963-70. The upgrade was revealed on 16 July 1986 with the unveiling of a two-seat Mirage IIID2Z, redesignated **Atlas Cheetah**. The Cheetah benefits from Israeli technology (not officially verified) and closely resembles the IAI Kfir.

Aerodynamic modifications include Kfir-style small nose side-strakes (to prevent yaw departure at high AOA), dog-tooth outboard leading-edge extensions, short fences replacing leading-edge slots, canards and fixed wing leading-edge droop. Two-seaters also have curved strakes below the cockpit along the lower fuselage.

Structural modifications are centred around increasing the minimum life of the wing main spar (originally set at 800 hours). Several progressive stages of modification are proposed, reducing fatigue problems and providing life extension of up to 1,250 hours (for a complete refurbishment with a newly-manufactured main spar).

Two-seaters and R2Zs are powered by an Atar 9K50 engine, for which Atlas has a manufacturing licence. Other conversions retain SNECMA Atar 9C/9D turbojets. Retention of the Atar engine is indicated by the absence of the large dorsal airscoop and smaller overfuselage airscoops of the Kfir (which is powered by the heavier, more powerful GE J79). Installation of the 9K50 (in the two-seaters) involves modifications to the inlets and fuselage frames; the R2Z already had this engine. The installation of an IFR probe permits take-off with a lower fuel load and a correspondingly higher warload. The probe is mounted to starboard immediately aft of the cockpit. In addition, a

The cruciform braking chute used by the Cheetah D has the advantages of ease of manufacture and packing over more common round chutes. Cheetah Ds were initially assigned to the SAAF's No. 89 CFS, but in recent times the fleet has been passed on to No. 2 Squadron.

single-point pressure refuelling system is fitted, enabling times to be reduced (a maximum of five minutes for a clean aircraft).

The performance improvements include a reduction in specific fuel consumption (four per cent), take-off distance (10-20 per cent), minimum speed (100 KIAS), time-to-height and increased SEP, sustained load factor and sustained turn rate (15 per cent). The canards permit MTOW to be increased by 700 kg (1,545 lb) for a penalty of under five per cent in level acceleration time and maximum level speed. The uprated engine also allows a possible growth in payload/fuel capability or MTOW.

The Cheetah introduces a new ECS providing adequate cooling for the revised avionics. The avionics upgrade may be based on the Elbit System 81 (or possibly upgraded System 82) weapons delivery and navigation system fitted to the Kfir C2 (or C7). The HUD, CTU (Computer Terminal Unit) and ACDP (Armament Control and Display Panel) function via a MIL-STD-1553B databus and allow for pre-flight programming and HOTAS pilot operation. The nav/attack system includes an inertial system and options include a helmet-mounted sight (of indigenous, or Israeli, origin) and a radar altimeter. The Kfir-type drooped nose houses an Elta EL/M-2001B I/J-band radar ranging unit. Like Kfirs, the Cheetah features a fuselage plug ahead of the windscreen to accommodate the extra avionics. An Israeli AOA sensor vane is fitted to the port side of the forward fuselage. Self-protection systems include an SPS-2000 RWR system with antennas in the nose and in the fin trailing edge (replacing the Mirage III ILS aerials) and a possible jammer system in the former rocket motor fairing.

The Cheetah DZ differs primarily from the EZ by having a longer nose (like that of the Kfir-T) with more pronounced droop, housing displaced avionics from the spine. An undernose fairing directly aft of the pitot boom contains two radar warning antennas and a large cooling intake.

Fixed armament of the Cheetah comprises two 30-mm DEFA cannon. All weaponry of the Cheetah has been officially stated to be of South African origin, including Armscor V3B Kukri/V3C Darter dogfight missiles. Air-to-ground weapons include AS30 ASMs (which also form the basis of a reported smart weapon with an indigenous designator pod), cluster bombs, rockets and combined fuel/rocket pods. Two Kfir-C7-type stores pylons have been introduced directly ahead of the wing/engine intake trunking.

The first Cheetah conversions comprised eight IIID2Z trainers to two-seat **Cheetah D** standard. Declared operational in 1987, the DZs were initially operated by No. 89 Combat Training School and may have a pathfinder role for the **Cheetah E**s. The SAAF has a total of 16 Mirage IIIDZ and D2Z two-seaters available for conversion. For economic reasons, conversions to Cheetah EZ standard may be limited to 14 surviving Mirage IIIEZ and four IIIR2Z single-seaters. These aircraft retain their original Atar 09C-3 or 9K50 powerplants and the reconnaissance models will retain recce capability. These initially equipped No. 5 Squadron, but were passed to No. 2 when it retired the Mirage IIICZs, IIIBZ s and IIIRZs operated by No. 2 ('Cheetah') Squadron at Hoedspruit which were considered not viable for conversion and were ultimately retired from service in 1990.

In April 1992, a further upgraded version of the Cheetah was revealed. Based on the single-seat Mirage IIIR2Z, this prototype features an advanced combat wing which reduces drag and increases lift. The wing also permits an increase in wing fuel tankage in its fixed leading edge and additional wing-tip missile stations. The modifications allow a 15 per cent increase in sustained turn performance, improved handling qualities for a small weight penalty, an increase in MTOW of 700 kg (1,545 lb) and a 55-nm (63-mile/101-km) improvement in tactical radius. There have been reports that IAI and Elta are further modifying the 12 lowest-houred Cheetah Es under a $1.8 billion programme, with a new Elta EL/M-2035 radar and more powerful engines taken from retired Mirage F1CZs, which may themselves receive Russian engines.

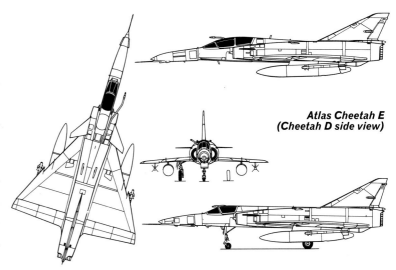

Atlas Cheetah E
(Cheetah D side view)

SPECIFICATION

Atlas Cheetah EZ
Wing: span 8.22 m (26 ft 11.6 in); aspect ratio1.94; area 34.80 m2 (374.60 sq ft); canard foreplane span 3.73 m (12 ft 3 in); canard foreplane area 1.66 m2 (17.87 sq ft)
Fuselage and tail: length including probe 15.65 m (51 ft 4.25 in); height 4.55 m (14 ft 11.25 in); wheel track 3.20 m (10 ft 6 in); wheel base 4.87 m

(15 ft 11.7 in)
Powerplant: one SNECMA Atar 9C rated at 41.97 kN (9.436 lb st) dry and 60.80 kN (13,668 lb st) with afterburning or, more probably, one SNECMA Atar 9K-50 rated at 49.03 kN (11,023 lb st) dry and 70.82 kN (15,873 lb st) with afterburning
Fuel and load: internal fuel 2288 litres (5,044 US gal); external fuel up to two 1700-, 1300-, 1100- or 625-litre (449-, 343-, 291- or 165-US gal) drop tanks; maximum ordnance about 4000 kg (8,818 lb)
Speed: maximum level speed 'clean' at 12000 m (39,370 ft) 2338 km/h (1,262 kt; 1,453 mph); maximum cruising speed at 11000 m (36,090 ft) 956 km/h (516 kt; 594 mph)

Above: Sometimes erroneously referred to as the Cheetah C, prototype aircraft No. 855 is the Mirage IIIR2Z Cheetah conversion and the first to carry the Advanced Combat Wing. This features a drooped leading edge, and plans exist for a wingtip launch rail.

Below: This Cheetah E wears the (toned-down) Pegasus badge of No. 5 Squadron, but all the SAAF's Cheetahs are now assigned to No. 2 Squadron.

Avions de Transport Régional ATR 42/52/72

Avions de Transport Régional
1 Allé Pierre Nadot
F-31712 Blagnac Cedex, France

A joint effort of Aérospatiale and Alenia, the ATR family serves the regional airline market. Two basic aircraft are available, the PW120 turboprop-powered **ATR 42** offering 40-50 seats, and the **ATR 72** offering 64-74 seats and PW124 power. An MPA version (**Petrel**) with nose search radar was proposed, but has found no buyers. Only one standard aircraft has been sold to the military: an **ATR 42F** freighter with port-side cargo door and strengthened floor to **Gabon**. Risk-sharing partners are now being sought for the rear-loading **ATR 52C Milfreighter**, a developed ATR-72-210.

SPECIFICATION

ATR 42F

Wing: span 24.57 m (80 ft 7.5 in); aspect ratio 11.08; area 54.50 m² (586.65 sq ft)

Fuselage and tail: length 22.67 m (74 ft 4.5 in); height 7.586 m (24 ft 10.75 in); elevator span 7.31 m (23 ft 11.75 in); wheel track 4.10 m (13 ft 5.5 in); wheel base 8.78 m (28 ft 9.75 in)

Powerplant: two Pratt & Whitney Canada PW120 each flat-rated at 1,800 shp (1342 kW)

Weights: operating empty 10285 kg (22,674 lb); maximum take-off 16700 kg (36,817 lb)

Fuel and load: internal fuel 4500 kg (9,921 lb); external fuel none; max payload 5375 kg (11,850 lb)

Speed: never exceed speed 250 kt (287 mph; 463 km/h) CAS; maximum cruising speed at 17,000 ft (5180 m) 267 kt (307 mph; 495 km/h); economical cruising speed at 25,000 ft (7620 m) 243 kt (279 mph; 450 km/h)

Range: 2,160 nm (2,487 miles; 4000 km) with a 2900-kg (6,393-lb) freight payload, or 1,250 nm (1,439 miles; 2316 km) with a 3800-kg (8,377-lb) freight payload or 42 passengers, or 540 nm (622 miles; 1000 km) with maximum freight payload

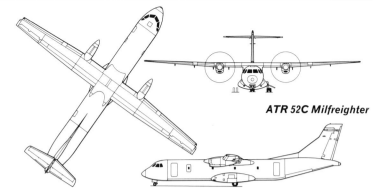

ATR 52C Milfreighter

Performance: maximum rate of climb at sea level 2,100 ft (640 m) per minute; maximum operating altitude 25,000 ft (7620 m); balanced take-off field length 3,576 ft (1090 m) at maximum take-off weight; landing field length 3,380 ft (1030 m) at maximum landing weight

---

Ayres **Turbo-Thrush (NEDS)**

Ayres Corporation
PO Box 3090, One Rockwell Ave, Albany
Georgia 31708-5201, USA

E volved from the long line of proven Turbo-Thrush agricultural aircraft for use as a **Narcotics Eradication Delivery System (NEDS)**, the two-seat **Ayres S2R-T65/400** was developed specifically for use by the State Department's International Narcotics Matters Bureau. Intended to dispense 'Roundup' herbicide from a hopper ahead of the cockpit, the NEDS Turbo-Thrush flies Operation Roundup narcotics plantation eradication missions in Colombia, Belize, Guatemala, Mexico, Myanmar and Thailand, targeting cocaine and marijuana.

The NEDS Turbo-Thrush, 19 examples of which were ordered by the **United States**

State Department between 1983 and 1985, has an armoured tandem two-seat cockpit, armour around its turboprop engine and a self-sealing fuel tank (additional to normal wing tankage) in a bullet-proof structure. Underwing hardpoints are fitted and theoretically allow gun or rocket pods to be carried.

SPECIFICATION

Ayres Turbo-Thrush S2R-T65 NEDS

Wing: span 44 ft 5 in (13.54 m); aspect ratio 6.04; area 326.60 sq ft (30.34 m²)

Fuselage and tail: length 33 ft 0 in (10.06 m); height 9 ft 2 in (2.79 m); tailplane span 17 ft 0 in (5.18 m); wheel track 9 ft 0 in (2.74 m); wheel base 8 ft 11 in (2.74 m)

Powerplant: one Pratt & Whitney Canada PT6A-65AG rated at 1,376 shp (1026 kW)

Weights: empty 3,600 lb (1633 kg) with standard hopper or 3,900 lb (1769 kg) with optional hopper; normal take-off 8,200 lb (3719 kg) with standard hopper or 8,500 lb (3856 kg) with optional hopper

Fuel and load: internal fuel 228 US gal (863 litres) plus provision for 20 US gal (75.7 litres) of auxiliary fuel in a bulletproof fuselage tank; external fuel none

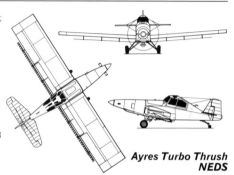

Ayres Turbo Thrush NEDS

Ayres **V-1-A Vigilante**

D eveloped as a low-cost surveillance and close-support aircraft based on the Turbo-Thrush NEDS, the **V-1-A Vigilante** was evolved in co-operation with the **US State Department** and in association with the **US Army** Electro-Optical Survivability Program. The prototype, first flown in May 1989, performed night surveillance trials along the Texas and Arizona borders on behalf of the US Border Patrol, successfully detecting groups of illegal immigrants.

Intended for marketing primarily in Latin America and North Africa, the Vigilante's turboprop has exhaust suppression and a hush kit. Its features include a two-seat armoured cockpit, a self-sealing auxiliary fuel tank, four standard NATO wing hardpoints and three stores stations under the fuselage. Stores may include 500-lb (227-kg) bombs, 2.75-in (70-mm) rockets, gun pods containing weapons ranging in calibre from 7.62 mm to 20 mm, and a variety of anti-armour missiles, sea mines and torpedoes.

SPECIFICATION

Ayres V-1-A Vigilante

generally similar to the Ayres Turbo-Thrush S2R-T65 NEDS except in the following particulars:

Fuselage and tail: tailplane span 16 ft 9 in (5.11 m); wheel base 17 ft 5 in (5.31 m)

Weights: empty 4,900 lb (2223 kg); maximum take-off 10,500 lb (4762 kg)

Fuel and load: external fuel 2,800 lb (1270 kg) in drop tanks; maximum ordnance 4,500 lb (2041 kg)

Speed: never exceed speed and maximum level speed clean at optimum altitude 191 kt (220 mph; 354 km/h); maximum cruising speed at optimum altitude 200 kt (230 mph; 370 km/h); economical cruising speed at optimum altitude 150 kt (173 mph; 178 km/h)

Range: ferry range 1,750 nm (2,015 miles; 3243 km) with drop tanks; range 900 nm (1,036 miles; 1667 km) with standard fuel; endurance 7 hours with standard fuel

Performance: maximum rate of climb at sea level

3,500 ft (1067 m) per minute; service ceiling 25,000 ft (7620 m); take-off run 1,250 ft (381 m) at maximum take-off weight; landing run 750 ft (229 m) at maximum landing weight

In its surveillance role the V-1-A can carry a Honeywell, Lockheed or Texas Instruments FLIR, Lockheed/Kollmorgen LLLTV and even a Honeywell IRLS.

Beech **Model 23/Musketeer III**

Beech Aircraft Corporation
9709 East Central, Wichita
Kansas 67201-0085, USA

F irst flown on 23 October 1961, the Beech Model 23 Musketeer was later adopted for primary tuition by two air arms, the **Mexican air force** and the Air Command of the **Canadian Forces**. The former procured 20 of the 112-kW (150-hp) Avco Lycoming O-320-E2C-powered Musketeer III (Sport) trainers in 1970, and the latter obtained 21 134-kW (180-hp) O-360-A4K-powered Beech Musketeer III (Sundowner) aircraft in 1981. The Canadian Musketeers were employed as **CT-134**s at No. 3 FTS at Portage la Prairie and gave place in mid-1992 to Slingsby T-67

Fireflies supplied by a private contractor (Canadair). The Mexican aircraft remain in service with the Escuela Militar de Aviación at Zapopán.

The Muskeeter was awarded its type certificate in February 1972. Initially a two-seat design, it was developed into a 200-hp (149-kW), six-seat aircraft with retractable undercarriage. Nearly 4,000 of all versions have been built, but military sales have been slight. This is a Canadian example, now retired.

SPECIFICATION

Beech Model C23 Sundowner
Wing: span 32 ft 9 in (9.98 m); aspect ratio 7.5; area 146.00 sq ft (13.57 m²)
Fuselage and tail: length 25 ft 8.5 in (7.84 m); height 8 ft 3 in (2.51 m); tailplane span 10 ft 8 in (3.25 m);
wheel track 11 ft 10 in (3.61 m); wheel base 6 ft 4 in (1.93 m)
Powerplant: one Textron Lycoming IO-360-A4J rated at 180 hp (134 kW)
Weights: basic empty 1,425 lb (646 kg); maximum take-off 2,450 lb (1111 kg)
Fuel and load: internal fuel 60 US gal (227 litres); external fuel none; maximum ordnance none
Speed: maximum level speed 'clean' at sea level 131 kt (151 mph; 243 km/h); maximum cruising speed at 7,000 ft (2135 m) 124 kt (143 mph; 230 km/h); economical cruising speed at 10,000 ft (3050 m) 107 kt (123 mph; 198 km/h)
Range: 747 nm (860 miles; 1384 km)
Performance: maximum rate of climb at sea level 888 ft (271 m) per minute; service ceiling 13,650 ft
(4160 m); take-off run 1,132 ft (345 m) at maximum take-off weight; take-off distance to 50 ft (15 m) 1,883 ft (574 m) at maximum take-off weight; landing distance from 50 ft (15 m) 1,493 ft (455 m) at normal landing weight; landing run 746 ft (227 m) at normal landing weight

Beech **Model 33/Bonanza**

Derived from the V-tailed Model 35, the **Model 33 Bonanza** differed in having a conventional tail, and was first flown on 14 September 1959 as the **Debonair**. Manufactured almost continuously since then, the Model 33 Bonanza has been adopted by a number of air arms in both standard **F33A** and aerobatic **F33C** forms. Of these, the **Mexican air force** has more than 30 F33Cs remaining from batches of 20 acquired in 1975 and 22 in 1986. These aircraft serve at the Escuela Militar de Aviación at Zapopán. The **Islamic Republic of Iran air force** may fly the survivors of 18 F33As and 27 F33Cs procured prior to the revolution of February 1979. The **Spanish air force** has 18 F33s with its 42 Grupo de Ensenanza at Getafe and half a dozen with the San Javier air academy, remaining from 12 F33As and 29

F33Cs originally purchased, and several of six F33Cs obtained in 1979 remain with the air arm of the **Ivory Coast**. Bonanzas are additionally flown by the air forces of **Haiti**, **Israel** and **Paraguay**.

SPECIFICATION

Beech Model F33A Bonanza
Wing: span 33 ft 5.5 in (10.20 m); aspect ratio 6.2; area 181.00 sq ft (16.81 m²)
Fuselage and tail: length 25 ft 6 in (7.77 m); height 8 ft 3 in (2.51 m); tailplane span 12 ft 2 in (3.71 m); wheel track 9 ft 6.75 in (2.91 m); wheel base 7 ft 5.75 in (2.27 m)
Powerplant: one Teledyne Continental IO-520-B rated at 285 hp (213 kW)
Weights: empty 2,000 lb (907 kg); maximum take-off 3,400 lb (1542 kg)

Production of the first Model 35 Bonanza commenced in 1946. Spain operates the IO-520-B-powered F33A and C under the designation E.24A and B.

Fuel and load: internal fuel 44 US gal (166.5 litres) plus provision for 30 US gal (113.5 litres) of auxiliary fuel; external fuel none; maximum ordnance none
Speed: maximum level speed 'clean' at sea level 182 kt (209 mph; 336 km/h); maximum cruising speed at 6,000 ft (1980 m) 174 kt (200 mph; 322 km/h); economical cruising speed at 10,000 ft (3050 m) 135 kt (156 mph; 251 km/h)
Range: ferry range 851 nm (980 miles; 1577 km);
range 433 nm (499 miles; 803 km)
Performance: maximum rate of climb at sea level 1,136 ft (346 m) per minute; service ceiling 17,500 ft (5335 m); take-off run 1,091 ft (333 m) at maximum take-off weight; take-off distance to 50 ft (15 m) 1,873 ft (571 m) at maximum take-off weight; landing distance from 50 ft (15 m) 1,500 ft (457 m) at normal landing weight; landing run 792 ft (242 m) at normal landing weight

Beech **Model 45 T-34A/B Mentor**

Derived from the Model 35 Bonanza commercial light cabin monoplane of 1945, the Beech **Model 45 Mentor** tandem two-seat trainer was first flown as a prototype on 2 December 1948. Early in 1950, the USAF initiated the selection process for a primary tuitional aircraft, evaluating three Model 45s as **YT-34**s. On 4 March 1953, the Beech trainer was announced the winning contender and ordered into production as the **T-34A**, the **USAF** eventually procuring 350 from the parent company and 100 from Canadian Car and Foundry. Deliveries to the USAF's Air Training Command began in 1954, in which year the **US Navy**, too, elected to adopt the Mentor as standard primary training equipment, deliveries of 423 similar **T-34B**s commencing on 17 December 1954. In 1955 the Model 73 Jet Mentor, developed from the Model 45 but powered by a YJ69 turbojet, first flew. It was soon abandoned in favour of the increasingly popular T-34.

Canadian Car and Foundry also manufactured 25 Mentors for the **Royal Canadian Air Force** (24 of these subsequently being transferred to **Turkey**), and 75 were assembled by the FMA at Cordoba for the **Argentine air force** (which also received 15 from the parent company), while Fuji in **Japan** built 124 under licence for the

national Air Self-Defence Force and 36 for the **Philippine air force**. In addition, the parent company exported T-34s to Japan (18), **Chile** (66), **Colombia** (41), **Mexico** (four), **El Salvador** (three) and **Venezuela** (41). The US government also supplied T-34s through the Military Assistance Program to **Spain** and **Saudi Arabia**. The Mentor became redundant in USAF service in 1960 with the introduction of all-through jet training while, in the US Navy, the Mentors were progressively phased out in favour of the **T-34C Turbo Mentor** (described separately) through the late 1970s and early 1980s. A small number of Mentors are still operated as hacks in support of recruitment efforts.

Of more than 1,300 Mentors manufactured, approximately 120 of these trainers – each averaging some 35 years of age – remain standard primary tuitional equipment with the air forces of Argentina, Colombia, **Dominica**, El Salvador, the Philippines, Turkey (air force and navy), **Uruguay** and Venezuela.

SPECIFICATION

Beech Model 45 (T-34A/B Mentor)
Wing: span 32 ft 10 in (10.01 m); aspect ratio 6.07;
area 177.60 sq ft (16.50 m²)
Fuselage and tail: length 25 ft 10 in (7.87 m); height 9 ft 7 in (2.92 m); wheel track 9 ft 6.5 in (2.91 m)
Powerplant: one Continental O-470-13 or, in T-34B, one Continental O-470-4, both rated at 225 hp (168 kW)
Weights: empty 2,055 lb (932 kg); normal take-off 2,600 lb (1179 kg); maximum take-off 2,900 lb (1315 kg)
Fuel and load: internal fuel 50 US gal (189 miles); external fuel none; ordnance none
Speed: maximum level speed 'clean' at sea level 163 kt (188 mph; 302 km/h); maximum cruising speed at 10,000 ft (3050 m) 145 kt (167 mph; 269 km/h)

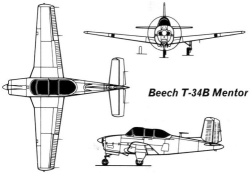

Beech T-34B Mentor

Range: 667 nm (770 miles; 11238 km)
Performance: maximum rate of climb at sea level 1,210 ft (369 m) per minute; service ceiling 21200 ft (6465 m)

The Mentor was licence-built by Fuji, in Japan, and was supplied to the Philippine air force in its T-34A form.

Beech **Model 45 (T-34C) Turbo Mentor**

In March 1973, almost 20 years after the service had selected the Model 45 as its standard primary trainer under the designation T-34B, the US Navy sought a single type of aircraft to replace both the *ab initio* Beech trainer and the North American T-28B and T-28C onto which students progressed from the T-34B. To meet this requirement, and under US Navy contract, Beech began adaptation of the basic Model 45 design to take a derated PT6A-25 turboprop, converting two T-34Bs to take this powerplant as **YT-34C**s, the first of these flying on 21 September 1973.

After an extended development programme, in April 1975 the USN ordered production of the **T-34C Turbo Mentor**. Since its earliest days in US Navy service the Turbo Mentor has been referred to as the 'Tormentor', and it is still the first aircraft encountered by prospective naval pilots. Successive contracts brought the total produced to 352 by April 1984, of which 19 were built as attrition replacements, with the final deliveries in April 1990. An armed version built solely for export carries the designation **T-34C-1.**

OPERATORS

The majority of USN T-34Cs are used in the primary training role and approximately 200 aircraft are shared by Training Wing Five's three squadrons: VT-2, VT-3 and VT-6 at Whiting Field, FL. Training Wing Four at Corpus Christi, TX, operates a smaller fleet of some 70 T-34Cs in a similar role; these aircraft being assigned to VT-27. VT-10 of Training Wing Six at Pensacola, FL, operates 20 aircraft to give limited flight instruction to naval flight officers.

In addition, the Turbo Mentor is operated in very limited numbers by USN fleet training units VA-42

(equipped with the A-6 Intruder), VFA-125 (F/A-18 Hornet), LAW-1 (F/A-18) and USMC attack squadron VMFAT-101 (F/A-18), on range clearance and spotting duties. VF-43 has at least three T-34Cs as spin trainers. One early production Turbo Mentor was assigned to permanent test duties at Patuxent River as an NT-34C. Six T-34Cs were transferred from US Navy stocks to the US Army to serve as chase and photographic aircraft for the Airborne Special Operations Test Board at Fort Bragg until replaced by Pilatus PC-9s (since disposed of also). It is intended to replace this veteran design with whatever aircraft is selected to fulfil the JPATS requirement, but probably not before fiscal year 2000.

Beech also built for export 129 T-34C-1 armament systems training models of the US Navy's T-34C, these being capable of forward air control and strike training missions in addition to basic flying tuition.

was supplied to the Argentine navy (15), the Ecuadorian air force (20), the Ecuadorian navy (three), the Gabonese Presidential Guard (four), the Indonesian air force (25), the Moroccan air force (12), the Peruvian navy (seven), the Nationalist Chinese air force (40) and the Uruguayan navy (three). A civil version is known as the Turbine Mentor 34C, six trainers of this type having been supplied to the Algerian national pilot training school in 1979.

SPECIFICATION

Beech T-34C Turbo Mentor
Wing: span 33 ft 4 in (10.16 m); aspect ratio 6.2; area 179.6 sq ft (16.69 m2)
Fuselage and tail: length 28 ft 8.5 in (8.75 m); height 9 ft 7 in (2.92 m); tailplane span 12 ft 2 in (3.71 m); wheel track 9 ft 8 in (2.95 m); wheel base 7 ft 11 in (2.41 m)
Powerplant: one Pratt & Whitney Canada PT6A-25 rated at 715 shp (533 kW)

Weights: empty 2,960 lb (1342 kg); maximum take-off 4,300 lb (1950 kg)
Fuel and load: internal fuel 130 US gal (492 litres); external fuel none; maximum ordnance none
Speed: never exceed speed 280 kt (322 mph; 518 km/h); maximum cruising speed at 17,000 ft (5180 m) 214 kt (246 mph; 396 km/h)
Range: 708 nm (814 miles; 1311 km) at 180 kt (207 mph; 333 km/h) at 20,000 ft (6095 m), or 427 nm (491 miles; 790 km) at 181 kt (208 mph; 335 km/h) at 1,000 ft (305 m)
Performance: maximum rate of climb at sea level 1,480 ft (451 m) per minute; service ceiling more than 30,000 ft (9145 m); take-off run 1,155 ft (352 m) at 4,210 lb (1588 kg); take-off distance to 50 ft (15 m)

1,920 ft (586 m) at 4210 lb (1588 kg); landing distance from 50 ft (15 m) 1,795 ft (547 m) at maximum landing

weight; landing run 740 ft (226 m) at maximum landing weight

Beech Model 50/Twin Bonanza/L-23/U-8 Seminole

The first post-World War II US light twin-engined aircraft to attain quantity production, the **Model 50 Twin Bonanza** six-seater first flew on 15 November 1949. Various examples of the progressively-refined series models were procured in small quantities for utility and liaison tasks

by several air forces. In addition, the **US Army** adopted the Twin Bonanza as the **L-23A Seminole**, 55 of which were followed by 40 examples of the generally similar **L-23B**. In November 1956 the US Army began to accept 85 **L-23D**s based on the commercial Model E50 and, during 1956

and 1958, the 93 surviving L-23As and Bs were remanufactured to the same standard with 340-hp (253-kW) Lycoming O-480-1 engines. Six Model D50s with 295-hp (220-kW) GO-480-G2D6 were acquired as **L-23E**s. In 1962, the L-23D and E were respectively redesignated **U-8D** and **U-8E**,

the last of these veterans being phased out of US Army service in the 1980s. One Twin Bonanza ostensibly remains in the inventory of the **Haitian air corps** and another continued in service until recently with the **Pakistan air force** alongside more modern Beech B55 Barons.

Beech Model Baron 55/T-42 Cochise

A development of the Model 95 Travel Air with two 260-hp (194-kW) Continental IO-470-L engines and swept vertical tail surfaces, the four/five-seat **Model 95-55**, or **Baron 55**, first flew on 29 February 1960. An optional sixth seat was introduced with the **Baron A55**, available from January 1962. The Baron was built in large numbers primarily for civil use in successively upgraded series (**B55**, **C55**, **D55** and **E55**), the provision of a 30-in (76-cm) longer cabin and 285-hp (213-kW) IO-520-C engines late in 1969 resulting in the **Baron 58**. Production continued until the early 1990s.

The Baron was procured for utility and liaison roles by various military forces and, in February 1965, was chosen by the **US Army** for use as a twin-engined instrument trainer. Seventy examples of the **Baron B55B** were ordered as the **T-42A Cochise**, five of these being for Military

Assistance Program delivery to **Turkey**.

Some 20 T-42As are currently included in the inventory of the US Army Reserve at Cairns Army Airfield, and three remain with the Turkish army. Various models of the Baron 55 and 58 serve with the **Argentine army** (two), the **Mexican navy** (three), the **Haitian air corps** (one), and the air forces of **Brazil** (one), **Paraguay** (one), **Spain** (five – local designation **E.20**) and **Togo** (two).

SPECIFICATION

Beech Baron Model D55
Wing: span 37 ft 9.75 in (11.52 m); aspect ratio 7.2; area 199.20 sq ft (18.51 m2)
Fuselage and tail: length 29 ft 0 in (8.84 m); height 9 ft 3 in (2.82 m); tailplane span 15 ft 11.25 in (4.86 m); track 9 ft 7 in (2.92 m); wheel base 8 ft 0 in (2.44 m)

Powerplant: two Teledyne Continental IO-520-C each rated at 285 hp (212 kW)
Weights: empty 3,075 lb (1395 kg); maximum take-off 5,300 lb (2404 kg)
Fuel and load: internal fuel 112 US gal (424 litres) standard or 142 US gal (536 litres) optional; external fuel none
Speed: maximum level speed clean at sea level 210

kt (242 mph; 390 km/h); maximum cruising speed at 7,000 ft (2135 m) 200 kt (230 mph; 370 km/h); economical cruising speed at 10,000 ft (3050 m) 169 kt (195 mph; 314 km/h)
Range: 993 nm (1,143 miles; 1840 km)
Performance: maximum rate of climb at sea level 1,670 ft (510 m) per minute; service ceiling 20,900 ft (6370 m); take-off run 596 ft (182 m) at maximum take-off weight; take-off distance to 50 ft (15 m) 968 ft (295 m) at maximum take-off weight; landing distance from 50 ft (15 m) 1,414 ft (431 m) at normal landing weight; landing run 868 ft (265 m) at normal landing weight

The Beech B55 Baron was a six-seat development of the A55, with a longer nose and increased MTOW. Nearly 2,000 were built.

Beech Model 65/80/Queen Air (Excalibur Queenaire)

A direct-growth version of the Model 50 Twin Bonanza embodying basic fuselage redesign, the **Model 65 Queen Air** was first flown on 28 August 1958. With a crew of one or two and accommodation for four to seven passengers, the Model 65 Queen Air or Queen Air 65 was ordered for evaluation by the **US Army**. The first example flew as the **L-23F Seminole** in January 1959. Subsequent contracts placed by the service brought total procurement of the L-23F to 68 aircraft. The type was redesignated as the **U-8F** in 1962, following rationalisation of all service designations.

The Queen Air 65 was also adopted by **Japan's Maritime Self-Defence Force** for navigational training and communications tasks, 19 being delivered from 1963 and known as the **B-65 Umibato** (Sea Dove). The JMSDF Queen Air 65s were later supplemented by nine **Queen Air A65**s introduced by the Beech company in 1966, featuring swept vertical tail surfaces

similar to those first employed by the Model 65-80 Queen Air 80, which had entered production in 1962. The A65 also embodied increased fuel capacity. Five of the JMSDF's Queen Airs were transferred to the Air Self-Defence Force in March 1980 and currently remain with that service. Only two are still in the inventory of the JMSDF, and these have relinquished their training role.

The **Queen Air 80** introduced a 300-lb (136-kg) weight increase – raising MTOW to 8,000 lb (3629 kg) and resulting in the numerical suffix – and IGSO-540-A1A engines. First flown on 22 June 1961, the Queen Air 80 was succeeded in 1964 by the **A80** with a modest wing span increase and certification for up to 11 passengers. With more minor changes, the **B80** followed in 1966, and the Queen Air 80 series proved popular with Latin American military services and is serving with the air forces of **Colombia** (four), **Dominica** (three), **Peru** (15), **Uruguay** (five) and **Venezuela** (four).

The air component of the **Ecuadorean army** operates two examples. The Queen Air 80 is also operated by **Israel's Heyl Ha'Avir**, which has some 20 for the twin-engine conversion role.

Beech designed the Queen Air to accommodate two main seating arrangements. The Airliner Package comprised seven seats with a baggage compartment. The Executive Package sat four passengers.

The Colombian air force operates a wide range of transports, from a Boeing 707 to the DHC-3 Otter. This is a Beech 65-B80 Queen Air attached to the liaison fleet of CACOM-3 at Barranquilla.

During 1981-83, the US Army purchased 11 ex-commercial Queen Air 65s, which, like the essentially similar aircraft originally built, were designated U-8F Seminole. More than 40 U-8Fs currently remain in service with Army Reserve and National Guard units after conversion to **Excalibur Queenaire 800** standard. This involved fitting new Lycoming IO-720 powerplants driving metal Hartzell props, revised engine nacelle design and a new exhaust system.

SPECIFICATION

Beech Queen Air Model A65
Wing: span 45 ft 10.5 in (13.98 m); aspect ratio 7.6; area 277.06 sq ft (25.73 m2)
Fuselage and tail: length 35 ft 6 in (10.82 m); height 14 ft 2.5 in (4.33 m); tailplane span 17 ft 2.75 in (5.25 m); wheel track 12 ft 9 in (3.89 m); wheel base 12 ft 3.5 in (3.75 m)
Powerplant: two Textron Lycoming IGSO-480-A1E6 each rated at 340 hp (253.5 kW)
Weights: empty 4,960 lb (2249 kg); maximum take-off 7,700 lb (3493 kg)
Fuel and load: internal fuel 214 US gal (811 litres) standard or 264 US gal (1000 litres) optional; external fuel none
Speed: maximum level speed 'clean' at 12,000 ft (3660 m) 208 kt (239 mph; 385 km/h); maximum cruising speed at 15,000 ft (4570 m) 186 kt (214 mph; 344 km/h); economical cruising speed at 15,000 ft (4570 m) 149 kt (171 mph; 275 km/h)
Range: range 1,442 nm (1,660 miles; 2671 km) with optional fuel
Performance: maximum rate of climb at sea level 1,300 ft (396 m) per minute; service ceiling 31,300 ft (9540 m); take-off run 1,180 ft (360 m) at maximum take-off weight; take-off distance to 50 ft (15 m) 1,560 ft (475 m) at maximum take-off weight; landing distance from 50 ft (15 m) 1,750 ft (533 m) at normal landing weight; landing run 1,330 ft (405 m) at normal landing weight

Beech **90 King Air/U-21 Ute/T-44**

One Queen Air 80 airframe was fitted with 500-hp (372-kW) Pratt & Whitney Canada PT6A-6 turboprops and flown on 15 May 1963, subsequently being delivered to the US Army as the NU-8F. The definitive model, which was developed from the **NU-8F**, featured a pressurised cabin and was first flown on 20 January 1964.

In October 1966, the **US Army** adopted an unpressurised version of the King Air as the **U-21A Ute** with 550-hp (409-kW) PT6A-20 engines. The first example flew in March 1967 and a total of 161 was eventually procured. The U-21A utility aircraft could accommodate 10 combat troops, six command personnel, or three stretcher patients and three seated casualties. Some 60 were adapted for special Elint tasks, designations ranging from **RU-21A** to **RU-21E** according to the equipment and powerplant installed. Many of these were upgraded to **RU-21H** standard with new wingtips and undercarriage, and this sub-type preponderates among the 40-plus RU-21s remaining in US Army service. About a dozen others have been reconverted for the utility role to join approximately 100 surviving U-21s.

In 1976, a **US Navy** advanced turboprop pilot training aircraft requirement was met by an off-the-shelf purchase of the **King Air 90** as the **T-44A**. This tuitional model entered service in 1977, with procurement totalling 61 aircraft for service at NAS Cor-

pus Christi, TX, with squadrons VT-28 and VT-31. A modestly stretched version of the basic King Air appeared in 1969. With a 4-ft 2-in (1.27-m) longer fuselage, a reduced wing span and 680-hp (507-kW) PT6A-28 engines, this **Model 65-100 King Air 100** had a crew of two and carried 13 passengers. Five examples were delivered to the US Army as **U-21F**s.

The King Air has been exported to a number of military services. The Model 65-90 is included in the air forces of **Bolivia**, **Colombia** (**C90**), **Ecuador** (**E90**), **Mexico** (and Mexican navy), **Peru** (**C90**) and **Thailand** (**E90**). The C90 version is operated additionally by the **Venezuelan army** and **navy**. Twenty-five **TC90** and **UC90** King Airs have been acquired by the **Japanese Maritime Self-Defence Force** for transport and multi-engine training, replacing Queen Air 65s. The larger Model 65-100 serves with the air forces of **Chile** (in the photo-survey role), **Ivory Coast** and **Morocco**. The **Jamaican Defence Force Air Wing** operates one King Air 100 for maritime patrol and transport duties.

SPECIFICATION

Beech King Air Model C90A
Wing: span 50 ft 3 in (15.32 m); aspect ratio 8.6; area 293.94 sq ft (27.31 m2)

Fuselage and tail: length 35 ft 6 in (10.82 m); height 14 ft 3in (4.34 m); tailplane span 17 ft 3 in (5.26 m); wheel track 12 ft 9 in (3.89 m); wheel base 12 ft 3 in (3.73 m)
Powerplant: two Pratt & Whitney Canada PT6A-21 each rated at 550 shp (410 kW)
Weights: empty 6,580 lb (2985 kg); maximum take-off 10,100 lb (4581 kg)
Fuel and load: internal fuel 384 US gal (1454 litres); external fuel none
Speed: maximum cruising speed at 12,000 m (3660 m) 241 kt (278 mph; 448 km/h) and at 16,000 m (4875 m) 247 kt (284 mph; 457 km/h)
Range: 1,277 nm (1,470 miles; 2336 km)
Performance: maximum rate of climb at sea level 2,000 ft (610 m) per minute; service ceiling 28,900 ft (8810 m); take-off run 1,885 ft (574 m) at maximum take-off weight; take-off distance to 50 ft (15 m) 2,577 ft

Beech T-44A Pegasus

(785 m) at maximum take-off weight; landing distance from 50 ft (15 m) 2,078 ft (633 m) at maximum landing weight with propeller reversal; landing run 1,036 ft (316 m) at maximum landing weight with propeller reversal

To the US Navy, the Beech T-44A is known as the Pegasus. All examples currently in service are based at NAS Corpus Christi, flown by Training Wing Four.

Beech **Model 99**

The prototype of the **Beech Model 99**, when flown for the first time during July 1966, represented the largest aircraft to be manufactured in quantity by the company. Intended for operators of commuter airlines, it was a low-wing monoplane powered by twin turboprop engines. The roomy fuselage incorporated a flight deck with side-by-side seats for pilot and co-pilot, and the cabin was equipped with easily removable seats in a 15-passenger high-density layout. A double-width door was optional, to simplify the loading of cargo, and a movable cabin divider was available so that the aircraft could operate in an all-passenger, all-cargo or combined passenger/cargo role. Initial reaction was favourable and there were plans to build 100 units per year by mid-1968 to meet strong initial demand.

Such enthusiasm was not ultimately justified and it was not until 2 May 1968 that the first production aircraft was delivered to Commuter Airliners Inc. in the USA. When production of what was then designated the **B99 Airliner** was suspended in 1977, a total of only 164 had been built.

Of this total, small numbers entered military service, and some of these were acquired secondhand. The Beech 99 was purchased by **Thailand** and **Peru**, the type remaining in service only with the Royal Thai army, which operates a single example for transport duties. By far the largest user is **Chile**, which had nine **Beech 99A**s built as new. Three aircraft are used as liaison and general transports, with one example configured for VIP duties. The transports serve with 10 Grupo at Merino Benitez.

Political friction with Argentina has led to modification of the remaining aircraft for electronic surveillance work. These serve with Grupo No. 2's Escuadrilla de Guerra Electronica at Los Cerillos. Three examples, known as **Petrel Alfa**, have been configured with surveillance radar for maritime patrol missions. The remaining aircraft, named **Petrel Beta**, are fitted with an ENAER ITATA electronic intelligence suite and are employed for classifying Argentina's radar systems. This enables determination of an electronic order of battle and development of countermeasures.

SPECIFICATION

Beech Model B99
Wing: span 45 ft 10.5 in (13.98 m); aspect ratio 7.51; area 279.70 sq ft (25.98 m2)
Fuselage and tail: length 44 ft 6.75 in (13.58 m); height 14 ft 4.25 in (4.37 m); tailplane span 22 ft 4.5 in

(6.82 m); wheel track 13 ft 0 in (3.96 m); wheel base 17 ft 11.75 in (5.48 m)
Powerplant: two Pratt & Whitney Canada PT6A-28 each rated at 680 shp (507 kW)
Weights: empty equipped 5,777 lb (2620 kg); maximum take-off 10,900 lb (4944 kg)
Fuel and load: internal fuel 368 US gal (1393 litres); external fuel none
Speed: maximum cruising speed at 16,000 ft (4875 m) 244 kt (281 mph; 452 km/h)
Range: 1,019 nm (1,173 miles; 1887 km)
Performance: maximum rate of climb at sea level 2,090 ft (637 m) per minute; service ceiling 26,215 ft (8020 m); take-off run 1,660 ft (506 m) at maximum take-off weight; take-off distance to 50 ft (15 m) 2,480 ft (756 m) at maximum take-off weight; landing distance from 50 ft (15 m) 2,793 ft (851 m) at normal landing weight without propeller reversal or 1,810 ft (552 m) at normal landing weight with propeller reversal; landing run 1,317 ft (401 m) at normal landing weight without propeller reversal or 850 ft (259 m) at normal landing weight with propeller reversal

Beech **King Air 100/Super King Air 200/C-12**

The **Beech King Air 100** was based on the King Air 90 but incorporated a 50-in (127-cm) fuselage stretch, two extra cabin windows, larger tail, increased MTOGW and a twin-wheel main undercarriage. Nearly 400 were built and several found their way into military service. The **Super King Air 200** evolved from the King Air 100 as an even more enlarged, more powerful derivative of the latter, a pro-

totype flying on 27 October 1972. Introducing a T-tail, increased wing span, extra fuel and improved pressurisation, the Super King Air was adopted by all US armed services, with more than 300 currently active.

The first three production Super King Airs were delivered in 1974 to the **US Army** as **RU-21J** (later redesignated **C-12L**) electronic warfare and intelligence-gathering equipment testbeds. In the same year, stan-

dard Super King Airs were obtained off-the-shelf as staff transports by all four US armed services simultaneously, the US Army and **USAF** aircraft being assigned the designation **C-12A**, and those for the **US Navy** and **Marine Corps** (with cargo doors, more powerful engines and high flotation undercarriages) being designated as **UC-12B**. All versions were given the name **Huron**.

The C-12A Huron was powered by 750-shp (560-kW) Pratt & Whitney Canada PT6A-38 turboprops and had provision for two pilots and eight passengers, the first of 60 entering US Army service in July 1975. The USAF received 30 identical aircraft. The Army later adopted the PT6A-41 engine for its C-12As, purchasing 14 additional aircraft with this powerplant as **C-12C**s. Twenty-nine of the USAF's C-12As were retrofitted

Beech King Air 100/Super King Air 200/C-12

with similar PT6A-42 engines as **C-12E**s.

Further production for the US Army comprised 55 **C-12D**s with side cargo doors, high flotation undercarriages and provision for wingtip tanks. Six of these were delivered (as **UC-12D**s) to the Army National Guard and six more to the USAF, while 18 were converted to **RC-12D Guardrail** (described seperately) Elint configuration. Five examples of this variant were for FMS supply to **Israel** and the remainder for the US Army, which purchased six more under a May 1983 contract. These were followed in 1986 by a US Army purchase of nine basically similar **RC-12K**s with PT6A-67 engines, large cargo door and oversize wheels, deliveries of this model continuing through 1992 against follow-on contracts.

Deliveries of the Super King Air 200 to the USAF as an operational support aircraft under the designation **C-12F** began in May 1984, these having side cargo doors and payload choices including two casualty litters plus attendants. Forty were purchased by the USAF after an initial five-year lease, six were supplied to the Air National Guard and 17 were delivered to the US Army. The designation **UC-12B** was applied to 49 Super King Air 200s ordered off-the-shelf for the US Navy, with a further 17 going to the US Marine Corps. The US Navy also obtained 12 **UC-12F**s (equivalent to the C-12F) and these, together with the UC-12Bs, became **UC-12M**s from 1987.

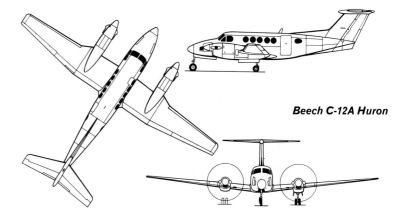

Beech C-12A Huron

OPERATORS

US Army: C-12 (all versions, 120)
USAF: C-12A, D and F (82)
USN and USMC: UC-12 B, F and M (100)
Algeria: A100 (1), 200 (5), 200T (2)
Argentina: 200 (7)
Bolivia: 200 (1), 200C (2)
Ecuador: 200 (2)
Greece: C-12A (1)
Guatemala: 200 (1)
Hong Kong: B200C (2)
India: B200 (3), B200C (2)
Ireland: 200 (1)
Israel: B200 (4), RC-12D (5)
Ivory Coast: 200 (1)
Japan: 200T (14)
Libya: 200C (2)
Morocco: 100 (5), B200 (3), B200C (1)
Peru: B200CT (3), B200T (3)
Sudan: 200C (1)
Sweden: 200 (3)
Thailand: 200 (1), B200 (1)
Togo: B200 (2)
Turkey: B200 (6)
Venezuela: B200 (3), 200C (2), B200C (1)
Yugoslavia: 200 (1)

SPECIFICATION

Beech C-12F

Wing: span 54 ft 6 in (16.61 m); aspect ratio 9.8; area 303.0 sq ft (28.15 m²)
Fuselage and tail: length 43 ft 9 in (13.34 m); height 15 ft 0 in (4.57 m); tailplane span 18 ft 5 in (5.61 m); wheel track 17 ft 2 in (5.23 m); wheel base 14 ft 11.5 in (4.56 m)
Powerplant: two Pratt & Whitney Canada PT6A-42 each rated at 850 shp (634 kW)
Weights: operating empty 8,060 lb (3656 kg); maximum take-off 12,500 lb (5670 kg)
Fuel and load: internal fuel 3,645 lb (1653 kg); external fuel none; maximum payload 2,647 lb (1201 kg)
Speed: never exceed speed 259 kt (298 mph; 480 km/h) IAS; maximum level speed at 25,000 ft (7620 m) 294 kt (339 mph; 545 km/h); maximum cruising speed at

25,000 ft (7620 m) 289 kt (336 mph; 536 km/h); economical cruising speed at 25,000 ft (7620 m) 282 kt (325 mph; 523 km/h)
Range: 1,965 nm (2,263 miles; 3641 km)
Performance: maximum rate of climb at sea level 2,450 ft (747 m) per minute; service ceiling more than 35,000 ft (10670 m); take-off run 1,856 ft (566 m) at maximum take-off weight; take-off distance to 50 ft (15 m) 2,579 ft (786 m) at maximum take-off weight; landing distance from 50 ft (15 m) 2,074 ft (632 m) at normal landing weight with propeller reversal or 2,845 ft (867 m) without propeller reversal; landing run 1,760 ft (536 m) at normal landing weight

The US Navy and Marine Corps purchased the UC-12B, a military version of the Super King Air A200C, with PT6A-41s and a rear cargo door.

Standard civil Super King Airs have been widely adopted as staff/VIP transports. This is one of three aircraft operated by the Swedish air force.

Beech RC-12

Versions of the U-21 configured for battlefield Sigint missions have served the **US Army** well for many years. The natural heir is the Beech RC-12, based on the Super King Air 200 airframe. Several versions are in use, the first of which was the **RC-12D**, which was produced under the programme name **Improved Guardrail V**. Thirteen of this variant were built, mostly for service with the 1st and 2nd Military Intelligence Battalions in Germany. With cabin windows faired over, the cabin of the RC-12D is packed with electronic recording equipment largely aimed at the gathering of Comint. The RC-12D operates in minimally-manned configuration, onboard receivers collecting and locating hostile communications, and relaying the data via a downlink to ground vehicles for further analysis and dissemination to ground commanders. RC-12Ds are characterised by a wide array of dipole and blade antennas, and large wingtip pods housing ESM.

Two similar versions are the **RC-12G**, of which three were delivered with higher gross weights and Sanders-installed electronics equipment, and the **RC-12H**, six of which were delivered to the 3rd Military Intelligence Battalion operating in Korea. These again have higher gross weights, but have the same ESL-installed Improved Guardrail V equipment as the RC-12D.

The current major model is the **RC-12K Guardrail Common Sensor**, which combines the Comint mission of the RC-12D with the Elint mission previously undertaken

The RC-12K succeeds the RU-21H and RC-12D as the US Army's prime D/F and voice intercept intelligence-gathering platform. This programme dates from the Korean War and the current aircraft were heavily utilised during Operation Desert Storm. Improved Guardrail aircraft are fitted with the Guardrail/Common Sensor System (G/CSS) combining a Comint and Elint sensor fit. They also carry the ASE/ACS self-protection jamming fit.

by the Grumman RV-1D. Thirty-four are on order for the US Army, and deliveries began to Europe. These aircraft feature even larger numbers of aerials than their predecessors, with radar receivers having been added. The **RC-12N** is believed to be a similar version with some upgrades. In 1995/96 the US Army will introduce the **RC-12P** into the Guardrail fleet but, beyond its name, little has been made public about this aircraft.

In addition to the US Army **Special Electronic Mission Aircraft (SEMA)**, there are two **US Navy** King Air versions with the RC-12 designation. Both are configured as **RANSAC** (range surveillance aircraft) platforms, and are distinguished by having a large radome under the centre-section. The two **RC-12F**s are employed at the Barking Sands Missile Range Facility in the Hawaiian islands, and a similar number of **RC-12M**s fly with the Naval Air Warfare Center/Weapons Division (formerly Pacific Missile Test Center) at NAS Point Mugu, CA, and with the base flight at NS Roosevelt Roads, PR. Their chief task is to clear the maritime ranges before missiles tests.

SPECIFICATION

Beech RC-12D

Wing: span 57 ft 10 in (17.63 m)
Powerplant: two Pratt & Whitney Canada PT6A-41 each rated at 850 shp (634 kW)
Weights: empty 7,334 lb (3327 kg)
Fuselage and tail: length 43 ft 9 in (13.34 m); height 15 ft 0 in (4.57 m); tailplane span 18 ft 5 in (5.61 m); wheel track 17 ft 2 in (5.23 m); wheel base 14 ft 11.5 in (4.56 m)
Fuel and load: internal fuel 3,540 lb (1606 kg); maximum payload more than 2,300 lb (1043 kg)
Speed: maximum level speed at 14,000 ft (4265 m) 260 kt (299 mph; 481 km/h); maximum cruising speed at 30,000 ft (9145 m) 236 kt (272 mph; 438 km/h)
Range: at maximum cruising speed 1,584 nm (1,824 miles; 2935 km)
Performance: service ceiling 30,900 ft (9420 m); take-off distance to 50 ft (15 m) 2,850 ft (869 m); landing distance from 50 ft (15 m) 2,514 ft (766 m)

Beech Super King Air 300/350

Following the success of its 200 series, Beech introduced the **Super King Air 300/350** series to continue the sales drive. The **King Air 300LW** is an improved Series 200, and this led to the **Super King Air 350**, which featured a stretched fuselage accommodating up to 12 passengers in standard configuration, useful for the staff transport/liaison mission. The 350 is also characterised by its drag-reducing winglets.

Raytheon undertook the conversion of the prototype 350 to **RC-350 Guardian** standard for the signals intelligence mission. In addition to ALQ-142 ESM equipment in wingtip pods and Watkins-Johnson communications intelligence receiver in an underbelly radome, the RC-350 also has accurate navigation gear including laser INS and GPS, and a secure datalink. As yet there are no military orders for the Guardian, which closely resembles the RC-12 in its mission and equipment, despite an impressive six-plus hour loiter time on-station. The government of **Morocco** operates a single Super King Air 300 for VIP duties.

SPECIFICATION

Beech Super King Air Model 300
Wing: span 54 ft 6 in (16.61 m); aspect ratio 9.8; area 303.00 sq ft (28.15 m²)
Fuselage and tail: length 43 ft 10 in (13.36 m); height 14 ft 4 in (4.37 m); tailplane span 18 ft 5 in (5.61 m); wheel track 17 ft 2 in (5.23 m); wheel base 14 ft 11.5 in (4.56 m)
Powerplant: two Pratt & Whitney Canada PT6A-60A each rated at 1,050 shp (783 kW)
Weights: empty 8,490 lb (3851 kg); maximum take-off 14,000 lb (6350 kg)
Fuel and load: internal fuel 539 US gal (2039 litres); external fuel none
Speed: maximum level speed 'clean' at optimum altitude 317 kt (365 mph; 587 km/h); maximum cruising speed at optimum altitude 315 kt (363 mph; 583 km/h); economical cruising speed at optimum altitude 307 kt (353 mph; 568 km/h)
Range: 1,959 nm (2,256 miles; 3630 km)
Performance: maximum rate of climb at sea level 2,844 ft (867 m) per minute; certificated ceiling 35,000 ft (10670 m); take-off run 1,350 ft (411 m) at maximum take-off weight; take-off distance to 50 ft (15 m) 1,992 ft (607 m) at maximum take-off weight; landing distance from 50 ft (15 m) 2,907 ft (886 m) at normal landing weight; landing run 1,686 ft (514 m) at normal landing weight without propeller reversal

This heavily retouched photograph illustrates Beechcraft's planned special mission Super King Air 350/RC-350 Guardian.

Beech Model 1900/C-12J

The **Beech Model 1900** commuter transport evolved as a stretched derivative of the Super King Air 200. The first Model 1900 flew on 3 September 1982, and made provision for a crew of either one or two on the flight deck and standard accommodation for 19 passengers. The Model 1900, of which only three examples were built, gave place to the **Model 1900C** as the standard production variant, differing only in having a starboard rear cargo door. This was powered by two 820-kW (1,100-shp) Pratt & Whitney Canada PT6A-65B turboprops, as was also the succeeding series version, the **Model 1900C-1** with a wet wing and redesigned fuel system. Production of the Beech 1900C ceased in 1991 after delivery of a total of 225 examples. A 'biz-prop' version, the **1900C/C-1 Exec-Liner**, was developed but fewer than 10 were sold, to civilian customers only.

The Model 1900C-1 was the first to receive military orders, a contract being placed in March 1986 by the **USAF** for six examples. Delivered from September 1987 as **C-12J**s, these replaced C-131s with the Air National Guard as mission support aircraft. From January 1988, 12 Model 1900C-1s were delivered to the **Republic of China air force**, the last of these being delivered in late 1989, and these serve with the VIP Transport Squadron of the Sungshan air base command. Eight were ordered for delivery to the **Egyptian air force** from 1989. Of these, six were delivered with electronic surveillance equipment and the remaining two, intended for maritime surveillance, were fitted with Litton search radar and Motorola side-looking airborne multi-mode radar (SLAMMR) and Singer-manufactured ESM equipment.

The Model 1900C was superseded in production by the **Model 1900D**. This version introduces a cabin with 28.5 per cent increased volume, swept tail surfaces with tailplane ventral fins, winglets, twin ventral strakes to improve directional stability and rear fuselage stabilons (additional fixed tail surfaces) to improve centre of gravity range. No military orders have yet been received.

The USAF and RoCAF operate the Beech 1900 in its intended transport role. The heavily modified Egyptian aircraft boast extensive aerial arrays.

SPECIFICATION

Beech C-12J
generally similar to the Beech C-12F except in the following particulars:
Fuselage and tail: length 57 ft 10 in (17.63 m); height 14 ft 11 in (4.55 m); tailplane span 18 ft 6 in (5.64 m); wheel track 17 ft 2 in (5.23 m); wheel base 7.26 m (23 ft 10 in)
Powerplant: two Pratt & Whitney Canada PT6A-65B each rated at 1,100 shp (820 kW)
Weights: typical empty 9,100 lb (4128 kg); maximum take-off 16,600 lb (7530 kg)
Fuel and load: internal fuel 4,470 lb (2027 kg); maximum baggage 1,910 lb (866 kg)
Speed: maximum cruising speed at 25,000 ft (7620 m) 254 kt (292 mph; 471 km/h)
Range: with 15 passengers at high-speed cruising power 1,286 nm (1,481 miles; 2383 km)
Performance: maximum rate of climb at sea level 2,330 ft (710 m) per minute; service ceiling more than 25,000 ft (7620 m); take-off run 2,200 ft (671 m) at maximum take-off weight; take-off distance to 50 ft (15 m) 3,250 ft (991 m) at maximum take-off weight; landing distance from 50 ft (15 m) 2,540 ft (774 m) at maximum landing weight; landing run 1,530 ft (466 m) at maximum landing weight

Beech 400/T-1A Jayhawk

Entering service in increasing numbers, the **Beech T-1A Jayhawk** provides the **USAF** with advanced training for aircrew destined for multi-engine tanker/transport aircraft. It is the first aircraft type to be delivered for the SUPT (Specialized Undergraduate Pilot Training) system, which is being implemented to make the USAF's aircrew training more efficient and to cover a shortfall in T-38 capability, the Talon previously being responsible for all advanced training. The arrival of the T-1A in the TTTS (Tanker/Transport Training System) role allows the advanced training of crews for large aircraft on a system more compatible with their intended operational aircraft (KC-10, KC-135 and C-17).

From the outset, the US Air Force was looking for an 'off-the-shelf' design. Proposals from British Aerospace, Cessna and Learjet were considered by the US Air Force before Beech was awarded the contract in February 1990, this also covering simulator and a syllabus as part of an overall package.

The Jayhawk is based on the **Beechjet 400**, itself based on the Mitsubishi Diamond biz-jet. The Jayhawk differs from its civil counterpart by having increased fuel capacity with single-point refuelling, strengthened leading edges and windscreen for low-level birdstrike protection, and increased air-conditioning capability. The Jayhawk also features six fewer cabin windows in total, plus strengthened wing carry-through structure and engine attachment points to meet low-level flight stresses. The cabin-mounted avionics (relocated from the nose) include Rockwell Collins five-tube EFIS, turbulence-detection radar and TACAN with air-to-air capability.

For the SUPT role the aircraft carries instructor (right) and student (left) pilots, with a third observer/second student seat immediately behind. The cabin has four seats for passenger carriage or for additional students awaiting instruction.

When Beech acquired the Diamond design from Mitsubishi, they built 65, progressed to the improved Model 400A then developed the 400T (T-1A) for the TTTS programme, then sold it back to Japan.

The first production T-1A took to the air at Wichita, Kansas, on 5 July 1991, and the first was formally handed over to the US Air Force on 17 January 1992. Instructor training began in March 1992 with the 64th FTW at Reese AFB, with the first student courses beginning in September. By early 1994, 148 Jayhawks had been ordered, with an eventual total of 180 planned.

Both name and designation duplicate those of other US aircraft: T-1A was the post-1962 designation of the Lockheed T2V SeaStar, while the HH-60J Coast Guard helicopter is also known as the Jayhawk.

In a somewhat ironic move, by early 1994 the **Japan Air Self-Defence Force** had also taken delivery of three Beech **400T**s (equivalent to the T-1A) for its Kawasaki C-1 pilot training. The Beech 400T features thrust-reversers, extra fuel and regeared trim (to simulate a heavier aircraft). Three more are on order.

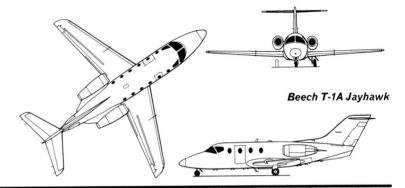

The Jayhawk features several changes over standard Beechjets. Featuring an additional fuel tank and a new fuel system, a strengthened undercarriage and only three windows (as opposed to six) 148 aircraft are currently on order. First deliveries went to Reese AFB.

Beech T-1A Jayhawk

SPECIFICATION

Beech T-1A Jayhawk
Wing: span 43 ft 6 in (13.25 m); aspect ratio 7.5; area 241.40 sq ft (22.43 m²)
Fuselage and tail: length 48 ft 5 in (14.75 m); height 13 ft 9 in (4.19 m); tailplane span 16 ft 5 in (5.00 m); wheel track 9 ft 4 in (2.84 m); wheel base 19 ft 3 in (5.86 m)
Powerplant: two Pratt & Whitney Canada JT15D-5B each rated at 2,900 lb st (12.9 kN) dry
Weights: operating empty 10,115 lb (4588 kg);

maximum take-off 15,780 lb (7157 kg)
Fuel and load: internal fuel 4,904 lb (2224 kg); external fuel none; maximum payload 2,400 lb (1089 kg)
Speed: never exceed speed Mach 0.785; maximum level speed at 29,000 ft (8840 m) 461 kt (531 mph; 854 km/h); typical cruising speed at 39,000 ft (11890 m) 447 kt (515 mph; 828 km/h); long-range cruising speed at 41,000 ft (12495 m) 388 kt (447 mph; 719 km/h)
Range: 1,930 nm (2,222 miles; 3575 km) with four passengers
Performance: maximum operating altitude 41,000 ft (12495 m); take-off distance to 35 ft (10.7 m) 3,950 ft (1204 m) at maximum take-off weight; landing distance from 50 ft (15 m) 2,830 ft (862 m) at maximum landing weight

Bell **Model 47/H-13 Sioux**

The comparatively small number of company personnel who witnessed on 8 December 1945 the first flight of the prototype **Bell Model 47**, a small two-seat utility helicopter, could not have expected that when production by Bell and its licensees ended well over 5,000 would have been built. However, the Model 47 was not only to prove a classic design, it was also the first helicopter to gain an Approved Type Certificate, and on 8 March 1946 was issued the first commercial helicopter licence (NC-1H) granted by the United States Civil Aeronautics Administration. It quickly proved both its reliability and simplicity of operation, and in 1947 the **USAAF** began procurement for evaluation of 28 improved Model 47A helicopters with the 157-hp (117-kW) Franklin O-335-1 piston engine. Of these, 15 were designated **YR-13**, three **YR-13A** models were for cold-weather testing, and the balance of 10 went to the US Navy as **HTL-1** trainers. In 1948 the US Army ordered the Model 47, acquiring 65 under the designation **H-13B**; all US Army versions were subsequently named **Sioux**. Later variants included the H-13B (15 conversions) to carry external

stretchers (redesignated **H-13C**); the two-seat **H-13D** with stretcher carriers and Franklin O-335-5 engines; the three-seat but similar dual-control **H-13E**; the **H-13G** which added a small elevator; and the **H-13H** with 250-hp (186-kW) Lycoming VO-435 engine. Some H-13Hs were used by the USAF, which also acquired two as **H-13J** helicopters for Presidential use, powered by derated VO-435 engines. The designation **H-13K** covered two trial H-13Hs with larger rotors and 225-hp (168-kW) Franklin 6VS-335 engines. In 1962 US Army H-13E/G/H/K Sioux were redesignated with prefix O, for observation; similarly, USAF H-13H/J helicopters were prefixed U, for utility. Later versions were the three-seat **OH-13S**, and the **TH-13T** instrument trainer. US Navy procurement included 12 **HTL-2** and nine **HTL-3** helicopters, but the **HTL-4** was the first major version; it was followed by the **HTL-5** (with O-335-5 engine), **HTL-6** (with elevator), **HTL-7** all-weather instrument trainer, and **HUL-1** for ice-breaking ships. In 1962 the HTL-4/6/7 and HUL-1 became, respectively, **TH-13U/M/N** and **UH-13P**.

Also licence-built by Agusta in Italy and Kawasaki in Japan, and by Westland Heli-

copters (under sub-licence from Agusta) as the **AB 47G-2** for the British army, Bell's Model 47 has seen widescale use by armed forces around the world. Today, numbers are dwindling, but an ever decreasing number still serve in the training or 'hack' roles with smaller air arms.

SPECIFICATION

Bell Helicopter Textron Model 47G-3B-2A
Rotor system: main rotor diameter 37 ft 2.5 in (11.32 m); tail rotor diameter 5 ft 10.125 in (1.78 m); main rotor disc area 1,082.49 sq ft (100.56 m²); tail rotor disc area 26.82 sq ft (2.49 m²)
Fuselage and tail: length overall, rotors turning 43 ft

7.5 in (13.30 m) and fuselage 31 ft 7 in (9.63 m); height overall 9 ft 3.875 in (2.84 m) to top of rotor head; skid track 7 ft 6 in (2.29 m)
Powerplant: one Textron Lycoming TVO-435-F1A rated at 280 hp (209 kW)
Weights: empty 2,893 lb (858 kg); maximum take-off 2,950 lb (1338 kg)
Fuel and load: internal fuel 57 US gal (216 litres); external fuel none; maximum payload 1,000 lb (454 kg)
Speed: maximum level speed at sea level 91 kt (105 mph; 169 km/h); recommended cruising speed at 5,000 ft (1525 m) 73 kt (84 mph; 135 km/h)
Range: 215 nm (247 miles; 397 km)
Performance: maximum rate of climb at sea level 990 ft (302 m) per minute; service ceiling 19,000 ft (5790 m); hovering ceiling 17,700 ft (5385 m) in ground effect and 12,700 ft (3870 m) out of ground effect

This Royal Malaysian Air Force Bell 47G is an ex-Indonesian aircraft and one of the few surviving US-built Model 47s still in service.

Bell **Model 204/UH-1 Iroquois**

Bell Helicopter Textron Inc.
PO Box 482, Fort Worth, Texas 76101
USA

In the early 1950s the **US Army** unveiled its requirement for a helicopter with a primary casevac mission, but suitable also for utility use and as an instrument trainer. In 1955 the design submitted by Bell was announced the winner, three prototypes of the **Bell Model 204** being ordered under the designation **XH-40**. The first of these (55-4459) was flown initially on 22 October 1956, its 825-shp (615-kW) Lycoming XT53-L-1 turboshaft engine, derated to 700 shp (522 kW), making it the first turbine-powered aircraft to be acquired by the US Army. The XH-40s were followed by six **YH-40** service trials aircraft with small changes,

the most important being a 1.0-ft (30.5-cm) fuselage 'stretch'. When ordered into production, the designation **HU-1A** was allocated, the HU prompting the 'Huey' nickname that survived the 1962 redesignation to **UH-1**, and which became far better known than the official title of l**Iroquois.** Initial production version was the HU-1A, with a crew of two, plus six passengers or two stretchers, and with the T53-L-1 engine. It was followed by the **HU-1B** with revised main rotor blades and an enlarged cabin seating two crew, plus seven passengers or three stretchers; early production helicopters had the 960-shp (716-kW)

Lycoming T53-L-5, late-production machines the 1,100-shp (820-kW) T53-L-11. In 1962, the HU-1A and HU-1B were redesignated **UH-1A** and **UH-1B** respectively, and in 1965 the UH-1B was superseded in production by the **UH-1C**.

Other military versions included the USMC's **UH-1E** (with rescue hoist, rotor brake and special avionics, and initially with a TAT-101 chin turret housing two 7.62-mm M60 machine-guns) and 20 similar dual-control-equipped **TH-1E** trainers; the USAF's 120 **UH-1F**s used for ICBM site support and 26 similar **TH-1F** trainers (both with uprated 1,290-shp/962-kW) General Electric

T58-GE-3 engines, and an increased-diameter Bell 540 rotor, 27 US Navy search and rescue **HH-1K**s (similar to the UH-1E but with a 1,400-shp/1044-kW) T53-L-13 engine and improved avionics, 90 **TH-1L** (training) and eight **UH-1L** (utility) both Navy versions of the UH-1E with T53-L-13 engine; and the US Army **UH-1M** with INFANT low-light-level TV equipment (three acquired for evaluation). In addition to production for the US armed forces, The Model 204B was extensively licence-built for both civil and military use by Agusta in Italy as the **Agusta-Bell AB 204** (described separately) and by Fuji in Japan, the latter also developing the

Fuji-Bell 204B-2 with increased engine power and a tractor tail rotor. In **Japanese Ground Self-Defence Force** service it was known as the **Hi'yodori** (meaning Bulbul – a type of finch).

OPERATORS

Austria: AB 204
Brazil: UH-1D
Indonesia: AB 204
Japan: UH-1B
Panama: UH-1B
Singapore: UH-1B
South Korea: UH-1B
Spain: UH-1C (HU.8)
Sweden: AB 204B (Hkp 3B)
Thailand: UH-1A, UH-1B
Uruguay: UH-1B
Yemen: AB 204B

SPECIFICATION

Bell Helicopter Textron Model 204 (UH-1C)
Rotor system: main rotor diameter 44 ft 0 in (13.41 m); tail rotor diameter 8 ft 6 in (2.59 m); main rotor disc area 1,520.53 sq ft (141.26 m2); tail rotor disc area 56.74 sq ft (5.27 m2)
Fuselage and tail: length overall, rotors turning 53 ft 0 in (16.15 m) and fuselage 42 ft 7 in (12.98 m); height overall 12 ft 7.25 in (3.84 m); stabiliser span 9 ft 4 in (2.84 m); skid track 8 ft 8 in (2.64 m)
Powerplant: one Textron Lycoming T53-L-11 rated at 1,100 shp (820 kW)
Weights: empty 5,071 lb (2300 kg); maximum take-off 9,500 lb (4309 kg)
Fuel and load: internal fuel 242 US gal (916 litres) plus provision for 350 US gal (1325 litres) of auxiliary fuel in a fuselage tank; external fuel none; maximum payload 3,000 lb (1361 kg)
Speed: maximum level and maximum cruising speed 'clean' at sea level 129 kt (148 mph; 238 km/h); economical cruising speed at 5,000 ft (1525 m) 124 kt (143 mph; 230 km/h)
Range: ferry range 332 nm (382 miles; 615 km) with auxiliary fuel
Performance: maximum rate of climb at sea level 1,400 ft (427 m) per minute; service ceiling 11,500 ft (3505 m); hovering ceiling 10,600 ft (3230 m) in ground effect and 10,000 ft (3050 m) out of ground effect

Bell Helicopter Textron Model 204 (UH-1E)
generally similar to the Model 204 (UH-1C Iroquois) except in the following particulars:
Weights: empty 5,055 lb (2292 kg); maximum take-off 9,500 lb (4309 kg)
Fuel and load: max payload 4,000 lb (1814 kg)
Speed: maximum level speed at sea level 140 kt (161 mph; 259 km/h); maximum cruising speed at sea level 120 kt (138 mph; 222 km/h)
Range: 248 nm (286 miles; 460 km)

Twenty-four Bell 204B Iroquois were delivered to Austria, though these have now largely been replaced by 24 Bell 212s. Eight 204Bs remain.

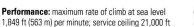

The hardworking Hkp 3Bs (AB 204Bs) of the Flygvapen (Swedish air force) are tasked mainly with SAR duties at bases throughout the country.

Performance: maximum rate of climb at sea level 1,849 ft (563 m) per minute; service ceiling 21,000 ft (6400 m); hovering ceiling 15,800 ft (4815 m) in ground effect and 11,800 ft (3595 m) out of ground effect

Bell Model 205/UH-1D/H Iroquois

Production of the Model 204 for the US armed services totalled some 2,500 examples, and Bell proposed an improved **Bell Model 205** to the US Army in 1960. A contract followed in July 1960 for seven service evaluation **YUH-1D** helicopters. These retained the Lycoming T53-L-11 turboshaft, but differed from the Model 204 by having a larger-diameter main rotor, and a lengthened fuselage for a pilot and 12-14 troops, or six stretchers and a medical attendant, or 4,000 lb (1814 kg) of freight. Additionally, the Model 205 featured increased fuel capacity and provision was made for auxiliary fuel. The prototype was flown on 16 August 1961 and the type was ordered into production for the US Army under the designation **UH-1D**, the first example being delivered on 9 August 1963. A total of 2,008 UH-1Ds was built for the US Army, followed by the generally similar **UH-1H**, which differed by introducing an uprated 1,400-shp (1044-kW) T53-L-13 turboshaft; final production of the UH-1H (40 for the Turkish army) occurred in 1986.

Variants of the Model 205 include three **EH-1H** ECM conversions from the UH-1H (with many more planned before the intended 'Quick Fix' ECM/Elint mission was taken over by the Sikorsky EH-60A), four **JUH-1H** testbeds for the radar intended for the EH-60B SOTAS, and some **220 UH-1V** medevac/rescue conversions from UH-1Hs, carried out by the US Army Electronics Command. One **EH-1X** was produced by marrying the airframe of an EH-1 jammer with the engine and IR jammer of an AH-1. Other military versions of the Model 205, generally similar to the UH-1H, have included 10 **CUH-1H** operational trainers for the Canadian Armed Forces (designated **CH-118**) and 30 **HH-1H** rescue helicopters for the USAF. Production of the UH-1H for the US Army totalled 3,573 examples, and it is planned to retain large numbers in service into the 21st century.

Under a product improvement programme, the US Army's Hueys have gained new avionics and equipment, and new composite main rotor blades are to be introduced, as well as Doppler navigation and an improved cockpit. Further radical upgrading seems increasingly likely. The US Army

requirement for 491 LUHs (Light Utility Helicopters) is unlikely to be funded, so many are pressing for the National Guard to take over the role with upgraded UH-1s or a new off-the-shelf type (the Vought Panther 800, MDH Explorer and Bell OH-58D all having been suggested). Thus, the Guard might gain more UH-1s to be upgraded alongside the 200 aircraft it already wants to replace or rebuild. Many export customers are also looking to upgrade their ageing Hueys.

Three companies are offering different UH-1 upgrades, all centred around re-engining the aircraft and upgrading its dynamic system. Avionics improvements are also incorporated and costs work out at between $750,000 and $1,000,000 per aircraft. Bell Helicopter itself offers the **UH-1HP Huey II** with an upgrade to the existing T53-13B engine (bringing it to T53-703 standard) during overhaul. This increases power by 400 shp (300 kW) and extends TBO by 600

hours (to 3,000 hours). If the 'new' engine is then derated to 13B levels, the airframe and dynamic system improvements necessary to use the extra power can be added in stages. All of these use existing Model 212 and UH-1N components, and include a strengthened tailboom, a tractor tail rotor, an uprated drive train and a 1,290-shp (960 kW) transmission, and the Model 212 main rotor hub and blades. The prototype first flew in August 1992. Gross weight is increased to 10,500 lb (4750 kg), allowing the aircraft to carry a 3,000-lb (1350-kg) payload over 200 nm (230 miles/370 km), where the original UH-1 would only carry 1,000 lb (450 kg). The T53-703 is marginally more fuel efficient than the original powerplant, offering a slight increase in range.

The fact that the Huey II carries Bell's 'seal of approval' has not deterred other companies from offering their own upgrades. Global Helicopter is promoting

the **Huey 800,** which replaces the T53 with an LHTEC T800-800 engine with an integral inlet particle separator and full authority digital engine controls. Engine life is extended to over 6,000 hours. Power output is actually reduced slightly, to 1,300 shp (985 kW), but the new engine is significantly lighter and much more fuel efficient. Power is not increased so the new aircraft requires no dynamic system changes, and the unchanged gross weight means that no airframe strengthening is necessary, although a speed reduction gearbox does need to be fitted. Range is increased dramatically, although maximum payload is not significantly increased. The prototype Huey 800 flew on 15 June 1992.

UNC Helicopter's upgraded aircraft is designated **UH-1/T700 Ultra Huey** and uses the same airframe/dynamic system improvements as the Huey II, but with a 1,900-shp (1400-kW) General Electric T700-GE-701C engine, with a life of 5,000 hours. The new engine requires a speed reduction gear box and vertical strip engine instruments, as found on the H-60. Performance

The Pakistan army was already operating helicopters of Soviet (Mil Mi-8), French (Sud Alouette III) and Romanian (CNIAR Lama) origin when it received its first American type in the form of the UH-1H. Six were delivered after the disastrous floods of 1973, with the strict proviso that they should be used only for humanitarian work. Allocated to No. 6 Emergency Relief Sqn they were later joined by 10 ex-Iranian AB 205As with No. 21 Sqn.

Bell Model 205/UH-1D/H Iroquois

benefits are almost identical to those enjoyed by the Huey II, though with better fuel burn figures.

In addition to military exports by Bell, a multi-role utility helicopter for both civil and military use has been extensively licence-built by Agusta in Italy as the **Agusta-Bell AB 205** (described separately); Fuji in Japan remains the only current production source of the Model 205 under the designation **HU-1H**. (The **AB 205A** and the improved **Advanced Model 205A-1** model are described separately.) Dornier in Germany completed 352 equivalent to the UH-1D model, which serve with the Luftwaffe and Heeresfliegertruppen, and in Taiwan AIDC built 118 similar to the UH-1H for the Chinese Nationalist army.

The Huey II is Bell's own entrant in the race for lucrative UH-1 upgrade contracts. Combining many of the advances found in the Model 212, it faces competition from the UNC Ultra Huey and Global Helicopter's Huey 800.

OPERATORS

Argentina: UH-1D, UH-1H
Australia: UH-1H
Bahrain: AB 205A-1
Bangladesh: AB 205A-1
Bolivia: UH-1H
Brazil: UH-1D, UH-1H
Brunei: B 205A-1
Canada: UH-1H (CH-118)
Chile: UH-1D, UH-1H
Colombia: UH-1H
Dominican Republic: B 205A-1
Dubai: B 205A-1
El Salvador: UH-1H
Germany: UH-1D
Greece: AB 205A, UH-1H
Guatemala: UH-1D
Honduras: UH-1H
Iran: AB 205A
Italy: AB 205
Jamaica : B 205
Japan: UH-1H, UH-1 Kai
Mexico: AB 205A-1, UH-1H
Morocco: AB 205A-1

Myanmar/Burma: UH-1H
New Zealand: UH-1H
Oman: AB 205A-1
Pakistan: AB 205, UH-1H
Panama: UH-1H
Peru: AB 205A-1
Philippines: UH-1H
Saudi Arabia: AB 205
Singapore: B 205, UH-1H
South Korea: UH-1H
Spain: UH-1H (HU.10B)
Taiwan/Republic of China: UH-1H
Tanzania: AB 205A
Thailand: UH-1H
Tunisia: AB 205A-1
Turkey: AB 205A, UH-1H
Uganda: AB 205
United Arab Emirates: B 205A
US Army UH-1H – chiefly special mission variants
Uruguay: UH-1H
Venezuela: UH-1D
Zambia: AB 205A
Zimbabwe: AB 205A

SPECIFICATION

Bell Helicopter Textron Model 205
Rotor system: main rotor diameter 48 ft 0 in (14.63 m); tail rotor diameter 8 ft 6 in (2.59 m); main rotor disc area 1,809.56 sq ft (168.11 m²); tail rotor disc area 56.74 sq ft (5.27 m²)
Fuselage and tail: length overall, rotors turning 57 ft 9.625 in (17.62 m) and fuselage 41 ft 10.25 in (12.77 m); height overall 14 ft 5.5 in (4.41 m) with tail rotor turning, and to top of rotor head 11 ft 9.75 in (3.60 m); stabiliser span 9 ft 4 in (2.84 m); skid track 9 ft 6.5 in (2.91 m)
Powerplant: one Textron Lycoming T53-L-13 rated at 1,400 shp (1044 kW)
Weights: empty equipped 5,210 lb (2363 kg); basic operating 5,557 lb (2520 kg) in the troop-carrying role; normal take-off 9,039 lb (4100 kg); maximum take-off 9,500 lb (4309 kg)
Fuel and load: internal fuel 223 US gal (844 litres)

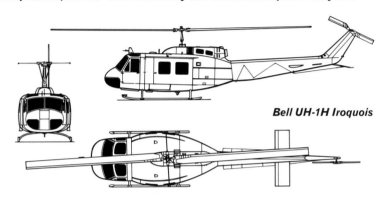

Bell UH-1H Iroquois

plus provision for 511 US gal (1935 litres) of auxiliary fuel in two tanks; external fuel none; maximum payload 3,880 lb (1759 kg)
Speed: never exceed, maximum level, maximum cruising and economical cruising speed at 5,700 ft (1735 m) 110 kt (127 mph; 204 km/h)

Range: 276 nm (318 miles; 511 km)
Performance: maximum rate of climb at sea level 1,600 ft (488 m) per minute; service ceiling 12,600 ft (3840 m); hovering ceiling 13,600 ft (4145 m) in ground effect and 4,000 ft (1220 m) out of ground effect

Bell **Model 206 JetRanger/TH-67/206L LongRanger**

The **Bell Model 206A JetRanger** was derived substantially from Bell's losing HO-4 submission for the **US Army**'s LOH competition. The JetRanger was fundamentally the same as the **OH-4A** (formerly HO-4) prototypes, except for modifications to provide seating for five. Flown on 10 January 1966 it was certificated nine months later as a general-purpose light helicopter. It was also built under licence by Agusta as the **AB 206** (described separately).

Bell began development of an improved version of the Model 206A in early 1971. The resulting **Model 206B JetRanger II** replaced the Model 206A in production, and introduced a more powerful 400-shp (298-kW) Allison 250-C20 turboshaft engine. The installation of this engine involved only minor airframe modification and made it possible for Bell to offer kits for the upgrading of earlier Model 206s to Model 206B standard.

Production of the JetRanger II ended in 1977 when it was replaced by the **Model 206B JetRanger III**. This introduced a

420-shp (313-kW) Allison 250-C20B turboshaft, derated to 317 shp (236 kW), which offered further improved performance. Manufacture was transferred in early 1987 to Bell's Mirabel plant in Canada, where production continues.

The JetRanger was subsequently sold, ostensibly in civil guise, to numerous military air arms. Current operators comprise **Brazil, Brunei, Chile, Colombia, Cyprus, Ecuador, Guatemala, Guyana, Indonesia, Israel, Ivory Coast, Mexico, Myanmar, Pakistan, Peru, South Korea, Sri Lanka, Thailand, United Arab Emirates** (Abu Dhabi) and **Venezuela**. The JetRangers are used in a variety of duties, primarily for training and liaison, but also for observation and VIP transport. The Chilean navy operates the **206AS** ASW variant armed with torpedoes. In March 1993 the US Army again selected the JetRanger, this time in the form of the JetRanger III-derived **TH-67 Creek** as its NTH (New Training Helicopter). Against bids from Eurocopter

(Astar/Ecureuil), Grumman/Schweizer/UNC (TH-330) and Enstrom (TH-28), Bell won an initial order for 29 aircraft (company designation **TH206**), with an eventual requirement for up to 102, with options on a further 55. Deliveries to Fort Rucker, Alabama, replacing existing UH-1s, commenced on 15 October 1993.

Bell developed a medium-lift version under the designation **Model 206L-1 LongRanger**. This retained the powerplant of the JetRanger III, but incorporated a fuselage stretch of 2 ft 1 in (0.63 m) to accommodate a total of five passengers and an increased cabin capacity of 83 cu ft (2.35 m³). A double door on the port side of the fuselage simplifies the loading of bulky cargo. Other improvements included the

use of an advanced main rotor, plus introduction of the company's patented Noda-Matic suspension system giving reduced cabin vibration levels.

Deliveries of the LongRanger commenced in 1975, superseded in mid-1978 by the **Model 206L-2 LongRanger II**. This differed by having an uprated Allison 250C-28B turboshaft with a maximum continuous rating of 489 shp (365 kW) and higher-rated transmission. The **Model 206L-3 LongRanger III** was introduced in 1981 and featured a 650-shp (485-kW)

The US Army's TH-67 (Bell TH206) will carry a pilot and student in the cockpit, with a second trainee observing by CCTV in the cabin.

Standard 'off-the-shelf' Bell JetRangers, like this Brunei air force example, are popular training helicopters and a useful transport asset.

Allison 250-C30P engine and detail modifications. The **206L-4 LongRanger IV** remains the current production variant at Mirabel and has been joined by the **206LT TwinRanger**, a newly developed twin-engined conversion. All Canadian-built Bells (except those bound for Canada) are sold to the parent company at Ft Worth for resale on the US and world market.

Military operators of the LongRanger comprise **Bangladesh**, **Cameroon**, **Guatemala**, **Mexico**, **United Arab Emirates** (Dubai air wing and Ras Al-Khaimah Mobile Force) and the **Venezuelan army**. The aircraft are used primarily for liaison/communications and exclusively non-combat duties.

In 1980 Bell began development of a military **Bell Model 206L TexasRanger**, which has not proceeded beyond a demonstration aircraft. Powered by a 500-shp (373-kW) Allison 250-C28B turboshaft, it incorporates the fuselage of the **Model 206L LongRanger** to seat a pilot and up to six passengers, but for anti-armour/armed reconnaissance sorties it has side-by-side armoured seats for the pilot and weapons operator. Weapons include air-to-air or TOW missiles, or two pods containing folding-fin rockets or 7.62-mm (0.3-in) machine-guns. Industrias Cardoen of Chile has developed a modified armed version of the LongRanger as the **Cardoen CB 206L-III** (described separately).

By 1994, overall production by Bell of members of the Model 206 family was considerably in excess of 7,000 examples. Italian production, for civil and military use, exceeds 1,000 aircraft.

SPECIFICATION

Bell Helicopter Textron Model 206B JetRanger III
Rotor system: main rotor diameter 33 ft 4 in (10.16 m); tail rotor diameter 5 ft 5 in (1.65 m); main rotor disc area 872.65 sq ft (81.07 m²); tail rotor disc area 23.04 sq ft (2.14 m²)
Fuselage and tail: length overall, rotors turning 38 ft 9.5 in (11.82 m) and fuselage 31 ft 2 in (9.50 m) including tailskid; height overall 9 ft 6.5 in (2.91 m)

and to top of fin 8 ft 4 in (2.54 m); stabiliser span 6 ft 5.75 in (1.97 m); skid track 6 ft 3.5 in (1.92 m)
Powerplant: one 420-shp (313-kW) Allison 250-C20J flat-rated at 317 shp (236 kW)
Weights: empty 1,635 lb (742 kg); maximum take-off 3,200 lb (1451 kg)
Fuel and load: internal fuel 91 US gal (344 litres); external fuel none; maximum payload 1,500 lb (680 kg)
Speed: never exceed speed at sea level 122 kt (140 mph; 225 km/h); maximum cruising speed 'clean' at 5,000 ft (1525 m) 116 kt (134 mph; 216 km/h)
Range: 404 nm (465 miles; 748 km)
Performance: maximum rate of climb at sea level 1,260 ft (384 m) per minute; service ceiling 13,500 ft (4115 m); hovering ceiling 12,800 ft (3900 m) in ground effect and 8,800 ft (2680 m) out of ground effect

---

Bell **Model 206/OH-58A/B/C Kiowa**

In 1960 the **US Army** launched a design competition for a new Light Observation Helicopter (LOH). The requirement was for a helicopter suitable not only for an observation role but for missions that included casevac, close support, photo-reconnaissance and light transport. The specification called for a four-seat helicopter, carrying a 400-lb (180-kg) payload at a cruising speed of approximately 120 mph (190 km/h). The competition elicited responses from 12 manufacturers, from which Bell, Hiller and Hughes were each contracted to build five prototypes for competitive evaluation. Hughes' HO-6 (later OH-6) contender was subsequently declared the winner and was chosen by the US Army. Nevertheless, convinced of the merit of its losing **HO-4** submission, Bell built a new five-seat prototype as the **Bell Model 206A JetRanger** (described separately).

In 1967 the US Army, worried by the delivery rate and rising costs of the OH-6A, reopened its LOH competition; on 8 March 1968 the Bell Model 206A was declared the winner and ordered into production as the **OH-58A Kiowa**. Deliveries to the US Army began on 23 May 1969 and over five years a total of 2,200 was procured. The **Canadian Armed Forces** also acquired 74 as **COH-58A** (later designated **CH-136 Kiowa**) helicopters. An additional US Army contract for 74 was issued in January 1973 to replace those supplied to Canada. This Canadian order was followed in 1980 by 14 JetRanger III (designated **CH-139**) helicopter trainers.

Licence-production over an eight-year period was also undertaken by Commonwealth Aircraft Corporation in Australia. A total of 56 helicopters, essentially similar to the JetRanger II, was produced as the **Model 206B-1 Kiowa**. Twelve helicopters were supplied by Bell and 44 were manufactured under a co-production agreement. CAC was responsible for final assembly, with avionics and powerplant of US origin. Forty-three survive with the **Australian army**, locally named **Kalkadoon**. Twelve Kiowas were also delivered to the **Austrian army** in 1976 under the designation **OH-58B**. These are operated by 3 Staffel of Hubschraubergeschwader 1 at Tulln, with a detachment at Klagenfurt.

On 30 June 1976 the US Army awarded Bell a development contract to convert the OH-58A to improved **OH-58C** standard. This version introduced a flat glass canopy to reduce glint, an uprated Allison T63-A720 turboshaft developing 420 shp (313 kW) and an installation for infra-red suppression. The final OH-58C configuration also included a new instrument panel, improved avionics and improved maintenance features. In addition, two OH-58As were modified to OH-58C standard for pre-production flight testing by the US Army and Bell. Production modification of 435 OH-58As to

OH-58C standard began in March 1978 and was completed in March 1985. Israeli Aircraft Industries completed an additional 150 conversions for the US Army in Germany.

Bell began delivery in September 1985 of kits for an improved tail rotor configuration for retrofitting to OH-58As and OH-58Cs. This modification increases the available tail rotor thrust, thus increasing directional controllability (such as uncommanded yaw at low speeds experienced during nap-of-the-earth (NOE) flying). The improved **OH-58D** scout is described in a separate entry.

SPECIFICATION

Bell Helicopter Textron Model 206A/OH-58A Kiowa
Rotor system: main rotor diameter 35 ft 4 in (10.77 m); tail rotor diameter 5 ft 2 in (1.57 m); main

rotor disc area 980.52 sq ft (91.09 m²); tail rotor disc area 20.97 sq ft (1.95 m²)
Fuselage and tail: length overall, rotors turning 40 ft 11.75 in (12.49 m) and fuselage 32 ft 3.5 in (9.84 m); height overall, rotors turning 9 ft 6.5 in (2.91 m); stabiliser span 6 ft 5.25 in (1.96 m); skid track 6 ft 3.5 in (1.92 m)
Powerplant: one Allison T63-A-700 rated at 317 shp (236.5 kW)
Weights: empty equipped 1,583 lb (718 kg); maximum take-off 3,000 lb (1361 kg)
Fuel and load: internal fuel 73 US gal (276 litres)
Speed: never exceed speed 130 kt (150 mph; 241 km/h); maximum cruising speed at sea level 106 kt (122 mph; 196 km/h); economical cruising speed at sea level 102 kt (117 mph; 188 km/h); loiter speed, for maximum endurance, 49 kts (91 km/h; 56 mph)
Range: maximum range at sea level with reserves 260 nm (299 miles; 481 km); endurance at sea level, no reserves 3 hours 30 minutes
Performance: maximum rate of climb at sea level 1,780 ft (543 m) per minute; service ceiling 19,000 ft (5790 m); hovering ceiling 13,750 ft (4190 m) in ground effect and 9,000 lb (2745 m) out of ground effect

Right: The Royal Australian Navy dubbed its Bell B 206B-1 Kiowas 'Battle Budgies'. The same legend was applied to armed AS 555 Squirrels serving in the Persian Gulf.

Left: To the Canadian Armed Forces the Kiowa is the CH-135. This float-equipped example also sports cable-cutters, above and below the cockpit, like most Kiowas worldwide.

Bell **Model 206/TH-57 SeaRanger**

The **US Navy** showed little interest in the US Army's light observation OH-58 Kiowa, but with a requirement identified in 1967 for a light turbine primary training helicopter it was decided, if possible, to procure an off-the-shelf aircraft. On 31 January 1968 the US Navy ordered from Bell 40 examples of a basically standard **Model 206A JetRanger II**; these differed only by having US Navy avionics and the optional

dual controls installed. Designated **TH-57A SeaRanger**, they were delivered during 1968 to training squadron HT-8 at NAS Whiting Field, Milton, FL. Utilised for the transition phase of helicopter training, the TH-57A served until the late 1980s. Today, almost all A models have been retired, although a few are still flown by the Naval Air Warfare Center/Aircraft Division at Patuxent River, MD, on test duties.

Initial helicopter training for both US Navy and Marine Corps aircrew is now accomplished on two developed variants of the TH-57A. Expanding requirements have led to 51 new production **TH-57B** primary trainers, the last of which was delivered in late 1985; these are based on the later **Model 206B JetRanger III**, and primarily differ from the TH-57A by having uprated Allison 250-C20 turboshafts, flat rated at

317 shp (236 kW), in addition to minor detail improvements. The TH-57B does retain, however, the dual controls of the TH-57A. Concurrent with the acquisition of the TH-57B, the US Navy ordered the **TH-57C**, a new production advanced instrument trainer, in January 1982. Also based on the JetRanger III, these are somewhat more sophisticated machines and feature full IFR instrumentation, thus allowing mastery of more complex skills in anticipation of moving on to operational type helicopters such as the SH-60B Seahawk and AH-1 SeaCobra. The initial order for 55 examples was

Bell Model 206/TH-57 SeaRanger

eventually raised to 89, the last of which was delivered in December 1984.

The SeaRanger serves exclusively with Training Wing Five at Whiting Field, FL. The TH-57B model is assigned to HT-8 and is operated as a primary and intermediate helicopter trainer. Following the initial six-week course, student pilots are subsequently assigned to HT-18, which operates the TH-57C model, for a 13-week advanced phase.

SPECIFICATION

Bell Helicopter Textron Model 206A (TH-57C SeaRanger)
Rotor system: main rotor diameter 33 ft 4 in (10.16 m); tail rotor diameter 5 ft 2 in (1.57 m); main rotor disc 873.0 sq ft (81.10 m2); tail rotor disc area 20.97 sq ft (1.95 m2)
Fuselage and tail: length overall, rotors turning 38 ft 9.5 in (11.82 m) and fuselage 31 ft 2 in (9.50 m); height 9 ft 6.5 in (2.91 m); stabiliser span 6 ft 5.25 in (1.96 m)
Powerplant: one 420-shp (313-kW) Allison 250-C20J flat-rated to 317 shp (236 kW)
Weights: empty 1,852 lb (840 kg); maximum take-off 3,350 lb (1520 kg)

Bell TH-57 SeaRanger

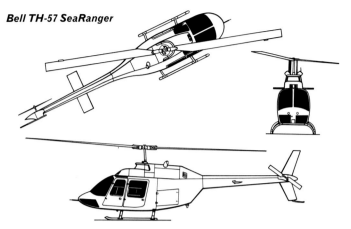

Fuel and load: internal fuel 76 US gal (288 litres)
Speed: never exceed speed 122 kt (140 mph; 225 km/h); maximum and economical cruising speed at sea level 115 kt (133 mph; 214 km/h)
Range: 458 nm (527 miles; 848 km)

Performance: max rate of climb at sea level 1,540 ft (469 m) per minute; service ceiling above 20,000 ft (6095 m); hovering ceiling 12,700 ft (3870 m) in ground effect, 6,000 ft (1830 m) out of ground effect

The US Navy's TH-57Bs are charged with basic rotary training, while the advanced classes of HT-18 are also allocated TH-57Cs.

Bell **Model 209/AH-1F/S HueyCobra**

Produced in 1965 as a private project, the **Bell Model 209 HueyCobra** was intended to fulfil an urgent requirement for an 'interim' armed helicopter escort pending service entry of the AAFSS winner (the AH-56). The latter project subsequently foundered, while Bell produced some 1,100 **AH-1G Cobra**s for the US Army.

Post-Vietnam, the Cobra was upgraded to carry TOW missiles, resulting in conversion of some to **AH-1Q** standard. This was underpowered and a sequence of improvements was initiated, intended to upgrade engine and transmission, armament, avionics, cockpit and rotors, all of which would culminate in a common standard known as **AH-1S(MC)**. This was never fully achieved and left the Army with a range of airframes all designated 'S' but in different modification states. In 1989 redesignations renamed the MC **AH-1F**, and the less advanced versions as **AH-1P**, **AH-1E** and **AH-1S**. The AH-1F is the current production configuration and so applies to most exports.

Unchanged structurally from the prototype to date, F models and all but the earliest S airframes are distinguishable by the 'flat-plate' canopy and nose turret for the M65 TOW sighting system. A modified aft cowling and prominent exhaust suppressor are also distinctive. A Lycoming T53-L-703 turboshaft rated at 1,800 shp (1342 kW) drives the K-747 composite rotor. This unit retains the characteristics of Bell's original 540 semi-rigid 'teetering' rotor but is lighter, with a much-improved life. The Dash 747 blade is distinguished by its tapered tips.

The updated cockpit is NVG-compatible with a HUD for the pilot, a new stores management system and a comprehensive nav/comms fit. The co-pilot's panel is dominated by the TOW sight so he is provided with 'sidestick' cyclic and collective controls. Extensive armour is provided around the seats and cockpit to give some protection from small-arms fire. Further upgrades centred on a four-bladed rotor and new stability augmentation system are available, adding 1,000 lb (454 kg) to the payload.

Notable items (along with the squadron badge) visible on this Israeli AH-1F are the low-speed sensor probe between the cockpits, bulge for the laser tracker (not fitted) forward of the rotor mast, exhaust suppressor, Kaiser HUD and wire cutters behind the cockpit.

Pakistani army AH-1s are spread between two squadrons, Nos 31 and 32, both based at Multan. All aircraft retain their standard US Army olive drab finish. Deliveries began in 1984. Despite the current US arms embargo, Pakistan is believed to have obtained further AH-1s during 1993, perhaps from a third party.

WEAPON OPTIONS

Primary armament is the TOW missile, four of which can be carried on each outboard pylon; 2.75-in FFARs with a variety of warheads are carried inboard in either seven- or 19-shot pods. Gun pods remain a seldom-seen option. Secondary armament is the M197 triple-barrelled 20-mm cannon in a chin turret. As part of the original AH-1S (later AH-1E) stage 2 upgrade, aircraft were fitted with this weapon along with a new wing stores management system, the Enhanced Cobra Armament System (ECAS). A maximum of 750 rounds can be carried and the gun, together with the M65 'bucket', can be slaved to the crew helmet sight system. The gun has a field of fire of 110° on either side of the nose, an elevation of 20.5° and a maximum depression of 50°. Accuracy of the ballistic weapons is greatly enhanced by an air data system (by GEC Avionics) supplying information to a weapons computer. Some aircraft are now receiving the CNITE thermal imaging system which provides a full night capability, and trials are underway to qualify the aircraft for Stinger missiles. Provision has also been made for a laser spot tracker.

Bell AH-1F Cobra

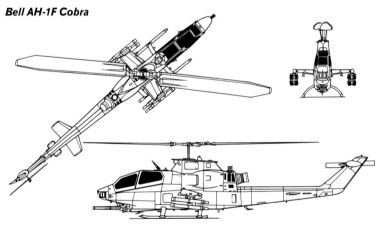

Passive defence starts with a special paint designed to be non-reflective of both visible and IR spectrum light. A suppressor cools and diffuses the exhaust plume and the Dash 747 blade reduces radar signature compared with the previous metal unit. Radar warning receivers give cockpit indication of hostile emissions. A laser detector has been trialled but is not currently fitted. Active defence is entrusted to a radar countermeasures/jammer set and the AN/ALQ-144 IR jammer. Army Cobras do not normally carry chaff/flare dispensers.

OPERATORS

The largest user of the AH-1F/S remains the US Army, with some 800 airframes still in service. Ninety-nine were built to Modernised AH-1S between 1979 and 1986, while 378 were rebuilt to the new standard from November 1979 to June 1982. This total includes 42 TAH-1S trainers. A handful of AH-1S aircraft (with the early canopy and XM-28 turret) remain in use, as well as some AH-1Ps (with XM-28 turret) and AH-1Es (which lack the low-speed sensor probe and some avionics equipment). The F is licence-built in Japan and has been exported to Jordan, South Korea, Pakistan, Israel, Thailand and, most recently, to Turkey.

Israel: AH-1F (30)
Japan: AH-1F (88 with 70 funded)
Jordan: AH-1F (24)
Pakistan: AH-1F (20 plus 10 options)
South Korea: (42 plus 28 options)
Thailand: AH-1F (4)
Turkey: AH-1S Mod/AH-1F (unknown)

Since the 1970s Turkish Army Aviation (Türk Kara Havaciligi) has had a requirement for an attack helicopter. Initially a $50 million order was placed for six Bell AH-1S in 1983, but no confirmation of delivery was ever announced. However, the Turkish army has joined the ranks of Cobra operators, flying an unknown number of single-engined AH-1Fs alongside its twin-engined ex-USMC AH-1Ws.

SPECIFICATION

Bell Helicopter Textron Model 209 (AH-1F HueyCobra)
Rotor system: main rotor diameter 44 ft 0 in (13.41 m); tail rotor diameter 8 ft 6 in (2.59 m); main rotor disc area 1,520.23 sq ft (141.26 m²); tail rotor disc area 56.75 sq ft (5.27 m²)
Wing: span 10 ft 9 in (3.28 m)
Fuselage and tail: length overall, rotors turning 53 ft 1 in (16.18 m) and fuselage 44 ft 7 in (13.59 m); height to top of rotor head 13 ft 5 in (4.09 m); stabiliser span 6 ft 11 in (2.11 m); skid track 7 ft 0 in (2.13 m)
Powerplant: one 1,800-shp (1342-kW) Textron Lycoming T53-L-703 transmission limited to 1,290 shp (962 kW) for take-off and 1,134 shp (845 kW) for continuous running
Weights: operating empty 6,598 lb (2993 kg); normal take-off 9,975 lb (4524 kg); maximum take-off 10,000 lb (4536 kg)
Fuel and load: internal fuel 259 US gal (980 litres);

external fuel none
Speed: never exceed speed 170 kt (195 mph; 315 km/h) in TOW configuration; maximum level speed at optimum altitude 123 kt (141 mph; 227 km/h) in TOW configuration
Range: 274 nm (315 miles; 507 km)
Performance: maximum rate of climb at sea level 1,620 ft (494 m) per minute; service ceiling 12,200 ft (3720 m); hovering ceiling 12,200 ft (3720 m) in ground effect

Bell Model 209/AH-1W SuperCobra

The lineage of the Whiskey model Cobra can be traced directly back to the Model 209 prototype and subsequent **AH-1G** service variant. Developed for the USMC, the **AH-1J** was essentially a twin-engined AH-1G to which was added the M197 20-mm turreted gun. Development thereafter followed its own path via the improved Iranian **AH-1J**, the **KingCobra** demonstrator, and the stretched **AH-1T** models.

The AH-1W had its origins in a paper proposal to the Iranian air force for an upgraded AH-1T with T-700 engines. A demonstrator (c/n 161022) was built and flown as the **'AH-1T+'** to qualify the engines. This aircraft accumulated various modifications and improvements until it fully represented the production aircraft, by which time it was known as **SuperCobra**. The designation **AH-1W** was adopted as the first production airframe rolled out for the USMC.

That the 'W' airframe is fundamentally unchanged from the 'T' is amply demonstrated by the fact that nearly 50 (from a total built of only 57) of the Ts are being rebuilt to incorporate the W improvements and will be indistinguishable from new-build. Compared to other Cobra variants, the T/W airframe features a lengthened tail boom and forward fuselage plug to accommodate the 48-ft (14.63-m) diameter/2-ft 9-in (0.84-m) chord main rotor, and to maintain aircraft CG in the manner of the Huey. Aside from the obvious redesign of the engine cowlings, the other external airframe change is the 'cheek bulge', which, together with a starboard shift of the ammunition box, allowed the TOW 'black boxes' to be moved from the tail boom.

T700-GE-401 turboshafts, each rated at 1,690 shp (1260 kW), are currently used, giving the Cobra one of the best thrust/weight ratios of any current attack helicopter and ensuring single-engine safety. Future upgrades will take the current 14,750 lb (6691 kg) gross weight to 16,000 lb (7258 kg). The two-bladed teetering rotor is retained at present, but a more advanced four-bladed design has been flown and par-

tially qualified, resulting in the **AH-1(4B) W Viper** designation. The USMC intends that it will be incorporated eventually.

The AH-1W forms the basis of the **Cobra Venom** offered by Bell and GEC to meet the British Army Air Corps' need for a battlefield helicopter. A new avionics suite incorporates night vision and all-weather sensors, with an autonomous navaid fit and digital mapping, colour CRT displays. It will also be Hellfire equipped, as standard.

During Operation Desert Storm AH-1Ws from HMLA-169, -269, -367, and -369 were deployed, with the two former units land-based and the remaining two sea-based. Flying with the 1st Marine Expeditionary Force from the start of the ground offensive on 24 February 1991, they provided air support for the advancing Marines, including an engagement at Al Jaber airfield which claimed 60 Iraqi tanks. Whiskey Cobras were deployed to Somalia in 1993. However, in 1993/94 a sizeable portion of the fleet was grounded with fatigue problems.

In 1990 the first of five former US Marine Corps AH-1W SuperCobras was delivered to the Turkish army. These were joined by at least a further five aircraft in 1993, to complement the AH-1s already in service. These Cobras have seen action in the fighting against Kurdish rebels on Turkey's southern borders. Turkish AH-1Ws do not carry the 'hot brick' IR jammer above the engines but do carry chaff and flare dispensers on the weapons pylons.

WEAPON OPTIONS

The Whiskey is qualified for most of the stores in the USMC inventory. Uniquely, it has a dual main armament, TOW or AGM-114 Hellfire ATGMs, which can be carried simultaneously if required. Up to four 19-round LAU-61A, LAU-86A, LAU-68A/A, or seven-round LAU-69A rocket pods can be carried. All pods utilise 2.75-in Hydra 70 rockets. The AIM-9L

Sidewinder (or AGM-122A Sidearm) is also routinely carried on one of the outboard pylons. An overwing mounting for this weapon has been successfully demonstrated but is not at present used operationally (wiring for a 'six-point' wing will be incorporated during the overhaul programme, allowing a later decision on this or wingtip mounting for AIM-9 or Stinger air-to-air missiles). The Shorts Starstreak short-range AAM was test-fired during 1993. In addition, Cobras often carry 5-in Zuni rockets, and have on occasion used CBUs, CBU-55B FAE and similar weapons. The aircraft is also qualified for the AGM-65D Maverick, various flare (SUU-44/A) and smoke systems, and even iron bombs. Two GPU-2A or

AH-1Ws from four USMC units saw action during Desert Storm. They were involved in the fighting for Khafji and later employed their Hellfire capability for the first time.

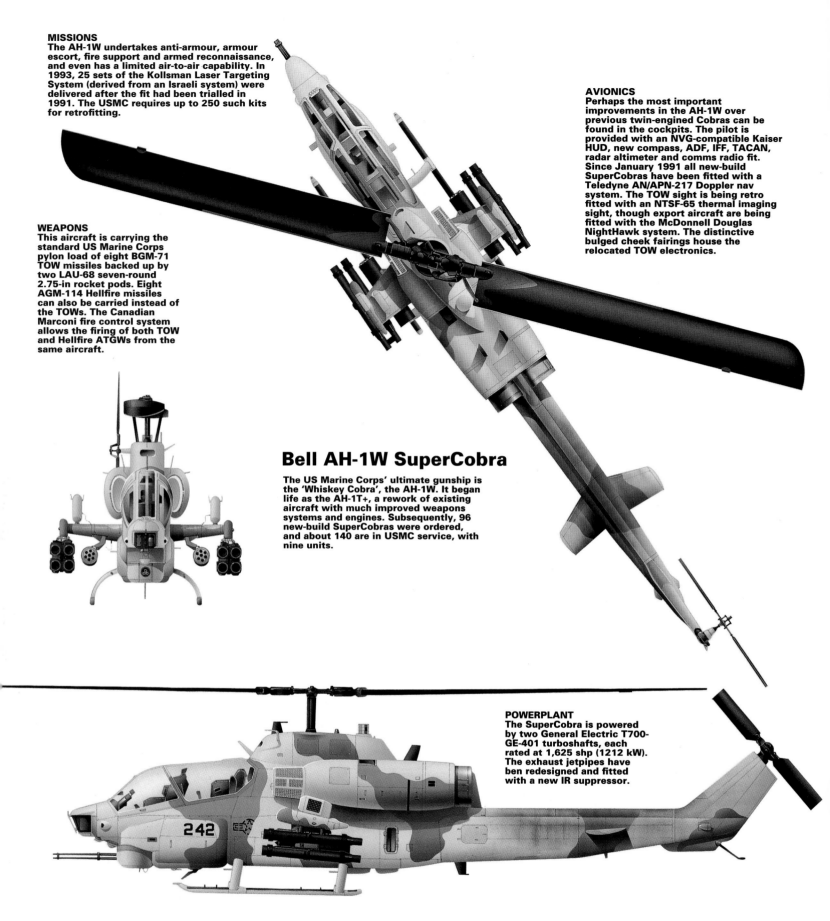

MISSIONS
The AH-1W undertakes anti-armour, armour escort, fire support and armed reconnaissance, and even has a limited air-to-air capability. In 1993, 25 sets of the Kollsman Laser Targeting System (derived from an Israeli system) were delivered after the fit had been trialled in 1991. The USMC requires up to 250 such kits for retrofitting.

WEAPONS
This aircraft is carrying the standard US Marine Corps pylon load of eight BGM-71 TOW missiles backed up by two LAU-68 seven-round 2.75-in rocket pods. Eight AGM-114 Hellfire missiles can also be carried instead of the TOWs. The Canadian Marconi fire control system allows the firing of both TOW and Hellfire ATGWs from the same aircraft.

AVIONICS
Perhaps the most important improvements in the AH-1W over previous twin-engined Cobras can be found in the cockpits. The pilot is provided with an NVG-compatible Kaiser HUD, new compass, ADF, IFF, TACAN, radar altimeter and comms radio fit. Since January 1991 all new-build SuperCobras have been fitted with a Teledyne AN/APN-217 Doppler nav system. The TOW sight is being retro fitted with an NTSF-65 thermal imaging sight, though export aircraft are being fitted with the McDonnell Douglas NightHawk system. The distinctive bulged cheek fairings house the relocated TOW electronics.

Bell AH-1W SuperCobra

The US Marine Corps' ultimate gunship is the 'Whiskey Cobra', the AH-1W. It began life as the AH-1T+, a rework of existing aircraft with much improved weapons systems and engines. Subsequently, 96 new-build SuperCobras were ordered, and about 140 are in USMC service, with nine units.

POWERPLANT
The SuperCobra is powered by two General Electric T700-GE-401 turboshafts, each rated at 1,625 shp (1212 kW). The exhaust jetpipes have ben redesigned and fitted with a new IR suppressor.

SUU-11A/A gun pods can also be fitted. Finally, the pylons are 'plumbed' for either 100-US gal (378-litre) ferry or 77-US gal (291-litre) combat fuel tanks.

As mentioned previously, the Cobra mounts the M197 cannon in a General Electric A/A49E-7(V4) turret as standard. This is qualified to fire the depleted uranium rounds used in the Navy's Phalanx close-in defence system for greater effectiveness out to ranges in excess of 1.8 miles (3 km). Both the turret gun and the M-65 sight system can be slaved to either crewman's helmet sight system. Seven hundred and fifty rounds are carried aft of the turret, and while the maximum rate of fire is 650 rpm, the gun is limited to single bursts of 16 rounds. An upgrade programme is

underway which will provide a night targeting system incorporating FLIR and laser designation/range finding. This is extremely significant as it means that the aircraft has a true night capability and can designate targets either for its own weapons or those carried by fixed-wing aircraft. Countermeasures systems consist of AN/APR-44 and AN/APR-39 passive radar warning and detector systems, while active countermeasures include AN/ALE-39 chaff/flare dispensers and an AN/ALQ-144 IR jammer.

Installation of the NTS has provided the opportunity to make considerable cockpit improvements. The front panel will be enlarged and improved. The addition of new multi-function displays,

a HUD, improved ANVIS displays and a radar altimeter will mean that both crewmen have full access to navigation and communication information. Other improvements include a five-point seat harness with inflatable head and body restraints to increase survivability.

OPERATORS

The USMC is the primary user of the AH-1W and will eventually receive 230 (including the rebuilt Tango model). These will equip the Marine Corps' light attack squadrons (HMLAs 167, 267, 367, 169, 269 and

369), the training squadron (HMT-303), and two reserve units (HMAs 773 and 775). Two HMLs may also receive Cobras (771 and 776). In March 1994 Bell withdrew 60 of the USMC's 128 aircraft, having discovered serious salt water corrosion of their main rotors. The AH-1Ws concerned had chalked up over 1,000 flying hours, and all rotors with over 400 hours now require attention. Foreign SuperCobra operators are Turkey (which is using five ex-USMC airframes on a loan basis pending delivery of a further five new-build machines), and Thailand, which took delivery of its first example in March 1993. Thailand had signed letter of acceptance in February 1992 for 18 AH-1W aircraft plus 24 options.

SPECIFICATION

Bell Helicopter Textron Model 209 (AH-1W SuperCobra)
Rotor system: main rotor diameter 48 ft 0 in (14.63 m); tail rotor diameter 9 ft 9 in (2.97 m); main rotor disc 1,809.56 sq ft (168.11 m2); tail rotor disc area 74.7 sq ft (6.94 m2)

Wing: span 10 ft 7 in (3.23 m); aspect ratio 3.74
Fuselage and tail: length overall, rotors turning 58 ft 0 in (17.68 m) and fuselage 45 ft 6 in (13.87 m); height overall 14 ft 2 in (4.32 m) and to top of rotor head 13 ft 6 in (4.11 m); stabiliser span 6 ft 11 in (2.11 m); skid track 7 ft 0 in (2.13 m)
Powerplant: two 1,625-shp (1212-kW) General Electric T700-GE-401 transmission, limited to a total of 2,032 shp (1515 kW) for take-off and 1,725 shp

(1286 kW) for continuous running
Weights: empty 10,200 lb (4627 kg); maximum take-off 14,750 lb (6691 kg)
Fuel and load: internal fuel 304.5 US gal (1153 litres); external fuel up to four 77-US gal (291-litre) or two 100-US gal (379-litre) drop tanks; maximum ordnance 2,466 lb (1119 kg)
Speed: never exceed speed 190 kt (219 mph; 352 km/h); maximum level speed 'clean' at sea level 152

kt (175 mph; 282 km/h) or at optimum altitude 150 kt (173 mph; 278 km/h)
Range: 343 nm (395 miles; 635 km) with standard fuel
Performance: maximum rate of climb at sea level, one engine out 800 ft (244 m) per minute; service ceiling more than 12,000 ft (3660 m); hovering ceiling 14,750 ft (4495 m) in ground effect and 3,000 ft (914 m) out of ground effect

Bell **Model 212/UH-1N**

Following negotiations in early 1968 between Bell Helicopters, the Canadian government and Pratt & Whitney Canada, it was mutually agreed to initiate a jointly-funded programme covering the development of a twin-turbine version of the Bell Model 205/UH-1H Iroquois (described separately). Selected as powerplant for this new venture was the PT6T Turbo Twin-Pac. It comprised two turboshaft engines mounted side-by-side to drive a single output shaft through a combining gearbox. An advantage was provided by sensing torquemeters in the gearbox which, in the event of an engine failure, could signal the still-operative turbine to develop either emergency or continuous power in order that the flight could be concluded in safety.

Adaptation of the initial production PT6T-3 Turbo Twin-Pac to the airframe of the Bell Model 205 proceeded without serious problems, and the first deliveries of the resulting **Bell Model 212** helicopters to the US Air Force began during 1970 under the tri-service designation **UH-1N**. The USAF acquired a total of 79 UH-1Ns, which saw service worldwide in support of Special Operations Force counter-insurgency activities. A larger number went to the US Navy and Marine Corps, which by 1978 had received a total of 221. Those of the US Marine Corps include two UH-1Ns converted to **VH-1N** VIP transports, plus six built as new to this configuration. The Canadian Armed Forces acquired 50 Bell 212s, the first of them handed over on 3 May 1971 and the last of them being delivered just over a year later. These were designated initially **CUH-1N**, but have since been redesignated **CH-135 Twin Huey**.

The improved safety offered by the Twin-Pac powerplant made this helicopter attractive to companies providing support to offshore gas/oil operations, and while Bell soon had a commercial **Twin Two-Twelve** in full-scale production, it also built small numbers of military helicopters for other nations. Agusta in Italy soon acquired a licence for the Model 212, producing the **AB 212** (described separately) for civil and military customers, and has developed a specialised maritime version as the AB 212ASW.

Lebanon: AB 212
Libya: AB 212
Malta: AB 212
Mexico: B 212
Morocco: AB 212
Panama: UH-1N, B 212
Philippines: UH-1N
Saudi Arabia: AB 212
Singapore: B 212
South Korea: B 212
Spain: AB 212 (HU.18B), AB 212ASW
Sri Lanka: B 212
Sudan: AB 212
Thailand: B 212
Tunisia: UH-1N
Turkey: AB 212, AB 212ASW
Uganda: B 212
Venezuela: AB 212ASW
Yemen: AB 212
Zambia: B 212

USAF: HH-1N, UH-1N, VH-1N
USMC: UH-1N, VH-1N
USN: HH-1N

SPECIFICATION

Bell Helicopter Textron Model 212 (UH-1N Iroquois)
Rotor system: main rotor diameter 48 ft 2.25 in (14.69 m) with tracking tips; tail rotor diameter 8 ft 6 in (2.59 m); main rotor disc area 1,871.91 sq ft (173.90 m2); tail rotor disc area 56.74 sq ft (5.27 m2)
Fuselage and tail: length overall, rotors turning 57 ft 3.25 in (17.46 m) and fuselage 42 ft 4.75 in (12.92 m); height overall 14 ft 10.25 in (4.53 m) and to top of rotor head 12 ft 10 in (3.91 m); stabiliser span 9 ft 4.5 in (2.86 m); skid track 8 ft 8 in (2.64 m)
Powerplant: one 1,800-shp (1342-kW) Pratt & Whitney Canada T400-CP-400 flat rated to 1,290 shp (962 kW) for take-off and 1,130 shp (842 kW) for continuous running
Weights: empty 6,143 lb (2787 kg); maximum take-off 11,200 lb (5080 kg)
Fuel and load: internal fuel 215 US gal (814 litres);

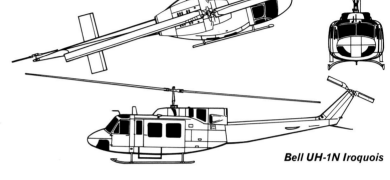

Bell UH-1N Iroquois

external fuel none; maximum payload 5,000 lb (2268 kg) externally or 4,000 lb (1814 kg)internally
Speed: never exceed speed at sea level 140 kt (161 mph; 259 km/h); maximum cruising speed at sea level 123 kt (142 mph; 230 km/h); economical cruising speed at sea level 100 kt (115 mph; 185 km/h)
Range: range 227 nm (261 miles; 420 km)
Performance: maximum rate of climb at sea level 1,320 ft (402 m) per minute; service ceiling 14,200 ft (4330 m); hovering ceiling 11,000 ft (3355 m) in ground effect

Right: The bright red UH-1Ns of VXE-6 (Antarctic Development Squadron 6) 'Puckered Penguins' operate alongside LC-130 Hercules of the same unit in support of US bases in the Antarctic.

Sri Lanka received 12 Bell 212s, nine of which have been fitted out as gunships. Three wear an IR-reflecting olive drab paint scheme but carry no nose radar.

Below: The Philippine air force has two VIP-configured Bell 212s on strength. The smartly painted aircraft are fitted out with much-improved radio equipment, and weather radar under the nose.

OPERATORS

Argentina: B 212
Austria: AB 212
Bangladesh: B 212
Brunei: B 212 Twin Pac
Canada: UH-1N (CH-135 Twin Huey)
Chile: B 212
Dominican Republic: B 212
Dubai: B 212
Ecuador: B 212
El Salvador: B 212
Ghana: B 212
Greece: B 212, AB 212, AB 212ASW
Guatemala: B 212
Guyana: B 212
Iran: AB 212, AB 212ASW
Iraq: AB 212ASW
Israel: AB 212
Italy: AB 212, AB 212ASW
Japan: B 212

Bell Model 214/Isfahan

Evolved via the Huey Plus (a privately-funded, improved version of the Model 205), the **Model 214A** 16-seat utility helicopter was, in late 1972, the subject of a major Iranian contract (worth upwards of $575,000,000). Featuring a more powerful engine to cater for high ambient temperatures, a larger main rotor and a strengthened airframe, the Model 214A was first flown on 13 March 1974. Two hundred and eighty-seven were delivered to **Iran**, primarily for use by the air component of the army as a troop carrier and supply transport helicopter, the Model 214A being assigned the name **Isfahan** in Iran. Isfahan (Esfahan) is an ancient town in central Iran, and was also home to the Iranian Army helicopter training school. It is uncertain how many Model 214A Isfahan helicopters remain in the inventory of the Islamic Republic of Iran army aviation, or the level of serviceability of those still considered operable, but more than 100 may still be active. Iranian Bell 214s were heavily involved in the fighting against Iraq as troop transports, alongside surviving CH-47Cs. Throughout the bitter fighting of the first Gulf war the Iranian aircraft faced Iraqi gunship Bell 214STs. Forty-five of these had been delivered to Saddam Hussein's forces from 1985, ostensibly for the civilian Ministry of Communications and Transport.

Iran was also the recipient of 39 **Model 214C** helicopters equipped for SAR tasks. A commercial derivative of the basic helicopter was designated **Model 214B** and dubbed **BigLifter**. The latter was subsequently sold in small numbers to several military operators, including **Dubai**,

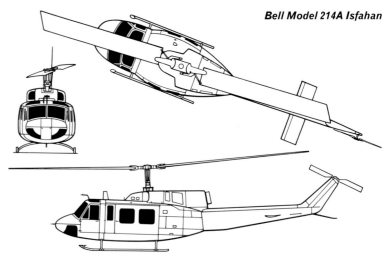

Prime mover behind the Bell 214's development was the Shah's Imperial Iranian Air Force. Two hundred and eighty-seven B 214As were ordered and a deal for a further 400 Isfahans had been signed when the 1978 revolution halted everything. This is the Philippine air force's sole Bell 214 in formation with a UH-1H.

Ecuador, **Oman** and the **Philippines**, all of which have small numbers in their respective inventories. The Iranian requirement for a transport version of the Bell 214 led to the development of a completely new version, the Model 214ST.

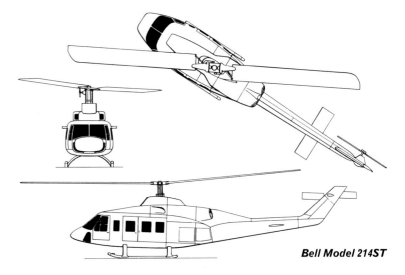

Bell Model 214A Isfahan

SPECIFICATION

Bell Helicopter Textron Model 214B BigLifter
Rotor system: main rotor diameter 50 ft 0 in (15.24 m); tail rotor diameter 9 ft 8 in (2.95 m); main rotor disc area 1,963.49 sq ft (182.41 m²); tail rotor disc area 73.39 sq ft (6.82 m²)
Powerplant: one 2,930-shp (2185-kW) Textron Lycoming T5508D flat-rated at 2,050 shp (1528 kW) for take-off and 1,850 shp (1379.5 kW) for continuous running
Weights: maximum take-off 16,000 lb (7257 kg)
Fuel and load: external fuel none; maximum payload 7,000 lb (3175 kg)
Speed: maximum cruising speed at optimum altitude 140 kt (161 mph; 259 km/h)

Bell Model 214ST

Despite retention of the type number of the preceding Model 214A, the **Model 214ST** possesses little commonality with the earlier helicopter, being twin-engined, with a stretched fuselage, composite rotor blades of greater diameter, and numerous other changes. The Model 214ST (the suffix originally signified Stretched Twin, then **SuperTransport**) was designed to an Iranian requirement calling for increased capacity, higher safety margins and improved 'hot-and-high' performance by comparison with the Model 214A Isfahan.

Plans for licence assembly of the Isfahan in Iran were changed when Bell proposed the more capable Model 214ST, the programme being revised to cover only 50 examples of the former and 350 of the latter. Bell initiated construction of three prototypes but, before the first of these flew on 21 July 1979, the Islamic revolution occurred and the licence plan was abandoned.

Having identified a market for a medium-lift helicopter in the Model 214ST category, Bell continued development and, in November 1979, launched production of a series of 100 aircraft, delivering the last in 1990. Of these, the majority found military customers, principal of which was the **Iraqi air force** which procured 45 during 1987-88. Other current operators of the Model 214ST are the air wing of the **Royal Brunei armed forces** (one), the air forces of **Oman**, **Peru** and **Venezuela** (each with three), and the **Royal Thai armed forces**, comprising the air force and army (each with two) and the navy (five).

SPECIFICATION

Bell Helicopter Textron Model 214ST
Rotor system: main rotor diameter 52 ft 0 in (15.85 m); tail rotor diameter 9 ft 8 in (2.95 m); main rotor disc area 2,123.71 sq ft (197.29 m²); tail rotor disc area 73.39 sq ft (6.82 m²)

Fuselage and tail: length overall, rotors turning 62 ft 2.25 in (18.95 m) and fuselage 49 ft 3.5 in (15.02 m); height overall 15 ft 10.5 in (4.84 m); skid track 8 ft 8 in (2.64 m) or wheel track 9 ft 3.5 in (2.83 m)
Powerplant: two General Electric CT7-2A each rated at 1,625 shp (1212 kW)
Weights: empty 9,445 lb (4284 kg); maximum take-off 17,500 lb (7938 kg)
Fuel and load: internal fuel 435 US gal (1647 litres) plus provision for 174 US gal (658 litres) of auxiliary fuel in two cabin tanks; external fuel none; maximum payload more than 7,700 lb (3493 kg)
Speed: maximum cruising speed at 4,000 ft (1220 m) 140 kt (161 mph; 259 km/h)
Range: ferry range 550 nm (633 miles; 1019 km) with auxiliary fuel; range 463 nm (533 miles; 858 km) with standard fuel
Performance: maximum rate of climb at sea level 1,780 ft (543 m) per minute; service ceiling 4,800 ft (1460 m) with one engine out; hovering ceiling 6,400 ft (1950 m) in ground effect

Bell Model 214ST

The Imperial Iranian Air Force took a decision in the mid-1970s to establish a sizeable air cavalry force, under the influence of US experience in Vietnam. This led to significant orders for types such as the Bell AH-1 and the initiation of a whole new type in the form of the Bell 214 Isfahan. The Bell 214ST design was led by the Iranian requirement and resulted in a $575 million contract, which was cancelled in 1978. Small numbers of B 214STs were sold elsewhere. The Royal Thai navy bought five Model 214STs from Bell in 1986, with deliveries taking place the following year. They operate alongside ASW Bell 212s and transport UH-1Hs.

Bell Model 230

An upgraded derivative of the Model 222, the **Model 230** light utility and transport helicopter is being offered for both military and commercial tasks. The responsibility of Bell's Canadian company at Mirabel, Quebec, the Model 230 was first flown on 12 August 1991, both first and second prototypes being converted Model 222s. Accommodating up to 10 persons, it is powered by two 700-shp (522-kW) Allison 250-C30G2 turboshafts and is available in both fixed-skid and retractable-wheel versions. Variants currently proposed include a medevac model with extra storage capacity for medical equipment, rupture-resistant fuel cells and self-sealing fuel fittings. It is anticipated that military models will have provision for externally-mounted weaponry. In 1993 one much modified aircraft was leased to the **Chilean navy**, which has several classes of helicopter-capable vessels, for SAR duties. Equipped with a hoist, Honeywell Primus 700 radar, Spectrolab SX-16 Nitesun searchlight, thermal imager, EFIS cockpit with GPS nav system, HUD and auxiliary fuel tanks it is also fitted out with an Indal ASIST deck landing system.

The twin-engined Bell 230 is the successor to Bell's Model 222, and is available with either a retractable wheeled undercarriage or skids. It is aimed primarily at the VIP and air ambulance market.

SPECIFICATION

Bell Helicopter Textron Model 230 Utility
Rotor system: main rotor diameter 42 ft 0 in (12.80 m); tail rotor diameter 6 ft 10.75 in (2.10 m); main rotor disc area 1,385.44 sq ft (128.71 m²); tail rotor disc area 37.35 sq ft (3.47 m²)
Fuselage and tail: length overall, rotors turning 50 ft 5.5 in (15.38 m) and fuselage 42 ft 6.75 in (12.97 m); height overall 12 ft 0.25 in (3.66 m) on skids; skid track 7 ft 10 in (2.39 m)
Powerplant: two Allison 250-C30G2 each rated at 700 shp (522 kW) for take-off and 622 shp (464 kW) for continuous running, or two Textron Lycoming LTS 101750C-1 each rated at 684 shp (510 kW)
Weights: manufacturer's empty 4,950 lb (2245 kg); maximum take-off 8,400 lb (3810 kg)
Fuel and load: internal fuel 246 US gal (931 litres) plus provision for 48 US gal (182 litres) of auxiliary

fuel; maximum payload 2,800 lb (1270 kg)
Speed: maximum cruising speed at sea level 137 kt (158 mph; 254 km/h); economical cruising speed at sea level 134 kt (154 mph; 248 km/h)

Range: range 379 nm (436 miles; 702 km)
Performance: service ceiling 15,000 ft (4570 m); hovering ceiling 12,300 ft (3750 m) in ground effect and 7,300 ft (2225 m) out of ground effect

Bell Model 406CS Combat Scout

A lighter and simplified export derivative of the US Army's OH-58D Kiowa (Model 406 AHIP) two-seat scout and attack helicopter, the **Model 406CS Combat Scout** entered flight test in June 1984, and that year entered a fly-off competition in **Saudi Arabia**. Retaining the main rotor, tail rotor and transmission of the OH-58D, and a similar powerplant, the Combat Scout was a nevertheless downgraded version of the OH-58D, as export of the mast-mounted sight, Hellfire missile and specialist cockpit electronics was prohibited. Armament choices include two GIAT 20-mm cannon pods, a quartet of TOW 2 or Hellfire anti-armour missiles, or combinations of Stinger missiles, 70-mm rockets, 7.62-mm or 12.7-mm guns. The Combat Scout successfully performed air-to-air combat trials, flown at NAS Patuxent River in 1987.

The Combat Scout is equipped with a SFENA hybrid cockpit with conventional instrumentation and electronic displays for TOW missiles and communications control. Other features include a roof-mounted Saab-Emerson HeliTOW sight with a folding overhead direct-view optics tube, folding rotor blades and tailplane, and a squatting undercarriage to facilitate rapid loading and redeployment from C-130 transports. Further upgrades are planned, including TOW armament, laser ranger and designator and an increase in gross weight of 500 lb (227 kg).

During autumn 1988, an order was placed on behalf of the Royal Saudi Land Forces Army Aviation Command for 15 Combat Scouts, these being delivered from June 1990. The first flight of a Saudi aircraft was made by Col Homood Al-Reshoodi at Arlington on 2 February of that year. These aircraft have frequently been referred to as **MH-58D**s, but this is inaccurate. Five of the 15 aircraft are now equipped with TOW missiles.

The Bell 406 was a result of the US Army's Advanced Helicopter Improvement Program of 1979. Having produced the OH-58D, Bell offered the downgraded Combat Scout for the export market. This is the company demonstrator, armed with a pair of GIAT M621 20-mm cannon.

Powerplant: one Allison 250-C30R rated at 650 shp (485 kW)
Weights: empty 2,271 lb (1030 kg); maximum take-off 5,000 lb (2268 kg)
Fuel and load: internal fuel 120 US gal (454 litres);

external fuel none; maximum payload 1,500 lb (680 kg)
Speed: never exceed speed 130 kt (150 mph; 241 km/h); maximum level speed 'clean' at optimum altitude 125 kt (144 mph; 232 km/h); max cruising speed at optimum altitude 120 kt (138 mph; 222 km/h)

Range: 218 nm (251 miles; 404 km); endurance 2 hours 48 minutes
Performance: hovering ceiling 20,500 ft (6250 m) in ground effect and 14,500 ft (4420 m) out of ground effect

The OH-58D was a cautious (pre-Reagan era) attempt to find a no-frills armed scout to complement the AH-64 force. The Bell 406CS has so far attracted only one customer, the Royal Saudi Land Forces, to back up its newly delivered Apaches. Taiwan is interested in acquiring the Combat Scout also, but only if it comes equipped with the Hellfire/mast-mounted sight combination, which does away with the 406CS's raison d'être.

SPECIFICATION

Bell Helicopter Textron Model 406CS Combat Scout
Rotor system: main rotor diameter 35 ft 0 in (10.67 m); tail rotor diameter 5 ft 5 in (1.65 m); main rotor disc area 962.00 sq ft (89.37 m²); tail rotor disc area 23.04 sq ft (2.14 m²)
Fuselage and tail: length overall, rotors turning 42 ft 2 in (12.85 m) and fuselage 34 ft 4.75 in (10.48 m); height overall 12 ft 10.625 in (3.93 m); stabiliser span 7 ft 6 in (2.29 m); skid track 6 ft 2 in (1.88 m)

Bell Model 406 (AHIP)/OH-58D Kiowa/Kiowa Warrior

In September 1981, the **Bell Model 406** proposal won the Army Helicopter Improvement Program (AHIP) to develop a near-term scout helicopter, capable of intelligence gathering and surveillance duties, in addition to the support of attack helicopters and directing artillery fire. After Bell was awarded a development contract, the first of five **OH-58D** prototypes made its first flight on 6 October 1983. Development and operational test programmes were conducted by the US Army at Yuma and Edwards AFB, and were completed in February 1985.

The Model 406 thus introduced a mast-mounted sight (developed by McDonnell Douglas Astronautics in association with Northrop's Electro-Mechanical Division), specialised avionics and a cockpit control and display sub-system developed by Sperry Flight Systems. In addition, the two-bladed rotor of the OH-58A was replaced with a four-bladed soft-in-plane rotor with composite blades, main rotor head yoke and elastomeric bearings.

Initial plans envisaged upgrading of 592 US Army OH-58As to 'D' standard in 1985-1991, but have been progressively reduced to the current total of 315 examples, with a further 12 Gulf War attrition replacements. Deliveries of two OH-58Ds commenced in December 1985, with the first Europe-based delivery taking place in June 1987. Under Operation Prime Chance, 15 OH-58Ds were modified from September 1987 for operations against Iranian fast-patrol boats in the Persian Gulf. Provision

The needle-nose and treated windscreen identify the Optimized Aircraft, or 'stealthy' OH-58D. Eighteen of these specialist conversions fly with the 82nd Airborne Division's 1/17th Cavalry.

With laser-protective windscreen coating, the 'OH-58X' is a one-off company demonstrator with a lengthened nose. The latter has been extended to accommodate avionics equipment, which is housed in the rear of the cabin of the OH-58D. This allows the use of the rear cabin seats for passengers.

An OH-58D launches Hydra-70 rockets. These weapons provide capability against soft targets, and are often used in conjunction with gun pods.

was made for Stinger and Hellfire missiles, in addition to 12.7-mm (0.50-in) machine-guns and seven-tube rocket pods.

The armament options of the Prime Chance OH-58Ds have been retained for an armed OH-58D, designated **Kiowa Warrior**, to which standard 243 planned OH-58Ds are to be modified. The major modifications include an integrated weapons pylon, uprated engine and transmission, increased gross weight, RWR, IR jammer, laser warning receiver, tilting vertical fin, integrated avionics and a lightened structure. Newly-converted Kiowa Warriors were delivered from the 208th aircraft in May 1991 and were delivered initially to 'C' and 'D' Troops of 4-17 Aviation, US Army.

Eighty-one Kiowa Warriors are to be modified further as **Multi-Purpose Light Helicopter**s (MPLH). This version features squatting landing gear and quick-fold rotor blades, horizontal stabiliser and tilting fin for

transportation in C-130s and speedy deployment for use by US Army rapid reaction forces. Later modifications envisaged include provision for a cargo hook for a slung load of up to 2,000 lb (907 kg) and fittings for external carriage of four stretchers or six troop seats. A further Kiowa Warrior upgrade is also offered by Bell, this version featuring new avionics including a FLIR,

DEFENCES
The OH-58D is fitted with various threat warning systems. These include APR-44(V)3 radar warning receiver, AVR-2 laser detection set and APR-39(V)1 radar warning. The principal anti-missile defence is the ALQ-144 infra-red countermeasures set. To counter small arms fire, the OH-58D uses nap-of-the-earth flying so that it is exposed for as short a time as possible.

10553

THUGS

UNITED STATES ARMY

GRANT RACE

THUGS

AIR TRANSPORTABILITY
Some Kiowa Warriors are completed with collapsible skids, folding stabiliser and fin, removable wire-cutter and MMS support frame for rapid air transportability in C-130s or C-141s.

Bell Model 406 (AHIP)/OH-58D Kiowa/Kiowa Warrior

WEAPON OPTIONS
The outrigger pylons can carry a maximum of four AGM-114C Hellfire anti-tank missiles. Each of these is 1.73 m (5 ft 8 in) long and has a launch weight of 48 kg (106 lb). Control is effected by surfaces on the aft wings, and homing is by either semi-active laser, RF/infra-red, or long-range infra-red depending on the seeker head fitted. Alternatively, seven-round launchers for rockets can be fitted, the Hydra-70 2.75-in FFAR rocket being the principal weapon. Alternative weapons include Stinger air-to-air missiles and podded machine-guns – either 7.62-mm Miniguns or 0.50-in M2s.

Bell OH-58D Kiowa Warrior

Fulfilling the primary mission of airborne scout and laser designator for close air support aircraft and AH-64 Apaches, the Kiowa Warrior can also undertake autonomous attacks using Hellfire missiles or area weapons such as unguided rockets or guns. These weapons also make it more survivable in its primary role. This aircraft is one of those assigned to the 4th Squadron, 17th Cavalry ('The Thugs'), a designated seagoing unit which is trained to deploy aboard US Navy warships. In this role the 4/17th is the successor to the Prime Chance aircraft which performed so well during Operation Earnest Will when they supported reflagged tanker escort duties in the Persian Gulf.

Honeywell helmet-mounted displays, ring laser gyros, colour digital map and GPS. In February 1992, **Taiwan** ordered 12 OH-58Ds, with 14 options, for delivery in June 1993.

SPECIFICATION

Bell Model 406/OH-58D Kiowa Warrior
Rotor system: main rotor diameter 35 ft 0 in (10.67 m); tail rotor diameter 5 ft 5 in (1.65 m); main rotor disc area 962.00 sq ft (89.37 m²); tail rotor disc area 23.04 sq ft (2.14 m²)
Fuselage and tail: length overall, rotors turning 42 ft 2 in (12.85 m) and fuselage 34 ft 4.75 in (10.48 m); height overall 12 ft 10.625 in (3.93 m); stabiliser span 7 ft 6 in (2.29 m); skid track 6 ft 2 in (1.88 m)
Powerplant: one Allison T703-AD-700 rated at 650 shp (485 kW)
Weights: empty 3,045 lb (1381 kg); maximum take-off 4,500 lb (2041 kg)
Fuel and load: internal fuel 752 lb (341 kg); external fuel none
Speed: never-exceed speed 130 kt (150 mph; 241 km/h); maximum level speed 'clean' at 4,000 ft (1220 m) 128 kt (147 mph; 237 km/h); maximum cruising speed at optimum altitude 118 kt (136 mph; 219 km/h); economical cruising speed at 4,000 ft (1220 m) 110 kt (127 mph; 204 km/h)
Range: 250 nm (288 miles; 463 km); endurance 2 hours 24 minutes
Performance: maximum rate of climb at sea level 1,540 ft (469 m) per minute; service ceiling more than 12,000 ft (3660 m); hovering ceiling more than 12,000 ft (3660 m) in ground effect and 11,200 ft (3415 m) out of ground effect

MAST-MOUNTED SIGHT
The key sensors of the OH-58D are located in the McDonnell Douglas-built Mast-Mounted Sight. This has two windows for a TV sensor and an imaging infra-red, which provide targeting and navigation information in all light and weather conditions. Boresighted with these sensors is a laser designator/rangefinder. The sight itself is mounted on a special bearing which does not transmit the vibrations from the helicopter. The entire sight can swivel 360° in azimuth and +/- 30° in elevation.

ROTOR
The four-bladed main rotor has composite blades and a carbon-fibre yoke. It turns at 395 rpm. The two-bladed tail rotor turns at 2,381 rpm.

EXHAUST
The exhaust is located in the upper decking of the engine fairing. Hot gases are ejected straight into the rotor downwash, where they are rapidly diffused to reduce infra-red signature.

CAVING LADDER
The boxes each side of the lower cabin house drop-down rope ladders. These allow the rapid retrieval of personnel from the ground, who climb on to the ladder and hang on while the Kiowa moves away.

POWERPLANT
The OH-58D is powered by a single Allison 250-C30R (military designation T703-AD-700). The power rating is 485 kW (650 shp) but the transmission is limited to 410 kW (550 shp).

Protection against heat-seeking missiles is provided by the ALQ-144 IRCM turret.

Bell Model 412

The success of the Bell Model 212 Twin Two-Twelve in both civil and military use led the company to consider how to improve its performance. Reliable and useful though it is, the Model 212 nevertheless has a sea-level maximum cruising speed of only 100 kt (115 mph; 185 km/h) and a maximum range of 261 miles (420 km). The aim was to increase both these parameters, as well as other aspects of performance, without any major structural change to the airframe or the introduction of an entirely different powerplant. With these factors in mind, two new production Model 212s were taken to serve as prototypes for the new helicopter.

As a beginning, the standard Pratt & Whitney Canada PT6T-3B Turbo Twin Pac of the Model 212 gave way to the PT6T-3B-1 version, which differs only by being rated to produce a maximum 1,400 shp (1044 kW) for take-off. To increase range the standard fuel capacity was increased from 215 US gal (814 litres) to 330 US gal (1249 litres). The most significant change was the introduction of a new advanced-technology foldable four-bladed main rotor, comprising a new hub with elastomeric bearings and rotor blades of composite construction. These blades each have a glass-fibre spar and, apart from a Nomex honeycomb filler between the spar and blade trailing edge, the basic blade is entirely of glass-fibre with a titanium abrasion strip and a stainless steel tip cap. Not only was this combination expected to give the desired performance improvements, but static testing had suggested that the new rotor would eliminate most of the induced vibration, avoiding costly structural changes to introduce a nodal suspension system.

The two **Bell Model 412** prototypes were flown first in 1979 and gained VFR and IFR certification in 1981, on 9 January and 13 February respectively. The first production deliveries were made in January 1981, and Bell is continuing production for both civil and military customers.

Norway operates the Bell 412SP Arapaho with 720 Skvadron. This example is seen operating from a portable landing pad. The Norwegians bought 18, of which 17 were assembled locally.

In 1989 Bell transferred its production to Quebec in Canada, although many components are still made at Fort Worth. Further developments are the **Bell 412SP**, which introduced increased gross weight and fuel capacity, itself superseded by the **Bell 412HP** with improved transmission. These variants have accounted for the majority of military sales, including a 1992 order from the Canadian Forces covering 100 examples as the **CH-146 Griffon**. IPTN manufactures the type under licence in Indonesia as the **NBell-412**, while Agusta continues its tradition of Bell licence-production by building the **AB 412**. The Italian company has developed its own **Grifone** (described separately), a dedicated military variant.

SPECIFICATION

Bell Helicopter Textron Model 412SP
Rotor system: main rotor diameter 46 ft 0 in (14.02 m); tail rotor diameter 8 ft 6 in (2.59 m); main rotor disc area 1,661.90 sq ft (154.40 m²); tail rotor disc area 56.74 sq ft (5.27 m²)
Fuselage and tail: length overall, rotors turning 56 ft 0 in (17.07 m) and fuselage 42 ft 4.75 in (12.92 m); height overall 14 ft 2.25 in (4.32 m) with tail rotor turning and to top of rotor head 10 ft 9.5 in (3.29 m); stabiliser span 9 ft 4.5 in (2.86 m); skid track 8 ft 6 in (2.59 m)
Powerplant: one 1,800-shp (1342-kW) Pratt & Whitney Canada PT6T-3B-1 Turbo Twin Pac flat-rated at 1,400 shp (1044 kW) for take-off and 1,130 shp (843 kW) for continuous running
Weights: empty 6,470 lb (2935 kg); maximum take-off 11,900 lb (5397 kg)
Fuel and load: internal fuel 330 US gal (1249 litres) plus provision for 164 US gal (621 litres) of auxiliary fuel; external fuel none
Speed: never-exceed speed at sea level 140 kt (161 mph; 259 km/h); maximum cruising speed at sea level 124 kt (143 mph; 230 km/h)
Range: 375 nm (432 miles; 695 km) with maximum payload
Performance: maximum rate of climb at sea level 1,350 ft (411 m) per minute; service ceiling 16,300 ft (4970 m); hovering ceiling 9,200 ft (2805 m) in and out of ground effect

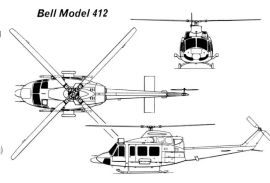

Bell Model 412

OPERATORS

Military versions of the Bell 412 are operated by Bahrain, Botswana, Canada, Colombia, Guatemala, Guyana, Honduras, Indonesia, Lesotho, Norway, Peru, Slovenia, South Korea, Sri Lanka, Thailand, Uganda, Venezuela and Zimbabwe, with the prospect of further sales.

Bell/Boeing V-22 Osprey

From research started by Bell with the tilt-rotor XV-3 in 1951 and Vertol in 1956 with the first tilt-wing VZ-2 (V-76) prototype, followed by Bell's development from 1973 of the highly successful XV-15 proof-of-concept tilt-rotor demonstrator, Bell Helicopter Textron and Boeing Vertol joined forces in the early 1980s to scale up and develop the XV-15 for the Joint Services Advanced Vertical Lift Aircraft (formerly JVX) programme. Combining the vertical lift capabilities of a helicopter with the fast-cruise (275 kt) forward flight efficiencies of a fixed-wing turboprop aircraft, the resulting **V-22 Osprey**, powered by tip-mounted 6,150-shp (4588-kW) Allison T406-AD-500 turboshaft engines driving three-bladed prop-rotors through interconnected drive shafts in nacelles which could be swivelled through 97.5°, was the subject of a US Navy-managed full-scale development contract awarded in June 1985.

Workshare

This included six prototypes, plus several static test airframes, for which Bell was responsible for design and construction of the wing, nacelles, transmissions, rotor and hub assemblies, and integration of the government-furnished engines. Boeing handled the fuselage, empennage, overwing fairings and avionics integration. Composite materials account for 59 per cent of the V-22's airframe weight. Both companies will compete for the major share of any future production lots. Initial joint service requirements were for 913 Ospreys, mostly for the US Army and **Marine Corps**, comprising 552 **MV-22A** USMC assault versions each carrying up to 24 fully-armed troops, as Boeing CH-46 replacements; 231 similar vari-

The first and second prototype V-22s in translational flight. The Osprey will revolutionise assault transport if it eventually succeeds in the budgetary battlefield.

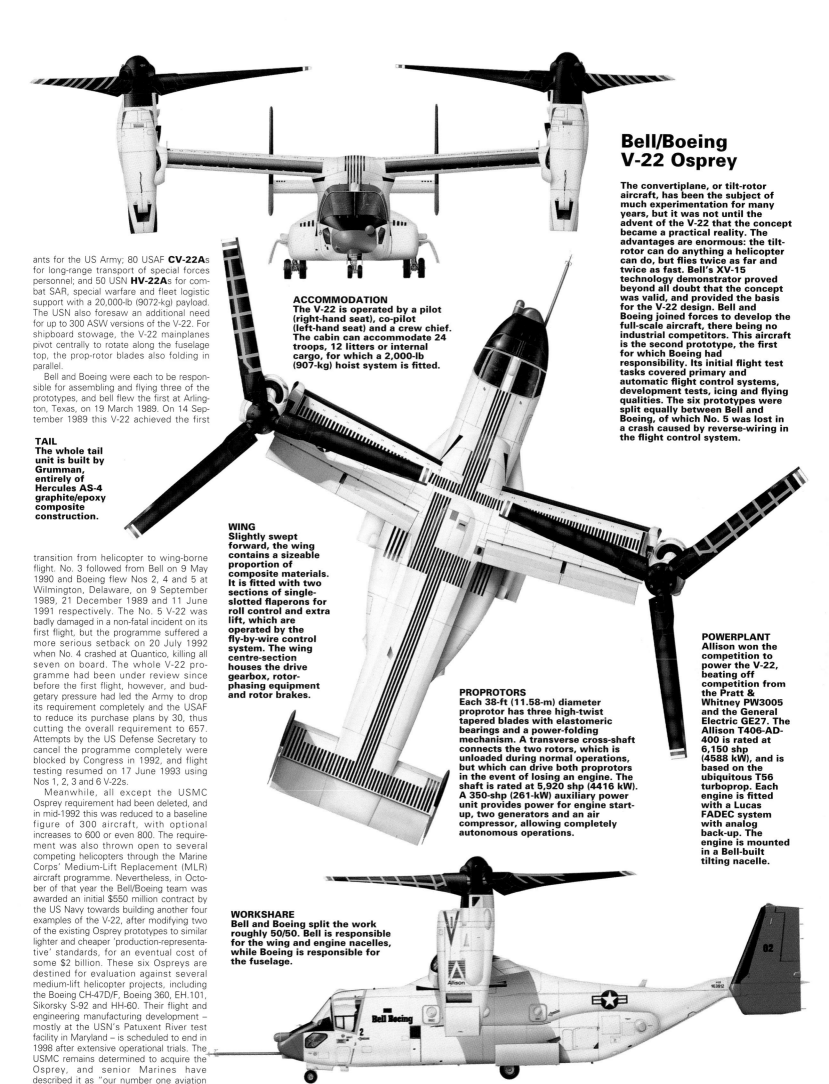

Bell/Boeing V-22 Osprey

The convertiplane, or tilt-rotor aircraft, has been the subject of much experimentation for many years, but it was not until the advent of the V-22 that the concept became a practical reality. The advantages are enormous: the tilt-rotor can do anything a helicopter can do, but flies twice as far and twice as fast. Bell's XV-15 technology demonstrator proved beyond all doubt that the concept was valid, and provided the basis for the V-22 design. Bell and Boeing joined forces to develop the full-scale aircraft, there being no industrial competitors. This aircraft is the second prototype, the first for which Boeing had responsibility. Its initial flight test tasks covered primary and automatic flight control systems, development tests, icing and flying qualities. The six prototypes were split equally between Bell and Boeing, of which No. 5 was lost in a crash caused by reverse-wiring in the flight control system.

ants for the US Army; 80 USAF **CV-22A**s for long-range transport of special forces personnel; and 50 USN **HV-22A**s for combat SAR, special warfare and fleet logistic support with a 20,000-lb (9072-kg) payload. The USN also foresaw an additional need for up to 300 ASW versions of the V-22. For shipboard stowage, the V-22 mainplanes pivot centrally to rotate along the fuselage top, the prop-rotor blades also folding in parallel.

Bell and Boeing were each to be responsible for assembling and flying three of the prototypes, and bell flew the first at Arlington, Texas, on 19 March 1989. On 14 September 1989 this V-22 achieved the first

transition from helicopter to wing-borne flight. No. 3 followed from Bell on 9 May 1990 and Boeing flew Nos 2, 4 and 5 at Wilmington, Delaware, on 9 September 1989, 21 December 1989 and 11 June 1991 respectively. The No. 5 V-22 was badly damaged in a non-fatal incident on its first flight, but the programme suffered a more serious setback on 20 July 1992 when No. 4 crashed at Quantico, killing all seven on board. The whole V-22 programme had been under review since before the first flight, however, and budgetary pressure had led the Army to drop its requirement completely and the USAF to reduce its purchase plans by 30, thus cutting the overall requirement to 657. Attempts by the US Defense Secretary to cancel the programme completely were blocked by Congress in 1992, and flight testing resumed on 17 June 1993 using Nos 1, 2, 3 and 6 V-22s.

Meanwhile, all except the USMC Osprey requirement had been deleted, and in mid-1992 this was reduced to a baseline figure of 300 aircraft, with optional increases to 600 or even 800. The requirement was also thrown open to several competing helicopters through the Marine Corps' Medium-Lift Replacement (MLR) aircraft programme. Nevertheless, in October of that year the Bell/Boeing team was awarded an initial $550 million contract by the US Navy towards building another four examples of the V-22, after modifying two of the existing Osprey prototypes to similar lighter and cheaper 'production-representative' standards, for an eventual cost of some $2 billion. These six Ospreys are destined for evaluation against several medium-lift helicopter projects, including the Boeing CH-47D/F, Boeing 360, EH.101, Sikorsky S-92 and HH-60. Their flight and engineering manufacturing development – mostly at the USN's Patuxent River test facility in Maryland – is scheduled to end in 1998 after extensive operational trials. The USMC remains determined to acquire the Osprey, and senior Marines have described it as "our number one aviation policy."

TAIL
The whole tail unit is built by Grumman, entirely of Hercules AS-4 graphite/epoxy composite construction.

ACCOMMODATION
The V-22 is operated by a pilot (right-hand seat), co-pilot (left-hand seat) and a crew chief. The cabin can accommodate 24 troops, 12 litters or internal cargo, for which a 2,000-lb (907-kg) hoist system is fitted.

WING
Slightly swept forward, the wing contains a sizeable proportion of composite materials. It is fitted with two sections of single-slotted flaperons for roll control and extra lift, which are operated by the fly-by-wire control system. The wing centre-section houses the drive gearbox, rotor-phasing equipment and rotor brakes.

PROPROTORS
Each 38-ft (11.58-m) diameter proprotor has three high-twist tapered blades with elastomeric bearings and a power-folding mechanism. A transverse cross-shaft connects the two rotors, which is unloaded during normal operations, but which can drive both proprotors in the event of losing an engine. The shaft is rated at 5,920 shp (4416 kW). A 350-shp (261-kW) auxiliary power unit provides power for engine start-up, two generators and an air compressor, allowing completely autonomous operations.

POWERPLANT
Allison won the competition to power the V-22, beating off competition from the Pratt & Whitney PW3005 and the General Electric GE27. The Allison T406-AD-400 is rated at 6,150 shp (4588 kW), and is based on the ubiquitous T56 turboprop. Each engine is fitted with a Lucas FADEC system with analog back-up. The engine is mounted in a Bell-built tilting nacelle.

WORKSHARE
Bell and Boeing split the work roughly 50/50. Bell is responsible for the wing and engine nacelles, while Boeing is responsible for the fuselage.

Bell/Boeing V-22 Osprey

The No. 1 V-22 in helicopter flight. This regime is controlled by normal rotary wing controls with cyclic and collective. As the aircraft translates to horizontal flight, the system automatically decreases these signals to the rotor swashplates, and increases those to the standard fixed-wing flying surfaces.

SPECIFICATION

Bell/Boeing V-22 Osprey
Wing and rotors: rotor diameter, each 38 ft 0 in (11.58 m); width overall, rotors turning 84 ft 6.8 in (25.78 m) and with rotors folded 18 ft 5 in (5.61 m); rotor disc area, total 2,268.23 sq ft (210.72 m²)
Wing: span 50 ft 11 in (15.52 m) including nacelles; aspect ratio 6.77; area 382.00 sq ft (35.59 m²)
Fuselage and tail: length, fuselage excluding probe

57 ft 4 in (17.47 m); height over fins 17 ft 7.8 in (5.38 m) and overall with nacelles vertical 20 ft 10 in (6.35 m); tailplane span over fins 18 ft 5 in (5.61 m); wheel track 15 ft 2 in (4.62 m); wheel base 21 ft 7.5 in (6.59 m)
Powerplant: two Allison T406-AD-400 each rated at 6,150 shp (4586 kW) for take-off and 5,890 shp (4392 kW) for continuous running
Weights: empty equipped 31,886 lb (14463 kg); normal mission take-off 47,500 lb (21545 kg) for VTO and 55,000 lb (24947 kg) for STO; maximum take-off

60,500 lb (27442 kg) for STO
Fuel and load: internal fuel 13,700 lb (6215 kg) standard and 30,074 lb (13641 kg) with self-ferry cabin tanks; maximum internal payload 20,000 lb (9072 kg); maximum external payload 10,000 lb (4536 kg) on a single hook or 15,000 lb (6804 kg) on two hooks
Speed: maximum cruising speed at optimum altitude 300 kt (345 mph; 556 km/h) in aeroplane mode; maximum cruising speed at sea level 100 kt (115 mph; 185 km/h) in helicopter mode and 275 kt (316 mph; 509 km/h) in aeroplane mode; maximum forward

speed with maximum slung load 200 kt (230 mph; 370 km/h)
Range: ferry range 2,100 nm (2,418 miles; 3892 km) after STO at 60,500 lb (27442 kg); tactical range 1,200 nm (1,382 miles; 2224 km) after VTO at 44,619 lb (21146 kg) with 12,000-lb (5443-kg) payload, or 1,800 nm (2,075 miles; 3336 km) after STO at 55,000 lb (24947 kg) with 20,000-lb (9072-kg) payload
Performance: service ceiling 26,000 ft (7925 m); take-off run less than 500 ft (152 m) at normal STO weight

Bellanca Citabria

A product of the Aeronca company with its origins in the wartime L-3 Grasshopper, the Model 7 Champion became a Bellanca property in 1970 after it had been further developed by Champion Aircraft Corp. An aerobatic version was named **Citabria** ('Airbatic' reversed), and in 1979 an order for 40 of these was placed by the Turkish army to serve as primary trainers. Known as the **Citabria 150S**, the chosen model was the Model 7GCBC powered by a 150-hp

(112-kW) Lycoming O-320-A2D engine. The Citabrias continue in service at the main army aviation base at Güverncinlik.

The Turkish army operates the Citabria in the primary trainer role and it is also used to screen potential students. The aircraft serve with the army aviation school.

Beriev Be-6 'Madge'

Beriev OKB
Taganrog Aviation Scientific-Technical Complex
Instrumentalniy Toupic 347927, Taganrog, Russia

Designed in 1945, and first flying in 1947, the Beriev LL-143 prototype was developed into the **Be-6** flying-boat, which first flew in 1949 and was assigned the NATO reporting name **'Madge'**. The aircraft was of classic Beriev design, with a long boat hull, gull wings and high-set engines. Power came from two Shvetsov ASh-73 radials. Initial production aircraft had a twin NS-23 cannon installation in the tail, but this gave way later to a MAD boom. Other weapons were a twin NS-23 dorsal barbette, and a bow-mounted single NS-23. Mines, depth charges or torpedoes could be carried. The 'Madge' remained in Soviet service into the 1970s, on second-line duties However, a small number were supplied to **China,** and it is believed that 10 of these continue to serve in the ASW role from the base at Tuandao.

Beriev Be-12 Tchaika 'Mail'

Developed as a successor to the Beriev Be-6, the **Be-12 Tchaika** (seagull) was designed primarily as an ASW and maritime patrol aircraft, although as land-based aircraft like the Il-38 and Tu-142 have taken over this role, SAR operations have become increasingly important.

Despite its anachronistic appearance, the Be-12 is a capable aircraft, and between 1964 and 1983 broke or set all 44 FAI world records for turboprop amphibians and flying-boats. The prototype first flew in 1960, and series production began during 1964, probably after competitive evaluation against the same bureau's jet-powered Be-10 'Mallow'.

The Be-12 is of very similar configuration and appearance to the 1949-vintage Be-6 flying-boat, with a cranked (gullwing) cantilever high wing, with considerable dihedral on the inner panels and slight anhedral on the outer wings. A 3124-kW (4,190-ehp) Ivchenko AI-20D turboprop is mounted on the top of each wing at the highest point, giving the AV-681 four-bladed propellers maximum clearance. The tailplanes also have considerable anhedral, and are tipped by vertical endplate fins. The aircraft has a single-step metal monocoque hull, with strakes on each side of the forward fuselage to minimise the amount of spray

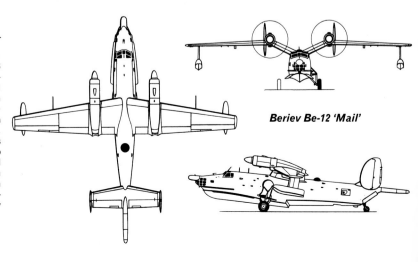

Beriev Be-12 'Mail'

The elderly Be-12 serves the Russian navy on coastal patrols. These cover ASW, SAR and fishery protection.

thrown up on take-off and landing. For operations from land, the Be-12 has a retractable tailwheel undercarriage, with the single mainwheels retracting upwards to lie flush in the sides of the hull. The five-man crew consists of pilot, co-pilot, navigator, radar operator and MAD operator.

A small search radar is carried, with a thimble radome directly above the glazing of the navigator's nose station, and there is a prominent magnetic anomaly detector 'stinger' projecting aft from the tailcone. The aircraft has an internal weapons bay in the hull, immediately aft of the step, and has two underwing pylons under each outer wing panel, and can reportedly also carry rocket rails farther outboard. Armament would usually consist of homing torpedoes and depth charges.

About 70 of the 100-200 Be-12 Tchaika amphibians built remain in service with the air forces of the **Russian Northern Fleet,** and almost certainly with the **Ukrainian** successor to the old Black Sea Fleet. About a dozen may also remain active with the **Vietnam People's Army Air Force,** and a handful more with **Syria,** serving on SAR and patrol duties.

Seven ex-AV-MF Be-12s were returned in 1993 to Taganrog for conversion to new roles. Two are serving as the prototypes for a proposed water-bomber, with twin water scoops behind the step, extra drop doors in the hull just behind the cockpit, and small overflow portholes in the upper fuselage

above all the water tanks. Three 1.5-ton tanks are fitted in the former rear weapons bay, and a single 3-ton tank in the stores position behind the cockpit. The 7½-ton load can be dropped simultaneously, or sequentially from fore and aft doors to cover a larger area. The Be-12's agility and powerful engines make it extremely suitable for the firefighting role, and Beriev expects an order in 1993 for six aircraft for service in the Russian Far East. A third aircraft is serving as the prototype for a cargo aircraft,

with an enlarged hatch and all ASW equipment removed.

SPECIFICATION

Beriev Be-12 Tchaika 'Mail'
Wing: span 29.71 m (97 ft 5.75 in); aspect ratio 8.4; area 105.00 m² (1,130.25 sq ft)
Fuselage and tail: length 30.17 m (99 ft 0 in); height 7.00 m (22 ft 11.5 in)
Powerplant: two ZMDB Progress (Ivchyenko) AI-20D

each rated at 3,124 ekW (4,190 ehp)
Weights: empty 21700 kg (47,840 lb); maximum take-off 31000 kg (68,342 lb)
Fuel and load: external fuel none; maximum ordnance about 5000 kg (11,023 lb)
Speed: maximum level speed 'clean' at optimum altitude 608 km/h (328 kt; 378 mph); normal operating speed at optimum altitude 320 km/h (173 kt; 199 mph)
Range: ferry range 7500 km (4,047 nm; 4,660 miles)
Performance: maximum rate of climb at sea level 912 m (2,990 ft) per minute; service ceiling 11280 m (37,000 ft)

Beriev **A-40 Albatros 'Mermaid'**

Development of the **A-40** began during 1983 as a successor to the Be-12 'Mail' in the ASW, maritime patrol, minelaying and secondary SAR roles. The prototype made its first flight during December 1986, and it became known to the West during 1987. In 1988 the director of US naval intelligence revealed that the provisional reporting name **'TAG-D'** (the fourth new experimental aircraft spotted at Taganrog) had been allocated to a new amphibian photographed by a US satellite. On 20 August 1989 the prototype made a flypast at the Aviation Day display at Tushino, and articles about the aircraft (described as being for SAR duties, and attributed to designer Alexei K. Konstantinov) began to appear in the Soviet press. The second prototype finally made the type's Western debut at the 1991 Paris air show at Le Bourget, by which time the

Beriev Design Bureau had been renamed as the Taganrog Aviation Scientific-Technical Complex, named after G. M. Beriev.

The A-40 is the largest amphibian ever built, and is of completely modern design. A pair of Perm/Soloviev D-30KPV turbofan engines is mounted on pylons above the wingroot, just aft of the trailing edge. An RD-60K turbojet take-off booster is fitted inside each pylon, with its nozzle usually

covered by a vertically split 'eyelid'. The wings themselves, along with small strakes on the nose, protect the engine intakes from spray.

The single-step hull is of revolutionary design, described by its creators as the world's first 'variable rise bottom', with unique double chines. This sets new standards of stability and controllability in the water and gives smaller g forces on take-off and landing. Small wedges help the aircraft to 'unstick'. The aircraft has a large stores bay in the hull, aft of the step, and the large pods which form the wingroots accommodate electronic equipment as well as the retracted four-wheel main undercarriage bogies. Slim ESM pods are carried on the wingtips, above the stabilising floats. A flight crew of eight would be carried, consisting of two pilots, a flight engineer, a radio operator, a navigator and three observers/equipment operators.

The basic A-40 ASW/patrol amphibian will probably bear the service designation **Be-44** (which may have been the subject of a lapsed 10-aircraft order for the **CIS navy**) if it ever enters production. The aircraft forms the basis for a number of as-yet unflown variants. A minimum-change SAR version, stripped of ASW equipment and without ESM wingtips, is designated **Be-42.** This will have a nine-man crew, with an additional technician and the three observer/operators replaced by medical attendants. The aircraft would carry two LPS-6 life rafts, blood transfusion equipment, ECG machines and other surgical equipment. Up to 54 survivors could be accommodated, entering the aircraft via two side hatches, each equipped with mechanised ramps. Searchlights and IR sensors

An impressive view of an A-40 Albatros launching during a test flight. The aircraft has excellent water characteristics, and good performance once it is airborne.

The A-40's strange configuration results from the conflicting demands of operations from both water and land. The engines are mounted high above the fuselage to avoid spray ingestion.

Fuselage and tail: length 43.839 m (143 ft 10 in) including probe; height 11.066 m (36 ft 3.75 in); tailplane span 11.87 m (38 ft 11.5 in); wheel track 4.96 m (16 ft 3.25 in); wheel base 14.835 m (48 ft 8 in)
Powerplant: two PNPP 'Aviadvigatel' (Soloviev) D-30KPV each rated at 117.68 kN (26,455 lb st) dry and two Klimov RD-60K each rated at 24.52 kN (5,511 lb st) dry
Weights: maximum take-off about 86000 kg (189,594 lb)
Fuel and load: internal fuel 35000 kg (77,160 lb); external fuel none; maximum ordnance 6500 kg (14,330 lb)
Speed: never-exceed speed 650 km/h (350 kt; 404 mph); maximum level speed 'clean' at 6000 m (19,685 ft) 760 km/h (410 kt; 472 mph); maximum cruising speed at 6000 m (19,685 ft) 720 km/h (388 kt; 447 mph)
Range: 5500 km (2,967 nm; 3,417 miles) with maximum fuel or 4100 km (2,212 nm; 2,547 miles) with maximum payload
Performance: maximum rate of climb at sea level 1800 m (5,906 ft) per minute with one engine inoperative; service ceiling 9700 m (31,825 ft); take-off run 1000 m (3,281 ft) at maximum take-off weight; take-off distance to 15 m (50 ft) 1100 m (3,609 ft) at maximum take-off weight; landing distance from 15 m (50 ft) 1450 m (4,757 ft) at normal landing weight; landing run 900 m (2,953 ft) at normal landing weight

would be used for locating survivors. The first Be-42 is already under construction, but the status of an order for 10 by the CIS navy (which originally wanted 10 ASW Be-44s) is very uncertain. The **Be-40P** is a projected 105-seat passenger aircraft, and the **Be-**

40PT a mixed passenger and cargo aircraft carrying between 37 and 70 people plus freight. The **Be-200** is a scaled-down version, powered by a pair of Lotarev D-436T turbofans and with passenger, cargo, ambulance and SAR versions projected.

SPECIFICATION

Beriev A-40 Albatros 'Mermaid'
Wing: span 41.62 m (136 ft 6.5 in); aspect ratio 8.6; area 200.00 m² (2,152.85 sq ft)

Boeing **B-52G Stratofortress**

Boeing Defense and Space Group
PO Box 3999, Seattle
WA 98124, USA

Backbone of Strategic Air Command until the organisation's demise on 31 May 1992, the mighty B-52 has been an icon of US military strength for nearly 40 years, having first entered service in June 1955. In today's streamlined **Air Combat Command**, the type still plays an important part in the power projection force, while also retaining its nuclear deterrent function. By the end of 1994 only the B-52H will be left in service.

One hundred and ninety-three **B-52Gs** were built, these introducing integral wing tanks and a shorter fin compared to earlier variants. Defensive armament remained as four 0.50-in machine-guns in a remotely-controlled turret, although in October 1991

the gunner was removed from the crew as an economy measure. Eighty G models remained in service in early 1993, but during the year most were retired to the boneyard.

In the initial ACC structure, B-52Gs served with the 2nd, 42nd, 93rd, 366th, 379th and 416th Bomb Wings. Power projection was the principal role for these veterans, using their enormous range and load-carrying ability to haul conventional bomb-loads to any point on the globe. Desert Storm missions were all assigned to the G model. Some aircraft were converted to carry 12 AGM-86 cruise missiles on the wing pylons, principally for the nuclear role with the AGM-86B. However, the conventional warhead AGM-86C is now in use,

launched operationally for the first time on the opening night of Desert Storm. Non-cruise configured B-52Gs were assigned a maritime role, including the launch of Harpoon anti-ship missiles. In the Gulf War these aircraft operated as free-fall bombers.

Internal configuration

Internally the B-52G has a large weapons bay occupying the central fuselage, which is capable of accommodating clips of conventional weapons or free-fall nuclear devices. The crew area is arranged on two levels, the lower deck housing the en route navigator and radar navigator/bombardier, while the upper deck has the two pilots and the electronic warfare officer, the latter facing

backwards in a seat next to the vacated gunner's position. Four main undercarriage units are staggered to retract sideways into the fuselage, and outriggers are provided in the tips of the drooping wings to maintain stability. The B-52G is well protected by numerous ECM systems, and two under-nose blisters house LLLTV and FLIR sen-

The B-52G is fast disappearing from service as Air Combat Command shrinks to a manned bomber force consisting of the B-52H and B-1B, with a 'silver bullet' fleet of B-2s. The 366th Wing at Mountain Home was the last user of the G model, receiving B-1Bs in 1994.

In its twilight years, the B-52G has become closely associated with conventional weapons. Here the load is low-drag general-purpose bombs, of which a great number can be carried. In the maritime role the B-52 can sow mines.

sors, which are used with terrain-avoidance radar to provide low-level penetration capability in bad weather or at night.

With the reduction in threat posed by the former Soviet Union, the nuclear deterrent requirement is considerably reduced, releasing B-52Hs to assume many of the conventional tasks previously undertaken by the B-52G. Consequently, the G model will be out of service by the mid-1990s. The final unit is the 366th Wing, the US Air Force's power projection unit headquartered at Mountain Home AFB, Idaho. This unit controls the 34th Bomb Squadron, stationed at Ellsworth AFB, SD (previously March AFB, CA). The squadron is converting to the B-1B, the first two of a planned six having been delivered by May 1994.

WEAPON OPTIONS

Tail turret with four 0.50-in machine-guns (not currently used), internal bomb bay and inboard wing pylons for carriage of offensive load. Up to 20 AGM-86 ALCM can be carried, eight internally and three on each wing pylon. Internal carriage for 'clip' of four B83 free-fall nuclear weapons. In the conventional role the B-52G can be configured with the Heavy Stores Adaptor Beam on the wing hardpoints so that nine 2,000-lb class Mk 84 bombs can be carried under each wing, with a further 27 internally. Alternatively 27 750-lb class M117 or 1,000-lb class Mk 83 bombs can be carried internally, with a further 24 on wing pylons fitted with the redundant Hound Dog pylon and multiple ejector racks. AGM-86C conventional-warhead cruise missiles provide long-range stand-off attack capability, and the AGM-142 Have Nap EO-guided missile can be carried on the HSABs. This missile has

a stand-off range of 80 km (50 miles) and features a 896-kg (1,975-lb) high-explosive warhead.

SPECIFICATION

Boeing B-52G Stratofortress
generally similar to the B-52H except in the following particulars:
Powerplant: eight Pratt & Whitney J57-P-43WB each rated at 13,750 lb st (61.16 kN) dry
Weights: maximum take-off more than 488,000 lb (221357 kg)
Range: range more than 6,513 nm (7,500 miles; 12070 km)
Performance: service ceiling 40,000 ft (12190 m)

Right: The B-52Gs of the 366th Wing have been issued with the AGM-142 EO/IR-guided Have Nap stand-off missile. This allows the B-52 to hit targets with great accuracy but without having to penetrate heavily-defended air space.

Boeing **B-52H Stratofortress**

Based on the preceding B-52G version, the **Boeing B-52H** was intended to serve as a carrier for the Douglas GAM-87A Skybolt air-launched ballistic missile under development in the early 1960s. The most significant of the changes for this mission was to ensure that the B-52H would be able to penetrate enemy air space at low level, below radar coverage, which required extensive structural modification to ensure the airframe would be able to withstand the effects of low-level turbulence. The changes were barely visible externally, but two other modifications were to provide external features that allowed identification. One of the early-build B-52Gs (57-6471) had flown in July 1960 as a testbed for the Pratt & Whitney TF33-P-1 turbofan, and more powerful versions of the same engine were installed in revised cowlings to enhance performance of the B-52H, giving a range increase of almost one third by comparison with the B-52G. The last externally noticeable change was replacement of the four 12.7-mm (0.5-in) machine-guns in the tail turret of the B-52G with a Vulcan cannon with six 20-mm barrels. Internal changes for the new role brought revised ECM equipment and the provision of terrain-avoidance radar.

A total of 102 B-52H Stratofortresses

was built, the first (60-006) being flown on 6 March 1961. Within 16 months, in June 1962, the last of them had been completed; six months later President John F. Kennedy cancelled the Skybolt programme for which the B-52H had been developed. Since that time the aircraft has been subject of many update programmes, which have added improved avionics, ECM protection and the ALQ-151 Electro-optical Viewing System (EVS). B-52Hs were configured to carry 20 AGM-86B cruise missiles (12 under the wing pylons and eight on an internal rotary launcher), and were employed mainly in the stand-off nuclear missile launch role until 1991, when the force began to adopt a wider brief including conventional bombing tasks. In the same time-frame, the H model began to be equipped with the AGM-129

Advanced Cruise Missile, a stealthy successor to the AGM-86. Further weapon options include AGM-86C conventional-warhead cruise missiles, B61 or B83 free-fall nuclear

Above: Operating in the conventional role, this B-52H is from the 5th Bomb Wing, seen participating in a Red Flag exercise.

A 416th BW B-52H displays the unique undercarriage arrangement of the Stratofortress. The tail gun may be replaced by Stinger missiles.

Boeing B-52H Stratofortress

FUEL
Internal fuel is housed in giant tanks between the spars of the wings and in the upper fuselage. This is augmented by two permanently fixed external tanks on the outer wings, raising total capacity to 48,030 US gal (181813 litres).

RADAR
Under the upward-hinging nose radome is the Norden APQ-156 multi-mode radar, which incorporates synthetic aperture technology. The principal function is targeting.

Boeing B-52H Stratofortress

Universally known throughout the US Air Force as the 'Cadillac', the B-52H introduced significant upgrades compared to the G model to make it a far more capable aircraft, especially in the areas of load/range performance and crew comfort. One hundred and two were built for Strategic Air Command, and the 90 remaining on charge are set to provide long-range power projection and cruise missile carriage for the foreseeable future. This aircraft carries the steer's head badge of the 7th Bomb Wing, based at Carswell AFB, Texas, now a B-1 operator.

TERRAIN AVOIDANCE
The radar presents a terrain trace on the TV screen displays of the pilot and co-pilot. Using this, the flight crew input control commands to avoid terrain. The process is not automatic as on TFR-equipped aircraft.

EVS
At the heart of the B-52's ability to fly and fight at low level in all weathers is the Electro-optical Viewing System, the sensors for which are located in two blisters under the nose. Forward-looking infra-red and low-light-level TV provide images on cockpit display screens of the view ahead of the bomber which, combined with the terrain-avoidance radar, allow the crew to navigate safely at low level, and to locate targets, with no outside visibility due to bad weather, night or the use of nuclear windscreen shielding.

weapons, AGM-142 Have Nap (Rafael Popeye) precision-guided attack missiles (originally procured for the B-52G), and up to 51 750-lb class iron bombs.

The first B-52H to be specifically modified to embrace full conventional warfare capability was delivered to Boeing's Wichita plant for the upgrade. This involves enabling the B-52H to carry the AGM-142 Have Nap missile, the AGM-84 Harpoon anti-ship missile and the universal bomb bay adaptor. Ninety B-52Hs remained in the inventory in early 1994 and no plans had then been announced for any retirements. So useful is the load-carrying/range performance of the B-52H that it has been mooted that they may even serve beyond the retirement date of the B-1B. Within Air Combat Command the B-52 force is being concentrated at three bases with the 2nd Bomb Wing (Barksdale AFB, LA), 5th Bomb Wing (Minot AFB, ND) and 92nd Bomb Wing (Fairchild AFB, WA – deactivating in late 1994). In addition there are two reservist squadrons, the 166th Bomb Squadron, Washington ANG, at Fairchild, and the 93rd Bomb Squadron, Air Force Reserve, at Barksdale, with more likely to form.

UNDERCARRIAGE
The four eight-wheel units are arranged in tandem pairs, the wheel wells being staggered to accommodate the gear within the narrow fuselage. Each unit swivels to allow the fuselage to crab during crosswind take-offs and landings. Small outriggers deploy from the outer wings to protect the wingtips, although these frequently do not touch the ground when the wing fuel tanks are less than full.

POWERPLANT
Giving the B-52H its excellent performance is the Pratt & Whitney TF33-P-3 turbofan, rated at 17,000 lb (75.65 kN) thrust for take-off. The extra power compared to earlier models adds a good safety margin for heavyweight launches, and the lower fuel burn considerably extends range. Cabin noise is significantly reduced, with a corresponding effect on crew fatigue. Water-methanol boosting is provided for take-off, the 1,200-US gal (4542-litre) saddle tank being located behind the crew compartment. Ducting takes the boost mixture along the leading edges and into the engine nacelles.

ECM
The B-52 is comprehensively equipped to handle hostile radar threats. Equipment includes an ALT-28 jammer in a fairing on top of the nose, ALQ-117 deception jammers facing sideways from the nose, ALQ-172 deception jammer forward of the gun-control radar and clusters of aerials for the ALQ-155 system under the forward and rear fuselage. Radar warning receivers are located in the tailcone and in blisters on the sides of the vertical fin.

CREW
The B-52H crew consists of two pilots and an electronic warfare officer on the upper deck, with a navigator and bombardier/radar navigator on the lower deck. The former gunner's station is now vacant.

WEAPON OPTIONS

In the nuclear role the B-52H can carry 20 cruise missiles (eight internally on rotary launcher and six under each wing pylon). These can either be AGM-86B ALCM or AGM-129 Advanced Cruise Missiles. Free-fall weapons such as B61 or B83 remain an option, but this capability is at present entrusted to the B-1 fleet (with B-2 assuming the role in the future). Conventional weapons are the same as for B-52G, namely AGM-86C cruise missiles, AGM-142 Have Nap and AGM-84 Harpoon. Free-fall bombs can be carried on HSABs or Hound Dog pylons,

to a maximum of 51 750-lb class weapons. Alternatives to general-purpose bombs include cluster munitions and mines. The M61A1 Vulcan 20-mm cannon in the tail turret is no longer used, and may be replaced by a Stinger air-to-air missile launcher.

SPECIFICATION

Boeing B-52H Stratofortress
Wing: span 185 ft 0 in (56.39 m); aspect ratio 8.56; area 4,000.00 sq ft (371.60 m2)
Fuselage and tail: length 160 ft 10.9 in (49.05 m); height 40 ft 8 in (12.40 m); tailplane span 55 ft 7.5 in

(16.95 m); wheel track 8 ft 3 in (2.51 m); wheel base 50 ft 3 in (15.48 m)
Powerplant: eight Pratt & Whitney TF33-P-3 each rated at 17,000 lb st (75.62 kN) dry
Weights: maximum take-off 505,000 lb (229088 kg)
Fuel and load: internal fuel 299,434 lb (135821 kg) plus provision for 9,114 lb (4134 kg) in two 700-US gal (2650-litre) non-jettisonable underwing tanks; external fuel none; maximum ordnance about 50,000 lb (22680 kg)
Speed: maximum level speed 'clean' at high altitude 516 kt (595 mph; 957 km/h); cruising speed at high altitude 442 kt (509 mph; 819 km/h); penetration speed at low altitude between 352 and 365 kt

These B-52Hs wear the 'Seattle Seahawks' badge of the 92nd Bomb Wing, based at Fairchild AFB, Washington. The aircraft are armed with AGM-86B ALCMs, six being carried on each wing pylon with a further eight inside.

(405 and 420 mph; 652 and 676 km/h)
Range: more than 6,865 nm (10,000 miles; 16093 km)
Performance: service ceiling 55,000 ft (16765 m); take-off run 9,500 ft (2896 m) at maximum take-off weight

Boeing C-135

Eight hundred and twenty of the C-135 family were built, all but 12 being for **USAF** service. Although the KC-135 tankers were the principal variants, 45 were built as **C-135A** (15) or **C-135B** (30) transports, with tanking equipment deleted. Several of these remain in limited service on specialised transport or test duties.

Having spent many years with the 89th MAW on staff transport duties, this C-135B is one of a small fleet assigned to general duties with the 55th Wing at Offutt AFB, where most 'special' C-135s are gathered.

J57 turbojets powered the C-135A, and only two of these remain in service under this designation, used by the 4950th Test Wing of Air Force Materiel Command and as a command transport/trials aircraft by the 55th Reconnaissance Wing. Further C-135A aircraft still serve as transports, upgraded to **C-135E** standard with TF33 turbofans and wide-span tailplanes, one flying with the 4950th TW and one operated by the 552nd AW&CW on behalf of the Commander, Space Command.

C-135Bs were built with TF33 turbofans and wide-span tailplanes from the outset, and a small number remains in service in

their original form, one serving with the 55th Wing on staff transport duties. The **C-135C** designation applies to three **WC-135B** weather reconnaissance aircraft which reverted to transport status. Most of the other C-135Bs were converted to various special mission variants following their service with Military Airlift Command.

SPECIFICATION

Boeing C-135A
Wing: span 130 ft 10 in (39.88 m); aspect ratio 7.04; area 2,433.00 sq ft (226.03 m2)
Fuselage and tail: length 136 ft 3 in (41.53 m); height 41 ft 8 in (12.70 m); tailplane span 40 ft 3 in (12.27 m); wheel base 46 ft 7 in (14.20 m)
Powerplant: four Pratt & Whitney J57-P-59W each

rated at 13,750 lb st (61.16 kN) dry
Weights: operating empty 106,306 lb (48220 kg); maximum take-off 316,000 lb (143335 kg)
Fuel and load: internal fuel 189,702 lb (86047 kg); external fuel none; maximum payload 83,000 lb (37650 kg)
Speed: maximum level speed at high altitude 530 kt (610 mph; 982 km/h); cruising speed at 35,000 ft (10670 m) 462 kt (532 mph; 856 km/h)
Range: ferry range 7,990 nm (9,200 miles; 14806 km); operational radius 3,000 nm (3,455 miles; 5560 km) to offload 24,000 lb (10886 kg) of fuel or 1,000 nm (1,151 miles: 1854 km) to offload 120,000 lb (54432 kg) of fuel
Performance: maximum rate of climb at sea level 1,290 ft (393 m) per minute; service ceiling 45,000 ft (13715 m); typical take-off run 10,700 ft (3261 m) increasing to 14,000 ft (4267 m) under 'hot and high' conditions at maximum take-off weight

Boeing **KC-135A/Q Stratotanker**

On 15 July 1954, Boeing's famous Model 367-80 prototype took to the air for the first time at the company's Renton plant. The four-jet swept-wing transport provided the basis for the prolific Model 707 civil airliner and Model 717 (C-135) tanker-transport families, and also set the design philosophy which extended throughout Boeing's hugely successful airliner dynasty.

In September 1955 Boeing received the first order for the **KC-135A** tanker, following successful trials with the 'Dash Eighty' prototype configured with a Boeing-designed flying boom under the rear fuselage. The first tanker (55-3118) flew from Renton on 31 August 1956, piloted by 'Dix' Loesch and 'Tex' Johnston. Flight tests revealed no serious flaws and the KC-135A entered service with the 93rd Air Refueling Squadron on 28 June 1957.

Seven hundred and thirty-two KC-135s were built in a long and efficient production run. The first 582 aircraft were built with a short fin, but from the 583rd today's taller fin was introduced to make the aircraft more stable during take-off, a feature retrofitted to all machines. An early modification was the addition of strengthening straps around the rear fuselage to dampen jet-induced resonance.

Internal configuration

Internally, the KC-135A features integral wing tanks between the spars, and further tanks in the lower lobe of the fuselage, making a total of 22. The main cabin provides a considerable volume for cargo carriage, for which a side-loading cargo door is fitted. Alternatively, seating can be provided for 80 troops. A crew of four comprises two pilots, a navigator and a boom operator. The latter is called upon to act as loadmaster and to aid the flight crew in navigation and with checklists, in addition to his primary task.

This is performed from a prone position in a fairing under the rear of the aircraft, from where the boomer has an excellent view of the boom and the receiver aircraft. A small control column is provided which is linked to control surfaces on the end of the boom. Further controls are provided for extending and retracting the boom, and the boomer also operates director lights which provide positional information for receiver pilots. The fuel system is managed by the co-pilot from a console between the two pilots.

Fifty-six of the tankers were converted as **KC-135Q**s, which featured additional navigation and communications equipment for the support of the now-retired Lockheed SR-71 fleet. These carried high-flashpoint JP-7 fuel in addition to the regular JP-4/5 used by the tanker itself. They remained capable of refuelling other receivers, but the JP-7 tanks had to be purged before they could carry regular fuel. Today the Q models are often involved in supporting F-117 operations, and are in the process of being re-engined to **KC-135T** standard (described separately). Other early tanker variants were the **C-135F** (a designation applied to 12 KC-135As which were supplied to France), and the **KC-135D**, four of which were converted from RC-135A survey aircraft.

Between 1975 and 1988, Boeing replaced the lower wing skins of all surviving KC-135s to extend their useful lives to beyond 2020. Work also began on re-engining a large portion of the fleet to replace the noisy and thirsty J57 engines.

Two major re-engining programmes reduced the numbers of KC-135As in the inventory considerably, and in 1993/94 large numbers were retired to AMARC at Davis-Monthan AFB, AZ. In early 1994 the only front-line units still operating the original J57-engined 'stovepipe' tankers were the 71st Air Refueling Squadron, 19th Air Refueling Wing at Barksdale AFB, LA, (inactivating 1994), 350th ARS/43rd ARW at Beale AFB, CA, and the 917th ARS/43rd ARW at Dyess AFB, TX. Each squadron was operating 15 KC-135Qs. Six KC-135As remained with the 93rd ARS, the training unit at Castle AFB, but were due for imminent retirement, while the training function was to transfer (with KC-135Rs) to Altus AFB, OK, under the auspices of Air Education and Training Command.

With the KC-135A retired to the boneyard, and the KC-135Q fleet being cycled through Boeing Wichita for conversion to KC-135T standard, the days of the 'stovepipe' are all but over.

SPECIFICATION

Boeing KC-135A Stratotanker
Wing: span 130 ft 10 in (39.88 m); aspect ratio 7.04; area 2,433.00 sq ft (226.03 m²)
Fuselage and tail: length 136 ft 3 in (41.53 m);

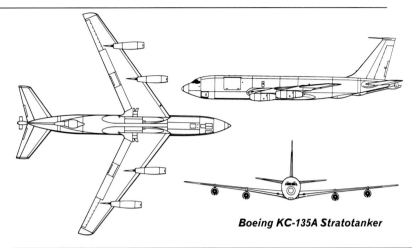

Boeing KC-135A Stratotanker

height 41 ft 8 in (12.70 m); tailplane span 40 ft 3 in (12.27 m); wheel base 46 ft 7 in (14.20 m)
Powerplant: four Pratt & Whitney J57-P-59W each rated at 13,750 lb st (61.16 kN) dry
Weights: operating empty 106,306 lb (48220 kg); maximum take-off 316,000 lb (143335 kg)
Fuel and load: internal fuel 189,702 lb (86047 kg); external fuel none; maximum payload 83,000 lb (37650 kg)
Speed: maximum level speed at high altitude 530 kt (610 mph; 982 km/h); cruising speed at 35,000 ft (10670 m) 462 kt (532 mph; 856 km/h)
Range: ferry range 7,990 nm (9,200 miles; 14806 km); operational radius 3,000 nm (3,455 miles; 5560 km) to offload 24,000 lb (10886 kg) of fuel or 1,000 nm (1,151 miles: 1854 km) to offload 120,000 lb

Having previously supported SR-71 operations, the KC-135Qs are often used to refuel Lockheed F-117s. The specialist aircraft are the last to undergo the F108 re-engining.

(54432 kg) of fuel
Performance: maximum rate of climb at sea level 1,290 ft (393 m) per minute; service ceiling 45,000 ft (13715 m); typical take-off run 10,700 ft (3261 m) increasing to 14,000 ft (4267 m) under 'hot-and-high' conditions at maximum take-off weight

The 'stovepipe' KC-135As are now retired from service. This example wears 379th BW markings.

Boeing **KC-135D/E Stratotanker**

Of the two re-engining programmes for the KC-135, the least ambitious was that to upgrade the KC-135A tankers of the Air National Guard and Air Force Reserve (together with a small number of special mission EC/RC/NKC-135 aircraft) with turbofans.

Large numbers of surplus 707 airliners were purchased by the US Air Force, and stripped of their JT3D (military designation TF33) engines for fitment to the tankers. At the same time the wide-span tailplanes of the airliners were also fitted to the tankers to maintain stability with the greater thrust of the new engines.

Fitment of the TF33s provides several important improvements over the J57. The greater thrust allows the **KC-135E** to operate on far greater safety margins than previously possible, and to use shorter runways. The fan engines are more efficient, offering cost-saving and greater fuel offloads on similar mission profiles. Noise pollution is considerably reduced, a major factor for Guard units operating from civilian airports, and lastly the TF33s incorporate thrust-reversers for greater landing safety.

Over one hundred and sixty ANG and AFRES KC-135s underwent the 'E' conver-

sion, including the four **KC-135D**s (although these retain their original designation), and were joined by 21 special mission aircraft. Current units are:

Air Force Reserve – 63rd ARS/434th ARW (Selfridge ANGB), 314th ARS/434th ARW (McClellan AFB) and 336th ARS/452nd ARW (March AFB);

Air National Guard – 168th ARS/Alaska ANG (Eielson AFB, operates all four KC-135Ds in addition to KC-135Es), 197th ARS/Arizona ANG (Sky Harbor IAP, Phoenix), 196th ARS/California ANG (March AFB), 108th ARS/Illinois ANG (O'Hare ARFF, Chicago), 117th ARS/Kansas ANG (Forbes Field, Topeka), 132nd ARS/Maine ANG (Bangor ANGB), 133rd ARS/New Hampshire ANG (Pease AFB – converting to KC-135R), 141st ARS and 150th ARS/New Jersey ANG (McGuire AFB), 146th ARS and 147th ARS/Pennsylvania ANG (Greater Pittsburgh IAP), 151st ARS/Tennessee ANG (McGhee Tyson AP, Knoxville), 191st ARS/Utah ANG (Salt Lake City IAP) and 116th ARS/Washington ANG (Fairchild AFB – converting to B-52H). Three more ANG tanker squadrons were due to form in 1994: 106th ARS/Alabama, 136th ARS/New York and 173rd ARS/Nevada.

SPECIFICATION

Boeing KC-135E Stratotanker
generally similar to the KC-135A
Powerplant: four Pratt & Whitney JT3D-3B each rated at 18,000 lb st (80.07 kN) dry

The KC-135E (and similar KC-135D illustrated) forms the main equipment of the Air National Guard and Air Force Reserve tanker units. The TF33 turbofans give increased performance and greater efficiency compared to the old J57s.

Boeing **KC-135R/T/C-135FR Stratotanker**

In 1980 Boeing announced a major upgrade programme for the KC-135 involving the fitment of high bypass-ratio turbofans to offer far greater fuel efficiency, noise reduction and operational flexibility. Under the company designation **KC-135RE**, the first conversion took to the air on 4 August 1982.

Designated **KC-135R** in service (the second time this had been applied, having previously been used by a reconnaissance variant of the KC-135A), the re-engined and

The KC-135R is the mainstream type in the USAF's tanker fleet, although further conversions have been cancelled. In addition to the obvious re-engining, the KC-135R has an APU added to allow autonomous operations. Most serve with CONUS units, but squadrons are assigned to PACAF (909th ARS at Kadena – illustrated) and USAFE (351st ARS at RAF Mildenhall).

upgraded tanker is now the mainstay of the US Air Force's tanker fleet, and as more conversions are completed more units are dispensing with their older variants in favour of the KC-135R.

CFM International's CFM56 engine (military designation F108) was chosen for the KC-135R, offering 22,000 lb (97.86 kN) of thrust. This allows an increase in maximum take-off weight and an increase in fuel carriage. An APU is fitted, characterised by intake and exhaust ports on the port side of the rear fuselage, which allows the KC-135R to undertake autonomous operations from austere locations. Many other systems are also upgraded during the conversion.

Air Force delivery

First delivery (to SAC's 384th Air Refueling Wing) took place in July 1984, and the 200th was delivered in April 1990. Three hundred and six conversions have been funded so far, with the prospect of the programme continuing to cover most of the

active-duty tanker fleet. The surviving 11 C-135Fs delivered to France were also upgraded under this programme, becoming **C-135FR**s, and were subsequently fitted with Adèle radar warning receivers and underwing pods for probe-and-drogue work.

Related variants include the **KC-135R(RT)**, the designation applied to a small number of aircraft fitted with a refuelling receptacle. Most of these are ex-special mission or trials aircraft. These have been joined by the survivors of the 56 KC-135Q aircraft, which are being fitted with refuelling receptacles as they undergo the re-engining conversion to emerge as **KC-135T**s, with a primary role of supporting F-117 attack aircraft and other covert programmes. A feasibility study has also been undertaken to fit the KC-135R with wing pods for the refuelling of probe-equipped aircraft from other US or foreign services. At present, this is only possible by fitting a short hose/drogue assembly to the end of the boom, as originally practised by

the French C-135FR aircraft.

Active-duty US Air Force units were first in line to receive the new tanker, but in 1991 the KC-135Rs were delivered to the Air National Guard. By 1994 five squadrons had re-equipped, with a sixth (Hawaii) being established to provide refuelling coverage for the Pacific islands. Following the 1 June 1992 reshuffle of Air Force units, KC-135R assignments remained roughly along the previous SAC lines, but were soon dramatically altered as all but the 366th Wing aircraft were transferred to Air Mobility Command and the two reservist organisations.

SPECIFICATION

Boeing KC-135R Stratotanker
generally similar to the KC-135A except in the following particulars:
Powerplant: four CFM International F108-CF-100 each rated at 22,000 lb st (97.86 kN) dry
Weights: maximum take-off 322,500 lb (146284 kg)
Fuel and load: internal fuel 203,288 lb (92210 kg)
Range: operational radius 2,500 nm (2,879 miles; 4633 km) to offload 150 per cent more fuel than the KC-135A

Boeing KC-135R/T/C-135FR Stratotanker

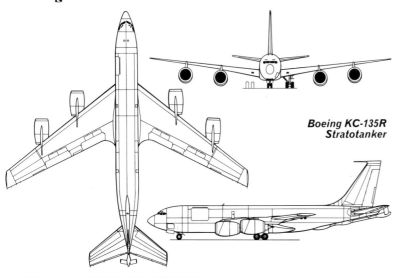

Boeing KC-135R Stratotanker

French C-135FR aircraft have been fitted with Adèle RWR, with distinctive antennas above the flight deck and on the fin.

ARS (Robins AFB), 11th and 306th ARS (Altus AFB)
22nd ARW: 384th ARS (McConnell AFB) – one more squadron to form
43rd ARW: 91st and 97th ARS (Malmstrom AFB), 28th ARS (Ellsworth AFB), 43rd and 92nd ARS (Fairchild AFB – 92nd ARW to form in 1994), 906th ARS (Minot AFB)
319th ARW: 905th ARS (Grand Forks AFB - one more squadron to form)
380th ARW: 310th and 380th ARS (Plattsburgh AFB), 42nd ARS (Loring AFB – deactivating), 509th ARS (Griffiss AFB)
398th OG: 93rd ARS (Castle AFB – KC-135 training unit. The task will move to Altus in 1994)
Pacific Air Forces – 906th ARS/18th Wing (Kadena AB, Okinawa)
US Air Forces in Europe – 351st ARS/100th ARW

OPERATORS

The following were KC-135R and C-135FR assignments in early 1994:
Air Combat Command – 22nd ARS/366th Wing (Mountain Home AFB – to get KC-10s in 1995)
Air Mobility Command – 19th ARW: 99th and 912th

(RAF Mildenhall, England)
Air Force Reserve – 72nd and 74th ARS/434th ARW (Grissom AFB). 77th and 465th ARS to convert in 1994.
Air National Guard – 153rd ARS/Mississippi ANG (Key Field, Meridian), 133rd ARS/New Hampshire ANG (Pease ANGB), 145th ARS and 166th ARS/Ohio ANG (Rickenbacker ANGB), 126th ARS/Wisconsin ANG (General Mitchell IAP, Milwaukee) and 203rd ARS/Hawaii ANG (Hickam AFB)
Armée de l'Air – Escadre de Ravitaillement en Vol 93 (HQ and ERV 1/93 'Aunis' at Istres, ERV 2/93 'Sologne' at Avord and ERV 3/93 'Landes' at Mont-de-Marsan)

Boeing EC-135

Under various EC-135 designations, the US Air Force flies a small fleet of aircraft dedicated to the airborne command post mission. As the Cold War has ended, this mission has assumed far less importance than in previous times, and the inventory has been reduced accordingly. EC-135s were previously assigned to theatre commanders, in addition to the major US Air Force commands, but are now centrally maintained by the 2nd Air Command and Control Squadron of the 55th Wing at Offutt AFB, with detachments made to commands who need their services.

Originally developed to provide an airborne command post for SAC's nuclear retaliation forces, the EC-135 fleet is equipped with comprehensive communications equipment, which allows the airborne commander to link with national command authorities, theatre forces, other airborne command posts (such as the Navy's TACAMO fleet) and with his assets on the ground. A trailing wire aerial deploys from the EC-135's belly, while the airframe is liberally covered with aerials for a wide range of frequency coverage. New to the aircraft is the ARC-208(V) Milstars satellite communications antenna, housed in a large dorsal fairing on some aircraft.

Backbone of the 2nd ACCS fleet is the **EC-135C** variant, which was previously dedicated to SAC support. Other similar variants are the **EC-135H**, **J**, **P** and **Y**, which were previously given a theatre assignment. The **EC-135A**, **G** and **L** are radio relay platforms used to extend the effective range of the main command post. By late 1992 most of the EC-135A/G/H/L and P aircraft were in open storage at Davis-Monthan AFB, along with two EC-135Cs and an EC-135J. Among future plans is the complete retirement of the USAF EC-135 fleet, with command post functions being performed by the US Navy's E-6 Mercury.

Further aircraft in the series include two **EC-135K** aircraft, which are used to provide navigation support to fighter deploy-

ments, and four **EC-135E** range support/test aircraft. The latter fly with the 4950th Test Wing, and are fitted with a telemetry-receiving dish antenna in a bulbous nose radome.

SPECIFICATION

Boeing EC-135C
Wing: span 130 ft 10 in (39.88 m); aspect ratio 7.04; area 2,433.00 sq ft (226.03 m²)
Fuselage and tail: length 136 ft 3 in (41.53 m); height 41 ft 8 in (12.70 m); tailplane span 45 ft 3 in (13.79 m); wheel base 45 ft 8 in (13.92 m)

Four of the 55th Wing's EC-135Cs are equipped with the Milstars satcom antenna on the spine.

Powerplant: four Pratt & Whitney TF33-P-9 each rated at 18,000 lb st (80.07 kN) dry
Weights: basic empty 102,300 lb (46403 kg); maximum take-off 299,000 lb (135626 kg)
Fuel and load: internal fuel 189,702 lb (86047 kg); external fuel none
Speed: maximum level speed at 25,000 ft (7620 m) 535 kt (616 mph; 991 km/h); cruising speed at 35,000 ft (10670 m) 486 kt (560 mph; 901 km/h)
Range: ferry range 4,910 nm (5,654 miles; 9099 km); operational radius 2,325 nm (2,677 miles; 4308 km)

Boeing NC/NKC/OC/WC-135

Under various designations, including **NC-135A**, **NKC-135A** and **NKC-135E**, the US Air Force operates a fleet of

Among the work undertaken by the NKC-135 test fleet is inflight refuelling trials. Shown here refuelling an Edwards AFB B-52 is an NKC-135E.

grossly modified C-135 airframes on development and trials work, mostly with the 4950th Test Wing at Wright-Patterson AFB, OH. The type of work performed by these aircraft is highly varied, but includes staff transport, refuelling tests with new aircraft types, airborne laser trials, weightlessness training for astronauts (the 'vomit comets' serving with NASA), and numerous pro-

grammes involving the testing of airborne equipment and space technology. A large portion of their work has been in support of the SDI programme. A single NKC-135A serves with the 55th Wing on command support transport duties.

Two further NKC-135A aircraft serve with the Fleet Electronic Warfare Support Group of the US Navy, maintained and flown by Chrysler at Waco, TX. These operate alongside a single DC-8, providing realistic electronic warfare environments for naval ships on exercise, and are consequently fitted with a wide range of jammers, resulting in numerous external fairings and antennas.

Unconnected with the test fleet, the

Chrysler operates two NKC-135As on behalf of the US Navy from Waco Field, alongside the single Douglas EC-24. These aircraft are packed with jammers to create a hostile ECM environment for fleet exercises.

WC-135B is a meteorological aircraft previously operated by the US Air Force's 55th Weather Reconnaissance Squadron at McClellan AFB, CA. Ten C-135B transports were converted to this standard, identified by having air scoops on either side of the fuselage. Today six of these aircraft remain in service, gathered with other C-135 specials at Offutt AFB with the 55th Wing. Two retain the WC-135B designation, while one has been redesignated the **TC-135B** to act as a crew trainer for the remaining three aircraft, which have been modified as **OC-135Bs** for the 'Open Skies' reconnaissance mission. These have a series of photographic sensors installed, including a

KA-91A panoramic camera for medium-altitude work, and two KS-87 oblique cameras and a single KS-87 vertical camera for low-altitude photography. The OC-135Bs can accommodate 38 crew, including maintenance personnel, foreign representatives and members of the On-Site Inspection Agency, the organisation responsible for providing sensors and linguists for the 'Open Skies' verification sorties. The OC-135Bs and TC-135B are assigned to the 24th Reconnaissance Squadron.

SPECIFICATION

Boeing NKC-135A
Wing: span 130 ft 10 in (39.88 m); aspect ratio 7.04; area 2,433.00 sq ft (226.03 m²)

The USAF's latest C-135 variant is the OC-135B, a dedicated platform for 'Open Skies' arms treaty verification flights. The aircraft is equipped with a battery of cameras.

Fuselage and tail: length 136 ft 3 in (41.53 m); height 41 ft 8 in (12.70 m); tailplane span 40 ft 3 in (12.27 m); wheel base 46 ft 7 in (14.20 m)
Powerplant: four Pratt & Whitney J57-P-59W each rated at 13,750 lb (61.1 kN) dry
Weights: operating empty 123,000 lb (55793 kg); maximum take-off 270,000 lb (122472 kg)
Fuel and load: internal fuel 189,702 lb (86047 kg); external fuel none
Speed: maximum level speed at high altitude 530 kt (610 mph; 982 km/h); cruising speed at 35,000 ft (10670 m) 462 kt (532 mph; 856 km/h)
Range: ferry range 7,990 nm (9,200 miles; 14806 km);

typical operational range 4,400 nm (5,057 miles; 8154 km)
Performance: maximum rate of climb at sea level

1,290 ft (393 m) per minute; service ceiling 41,000 ft (12495 m); typical take-off run 10,700 ft (3260 m) at maximum take-off weight

Boeing **RC/TC-135**

From an early date, the Boeing C-135 was recognised as an excellent airframe for various special missions. One of these was strategic reconnaissance, using the aircraft's capacious cabin to house large amounts of electronic equipment. Designated RC-135, several versions of reconnaissance Stratotankers are used today.

All RC-135s serve with the 55th Wing at Offutt AFB, previously the headquarters of Strategic Air Command, from where they are detached on a global basis to cover areas of the world where intelligence-gathering is required. Regular detachments are made to RAF Mildenhall in England, Souda Bay on Crete, Kadena AB on Okinawa and Shemya AB on the Aleutians.

Among the current versions are three dedicated to general Sigint gathering. All feature large amounts of electronic recording and analysing equipment on board, and have many aerials on the airframe. All three have slab-sided cheek fairings where many of the side-facing antennas are grouped. These serve the Automatic Elint Emitter Locator System (AEELS), which gathers signals from across the frequency spectrum, sifts out those of particular interest and

Fourteen RC-135s are Rivet Joint aircraft, eight being RC-135Vs (illustrated) and six being RC-135Ws. These are the backbone of the Sigint-gathering fleet.

relays data to operator stations in the cabin. Many other antennas, notably the farm of 'MUCELS' under the fuselage, supply data for other systems.

Two aircraft are to **RC-135U** standard, these characterised by cheek fairings and additional fairings in the chin, boomer, wingtip, tailcone and fin-top positions. Until 1991 they were fitted with 'towel rail' antennas above the cheek fairings, but these have been removed. Known as **Combat Sent** aircraft, the pair of RC-135Us is believed to have special purposes within the Sigint fleet, and may also be used to trial new equipment.

Eight aircraft are to **RC-135V Rivet Joint** standard, and six are the essentially similar **RC-135W** variant. These are the workhorses of the Sigint fleet, and are distinguished by having extended 'thimble' noses and large plate aerials under the centre-section. External differences between the two variants are restricted to a lengthened cheek fairing on the W model, which also lacks auxiliary air intakes on its engine pods. A related variant is the **TC-135W**, which is based at Offutt to provide crew training for the RC-135U/V/W fleet. This has the 'thimble' nose and cheek fairing, but does not have mission equipment.

An altogether more specialised role is undertaken by two **RC-135S Cobra Ball** aircraft which normally operate from Shemya. In addition to 'thimble' noses, elec-

Above: Two RC-135U Combat Sent aircraft serve with the 55th Wing. They have now had the fuselage side 'towel rail' removed.

Below: The TC-135W is used as an aircrew trainer for the RC-135U/V/W. The 55th Wing also flies TC-135B and TC-135S trainers.

Boeing RC/TC-135

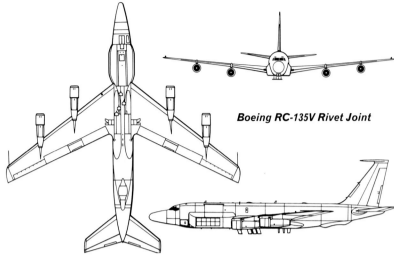

Boeing RC-135V Rivet Joint

Two RC-135S Cobra Balls fly with the 55th Wing. Their role is to record foreign missile tests, but they may be assigned a 'Scud'-hunting theatre missile reconnaissance role.

tronic receivers mounted in cheek fairings and a teardrop-shaped fairing on the aft fuselage, these have large circular windows in the fuselage for the photography of foreign missile tests. The equipment is known as the Real Time Optical System (RTOS). The wings and engine nacelles on the starboard side were painted black to reduce glare for re-entry vehicle photography (in the process of being removed), while the aerials are used to gather telemetry data from the

test launches and re-entries.

Telint (telemetry intelligence) is the role of the RC-135S, and it serves with the 24th Reconnaissance Squadron. With the decrease in foreign ICBM tests following the end of the Cold War, the Cobra Balls may adopt a theatre role spotting battlefield missiles. This is in response to the difficulties caused by the Iraqi 'Scud' missiles during the Gulf War. Until February 1993 the pair was augmented by the sole **RC-135X Cobra Eye**, which had a single camera window behind a sliding door for missile photography, and fewer antennas. A single **TC-135S**, without mission equipment, provides aircrew training for the Telint fleet.

The RC-135 fleet has consistently proved

of great value, both as a strategic reconnaissance tool during peacetime and as a more tactical asset during times of tension. The 55th Wing has been highly active in all the world's troublespots, and played an instrumental part in Desert Storm and subsequent operations in the Gulf. Two more airframes are earmarked for conversion to

RC-135W standard to swell the 'Rivet Joint' fleet.

SPECIFICATION

Boeing RC-135/TC-135
generally similar to the Boeing KC-135E Stratotanker

Boeing C-137/C-18

Derived from the same Model 367-80 prototype as the KC-135, the Boeing 707 proved to be one of the most successful airliners of all time, with 916 sales of civil models. 707s in **USAF** service received the C-137 designation, and comprised three 707-153s delivered in 1959 as **VC-137A**s. These were subsequently re-engined with TF33 turbofans, becoming **VC-137B**s in the process. The 'V' was dropped from the prefix in the late 1970s. The trio is still in use with the 89th Airlift Wing at Andrews AFB, and has been joined by four more aircraft.

The first pair were 707-353Cs procured for use as Presidential transports under the **VC-137C** designation. On replacement by the VC-25As currently in use as 'Air Force One' aircraft, the two C-137s joined the first three on general staff and VIP transport duties. In the late 1980s, two more C-137Cs were added to the 89th Airlift Wing fleet. In 1991 a 707-355C was issued to Central Command as a transport under the **EC-137D** designation (used for the second time, having previously been applied to the test aircraft for the E-3 programme).

Under the designation **C-18A**, eight ex-American Airlines Boeing 707s were purchased in 1981 for the 4950th Test Wing fleet at Wright-Patterson AFB, OH (subsequently moved to Edwards AFB, CA). Two were left in their original configuration, although one was broken up for spares and

the other used for general trials and training work. Of the other six, four were modified to **EC-18B** standard, for the **ARIA** (Advanced Range Instrumentation Aircraft) role, which involves the fitment of a large steerable telemetry-receiving antenna in a giant nose radome, as fitted to the EC-135E. The final pair are equipped as **EC-18D** Cruise Missile Mission Control Aircraft, with APG-63 radar (as fitted to the F-15) and telemetry receiver.

SPECIFICATION

Boeing C-137C
Wing: span 145 ft 9 in (44.42 m); aspect ratio 7.056; area 3,010.00 sq ft (279.63 m²)
Fuselage and tail: length 152 ft 11 in (46.61 m); height 42 ft 5 in (12.93 m); tailplane span 45 ft 9 in (13.94 m); wheel track 22 ft 1 in (6.73 m); wheel base 59 ft 0 in (17.98 m)
Powerplant: four Pratt & Whitney TF33 (JT3D-3) each rated at 18,000 lb st (80.07 kN) dry
Weights: maximum take-off 327,000 lb (148325 kg)
Fuel and load: internal fuel 23,855 US gal (90299 litres); external fuel none; maximum payload 51,615 lb (23413 kg)
Speed: maximum level speed at high altitude 545 kt (628 mph; 1011 km/h); maximum cruising speed at 25,000 lb (7620 m) 520 kt (599 mph; 964 km/h); economical cruising speed at optimum altitude 478 kt (550 mph; 886 km/h)
Range: 6,610 nm (7,611 mph; 12248 km)

A few C-137s remain in service with the 89th Airlift Wing on VIP transport duties.

Below: The EC-18B has a telemetry receiver antenna in the giant nose radome for supporting missile tests.

Performance: maximum rate of climb at sea level 3,550 ft (1082 m) per minute; service ceiling 42,000 ft (12800 m); take-off distance to 35 ft (10.7 m) 10,350 ft (3155 m) at maximum take-off weight; landing distance from 50 ft (15 m) 5,930 ft (1807 m) at normal landing weight

---

Boeing E-3 Sentry

The **Boeing E-3 Sentry** is the West's principal AWACS (airborne warning and control system) platform. Using the airframe of a Boeing 707-320B airliner and a massive payload of radar and electronic sensors, the E-3/AWACS is a flying headquarters for C³I (command, control, communications and intelligence), employed near a combat zone to monitor aircraft and missiles and to direct friendly warplanes.

On a typical mission, an E-3, which has

an unrefuelled endurance of 11 hours, routinely refuels and stays aloft for up to 18 hours, carrying a crew of 20 including 16 mission specialists such as weapon controllers, radar operators and communications specialists. Heart of the AWACS system is its Westinghouse AN/APY-2 Overland Downlook Radar (ODR), which, with other sensors and instrumentation, is mounted in a saucer-like rotodome mounted on two 3.35-m (11-ft) struts above

the rear fuselage. The AN/APY-2 replaced the AN/APY-1 system from the 25th aircraft onwards and is fitted to all export E-3s. The deep circular rotodome is some 9.14 m (30 ft) in diameter, weighs 1540 kg (3,395 lb) and is canted 2.5° downward. In operation, the dome rotates six times per minute. The radar is capable of tracking up to 600 low-flying aircraft.

The **EC-137D** prototype for the AWACS series first flew on 5 February 1972. The first E-3A Sentry, of a total of 34 (including two EC-137Ds) procured by the **USAF**, made its maiden flight on 31 October 1975, and following completion of full-scale devel-

opment in 1976, the first operational example was delivered to the 552nd AC&CW at Tinker AFB, OK, in March 1977. IOC (initial operating capability) was gained in April 1978 and E-3s assumed a US continental air defence role in January 1979. Since then, AWACS aircraft have been involved in all American combat operations in Grenada (1983), Lebanon (1983), Panama (1989) and Iraq (1991).

Twenty-two **E-3A** and two EC-137D aeroplanes, collectively termed 'core' aircraft when they were standardised in the late 1970s, were upgraded to **E-3B** standard. The first was converted by Boeing,

Boeing E-3D Sentry AEW.Mk 1

After a protracted procurement programme, including the development and cancellation of the Nimrod AEW.Mk 3, the RAF was eventually able to retire its vintage Shackletons in 1991. Seven Sentry AEW.Mk 1s were procured for No. 8 Squadron at RAF Waddington, which supports the NATO Airborne Early Warning Force, itself an E-3 operator. RAF aircraft have been active on Deny Flight operations over Bosnia.

ESM
The RAF Sentries featured wingtip pods from the outset, containing Loral 1017 'Yellow Gate' ESM equipment for passive radar detection. ESM equipment has been tested on USAF E-3s, housed in fairings on each side of the forward fuselage.

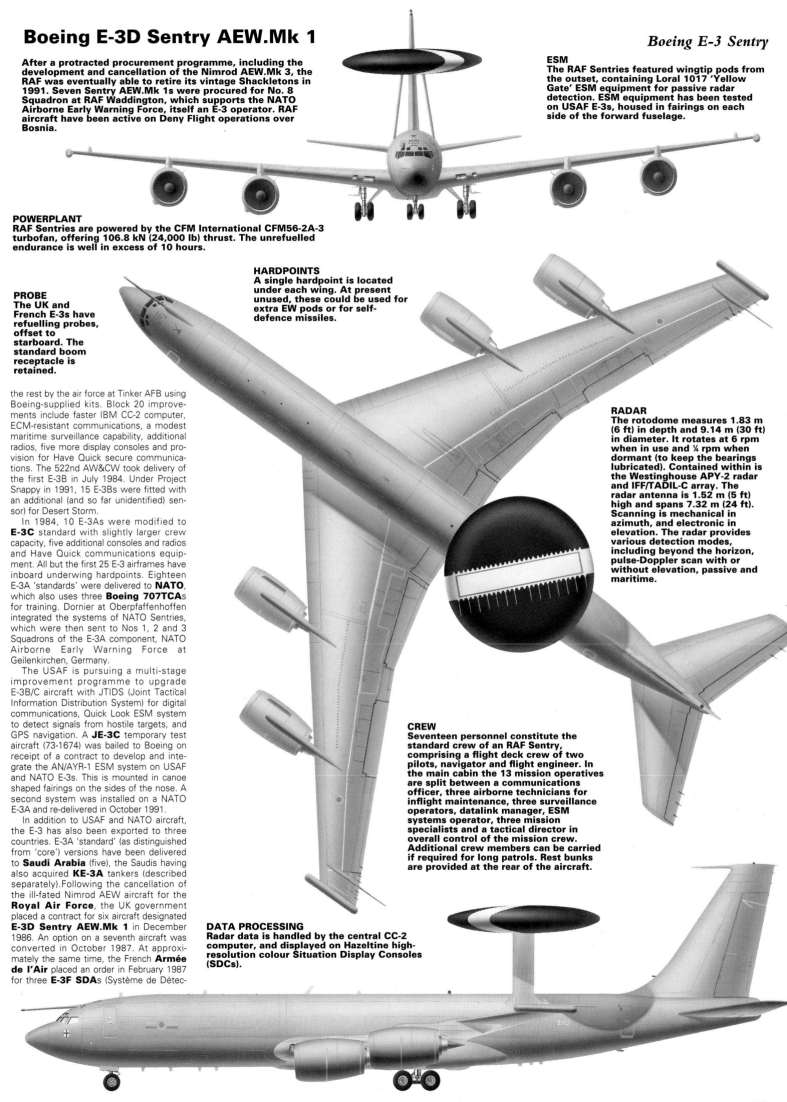

POWERPLANT
RAF Sentries are powered by the CFM International CFM56-2A-3 turbofan, offering 106.8 kN (24,000 lb) thrust. The unrefuelled endurance is well in excess of 10 hours.

HARDPOINTS
A single hardpoint is located under each wing. At present unused, these could be used for extra EW pods or for self-defence missiles.

PROBE
The UK and French E-3s have refuelling probes, offset to starboard. The standard boom receptacle is retained.

RADAR
The rotodome measures 1.83 m (6 ft) in depth and 9.14 m (30 ft) in diameter. It rotates at 6 rpm when in use and ¼ rpm when dormant (to keep the bearings lubricated). Contained within is the Westinghouse APY-2 radar and IFF/TADIL-C array. The radar antenna is 1.52 m (5 ft) high and spans 7.32 m (24 ft). Scanning is mechanical in azimuth, and electronic in elevation. The radar provides various detection modes, including beyond the horizon, pulse-Doppler scan with or without elevation, passive and maritime.

the rest by the air force at Tinker AFB using Boeing-supplied kits. Block 20 improvements include faster IBM CC-2 computer, ECM-resistant communications, a modest maritime surveillance capability, additional radios, five more display consoles and provision for Have Quick secure communications. The 522nd AW&CW took delivery of the first E-3B in July 1984. Under Project Snappy in 1991, 15 E-3Bs were fitted with an additional (and so far unidentified) sensor) for Desert Storm.

In 1984, 10 E-3As were modified to **E-3C** standard with slightly larger crew capacity, five additional consoles and radios and Have Quick communications equipment. All but the first 25 E-3 airframes have inboard underwing hardpoints. Eighteen E-3A 'standards' were delivered to **NATO**, which also uses three **Boeing 707TCA**s for training. Dornier at Oberpfaffenhoffen integrated the systems of NATO Sentries, which were then sent to Nos 1, 2 and 3 Squadrons of the E-3A component, NATO Airborne Early Warning Force at Geilenkirchen, Germany.

The USAF is pursuing a multi-stage improvement programme to upgrade E-3B/C aircraft with JTIDS (Joint Tactical Information Distribution System) for digital communications, Quick Look ESM system to detect signals from hostile targets, and GPS navigation. A **JE-3C** temporary test aircraft (73-1674) was bailed to Boeing on receipt of a contract to develop and integrate the AN/AYR-1 ESM system on USAF and NATO E-3s. This is mounted in canoe shaped fairings on the sides of the nose. A second system was installed on a NATO E-3A and re-delivered in October 1991.

In addition to USAF and NATO aircraft, the E-3 has also been exported to three countries. E-3A 'standard' (as distinguished from 'core') versions have been delivered to **Saudi Arabia** (five), the Saudis having also acquired **KE-3A** tankers (described separately).Following the cancellation of the ill-fated Nimrod AEW aircraft for the **Royal Air Force**, the UK government placed a contract for six aircraft designated **E-3D Sentry AEW.Mk 1** in December 1986. An option on a seventh aircraft was converted in October 1987. At approximately the same time, the French **Armée de l'Air** placed an order in February 1987 for three **E-3F SDA**s (Système de Détec-

CREW
Seventeen personnel constitute the standard crew of an RAF Sentry, comprising a flight deck crew of two pilots, navigator and flight engineer. In the main cabin the 13 mission operatives are split between a communications officer, three airborne technicians for inflight maintenance, three surveillance operators, datalink manager, ESM systems operator, three mission specialists and a tactical director in overall control of the mission crew. Additional crew members can be carried if required for long patrols. Rest bunks are provided at the rear of the aircraft.

DATA PROCESSING
Radar data is handled by the central CC-2 computer, and displayed on Hazeltine high-resolution colour Situation Display Consoles (SDCs).

A USAF E-3 approaches a KC-135. USAF E-3s proved their worth in Desert Storm, during which they controlled all coalition attacks.

tion Aéroportée). An order for a fourth aircraft was added later, but options on a further two E-3s were dropppped in 1988. Both European versions differ markedly from other E-3s, with Boeing giving each nation a 130 per cent industrial offset. The primary difference is the replacement of TF33 turbofans with 106.8-kN (24,000-lb st) CFM56-2A-3 turbofans, and installation of an upper forward fuselage-mounted SOGERMA inflight-refuelling probe in additon to the refuelling receptacle. RAF aircraft also have wingtip-mounted Loral 1017 'Yellow Gate' ESM pods. The RAF's first E-3D (ZH101) was first flown on 11 September 1989, and made its initial flight in fully-equipped mode in 5 January 1990. It preceded the French E-3F which first flew on 27 June 1990. The last RAF aircraft was the ultimate Boeing 707 airframe produced, after which the production line was closed, forcing Japan to opt for an AEW version of the much newer twin-engined Boeing 767, using essentially E-3C equipment. Planned improvements for the E-3 include the Block 30/35 programme

Designated JE-3C, this aircraft was bailed back to Boeing for integration of an ESM system, with antennas mounted in two fuselage bulges and an undernose fairing.

with radar improvements, an upgrade of JTIDS to TADIL-J standards, improved memory and compatibility with GPS. A further improvement may be funded, which will give a radar upgrade for USAF aircraft, with new processors and displays and pulse compression for enhanced performance against small targets.

SPECIFICATION

Boeing E-3C Sentry
Powerplant: four Pratt & Whitney TF33-P-100/100A turbofans each rated at 93.41 kN (21,000 lb st)
Dimensions: wing span 145 ft 9 in (44.42 m); length 46.61 m (152 ft 11 in); height 12.73 m (41 ft 9 in); wing area 283.35 m² (3,050.00 sq ft)
Weights: operating empty 77996 kg (171,950 lb); maximum take-off 147420 kg (325,000 lb)
Performance: maximum level speed at high altitude 853 km/h (530 mph; 460 kt); operating ceiling 8840 m (29,000 ft); operational radius 1612 km (1,002 miles; 870 nm) for a 6-hour patrol without flight refuelling; endurance more than 11 hours without flight refuelling

France's four E-3F Sentries are similar to those of the RAF, except that they lack the wingtip ESM pods. The E-3Fs serve with EDA 36, and are the only aircraft assigned to the French air defence command CAFDA. They are based at Avord.

Boeing KE-3

The **Boeing KE-3A/B** is an air-refuelling tanker for **Saudi Arabia**. Eight 'new build' KE-3A models were delivered to the Royal Saudi air force in 1987 under the Peace Shield programme and are operated by the RSAF's No. 18 Squadron at Riyadh.

Manufactured with the E-3A Sentry AWACS aircraft, and using the same Boeing 707-320B airframe, the KE-3A has a dedicated tanker mission and lacks AWACS sensors or capability. Although other countries operate tanker versions of the veteran 707, none employs the KE-3A designation.

As part of its ongoing military build-up, Saudi Arabia would like to obtain seven further KE-3As to refuel its F-15s and Tornados. Prompted by Israel's dual-role use of the Boeing 707 as a tanker and intelligence gatherer, the RSAF is also expected to add

an Elint function with cabin consoles.

Since the 707 production line will not be reopened, additional KE-3s will be obtained by purchasing and modifying existing 707s. At the beginning of 1993, a single, previously-owned 707 airframe was being modified by E-Systems at Greenville, TX, to become the RSAF's first **KE-3B** tanker.

SPECIFICATION

Boeing KE-3A
Wing: span 145 ft 9 in (44.42 m); aspect ratio 7.056; area 3,050.00 sq ft (283.35 m²)
Fuselage and tail: length 152 ft 11 in (46.61 m); height 41 ft 9 in (12.73 m); tailplane span 45 ft 9 in (13.94 m); wheel track 22 ft 1 in (6.73 m); wheel base 59 ft 0 in (17.98 m)

Powerplant: four CFM International CFM56-2A2 each rated at 24,000 lb st (106.76 kN) dry
Weights: maximum take-off 342,000 lb (155131 kg)
Fuel and load: internal fuel 23,855 US gal (90299 litres) plus provision for 5,030 US gal (19040 litres) of transfer fuel in in the rear lower cargo hold; external fuel none
Speed: never-exceed speed Mach 0.95; maximum

Despite the designation KE-3A, the aircraft is simply a tanker 707 powered by CFM56 turbofans.

level speed at high altitude 460 kt (530 mph; 853 km/h)
Range: operational radius 1,000 nm (1,151 miles; 1853 km) to offload 123190 lb (55878 kg) of fuel

---

Boeing E-4

Based on the successful 747-200B airframe, the **E-4B** serves the **United States** as an AABNCP (Advanced Airborne National Command Post). The main purpose is to provide an aerial platform for the national command authority during time of (nuclear) war, from which the President and his key staff can lead the chain of command of the nation and its forces. Known alternatively as the National Emergency Airborne Command Post (NEACP, inevitably 'kneecap', or in popular parlance the 'Doomsday Plane'), four E-4Bs serve with the 1st Airborne Command and Control Squadron of the 55th Wing, headquartered at Offutt AFB, NE, but with one aircraft always deployed to an airfield near to the President's location when he is overseas. The practice of maintaining one E-4B on alert at Andrews AFB near the White House was discontinued in the late 1980s as global tensions reduced.

Using the 747-200B airframe, the E-4B is adapted internally for its mission. Five operating compartments on the main deck are a flight crew station (the E-4 carrying two complete crews of aircraft commander, copilot, navigator and flight engineer), NCA area (equivalent to a 'flying White House Situation Room'), conference room, battle staff area and C³I area, from where the communications equipment is operated. The top deck provides crew rest facilities.

Hardening against electro-magnetic pulse and thermal shielding from nuclear blast is incorporated, and the comprehensive communications suite covers the frequency range. A feature of the E-4B is the SHF (super high frequency) communications aerial in a large dorsal fairing, and the capability to break in to civilian radio/TV networks for direct broadcasts to the population.

Inflight refuelling is possible through a receptacle mounted in front of the flight deck, and the systems of the E-4B are optimised for long endurance. A minimum requirement of 72 hours aloft is accepted, and the mission could theoretically last for a week. Barring other malfunctions, the limiting factor is the availability of lubrication for the engines.

Three of the four aircraft were delivered as **E-4A**s in late 1974 following a first flight on 13 June 1973. Initially the equipment was that ripped from the aircraft's predecessor, the EC-135J. The fourth aircraft was

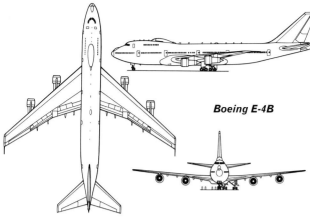

Boeing E-4

Boeing E-4B

In terms of communications, the E-4B is the best-equipped aircraft in the world.

completed as an E-4B, and was first delivered in December 1979 with vastly updated systems including SHF, better engines and revised accommodation. The E-4As were subsequently upgraded to this standard.

SPECIFICATION

Boeing E-4B
Wing: span 195 ft 8 in (59.64 m); aspect ratio 6.96; area 5,500.00 sq ft (510.95 m²)
Fuselage and tail: length 231 ft 4 in (70.51 m); height 63 ft 5 in (19.33 m); tailplane span 72 ft 9 in (22.17 m); wheel track 36 ft 1 in (11.00 m); wheel base 84 ft 0 in (25.60 m)
Powerplant: four General Electric F103-GE-100 (CF6-50E2) each rated at 52,500 lb st (233.53 kN) dry
Weights: maximum take-off 800,000 lb (362874 kg)
Fuel and load: internal fuel 331,565 lb (150395 kg); external fuel none
Speed: maximum level speed at 30,000 ft (9145 m) 523 kt (602 mph; 969 km/h)
Range: ferry range 6,800 nm (7,830 miles; 12600 km); mission endurance 12 hours without flight refuelling or 72 hours with flight refuelling
Performance: cruise ceiling 45,000 ft (13715 m); take-off distance to 35 ft (10.7 m) less than 10,820 ft (3298 m) at maximum take-off weight; landing field length 6,920 ft (2109 m) at maximum landing weight

Boeing **E-6 Mercury**

Procured to replace the Lockheed EC-130Q Hercules, the **E-6A Mercury** performs the TACAMO (Take Charge And Move Out) role, maintaining communications links with the **US Navy**'s ballistic missile submarine force. Two US Navy squadrons are active with the aircraft.

A decision to acquire a new TACAMO platform was taken as the Hercules airframes were getting old, and the Lockheed aircraft did not offer much endurance. On 29 April 1983 Boeing was given the contract to develop TACAMO II, and naturally chose its Model 707 airframe, offering commonality with the E-3 Sentry. CFM F108 turbofans were chosen for outstanding fuel efficiency, resulting in ultra-long endurance while on patrol, which can be further extended by inflight refuelling.

The first E-6A took to the air at Renton, WA, on 19 February 1987. Flight trials revealed a flaw in the structure which caused part of the fin to be lost in a high-speed dive. With suitable remedies, the first pair of E-6s was delivered to NAS Bar-

An E-6A displays the two trailing wire aerials (TWAs) which deploy from the tailcone and rear fuselage. These are for VLF communications.

ber's Point on 2 August 1989. The name **Hermes** was initially assigned, but this was changed to Mercury.

Internally the E-6 is arranged in three sections, comprising a forward crew area with eight rest bunks for spare crew members, galley and other facilities. Over the wing is the mission compartment, with five communications stations. In the rear is the equipment compartment, with access for inflight maintenance. The Mercury is packed with communications equipment operating across the frequency spectrum. Three VHF/UHF and five HF radio systems are carried and UHF satellite communications antennas are housed in the wingtip pods (along with ALR-66(V)4 ESM antennas), with prominent HF probes underneath. All communications equipment is secure against eavesdropping, and is hardened against the effects of EMP.

Principal task of the E-6 is to provide a link between various national and military commands, including the Presidential Boeing E-4B, and the US Navy's submarines. In order to communicate with the subs, the E-6 uses two trailing wire antennas which deploy from the tailcone (4,000 ft/1220 m long) and under the rear fuselage (26,000 ft/ 7925 m long). When the aircraft flies in a

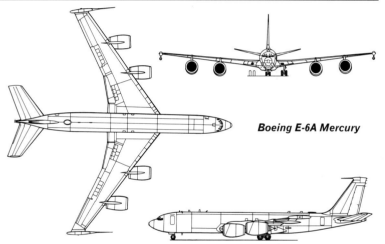

Boeing E-6A Mercury

tight orbit, the aerials hang vertically, allowing VLF communications to be transmitted to submarines, which have a towed aerial array.

Training support

Training for the Mercury fleet is undertaken at Waco, TX, by civilian contractor Chrysler using two standard 707s with E-6 cockpit systems. VQ-3 (initially 'Tacamopac' but now known as 'Iron Men') was the first operator, and deliveries followed to East Coast operator VQ-4 'Shadows' in early 1991. Each squadron is assigned eight aircraft. As part of the rationalisation of US command assets, both squadrons have consolidated under Strategic Wing One at Tinker AFB, OK, where they enjoy central maintenance with the USAF's E-3 Sentry fleet. Further cost-saving may be possible in an era of reduced threat by moving the USAF's strategic command post function aboard the E-6s and retiring the current fleet of EC-135Cs.

Boeing E-6A Mercury
Wing: span 148 ft 2 in (45.16 m); aspect ratio 7.2; area 3,050.00 sq ft (283.35 m²)
Fuselage and tail: length 152 ft 11 in (46.61 m); height 42 ft 5 in (12.93 m); tailplane span 45 ft 9 in (13.94 m); wheel track 22 ft 1 in (6.73 m); wheel base 59 ft 0 in (17.98 m)
Powerplant: four CFM International F108-CF-100 (CFM56-2A-2) each rated at 22,000 lb st (97.9 kN) dry
Weights: operating empty 172,795 lb (78378 kg); maximum take-off 342,000 lb (155128 kg)
Fuel and load: internal fuel 155,000 lb (70308 kg); external fuel none
Speed: dash speed at optimum altitude 530 kt (610 mph; 981 km/h); maximum cruising speed at 40,000 ft (12190 m) 455 kt (523 mph; 842 km/h)
Range: mission range 6,350 nm (7,307 miles; 11760 km) without flight refuelling; operational radius 1,000 nm (1,152 miles; 1854 km) for a patrol of 10 hours 30 minutes without flight refuelling, or of 28 hours 54 minutes with one flight refuelling, or of

72 hours with multiple flight refuellings; endurance 15 hours 24 minutes without flight refuelling
Performance: service ceiling 42,000 ft (12800 m); patrol altitude between 25,000 and 30,000 ft (7620

and 9145 m); maximum effort take-off run with fuel for 2,500 nm (2,875 miles; 4630 km) 2,400 ft (732 m); maximum effort take-off distance 5,400 ft (1646 m); landing run 2,600 ft (793 m) at max landing weight

Initially based on both East and West Coasts, the E-6 fleet is now centrally located at Tinker AFB, Oklahoma, alongside USAF E-3s.

Boeing 707

Boeing Commercial Airplane Group
PO Box 3707, Seattle,
WA 98124-2207, USA

USAF versions of this popular airliner are described under the C-137/C-18 entry, but many others are in service with air arms as transports, tankers and special mission aircraft. Transport tasks include both passenger and cargo carriage, and some aircraft can be reconfigured for either. Tanker conversions are usually restricted to wingtip refuelling pods, although KC-135-style flying booms or fuselage HDUs (hose-drum units) have been installed on some tankers. Special mission aircraft are used by Israel and South Africa, who have several versions of Sigint-gathering aircraft, radar reconnaissance aircraft and jamming platforms based on the 707 airframe, some of them with RC-135-style antenna arrays.

In alphabetical order, the current military users are: **Argentina** has two **707-372C**s and three **707-387B**s serve with 1 Escuadrón de Transporte at BAM El Palomar, Buenos Aires, used for general transport tasks although they were pressed into long-range maritime patrol duties during the Falklands War. **Australia** flies a single **707-368C** on transport duties, and three of four **707-338C**s converted to tanker standard by ASTA with Flight Refuelling Ltd

An Israeli 707 in full tanker configuration, with Sargent Fletcher 34-000 wingtip pods and a fuselage boom. Other Israeli aircraft feature electronic intelligence/command post equipment.

(FRL) Mk 32 wing pods (the fourth was lost in a fatal crash). They serve with No. 34 Sqn, RAAF, at Fairbairn. **Brazil** operates two **707-324C**s and two **707-345C**s, all converted to tanker status with Beech 1800 wing pods. Service designation is **KC-137**. **Canada** flew five **707-347C**s (local designation **CC-137**) on transport duties with No. 437 Sqn, RCAF, at Ottawa. Two have been converted to tankers with Beech 1800 wing pods, while the other three have been retired in favour of Airbus A310s.

Chile has four 707s, a **-321B** and **-330B** for staff transport, and a **-351C** and **-385C** for freight duties. **Colombia** flies a single **707-373C** on transport flights from Bogotá-El Dorado. **Germany**'s Köln-Bonn-based Flugbereitschaftsstaffel has four **707-307C**s for passenger transport, although these may be converted to tankers from 1995. **India** flies two **707-337C**s with the Aviation Research Centre at Palam. **Indonesia** has a single **707-3M1C** flying on long-range VIP missions. **Iran** received 14 new-build **707-3J9C**s, four of which were completed by Boeing as tankers with booms and Beech 1800 wing pods. One further **707-386C** has been added, and further tanker conversions may have been undertaken.

Israel operates a large fleet of aircraft, some sources suggesting a number of 17, although only four **-328**s, three **-329**s, one **-328B**, two **-331C**s, two **-344C**s and a **-3H7C** are positively identified. Most have

been modified to various standards by IAI's Bedek Aviation Division. At least six are tankers, with Sargent Fletcher 34-000 wing pods and centreline booms. Several Sigint versions have been noted, including a dual-role Sigint/tanker platform with wing pods and Elta EL/L-8300 Sigint system on board, with corresponding aerials and main cabin configured for operator stations. An unknown number have the Elta Phalcon

Boeing Model 707-320C (C-137C)

L-band conformal phased-array radar system scabbed on to the fuselage sides (described separately under IAI/Elta). Further machines retain a transport function, and it is believed that there is an active jamming system. IAI retains several withdrawn airframes which may be the subject for further special mission conversions.

Italy has recently joined the ranks of 707 operators, and now flies four **707-382B** tankers, converted by Alenia with Sargent Fletcher 34-000 wing pods and a Flight Refuelling 480C fuselage HDU. **Morocco** flies a single transport **707-3W6C**, which was the last civil 707 built and originally constructed as the **707-700** with CFM56

The Beech 1800 is one of three types of pod fitted to 707 tankers, seen here on a Brazilian KC-137. The drogue is trailed from a section which hinges down from the pod.

engines, and a **707-138B** tanker with Beech 1800 wing pods. **NATO** relieves the pressures on its E-3A Sentry fleet by employing three **707-329C**s for crew training, these based at Geilenkirchen in Germany. **Pakistan** has a **707-340C** for freight carriage, and a **707-351C** for VIP transport. **Peru** has recently acquired a single **707-323C** tanker, with FRL wing pods fitted by IAI.

Saudi Arabia stands alone in operating the **KE-3A** variant (described separately), which is a pod- and boom-equipped tanker powered by CFM56 engines. These serve with 18 Squadron alongside E-3A AWACS platforms. **South Africa** has recently added four 707s to its inventory, which are believed to include two Phalcon-equipped radar platforms and two dual-role Sigint/tanker aircraft, all fitted out by IAI. **Spain**'s single examples of **707-331B**, **-331C** and **-368C** are locally designated **T.17**, and two are configured with Sargent Fletcher 34-000 wing pods. **Venezuela** has a pair of **707-394C** tankers, both converted by IAI with SFC pods and fuselage boom. The former **Yugoslavia** now operates a single ex-Ugandan Airlines **707-324C**, which was seized on 31 August 1991 while it was allegedly on an arms supply flight.

Several other nations also fly the 707 on government transport tasks, but with civil registrations. These are Abu Dhabi, Dubai, Egypt, Libya, Saudi Arabia, Togo and Zaïre. There is every likelihood of more 707s joining air arms as they are retired from commercial service, and conversions to tanker and special mission configurations will continue, mostly under the auspices of IAI.

SPECIFICATION

Boeing Model 707-320B
Wing: span 145 ft 9 in (44.42 m); aspect ratio 7.06; area 3,010.00 sq ft (279.64 m²)
Fuselage and tail: length 152 ft 11 in (46.61 m); height 42 ft 5 in (12.93 m); tailplane span 45 ft 9 in (13.94 m); wheel track 22 ft 1 in (6.73 m); wheel base 59 ft 0 in (17.98 m)
Powerplant: four Pratt & Whitney JT3D-3/3B each rated at 18,800 lb st (80.07 kN) dry
Weights: operating empty 138,385 lb (62771 kg) standard or 140,524 lb (63740 kg) optional; maximum take-off 327,000 lb (148325 kg) standard or 333,600 lb (151315 kg) optional
Fuel and load: internal fuel 23,855 US gal (90299 litres); external fuel none; maximum payload 51,615 lb (23413 kg) standard or 54,476 lb (24709 kg) optional
Speed: maximum level speed 'clean' at optimum altitude 545 kt (627 mph; 1010 km/h); maximum cruising speed at 25,000 ft (7620 m) 521 kt (600 mph; 966 km/h); economical cruising speed at optimum altitude 478 kt (550 mph; 886 km/h)
Range: range 6,610 nm (7,611 miles; 12249 km) with maximum fuel or 5,350 nm (6,161 miles; 9914 km) with maximum payload
Performance: maximum rate of climb at sea level 3,550 ft (1082 m) per minute; service ceiling 42,000 ft (12800 m); take-off distance to 35 ft (10.7 m) 10,350 ft (3155 m) at maximum take-off weight; landing distance from 50 ft (15 m) 5,930 ft (1807 m) at normal landing weight; landing run 2,455 ft (750 m)

Above: Italy's four tankers have SFC 34-000 wing pods, but also have a Flight Refuelling HDU in the lower rear fuselage.

Below: India is among the users of unmodified 707s, which are used on both passenger and cargo transport duties.

Boeing 720

The Model 720 was developed by Boeing as a short/medium-haul derivative of the successful 707 airliner. It was shorter, and featured a reduced-strength structure and revised aerodynamics. Only one aircraft serves in military colours, an ex-Northwest 720-051B flying with the Presidential Flight of the **Republic of China Air Force**. It was purchased in 1971, and flies with a luxury interior fitting from Sungshan Air Base, outside the capital, Taipei.

Believed to be the only military 720, this aircraft flies with Taiwan's Presidential Flight. A civil-registered aircraft is used for engine tests by Pratt & Whitney.

Boeing 727/C-22

As the **Boeing 727** was one of the world's most popular airliners, with 1,832 built, it is no surprise that small numbers have found their way into military service, mostly in a passenger transport role. Additionally, the governments of several other nations operate the 727 on similar tasks but in civil markings.

In US service, the 727 is designated **C-22**, this covering six aircraft of three variants. The **C-22A** was a single 727-030 which had previously served with Lufthansa and the FAA, before being purchased for US Southern Command. It has been withdrawn from use at Davis-Monthan AFB. Four **C-22B**s were ex-National/Pan Am Srs 100s, purchased by the US Air Force in 1985. These flew on behalf of the Air National Guard Bureau with Det 1, 121st TFW, DC ANG at Andrews AFB, MD. The detachment has been raised to squadron level as the 201st Airlift Squadron, and the four continue their staff transport mission, internally configured with 24 leather first-class seats and 66 fabric seats, all rear-facing. The single **C-22C** is an ex-Singapore Airlines 727-212 which flies from Andrews AFB on behalf of Central Command.

SPECIFICATION

Boeing Model 727-200 (C-22C)
Wing: span 108 ft 0 in (32.92 m); aspect ratio 7.07; area 1,700.00 sq ft (157.93 m²)
Fuselage and tail: length 153 ft 2 in (46.69 m); height 34 ft 0 in (10.36 m); tailplane span 35 ft 9 in (10.90 m); wheel track 18 ft 9 in (5.72 m); wheel base 63 ft 3 in (19.28 m)
Powerplant: three Pratt & Whitney JT8D-9A each rated at 14,500 lb st (64.50 kN) dry
Weights: operating empty 102,900 lb (46675 kg); maximum take-off 209,500 lb (95027 kg)
Fuel and load: internal fuel 8,090 US gal (30623 litres); external fuel none; maximum payload typically 40,000 lb (18144 kg)
Speed: maximum level speed 'clean' at 20,500 ft (6250 m) 540 kt (622 mph; 1001 km/h); maximum cruising speed at 24,700 ft (7530 m) 520 kt (599 mph; 964 km/h); economical cruising speed at 30,000 ft (9145 m) 470 kt (541 mph; 871 km/h)
Range: range 2,362 nm (2,720 miles; 4392 km) with a 27,500-lb (12474-kg) payload or 2,160 nm (2,487 miles; 4003 km) with maximum payload
Performance: initial cruise ceiling 33,000 ft (10060 m); take-off distance to 35 ft (10.7 m) 9,200 ft (2804 m) at maximum take-off weight; landing distance from 50 ft (15 m) 4,690 ft (1430 m) at normal landing weight

OPERATORS

In addition to the United States, other military operators are Belgium (one remaining of two **727-29C**s bought from SABENA serves with 21 Smaldeel/Escadrille but is due for sale), Mexico (one **727-51** of Presidential Flight and three **727-14**s), New Zealand (two **727-22C**s serving with No. 40 Sqn at Whenuapai), Panama (one **727-44**), and Taiwan (two **727-109**, one **727-109C** and one **727-121C** with VIP squadron at Sungshan AB).

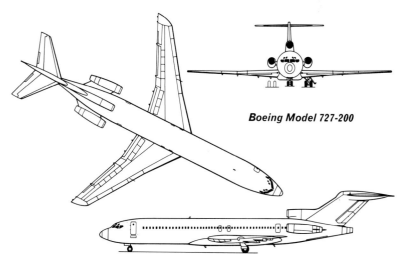

Boeing Model 727-200

Taiwan flies a quartet of Boeing 727s with its VIP squadron. All operators of the type use it purely as a passenger transport.

Boeing 737/CT-43

Boeing's **Model 737** is the world's best-selling airliner, and has notched up over 3,000 sales. Apart from two special military variants, surprisingly few serve with air forces in staff transport roles.

The major military variant is the **CT-43A**, originally delivered as the **T-43A**. This is a dedicated navigation trainer for the **US Air Force**. Derived from the **737-200**, the CT-43 has a standard flight deck, but with the main cabin configured for 12 student navigators, four advanced students and three instructors. Each station has a complete range of navigation instruments, allowing students to plot courses and monitor the aircraft's path during each mission. The stations are arranged in bays along the starboard side of the cabin, the port side being a walkway which also contains sighting platforms for portholes in the ceiling for celestial navigation using sextants.

Nineteen navigation trainers were delivered from July 1973 to the 323rd Flying Training Wing at Mather AFB, CA, the remainder having moved to Randolph AFB, TX. One aircraft was seen operating in Europe with civilian registration, allegedly on CIA business. It then joined the 58th MAS at Ramstein, from where it flew on regular duties. Three ex-USAF CT-43s now serve with Las Vegas-based EG&G, ferrying personnel to test-sites in Nevada.

The other four aircraft were diverted to Air National Guard support duties, initially with Det 1, 121st TFW, DC ANG at Andrews AFB (two aircraft) and Det 1, 140th TFW, Colorado ANG at Buckley ANGB (two aircraft). The latter took over the East Coast aircraft in the 1980s, and in 1992 upgraded to squadron status as the 200th Airlift Squadron. It has two tasks: to provide navigation training for cadets at the USAF Academy at Colorado Springs, and to provide general staff transport for West Coast ANG units.

Indonesia was the only customer for the second military variant, the **737-200**

The T-43 was originally procured for the navigation training role, with a cabin given over to navigator stations. Some aircraft were subsequently converted for transport use, and the type redesignated CT-43 to reflect the new tasking.

Surveiller. The main features of this maritime reconnaissance variant are two blade antennas on the upper fuselage forward of the fin, each 16 ft (4.87 m) in length. These serve a Motorola SLAMMR (side-looking airborne modular multi-mission radar), which can spot a small ship in heavy seas at a range of 115 miles (185 km) from an altitude of 30,000 ft (9150 m). The interior retains seating for 14 in first class and 88 in tourist class, allowing the 737s to be used for standard passenger transport tasks. Two aircraft were delivered to the TNI-AU's 32 Skwadron at Malang. Other aircraft in military service are civilian variants, the **Series 300** featuring a lengthened fuselage and CFM56 engines.

OPERATORS

In addition to those flying with the USAF and Indonesia, other 'airliner' 737s in military service fly with Brazil (two **737-2N3**s), India (two **737-2A8 Advanced** with Air Headquarters Communications Squadron at Palam), South Korea (one **737-3Z8**), Mexico (one **737-112** and one **737-247**), Thailand (one **737-2Z6 Advanced** and one **737-3Z6** with the Royal Flight at Bangkok-Don Muang) and Venezuela (one **737-2N1 Advanced**).

SPECIFICATION

Boeing Model T-43A (737-200)
Wing: span 93 ft 0 in (28.35 m); aspect ratio 8.8; area 980.00 sq ft (91.05 m2)
Fuselage and tail: length 100 ft 0 in (30.48 m);

height 37 ft 0 in (11.28 m); tailplane span 36 ft 0 in (10.97 m); wheel track 17 ft 2 in (5.23 m); wheel base 37 ft 4 in (11.38 m)
Powerplant: two Pratt & Whitney JT8D-9 each rated at 14,500 lb st (64.4 kN) dry
Weights: operating empty 60,210 lb (27311 kg); maximum take-off 115,500 lb (52391 kg)
Fuel and load: internal fuel 5,151 US gal (19498 litres) plus provision for 800 US gal (3028

Indonesia is the only user of the 737 Surveiller, equipped with side-looking radar for maritime patrol.

litres) of auxiliary fuel; external fuel none; maximum payload 34,790 lb (15780 kg)
Speed: never-exceed speed at 20,000 ft (6095 m) 545 kt (628 mph; 1010 km/h); maximum level speed at 23,500 ft (7165 m) 59 kt (586 mph; 943 km/h); maximum cruising speed at 22,600 lb (6890 m) 500 kt (576 mph; 927 km/h)
Range: range 2,600 nm (2,994 miles; 4818 km); endurance 6 hours
Performance: maximum rate of climb at sea level 3,760 ft (1146 m) per minute; take-off distance to 35 ft (10.7 m) 6,700 ft (2042 m) at 109,000 lb (49442 kg); landing distance from 50 ft (15 m) 4,300 ft (1311 m)

Boeing 747/C-19/VC-25

The **Boeing 747**, acclaimed as an airline pioneer, has proven highly adaptable to military roles. Derivatives of the 747 serve as VIP transports (the **United States**, **Japan**) and as dual-role cargo/tanker aircraft (**Iran**). Conceived as a military aircraft for the requirement which produced the Lockheed C-5A Galaxy in the late 1960s, the 747 was developed by Boeing as a departure in commercial airliners, introducing the 'wide body' and carrying 400 or more passengers. The first Boeing 747 flew on 9 February 1969. Variants, including long-range and 'stretched' versions, are credited with nothing less than a revolution, bringing air travel to vast numbers for the first time. A civilian **747-123** is used by NASA as a 'piggy-back' transport for the Space Shuttle orbiter.

American-owned 747 airliners are part of

the Civil Reserve Aircraft Fleet which is impressed into military service when needed to supplement USAF Air Mobility Command. The designation **C-19A** was applied to a military **747-200** once planned for a single Air National Guard squadron but never purchased.

The designation **VC-25A** applies to two specially-equipped Boeing **747-200B** presidential aircraft, referred to as 'Air Force One' when the President is on board. The VC-25A can carry president and staff, with 70 passengers and 23 crew members, 7,140 miles (11490 km) without refuelling.

Iran acquired three **747-100** tanker-transports and four **747F** freighters for military use. Two **747-47C**s were delivered to Japan as VIP transports and have been operated by the Japan Air Self-Defence Force since 1 April 1992.

SPECIFICATION

Boeing Model 747-200F
Wing: span 195 ft 8 in (59.64 m); aspect ratio 7.0; area 5,500.00 sq ft (510.95 m2)
Fuselage and tail: length 231 ft 10 in (70.66 m); height 63 ft 5 in (19.33 m); tailplane span 72 ft 9 in (22.17 m); wheel track 36 ft 1 in (11.00 m); wheel base 84 ft 0 in (25.60 m)
Powerplant: four Pratt & Whitney JT9D-7R4G2 each rated at 54,750 lb st (243.54 kN) dry, or General Electric CF6-50E2 (F103-GE-102) each rated at 52,500 lb st (233.53 kN) dry, or General Electric CF6-80C2 each rated at 56,700 lb st (252.21 kN) dry, or Rolls-Royce RB211-524D4-B each rated at 53,110 lb st (236.24 kN) dry
Weights: operating empty 342,200 lb (155219 kg) with JT9D engines, or 345,700 lb (156807 kg) with CF6-50 engines, or 348,300 lb (157986 kg) with CF6-80 engines, or 351,100 lb (159256 kg) with RB211 engines; maximum take-off 775,000 lb (351525 kg) with options at 785,000 lb (356070 kg), 800,000 lb (362875 kg), 820,000 lb (371945 kg) and 833,000 lb (377840 kg)
Fuel and load: internal fuel 364,400 lb (165289 kg)

The JASDF operates a pair of 747-400s on governmental transport duties.

Two 747s serve as Presidential transports, designated VC-25A.

with JT9D and RB211 engines, or 361,870 lb (164141 kg) with both CF6 engine variants; external fuel none; maximum payload 247,800 lb (112400 kg) with JT9D , or 244,300 lb (110812 kg) with CF6-50, or 348,300 lb (109633 kg) with CF6-80, or 238,900 lb (108363 kg) with RB211
Speed: maximum level speed 'clean' at 30,000 ft (9145 m) between 522 and 530 kt (601 and 610 mph; 967 and 981 km/h) depending on engine type
Range: ferry range 7,900 nm (9,091 miles; 14630 km) with JT9D engines, or 7650 nm (8,803 miles; 8426 km) with CF6-50 engines, or 8,300 nm (9,551 miles; 15371 km) with CF6-80 engines, or 7,950 nm (9,148 miles; 14723 km); range with a 200,000-lb (90720-kg) payload 4,700 nm (5,408 miles; 8704 km) with JT9D engines, or 4,550 nm (5,236 miles; 8426 km) with CF6-50 engines, or 4,900 nm (5,639 miles; 9075 km) with CF6-80 engines, or 4,650 nm (5,351 miles; 8612 km) with RB211 engines
Performance: cruise ceiling 45,000 ft (13715 m); take-off distance to 35 ft (10.7 m) at 833,000 lb (377840 kg) 10,400 ft (3170 m) with JT9D engines, or 10,800 ft (3292 m) with CF6-50 engines, or 10,100 ft (3078 m) with CF6-80 engines, or 10,350 ft (3155 m) with RB211 engines; landing field length 6,170 ft (1881 m) at 564,000 lb (255825 kg) increasing to 6,930 ft (2112 m) at 630,000 lb (285765 kg)

Boeing 757

The **Boeing 757** is a third-generation workhorse for commercial carriers. The first aircraft, a Boeing **757-200**, flew on 18 February 1982. The type has good potential for the military passenger-carrying role; the **Fuerza Aérea Mexicana** operates a **757-225** delivered in October 1987 and returned to the US in March 1988 for conversion to a presidential aircraft. One also serves with **Argentina**. Boeing uses the prototype for testing F-22 systems, currently being modified to **'Catfish'** configuration with an F-22 nose and a wing section above the flight deck to test conformal avionics.

SPECIFICATION

Boeing Model 757-200
Wing: span 124 ft 10 in (38.05 m); aspect ratio 7.8; area 1,994.00 sq ft (185.24 m2)
Fuselage and tail: length 155 ft 3 in (47.32 m); height 44 ft 6 in (13.56 m); tailplane span 49 ft 11 in (15.21 m); wheel track 24 ft 0 in (7.32 m); wheel base 60 ft 0 in (18.29 m)
Powerplant: two Rolls-Royce 535C each rated at 37,400 lb st (166.36 kN) dry, or Pratt & Whitney PW2037 each rated at 38,200 lb st (169.92 kN) dry, or Rolls-Royce 535E4 each rated at 40,100 lb st (178.37 kN) dry, or Pratt & Whitney PW2040 each rated at 41,700 lb st (185.49 kN) dry
Weights: operating empty 126,060 lb (57180 kg) with 535E engines, or 125,750 lb (57039 kg) with PW engines; maximum take-off 250,000 lb (113395 kg)
Fuel and load: internal fuel 11,253 US gal (42597 litres); external fuel none; maximum payload 57,530 lb (26096 kg)
Range: range 3,820 nm (4,399 miles; 7070 km) with 535E engines, or 4,000 nm (4,603 miles; 7408 km) with PW engines

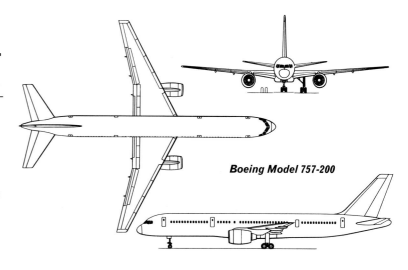

Boeing Model 757-200

Performance: initial cruise ceiling 38,970 ft (11880 m) with 535 engines, or 38,300 ft (11675 m) with PW engines; take-off field length at maximum take-off weight 7,000 ft (2134 m) with 535E engines, or 9,160 ft (2792 m) with PW2037 engines, or 6,950 ft (2118 m) with PW2040 engines; landing field length at maximum landing weight 4,630 ft (1411 m) with 535E engines, or 4,790 ft (1460 m) with PW engines

Boeing 767

The **Boeing 767** is a third-generation jetliner sharing features with the 757 but with a wider-body fuselage. The US Army operates the prototype Boeing 767-200 (no military designation) with a dorsal cupola, giving the aircraft a 'humpbacked' configuration. It was converted as the Airborne Optical Adjunct laboratory with a unique long-wavelength infra-red sensor as part of the Air Defence Initiative and the Strategic Defense Initiative programmes. The extra keel area forward is compensated for by a pair of enormous ventral fins.

Boeing is promoting the **767-200ER** as an AWACS platform, and plans are well advanced to supply two AWACS 767s to **Japan** under the designation **E-767**. Japan has an eventual requirement for four large AWACS platforms, but did not act on this before the E-3 production line closed. Two Boeing 767s will therefore be built at Seat-tle and then flown to Wichita for structural modifications in January 1995. They will then return to Seattle for equipment installation and flight test (a seven-month process) before being handed over to the JASDF from January 1998.

SPECIFICATION

Boeing Model 767-200
Wing: span 156 ft 1 in (47.57 m); aspect ratio 7.9; area 3,050.00 sq ft (283.35 m2)
Fuselage and tail: length 159 ft 2 in (48.51 m); height 52 ft 0 in (15.85 m); tailplane span 61 ft 1 in (18.62 m); wheel track 30 ft 6 in (9.30 m); wheel base 64 ft 7 in (19.69 m)
Powerplant: typically two Pratt & Whitney JT9D-7R4D or General Electric CF6-80A each rated at 48,000 lb st (213.51 kN) dry
Weights: manufacturer's empty 164,800 lb (74752 kg) with JT9D engines or 163,900 lb (74344 kg) with CF6 engines; operating empty 178,400 lb (80921 kg) with JT9D engines or 177,500 lb (80512 kg) with CF6 engines; maximum take-off 300,000 lb (136078 kg)
Fuel and load: internal fuel 112,725 lb (51131 kg); external fuel none; maximum payload 43,200 lb (19595 kg)
Speed: maximum cruising speed at optimum altitude Mach 0.80
Range: range 3,160 nm (3,639 miles; 5856 km) with

The prototype 767 is used as an airborne laboratory for strategic defence programmes.

JT9D engines or 3,220 nm (3,708 miles; 5967 km) with CF6 engines
Performance: initial cruise ceiling 39,200 ft (11950 m) with JT9D engines or 39,700 ft (12100 m) with CF6 engines; take-off field length 5,900 ft (1798 m) at maximum take-off weight

Boeing Helicopters (Boeing Vertol) CH-46 Sea Knight

Boeing Helicopters
Boeing Center, PO Box 16858,
Philadelphia, PA 19142, USA

Still the backbone of the **US Marine Corps** medium assault helicopter fleet, the **CH-46 Sea Knight** dates back to the commercial Vertol Model 107 which first flew in April 1958. The first military interest came from the US Army, which ordered three **YHC-1As** for evaluation but in the event bought the larger Chinook. However, further interest was expressed by the USMC, which needed a turbine-powered helicopter to replace its fleet of UH-34s.

Initial USMC aircraft were designated **HRB-1** (**CH-46A** after 1962), and the first entered service with HMM-265 in June 1964. One hundred and sixty CH-46As were built, along with 14 **UH-46As** for the **US Navy**, which used the type for vertical replenishment tasks. These were followed in production by 266 **CH-46Ds** and 10 **UH-46Ds**, which introduced the more powerful T58-GE-10 turboshaft and cambered rotor blades. The final production variant was the **CH-46F**, of which 174 were built and delivered between July 1968 and February 1971.

Today the principal variant is the **CH-46E**, the result of an update programme applied to both Ds and Fs to improve safety and crashworthiness. Glass-fibre rotor blades were fitted, in addition to other strengthening, while the engines were replaced with the further-uprated T58-GE-16. The 'Bullfrog' conversion has further enhanced the capability of the type, this programme adding more fuel in enlarged fuselage sponsons.

Marine Corps users

In service with the USMC, the CH-46E serves with 17 medium assault squadrons and a training unit at Tustin, CA (HMM-161, 163, 164, 166, 268 and HMT-301), New River, NC (HMM-162, 204, 261, 263, 264, 266 and 365), Kaneohe Bay, HI (HMM-165, 265, 364), Norfolk, VA (HMM-774), and El Toro, CA (HMM-764). The standard load is 17 fully-equipped troops or 15 casualty litters. Small cargo can be admitted through the rear loading ramp although in practice the aircraft are usually used for troop transport, while CH-53s undertake the heavy supply role. Typically 12 CH-46s will deploy aboard an amphibious assault ship, supported by AH-1s, CH-53s and AV-8Bs. Once they have been used to establish a beach-head, they will continue a shuttle between ship and shore, bringing in extra forces and supplies. CH-46s are also used in a Special Forces support role, and have been active on evacuation duties. Five aircraft serve with HMX-1 at MCAS Quantico in VH-46F configuration for VIP transport. A small number serve as HH-46D SAR aircraft at USMC bases at Beaufort, Cherry Point, Iwakuni and Kaneohe Bay, equipped for the role with a winch.

Navy Sea Knights serve with HC-3 and HC-11 at North Island, CA, HC-5 at Agana, Guam, and HC-6 and HC-8 at Norfolk, VA. These units fly the CH/HH/UH-46D on a variety of fleet support duties, including vertical replenishment of vessels and rescue. The latter role is performed by **HH-46Ds** assigned to the base flight at NAS Point Mugu, CA.

Export orders were restricted to **Canada** and **Sweden**, although the design was licence-built, and subsequently improved, by Kawasaki in Japan as the **KV-107** (described separately). A small number of Vertol 107s was sold to Sweden as **Hkp 4As** for use by the air force in a SAR role, although subsequent Swedish

Canada uses its aircraft in the SAR role, locally designated CH-113 Labrador. The yellow and red high-conspicuity scheme is applied fleet-wide.

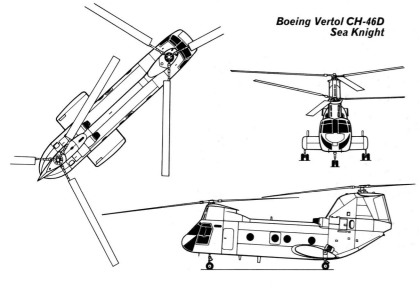

*Boeing Vertol CH-46D
Sea Knight*

The CH-46E/F is the backbone of the Marine Corps assault transport fleet. The aircraft sport a variety of schemes to match different terrains.

machines were all KV-107s. Canada's **CH-113 Labradors** were procured from Boeing Vertol. Thirteen (of 18) remain in service for SAR duties, but are being replaced by Bell 412HPs.

SPECIFICATION

Boeing Vertol UH-46A Sea Knight
Rotor system: rotor diameter, each 50 ft 0 in (15.24 m); rotor disc area, total 3,926.99 sq ft (364.82 m²)

Fuselage and tail: length overall, rotors turning 83 ft 4 in (25.40 m) and fuselage 44 ft 10 in (13.66 m); height 16 ft 8.5 in (5.09 m) to top of rear rotor head; wheel track 12 ft 10.5 in (3.92 m); wheel base 24 ft 10 in (7.57 m)
Powerplant: two General Electric T58-GE-8B each rated at 1,250 shp (932 kW)
Weights: empty equipped 12,406 lb (5627 kg); maximum take-off 21,400 lb (9706 kg)
Fuel and load: internal fuel 380 US gal (1438 litres); external fuel none; maximum payload 4,000 lb (1814 kg) carried internally or 6,330 lb (2871 kg)

carried externally
Speed: never-exceed speed 138 kt (159 mph; 256 km/h); maximum cruising speed at optimum altitude 135 kt (155 mph; 249 km/h); economical cruising speed at optimum altitude 131 km/h (151 mph; 243 km/h)
Range: range 230 nm (265 miles; 426 km) with maximum internal payload or 200 nm (230 miles; 370 km) with a 6,070-lb (2753-kg) external payload
Performance: maximum rate of climb at sea level 1,440 ft (439 m) per minute; service ceiling 14,000 ft (4265 m); hovering ceiling 9,070 ft (2765 m) in ground

effect and 5,600 ft (1707 m) out of ground effect

Boeing Vertol CH-46E Sea Knight
generally similar to the UH-46A Sea Knight except in the following particulars:
Powerplant: two General Electric T58-GE-16 each rated at 1,870 shp (1394 kW)
Weights: empty 11,585 lb (5255 kg); maximum take-off 24,300 lb (11022 kg)
Fuel and load: internal fuel 350 US gal (1323 litres); maximum payload 7,000 lb (3175 kg)
Speed: maximum speed at sea level 144 kt (166 mph; 267 km/h); maximum cruising speed at sea level 143 kt (165 mph; 266 km/h)
Range: ferry range 600 nm (691 miles; 1112 km); range with 2,400-lb (1088-kg) payload 550 nm (633 miles; 1019 km)
Performance: maximum rate of climb at sea level 1,715 ft (523 m) per minute; service ceiling 9,400 ft (2865 m); hovering ceiling 9,500 ft (2895 m) in ground effect and 5,750 ft (1753 m) out of ground effect

Boeing Helicopters (Boeing Vertol) CH-47 Chinook

In widespread service with the **US Army** and other air arms around the world, the **Chinook** rivals the Sikorsky CH-53 as the world's leading medium-lift helicopter. This workhorse of the modern army won its spurs in Vietnam, and has been the subject of continual upgrading since.

Developed along Vertol's proven twin-rotor concept, the Chinook began life under the company designation **V-144**. Initially assigned the US Army designation **YHC-1B**, it was retitled **CH-47** in 1962.

First flight occurred on 21 September 1961, and the first **CH-47A** was delivered to the US Army on 16 August 1962.

By mounting the engines externally above the rear fuselage, and by placing the three-bladed rotors high above either end of the fuselage, Vertol's designers left the cabin completely clear for the carriage of troops, cargo or small vehicles. Fuselage-side sponsons provided mountings for the four-unit undercarriage and space for fuel carriage. A rear-loading ramp and slightly

tilted fuselage combine to make loading and unloading extremely easy, an important factor for combat operations under fire.

A standard crew comprises two pilots and a loadmaster/crew chief, who has a jump seat between the pilots. Guns can be mounted in the starboard entry door or the rear ramp. A normal load of up to 55 troops can be carried, or 24 litters, while the cabin has tie-down cleats for the carriage of cargo. The initial CH-47A had one cargo hook for the carriage of underslung loads,

but in modern Chinooks the number is increased to three. The rotors are counter-rotating, obviating the need for a tail rotor, and the engines are geared so that either one can drive both rotors in the event of an engine failure. As the blades are intermesh-

The Chinook is the standard workhorse of the US Army, used primarily for battlefield mobility of vehicles, artillery, supplies and large numbers of troops.

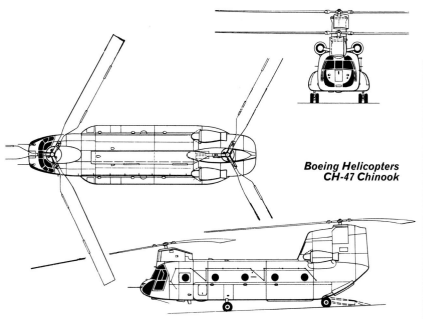

**Boeing Helicopters
CH-47 Chinook**

ing, a synchronisation unit is required to keep them at 60° to each other. The fuselage is waterproofed for emergency ditchings, although this is rarely demonstrated.

A total of 354 CH-47As was built for the US Army, and these were rapidly deployed to Vietnam where they immediately established a reputation for versatility, reliability, strength and the ability to carry out Herculean tasks of lifting. One hundred and eight **CH-47B**s followed, these having extra power and increased-diameter rotor blades. The third Chinook model, the **CH-47C**, introduced greater improvements, including further uprated engines for better lifting power and extra fuel (although not in the 'crashworthy' version ordered by some export customers). A total of 270 was built for the US Army, of which 182 were retrofitted with composite blades, integral spar inspection systems and crashworthy fuel systems.

The C model first flew on 14 October 1967, and in the early 1970s was the subject of the first export orders. **Thailand** received ex-US Army CH-47As, but **Australia** was the first foreign customer, buying 12 CH-47Cs for 'hot-and-high' operations within Papua New Guinea. **Spain**, **Canada** and the **Royal Air Force** followed, identifying their aircraft as **HT.17**, **CH-147** and **Chinook HC.Mk 1**, respectively. The British machines were the first to introduce triple-hook capability, a rotor brake, NVG-compatible cockpit, automatic fuel fire suppression system and pressure refuelling. They were retrofitted with glass-fibre blades as **Chinook HC.Mk 1B**s. In 1970, the Italian company Elicotteri Meridionali began licence-production of the CH-47C for the **Italian army** and Mediterranean customers.

Many of the improvements specified by export customers found their way to the US Army fleet, which is now to **CH-47D** standard. This version is a mix of conversions from all three former variants and some new-build machines. The first flight of a production CH-47D was on 26 February 1982, with service entry (with the 101st Airborne Division) achieved on 20 May. The full programme covers 472 aircraft (including **MH-47E**s, described separately) and entails the complete reworking of the aircraft for service into the next century. T55-L-712 turboshafts are fitted, these offering the same power as the C model's powerplant, but with a greater power reserve for emergencies and far greater battle damage resistance. Numerous other systems are improved or added, including a new NVG-

The RAF has a large force of Chinooks, currently being reworked to HC.Mk 2 standard. Some operate in a Special Forces role.

compatible flight deck, triple cargo hooks and pressure refuelling. In a similar programme, the RAF is returning its Chinooks to Boeing for rework to CH-47D standard, aircraft emerging as **Chinook HC.Mk 2**s.

In operation, the CH-47D can carry a wide variety of loads up to a maximum of 22,798 lb (10341 kg) externally or 13,907 lb (6308 kg) internally. Typical external loads include vehicles, howitzer crews and ammunition, supply containers or fuel blivets. Chinooks of both the RAF and US Army were heavily involved in the Desert Storm, several in Special Forces support roles (see following entry). Some US Army CH-47Ds, notably those of the 228th Aviation Regiment at Fort Wainwright, AK, operate on skis.

Following the US Army's CH-47D is the **CH-47D International Chinook (Model 414)**, which is tailored to the export market. The first customer was **Japan** which, after the supply of two pattern aircraft and one in kit form, is now building the aircraft under licence.

US Army re-equipment with the CH-47D is largely complete, the variant having been supplied to 17 active-duty units and several within the Army National Guard and Reserve organisations. Foreign operators, including those which fly licence-built aircraft, are as follows: **Argentina** received three CH-47Cs, of which one is believed to continue on Antarctic support duties with the air force. The Royal Australian Air Force

purchased 12 CH-47Cs for army support, and the 11 survivors were later transferred to that service but subsequently grounded. Four CH-47Ds are on order for 1995 delivery. Canada's CH-147 fleet numbered nine, but the aircraft have since been withdrawn and may be sold to the Netherlands. An order for six CH-47Ds placed by China is still embargoed by the US government. **Egypt** operates 15 Italian-built CH-47Cs from Kom Amshim, the aircraft being part of a cancelled Iranian order. The **Greek army** also received CH-47Cs from Meridionali, the nine remaining (of 10 delivered) being returned to Boeing for CH-47D conversion. Sixty-eight Meridionali CH-47Cs were delivered to **Iran**, which made heavy use of them during the war with Iraq. An unknown number remains serviceable.

Italy itself received 38 CH-47Cs from home production to serve with the 11° and 12° Gruppi Squadroni at Viterbo. Twenty-six now serve with the army, upgraded to **CH-47C Plus** standard with T55-L-412E engines and composite blades. One is in ESFC (emergency surgery flying centre) configuration as a flying hospital, while others are able to conduct firefighting and disaster relief operations. The Japanese Ground Self-Defence Force is in the process of acquiring **CH-47J**s (Kawasaki-built CH-47D), an eventual total of 42 being

All of Spain's Chinooks are to CH-47D standard. Some were built as such from new, while the remainder were modified from CH-47C standard.

expected. The JASDF wishes to acquire a total of 16. Another recipient of Italian machines was **Libya**, which split its purchase of 20 into six for the air force and 14 for the army, of which one has crashed. **Morocco** also received CH-47Cs from Meridionali, 12 serving with the Royal Moroccan air force. **Nigeria** is believed to have five CH-47s on order, but funding difficulties may halt delivery. **Singapore** has ordered six CH-47Ds.

South Korea has 24 International Chinooks, of which six serve with the air force and the remainder with the army. The Spanish army's BHelTra V at Colmenar Viejo operates 18 CH-47Ds, of which nine have been upgraded from C-model standard. **Taiwan** has a trio of civilian **Boeing 234MLR** models for its army's heavylift requirements, while Thailand has 12 International Chinooks on order, to add to the two survivors of the CH-47As first supplied. Finally, the RAF's Chinook force now numbers 35 aircraft, which are in the process of becoming HC.Mk 2s, serving with Nos 7, 18, 27(R) and 78 Sqns.

Boeing Helicopters (Boeing Vertol) CH-47 Chinook

Boeing Helicopters has further plans for the development of the Chinook design, including a study for the **Advanced Chinook** with 5,000 shp-class engines, redesigned rotors and additional fuel.

SPECIFICATION

Boeing Vertol CH-47D Chinook
Rotor system: rotor diameter, each 60 ft 0 in (18.29m); rotor disc area, total 5,654.86 sq ft (525.34 m²)
Fuselage and tail: length overall, rotors turning 98 ft 10.75 in (30.14 m) and fuselage 51 ft 0 in (15.54 m); height 18 ft 11 in (5.77 m) to top of rear rotor head; wheel track 10 ft 6 in (3.20 m); wheel base 22 ft 6 in (6.86 m)
Powerplant: two Textron Lycoming T55-L-712 each rated at 3,750 shp (2796 kW) for take-off and 3,000 shp (2237 kW) for continuous running, or two
Textron Lycoming T55-L-712 SSB each rated at 4,378 shp (3264 kW) for take-off and 3,137 shp (2339 kW) for continuous running, in both cases driving a transmission rated at 7,500 shp (5593 kW) on two engines and 4,600 shp (3430 kW) on one engine
Weights: empty 22,379 lb (10151 kg); normal take-off 46,000 lb (20866 kg); maximum take-off 50,000 lb (22679 kg)
Fuel and load: internal fuel 1,030 US gal (3899 litres); external fuel none; maximum payload 22,798 lb (10341 kg)
Speed: maximum level speed at sea level 161 kt (185 mph; 298 km/h); maximum cruising speed at optimum altitude 138 kt (159 mph; 256 km/h)
Range: ferry range 1,093 nm (1,259 miles; 2026 km); operational radius between 100 and 30 nm (115 and 35 miles; 185 and 56 km) with maximum internal and maximum external payloads respectively
Performance: maximum rate of climb at sea level 2,195 ft (669 m) per minute; service ceiling 22,100 ft (6735 m); hovering ceiling 10,550 ft (3215 m)

Argentina bought three CH-47Cs for Antarctic support, but one was captured in the Falklands. This survivor wears a 'Malvinas' campaign badge.

Boeing Helicopters **Chinook (Special Forces)**

As part of the upgrade to the US Army's Special Operations Forces (SOF) capabilities, the service has ordered 12 (of a total requirement of 51) **MH-47E SOA**s (Special Operations Aircraft) to augment MH-60s also being procured for the role. These are based on the CH-47D airframe, but feature a full range of features to aid covert infil/exfil work.

The cockpit is fitted with a four-screen NVG-compatible EFIS, while the avionics include dual MIL-STD-1553 databuses, automatic target hand-off system, jam-resistant communications, GPS receiver, APQ-174 radar for mapping and terrain-following flight down to 30 m (100 ft) in a pod on the port side of the nose, and AAQ-16 FLIR in an undernose turret. Comprehensive defences include missile-, laser- and radar-warning receivers, pulse and CW jammers and chaff/flare dispensers. Armament consists of two window-mounted M2 0.50-in machine-guns, and Stinger air-to-air missiles.

Optional equipment includes extra bolt-on fuel tanks which double fuel capacity, although this fitment requires moving the nosewheels forward to accommodate the tanks. A refuelling probe allows the **MH-47E** to refuel from HC/KC/MC-130 Hercules, and a typical deep-penetration mission lasts for 5-6 hours, to a radius of some 350 miles (565 km). Units which are due to be equipped with the MH-47E are the 2nd Battalion, 160th Special Operations Aviation Group at Fort Campbell, KY (first delivery

late 1992), to be followed by the 3rd Battalion/160th SOAG at Hunter AAF, GA, and the 1/245th Aviation Battalion (SOA), of the Oklahoma Army National Guard.

Pending delivery of the MH-47Es, the 160th SOAG made use of 32 Chinooks temporarily upgraded to **CH-47D SOA** standard with refuelling probes, thermal imaging equipment, weather radar, improved nav/comms and door-mounted 7.62-mm machine-guns. During the Gulf War, the Royal Air Force upgraded a handful of its **Chinook HC.Mk 1B** aircraft with better navigation equipment, NVG-compatible cockpits, IR searchlight and missile warning/countermeasures for Special Forces support.

SPECIFICATION

Boeing Vertol MH-47E Chinook
generally similar to the Boeing Vertol CH-47D Chinook except in the following particulars:
Fuselage and tail: length overall, rotors turning 98 ft 10.75 in (30.14 m) and fuselage 52 ft 1 in (15.87 m); height 18 ft 4 in (5.59 m) to top of rear rotor head; wheel track 11 ft 11 in (3.63 m); wheel base 25 ft 10 in (7.87 m)
Powerplant: two Textron Lycoming T55-L-712 SSB each rated at 4,378 shp (3264 kW) for take-off and 3,137 shp (2339 kW) for continuous running, in both cases driving a transmission rated at 7,500 shp (5593 kW) on two engines and 4,600 shp (3430 kW) on one engine

Weights: empty 26,918 lb (12210 kg); maximum take-off 54,000 lb (24494 kg)
Fuel and load: internal fuel 15,025 lb (6815 kg); external fuel none
Speed: maximum level speed at sea level 154 kt (177 mph; 285 km/h); maximum cruising speed at sea level 140 kt (161 mph; 259 km/h)
Range: ferry range 1,200 nm (1,382 miles; 2224 km) fuel; typical range 613 nm (706 miles; 1136 km); operational radius 300 nm (345 miles; 560 km); endurance 5 hours 30 minutes
Performance: maximum rate of climb at sea level 1,840 ft (561 m) per minute; service ceiling 10,150 ft (3095 m); hovering ceiling 9,800 ft (2990 m) in ground effect and 5,500 ft (1675 m) out of ground effect

Above: The MH-47E features a full Special Ops kit, including APQ-174 radar in a nose-mounted pod and inflight-refuelling probe. Under the nose is a FLIR sensor.

Below: Known as the CH-47D SOA or MH-47D, a number of CH-47Ds was given FLIRs for the SOF role.

Boeing Helicopters/Sikorsky **RAH-66 Comanche**

The US Army announced its LHX (Light Helicopter Experimental) requirement in 1982, with an initial requirement for 5,000 helicopters to replace UH-1, AH-1, OH-6 and OH-58 scout/attack/assault aircraft. This has since been scaled down to 1,292 for the scout/attack role only. Boeing/Sikorsky's 'First Team' was awarded the contract for three dem/val aircraft on 5 April 1991.

The First Team's aircraft is known as the **RAH-66 Comanche**, and is expected to fly in August 1995. The Comanche has a five-bladed main rotor and a shrouded tail rotor. The fuselage is designed for low observability, employing some degree of faceting and sunken notch intakes for the two LHTEC T800 turboshafts. Flight control is by a triplex fly-by-wire system. The undercarriage is retractable, and missiles are housed in bays on the fuselage sides, directly attached to the bay doors which act as pylons when they are open. A chin turret houses a three-barrelled 20-mm cannon,

and in the extreme nose is a sensor turret for FLIR and laser. The RAH-66 also features a wide array of defensive equipment, including laser-, IR- and radar-warning receivers. A third of the fleet will have miniaturised Longbow radar.

SPECIFICATION

Boeing/Sikorsky RAH-66 Comanche
Rotor system: main rotor diameter 39 ft 0.5 in (11.90 m); fantail rotor diameter 4 ft 6 in (1.37 m); main rotor disc area 1,197.14 sq ft (111.21 m²); fantail rotor disc area 15.90 sq ft (1.48 m²)
Fuselage and tail: length overall, rotor turning 46 ft 10.25 in (14.28 m) and fuselage 43 ft 4.5 in (13.22 m) excluding gun barrel; height overall 11 ft 1.5 in (3.39 m) over stabiliser; stabiliser span 9 ft 3 in (2.82 m)
Powerplant: two LHTEC T800-LHT-800 each rated at 1,344 shp (1002 kW)
Weights: empty equipped 9,187 lb (4,167 kg); normal

take-off 10,112 lb (4587 kg); maximum take-off 17,174 lb (7790 kg)
Fuel and load: internal fuel 260 US gal (984 litres); external fuel up to two 460-US gal (1741.5-litre) auxiliary tanks

Speed: maximum level speed 'clean' at optimum altitude 177 kt (204 mph; 328 km/h)
Range: ferry range 1,260 nm (1,451 miles; 2335 km) with external fuel; endurance 2 hours 30 minutes
Performance: maximum vertical rate of climb at sea level 1,182 ft (328 m) per minute

A mock-up of the RAH-66 reveals its futuristic lines.

Boeing/Grumman E-8 J-STARS

Making a 'star' appearance in Operation Desert Storm long before it was considered operational, the Boeing/Grumman E-8 represents a major advance in battlefield control, introducing the kind of capability for monitoring and controlling the land battle that the E-3 provides for the air battle. Like the E-3, the E-8 is based on the tried and trusted Boeing 707-320 airframe, and no new-build aircraft are envisaged.

Two **E-8A** prototypes were converted, Grumman being the prime contractor for the system. A ventral canoe fairing houses a Norden multi-mode side-looking radar, while the cabin is configured with operator consoles. A datalink provides the means to transmit gathered intelligence to the ground in near real-time. The radar can operate in synthetic aperture mode, which gives a high-resolution radar picture out to 160 miles (257 km) from the orbiting aircraft, while two pulse-Doppler modes give moving target information, allowing the controllers to monitor the positions and movements of all ground vehicles. Wide area search/moving target indicator (WAS/MTI) mode monitors a large sector of land, while sector search mode (SSM) is used on much smaller areas to follow individual vehicles. The radar can differentiate

between wheeled and tracked vehicles.

Using the various modes, the J-STARS (Joint Surveillance Target Attack Radar System) can be used for general surveillance and battlefield monitoring to provide the 'big picture' to commanders, stand-off radar reconnaissance or individual targeting functions for attacking vehicles and convoys. A replay function is available so that several hours of returns can be run on fast-forward to spot overall trends in vehicle movements. A velocity threshold on the moving target modes can filter out fast-moving vehicles (i.e. private cars).

Although data can be interpreted on board, the datalink allows gathered data to be relayed immediately to mobile ground consoles. The ground systems are truck-mounted and contain similar consoles to those found on the aircraft, allowing operators on the ground to directly access the J-STARS system with their own requirements.

December 1988 saw the first J-STARS-configured E-8 take to the air for the first time, followed by a second development machine. In January 1991 both E-8As deployed to Riyadh to fly combat missions under the control of the hastily-organised 4411th Joint STARS Squadron. Forty-nine

war missions were flown, for a total of 535 hours, a sizeable portion of which was spent on the search for Iraqi 'Scud' missiles. Desert Storm operations provided ground and air commanders with a wealth of material, and fully validated the concept.

In service, the system was to be have been carried on the new-build **E-8B** aircraft with F108 turbofans, but despite one **YE-8B** being procured (later sold), the carrier will now be the **E-8C** based on converted 707 airliner airframes. A total of 20 is required, the first of which flew in April 1994. Deliveries are expected from 1995, with IOC in 1997.

The two E-8As carried far more test equipment than the E-8C production aircraft. The latter also has more sensor operator stations inside the cabin.

SPECIFICATION

Boeing/Grumman E-8A

Wing: span 145 ft 9 in (44.42 m); aspect ratio 7.056; area 3,050.00 sq ft (283.35 m²)

Fuselage and tail: length 152 ft 11 in (46.61 m); height 42 ft 5 in (12.93 m); tailplane span 45 ft 9 in (13.94 m); wheel track 22 ft 1 in (6.73 m); wheel base 17.98 m (59 ft 0 in)

Powerplant: four Pratt & Whitney JT3D-7 each rated at 19,000 lb (84.52 kN) dry

Weights: maximum take-off 333,600 lb (151315 kg)

Fuel and load: internal fuel 159,560 lb (72375 kg); external fuel none; maximum theoretical payload 96,126 lb (43603 kg)

Speed: maximum cruising speed at 25,000 ft (7620 m) 525 kt (605 mph; 973 km/h); economical cruising speed at 35,000 ft (10670 m) 464 kt (534 mph; 860 km/h)

Range: range with maximum fuel 5,000 nm (5,758 miles; 9266 km)

Performance: maximum rate of climb at sea level 4,000 ft (1219 m) per minute; service ceiling 39,000 ft (11890 m)

AIRFRAME
The E-8 is based on the 707-320C airframe, the final and definitive version of the airliner. This is distinguished from earlier variants by the lack of ventral fin.

'FIDDLE'
The large teardrop fairing under the centre-section houses the antenna for the Flight Test Data Link, fitted to the E-8As only. This was used during Desert Storm for transmitting data over long distances back to central commands in Riyadh.

Boeing/Grumman E-8A

RADAR
The Norden multi-mode radar offers an imaging range in synthetic aperture radar mode of up to 175 km (100 miles). In an eight-hour sortie one million km² (386,100 sq miles) can be surveyed. The radar fitted to the E-8C features resolution three times better than that of the two E-8As.

CONSOLES
The E-8A carried 10 operator consoles and various test stations. The production E-8C has 17 operator consoles and one dedicated to defensive electronics.

'SKITTLE'
Aft of the 'Fiddle' radome is a small antenna for the Surveillance and Control Data Link, the primary means of downlinking information to Ground Station Modules. Data is linked to other aircraft by the JTIDS network.

Breguet (Dassault Aviation) Br.1150 Alizé

In December 1971 Breguet Aviation merged with Avions Marcel Dassault, resulting in Avions Marcel Dassault-Breguet Aviation

Now the most elderly combat aircraft regularly operating from aircraft-carrier decks, the **Breguet Alizé** was produced to meet a French naval requirement in the early 1950s and is expected to serve with the **Aéronavale** beyond the year 2000. Breguet proposed to use a Nene turbojet in the tail to boost performance, but after tests with this configuration in the Vultur prototype only the turboprop was retained in the definitive Alizé, with a retractable radome for sea-search radar replacing the turbojet in the rear fuselage. After two prototypes – the first of which flew on 6 October 1956 – and three pre-production aircraft, Breguet built a total of 75 Alizés for the Aéronavale and 12 for the **Indian navy**.

Service use in France has been reduced from three to two *flottilles*, 4F and 6F, for use in the anti-submarine role from the aircraft-carriers *Foch* and *Clemenceau*. An upgrade programme initiated in 1980 introduced Thomson-CSF Iguane radar in the ventral radome, Omega Equinox navigation system, new communications equipment and ESM in the noses of the underwing

stores panniers. This added 15 years to the expected service life, but a further modification programme for 24 surviving aircraft began in 1990 to introduce datalink, better decoy capability and other improvements to give a further service life extension. A few Alizés fly with Escadrille 59E at Hyères for training and SAR, and with 10S at St Raphael on miscellaneous test tasks along with Nord 262s and Xingus.

With the Indian navy, the original Alizés (supplemented by later purchase of about a dozen ex-Aéronavale aircraft) served with INAS 310 'Cobras' squadron from the *Vikrant*. The addition of ski-ramps to that carrier forced the remaining five Alizés ashore in 1987; a dwindling number continued in service until late 1992 from Dabolin, when the last example was withdrawn from service.

The elderly Breguet Alizé continues to fly with the French Aéronavale on carrier-based ASW duties and shore-based patrols with two front-line units.

SPECIFICATION

Breguet (Dassault Aviation) Br.1150 Alizé
Wing: span 15.60 m (51 ft 2 in); width folded 7.00 m

(22 ft 11.5 in); aspect ratio 6.76; area 36.00 m² (387.51 sq ft)
Fuselage and tail: length 13.86 m (45 ft 6 in); height 5.00 m (16 ft 4.75 in)
Powerplant: one Rolls-Royce Dart RDa.7 Mk 21 rated at 1,975 ehp (1473 ekW)
Weights: empty 5700 kg (12,566 lb); maximum take-off 8200 kg (18,078 lb)
Fuel and load: external fuel none; maximum ordnance about 1250 kg (2,756 lb)
Speed: maximum level speed 'clean' at 3000 m

(9,845 ft) 520 km/h (281 kt; 323 mph); cruising speed at optimum altitude 370 km/h (200 kt; 230 mph); patrol speed at optimum altitude 232 km/h (125 kt; 144 mph)
Range: ferry range 2870 km (1,550 nm; 1,785 miles) with auxiliary fuel; range 2500 km (1,349 nm; 1,553 miles) with standard fuel; 7 hours 40 minutes with auxiliary fuel or endurance 5 hours 5 minutes with standard fuel
Performance: maximum rate of climb at sea level 420 m (1,380 ft) per minute; service ceiling more than 6250 m (20,505 ft)

British Aerospace/Raytheon (Hawker Siddeley) 125

*British Aerospace Corporate Jets Ltd
3 Bishop Square, St Albans Road West, Hatfield
Hertfordshire AL10 9NE, UK*

An early entrant into the executive jet field, the **de Havilland D.H.125** first flew on 13 August 1962, with the first production example flying the following February. Its configuration is similar to that adopted for other conventional executive jets, with a mid-mounted tailplane to keep the control surfaces out of the jet efflux. The engines (originally Viper 520 turbojets each rated at 3,000 lb/13.35 kN thrust) are mounted on pylons each side of the rear fuselage, resulting in a clean wing. The roomy cabin is of constant circular cross-section over much of its length, and can be fitted out in various degrees of comfort, from standard airliner-type seating to full-scale VIP configuration. The type was also designed from the outset to be able to operate from unpaved runways without special modification.

Following the maiden flight, the **RAF** ordered 20, named **Dominie** navigaton trainers (described separately). Following DH's incorporation into the Hawker Siddeley Group, four **H.S. 125 CC.Mk. 1** aircraft were procured by the RAF in March 1971 for communications and transport duties. These were based on the **Series 400** with 3,000-lb (13.35-kN) Rolls-Royce Viper 301 turbojets. Today they are operated by No. 32 Sqn, at Northolt. The type's high speed and good payload-range capability resulted in additional orders. These comprise two **BAe 125 CC.Mk 2s** comparable to the civil **Series 600** with stretched fuselage and 3,750-lb (16.68-kN) static thrust Viper 601-22 turbojets, and six **BAe 125 CC.Mk 3s**, similar to the **Series 700** with Garrett TFE731 turbofans of 3,700 lb (16.46 kN) thrust. Turbofans were introduced to improve airfield/climb performance and to increase range and maximum speed. For commonality and economy the first six aircraft were re-engined with the TFE731,

but were retired by No. 32 Sqn in May 1994. From 1988, four CC.Mk 3s received an overall grey low-visibility colour scheme and Northrop MIRTS infra-red countermeasures fitted in an extended tail fairing. An additional aircraft (BAe 125-600B 'ZF130') is operated by BAe Dunsfold as an airborne radar testbed. Fitted with Blue Vixen radar and a full Sea Harrier FRS.Mk 2 weapons system, the aircraft has since flown with an underwing Sidewinder acquisition round.

The BAe 125 also serves in small numbers with the air forces of **Botsawana**, **Brazil**, **Malawi**, **Malaysia** and **South Africa**. Of these, Brazil is the largest user with 12 aircraft, 10 serving on VIP duties (as the **VC-93**) and two **EC-93**s for radar calibration. In 1983 production moved on to the **BAe 125 Series 800**, with a new wing, uprated engines and avionics improvements. Six have been acquired for the Royal Flight of the **Royal Saudi air force**. Options exist for a further six aircraft under Phase Two of the Al Yamamah contract.

In 1990, the **USAF** took delivery of six 125-800s for combat flight inspection and navigation (C-FIN) duties. The aircraft were delivered 'green' by BAe and fitted with LTV Sierra Research Division equipment. Designated **C-29A**, the type first flew on 11 May 1989 and replaced CT-39A and C-140As serving with the 1866th FCS at Scott AFB, IL. In September 1991, control of these passed to the FAA at Oklahoma City. They are no longer designated C-29, simply 125-800.

In 1989, the JASDF announced the procurement of three aircraft similar to the C-29A. The first Sierra-equipped example made its maiden flight on 4 March 1992 and was delivered in December 1992. The JASDF has a further requirement for 27 BAe 125-800s for SAR duties. Designated **U-125A** for delivery from 1995, these will be equipped with a 360° scan radar and FLIR

sensor, with provision for dropping marker flares and rescue equipment. Any further aircraft will not be sold as a British Aerospace type. In June 1993 BAe Corporate jets was acquired by the Raytheon company in the USA, which now markets the aircraft as the **Raytheon Hawker 800**. The stretched **Hawker 1000** (BAe 125-1000) long-range business jet has so far sold only to commercial customers.

SPECIFICATION

British Aerospace (de Havilland/Hawker Siddeley) 125 Series 800 (C-29A)
Wing: span 51 ft 4.5 in (15.66 m); aspect ratio 7.06; area 474.00 sq ft (34.75 m²)
Fuselage and tail: length 51 ft 2 in (15.60 m); height 17 ft 7 in (5.36 m); tailplane span 20 ft 0 in (6.10 m); wheel track 9 ft 2 in (2,79 m)
Powerplant: two Garrett TFE731-5R-1H each rated at 4,300 lb st (19.13 kN) dry
Weights: typical operating empty 15,120 lb (6858 kg); maximum take-off 27,400 lb (12429 kg)
Fuel and load: internal fuel 1,248 Imp gal (1,499 US gal; 5674 litres); maximum payload 2,400 lb (1088 kg)
Speed: never-exceed speed Mach 0.87; economical cruising speed between 39,000 and 43,000 ft (11900 and 13100 m) 400 kt (461 mph; 741 km/h)
Range: 3,000 nm (3,454 miles; 5560 km) with maximum fuel or 2,870 nm (3,305 miles; 5318 km) with maximum payload
Performance: maximum rate of climb at sea level 3,100 ft (945 m) per minute; climb to 35,000 ft (10670 m) in 19 minutes; service ceiling 43,000 ft (13100 m); take-off balanced field length 5,620 ft (1713 m) at maximum take-off weight

For a brief period, the USAF operated its C-29As in the European One 'lizard' scheme, before their transferral to the Federal Aviation Authority as Sabre 75 replacements.

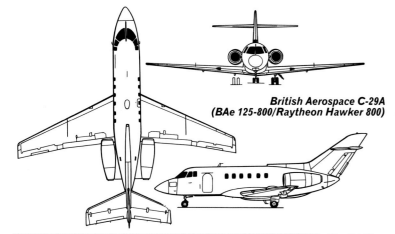

British Aerospace C-29A (BAe 125-800/Raytheon Hawker 800)

The RAF's BAe-125 CC.Mk 3s adopted this low-vis 'barley' scheme along with tail-mounted Northrop MIRTS infra-red counter measures.

British Aerospace/Avro (Hawker Siddeley) 146/RJ

Avro International Aerospace
Woodford Aerodrome, Chester Road, Stockport
Cheshire SK7 1QR, UK

In August 1973 Hawker Siddeley announced government backing for design and development of a new short-range civil transport which it identified as the HS.146. This was to be powered by four turbofan engines and would have operational noise levels considerably below announced future legislation on noise emission. This project had hardly gotten under way before nationalisation led to the shelving of the scheme. On 10 July 1978 the board of British Aerospace gave approval for a resumption of the programme. This involved not only British Aerospace, but also risk-sharing partners Avco (now Textron) Corporation in the USA and Saab-Scania in Sweden. Textron supplies the ALF502R turbofan engines (the R of the designation signifying reduced rating, which ensures that the already quiet engines have an even lower noise signature) and through its Textron Aerostructures division manufactures the wing boxes. Saab is responsible for the tailplanes and all movable control surfaces, while in the UK Short Brothers was subcontracted to fabricate pods for the ALF502 .

Production of three basic passenger versions continued until 1992. The **BAe 146-100** was designed specifically to operate from semi-prepared airstrips. Following demands for versions with less rigorous STOL capabilities and increased accommodation/payload, subsequent variants (designated **BAe 146-200** and **BAe 146-300**) featured progressively stretched fuselages and uprated engines and were optimised for operations from paved surfaces. Relaunch of the BAe 146 was announced in June 1992, with new **RJ (Regional Jet)** designations followed by numbers denoting passenger capacities (RJ 70, RJ 85 and RJ 100/RJ 115) The hallowed name of Avro was also revived to market the aircraft, the proposed joint UK/Taiwanese operation (with Taiwan Aerospace – TAC) becoming known as Avro International Aerospace. The new RJ series features more powerful Textron Lycoming LF-507-1H engines, with structural strengthening permitting increased weights. Production was to take place in Taiwan under a risk-sharing agreement, but the deal foundered in 1993, with recriminations on both sides.

In June 1983, two **BAe 146-100**s were leased as **BAe 146 CC.Mk 1**s by the **RAF**. These were evaluated at Brize Norton

for suitability as replacements for the ageing Andovers of The Queen's Flight. Designated **BAe 146 CC.Mk 2**, three aircraft have been subsequently acquired for this unit. Two BAe 146-200s were delivered in mid-1986 and were followed by a further example in early 1991. All aircraft have been fitted with Loral Matador infra-red jamming systems. Four dedicated VIP/executive **Statesman** aircraft are operated by No. 1 Squadron (Royal Flight) of the **Royal Saudi Air Force** at Riyadh.

Military developments of the BAe 146 as a multi-role transport were announced in 1987. These include the **BAe 146STA** (Small Tactical Airlifter), **BAe 146MT** (Military Tanker), **BAe 146MRL** (Military Rear Loader) and **BAe 146MSL** (Military Side Loader). The BAe 146STA is based on the **BAe 146-QT** Quiet Trader freighter and features a 14-ft 7-in (4.44-m) wide rear fuselage cargo door in the port side. Loading flexibility is further enhanced by optional roller tracks which permit the movement of pallets. A sliding door set within the main cargo hold permits paradropping. This may include air-dropping of standard military pallets or up to 60 fully-equipped paratroops. Variations include options for up to 24 stretchers in the casevac role. The variant may also be fitted with an optional refuelling probe. The prototype BAe 146STA first flew in August 1988, and undertook a sales tour of Australasia and the Far East. No orders for military versions had been announced by early 1994.

SPECIFICATION

British Aerospace (Hawker Siddeley) 146 Series 100

Wing: span 86 ft 5 in (26.34 m) including 2.5-in (6.3-cm) static dischargers on each wingtip; aspect ratio 8.97; area 832.00 sq ft (77.29 m2)
Fuselage and tail: length 85 ft 11.5 in (26.20 m); height 28 ft 3 in (8.61 m); tailplane span 36 ft 5 in (11.09 m); wheel track 15 ft 6 in (4.72 m); wheel base 33 ft 1.5 in (10.09 m)
Powerplant: four Textron Lycoming ALF502R-5 each rated at 6,970 lb st (31.00 kN) dry
Weights: operating empty 49,000 lb (22226 kg); maximum take-off 84,000 lb (38102 kg)
Fuel and load: internal fuel 20,640 lb (9362 kg) standard and 22,704 lb (10298 kg) optional; external fuel none; maximum payload 19,500 lb (8845 kg)
Speed: economical cruising speed at 30,000 ft (9145 m) 382 kt (440 mph; 709 km/h)
Range: 1,672 nm (1,924 miles; 3096 km) with maximum standard fuel or 935 nm (1,077 miles; 1733 km) with maximum payload
Performance: take-off distance to 35 ft (10.7 m) 4,000 ft (1219 m) at maximum take-off weight; landing distance from 50 ft (15 m) 3,500 ft (1067 m) at normal landing weight

The British Aerospace BAe 146 CC.Mk 2 finally replaced the Andover CC.Mk 2 in RAF Queen's Flight service with the arrival of a third aircraft in December 1990. By then, the Andover had been in service for 26 years.

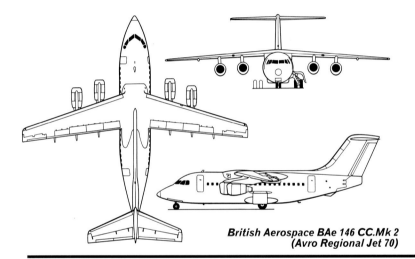

British Aerospace BAe 146 CC.Mk 2
(Avro Regional Jet 70)

British Aerospace (Avro/Hawker Siddeley) 748

British Aerospace plc
Warwick House, PO Box 87, Farnborough Aerospace Centre
Farnborough, Hampshire GU14 6YU, UK

Design of the Avro 748 twin-turboprop airliner was begun in January 1959. Representing the last identifiable product of the Avro (A. V. Roe) company, the aircraft was subsequently designated HS.748, following incorporation of Avro into the Hawker Siddeley Group. The Avro 748 prototype (G-APZV) was flown for the first time on 20 June 1960. Initial production models were the HS.748 Series 1, followed by the HS.748 Series 2 and HS.748 Series 2A, featuring uprated engines. Licence-production of Series 1s and 2s from 1961 was carried out by HAL in Kanpur, India, with a total of 72 aircraft delivered to the Indian Air Force. This figure includes 20 HAL-developed HAL (BAe) 748(M) dedicated military freighters with large cargo door, the final example

being delivered in 1984. Persistent reports suggest that one Indian 748 has been converted to serve as an AEW testbed, with a rotodome above the rear fuselage. Eyewitnesses report seeing such an aircraft flying over Bangalore during 1990-92, presumably on test from HAL's nearby facility. Whether this aircraft is any more than an aerodynamic prototype is unknown.

From 1979, production commenced of a new basic model. Following the formation of British Aerospace, the designation became **BAe (HS) 748 Series 2B**. This featured uprated Dart turboprops for improved 'hot-and-high' performance, an extended span wing, modified tail surfaces and other refinements. The **BAe 748 Military Transport** version incorporated a

reinforced floor and large rear freight door and could accommodate 58 troops, or 48 paratroops and dispatchers, or 24 stretchers and nine medical attendants.

The final production version was designated **BAe Super 748**. Based on the Series 2B, this model introduced significant new developments, including an advanced flight deck, Dart RDa.7 Mk 552 turboprops offering a 12 per cent reduction in fuel consumption and engine hush kits. British Aerospace also developed the **BAe 748 Coastguarder** dedicated maritime patrol aircraft, based on the BAe 748. This version was equipped for maritime surveillance, search and rescue and fishery protection, and had a moderate ASV/ASW capability. For these roles, it was fitted with a comprehensive

avionics suite including search radar, high accuracy navigation aids (INS and Omega) with options for ECM, ESM, IFF and MAD gear. This version did not receive any orders, however.

OPERATORS

The Royal Air Force is among the armed forces which have procured the 748, operating it as the Andover (described separately). Production of the Super 748 variant ceased in 1988, by which time production of all series totalled 382, including licence-produced aircraft and Andovers. The BAe 748 is currently operated by the air forces of the following nations: Australia (10 Series 2, including two navigation trainers), the Royal Australian Navy (two operated as EW trainers),

Operating from Don Muang Airport alongside a very varied transport force are the two HS.748s of the Royal Thai Air Force.

Sanders Associates converted a single Royal Australian Navy HS.748 as an EW trainer in 1977. It now serves with HC-723 at Nowra.

British Aerospace (Avro/Hawker Siddeley) 748

Belgium (three Series 2A), Brazil (six Series 2 and six Series 2A, local designation C-91), Colombia (two Series 2A jointly operated with the airline SATENA, one example converted to Series 2B), Ecuador (five Series 2A operated jointly with TAME), Nepal (one ex-Royal Flight Series 2A), South Korea (two Series 2A), Sri Lanka (five ex-civil Series 2, including the Coastguarder demonstrator, reconfigured for the transport role), Tanzania (three Series 2A), and Thailand (five Series 2 and one Series 2A). The BAe 748 has been withdrawn in Argentina, Brunei, Venezuela and Zambia.

SPECIFICATION

British Aerospace (Avro/Hawker Siddeley) 748 Series 2B Military Transport
Wing: span 102 ft 5.5 in (31.23 m); aspect ratio 12.668; area 828.87 sq ft (77.00 m²)
Fuselage and tail: length 67 ft 0 in (20.42 m); height 24 ft 10 in (7.57 m); tailplane span 36 ft 0 in (10.97 m); wheel track 24 ft 9 in (7.54 m); wheel base 20 ft 8 in (6.30 m)
Powerplant: two Rolls-Royce Dart RDa.7 Mk 536-2

each rated at 2,280 ehp (1700 kW)
Weights: operating empty 25,730 lb (11671 kg); maximum take-off 46,500 lb (21092 kg) standard or 51,000 lb (23133 kg) optional
Fuel and load: internal fuel 1,441 Imp gal (1,730 US gal; 6550 litres); external fuel none; maximum payload 12,829 lb (5819 kg) standard or 17,270 lb (7833 kg) optional
Speed: cruising speed at optimum altitude 244 kt (281 mph; 452 km/h)
Range: 1,420 nm (1,645 miles; 2630 km) with maximum fuel and an 8,070-lb (3660-kg) payload, or

1,280 nm (1,474 miles; 2372 km) with maximum fuel and a 14,027-lb (6363-kg) payload, or 785 nm (904 miles; 1455 km) with maximum payload
Performance: maximum rate of climb at sea level 1,420 ft (433 m) per minute; service ceiling 25,000 ft (7620 m); take-off run 3,720 ft (1134 m) at maximum take-off weight; take-off distance to 50 ft (15 m) 3,800 ft (1158 m) at maximum take-off weight; landing distance from 50 ft (15 m) 2,050 ft (625 m) at normal landing weight; landing run 1,270 ft (387 m) at normal landing weight

British Aerospace (Avro/Hawker Siddeley) Andover

The **Andover** was the dedicated military assault transport version of the Avro 748, and was sufficiently redesigned to warrant allocation of the new type number **Avro 780**. It was designed to meet an RAF requirement for a STOL multi-role transport able to operate from rough airstrips or 300-yd (275-m) lengths of ploughed field or desert, even with obstacles on the approach. The fuselage was lengthened and the entire rear section was redesigned to incorporate a 'beaver tail' rear loading ramp, which also allowed loads to be air-dropped. Lightweight Hawker Siddeley Skydel removable roller track was provided to ease loading, and the new Dowty Rotol 'kneeling' main undercarriage allows the cabin floor 'sill' to be moved vertically or horizontally to align with the tail board of a vehicle loading freight. The main cabin could accommodate up to three Land Rovers, or a Land Rover and a Ferret armoured car, or alternatively could seat up to 58 troops, 40 paratroops or 24 stretchers.

Power was provided by a pair of 3,245-eshp (2420-kW) Rolls Royce Dart R.Da12 Mk 201C turboprops. The extra 2-ft 6-in (0.76-m) propeller diameter (by comparison with the 748 model) necessitated moving the engines further outboard, although overall wingspan was actually reduced by 3 in (7.6 cm). The upswept rear fuselage meant relocating the tail unit, and the tailplane gained dihedral. The Andover prototype (converted from the first Avro 748) made its maiden flight on 21 December 1963, and 31 were manufactured for the **RAF**'s Air Support Command. The aircraft proved rugged

and dependable, and was as a result extremely popular, serving with squadrons in the UK, Singapore and Aden.

The withdrawal from east of Suez reduced the Andover force to a single squadron, and the 1975 defence cuts led to the disbandment of this unit. Ten of the 29 survivors were sold to the **Royal New Zealand Air Force** (nine remain in use), five were relegated to ground training duties, and four were transferred to RAF Germany for communications use, three to the **MoD Procurement Executive** and six to No. 115 Squadron for calibration duties. A single aircraft was also used by No. 51 Squadron (the RAF's Elint unit) for trials for some years, before it too joined No. 115.

Four of No. 115 Squadron's aircraft were designated **Andover E.Mk 3**, and are fitted with a nose-mounted Milligan light (to enable engineers on the ground to calibrate ILS equipment). The E.Mk 3s received a new Litton Inertial Referenced Flight Inspection System during 1983, which cross-checks the changing sight angle of lights on the ground to work out the aircraft's glideslope, instead of relying on a ground party with theodolites. Three aircraft without Milligan lights were designated **Andover E.Mk 3A** and had a limited calibration fit, allowing them to inspect TACAN and radars, but not ILS systems. These aircraft would have had a wartime communications relay role. These three Andovers were reassigned to No. 32 Squadron for communications duties in late 1992. No.115 Sqn disbanded in October 1993 handing

over their role to a civilian contractor, a subsidiary of Hunting plc. The Andover E.Mk 3s have been retained and operate from East Midlands Airport. No. 32 Sqn's Andovers are slated for retirement during 1994.

Under Modification 207, two of No. 60 Squadron's Andovers had their forward freight doors removed and were fitted with an underfuselage camera, for an undisclosed reconnaissance role believed to be connected with flights along the Berlin corridor. They were then redesignated **Andover C.Mk 1(PR)**. One of these aircraft later passed to the A&AEE at Boscombe Down, and has been used for Open Skies arms limitation verification flights over the former USSR.

The RAF also received six Series 2 Avro 748s (XS789-XS794) under the designation Andover **CC.Mk 2** (though they had none of the features of 'real' Andovers) and these served with the Queen's Flight, at RAF Benson, and a variety of other VIP and communications units. Four survivors now fly with No. 32 Squadron at RAF Northolt, and a fifth is with the Defence Research Agency at Bedford. Another RAF 748 is also used by the DRA, this one a Series 1 previously operated by Smiths Industries.

The Royal New Zealand Air Force's Andovers are split between five camouflaged tactical transports and four more distinguished looking VIP aircraft.

SPECIFICATION

British Aerospace (Avro/Hawker Siddeley) Andover C.Mk 1
generally similar to the British Aerospace HS 748 Series 2B Military Transport except in the following particulars:
Wing: span 98 ft 0 in (29.87 m); aspect ratio 11.552; area 831.00 sq ft (77.20 m²)
Fuselage and tail: length 77 ft 1 in (23.75 m); height 29 ft 3 in (8.92 m); wheel base 23 ft 8 in (7.21 m)
Powerplant: two Rolls-Royce Dart RDa.12 Mk 201C each rated at 2,305 shp (1719 kW) without water/methanol injection and 2,970 shp (2214 kW) with water/methanol injection
Weights: basic empty 27,709 lb (12569 kg); operating empty 28,250 lb (12814 kg); maximum take-off 50,000 lb (22680 kg)
Fuel and load: internal fuel 1,441 Imp gal (1,730 US gal; 6550 litres) plus provision for 1,700 Imp gal (2,041 US gal; 7728 litres) of auxiliary fuel in fuselage tanks; maximum payload 14,750 lb (6691 kg)
Speed: cruising speed at 20,000 ft (6095 m) 224 kt (258 mph; 415 km/h)
Range: 1,020 nm (1,175 miles; 1891 km) with a 10,000-lb (4536-kg) payload or 325 nm (374 miles; 602 km) with maximum payload
Performance: maximum rate of climb at sea level 1,170 ft (357 m) per minute; service ceiling 24,000 ft (7315 m); take-off distance to 50 ft (15 m) 1,300 ft (369 m) at maximum take-off weight; landing distance from 50 ft (15 m) 1,300 ft (369 m) at normal landing weight

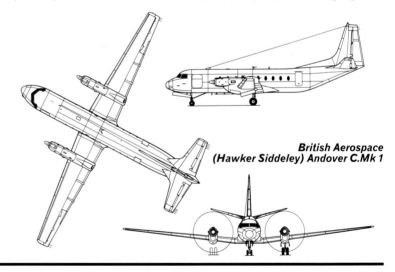

British Aerospace (Hawker Siddeley) Andover C.Mk 1

British Aerospace (Beagle/Scottish Aviation) Bulldog

Originally designed as a military trainer version of the civil Pup, the **Beagle Bulldog** was produced by Scottish Aviation (later BAe) from 1971 until 1982. An all-metal stressed-skin machine with fixed tricycle gear, the Bulldog has side-by-side dual controls, with rear space for an observer or a 220-lb (100-kg) load. The canopy slides to the rear, and other features include cockpit heating, electrically-driven slotted flaps, hydraulic wheel brakes (or optional skis), comprehensive avionics for communication and navigation, an optional glider tow hook and provision for rocket- and gun-pods.

All production Bulldogs have the same basic engine (though the AEIO-360 was offered for customers requiring 20 seconds of inverted flight at full power), driving a Hartzell constant-speed propeller. Four removable metal tanks in the wings hold 32 Imp gal (146 litres) of fuel. The Bulldog gained its popularity from a combination of low costs, robust simplicity and flawless handling in its primary training role.

The initial version was exported to **Malaysia** (15 **Bulldog Model 102**) and **Kenya** (five **Bulldog Model 103**). The chief order for this version was 78 placed by

Sweden, which designates the type as the **Sk 61**. The majority of these are operated by the Swedish army as the **Fpl 61**, as its fixed-wing training and liaison aircraft (though they were trialled with armament). Following plans to convert the army to a wholly rotary-wing force, army Bulldogs will be transferred to the Flygvapen to replace Saab Safirs. The Flygvapen already operates Bulldogs with its F5 flying school, and others are allocated to operational wings as liaison and IFR training aircraft.

In 1973 production switched to the **Bulldog Model 120**, with increased aerobatic

capability at maximum weight and a full clearance at increased weight. Orders for this comprised 130 **Bulldog Model 121** aircraft for the **RAF**, designated **Bulldog T.Mk 1**. The majority of the RAF's 118 surviving Bulldogs continue to serve with 15 University Air Squadrons (namely Aberdeen, Dundee and St Andrews; Birmingham; Bristol; Cambridge; East Lowlands; East Midlands; Glasgow and Strathclyde; Liverpool; London; Manchester; Northumbrian, Oxford; Queens; Southampton; Wales; Yorkshire), providing training to sponsored undergraduates and potential graduate entrants. Examples also fly with the College Air Squadron (Cranwell), Central Flying School (Scampton) and No.6 FTS (Finningley).

Exports include 12 **Bulldog Model 122**

aircraft for **Ghana**, 37 **Bulldog Model 123** aircraft for **Nigeria**, one **Bulldog Model 124** demonstrator and 22 **Bulldog Model 125** aircraft for **Jordan**, six **Bulldog Model 126** aircraft for **Lebanon**, nine **Bulldog Model 127** aircraft for **Kenya**, two **Bulldog Model 128** aircraft for **Hong Kong**, one **Bulldog Model 129** for a civil customer in **Venezuela**, and six **Bulldog Model 130** aircraft for **Botsawana**. In 1974 a retractable-gear **Bulldog Series 200** (**Bullfinch**) was flown, but this was not put into production . The type has since been withdrawn from service with the Royal Hong Kong Auxiliary Air Force and Botsawana. Malaysian Bulldogs have been relegated to the training of reserve pilots.

SPECIFICATION

British Aerospace (Beagle/Scottish Aviation) Bulldog T.Mk 1
Wing: span 33 ft 0 in (10.06 m); aspect ratio 8.4; area 129.40 sq ft (12.02 m²)
Fuselage and tail: length 23 ft 3 in (7.09 m); height 7 ft 5.75 in (2.28 m); tailplane span 11 ft 0 in (3.35 m); wheel track 6 ft 8 in (2.03 m); wheel base 4 ft 7 in (1.40 m)
Powerplant: one Textron Lycoming IO-360-A1B6 rated at 200 hp (149 kW)
Weights: empty equipped 1,430 lb (649 kg); operating empty 1,475 lb (669 kg); normal take-off 2,238 lb (1015 kg) for aerobatics; maximum take-off 2,350 lb (1066 kg)
Fuel and load: internal fuel 32 Imp gal (38.4 US gal;

145.5 litres); external fuel none; provision for light armament
Speed: never exceed speed 209 kt (241 mph; 389 km/h); maximum level speed 'clean' at sea level 130 kt (150 mph; 241 km/h); maximum cruising speed at 4,000 ft (1220 m) 120 kt (138 mph; 222 km/h); economical cruising speed at 4,000 ft (1220 m) 105 kt (121 mph; 194 km/h)
Range: standard range 540 nm (622 miles; 1001 km)

Performance: maximum rate of climb at sea level 1,035 ft (315 m) per minute; service ceiling 16,000 ft (4875 m); take-off run 900 ft (274 m) at maximum take-off weight; take-off distance to 50 ft (15 m) 1,400 ft (427 m) at maximum take-off weight; landing distance from 50 ft (15 m) 1,190 ft (363 m) at normal landing weight; landing run 500 ft (152 m) at normal landing weight
g limits: -3 to +6 aerobatic and -1.8 to +4.4 utility

British Aerospace (Scottish Aviation) Bulldog T.Mk 1

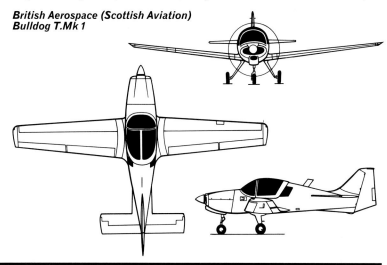

Most RAF Bulldogs serve with 16 University Air Squadrons training sponsored students and VR members, many of whom later join up.

British Aerospace (English Electric/BAC) Canberra

Britain's first jet bomber, the **Canberra**, was widely exported and was built under licence in Australia, and as the Martin B-57 in the USA. Australia, New Zealand, Ecuador, Venezuela, South Africa, Zimbabwe, France and Ethiopia have all retired their Canberras, but the type remains active in small numbers with **India**, **Peru**, **Argentina**, **Chile** and **Germany**, and in **Britain** with the RAF, Defence Research Agency and Flight Refuelling Ltd, mainly in second-line roles. The Royal Navy retired its last Canberras at the end of 1992.

The Canberra remains active in its country of birth, with several serving as testbeds and research aircraft with the Defence Research Agency now at Boscombe Down, and as target tugs/drone-launchers with Flight Refuelling Ltd at Llanbedr. Defence cuts at the end of the Cold War led to a rapid rundown in the Canberra force, which had stabilised at a full three squadrons, even though most airframes had been refurbished for service into the next century. Target facilities and ECM training is being taken over by cheaper-to-operate business jets, which will be unable to offer the Canberra's challenging handling characteristics and 'fast jet', high workload cockpit environment, which have made the type invaluable for upgrading young pilots who drop out of advanced fast jet training. Some **T.Mk 17**s and **T.Mk 17A**s are used for ECM training but are due to be retired by mid-1994, but five **PR.Mk 9**s will soldier on in the survey role into the next century, with three **T.Mk 4** dual control trainers and a pair of chaff-laying **PR.Mk 7**s.

In Peru and Argentina the Canberra remains active as a bomber, Peru having expanded its fleet to about 25 by purchasing five aircraft from South Africa. Chile and Germany both operate Canberras (two PR.Mk 9s and a single **B.Mk 2** respectively) in the survey role. The largest operator of the Canberra today is India, with about 45 aircraft still in use. A mix of **TT.Mk 4**s, **T.Mk 13**s, **B(I).Mk 12**s, **PR.Mk 57**s, **B(I).Mk 58**s, and **B(I).Mk 66**s equip No. 6 Squadron (in the anti-shipping and fleet requirements roles), No. 35 Squadron (in the ECM role), and No. 106

Squadron in the strategic reconnaissance and survey roles. No. 6 and No. 106 Squadrons each parent a target towing flight.

The prototype English Electric A1 made its maiden flight on 13 May 1949, and was followed by the production B.Mk 2 with 6,500-lb (28.9-kN) RA3 Avon Mk 101 engines. The T.Mk 4 was the training version of the B.Mk 2, lacking the latter aircraft's transparent nosecone and visual bombing system. With 7,500 lb st (33.36-kN) RA7 Avon Mk 109s and integral fuel tanks in the wings, the basic bomber became the **B.Mk 6**, and with an underfuselage gun pack, the **B(I).Mk 6**. The dedicated interdictor Canberra variant was the **B(I).Mk 8**, which was based on the B.Mk 6 but had a new nose, with the pilot sitting under a fighter-type canopy offset to port. Export versions of the Canberra B.Mk 2 included the **B.Mk 20**, **B.Mk 52**, **B.Mk 62**, and **B.Mk 82**, while the B(I).Mk 6 became the **B.Mk 56** and B(I).Mk 66. The B(I).Mk 8 was exported as the **B(I).Mk 12**, **B(I).Mk 58**, **B(I).Mk 68** and **B(I).Mk 88**. Export versions of the T.Mk 4 included the **T.Mk 13**,

T.Mk 21, **T.Mk 64** and **T.Mk 84**.
The Canberra has also been used for photo reconnaissance duties, with a 14-in (35-cm) forward fuselage stretch aft of the cockpit to accommodate camera stations and with the bomb bay replaced by a separate flare bay and fuel tank. The basic RA3-engined recce aircraft was the **PR.Mk 3**, while the **PR.Mk 7** had RA7s and integral wing tanks. The PR.Mk 9 is a dedicated high-altitude version with 11,250-lb (50-kN)

RA24 Avon Mk 206 engines and an extended-chord inner wing, and extended-span outer wing panels. The ailerons are hydraulically boosted and a new nose section is fitted, with an opening version of the B(I).Mk 8-style canopy for the pilot and with the navigator gaining access to his position via the hinged nose. The **PR.Mk 57** is an export version of the PR.Mk 7.

A plethora of variants was produced for other tasks, including Elint, the training of all-weather fighter crews and target facilities, while others were converted as unmanned target drones, and as test and research aircraft of every description.

With the rapid reduction in the RAF's Canberras (once thought to be ready to soldier on into the next century), only the PR.Mk 9 seems safe.

India's sizeable Canberra force has a more assured future with three units operating aircraft in the target-towing, electronic warfare and photo-reconnaissance roles. This Dayglo B(I).Mk 8 target tug (note black and yellow stripes underneath) performs a dirty, noisy cartridge start.

British Aerospace (English Electric/BAC) Canberra

SPECIFICATION

British Aerospace (English Electric/BAC) Canberra B(I).Mk 8

Wing: span 63 ft 11.5 in (19.50 m) without tip tanks and 65 ft 6 in (19.96 m) with tip tanks; aspect ratio 4.26; area 960.00 sq ft (89.19 m2)

Fuselage and tail: length 65 ft 6 in (19.96 m); height 15 ft 8 in (4.77 m); tailplane span 27 ft 5 in (8.36 m); wheel track 15 ft 9 in (4.80 m); wheel base 15 ft 2.75 in (5.64 m)

Powerplant: two Rolls-Royce Avon RA.7 Mk 109 each rated at 7,400 lb st (32.92 kN) dry

Weights: operating empty 27,950 lb (12678 kg); normal take-off 43,000 lb (19505 kg); maximum take-off 54,950 lb (24925 kg)

Fuel and load: internal fuel 2,457 Imp gal (2,951 US gal; 11170 litres); external fuel up to two 244-Imp gal (293-US gal; 1109-litre) wingtip tanks; maximum ordnance 8,000 lb (3629 kg)

Speed: maximum level speed 'clean' at 40,000 ft (12190 m) 470 kt (541 mph; 871 km/h) or at sea level 449 kt (517 mph; 832 km/h)

Range: ferry range 3,152 nm (3,630 miles; 5842 km); combat range 700 nm (806 miles; 1297 km) on a lo-lo-lo attack mission with maximum warload

Performance: maximum rate of climb at sea level 3,400 ft (1036 m) per minute; service ceiling 48,000 lb (14630 m); take-off distance to 50 ft (15 m) 6,000 ft (1829 m) at maximum take-off weight; landing distance from 50 ft (15 m) 3,900 ft (1189 m) at normal landing weight

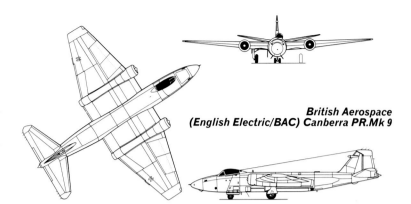

British Aerospace (English Electric/BAC) Canberra PR.Mk 9

British Aerospace (de Havilland/Hawker Siddeley) Dominie

Directly derived from one of the earliest production models of the de Havilland 125 (BAe 125), the **Dominie T.Mk 1** has been the **RAF**'s standard navigator trainer since 1966. Based on the Hawker Siddeley 125 Series 1A/B, the type was first flown on 30 December 1964. External changes included a ventral fairing extending forward of the wing, housing Doppler and Decca aerials. A revised cabin made provision for two students sitting in rearward-facing seats opposite an instructional console. The standard crew of six comprised a single pilot, two students and up to three supernumary crew members (instructors and pilot assister). The Dominie's navigation equipment included three types of communications, R/T, VOR/ILS, gyro-magnetic compass, weather radar, ground position indicator and facility for taking astro shots through a periscopic sextant.

Production of the Dominie totalled 20 aircraft, almost all of which have served with No. 6 FTS at Finningley. Initially supplementing the Vickers Varsity (withdrawn in 1976), the Dominie has accrued over 25 years' service. As the RAF has re-equipped with progressively complex aircraft, much of the equipment and techniques associated with Dominie training (originally optimised for V-Force backseaters) have

become increasingly unrepresentative, this problem being particularly acute with respect to low-level fast-jet navigator training.

To resolve this problem, the RAF initiated an update programme in 1993 involving a total of 11 aircraft. The programme is carried out by Thorn EMI in association with Marshall of Cambridge and involves installation of a Super Searcher maritime surveillance radar with associated radio, avionics and navigation mission computing systems improvements. The radar has been enhanced to provide a long/short-range ground-mapping capability at both high and low altitudes. The high-resolution radar, which is fitted with three-axis stabilisation, is unaffected by high angles of attack and rectifies a shortfall in the performance of previous Dominie equipment. The radar is integrated with tactical processing equipment and information is fed to multi-function, multi-colour displays in both cockpit and instructional installations. This enables other sensors to be incorporated, such as navaids, IFF, ESM, IRDS and acoustic devices; further extensions include facilities for datalink and surface-based command and control centres.

The update has also resulted in a rationalisation of the training programme. The normal crew complement of six or seven com-

The RAF's Dominie T.Mk 1 is derived from the HS.125 Srs 2, but with a restyled ventral fairing, originally housing Decca and Doppler.

prises two pilots, one senior instructor and three student navigators, with an additional air electronics officer when required. The updated Dominie is currently the common training vehicle for all RAF navigators, and flies an equal mix of high- and low-level training missions.

SPECIFICATIONS

British Aerospace (de Havilland/Hawker Siddeley) Dominie T.Mk 1

Wing: span 47 ft 0 in (14.33 m); aspect ratio 6.26; area 353.00 sq ft (32.79 m2)

Fuselage and tail: length 47 ft 5 in (14.45 m); height 16 ft 6 in (5.03 m); tailplane span 20 ft 0 in (6.10 m); wheel track 9 ft 2 in (2.80 m); wheel base 18 ft 8.5 in (5.70 m)

Powerplant: two Rolls-Royce (Bristol Siddeley) Viper Mk 301 each rated at 3,120 lb st (13.88 kN) dry

Weights: empty equipped 10,100 lb (4581 kg); maximum take-off 21,200 lb (9616 kg)

Fuel and load: internal fuel 1,025 Imp gal (1,231 US gal; 4660 litres); maximum ordnance none

Speed: maximum cruising speed at 25,000 ft (7620 m) 410 kt (472 mph; 760 km/h); economical cruising speed at 38,000 ft (11580 m) 365 kt (420 mph; 676 km/h)

Range: 1,162 nm (1,338 miles; 2153 km)

Performance: maximum rate of climb at sea level 2,000 ft (610 m) per minute; service ceiling 40,000 ft (12190 m)

British Aerospace Harrier GR.Mk 3/T.Mk 4

The **British Aerospace Harrier** was the world's first practical operational V/STOL strike fighter and was developed from six years of experience with the Hawker P.1127/Kestrel series of demonstrators. The first production **Harrier GR.Mk 1** made its maiden flight on 28 December 1967, entering service on 1 April 1969 with the No. 233 OCU at Wittering. Survivors were subsequently retrofitted with progressively uprated engines, resulting in the **Harrier GR.Mk 1A** (with 20,500-lb/91.2-kN thrust Pegasus Mk 102) and the **Harrier GR.Mk 3** (with 21,500-lb/95.6-kN thrust Pegasus Mk 103). A total of 118 single-seat Harriers (61 GR.Mk 1s, 17 GR.Mk 1As and 40 GR.Mk 3s) was acquired by the **RAF**.

From 1976, production GR.Mk 3s were fitted with a Marconi LRMTS (laser ranger and marked target seeker) contained in a 'thimble' nose fairing. A Marconi ARI 18223 E/J band radar warning receiver was added at the same time. A single oblique F95 70-mm camera was fitted and recce capability was further enhanced by an underfuselage camera pod. This 410-lb (186-kg) centreline pod contained a fan of four 70-mm F95 Mk 7 cameras and a single 127-mm F135 camera. No. IV Squadron had a 40 per cent commitment to recce operations.

Fourteen GR.Mk 3s were dispatched for Operation Corporate in 1982 and were fitted with radar transponders (identified by a nose bulged fairing and blade aerial). Self-

defence capability was enhanced by a Tracor AN/ALE-40 chaff/flare dispenser fitted in the rear fuselage and provision for AIM-9L AAMs on the outer two wing pylons. In 1984, Philips-MATRA Phimat chaff dispenser pods were also issued for outboard fitment. Following recapture of the Falkland Islands, a HarDet (Harrier Detachment), later renamed No. 1453 Flight, was established at Port Stanley airfield and assigned an air-defence role with AIM-9Ls, and was subsequently disbanded after the opening of Mount Pleasant airfield. The addition of four attrition replacements ordered for aircraft lost in the Falklands conflict brought total RAF single-seat Harrier procurement to 118.

Conversion of RAF units to Harrier GR.Mk 5/7s began in 1988, leaving only a few Mk 3s with No. 233 OCU (now renumbered as No. 20(R) Squadron) and No. 1417 Flight in Belize. The latter was the last front-line operator of the GR.Mk 3, bringing its aircraft home in July 1993. No. 20 (R) Sqn at Wittering maintain a handful into 1994, for instructor training and chase duties.

The first of two **Harrier T.Mk 2** prototypes was flown on 24 April 1969, and a total of 27 was delivered (23 RAF, 4 RN). To accommodate the second seat, some redesign was required, including repositioning of avionics and the port oblique camera.

The aft reaction control jet was housed in an extended fairing. The forward fuselage was extended by 3 ft 11 in (1.19 m), the ventral strake enlarged and fin moved rearwards and extended 11 in (28 cm) by a base insert. This was deemed insufficient for lateral stability at AoA exceeding 15° and the tip extension was increased to 18 in (46 cm).

These aircraft received the subsequent designations **T.Mk 2A** and **T.Mk 4** in parallel with the engine upratings fitted to the single-seaters. Lasers and RWRs were retrospectively installed on most. The LRMTS of some aircraft used exclusively for OCU training was removed, resulting in pointed noses and the designation **T.Mk 4A**. T.Mk 4s are currently operated at Wittering by Nos 1 and 20 Squadrons. One of the latter unit's T.Mk 4s is temporarily assigned to the College of Aeronautics, Cranfield. A further two are on strength with the Strike/Attack Operational Evaluation Unit at Boscombe Down for weapons and systems testing, including the so-called 'Nightbird Harrier'. The RAF Germany Harrier squadrons (Nos 3 & IV) have no two-seaters permanently assigned.

One Harrier T.Mk 4 was converted at Cranfield to serve as a testbed for advanced control systems for VTOL aircraft, and was designated VAAC (Vectored-thrust Aircraft Advanced flight Control) Harrier. The aircraft is fitted with a Smiths Industries flight management computer based on equipment developed for the Airbus A310. Conventional controls are retained in the front seat,

No longer in front-line service, small numbers of GR.Mk 3s serve with No. 20(R) Sqn, the Harrier OCU, along with several T.Mk 4As.

with navigation controls in the rear seat linked by computer to the aircraft's control circuits, rather than being mechanically connected. The aircraft is operated by the DRA's Flight Systems Dept at Bedford.

SPECIFICATION

British Aerospace (Hawker Siddeley) Harrier GR.Mk 3

Wing: span 25 ft 3 in (7.70 m) with combat tips or 29 ft 8 in (9.04 m) with ferry tips; aspect ratio 3.175 with combat tips or 4.08 with ferry tips; area 201.10 sq ft (18.68 m²) with combat tips or 216.00 sq ft (20.07 m²)
Fuselage and tail: length 46 ft 10 in (14.27 m) with laser nose; height 11 ft 11 in (3.63 m); tailplane span 13 ft 11 in (4.24 m); outrigger track 22 ft 2 in (6.76 m); wheel base about 11 ft 4 in (3.45 m)
Powerplant: one Rolls-Royce Pegasus Mk 103 rated at 21,500 lb st (95.64 kN) dry
Weights: empty equipped 12,300 lb (5579 kg); operating empty 13,535 lb (6139 kg); normal take-off

23,500 lb (10660 kg); max take-off 25,200 lb (11431 kg)
Fuel and load: internal fuel 5,060 lb (2295 kg); external fuel up to two 330-Imp gal (1500-litre) ferry tanks or two 190- or 100-Imp gal (228- or 120-US gal; 864- or 455-litre) drop tanks; maximum ordnance 5,000 lb (2268 kg) authorised or 8,000 lb (3269 kg) demonstrated
Speed: maximum level speed 'clean' at sea level 635 kt (730 mph; 1176 km/h)
Range: ferry range 1,850 nm (3,130 miles; 3428 km) with two ferry tanks; combat radius 360 nm (415 miles; 667 km) on a hi-lo-hi attack mission with a 4,400-lb (1996-kg) warload, or 200 nm (230 miles; 370 km) on a lo-lo-lo attack mission with a 4,400-lb (1996-kg) warload
Performance: maximum rate of climb at sea level 29,000 ft (8840 m) per minute; climb to 40,000 ft (12190 m) in 2 minutes 23 seconds after VTO; maximum speed in a dive, from height Mach 1.3: service ceiling 51,200 ft (15605 m); take-off run about 1,000 ft (305 m) at maximum take-off weight with a 5,000-lb (2268-kg) warload; landing run 0 ft (0 m) at normal landing weight

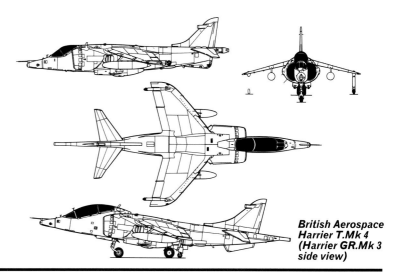

British Aerospace Harrier T.Mk 4 (Harrier GR.Mk 3 side view)

British Aerospace (Hawker Siddeley) **Hawk**

British Aerospace Defence
Warton Aerodrome, Preston,
Lancashire PR4 1AX, UK

When Air Staff Target (AST) 362 was issued in 1964 for a new RAF trainer to replace the Gnat, the requirement was only partially filled by a small number of two-seat Jaguars. By 1968 the shortfalll remained, and that year Hawker Siddeley Aviation initiated studies for a subsonic trainer, the original high performance criteria for such an aircraft having been waived in the interim. The company's private venture P.1182 (later HS.1182) evolved into an advanced trainer formalised as AST 397 in January 1970, HSA being awarded a production contract the following October. HSA chose a simple but robust low-wing layout for an aircraft of modest dimensions – although it was appreciably larger than the tiny Gnat – powered by a single Rolls-Royce Adour turbofan delivering 5,200 lb (23.1 kN) thrust. It was in cockpit design that the aircraft most impressed observers, this providing the instructor with forward visibility.

The name **Hawk** was chosen in 1973 and the first **Hawker Siddeley Hawk T.Mk 1** made its maiden flight on 21 August 1971. An indication of the integrity of the Hawk design was the fact that there were no prototypes or pre-production aircraft, and five of the six aircraft used for flight development were subsequently delivered to the RAF as part of the service order which totalled 175 T.Mk 1s.

Construction of the Hawk is entirely conventional. The fuselage incorporates skin, stringer and frame components. Its one-piece wing is attached by three bolts on either side, which places the associated structure under compression for integral strength. Inboard of the 'kink', the wing encloses an integral fuel tank and pick-up points for the main undercarriage. Three hardpoints were fitted as standard on RAF machines. The Hawk's RAF service began in April 1976 with delivery of the first production aircraft to No. 4 FTS at Valley. Students were given a total of 75 hours dual and solo instruction on the Hawk, about 10 hours being eliminated from the advanced stages as the new aircraft was able to undertake the weapons phase previously handled by the Hawker Hunter. Valley's initial course of Hawk pilots trained on the Hawk graduated in November 1977. BAe completed RAF deliveries by the end of 1976, other user units being No. 1 Tactical Weapons Unit at Brawdy, No. 2 TWU (Lossiemouth and later Chivenor), CFS (Valley and Scampton), ETPS (Boscombe Down) and the 'Red Arrows' aerobatic team based at Scampton.

In order to expand the Hawk's capability in the weapons training role the MoD contracted for the modification of 88 aircraft in January 1983. The resulting aircraft was designated **Hawk T.Mk 1A**, the most significant difference to the earlier trainer variant being its ability to carry a pair of AIM-9L Sidewinder AAMs on underwing launchers. For close-in air combat or ground strafing, a single 30-mm gun pod could also be fitted under the fuselage. The T.Mk 1A conversion programme was completed in May 1986, and the aircraft were intended as limited-role point-defence fighters for emergency use in the UK Defence Region, to augment Phantoms and Tornados in the 'mixed fighter force'. In such a situation they would have been flown by instructors of No. 1 TWU at Brawdy as Nos 79 and 234 shadow squadrons and by No. 2 TWU at Chivenor as Nos 63 and 151 shadow squadrons. Under the Options for Change policy, No. 1 TWU was disbanded on 31 July 1992. The Hawk T.Mk 1s and 1As currently operate as advanced trainers and weapons trainers with, respectively, Nos 19 and 92 Reserve Squadrons (formerly Nos 63 and 151) of No. 7 FTS at Chivenor (to disband at the end of 1994), Nos 74 and 208 Sqn (formerly No. 234 Sqn) of No. 4 FTS at Valley, and with No. 100 Sqn at Finningley (formerly Wyton) for target towing. Hawks are also in use with the Central Flying School, the Red Arrows (RAF Scampton), and No. 6 FTS at RAF Finningley.

The Hawk's considerable development and export potential was realised in 1977

Several famous RAF squadron identities are allocated to Hawk units, such as 4 FTS, whose shadow identity is No. 74 ('Tiger') Sqn.

Finland's Fouga (Valmet) Magisters were replaced by BAe Hawk T.Mk 51s (also assembled largely by Valmet) as the primary jet trainer for the Suomen Ilmavoimat (Finnish air force). Aircraft are largely assigned to training units within each of the tactical wings, but some aircraft are tasked with a reconnaissance role using podded equipment, replacing early MiG-21F13s.

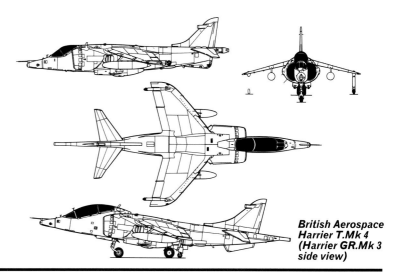

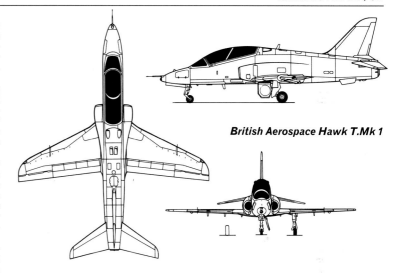

British Aerospace Hawk T.Mk 1

British Aerospace Hawk

when BAe introduced the **Series 50** upgrade for an initial sale to Finland of 50, deliveries beginning in December of that year. Forty-six were assembled by Valmet and a follow-on order for seven was placed in December 1990. In 1978, Kenya and Indonesia also purchased Hawks. The follow-on **Series 60** introduced an uprated Mk 861 Adour engine of 5,700 lb st (25.4 kN), additional wing leading-edge fences and four-position flaps to improve lift, anti-skid brakes and revised wheels and tyres. It was the subject of a series of foreign orders commencing in July 1982 to Zimbabwe, Dubai, Abu Dhabi, Kuwait, Saudi Arabia, Switzerland (19 assembled by F+W), and South Korea. ('long-nosed' version equipped with ranging radar and nosewheel steering).

OPERATORS

Abu Dhabi: Mk 60 – 16 (15 to Mk 63A)
Dubai: Mk 61 – 9
Finland: Mk 51 – 50, Mk 51A – 7
Indonesia: Mk 53 – 20
Kenya: Mk 52 – 12
Kuwait: Mk 64 – 12
Saudia Arabia: Mk 65 – 30
South Korea: Mk 67 – 20
Switzerland: Mk 66 – 20
United Kingdom: T.Mk 1 – 175 (88 to T.Mk 1A)
Zimbabwe: Mk 60 – 8, Mk 60A – 5

SPECIFICATION

British Aerospace (Hawker Siddeley) Hawk T.Mk 1
Wing: span 30 ft 9.75 in (9.39 m); aspect ratio 5.28; area 179.60 sq ft (16.69 m2)
Fuselage and tail: length 36 ft 7.75 in (11.17 m) excluding probe or 38 ft 11 in (11.86 m) including probe; height 13 ft 1.25 in (3.99 m); tailplane span 14 ft 4.75 in (4.39 m); wheel track 11 ft 5 in (3.47 m); wheel base 14 ft 9 in (4.50 m)
Powerplant: one Rolls-Royce/Turboméca Adour Mk 151-01 rated at 5,200 lb st (23.13 kN) dry
Weights: empty equipped 8,040 lb (3647 kg); normal take-off 11,100 lb (5035 kg); maximum take-off 12,566 lb (5700 kg)
Fuel and load: internal fuel 375 Imp gal (450 US gal; 1704 litres); external fuel up to two 190-, 130- or 100-Imp gal (228-, 156- or 120-US gal; 864-, 592- or 455-litre) drop tanks; maximum ordnance 1,500 lb (680 kg) in RAF service though a load of 6,800 lb (3084 kg) is possible
Speed: maximum level speed 'clean' at 11,000 ft (3355 m) 560 kt (645 mph; 1038 km/h)
Range: ferry range 1,670 nm (1,923 miles; 3094 km) with two drop tanks; standard range 1310 nm (1,509 miles; 2428 km); combat radius 300 nm (345 miles; 556 km) with a 5,600-lb (2540-kg) warload, or 560 nm (645 miles; 1038 km) with a 3,000-lb (1361-kg) warload
Performance: maximum rate of climb at sea level 9,300 ft (2835 m) per minute; climb to 30,000 ft (9145 m) in 6 minutes 6 seconds; service ceiling 50,000 ft (15240 m); take-off run 1,800 ft (549 m) at maximum take-off weight; landing run 1,600 ft (488 m) at normal landing weight
g limits: -4 to +8

Nine Hawk T.Mk 1As make up the 'Red Arrows', the RAF's display team. As AIM-9-capable aircraft, these Hawks have a wartime role as part of the RAF's mixed-fighter force.

British Aerospace **Hawk 100**

Having already developed an 'advanced' wing for the Hawk, BAe was able during the mid-1980s to offer the type as a relatively cheap dedicated dual-role weapon systems trainer and fully combat-capable ground attack aircraft based on the Hawk 60. Powerplant was an uprated RR Adour turbofan delivering 5,730 lb (25.5 kN) thrust compared to 5,700 lb (25.4 kN) thrust for the Hawk 60. Otherwise dimensionally similar, the new model had an overall wing span of 32 ft 7 in (9.93 m) as opposed to 30 ft 10 in (9.40 m) for all other Hawks. The extra 21 in (53 cm) was taken up by wingtip AIM-9 missiles and launch rails. Adapting the Hawk wing to take a full warload was aided by the modest degree of sweepback (21.5° at the leading edge), which meant that the additional pylons to accommodate heavier ordnance loads necessary for the ground attack role did not affect the aircraft's centre of gravity. With the addition of an elongated nose housing an optional FLIR and/or laser sensors, an advanced cockpit with multi-functional displays and HOTAS, plus more sophisticated avionics to exploit its enhanced combat potential, the resulting **BAe Hawk 100** (a converted development airframe) first flew in October 1987. The wing, which is stressed for six ordnance pylons enabling up to a maximum of 6,614 lb (3000 kg) of stores to be carried, incorporates combat manoeuvre flaps. As well as wingtip AAMs, a single 30-mm ADEN gun pod is an optional fitting on the fuselage centreline in place of a further stores station.

Abu Dhabi was the initial customer for the Series 100 (known as the **Series 102** with RWR, wingtip launch rails and laser designator), with 18 aircraft. **Oman** ordered four **Series 103**s in July 1990, and in December that year **Malaysia** ordered 10 Hawk **Series 108**s, the first example of which was handed over in February 1994.

South Korean aircraft are a Mk 60/ 100 hybrid which combines the avionics and systems improvements of the Hawk 100, with the basic airframe of the Hawk 60 trainer.

The most substantial order for the Hawk Series 100 came from **Saudi Arabia,** which under the post-Gulf War Al-Yamamah II contract signed for approximately 60 Hawks. **Brunei** has also ordered 19 aircraft, and **Indonesia** 12.

SPECIFICATION

British Aerospace Hawk Mk 100 (Enhanced Ground Attack Hawk)
Wing: span 30 ft 9.75 in (9.39 m) with normal tips or 32 ft 7.875 in (9.94 m with tip-mounted AIM-9 Sidewinder AAMs); aspect ratio 5.28; area 179.60 sq ft (16.69 m2)
Fuselage and tail: length 38 ft 4 in (11.68 m) excluding probe or 40 ft 9 in (12.42 m) including probe; height 13 ft 1.25 in (3.99 m); tailplane span 14 ft 4.75 in (4.39 m); wheel track 11 ft 5 in (3.47 m); wheel base 14 ft 9 in (4.50 m)
Powerplant: one Rolls-Royce/Turboméca Adour Mk 871 rated at 5,845 lb st (26.00 kN) dry
Weights: empty 9,700 lb (4400 kg); normal take-off about 11,350 lb (5148 kg); maximum take-off 20,061 lb (9100 kg)
Fuel and load: internal fuel 2,875 lb (1304 kg); external fuel up to 2,055 lb (932 kg) in two 190-, 130- or 100-Imp gal (228-, 156- or 120-US gal; 864-, 592- or 455-litre) drop tanks; maximum ordnance 6,614 lb (3000 kg)
Speed: never exceed speed 575 kt (661 mph; 1065 km/h) corresponding to Mach 0.87 at sea level and Mach 1.2 above 17,000 ft (5180 m); maximum level speed 'clean' at 36,000 ft (10975 m) 560 kt (645 mph; 1038 km/h)
Range: ferry range more than 1,400 nm (1,612 miles; 2594 km) with two 190-Imp gal (228-US gal; 864-litre) drop tanks; combat radius 660 nm (760 miles; 1223 km) on a hi-lo-hi attack mission with two 1,000-lb (454-kg) bombs, or 275 nm (317 miles; 510 km) on a hi-lo-hi attack mission with seven BL755 cluster bombs, or 140 nm (161 miles; 259 km) on a hi-hi-hi CAP with one 30-mm cannon and two AIM-9 Sidewinder AAMs for a loiter of 3 hours 30 minutes
Performance: maximum rate of climb at sea level 11,800 ft (3597 m) per minute; climb to 30,000 ft (9145 m) in 7 minutes 30 seconds; service ceiling 44,500 ft (13545 m); take-off run 2,100 ft (640 m) at maximum take-off weight; landing run 1,980 ft (605 m) at maximum landing weight

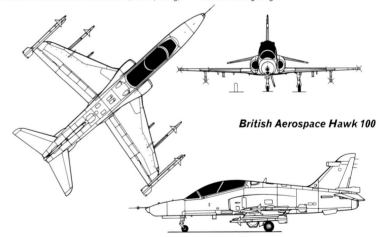

British Aerospace Hawk 100

British Aerospace Hawk 200

The international success of the two-seat Hawk models led British Aerospace to develop a single-seat variant which would attract new customers, particularly the smaller air arms requiring a relatively cheap air superiority fighter and ground attack aircraft. The BAe Hawk 200 is said to represent a far more cost-effective package in the long term, compared to the short-term option of continual refurbishment of older aircraft. A single-seater is more practical and desirable in some respects, not least because there is simply not a pool of trained navigators to occupy second seats.

By redesigning the Hawk's forward fuselage to accommodate a single cockpit, and adding a modern radar, there was still room enough to fit a pair of integral 25-mm ADEN cannon under the cockpit floor. These new guns represent a significant increase in combat capability. A seven-station wing (including wingtip AAM launchers) enables the carriage of up to 6,614 lb (3000 kg) of stores, the same as that of the Hawk 100. Constructed of conventional aluminium alloy and having about 80 per cent commonality with the two-seat models, the Hawk 200 is also powered by a single Adour Mk 871 turbofan. Even with additional equipment to tailor it for a multi-mission combat task, the aircraft has a maximum take-off weight of less than 21,000 lb (9527 kg).

The Westinghouse APG-66H radar is a multi-mode, modified version of that fitted in the F-16. With his seat set further aft than the forward seat position of the other Hawks, the pilot faces a main instrument panel which includes a comms/navigation integration panel, HUD, a multi-function CRT display, a radar display configured for the most modern symbology and a RHAW receiver. The Hawk 200 demonstrator (ZG200) made its maiden flight on 19 May 1986. Two months into the flight test programme this aircraft was destroyed in a crash, killing test pilot 'Jim' Hawkins. The probable cause of the crash was determined as pilot disorientation rather than any inherent fault, which had made 28 flights before it was lost. The second Hawk 200 (ZH200) flew on 24 April 1987. Unlike the first aircraft, ZH200 was fitted with full avionics (but no radar) and, later, a number of small but significant airframe revisions were made.

To counteract any tendency for the tailplane of the Hawk 200 to stall, a condition belatedly revealed on the trainer in 1975, the aircraft eventually received the fuselage-mounted tailplane vanes, or SMURFs (Side-Mounted Unit, horizontal tail Root Fins) developed for the US Navy's T-45 Goshawk trainer. These vanes throw a vortex over the tailplane to prevent undue travel caused by downwash from the flaps when the aircraft is in the low-speed configuration. In addition, an RWR was fitted to the fin leading edge, and the rear fuselage brake chute 'box' was deepened to house a chaff/flare dispenser and rearward-facing RWR antenna. The first APG-66-equipped Hawk 200RDA (Radar Development Aircraft) flew on 13 February 1992.

Oman became the launch customer for the Hawk 200 when 12 aircraft were ordered on 31 July 1990 as Series 203s, primarily to replace ageing Hunters. Malaysia followed suit on 10 December 1990 with an order for 18 aircraft identified as Series 208s. The Malaysian buy is for a mix of Series 100 and 200 aircraft but became embroiled in controversy after UK press speculation regarding the support of the deal with economic assistance for the controversial Pergau dam project. The first aircraft (a Series 100) was delivered in February 1994. Saudi Arabia's Al Yamamah II order may include an unconfirmed number of single-seaters within an overall buy of approximately 60 Hawks. Saudi aircraft would be APG-66H-equipped Hawk Series 205s. The Indonesian Hawk buy, of June 1993, combines both two-seat aircraft with 12 Hawk 200s reaching a confirmed total of 24 aircraft. It has been suggested that this number could rise to over 90.

SPECIFICATION

British Aerospace Hawk Mk 200

Wing: span 30 ft 9.75 in (9.39 m) with normal tips or 32 ft 7.875 in (9.94 m) with tip-mounted AIM-9 Sidewinder AAMs; aspect ratio 5.28; area 179.60 sq ft (16.69 m²)

Fuselage and tail: length 37 ft 2 in (11.33 m) without probe; height 13 ft 8 in (4.16 m); tailplane span 14 ft 4.75 in (4.39 m); wheel track 11 ft 5 in (3.47 m); wheel base 11 ft 8 in (3.56 m)

Powerplant: one Rolls-Royce/Turboméca Adour Mk 871 rated at 5,845 lb st (26.00 kN) dry

Weights: basic empty 9,810 lb (4450 kg); normal take-off 16,565 lb (7514 kg); maximum take-off 20,061 lb (9100 kg)

Fuel and load: internal fuel 3,000 lb (1361 kg); external fuel up to 4,080 lb (1851 kg) in three 190-, 130- or 100-Imp gal (228-, 156- or 120-US gal; 864-, 592- or 455-litre) drop tanks; maximum ordnance 7,700 lb (3493 kg)

Speed: never exceed speed 575 kt (661 mph; 1065 km/h) corresponding to Mach 0.87 at sea level and Mach 1.2 above 17,000 ft (5180 m); maximum level speed 'clean' at sea level 549 kt (632 mph; 1017 km/h); maximum cruising speed at sea level 550 kt (633 mph; 1019 km/h); economical cruising speed at 41,000 ft (12495 m) 430 kt (495 mph; 796 km/h)

Range: ferry range 1,950 nm (2,244 miles; 3610 km) with three drop tanks, or 482 nm (554 miles; 892 km) on internal fuel; combat radius 666 nm (767 miles; 1234 km) on a hi-lo-hi anti-ship mission with one Sea Eagle missile and two drop tanks, or 862 nm (993 miles; 1598 km) on a hi-hi-hi reconnaissance mission with one reconnaissance pod and two drop tanks, or 510 nm (586 miles; 945 km) on a lo-lo-lo reconnaissance mission with one reconnaissance pod and two drop tanks, or 510 nm (587 miles; 945 km) on a hi-lo-hi battlefield interdiction mission with a 3,000-lb (1361-kg) warload, or 104 nm (120 miles; 192 km) on a lo-lo-lo close support mission with five 1,000-lb (454-kg) and four 500-lb (227-kg) bombs, or 550 nm (633 miles; 1018 km) on a hi-hi-hi airspace denial mission with two AIM-9 Sidewinder AAMs and two drop tanks for a loiter of 1 hour, or 100 nm (115 miles; 185 km) on a hi-hi-hi airspace denial mission with two AIM-9 Sidewinder AAMs and two drop tanks for a loiter of

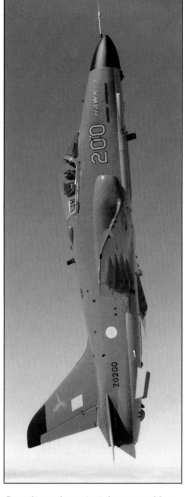

Despite a slow start, hampered by the loss of this, the prototype, sales of the Hawk 200 are now building.

3 hours 30 minutes, or 720 nm (828 miles; 1333 km) on a hi-hi-hi interception mission with two AIM-9 Sidewinder AAMs and two drop tanks

Performance: maximum rate of climb at sea level 11,510 ft (3508 m) per minute; service ceiling 45,000 ft (13715 m); take-off run 2,070 ft (630 m) 'clean' or 5,200 ft (1585 m) with maximum warload; take-off distance to 50 ft (15 m) 7,000 ft (2134 m) with maximum warload; landing distance from 50 ft (15 m) 2,800 ft (854 m) at 10,030 lb (4550 kg) with brake chute or 4,100 ft (1250 m) at 10,030 lb (4550 kg) without brake chute; landing run 1,960 ft (598 m) at normal landing weight

g limits: -4 to +8

British Aerospace Hawk 200

British Aerospace (Hawker/Hawker Siddeley) Hunter

British Aerospace Defence
Dunsfold Aerodrome, Godalming,
Surrey GU8 4BS, UK

The **Hawker Hunter** was originally designed as a day fighter replacement for the Gloster Meteor in RAF service, but was later developed to fulfil the ground attack role. The prototype first flew on 20 July 1951, giving Britain its first indigenous swept-wing fighter, and giving young RAF pilots an aircraft that was the equal to anything in the world. Production eventually reached 1,927, including some licence-production in the Low Countries. In the hands of a skilled pilot, the Hunter remained a competitive fighter well into the 1970s, with Indian, Jordanian and Iraqi pilots downing more modern fighter opponents when they took the Hunter to war.

With the Hunter **F.Mk 6** (and numerous export equivalents), the Hunter received the more powerful 200 series Avon engine, an all-flying tail, and a dogtooth wing leading edge. The externally similar **FGA.Mk 9** was designed from the outset as a fighter-bomber, with provision for a greater underwing weapon load, including up to four fuel tanks. The new variant (which spawned more export variants) received a strengthened landing gear and a brake chute to cope with the higher weights. A fighter reconnaissance variant, with a fan of forward- and sideways-looking oblique cameras in the nose, was closely based on the FGA.Mk 9, and designated **FR.Mk 10**. A handful of similar aircraft were delivered to export customers.

India's sole remaining Hunter squadron, No. 20 Sqn 'The Thunderbolts', functions as a lead-in training unit and also fields the 'Thunderbolts' aerobatic team.

British Aerospace (Hawker/Hawker Siddeley) Hunter

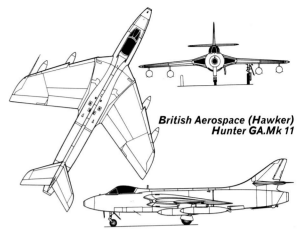

British Aerospace (Hawker) Hunter GA.Mk 11

Switzerland has long been the world's most active Hunter user, but the fighter's long career largely comes to an end in 1994. A replacement is due in the shape of the F/A-18.

Single-seat Hunters (most of them based on the FGA.Mk 9) remain in service in **Switzerland**, **Chile** and **Oman**, and as advanced trainers in **India**. In 1993 Switzerland began withdrawing Hunters in large numbers, while Oman's aircraft may have a limited service life once Hawk 200s are delivered. **Singapore** retains its Hunters, in flyable storage, while Chile is actively seeking a replacement. A handful of Hunters may also remain in service in **Zimbabwe**. The Hunter's original strengths remain important, and operators still prize its straightforward handling characteristics, easy maintenance, turn performance and powerful built-in armament of four 30-mm ADEN cannon. These are mounted in a pack, with their 540 rounds of ammunition, which can be replaced as a unit in minutes, allowing very quick turnaround times. All current front-line Hunters have been modernised with radar warning receivers and

provision for AIM-9 Sidewinder AAMs, and most also have chaff/flare dispensers and modern avionics. Swiss Hunters are compatible with a variety of modern air-to-ground weapons, including the AGM-65.

RAF two-seaters were designated **T.Mk 7** and were followed by a variety of **T.Mk 8** sub-variants for the RN. The last four RAF T.Mk 7s (used for training Buccaneer aircrew) were retired with the disbandment of No. 208 Sqn, on 31 March 1994. Seven Hunter **GA.Mk 11**s remain in use with the **Royal Navy**'s Fleet Requirements and Air Directions Unit (FRADU) in the target facilities role. These are based on the 'small-bore' Avon Mk 113-powered F.Mk 4. FRADU is also responsible for the eight surviving Hunter T.Mk 8Cs, which were shared with No. 899 Sqn until October 1993. A single Hunter FGA.9 serves with the A&AEE at Boscombe Down, largely for spray tank trials, and also to keep RNR pilots current. The

two DRA T.Mk 7s have also moved to Boscombe from Farnborough, joining T,Mk 7s used by the ETPS for inverted spinning. A single T.Mk 8M survives with BAe Dunsfold.

Most export two-seaters have the 'big bore' Avon 200 series engine, and small numbers remain in service with all users.

SPECIFICATION

British Aerospace (Hawker/Hawker Siddeley) Hunter FGA.Mk 9
Wing: span 33 ft 8 in (10.26 m); aspect ratio 3.25; area 349.00 sq ft (32.42 m²)
Fuselage and tail: length 45 ft 10.5 in (13.98 m); height 13 ft 2 in (4.01 m); tailplane span 11 ft 10 in (3.61 m); wheel track 14 ft 9 in (4.50 m); wheel base 15 ft 9 in (4.80 m)
Powerplant: one Rolls-Royce Avon RA.28 Mk 207 rated at 10,150 lb st (45.15 kN) dry
Weights: empty equipped 14,400 lb (6532 kg); normal

take-off 18,000 lb (8165 kg); maximum take-off 24,600 lb (11158 kg)
Fuel and load: internal fuel 3,144 lb (1426 kg); external fuel up to two 230 or 100-Imp gal (276- or 120-US gal; 1045- or 455-litre) drop tanks; maximum ordnance 7,400 lb (3357 kg)
Speed: maximum level speed 'clean' at 36,000 ft (10975 m) 538 kt (620 mph; 978 km/h) or at sea level 616 kt (710 mph; 1144 km/h); maximum cruising speed at 36,000 ft (10975 m) 481 kt (554 mph; 892 km/h); economical cruising speed at optimum altitude 399 kt (460 mph; 740 km/h)
Range: ferry range 1,595 nm (1,840 miles; 2961 km) with two drop tanks; combat radius 385 nm (443 miles; 713 km) on a hi-lo-hi attack mission with typical warload and two drop tanks
Performance: maximum rate of climb at sea level about 8,000 ft (2438 m) per minute; service ceiling 50,000 ft (15240 m); take-off run 2,100 ft (640 m) at normal take-off weight; take-off distance to 50 ft (15 m) 3,450 ft (1052 m) at normal take-off weight; landing run 3,150 ft (960 m) at normal landing weight

---

BAe (Hunting/BAC) Jet Provost

The **Percival** (later **Hunting Percival**) P.84 **Jet Provost** was a development of the Provost piston-engined trainer. Intended as a minimum-change private venture, the Jet Provost was in fact largely a redesigned aircraft. Its maiden flight took place on 26 June 1954 and was followed by nine production aircraft (**Jet Provost T.Mk 1**) and a single **Jet Provost T.Mk 2**. This version introduced a 1,753-lb (7.8-kN) Viper ASV.8 engine and shortened undercarriage. Provision was also made for wingtip tanks, pylons and two nose machine-guns.

From 1958 Hunting Aircraft delivered 201 **T.Mk 3** trainers with Martin-Baker ejection

seats, a clear-view canopy, tip tanks and updated avionics. BAC, which took over Hunting, continued development by fitting the much more powerful Viper 11 engine, rated at 2,500 lb (11.1 kN) thrust. One hundred and ninety-eight of the resulting **Jet Provost T.Mk 4** version were delivered to the **RAF** in 1961-64. Emphasis on high-altitude sorties had highlighted the need for cockpit pressurisation. This requirement led to the **Jet Provost T.Mk 5**, first flown on 28 February 1967, an almost completely redesigned T.Mk 4. The new front fuselage incorporated a pressurised cabin, a redesigned windscreen with sliding canopy

and a lengthened nose. A redesigned wing with a fatigue life of 5,000 hours permitted an increased internal fuel capacity. Provision was also made for wingtip tanks and underwing weapons load . These modifications led to a weight increase of more than 1,000 lb (454 kg), and a reduction in performance. BAC delivered 110 of this final version.

By the mid-1970s, the 'high performance' T.Mk 4s were phased out from the training role with exhausted airframe lives. A small number served until 1988 on ATC and FAC training. In 1973 BAC began conversion of 70 T.Mk 3s and 107 T.Mk 5s to **T.Mk 3A** and **T.Mk 5A** standard. This involved installation of VOR and DME with modifications to achieve cockpit commonality. Both are distinguished by a small 'hook' aerial at the extreme nose. Many T.Mk 5As have been further modified by the addition of lower forward fuselage strakes, in place of tip tanks. Such aircraft were loaned to units (chiefly Phantom) for spin training. The (unofficial) designation **Jet Provost T.Mk 5B** was given to aircraft equipped with tip-tanks for navigator training at No. 6 FTS. The last four RAF Jet Provosts were retired on 20 September 1993 from 6 FTS, giving way to the Shorts Tucano. One T Mk 5 remains in the hands of the ETPS at Boscombe Down.

Exports comprised 22 **Jet Provost T.Mk 51** trainers based on the T.Mk 3 but with weapons for **Sri Lanka**, **Kuwait** and the **Sudan**, 43 **Jet Provost T.Mk 52** trainers based on the T.Mk 4 for **Iraq**, **South Yemen**, the **Sudan** and **Venezuela**, and five **Jet Provost T.Mk 55**

No. 1 FTS flew its last 'JP' course in June 1993, ending their 33-year association. No. 6 FTS followed.

trainers based on the T.Mk 5 for the Sudan. The Jet Provost has been withdrawn by all foreign operators. Venezuelan Jet Provosts were replaced by a mid-1984 EMBRAER Tucano order. Three Sudanese Jet Provost T.Mk 55s are reported to remain but are believed to be non-serviceable.

SPECIFICATION

British Aerospace (Hunting/BAC) Jet Provost T.Mk 5
Wing: span 35 ft 4 in (10.77 m) without tip tanks and 36 ft 11 in (11.25 m) with tip tanks; aspect ratio 5.84; area 213.70 sq ft (19.85 m²)
Fuselage and tail: length 33 ft 7.5 in (10.25 m); height 10 ft 2 in (3.10 m); tailplane span 13 ft 6 in (4.11 m); wheel track 10 ft 8.9 in (3.27 m); wheel base 9 ft 7.4 in (2.93 m)
Powerplant: one Rolls-Royce (Bristol Siddeley) Viper Mk 202 rated at 2,500 lb st (11.12 kN) dry
Weights: empty equipped 4,888 lb (2271 kg); normal take-off 7,629 lb (3460 kg); maximum take-off 9,200 lb (4173 kg)
Fuel and load: internal fuel 262 Imp gal (315 US gal; 1191 litres) plus provision for 192 Imp gal (230.5 US gal; 873 litres) in two non-jettisonable tip tanks; external fuel none; maximum ordnance none
Speed: maximum level speed 'clean' at 25,000 ft (7620 m) 382 kt (440 mph; 708 km/h) and at sea level 355 kt (409 mph; 658 km/h)
Range: ferry range 782 nm (901 miles; 1450 km)
Performance: maximum rate of climb at sea level 4,000 ft (1219 m) per minute; service ceiling 36,750 ft (11200 m); take-off run 1,340 ft (408 m) at normal take-off weight; take-off distance to 50 ft (15 m) 2,070 ft (631 m) at normal take-off weight; landing distance from 50 ft (15 m) 2,560 ft (780 m) at normal landing weight; landing run 1,740 ft (530 m) at normal landing weight

British Aerospace (Handley Page/Scottish Aviation) Jetstream

Jetstream Aircraft
Prestwick Intl Airport
Ayrshire KA9 2RW, UK

The original prototype of the **Handley Page H.P.137 Jetstream** flew on 18 August 1967. A pressurised third-level and executive transport, it featured a circular-section fuselage offering stand-up head-room and large elliptical passenger windows. Powered by two 965-shp (720-kW) Turboméca Astazou XVI turboprops, it had a maximum weight of 12,500 lb (5670 kg) and could seat up to 18 and cruise at 241 kt (278 mph; 447 km/h). The factory was in full production when the firm went bankrupt in 1970, but many Jetstreams were completed by Scottish Aviation, among them 26 ordered by the **RAF** as **Jetstream T.Mk 1** MEPTs (multi-engined pilot trainers). The first was delivered to No. 5 FTS in June 1973. Policy then changed and the aircraft were stored during 1974.

Following their 1977 restoration to service after storage, 12 aircraft were returned to the RAF. Eleven Jetstream T.Mk 1s are currently on strength with No. 45(R) Sqn (No. 6FTS) at Finningley and are used in the multi-engine training role for pilots destined for tankers and transports. Fourteen of the remaining RAF aircraft were transferred to the **Fleet Air Arm** in 1978, and were converted to **Jetstream T.Mk 2** standard. These aircraft are similar in configuration to the T.Mk 1, but are equipped with MEL E.190 nose radar (used in weather and mapping modes) for observer training.

After Scottish Aviation was absorbed into BAe the decision was taken in 1978 to develop an improved version of the Jetstream. The resulting **BAe Jetstream Mk 31**, the first production example of which flew on 28 March 1980, introduced 900-shp (671-kW) Garrett TPE 331 turboprop engines, driving four-bladed Dowty Rotol propellers. This variant offered field performance and improved payload capability superior to the previous Astazou-powered versions. The Jetstream Mk 31 has

proved commercially successful, with 220 deliveries by late 1991. With numerous interior configurations available, the Jetstream is an ideal candidate for various paramilitary roles such as casevac, airfield calibration and patrolling of economic exclusion zones.

The Fleet Air Arm is one of two military customers which operate specialist applications versions of the Jetstream Mk 31, procuring four **Jetstream T.Mk 3** trainers for training helicopter observers in 1986. These are operated alongside the T.Mk 2 variant by No. 750 Squadron at RNAS Culdrose. A totally updated aircraft, the T.Mk 3 features eyebrow windows above the flight deck windscreen to improve all-round view. The interior is equipped with two observer training consoles with radar indicator, Doppler and TANS computer. A Racal ASR.360 multi-mode search radar is mounted in a ventral blister. The remaining customer, the **Royal Saudi Air Force**, took delivery in 1987 of two Jetstream Mk 31 navigator trainers equipped with Tornado IDS avionics. One aircraft has since been lost on approach to Dhahran in 1989.

SPECIFICATION

British Aerospace (Handley Page/Scottish Aviation) Jetstream T.Mk 1
Wing: span 52 ft 0 in (15.85 m); aspect ratio 10.0; area 270.00 sq ft (25.08 m²)
Fuselage and tail: length 47 ft 1.5 in (14.37 m); height 17 ft 5.5 in (5.32 m); tailplane span 21 ft 8 in (6.60 m); wheel track 19 ft 6 in (5.94 m); wheel base 15 ft 1 in (4.60 m)
Powerplant: two Turboméca Astazou XVID each rated at 681 kW (913 shp)
Weights: basic empty 7,683 lb (3485 kg); maximum take-off 12,566 lb (5700 kg)
Fuel and load: internal fuel 384 Imp gal (461 US gal; 1745 litres); external fuel none
Speed: never exceed speed 300 kt (345 mph; 555 km/h);

maximum level and maximum cruising speed 'clean' at 10,000 ft (3050 m) 245 kt (282 mph; 454 km/h); economical cruising speed at 15,000 ft (4575 m) 234 kt (269 mph; 433 km/h)
Range: 1,200 nm (1,382 miles; 2224 km)
Performance: maximum rate of climb at sea level

2,500 ft (762 m) per minute; service ceiling 25,000 ft (7620 m); take-off run 1,900 ft (579 m) at maximum take-off weight; take-off distance to 50 ft (15 m) 2,500 ft (762 m) at maximum take-off weight; landing distance from 50 ft (15 m) 2,310 ft (702 m) at normal landing weight

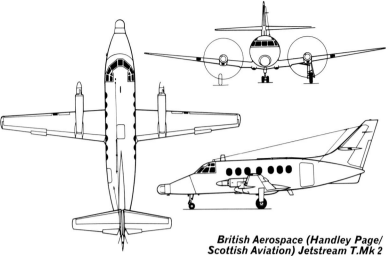

British Aerospace (Handley Page/ Scottish Aviation) Jetstream T.Mk 2

The Astazou-powered Jetstreams of No. 6 FTS (45 (Reserve) Sqn) provide multi-engined/ training for the RAF.

British Aerospace (Hawker Siddeley) Nimrod

The **Nimrod** began life as the **Hawker Siddeley 801**, a maritime reconnaissance derivative of the de Havilland Comet intended as a replacement for **RAF Coastal Command**'s ageing fleet of piston-engined Shackletons. Development began in 1964, and two unsold Comet 4Cs were converted to serve as prototypes. A MAD 'stinger' was added to the tailcone, a search radar was added in the nose, and a fin-tip radome ('football') was fitted to

While the Nimrod fleet is progressing towards retirement, it remains probably the world's most capable ASW aircraft.

accommodate ESM equipment. A new ventral weapons pannier was added beneath the cabin, giving a distinctive 'double-bubble' cross-section, these changes necessitating an increase in fin area. The first prototype was powered by the production Nimrod's intended Rolls-Royce Spey engines and made its maiden flight on 23 May 1967, serving as an aerodynamic testbed and for airframe/engine integration. The second prototype flew on 31 July, serving as the avionics development aircraft.

The first of 46 production **MR.Mk 1s** flew on 28 June 1968, entering service with No. 236 OCU in October 1969, eventually equipping five squadrons, one based at RAF

Luqa, Malta. The British withdrawal from Malta rendered the last batch of eight Nimrods surplus to requirements, although they could usefully have been used to spread hours more evenly across the fleet, extending the Nimrod's life. Five were delivered to the RAF, and the others were retained by BAe for trials, but their useful life was short, seven of them being selected for conversion to **AEW.Mk 3** standards, along with four earlier **MR.Mk 1s**. All of these airframes were effectively wasted, since the Nimrod AEW.Mk 3 never entered productive service, defeated by technical problems, and all but one were scrapped (the survivor becoming an instructional airframe).

From 1975 the 35 remaining MR.Mk 1s were upgraded to **MR.Mk 2** configuration, the first MR.Mk 2 being redelivered to the RAF in August 1979. The MR.Mk 2 had a completely new avionics and equipment suite, in which all major sensors and equipment items were changed. The aircraft received a new GEC central tactical system, based on a new computer and three separate processors for navigation systems, radar and acoustic sensors. The old ASV-21D radar is replaced by a Thorn EMI Searchwater, which now has a colour display. The acoustics system is compatible with BARRA, SSQ-41 and SSQ-53, TANDEM, and Ultra active and passive sonobuoys. Communications equipment is similarly upgraded.

The addition of inflight-refuelling probes (initially to 16 aircraft for participation in

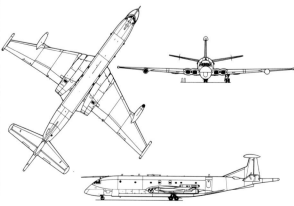

British Aerospace (Hawker Siddeley) Nimrod MR.Mk 2P

British Aerospace (Hawker Siddeley) Nimrod

Operation Corporate) changed the aircraft designation to **MR.Mk 2P** and necessitated the addition of tiny swept finlets on the tailplanes. The Falklands War also resulted in the underwing hardpoints being used by front-line Nimrods for the first time, giving the ability to carry AIM-9 Sidewinders for self-defence, or anti-ship Harpoon missiles, Stingray torpedoes, bombs or depth charges. The planned wingtip Loral ARI.18240/1 ESM pods were added later, these requiring larger rectangular finlets. All aircraft now have both refuelling probes and ESM pods. For operations from Seeb in Oman, during Operation Desert Storm, a

number of aircraft were drawn from Nos 120 (lead), 42 and 206 Sqns to form the Nimrod MR Detachment. Several were modified to what was (unofficially) referred to as **Nimrod MR.Mk 2P(GM)** (Gulf Mod) through the addition of an underwing FLIR turret on the starboard wing, BOZ pods and a TRD (Towed Radar Decoy).

SPECIFICATION

British Aerospace (Hawker Siddeley) Nimrod MR.Mk 2
Wing: span 114 ft 10 in (35.00 m); aspect ratio 6.2;

area 2,121.00 sq ft (197.04 m²)
Fuselage and tail: length 126 ft 9 in (38.63 m); height 29 ft 8.5 in (9.08 m); tailplane span 47 ft 7.25 in (14.51 m); wheel track 28 ft 2.5 in (8.60 m); wheel base 46 ft 8.5 in (14.24 m)
Powerplant: four Rolls-Royce RB.168-20 Spey Mk 250 each rated at 12,140 lb st (54.00 kN) dry
Weights: typical empty 86,000 lb (39010 kg); maximum normal take-off 177,500 lb (80514 kg); maximum overload take-off 192,000 lb (87091 kg)
Fuel and load: internal fuel 85,840 lb (38937 kg) plus provision for 15,100 lb (6849 kg) of auxiliary fuel in six weapon-bay tanks; external fuel none; maximum ordnance 13,500 lb (6124 kg)
Speed: maximum necessity speed at optimum

altitude 500 kt (575 mph; 926 km/h); maximum cruising speed at optimum altitude 475 kt (547 mph; 880 km/h); economical cruising speed at optimum altitude 425 kt (490 mph; 787 km/h); typical patrol speed at low level 200 kt (230 mph; 370 km/h) on two engines
Range: ferry range 5,000 nm (5,758 miles; 9266 km); endurance 12 hours 0 minutes typical, 15 hours 0 minutes maximum and 19 hours 0 minutes with one refuelling
Performance: service ceiling 42,000 ft (12800 m); take-off run 4,800 ft (1463 m) at normal maximum take-off weight; landing run 5,300 ft (1615 m) at normal landing weight

---

British Aerospace (Hawker Siddeley) Nimrod R.Mk 1

In addition to the 46 Nimrod MR.Mk 1s ordered as Shackleton replacements, three further aircraft (XW664-666) were ordered as replacements for No. 51 Squadron's specially modified intelligence-gathering Comets and Canberras. This role had never been formally admitted, and references to the squadron (which still shuns publicity) usually described it as a calibration unit. The three aircraft were designated **Nimrod R.Mk 1** and were delivered to RAF Wyton for fitting out in 1971. Security surrounding the aircraft was such that they were delivered as little more than empty shells, the RAF then fitting virtually all mission equipment. As a result, flight trials did not begin until late 1973, and the first operational flight took place on 3 May 1974. On 10 May 1974 the type was formally commissioned, bringing the Comet era to a close. A handful of Canberras remained on charge until mid-1976, and there are persistent rumours that the squadron 'borrowed' other Canberras for many years following.

Initially the Nimrod R.Mk 1s differed from their maritime cousins in having no MAD tailboom and no searchlight, instead having dielectric radomes in the nose of each

external wing tank and on the tail. The aircraft have been progressively modified since they were introduced, gaining more and more antennas above and below the fuselage and wing tanks, as well as Loral ARI.18240/1 wingtips ESM pods. With inflight-refuelling probes (first fitted to XW664 just before the Falklands War) the designation changed to **Nimrod R.Mk 1P**. Increased equipment has led to the deletion of several cabin windows, and in recent years the aircraft have started carrying underwing chaff/flare dispensers.

The main receivers cover the widest possible range of frequencies, with DF (direction finding) and ranging, and are thus able to record and locate the source of hostile radar and radio emissions. The aircraft almost certainly have a computerised 'threat library', allowing a detailed 'map' of potential enemy radar stations, navaids and air defence systems to be built up. Emissions from hostile fighters can also be recorded and analysed. During Cold War operations, the aircraft frequently operated in international airspace around the peripheries of the Soviet Union, necessitating extremely accurate navigation. One LORAN towel rail

antenna has thus been removed, and the aircraft has received a Delco AN/ASN-119 Carousel Mk IVA INS. The ASV21 nose radar was replaced by an EKCO 290 weather radar during the early 1980s. The Nimrod's predecessors are believed to have made 'feints' at Soviet airspace to provoke a reaction which could then be recorded.

Occasional reports of No. 51 Squadron's aircrew retiring, or reaching a landmark number of flying hours, sometimes appear in the *RAF News*, and from such reports an intriguing picture begins to emerge. The Nimrod R.Mk 1Ps seem to fly with very large crews (26-28 seems by no means extraordinary), the majority obviously being equipment operators. Most of the aircrew are extremely experienced, and are obviously hand-picked for their skill and discretion.

No. 51 Sqn gained a Battle Honour after the Falklands War in 1982 and, more recently, the squadron commander confirmed in a book that his three aircraft had operated from RAF Akrotiri in support of Operations Granby and Desert Storm, but maintained the fiction that this support took the form of radar and radio aid calibration. Daily newspapers have been more accurate, if a little sensationalist in tone, describing the aircraft as 'GCHQ's secret squadron of Nimrods', 'funded by the Foreign Office'. Other speculation has included the contention that R.Mk 1s operated from Chilean or Brazilian bases during the Falklands War. The low utilisation and lack of low-level flying has ensured that the Nimrod R.Mk 1s have not suffered the same corrosion and fatigue problems as the MR.Mk 2s, and they have a long life ahead of them.

The three Nimrod R.Mk 1s of No. 51 Sqn will leave their Wyton home for Waddington in 1995. The RAF's EW/AEW force will be centred at that base.

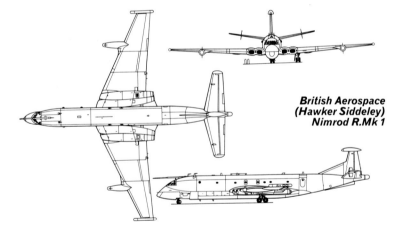

British Aerospace (Hawker Siddeley) Nimrod R.Mk 1

British Aerospace (BAC) One-Eleven

Developed as a company-funded venture by the newly formed British Aircraft Corporation, the **BAC One-Eleven** was planned as a short-haul airliner to succeed the Vickers Viscount. Launched on the basis of an order for 10 aircraft from British United, it first flew in August 1963. The basic design was entirely conventional, with two of the newly developed Spey engines mounted on the rear of a circular-section fuselage with small elliptical passenger windows and seating for 65 to 89 passengers who board via a stairway under the tail. Features included manual ailerons but powered tail surfaces, short undercarriage, engine bleed-air de-icing of wings and tail, thrust reversers and a gas-turbine APU (auxiliary power unit) in the tailcone.

Almost all production went to commercial operators. BAC built 56 **Series 200,** nine **Series 300,** 69 **Series 400** (origi-

nally developed for the US market), nine **Series 475** specially equipped for operations from short unpaved airstrips, and 87 of the stretched **Series 500** seating up to 109. All production has now been transferred to ROMAERO SA (formerly IAv Bucuresti) in Romania, where the **Rombac One-Eleven Series 495** and stretched **Series 560** were produced until 1991 for use within Romania and for export. A corresponding programme permits licence production of Rolls-Royce Spey engines. Romanian One-Eleven versions have been equipped with engine hushkits to enable the ageing One-Eleven to meet more stringent noise requirements. One of the first Romanian-assembled aircraft (at that time, 1984, still incorporating British parts) was used as a VIP transport by the Romanian President. This aircraft has since been withdrawn from service.

There are also mixed-traffic and cargo versions, and one of the few military customers, the **Royal Air Force of Oman,** continues to operate three **Series 485**s with forward freight doors, quick-change

interiors and rough-field capability. Two early Series 217s had a long career with No. 34 (VIP) Squadron, RAAF, at Canberra. Disposal of these aircraft was arranged in January 1990. Two Series 423s were delivered to the Brazilian air force in 1969 and were subsequently sold to civilian operators. A specially modified variant of the Series 475 was offered to Japan as replacement for

RAE (now DRA) One-Elevens have been heavily used as radar testbeds and played a major part in development of the EFA's Ferranti-built ECR-90, flying from Prestwick.

the NAMC YS-11. Known as the **Series 670**, this (eventually unproduced) version featured extended wingtips and modified flaps to meet the requirement for 1,220-m (4,000-ft) field capability.

A handful of former One-Eleven airliners have been acquired for the MoD. One **Series 479** (ZE432) is on strength with the Empire Test Pilots School for training purposes, where it has replaced the Vickers Viscount for heavy type handling. The Defence Research Agency operates two One-Elevens (XX105, XX919) for a variety of

test purposes. One Series 479 (ZE433) has been fitted with Sea Harrier FRS.Mk 2 Blue Vixen radar in the nose. Similarly, a BAC One-Eleven **Series 401** (N162W) was acquired in 1989 by Westinghouse for YF-23 systems integration. Northrop and McDonnell Douglas, the prime contractors for the YF-23, built a complete prototype avionics system. The avionics systems, comprising radar, infra-red search-and-track (IRST) system and electronic warfare suite, successfully demonstrated their ability to track real targets.

SPECIFICATION

British Aerospace (BAC) One-Eleven Series 479
Wing: span 93 ft 6 in (28.50 m)
Fuselage and tail: length 93 ft 6 in (28.50 m); height 24 ft 6 in (7.47 m); tailplane span 29 ft 6 in (8.99 m); wheel base 33 ft 1 in (10.08 m)
Powerplant: two Rolls-Royce Spey Mk 512 DW each rated at 12,550 lb (55.8 kN) dry
Weights: operating empty 51,731 lb (23464 kg); maximum take-off 98,500 lb (44,678 kg)
Fuel and load: internal fuel 3,080 Imp gal (3,700 US gal;

14006 litres); external fuel none; maximum payload 21,269 lb (9647 kg)
Speed: maximum cruising speed 470 kt (541 mph; 871 km/h); economical cruising speed 400 kt (461 mph; 742 km/h); stalling speed 111 kt (128 mph; 206 km/h)
Range: still air with maximum fuel and reserves 1,985 nm (2,285 miles; 3677 km)

Northrop relied on this BAC One-Eleven for systems development on the YF-23 ATF programme, whereas the (successful) YF-22 partners used the Boeing 757 prototype.

British Aerospace Sea Harrier FRS.Mk 1

Developed from the world's first and, at that time, only V/STOL fighter for the RAF, the **BAe Sea Harrier** fortuitously filled the gap left by the phase-out of the Phantom FGR.Mk 2 and the 1979 decommissioning of HMS *Ark Royal*, the last conventional Royal Navy carrier. It coincided with the introduction of a new generation of small, 20,000-ton ASW carriers. These were intended to embark only helicopters, and the Sea Harrier was instrumental in retaining some fixed-wing strike capability when the entire Fleet Air Arm was otherwise destined to become an all-helicopter force. Concurrent with the Navy taking delivery of HMS *Invincible*, dubbed a 'through deck cruiser' rather than an aircraft-carrier to get it past UK Treasury scrutiny, the Sea Harrier became one of the most important types ever procured by the FAA. Conflict in the Falklands was to prove the prudency of the decision to adopt the Sea Harrier.

Although a Harrier, in P.1127 form, had landed aboard *Ark Royal* as early as 8 February 1963, the RN evinced little interest in the programme despite the manufacturer's assurances that the engineering changes required to produce a navalised Harrier would be minimal. Navy interest gradually increased, spurred by the knowledge that no other fixed-wing aircraft could be ordered, and by a series of successful Harrier test deployments from seagoing platforms. This culminated in May 1975 in an initial order for 24 **Sea Harrier FRS.Mk 1**s and a single **T.Mk 4A** trainer, followed by a further 10 FRS.Mk 1s in May 1978. The designation reflected the Sea Harrier's dual capability as a fleet defence fighter, reconnaissance platform and strike aircraft. On 31 March 1980, the trials unit (No. 700A Sqn), was redesignated No. 899 Sqn as the HQ unit. On the same day No. 800 Sqn formed, with four aircraft, aboard HMS *Invincible*.

The main differences between the Harrier GR.Mk 3 (described separately) and Sea Harrier were the latter's front fuselage contours, with a painted radome covering a Ferranti Blue Fox pulse-modulated radar and its associated avionics bay. The cockpit was raised 10 in (25 cm) and the canopy revised for improved pilot view. An improved Pegasus Mk 104 engine of 21,492 lb (96.3 kN) thrust was fitted. Wing pylons were stressed to take a wide variety of loads up to and including a lightweight version of the WE177 nuclear weapon. An autopilot was added, as was a revised nav-attack system and a new HUD. Magnesium was deleted from all airframe areas likely to be exposed to corrosion from salt water. Embarking aboard HMS *Hermes* in June 1981, No. 800 Sqn had by then been joined by the second Sea Harrier unit, No. 801 Sqn, which had commissioned that February. Both squadrons were subsequently deployed as

part of the RN's modest fixed-wing air assets during the Falklands conflict. The Sea Harriers served with distinction, achieving a commendable 80 per cent serviceability record in an arduous operating environment.

Expanded capability was provided for the Sea Harriers of both squadrons (and hastily reformed No. 809 Sqn) aboard *Hermes* and *Invincible* for Operation Corporate. Particularly significant was the supply of AIM-9L Sidewinders, nullifying any disadvantage the Sea Harriers suffered compared to the higher-performance equipment of the Argentinian air force. Scoring 22 confirmed victories, the Sea Harrier force lost six aircraft, all of them to causes other than aerial combat. Contributing greatly to the weapons load with which Sea Harriers were launched was the 'ski jump', an ramp fitted to carrier bows. First tested on land at an angle of 7°, it was found that a laden Harrier could use inclines of up to 13° which allowed an additional 2,500 lb (1134 kg) to be added to the MTOW. Following the South Atlantic operation, 14 Sea Harrier FRS.Mk 1s were ordered as attrition replacements and, in 1984, nine more single-seaters plus three **T.Mk 4(N)**s were added, bringing RN procurement up to 57 single-seaters and four trainers.

Combat operations had highlighted areas where the Sea Harrier could be improved, and all these have been addressed. These included the capability to carry up to four AIM-9Ls, installation of an improved radar and radar warning receiver, and stronger wing pylons to take larger-capacity drop tanks. At that time it appeared that the Soviet navy's growing carrier-building programme might require NATO-assigned forces to be capable of launching ever more powerful AAMs to block any threat posed by low-flying bombers. An important addition to the Sea Harrier's inventory in this combat scenario was a current-generation fire-and-forget missile. These coincided with a mid-life update for the Sea Harrier, and the majority of the improvements recommended for the FRS.Mk 1 were carried over to the new **FRS.Mk 2** (described separately).

In late 1978 the Indian navy became the second Sea Harrier operator, budgeting for up to 48 aircraft designated **FRS.Mk 51** (single-seater) and **FRS.Mk 60** (trainer). Six single-seaters and two trainers were ordered in December 1979. A second batch

After Operation Corporate, the retaking of the Falkland Islands in 1982, twin AIM-9 Sidewinder launch rails became the standard fit across the entire Sea Harrier FRS.Mk 1 force. This increase in combat effectiveness went hand in hand with the adoption of a toned-down grey scheme. During the Falklands fighting, differing hastily-applied grey colour schemes were worn.

POWERPLANT
The Sea Harrier FRS.Mk 1 is powered by a single Rolls-Royce Pegasus Mk 104, rated at 21,500 lb st (95.64 kN). This maritime version of the Mk 103 has sacrificial protective coatings on various ferrous components, and all the low-pressure and intermediate castings are also made of a different alloy.

TAILPLANE AND RWR
The Kestrel introduced the familiar extended tailplane associated with the first-generation Harriers, with its distinctive kinked leading edge. The one-piece variable-incidence tailplane incorporates 15° of anhedral. The prominent housing on the leading edge is for the Marconi ARI.18223 radar warning receiver (RWR), sensitive to emitters in the 2 to 20 GHz band. Receiver aerials are also located in the tailcone.

RADIO AND NAVAIDS
Apart from the Ferranti self-aligning platform and Decca Doppler, the Sea Harrier has UHF homing and a GEC Avionics AD 2770 TACAN, plus I-band transponder for navigation. Communications are handled by a Plessey PTR 377 U/VHF transceiver, with D403M transceiver for a standby VHF.

British Aerospace Sea Harrier FRS.Mk 1

On top of its overall dark sea grey finish, this Sea Harrier wears the checkerboard rudder markings and winged trident badge of No. 801 Sqn, shore-based at RNAS Yeovilton (known as HMS *Heron* in naval parlance). The aircraft's 'triple zilch' code signifies its assignment to the squadron commander.

MISSILES
As the first and (until the advent of the FRS.Mk 2) the only Harrier with a primary air-to-air role, the Sea Harrier FRS.Mk 1 is the only member of the family to be fitted with twin Sidewinder launch rails.

DECCA DOPPLER 72
Flush Doppler aerials serve the Ferranti HARS (Heading and Attitude Reference System), a twin gyro platform which provides greater accuracy than a normal INAS, and can be aligned on a moving deck.

COCKPIT
The cockpit of the Sea Harrier was raised to provide room 'under-floor' for avionics, this incidentally resulting in much-improved all-round view for the pilot. The canopy still slides to the rear for access.

RADAR
The Ferranti Blue Vixen multi-mode radar, as fitted to the Sea Harrier, is a development of the Seaspray search radar carried by RN Lynx helicopters, with new air-to-air modes added. It is frequency-agile and operates in the I-band. As the Sea Harrier is a single-seat aircraft, essential flight information (speed, altitude, heading) can be overlaid on the radar's CRT, saving the pilot from having to constantly scan instruments while using the radar. Blue Vixen operates in four modes: search, attack, boresight (for target ranging) and transponder identification.

of 10 single-seaters and one trainer followed in November 1985, and a third batch, ordered in October 1986, comprised seven FRS.Mk 51s and a further FRS.Mk 60. India's carriers, *Vikrant* and *Viraat*, both currently deploy a Sea Harrier/Sea King air group.

WEAPON OPTIONS

Underfuselage mounts for two 30-mm ADEN cannon, and four underwing hardpoints stressed for up to 8,000 lb (3628 kg . Nominal carrying capabilities as follows – underfuselage and inboard wing hardpoints 2,000-lb (907 kg), outboard wing pylons 650 lb (295 kg) each. Cleared for carriage of WE177 free-fall nuclear bomb (withdrawn from inventory), standard UK 1,000-lb

(454-kg) free-fall and retarded HE bombs, BAe Sea Eagle ASM, AGM-84 Harpoon ASM, Lepus flare units, CBLS 100 practice bomb dispenser and most NATO-standard bombs, rockets and flares. Air-to-air armament can comprise four AIM-9L Sidewinders on twin-rail launcher, or MATRA Magic on Indian aircraft.

OPERATORS

Fleet Air Arm: 35 in service
     No. 800 Sqn – FRS.Mk 1
     No. 801 Sqn– FRS.Mk 1
     No. 899 Sqn (OCU) – T.Mk 4A/4N

Indian Naval Aviation: 26 delivered
     INAS 300 'White Tigers'
     INAS 551 'B' Flight
     – FRS.Mk 51 and T.Mk 60

SPECIFICATION

British Aerospace (Hawker Siddeley) Sea Harrier FRS.Mk 1
Wing: span 25 ft 3 in (7.70 m) with normal tips or 29 ft 8 in (9.04 m) with ferry tips; aspect ratio 3.175; area 202.10 sq ft (18.68 m²)
Fuselage and tail: length 47 ft 7 in (14.50 m) or with nose folded 41 ft 9 in (12.73 m); height 12 ft 2 in (3.71 m); tailplane 13 ft 11 in (4.24 m); outrigger wheel track 22 ft 2 in (6.76 m); wheel base about 11 ft 4 in (3.45 m)
Powerplant: one Rolls-Royce Pegasus Mk 104 rated at 95.64 kN (21,500 lb st) dry
Weights: basic empty 13,000 lb (5897 kg); operating empty 14,052 lb (6374 kg); maximum take-off 26,200 lb (11884 kg)
Fuel and load: internal fuel 5,060 lb (2295 kg);

external fuel up to 5,300 lb (2404 kg) in two 100-Imp gal (120-US gal; 455-litre) drop tanks or two 330- or 190-Imp gal (396- or 228-US gal; 1500- or 864-litre) ferry tanks; maximum ordnance 8,000 lb (3629 kg)
Speed: never exceed speed at high altitude 716 kt (825 mph; 1328 km/h); maximum level speed 'clean' at sea level more than 639 kt (736 mph; 1185 km/h); cruising speed at 36,000 ft (10975 m) 459 kt (528 mph; 850 km/h)
Range: combat radius 400 nm (460 miles; 750 km) on a hi-hi-hi interception mission with four AAMs, or 250 nm (288 miles; 463 km) on a hi-lo-hi attack mission
Performance: maximum rate of climb at sea level about 50,000 ft (15240 m) per minute; service ceiling 51,000 ft (15545 m); take-off run about 1,000 ft (305 m) at maximum take-off weight without 'ski jump'; landing run 0 ft (0 m) at normal landing weight
***g* limits:** -4.2 to +7.8

British Aerospace **Sea Harrier FRS.Mk 2**

In refining the Sea Harrier as a more capable interceptor, while retaining its reconnaissance and strike capability, British Aerospace made some significant changes to the airframe. The company received a contract in January 1985 for project definition phase of the programme, which included two conversions of the Sea Harrier FRS.Mk 1 to **FRS.Mk 2** standard. Initially (in 1984) it was reported the MoD planned to award a £200 million contract to BAe and Ferranti to cover a mid-life update of the entire Sea Harrier fleet, but these plans were substantially revised (in 1985) to cover an upgrade of some 30 airframes. The upgrade would include Blue Vixen radar, JTIDS, AIM-120 AMRAAM provision and an enhanced RWR fit. The original BAe proposal also covered the installation of wingtip Sidewinder rails. These additions, along with several other aerodynamic refinements, were eventually cut from the project, but a kinked wing leading edge and wing fence were retained. The first of these test aircraft (ZA195) was flown on 19 September 1988, followed by the second (XZ439) on 8 March 1989. Despite the addition of an extra equipment bay and a recontoured nose to house the Blue Vixen radar which gives it more of an elongated appearance than its predecessor, the FRS.Mk 2 is actually nearly 2 ft (0.61 m) shorter overall due to the elimination of the extended pitot head probe of the earlier variant. No increase in wingspan was found to be necessary to carry additional stores, including a pair of 190-Imp gal (864-litre) drop tanks plus Hughes AIM-120 AMRAAMs (or BAe Alarms) on each of the outer pylons, although ferry tips are available to increase span to 29 ft 8 in (9.04 m).

Two pre-production Sea Harrier FRS.Mk 2s took part in sea trials aboard HMS Ark Royal in November 1990. This, the second aircraft (ZA195), was not fitted with Blue Vixen radar and carried an instrumentation pitot instead.

A Sea Harrier FRS.Mk 2 Operational Evaluation Unit formed during June 1993 at Boscombe Down, as a sub-division of No.899 Sqn at RNAS Yeovilton. Some of its aircraft wear a new darker grey overall finish.

British Aerospace Sea Harrier FRS.Mk 2

The FRS.Mk 2 cockpit introduced new multi-function CRT displays and HOTAS controls to reduce pilot workload. The FRS.Mk 2 is powered by a Pegasus Mk 106 turbofan, a navalised version of the Mk 105 as fitted to the AV-8B but with no magnesium in its construction. On 7 December 1988 a contract was awarded for the conversion of 31 FRS.Mk 1s to Mk 2 standard. On 6 March 1990 an order was placed for 10 new-build FRS.Mk 2s to augment the conversions, attrition having by that time reduced the RN's Sea Harrier inventory to 39 aircraft. A further contract in January 1994 covered 18 more FRS.Mk 2s and an additional five FRS.MK 1 conversions.

Airframes undergoing conversion are stripped down at Dunsfold, before being delivered by road to Brough for the fundamental structural work. The upgraded aircraft are then returned to Dunsfold for final assembly.

Carrier qualification trials were conducted aboard HMS Ark Royal during November 1990 and, among other favourable factors, these proved the FRS.Mk 2 capable of operating safely from a 12° ramp. The two aircraft involved in the late 1990 trials were configured as per production aircraft, although there was only one radar between the two. In order to enhance pilot conversion training, a new two-seat trainer conversion, designated **T.Mk 8N**, is to be provided with four aircraft replacing T.Mk 4Ns in 1996. Essentially a reconfigured T.Mk 4N, this variant will duplicate FRS.Mk 2 systems, apart from radar.

The primary air-to-air missile for the Sea Harrier FRS.Mk 2 will be the Hughes AIM-120 AMRAAM. A successor to the AIM-9 for the RAF (and presumably the Navy) remains undecided. Delays, particularly in successfully marrying the aircraft to the Blue Vixen radar, have already put back the FRS.Mk 2 programme by five years and increased costs by some 20 per cent. Blue Vixen was test flown in a Sea Harrier for the first time on 24 May 1990. The Blue Vixen radar (A version) has been extensively flight tested in a BAe-operated BAC One-Eleven in a 114-hour flight programme which ended in November 1987, and again in a BAe 125 (XW930) until August 1988. Another BAe 125 (ZF130) was fitted with a complete

FRS.Mk 2 cockpit in the right-hand seat and later gained a B version radar in 1989. The next hurdle to be overcome was live firing trials of the AIM-120 primary armament. Originally scheduled for mid-1991, it was not until January 1993 that the second, radar-bearing prototype (XZ439) arrived at Norfolk Virginia, aboard the new Atlantic Conveyer. The aircraft was flown ashore, refuelled and then carried on to Eglin AFB. The trials included 10 live firings against sub-scale MQM-107 drones and full-scale supersonic QF-106 drones, commencing on 29 March 1993. A serious setback occurred with the loss of one of two radar-equipped aircraft (XZ495) in a crash in the Bristol Channel on 5 January 1994.

A trials unit formed at Boscombe Down in June 1993 receiving the first production FRS.Mk 2 (XZ497), on the 21st of that month. The Sea Harrier FRS.Mk 2 'OEU', currently undertaking trials at Boscombe is an off-shoot of No. 899 Sqn. and some aircraft already wear this unit's insignia.

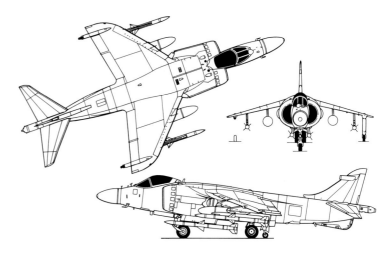

British Aerospace Sea Harrier FRS.Mk 2

SPECIFICATION

British Aerospace Sea Harrier FRS.Mk 2
generally similar to the British Aerospace Sea Harrier FRS.Mk 1 except in the following particulars:
Fuselage and tail: length 46 ft 6 in (14.17 m) or with nose folded 43 ft 2 in (13.16 m); wheel base about 12 ft 5.5 in (3.80 m)
Powerplant: one Rolls-Royce Pegasus Mk 104 rated

at 21,500 lb st (95.64 kN) dry
Fuel and load: external fuel up to 5,300 lb (2404 kg) in two 100-Imp gal (120-US gal; 455-litre) drop tanks or two 330- or 190-Imp gal (396- or 228-US gal; 1500- or 864-litre) ferry tanks; max ordnance 8,000 lb (3629 kg)
Speed: never exceed speed at high altitude 716 kt (825 mph; 1328 km/h); maximum level speed 'clean' at sea level more than 639 kt (736 mph; 1185 km/h); cruising speed at 36,000 ft (10975 m) 459 kt (528 mph; 850 km/h)

Range: combat radius 100 nm (115 miles; 185 km) on a 90-minute CAP with four AIM-120 AMRAAMs (or two AMRAAMs and two 30-mm cannon) and two 190-Imp gal (228-US gal; 864-litre) drop tanks, or 525 nm (600 miles; 970 km) on a hi-lo-hi reconnaissance mission with two 190-Imp gal (228-US gal; 864-litre) drop tanks, or 200 nm (230 miles; 370 km) on a hi-lo-hi attack mission with two Sea Eagle missiles and two 30-mm cannon, or 116 nm (133 miles; 215 km) on a hi-hi-hi interception mission with two AMRAAMs

For its detachment to Eglin, XZ439 received this ferocious sharkmouth. An AIM-120 is mounted under the starboard wing, with a Sidewinder 'tube' converted to an instrumentation pod just visible to port.

British Aerospace (BAC) 167 Strikemaster

The obvious appeal of the Jet Provost as a highly developed and economical trainer prompted BAC to develop the type into a tactical multi-role aircraft able to fly both pilot training and weapon training sorties, in addition to performing light-attack and reconnaissance roles. The **BAC.167 Strikemaster** was developed from the **BAC.145**, virtually an armed version of the pressurised Jet Provost T.Mk 5, by fitting a more powerful engine (a Viper Mk 535 developing 3,410 lb/15.2 kN thrust) and increasing the number of stores hardpoints to eight. The airframe had been strengthened several times in the course of development of the Jet Provost and BAC.145, and in the BAC.167 it was further reinforced for operations in rigorous environments.

The Strikemaster featured side-by-side Martin-Baker Mk PB4 ejection seats, short landing gear suitable for operation from rough airstrips, fuel housed entirely in integral and bag tanks in the wings and in fixed tip tanks, hydraulic spoiler/airbrake surfaces

above the wings, manual flight controls, a pressurised and air-conditioned cockpit, and comprehensive navigation and communications equipment (including VOR/ILS, DME and TACAN).

The first Strikemaster flew in October 1967 and the **Strikemaster Mk 80** series entered production a year later. Customers comprised Ecuador, Kenya, Kuwait, New Zealand, Oman, Saudi Arabia, Singapore, the Sudan and South Yemen. The final batch of new **Strikemaster Mk 90** aircraft was delivered to the Sudan in 1984, assembly of this batch having been relocated from Warton to Hurn. Sudan had previously been a customer for the less powerful BAC.145. Many Strikemasters have seen prolonged active service; for example, all 20 of the Sultan of Oman's **Strikemaster Mk 82** and **Mk 82A** aircraft have sustained battle damage. Surviving Omani Strikemasters have been fitted with LORAN navigation equipment and are distinguished by a large ventral 'towel-rack' aerial.

OPERATORS

Survivors continue to serve with the air arms of Kenya (five – refurbished Kuwaiti aircraft), Oman (13), Saudi Arabia (35) and Sudan (three). In 1988, the attack capability of the Botsawana air force was significantly enhanced with the delivery of nine ex-Kuwaiti Strikemaster Mk 83s, refurbished by BAe at Warton,

of which seven are still operational.

New Zealand's Strikemasters (colloquially known as 'Bluntys'), were finally retired by No. 75 Sqn in January 1993, replaced by the Aermacchi M.B.339C. Following replacement by Pilatus PC-9s (said by many to have been the RAF's preferred choice) and BAe Hawks, Saudi Strikemasters serve in refresher training and liaison duties. Ecuadorean Strikemasters, 16 of which were delivered to Taura-based Escuadrilla de Ataque 21, were finally retired in 1984 in favour of the EMB-312 Tucano. Singapore was also a major Strikemaster operator with 16 aircraft delivered during 1969, equipping No. 130 Sqn at Seletar. These were

The Strikemaster proved popular in Royal New Zealand Air Force service, but structural problems forced their premature retirement in 1992/93.

augmented by four former South Yemen aircraft and five from Oman. All have now been replaced by locally-assembled Agusta (SIAI-Marchetti) S.211s.

SPECIFICATION

British Aerospace (BAC) Strikemaster Mk 88
Wing: span 36 ft 10 in (11.23 m) over tip tanks; aspect ratio 6.35; area 213.70 sq ft (19.85 m²)
Fuselage and tail: length 34 ft 0 in (10.36 m); height 10 ft 2 in (3.10 m); tailplane span 13 ft 6 in (4.11 m); wheel track 10 ft 8.9 in (3.27 m); wheel base 9 ft 7.4 in (2.93 m)
Powerplant: one Rolls-Royce (Bristol Siddeley) Viper 20 Mk 525 rated at 3,410 lb st (15.17 kN) dry
Weights: operating empty 6,195 lb (2810 kg); normal take-off 10,500 lb (4762 kg); maximum take-off 11,500 lb (5216 kg)
Fuel and load: internal fuel 366 Imp gal (440 US gal; 1664 litres); external fuel up to two 75-Imp gal (90-US gal; 341-litre) and two 50-Imp gal (60-US gal; 227-litre) drop tanks; maximum ordnance 3,000 lb (1361 kg)
Speed: never exceed speed 450 kt (518 mph;

834 km/h); maximum level speed 'clean' at 20,000 ft (6095 m) 410 kt (472 mph; 760 km/h) and at sea level 391 kt (450 mph; 724 km/h)
Range: ferry range 1,200 nm (1,382 miles; 2224 km) with four drop tanks; combat radius 215 nm (247 miles; 397 km) on a hi-lo-hi close support mission with a 3,000-lb (1361-kg) warload, or 355 nm (408 miles; 656 km) on a hi-lo-hi close support mission with a 2,000-lb (907-kg) warload, or 500 nm (575 miles; 925 km) on a hi-lo-hi close support mission with a 1,000-lb (454-kg) warload, or 126 nm (145 miles; 233 km) on a lo-lo-lo close support mission with a 3,000-lb (1361-kg) warload, or 175 nm (201 miles; 323 km) on a lo-lo-lo close support mission with a 2,000-lb (907-kg) warload, or 240 nm (276 miles; 444 km) on a lo-lo-lo close support mission with a 1,000-lb (454-kg) warload, or 300 nm (345 miles; 555 km) on a reconnaissance mission
Performance: maximum rate of climb at sea level 5,250 ft (1600 m) per minute; climb to 30,000 ft (9145 m) in 8 minutes 45 seconds; service ceiling 40,000 ft (12190 m); take-off distance to 50 ft (15 m) 3,500 ft (1067 m) at maximum take-off weight; landing distance from 50 ft (15 m) 2,400 ft (732 m) at normal landing weight

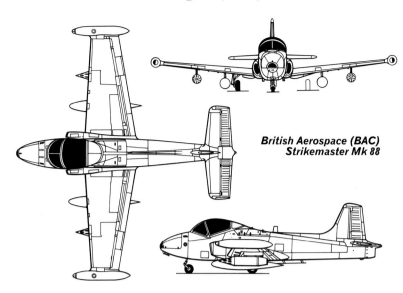

British Aerospace (BAC) Strikemaster Mk 88

British Aerospace (Vickers/BAC) **VC10**

Modification of the **Vickers (BAe) VC10** airliner into a transport gave the RAF useful passenger and cargo-carrying capacity at lower cost compared to development of a new aircraft. Meeting specification C 239 of 1960 for a strategic long-range transport for what was then Transport Command, the first military VC10s were similar to the civil Standard VC10 but had uprated Rolls-Royce Conway engines and the additional fin fuel cell of the Super VC10. Rearward-facing seats were fitted, as was a side-loading freight door and refuelling probe on the nose centreline forward of the cockpit windows. In addition, a Bristol Siddeley Artouste auxiliary power unit was located in the tailcone. As the **VC10 C.Mk 1**, the aircraft incorporated a strengthened floor and seating capacity for up to 150 passengers, or 76 stretcher cases and six medical attendants. A flight crew of four was carried.

The first RAF VC10 made its maiden flight on 26 November 1965 with initial deliveries to No. 10 Squadron at Fairford in July 1966. Subsequent procurement was five in September 1961, six in 1962 and three in July 1964. No. 10 Sqn was the sole operator of the transport version and undertook the first overseas training flight to Hong Kong in August 1966, regular route flights beginning on 4 April 1967. The squadron increased its VC10 flights to 27 a month to the Far East via the Persian Gulf, No. 10 sharing the main RAF transport base at Brize Norton with the Belfasts of No. 53 Sqn. Despite clipping 4½ hours off the flight time of the Comet and 12 hours off that of the Britannia, the VC10's Far East destinations meant a long haul of just over 19 hours to Singapore and 22 hours to Hong Kong. Carrying less than half its full payload, the VC10 had a range exceeding 5,000 miles (8047 km).

In 1978 a programme of converting VC10s to tankers to augment the Victor K.Mk 2 fleet was initiated with five ex-Gulf Air Standard VC10 Series 101s (which became **VC10 K.Mk 2**s) and four Super VC10 Series 1154s from East African Airways (**VC10 K.Mk 3**s). Carried out by BAe at Filton, the VC10 K.Mk 2/3 conversion work included the installation of extra fuel tanks in the cabin, three hose drum units (two under the wings and one in the rear fuselage) and a closed-circuit television system to enable the flight crew to monitor refuelling operations.

The first VC10 K.Mk 2s joined No. 101 Squadron at Brize Norton in May 1984, the first K.Mk 3s following in 1985. Four years later a further variant was ordered to meet Air Staff Requirements 415 and 416. These called for the conversion of five Super VC10s to short-range **VC10 K.Mk 4**s. These aircraft will be identical to the K.Mk 3 but with only the standard wing and fin fuel tankage. The first K.Mk 4 flew, after conversion at Filton, on 30 July 1993. The other current project is the upgrading of eight of No. 101 Sqn's machines to **VC10 C.Mk 1(K)** standard, retaining full passenger and freight capability but with the addition of two underwing fuel pods. BAe secured the contract and offset 40 per cent of the work to Flight Refuelling Aviation for the C.Mk 1(K)s. The K.Mk 4s will have Mk 17 and Mk 32 fuel pods, closed-circuit TV, air-to-air TACAN, avionics systems and engines of the K.Mk 3, but no cabin fuel tanks.

In 1992 it was decided to convert 13 C.Mk 1s to C.Mk 1(K) configuration under a

programme expected to last into 1995. All VC10 tankers are also to be fitted with JTIDS. Unexpectedly, No. 101 Squadron found itself preparing to go to war in August 1990, when it dispatched two aircraft to Seeb in Oman. When hostilities with Iraq began, the squadron sent further detachments to Bahrain and Saudi Arabia, all of its then-current fleet of nine VC10 K.Mks 2 and 3 eventually being committed. Primarily tasked to support RAF Desert Storm strike missions, each VC10 was able to refuel a

flight of four Tornados or Jaguars. The former required two refuellings on inbound flights and one on the return leg, and each tanker sortie usually involved the VC10 orbiting over Iraqi territory for up to one hour. Having completed 381 war sorties, No. 101 Sqn returned to the UK in March 1991 and currently remains at Brize Norton as part of No. 1 Group RAF, sharing the tanker task with No. 216's TriStar K.Mk 1s and the newly converted C.Mk 1(K)s of No. 10 Sqn. The ongoing tanker conversion programme will bring the RAF's VC10 strategic tanker force up to 27 aircraft, comprising 13 C.Mk 1(K)s, five K.Mk 2s, four K.Mk 3s and five K.Mk 4s.

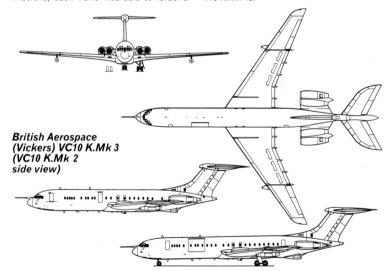

British Aerospace (Vickers) VC10 K.Mk 3 (VC10 K.Mk 2 side view)

Right: Clearly visible on the underside of this 101 Sqn VC10 K.Mk 3 are the positioning marks for the HDUs and ventral refuelling position.

Thirteen C.Mk 1s are in service with 'Shiny 10', No. 10 Squadron based at Brize Norton. They have been fitted with Loral Matador IRCM.

British Aerospace (Vickers/BAC) VC10

SPECIFICATION

British Aerospace (Vickers/BAC) VC10 C.Mk 1
Wing: span 146 ft 2 in (44.55 m); aspect ratio 7.29; area 2,932.00 sq ft (272.38 m2)
Fuselage and tail: length 158 ft 8 in (48.38 m) excluding probe; height 39 ft 6 in (12.04 m); tailplane span 43 ft 10 in (13.36 m); wheel track 21 ft 5 in (6.53 m); wheel base 65 ft 10.5 in (20.08 m)
Powerplant: four Rolls-Royce Conway RCo.43 Mk 301 each rated at 21,800 lb st (96.97 kN) dry
Weights: empty 146,000 lb (66224 kg); maximum take-off 323,000 lb (146510 kg)
Fuel and load: internal fuel 19,365 Imp gal (23,256 US gal; 88032 litres); external fuel none; maximum payload 57,400 lb (26037 kg)
Speed: maximum cruising speed 31,000 ft (9450 m)

The obvious addition of a Flight Refuelling Mk 32/2800 hose-drum unit beneath each wing points to the significant increase in capability provided for the RAF through the VC10 C.Mk 1(K) programme. All aircraft retain their transport role. The C.Mk 1 was delivered originally without a nose probe, but these (removable) units had been added by the mid-1980s.

505 kt (581 mph; 935 km/h); economical cruising speed at 30,000 ft (9145 m) 370 kt (426 mph; 684 km/h)
Range: 3,385 nm (3,898 miles; 6273 km) with maximum payload
Performance: maximum rate of climb at sea level 3,050 ft (930 m) per minute; service ceiling 42,000 ft

(12800 m); take-off distance to 35 ft (10.7 m) 8,300 ft (2530 m) at maximum take-off weight; balanced

landing field length 7,000 ft (2134 m) at normal landing weight

British Aerospace/McDonnell Douglas AV-8A/C/S Harrier

Throughout the early 1960s the US Marine Corps had an urgent requirement for an aircraft that could provide close support for amphibious landings. The choices seemed to be an armed helicopter, or ship loads of complex pre-fabricated airfield hardware, or total reliance on US Navy carriers. In 1968 the USMC evaluated the Hawker Siddeley Harrier, then still immature, and found it eminently suitable for their requirements. Plans were established to purchase 114 aircraft, designated **AV-8A**, although this was reduced to 102 and eight **TAV-8A** two-seat trainers because of the higher price of the two-seaters.

All AV-8As were built at Kingston, testflown at Dunsfold and delivered as air

freight. The first USMC production Harrier was flown on 20 November 1970 and deliveries commenced in January 1971. Allocated the Hawker Siddeley designation **Harrier Mk 50**, the aircraft initially resembled the GR.Mk 1A, with subsequent introduction of the Pegasus Mk 11 engine (which was given the US DoD designation F402-RR-402). The first 59 USMC Harriers had the FE451 nav/attack system, which was deleted and replaced by a simpler Smiths I/WAC attitude and reference heading system. In 1972 all were recycled through NAS Cherry Point to bring them to a common US standard, and without the inertial system, LRMTS laser nose or British radar warning receiver which distinguished

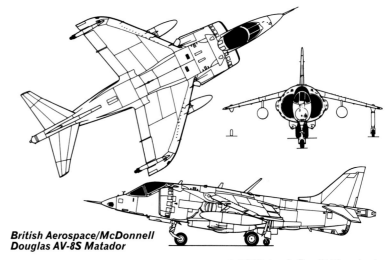

British Aerospace/McDonnell Douglas AV-8S Matador

Left: In addition to the surviving YAV-8B prototype, now serialled 704, NASA also operates this standard AV-8A, NASA 718 (N718NA). Both aircraft wear the blue and white NASA 'house colours'.

upgraded RAF aircraft. The AV-8As gained a manual fuel control (later fitted to RAF Harriers) to keep the engine running after birdstrike, and achieved clearance for US weapons including wiring and racks for AIM-9E Sidewinder AAMs (which were specified from the outset). The American Stencel SIII-S3 seat was fitted on US policy grounds, a non-toppling attitude/heading system was installed, together with tactical VHF radio using a large inclined mast aerial amidships, and the TAV-8As also received UHF for airborne command of ground forces. The Harrier equipped four USMC squadrons: VMA-513, VMA-542, VMA-231 and the conversion unit VMAT-203.

The Marines pioneered the VIFFing (vectoring in forward flight) technique, and achieved some measure of success with the relatively difficult and limited-capability AV-8A, although a large number of attrition losses occurred initially until the introduction of the trainer variant. From 1979, pending availability of a second-generation Harrier, a total of 47 aircraft (of 60 planned) was reworked to **AV-8C** standard with airframe life extension to 4,000 hours, lift-improvement devices developed for the AV-8B, Litton AN/ALR-45F radar warning receiver with wingtip and tail cone antenna, AN/ALE-39 chaff/flare dispenser, on-board oxygen generation, secure voice link and new UHF

A pair of AIM-9P-armed Armada AV-8A(S)s is here ranged on the deck of Principe de Asturias. The local designation is VA.1 Matador, but this goes largely ignored. Spanish AV-8As can carry twin Sidewinder launch rails, in the same way as FAA Sea Harrier FRS.Mk 1s, but these are rarely seen.

Spain ordered its Harriers from the US to circumvent a UK arms embargo on General Franco's regime. This is a two-seat Harrier Mk 56/TAV-8A(S).

secure radios. The F95 port oblique camera was deleted. The AV-8Cs flew alongside unconverted AV-8As until their withdrawal in February 1987, followed by the placement in storage of the last TAV-8A in November.

A Spanish naval order was placed for the AV-8A via the US government, with final assembly by McDonnell at St Louis. The purchase comprised 11 **AV-8A(S)** (Spanish designation **VA.1 Matador**) to **AV-8A Mod** standard, and two **TAV-8A(S)** (**VAE.1**) trainers, to **TAV-8A Mod** standard, again with tactical VHF. These aircraft were given the BAe designation **Harrier Mk 55/T.Mk 56** and were operated by Escuadrilla 008 from the wooden-decked carrier *Dédalo* (retired in 1988) and shore-based at Cádiz/Rota. In 1987 aircraft were rotated through RNAS Yeovilton to be fitted

with Sky Guardian RWR. Despite the introduction of second-generation **EAV-8B Matador II**s and the new carrier *Principe de Asturias*, the Arma Aérea de la Armada intends to operate its comparatively low-fatigued AV-8Ss until the mid-1990s.

SPECIFICATION

British Aerospace AV-8S (VA-1 Matador)
generally similar to the British Aerospace Harrier GR.Mk 3 except in the following particulars:

Fuselage and tail: length 45 ft 6 in (13.87 m)
Weights: empty equipped 12,190 lb (5529 kg); normal take-off 17,050 lb (7734 kg) for VTO; maximum take-off 22,300 lb (10115 kg) for STO
Fuel and load: maximum ordnance 5,300 lb (2404 kg)

British Aerospace/McDonnell Douglas **Harrier GR.Mk 5/5A**

BAe initiated independent development of an advanced Harrier during the late 1970s. This big-wing Harrier was known as the 'tin wing' Harrier due to the fact that its wing was of conventional alloy construction, and did not incorporate carbon-fibre. Purely a private venture, this wing might possibly have formed the basis of a new 'all-British' Harrier, although at that time the **RAF** was looking elsewhere for a Harrier successor under Air Staff Target 403. This sought a European combat aircraft to combine both Harrier and Jaguar roles while retaining a V/STOL capability. The requirement was revised as AST 409 in 1980, and a revised version of the tin-wing upgrade was designated **Harrier GR.Mk 5**. A working plan was proposed to retrofit 40 existing GR.Mk 3s with the new wing and build 60 more as GR.Mk 5s incorporating a new forward fuselage with a raised cockpit similar to that of the Sea Harrier.

At this point US government directives that the Harrier programme should proceed in co-operation with a foreign partner renewed the BAe and McDonnell Douglas partnership, with the British company becoming a sub-contractor rather than a full equal partner. Nevertheless, the work share offered to BAe under this new agreement was considerably larger than the entire British 'tin-wing' GR.Mk 5 programme, and it was instrumental in keeping the Harrier project alive and ensuring its continued RAF service. BAe consequently abandoned its own GR.Mk 5 and used the designation for

a licence-built version of the McDonnell Douglas/British Aerospace AV-8B Harrier II (described separately).

A 1982 agreement between the two companies led to the first 62 aircraft (two pre-series plus 60 production examples) of an initial RAF allocation of 100 Harrier IIs being test flown at Dunsfold on 30 April 1985. Numerous detail differences required by the GR.Mk 5 led to some delays in the programme, including the need to replace the newly specified Ferranti FIN 1057 INS with the original AV-8B Litton AN/ASN-130A system, to modify the tyres and ejection seats, and to fit extensions to the AIM-9L launch rails to accommodate Bofors chaff dispensers. That such seemingly minor changes could cause major problems was revealed in a 1988 inquiry which cited that £40 million extra funding had been needed to change just seven key systems from US to British equivalents. A two-year delay in RAF service entry was even more serious, and the delay would have been longer had aircraft not been accepted lacking major equipment items, including the new Royal Ordnance 25-mm cannon, Marconi Zeus ECM system and Plessey MAWS. Fortunately, other UK specific modifications were less troublesome, most notably the improved birdstrike resistance endowed by the RAF aircraft's thicker windscreen and reinforced leading edges.

Initial GR.Mk 5 deliveries to RAF Wittering for engineer familiarisation took place in May 1987, following establishment of the

Above right: A Harrier GR. Mk 3 of No. 233 OCU breaks from one of the unit's newly-delivered GR.Mk 5s, soon after the latter's introduction to service. The Harrier GR.Mk 5 originally wore this pale green finish, before adopting a darker finish.

Right: Not to be confused with Kingston's original (unflown) 'tin wing' Harrier GR. Mk 5, the British version of the AV-8B (also dubbed GR.Mk 5) made its maiden flight on 30 April 1985. The yellow primer-painted area approximates to the sections built by BAe.

British Aerospace Harrier GR.Mk 5

SPECIFICATION

British Aerospace/McDonnell Douglas Harrier GR.Mk 5

Wing: span 30 ft 4 in (9.25 m); aspect ratio 4.0; area 238.70 sq ft (22.18 m²) including 8.70 sq ft (0.81 m²) for the two LERXes

Fuselage and tail: length 47 ft 1.5 in (14.36 m); height 11 ft 7.75 in (3.55 m); tailplane span 13 ft 11 in (4.24 m); outrigger wheel track 17 ft 0 in (5.18 m)

Powerplant: one Rolls-Royce Pegasus Mk 105 rated at 21,750 lb st (96.75 kN) dry

Weights: operating empty 13,948 lb (6343 kg); normal take-off 22,950 lb (10410 kg) for STO; maximum take-off 31,000 lb (14061 kg) for STO or 18,950 lb (8595 kg) for VTO

Fuel and load: internal fuel 7,759 lb (3519 kg); external fuel up to 8,071 lb (3661 kg) in four 250-Imp gal (300-US gal; 1136-litre) drop tanks; maximum ordnance 9,200 lb (4173 kg)

Speed: maximum level speed 'clean' at 36,000 ft (10975 m) 522 kt (601 mph; 967 km/h) and 575 kt (661 mph; 1065 km/h) at sea level

Range: ferry range 2,100 nm (2,418 miles; 3891 km) with empty tanks dropped or 1,750 nm (2,015 miles; 3,243 km) with empty tanks retained; combat radius 90 nm (103 miles; 167 km) on a lo-lo-lo attack mission with a 1-hour loiter carrying 12 500-lb (227-kg) bombs, or 480 nm (553 miles; 889 km) after STO on a hi-lo-hi attack mission with seven 500-lb (227-kg) bombs, or 627 nm (722 miles; 1162 km) on a hi-hi-hi interception mission with two AIM-9 Sidewinder AAMs and two drop tanks, or 100 nm (115 miles; 185 km) for a 3-hour CAP

Performance: take-off run 1,330 ft (405 m) at maximum take-off weight; landing run 0 ft (0 m) at normal landing weight

g limits: -3 to +8

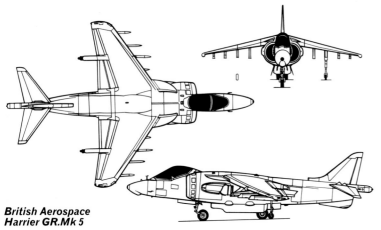

British Aerospace Harrier GR.Mk 5

Harrier Conversion Team on 1 March 1987, although delays in refining the INS and clearing the ejection seat prevented the team (later absorbed into No. 233 OCU) from beginning conversion until July 1988. No. 1 Squadron was declared operational on the GR.Mk 5 in November 1989, with No. 3 Sqn following suit in April 1990. GR.Mk 5s were also delivered to the SAOEU at Boscombe Down, for tactical and operational trials and development work.

Aircraft Nos 42-60 were completed to an interim **GR.Mk 5A** standard, with provision for GR.Mk 7 avionics, and were delivered straight into storage to await conversion to full night-attack standard. Surviving GR.Mk 5s are also being converted to the same standard. A handful of GR.Mk 5s remain with the OCU, now known as No. 20 (Reserve) Squadron at RAF Wittering (formerly 233 OCU), but are being returned to BAe for GR.Mk 7 conversion.

British Aerospace/McDonnell Douglas **Harrier GR.Mk 7**

The **Harrier GR.Mk 7** is basically the **RAF** equivalent of the night attack AV-8B, using much of the same equipment and avionics. It has the same overnose bulge housing the same GEC Sensors FLIR, but lacks the rear fuselage chaff/flare dispensers. The redundant fairing for MIRLS is

also absent, and is replaced by the definitive undernose forward hemisphere antennas for the Marconi Zeus ECM system, which will replace the USMC's AN/ALR-67 when it is finally cleared for service. The Harrier GR.Mk 7 also has an NVG-compatible cockpit, allowing use of Ferranti Night-Owl NVGs

instead of the GEC Cat's Eyes NVGs used by the USMC. A GEC digital colour map is fitted, in place of the old projected moving map. The first GR.Mk 7s ordered as such were the 34 aircraft requested during 1988, which took total RAF Harrier II procurement to 94 (plus two prototype/pre-series air-

craft). To serve as GR.Mk 7 prototypes, both pre-series aircraft were adapted to accommodate the overnose FLIR and undernose Zeus antennas, the first flying in its new guise on 20 November 1989.

The additional capability offered by the GR.Mk 7 was such that it was soon decided

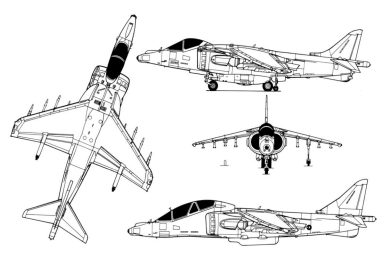

that all RAF Harriers would be retrofitted to this configuration, and to ease this process aircraft Nos 42-60 were completed as GR.Mk 5As with provision for GR.Mk 7 avionics (with an empty FLIR hump and Zeus antenna fairings) and were delivered straight to storage to await conversion. Conversions of these aircraft (and a damaged GR.Mk 5) began during December 1990, most of the former GR.Mk 5As going to No. 1 Squadron and No. 20 Squadron.

The first production GR.Mk 7 was delivered in May 1990, with service deliveries beginning in August 1990 to the Strike Attack OEU at Boscombe Down, which has used a handful of GR.Mk 7s to develop and refine operational procedures, tactics and equipment. The OEU's work has, by necessity, been largely unsung, but it has been their efforts that have enabled a much-troubled new aircraft, hampered by the non-availability of many important equipment items, to enter productive service. The unit's work with NVGs and FLIR has opened up a whole new range of possibilities for the Harrier force. Production GR.Mk 7s were delivered to No. IV Squadron (to replace first-generation GR.Mk 3s) from September 1990, and began to supplant GR.Mk 5s with No. 3 Squadron in November 1990.

From aircraft No. 77 (ZG506) all RAF Harriers have been fitted with the so-called 100 per cent LERX, which further delays the onset of wing rock and improves turn performance. These are similar to the LERXes originally designed for BAe's 'big wing' second-generation Harrier, and will replace the smaller compromise LERX on earlier aircraft by retrofit.

The failure of the MIRLS recce system designed for the Harrier GR.Mk 5 resulted in the GR.Mk 7 totally lacking any reconnaissance capability, although installation of a US Navy linescan housed in an external pod is a possible later upgrade. The Vinten Vicon 18 Srs 403 recce pod and Vicon 57 multisensor pod have also both been evaluated. When the RAF needed to replace Jaguars being used in Turkey to police the northern 'No-Fly Zone' over Iraq (Operation Warden), Harrier GR.Mk 7s were selected. In order to

Above: Harrier GR.Mk 7s were deployed to Incirlik, replacing Jaguars as part of Operation Warden in April 1993. They carried GR.Mk 3-vintage Vinten recce pods.

Right: Operation Warden aircraft are mix of GR.Mk 7s from Nos 3 and IV Sqns (which replaced Jaguars in April 1993). Up to 15 aircraft have been deployed from RAF Laarbrüch as No. 4 Composite Sqn.

give some recce capability, at least nine aircraft were rewired (at a cost of 600 man-hours per aircraft) to carry the old Harrier GR.Mk 3 recce pod, which contained only optical cameras, comprising a fan of four F95 cameras with 70-mm lenses and a single F135 with a 127-mm lens. No. IV Squadron had to hurriedly retrain in the recce role (which had been dropped when the GR.Mk 3 had been relinquished). Eight of the aircraft (all with the original 65 per cent LERX) were flown out to Turkey on 2 April 1993. Aircraft from No.IV Sqn have been fitted with the 100 per cent unit.

By the time some minor problems have been ironed out, the GR.Mk 7 will be an extremely versatile and effective aircraft. The twin Royal Ordnance Factory ADEN 25-mm pneumatically-cocked revolver cannon promises lower recoil, much faster initial rate of fire (important when firing short bursts) and lighter weight than the single GAU-12A fitted to US aircraft. The Plessey Missile Approach Warning System will automatically activate appropriate countermeasures and will augment Zeus, which consists of an indigenous RWR and a Northrop jammer and which will jam CW and pulse radars. Provision of a dedicated Sidewinder pylon (when cleared for use) will allow adequate defensive capability even when carrying a full offensive load. The eventual provi-

British Aerospace Harrier GR.Mk 7 (Harrier T.Mk 10 side view)

sion of an integral BOL chaff dispenser in these pylons will finally free the aircraft from having to 'loose' a pylon in order to carry a standard Phimat pod.

Some No. 1 Squadron aircraft have already had their FIN1075 INAS upgraded to FIN1075G standards, with the incorporation of a GPS receiver. The first aircraft so equipped (ZD437) flew with the new kit on 19 November 1992. The presence of GPS can be discerned by the addition of a small circular antenna on the aircraft spine. The armament of 1,000-lb (454kg) bombs, BL755s and 68-mm SNEB rocket pods is being augmented by CRV-7 rockets and CBU-87 cluster bombs, as used by RAF Jaguars during the Gulf War.

No. 1 Squadron received GR.Mk 7s during late 1992, and became the first front-line

unit to start night-attack training in earnest. Co-located No. 20 Reserve Squadron (the renumbered No. 233 OCU) also now flies GR.Mk 7s, while fully-equipped Nos 3 and IV Squadrons moved to Laarbrüch and the control of NATO's Rapid Reaction Force when RAF Gütersloh, Germany, closed in 1993.

SPECIFICATION

British Aerospace/McDonnell Douglas Harrier GR.Mk 7
generally similar to the British Aerospace/McDonnell Douglas Harrier GR.Mk 5 except in the following particulars:
Weights: operating empty 15,542 lb (7050 kg) including pilot and unused fuel

Left: A Harrier GR.Mk 7 of No. IV(AC) Squadron formates with one of its Harrier GR.Mk 3 siblings. As delivered, the RAF's GR.Mk 7s lacked the undernose fairing for the MIRLS (Miniature Infra-Red LineScan) provided for on the GR.Mk 5, and instead have two undernose Zeus ECM antennas and a FLIR housing above the nose. Note the lack of cannon.

Right: This No. 20 Sqn aircraft displays the '100 per cent LERX' which is being retrofitted to the entire fleet.

British Aerospace/McDonnell Douglas Harrier T.Mk 10

Having amply confirmed the usefulness of the two-seat **Harrier T.Mk 4** to expedite the demanding conversion from conventional fixed-wing aircraft to V/STOL's unique technique, the RAF sought to purchase a trainer fully representative of the second-generation Harrier GR.Mk 5/7's performance, equipment and capability. An interim solution of bringing existing T.Mk 4s up to **T.Mk 6** standard by fitting night-

attack avionics would not have fully simulated GR.Mk 5 or GR.Mk 7 performance, and was abandoned in favour of a version based on the American TAV-8B. An additional disadvantage of the T.Mk 6 was that all existing T.Mk 4 airframes are now quite old, and are becoming structurally tired. New production of two-seat first-generation Harriers would have been possible, but offered few advantages and many disadvan-

tages. A decision to proceed with what is now designated the **Harrier T.Mk 10** was taken in February 1990 and an order for 13 was confirmed early in 1992. Powered by the Pegasus Mk 105 engine, the T.Mk 10, which first flew on 7 April 1994, will be fully combat-capable with standard avionics and an ability to use a variety of weapons. In this respect it differs from its US counterpart, which carries only training armament.

SPECIFICATION

British Aerospace/McDonnell Douglas Harrier T.Mk 10
generally similar to the Harrier GR.Mk 5/7 except in the following particulars
Fuselage and tail: length 51 ft 9.5 in (15.79 m)
Fuel and load: internal fuel 7,306 lb (3314 kg)

Canadair CF-5/NF-5 Freedom Fighter

Canadair Group, Bombardier Inc., Cartierville Airport
1800 Laurentian Boulevard
St Laurent, Quebec, Canada H4R 1K2

In 1965 the Northrop F-5 was selected for what in 1968 became the NATO Canadian Forces (Air Element). Canadair Ltd at Montreal was chosen to build the aircraft under licence in two versions: the single-seat Canadair **CF-5A** and dual-control tandem-seat **CF-5D**.

Several major improvements were incorporated, the most important being uprated engines (licence-manufactured by Orenda Engines, also of Montreal) and the fitting of an inflight-refuelling probe. Soon after manufacture started, the **Royal Netherlands air force** placed an order with Canadair for 105 of the single-seater, under the local designation **NF-5A**. This had automatically-scheduled leading-edge manoeuvre flaps, Doppler navigation radar and 229-Imp gal (1041-litre) drop tanks. Manufacture involved participation of Netherlands companies but was integrated with CF-5 production, all assembly being by Canadair. In addition, four CF-5Ds, designated **VF-5**, were built for **Venezuela** in a government-to-government transaction which also included 16 ex-RCAF CF-5As.

The first CF-5A flew at Cartierville on 6 May 1968, and the type entered service with the **Canadian Armed Forces** later in the same year. The NF-5 entered Dutch service in 1969. To bring the CAF (Air Element) back up to full strength a follow-on order was placed for 20 additional CF-5Ds, and these brought the CF-5 total of all versions up to 240. The last example was delivered in 1975, the CAF designation being **CF-116**.

Replaced in the fighter-bomber role by Hornets, Canada's Freedom Fighters (14 CF-5As and 23 CF-5Ds) equip No. 419 Squadron, which functions as an advanced jet/tactical training pre-OCU unit. Detachable inflight-refuelling probes once fitted for rapid deployment/NATO reinforcement exercises now allow the aircraft to be used to teach students the rudiments of inflight refuelling.

The CF-5A can be fitted with a camera nose, containing three Vinten cameras, each with a 70-mm lens. When so fitted the aircraft are known as **CF-5A(R)s** or **CF-116A(R)s**. In Canadian service, these aircraft are retained mainly to allow a few instructors to remain recce qualified. Two-seaters cannot be fitted with the camera nose, or the inflight-refuelling probe.

After nearly 25 years' service, a comprehensive upgrade programme was authorised in 1991 by the Canadian government,

with Bristol Aerospace responsible for the two-part programme. Modified aircraft serve as lead-in weapons trainers for the CF-18 Hornet force. The first stage involves airframe refurbishment and strengthening (wings, fins, control surfaces and replacement of undercarriages) to give a progressive extension of up to 2,000 flying hours. The avionics upgrade includes a GEC-Ferranti HUD/weapons aiming system featuring Hornet symbology, Litton laser INS, GEC Avionics air data computer, MIL STD 1553B digital databus, HOTAS controls, radar altimeter and new radio. Following the maiden flight of a refurbished two-seat CF-5D on 14 June 1991, a total of 11 CF-5As and all 33 CF-5Ds are scheduled to be modified.

A number of military customers have purchased the CF-5 and NF-5 following their retirement from the active inventories of the CAF and the Dutch KLu. Of these, **Turkey** is by far the largest operator, receiving at least 60 ex-Canadian CF-5s, and additional ex-Dutch NF-5As from 1992 to augment its already substantial F-5 fleet. The **Greek** F-5 fleet has also been supplemented by some 12 ex-Royal Netherlands air force NF-5s delivered in March 1991.

Venezuela's surviving 13 CF-5As and single CF-5D have not flown since May 1990, but have been augmented by a single NF-5A and five NF-5Bs, refurbished by Fokker before delivery. The CF-5D and one CF-5A were sent to Singapore for upgrade by Singapore Aerospace, and seven more are due to be upgraded and refurbished in-country in

association with Singapore Aerospace. After upgrade, the aircraft will rejoin 36 Escuadrón. Three Venezuelan F-5s were reported destroyed when their Barquisimeto base was strafed during the 1992 coup.

SPECIFICATION

Canadair CF-5A
generally similar to the Northrop F-5A Freedom Fighter except in the following particulars:
Wing: span 25 ft 3 in (7.70 m) without tip tanks and 25 ft 9 in (7.85 m) with tip tanks; aspect ratio 3.67; area 174.00 sq ft (16.16 m2)
Powerplant: two Orenda (General Electric) J85-CAN-15 each rated at 4,300 lb st (19.13 kN) with

afterburning
Weights: empty equipped 8,681 lb (3938 kg); normal take-off 14,150 lb (6418 kg); maximum take-off 20,390 lb (9249 kg)
Speed: maximum level speed 'clean' at 36,000 ft (10975 m) 848 kt (977 mph; 1572 km/h)
Performance: maximum rate of climb at sea level 33,000 ft (19958 m) per minute; take-off run 1,900 ft (579 m) at 13,400 lb (6078 kg)

One of No. 419 Squadron's CF-5A(R)s in flight, showing to advantage its camera nose and optional inflight-refuelling probe. The three-tone grey/blue air superiority camouflage is typical of current CAF Freedom Fighters.

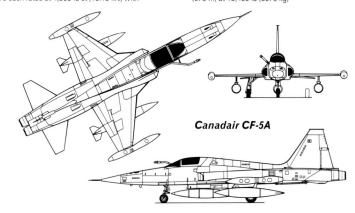

Canadair CF-5A

Canadair CL-66 (CC-109) Cosmopolitan

Canadian production of the Convair 540 began in 1960 (as the **Canadair CL-66 Cosmopolitan**) using Convair-supplied jigs and tools. It was powered by 3,500-eshp (2612-kW) Napier Eland NEl 6 turboprops. Ten aircraft for the Royal Canadian Air Force were designated **CC-109**. Eight aircraft were re-engined in 1966 with 3,750-eshp (2798-kW) Allison 501D-13

turboprops (to CV-580 standard), and were being withdrawn prematurely at Ottawa during 1994.

Six surviving CL-66s serve with No. 412 Squadron at Uplands in the VIP role, having had EFIS (Electronic Flight Instrumentation System) cockpits added in the late 1980s.

SPECIFICATION

Canadair CL-66 Cosmopolitan
Wing: span 105 ft 4 in (32.11 m); aspect ratio 12.06; area 920.00 sq ft (89.54 m²)

Fuselage and tail: length 81 ft 6 in (24.85 m); height 28 ft 2 in (8.59 m)
Powerplant: two Allison 501-D13 each rated at 3,750 ehp (2796 ekW)
Weights: basic empty 32,333 lb (14666 kg); maximum take-off 53,200 lb (24130 kg)
Fuel and load: external fuel none; maximum payload

14,300 lb (6486 kg)
Speed: maximum level speed 'clean' at optimum altitude 295 kt (340 mph; 547 km/h); maximum cruising speed at 20,000 ft (6095 m) 280 kt (322 mph; 518 km/h)
Range: ferry range 1,975 nm (2,274 miles; 3660 km) with auxiliary fuel; range 1,080 nm (1,244 miles;

1996 km) with 48 passengers
Performance: climb to 20,000 ft (6095 m) in 15 minutes 36 seconds; take-off run 4,550 ft (1388 m) at maximum take-off weight; landing run 4,020 ft (1226 m) at maximum landing weight

Canadair **CL-41 (CT-114) Tutor**

One of the first generation of pure jet aircraft designed from the outset as a trainer, the **Canadair CL-41 Tutor** side-by-side two-seat basic trainer is expected to remain in the active inventory of the Air Command of the **Canadian Forces** past the year 2000. Conceived as a private venture and adopted by the then Royal Canadian Air Force after evaluation of all contemporary Western aircraft in its category, the Tutor was first flown on 13 January 1960, two prototypes being followed by delivery of the first series aircraft on 16 December 1963. A total of 190 was built for the Canadian service and, of these, about 130 currently remain – including some in storage – all having undergone progressive avionics and equipment updating.

Allocated the service designation **CT-114**, the Tutor equips No. 2 Flying Training School at Moose Jaw. Students receive 140 hours on this type to wings standard, while future combat pilots undergo a further 60 Tutor hours. Moose Jaw is also the home of the Tutor-equipped national aerobatic team, the 'Snowbirds', and, at Winnipeg, the Central Flying School utilises the Tutor for instructor training.

Production deliveries of the Tutor to the Canadian service, completed on 28 September 1966, were followed by 20 examples of an export model, the **CL-41G**, supplied to the Royal Malaysian air force between 17 May and 30 November 1967. Dubbed **Tebuan** (Wasp) in Malaysian service, the CL-41G was a dual-role aircraft, combining training and light attack tasks. Powered by a 2,950-lb st (13.12-kN) General Electric J85-J4 turbojet, it featured six wing stations for

up to 3,500 lb (1590 kg) of ordnance. It equipped No. 9 'Jebat' (Civet) Squadron for training and No. 6 'Naga' (Dragon) Squadron for light strike duties. The Tebuan was withdrawn in the mid-1980s, as a result of fatigue and corrosion problems, although six were retained in flyable storage.

The second prototype Tutor was adapted as an experimental systems trainer under the designation **CL-41R**, and possessed a standard of avionics fit similar to the F-104G Starfighter.

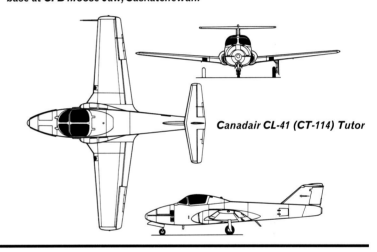

No. 2 Canadian Forces Flying Training School (CFFTS) operates the majority of Canada's surviving Tutors from its base at CFB Moose Jaw, Saskatchewan.

SPECIFICATION

Canadair CL-41A Tutor
Wing: span 36 ft 5.9 in (11.13 m); aspect ratio 6.06; area 220.00 sq ft (20.44 m²)
Fuselage and tail: length 32 ft 0 in (9.75 m); height 9 ft 3.75 in (2.84 m); tailplane span 13 ft 7 in (4.16 m); wheel track 13 ft 2.25 in (4.02 m); wheel base 11 ft 1 in (3.38 m)
Powerplant: one Orenda (General Electric) J85-CAN-J4 rated at 2,950 lb st (13.12 kN) dry
Weights: empty equipped 4,895 lb (2220 kg); normal take-off 7,397 lb (3355 kg); maximum take-off 7,788 lb (3532 kg)
Fuel and load: internal fuel 309 US gal (1170 litres); external fuel none; maximum ordnance none
Speed: maximum level speed 'clean' at 28,500 ft (8685 m) 432 kt (498 mph; 801 km/h)
Range: 541 nm (623 miles; 1002 km)
Performance: service ceiling 43,000 ft (13105 m); take-off distance to 50 ft (15 m) 2,250 ft (686 m) at maximum take-off weight; landing distance from 50 ft (15 m) 2,200 ft (671 m) at normal landing weight

Canadair CL-41 (CT-114) Tutor

Canadair **CL-215/215T/415**

Intended as a dedicated fire-fighter, the **Canadair CL-215** has served in a variety of other roles. Following its maiden flight on 23 October 1967, the aircraft was initially built in four production batches totalling some 80 aircraft. The majority of orders were for the fire-fighting variant, comprising eight Canadian provinces (49), France's Sécurité Civile (15), the **Italian air force**'s 15° Stormo (five, later transferred to a nominally civilian unit) and **Venezuela** (two equipped as passenger transports). The CL-215 was also delivered to the **Greek air force**, with 19 aircraft currently serving with 355 Mira at Elefsis, and to the former **Yugoslav air force**, the current status of whose five aircraft is uncertain. In addition, a number of aircraft fully configured for the SAR role have been delivered to the **Spanish air force** (eight of a total of 26 delivered) and the **Royal Thai navy** (two).

The aircraft is a boat-type amphibian, with two piston engines mounted on an untapered high wing. The interior may be used to carry 8,000 lb (3629 kg) of cargo, 26 passengers, or, in the fire-fighting version, two 588-Imp gal (2573-litre) water tanks (this water load weighs about 13,228 lb/6000 kg). The tanks may be replenished by retractable 'pickup probes' (similar to air inlets) on each side of the hull bottom. The

aircraft can be loaded initially with water or chemical retardants at its home base, which may be on water or a land airfield. When this load has been expended, the aircraft skims across the nearest moderately smooth body of water (fresh or salt), refilling the tanks in 10 seconds. This load is then dropped and the aircraft returns for another load. Full loads have been collected in runs across 6-ft (1.8-m) waves. In 1983 a Yugoslav CL-215 made 225 drops on fires in a single day.

When the last CL-215 (of 125 built) was delivered in May 1990 to the Greek air force, plans were already underway at Canadair for the development of a turboprop variant. Two Quebec CL-215s were modified as **CL-215T** prototypes, the first

of these making its initial flight on 8 June 1989. This version utilises the well-proven airframe of the piston-engined CL-215, but replaces scarce Pratt & Whitney R-2800 radial engines with more efficient and lighter P&W Canada PW123 turboprops. These necessitate the fitment of wingtip endplates and auxiliary finlets for increased lateral stability. Other modifications include powered flying controls, a new electrical system, pressure refuelling and an upgraded flight deck. The Spanish air force has been the sole military customer for this version, receiving a total of 15 conversion kits for the aircraft of Grupo 43 at Torrejon.

Following the receipt in 1991 of a firm order from the French government for 12 new-production aircraft, the formal launch

took place of the **CL-415**. This designation has been introduced to distinguish new-build aircraft from retrofitted CL-215Ts. First deliveries, initially in firefighting configuration, are scheduled to take place during 1994 and it is envisaged that the aircraft will then be developed for utility transport, passenger and maritime reconnaissance/ASW applications. The first CL-415 flew on 8 December 1993.

A Hellenic air force CL-215 in flight, wearing the standard bright yellow and orange colour scheme applied to most examples of this versatile twin-engined amphibian. Greek CL-215s are used primarily as water bombers.

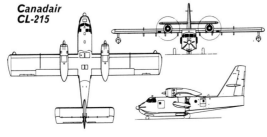

Canadair CL-215

SPECIFICATION

Canadair CL-415

Wing: span 93 ft 11 in (28.63 m); aspect ratio 8.2; area 1,080.00 sq ft (100.33 m2)

Fuselage and tail: length 65 ft 0.5 in (19.82 m); height 29 ft 5.5 in (8.98 m) on land or 22 ft 7 in (6.88 m) on water; tailplane span 36 ft 0 in (10.97 m); wheel track 17 ft 4 in (5.28 m); wheel base 23 ft 9 in (7.23 m)

Powerplant: two Pratt & Whitney Canada PW123AF each rated at 2,380 shp (1775 kW)

Weights: operating empty 27,190 lb (12333 kg) as a water bomber or 26,630 lb (12079 kg) as a utility aeroplane; maximum take-off 43,850 lb (19731 kg) as a land-based water bomber or 37,850 lb (17168 kg) as a water-based water bomber or as a land/water-based utility aeroplane

Fuel and load: internal fuel 10,250 lb (4649 kg);

Thailand's CL-215s serve with the navy's No. 2 Squadron, based at U-Tapao alongside Lake Buccaneers, GAF Nomads (Searchmasters) and Fokker F27s in the sea search, transport and surveillance roles.

external fuel none; maximum payload (waterbomber) 13,500 lb (6123 kg) or 9,770 lb (4431 kg) as a utility aeroplane

Speed: maximum cruising speed at 10,000 ft (3050 m) 203 kt (234 mph; 376 km/h); economical cruising speed at 10,000 ft (3050 m) 145 kt (167 mph; 269 km/h)

Range: ferry range 1,300 nm (1,497 miles; 2409 km) with a 1,000-lb (454-kg) payload

Performance: maximum rate of climb at sea level 1,375 ft (419 m) per minute; take-off run 2,700 ft (823 m) from land and 2,670 ft (814 m) from water at maximum take-off weight; landing run 2,210 ft (674 m)

on land and 2,180 ft (665 m) on water at 37,000 lb (16783 kg)

g limits: -1 to +3.25

Canadair **CL-600/-601 Challenger 600/601**

The Challenger business jet was designed by Bill Lear, of Learjet fame. It began life as the Learstar 600 but was to be much larger than any of his previous executive jets. Intended as a 14-seat aircraft, it would be able to accommodate up to 30 in a high-density configuration. The Learstar 600 was not built and, instead, Canadair bought the rights to the aircraft in 1976. The Canadian company carried out some extensive redesign (including the addition of a T-tail) and it was another two years before the maiden flight of the revised aircraft, known as **Challenger**. Deliveries began soon after type certification in November 1978.

The initial model, the **Challenger 600**, was powered by two 7,500-lb (33.36-kN) Avco Lycoming ALF-502 turbofans. It was followed by the **Challenger 601**, externally identifiable by its distinctive winglets and powered by uprated General Electric CF34 engines. Both variants are in military service. The first military customer was **Canada**, with an order for 12 Model 600s. Seven of these airframes were extensively re-equipped to serve as **CE-144** electronic support and training aircraft to replace the Dassault Falcon 20 (CC-117) with No. 414 Squadron at Cold Lake, Alberta, and these wear a toned-down tactical grey colour scheme. The eighth aircraft is used as an avionics and electronic systems testbed, under the designation **CX-144**.

Four further Challenger 600s are operated by No. 412 Squadron at Edmonton as VIP transports under the designation **CC-144**, wearing overall gloss white with a red

lightning flash along the fuselage. All of these Challengers have since been upgraded to **Challenger 600S** standard with the addition of winglets, but there is no associated change in their Canadian Armed Forces designation. In 1985 four Model 601s (still CC-144s) were delivered to supplement the VIP fleet.

Challenger 601s also fly missions for the Luftwaffe VIP transport unit, the FBS. The first of seven aircraft was delivered 'green' to Dornier for outfitting in 1986. Five are configured as 12-16 passenger transports, one as a passenger-cargo combi aircraft and one as an air ambulance with accommodation for stretchers. A pair of Challenger 600s serves as VIP aircraft with No. 2 Squadron of the **Royal Malaysian Air Force** at Kuala Lumpur. Three Challenger 601s have also been delivered to the **People's Liberation Army Air Force in China**.

SPECIFICATION

Canadair Challenger 601

Wing: span 64 ft 4 in (19.61 m) including winglets; aspect ratio 8.5; area 520.00 sq ft (48.31 m2) excluding winglets

Powerplant: two General Electric CF34-1A each rated at 8,650 lb st (38.48 kN) dry without automatic power reserve and 9,140 lb st (40.66 kN) dry with automatic power reserve

Weights: manufacturer's empty 19,950 lb (9049 kg); operating empty 24,585 lb (11151 kg); maximum take-off 43,100 lb (19950 kg)

Fuel and load: internal fuel 16,665 lb (7559 kg); external fuel none; maximum payload 4,915 lb

One of No. 2 Squadron, Royal Malaysian Air Force's two Canadair CL-600s, used primarily for transporting government VIPs. The aircraft thus carry a semi-military scheme, using the national flag instead of the simplified air force insignia.

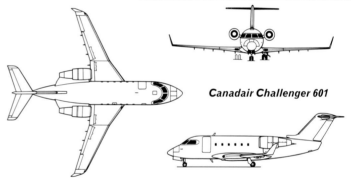

Canadair Challenger 601

(2229 kg) declining to 2,000 lb (907 kg) with maximum fuel

Speed: maximum cruising speed at optimum altitude 459 kt (529 mph; 851 km/h); normal cruising speed at optimum altitude 442 kt (509 mph; 819 km/h); economical cruising speed at optimum altitude 424 kt (488 mph; 786 km/h)

Range: 3,440 nm (3,961 miles; 6375 km) with five passengers

Performance: climb to initial cruising altitude in 21 minutes; maximum operating altitude 45,000 ft (12495 m); balanced take-off field length 5,400 ft (1646 m) at maximum take-off weight; landing run 3,550 ft (1082 m) at normal landing weight

---

Cardoen **CB 206L-III**

Industrias Cardoen LTDA, Aeropuerto Los Cerrillos Los Conquistadores 1700, Piso 28 Santiago, Chile

Industrias Cardoen in Chile initiated development in 1988 of an adaptation of the Bell 206L-III LongRanger transport helicopter (described separately) as a multi-role military helicopter. Based on imported commercial LongRangers, two prototypes of the multi-purpose **CB 206L-III** have been produced, the first of which entered flight test on 8 December 1989.

Cardoen's CB 206L-III differs from the LongRanger primarily in having a front fuselage of narrower cross-section featuring flatplate cockpit transparencies. Intended primarily as a gunship, the CB 206L-III is armed with gun or rocket pods, or anti-armour missiles mounted on pylons above the skid-type undercarriage, although it may be additionally configured for FLIR training, anti-drug patrol, crop spraying and police work.

A prototype was sent to the USA for FAA certification, under the auspices of Global Helicopter Technologies in Texas. Flight trials were successful but certification was witheld because of suspected Iraqi involvement in the programme.

SPECIFICATION

Cardoen CB 206L-III

Rotor system: main rotor diameter 37 ft 0 in (11.28 m); tail rotor diameter 5 ft 5 in (1.65 m); main rotor disc area 1,075.21 sq ft (99.89 m2); tail rotor disc area 23.04 sq ft (2.14 m2)

Fuselage and tail: length overall, rotors turning 42 ft 8.5 in (13.02 m); height overall 10 ft 3.75 in (3.14 m) to top of rotor head; stabiliser span 6 ft 6 in (1.98 m); skid track 7 ft 8.25 in (2.34 m)

Powerplant: one Allison 250-C30P rated at 650 shp

(485 kW) for take-off and 557 shp (415 kW) for continuous running

Weights: maximum take-off 4,250 lb (1927 kg)

Speed: never-exceed speed at sea level 130 kt (150 mph; 241 km/h); maximum cruising speed at 5,000 ft (1525 m) 110 kt (126 mph; 203 km/h)

Performance: maximum rate of climb at sea level 1,340 ft (408 m) per minute; service ceiling 20,000 ft (6,095 m); hovering ceiling 16,500 ft (5030 m) in ground effect and 5,400 ft (1645 m) out of ground effect

Cardoen CB 206L-III

CASA/SIAT 223 Flamingo

Construcciones Aeronauticas SA
Avenida de Aragón 404 (PO Box 193)
E-28022 Madrid, Spain

Siebelwerke-ATG (SIAT) was formed in 1952, and later became part of the MBB concern. Its first design was a four-seat touring aircraft, followed by the **SIAT 223 Flamingo**, which first flew on 1 March 1967. This all-metal side-by-side two-seat trainer had a tricycle undercarriage, and was offered in two versions, the utility **SIAT 223A1** 2+2 trainer and the single/two-seat **SIAT 223K1** aerobatic version. SIAT/MBB built 50 aircraft (including 15 for the Turkish air force) before pro-duction was transferred to Hispano (subse-quently CASA) in Spain. The first Spanish Flamingo flew on 14 February 1972 and a further 49 were built. **Syria** reportedly took 48, and about 30 are believed to remain in service for primary training.

SPECIFICATION

SIAT 223A1 Flamingo
Wing: span 8.28 m (27 ft 2 in); aspect ratio 5.96; area 11.50 m² (123.79 sq ft)
Fuselage and tail: length 7.43 m (24 ft 4.5 in); height 2.70 m (8 ft 10.25 in); tailplane span 3.20 m (10 ft 6 in); wheel track 2.75 m (9 ft 0 in); wheel base 1.82 m (5 ft 11.5 in)
Powerplant: one Textron Lycoming IO-360-C1B rated at 200 hp (149 kW)
Weights: empty equipped 685 kg (1,510 lb); normal take-off 1050 kg (2,315 lb); maximum take-off 980 kg (2,160 lb)
Fuel and load: internal fuel 220 litres (58 US gal); external fuel none; ordnance none
Speed: maximum level speed 'clean' at optimum altitude 132 kt (153 mph; 245 km/h); cruising speed at optimum altitude 118 kt (136 mph; 219 km/h)
Range: 475 nm (547 miles; 880 km)
Performance: maximum rate of climb at sea level 270 m (886 ft) per minute; service ceiling 4300 m (14,110 ft); take-off run 705 ft (215 m) at maximum take-off weight

CASA 101 Aviojet

Designed by CASA with assistance from MBB and Northrop (which provided the Norcasa wing section and inlet design) the **CASA C.101 Aviojet** has been built as a trainer and light strike aircraft, winning orders from Spain, Chile, Honduras and Jordan. A development contract was signed on 16 September 1975 covering the design, development and construction of four flying prototypes of a new jet trainer for the Spanish air force. It was intended as a replace-ment for the Hispano HA200/HA220 Saeta, and an eventual requirement for 120 was outlined. The first prototype made its maiden flight on 27 June 1977, and the last on 17 April 1978. All four were handed over to the air force for trials at the end of 1978.

The C.101 is of modular construction, to reduce cost and complexity, and ample space was deliberately left for avionics and equipment to meet any conceivable require-ment. Features include a single turbofan of high bypass ratio for good fuel economy, fed by lateral inlets above the unswept wing, stepped tandem Martin-Baker Mk 10L zero/zero ejection seats, a pres-surised cockpit with separate canopies which hinge to the right, levered-suspen-sion landing gear with a non-steerable nose-wheel, fuel contained in integral tanks in the wings and a flexible cell in the fuselage with pressure fuelling, fixed wing leading edge, slotted flaps, powered ailerons but manual elevators and rudder, and a tailplane with electric variable incidence for trimming.

The most unusual feature is that not only is there provision for underwing stores but all versions have a large fuselage bay beneath the rear cockpit in which can be housed armament (see specification) or a reconnaissance camera, ECM jammer, laser designator or other devices.

An initial contract from the **Spanish air force** covered the purchase of 60 **C.101EB-01** trainers, which were given the local designation and name **E.25 Mirlo** (Blackbird). They are powered by the 3,500-lb st (15.57-kN) Garrett TFE731-2-2J turbofan. A second contract covered another 28 aircraft, the requirement being reduced by adoption of the Chilean ENAER Pillan for basic training. Spanish C.101s are operated by the General Air Academy at San Javier and by the two squadrons of Grupo 74 at Matacan, which provide refresher flying for 'ground tour' pilots, and by trials unit Grupo 54 at Torrejon. C.101s of the Air Academy form the national 'Team Aguila' formation aerobatic display team. All aircraft received a nav/attack system mod-ernisation between 1990 and 1992.

The **C.101EB** proved to have a better-than-predicted performance at low level, but was disappointing at higher altitude. Thus the export **C.101BB** attack/trainer was powered by a TFE731-3-1J giving an extra 200 lb (0.89 kN) of thrust, and uses the aircraft's built-in provision for armament (Spanish C.101EBs have hardpoints, but these are not used). Six underwing pylons are provided for loads of up to 500 kg (1,100 lb), 375 kg (825 lb) and 250 kg (550 lb) going from wingroot to tip. The aircraft uses the underfuselage bay for quick-change pack-ages of recce pack, ECM, laser designator or twin 12.7-mm machine-gun pack, as an alternative to the DEFA 30-mm cannon pod mounted on the centreline.

The **C.101BB-02** was exported to Chile, who received four CASA-built aircraft and eight built by ENAER. All are desig-nated as **T-36** in service, and although intended for advanced training were modi-fied with ranging radar in the nose and serve as tactical weapons trainers with 1 Grupo, Ala 4 of I Brigada. A 1984 order for five further ENAER-built aircraft, with options on 23 more, is believed to have been converted to an order for **C.101CC**s. Four very similar **C.101BB-03**s were deliv-ered to **Honduras**.

The **C.101CC** first flew on 16 Novem-ber 1983 and is a dedicated attack aircraft, powered by the 4,300-lb st (19.13-kN) TFE731-5-1J engine. The engine has a mili-tary power reserve (available for periods of up to five minutes) of 4,700 lb st (20.91 kN). There is no increase in maximum weapon load, since the pylons have not been changed, but an increase in maximum take-off weight allows more fuel to be carried with a given weapon load.

The **C.101CC-02** was ordered by **Chile** as the **A-36 Halcon** (Hawk). A first example was CASA-built, and was followed by an initial 19 ENAER-assembled aircraft, which incorporated a progressively increas-ing proportion of locally manufactured sys-tems and components, which may eventu-ally include entire forward fuselages. The aircraft serves alongside the T-36 with 1 Grupo, and with 12 Grupo, Ala 3, IV Brigada. The first A-36 briefly served as a demon-strator for the proposed **A-36M**, with dummy BAe Sea Eagle missiles underwing, but this project floundered. Sixteen exam-ples of the **C.101CC-04** have also been delivered to **Jordan** to serve as advanced trainers with the King Hussein Air College at Mafraq.

On 25 May 1985 CASA flew the proto-type **C.101DD**, powered by the TFE731-5-1J engine and with new avionics, including a GEC Doppler, inertial platform and weapon aiming computer, and a Ferranti HUD. The aircraft also has HOTAS controls, an ALR-66 RWR and a Vinten chaff/flare dispenser, and is compatible with the AGM-65 Maver-ick missile. Intended as an improved trainer and light strike aircraft, the new variant has yet to attract any orders. A similar aircraft has been submitted as a contender for the **USAF/USN** JPATS requirement.

Spanish CASA C.101s are used for training, refresher flying and to equip the national aerobatic team ('Team Aguilla').

SPECIFICATION

CASA C.101CC Aviojet
Wing: span 10.60 m (34 ft 9.375 in); aspect ratio 5.6; area 20.00 m² (215.29 sq ft)
Fuselage and tail: length 12.50 m (41 ft 0 in); height 4.25 m (13 ft 11.25 in); tailplane span 4.32 m (14 ft 2 in); wheel track 3.18 m (10 ft 5.25 in); wheel base 4.77 m (15 ft 7.75 in)
Powerplant: one Garrett TFE731-5-1J rated at 4,300 lb st (19.13 kN) dry normal and 4,700 lb st (20.91 kN) dry with military power reserve
Weights: empty equipped 3500 kg (7,716 lb); normal take-off 5000 kg (11,023 lb); maximum take-off 6300 kg (13,889 lb)
Fuel and load: internal fuel 1822 kg (4,017 lb); external fuel none; maximum ordnance 2250 kg (4,960 lb)
Speed: never-exceed speed 450 kt (518 mph; 834 km/h); maximum level speed 'clean' at 20,000 ft (6,095 m) 435 kt (501 mph; 806 km/h) and at sea level 415 kt (478 mph; 769 km/h); economical cruising speed at 30,000 ft (9145 m) 354 kt (407 mph; 656 km/h)
Range: ferry range 2,000 nm (2,303 miles; 3706 km); combat radius 280 nm (322 miles; 519 km) on a lo-lo-lo interdiction mission with one cannon pod and four 250-kg (551-lb) bombs, or 200 nm (230 miles; 370 km) on a lo-lo-lo close support mission with cannon pack and four rocket launchers, or 170 nm (196 miles; 315 km) on a lo-lo-lo close support mission with cannon pack, four rocket launchers and two 125-kg (276-lb) bombs, or 325 nm (374 miles; 602 km) on a lo-lo-lo attack mission with cannon pack and two AGM-65 Maverick ASMs, or 520 nm (599 miles; 964 km) on a hi-lo-hi photo-reconnaissance mission, or 330 nm (380 miles; 611 km) on an ECM mission with a loiter of 3 hours 15 minutes, or 200 nm (230 miles; 370 km) on an armed patrol with gun pack and a loiter of 3 hours 30 minutes
Performance: maximum rate of climb at sea level 4,900 ft (1494 m) per minute at normal power and 6,100 ft (1859 m) per minute with MPR; climb to 25,000 ft (7620 m) in 6 minutes 30 seconds; service ceiling 42,000 ft (12800 m); take-off run 1,835 ft (559 m) at 4500 kg (9,921 lb); take-off distance to 50 ft (15 m) 2,460 ft (750 m) at 4500 kg (9,921 lb); landing distance from 50 ft (15 m) 2,625 ft (800 m) at 4700 kg (10,361 lb); landing run 1,575 ft (480 m) at 4700 kg (10,361 lb)
g limits: -3.9 to +7.5 at 4800 kg (10,582 lb) or -1 to +5.5 at 6300 kg (13,889 lb)

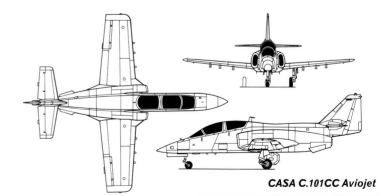

CASA C.101CC Aviojet

CASA 212 Aviocar

The dumpy **Aviocar** has developed into more than the useful light STOL trans-port conceived in Spain during the late 1960s. Intended to carry 16 equipped troops or 19 passengers, and able to load cargo rapidly via its rear ramp, the prototype flew on 26 March 1971. Production began in the following year of the **Series 100**, powered by two Garrett TPE331-5 turbo-props of 533 kW (715 shp) each. The Span-ish air force was, naturally, an early cus-tomer and eventually received 79 of this variant, mainly the **T.12B (C.212A)** trans-port, but also a few **T.12C (C.212AV)** VIP aircraft, **TE.12B (C.212E1)** dual control trainers and **TR.12A (C.212B1)** survey machines. Exports ranged between **Chile**, **Indonesia** and **Portugal**, where IPTN launched licensed production for Far East customers. Portugal has two **EC.212**s for

CASA 212 Aviocar

electronic intelligence gathering and ECM duties, these readily identifiable by their blunt noses and fin-tip pods containing antennas.

Installation from 1979 onwards of TPE331-10s rated at 679 kW (900 shp) resulted in the **C.212 Series 200**, which increases the earlier aircraft's 6500-kg (14,330-lb) maximum take-off weight to 7700 kg (16,975 lb) for normal operations or 8000 kg (17,637 lb) in military overload conditions. Spain bought three Series 200s for ECM training as the **TR.12D** and seven for SAR as the **D.3B**, The **D.3A** designation covered two T.12Bs converted for medevac. The SAR version, fitted with a prominent nose radome for an AN/APS-128 search radar (270° scan), is similar to the maritime patrol model used by **Mexico**, **Sweden** (designated **Tp 89**), **Sudan** and **Venezuela**.

Operational equipment is installed to meet individual requirements, but typically includes ESM equipment, MAD, sonobuoy launcher, sonobuoy data processing equipment, searchlight, FLIR and an underfuselage radome for 360° scanning radar. Homing torpedoes can be dropped, although no customer is confirmed as having taken up the option of Sea Skua or AS 15TT anti-ship missiles. Fisheries protection variants have less offensive equipment such as SLAR and pollution-detecting IR/UV sensors, such operators including **Sweden** and **Spain**. Transport Series 200 operators include **Abu Dhabi**, **Chad**, **Colombia**, **Djibouti**, **Equatorial Guinea**, **Ghana**, **Indonesia**, **Jordan**, **Myanmar**, **Nicaragua**, **Panama**, **Paraguay**, **Transkei**, **Uruguay**, **Venda**, **Venezuela** (navy) and **Zimbabwe**.

In **Series 300** form, flown in September 1984, the Aviocar has winglets but retains the -10 engines. The military **Series 300M**

has been bought in small numbers by **Angola**, **Bolivia**, **Bophuthatswana**, **Colombia**, **France** (**C.212C** civil version), **Lesotho**, **Panama**, **Venda** and the **US Coast Guard**, complemented by sales of the maritime patrol **300MP** to **Angola**, **Argentina** (coast guard), and the **Spanish** government. One standard transport Series 300 was modified for the **US Army** with undisclosed sensors as the prototype 'Grisly Hunter' drug interdiction aircraft; production conversions are based on the de Havilland Canada Dash 7 transport. At least four further Series 300s are used by the USAF for undisclosed missions, two operating in 1992 from Incirlik, Turkey, possibly into northern Iraq. **Chile** is also an operator but the sub-variant is not known. Sales of all C.212s had reached about 450 by 1993, including 155 Series 100s and 209 Series 200s. **Indonesia** contributed 126 to this total. Almost half have gone to civil customers.

SPECIFICATION

CASA C.212 Series 300 Aviocar
Wing: span 20.28 m (66 ft 6.5 in); aspect ratio 10.0; area 41.00 m² (441.33 sq ft)
Fuselage and tail: length 16.15 m (52 ft 11.75 in); height 6.60 m (21 ft 7.75 in); tailplane span 8.40 m (27 ft 6.75 in); wheel track 3.10 m (10 ft 2 in); wheel base 5.55 m (18 ft 2.5 in)
Powerplant: two Garrett TPE331-10R-513C each flat-rated at 900 shp (671 kW) without automatic power reserve and 925 shp (690 kW) with auto reserve
Weights: manufacturer's empty 3780 kg (8,333 lb); empty equipped 4400 kg (9,700 lb) in freight configuration; normal take-off 7700 kg (16,975 lb); maximum take-off 8000 kg (17,637 lb)
Fuel and load: internal fuel 1600 kg (3,527 lb) plus provision for one 1000-litre (264-US gal) or two 750-litre (198-US gal) ferry tanks in the cabin; external fuel

This CASA C.212-300 serves with the tiny air arm of Bophuthatswana. Other customers for this extraordinarily versatile light transport include the US Army National Guard and US Coast Guard.

CASA C.212 Series 300 Aviocar

up to 800 kg (1,764 lb) in two 500-litre (132-US gal) underwing tanks; maximum payload 2820 kg (6,217 lb)
Speed: maximum operating speed 'clean' at optimum altitude 200 kt (230 mph; 370 km/h); maximum cruising speed at 10,000 ft (3050 m) 191 kt (220 mph; 354 km/h); economical cruising speed at 10,000 ft (3050 m) 162 kt (186 mph; 300 km/h)
Range: range 1,446 nm (1,665 miles; 2680 km) with maximum standard and auxiliary fuel and a 1192-kg (2,628-lb) payload, or 907 nm (1,045 miles; 1682 km)

with maximum standard fuel and a 2120-kg (4,674-lb) payload, or 450 nm (519 miles; 1433 km) with maximum payload
Performance: maximum rate of climb at sea level 1,630 ft (497 m) per minute; service ceiling 26,000 ft (7925 m); take-off distance to 50 ft (15 m) 2,000 ft (610 m) at maximum take-off weight; landing distance from 50 ft (15 m) 1,516 ft (462 m) at normal landing weight; landing run 935 ft (285 m) at normal landing weight

---

CATIC J-9

China National Aero-Technology Import and Export Corporation
5 Liangguochang Road (PO Box 647)
Beijing 100010, People's Republic of China

The **CATIC J-9**, seen only in model form, and probably unbuilt, is an advanced tactical fighter aircraft apparently loosely based on **Mikoyan MiG-23** technology. MiG-23s were reportedly acquired from Egypt for evaluation in return for Chengdu F-7s and MiG-21/F-7 spare parts and support. The J-9 project is probably waiting for firm orders or funding prior to prototype construction. Two slightly different J-9 configurations have been observed, each with a revised wing and with quite different intakes. The J-9 seems to combine a standard MiG-23 type fuselage with a new low-set fixed delta wing and with canard foreplanes on the engine intakes. This gives the aircraft a configuration reminiscent of the Saab 37 Viggen. Compared to the standard MiG-23, the J-9 has a slightly recontoured fin, with a square top, reduced leading-edge sweep and an abbreviated dorsal fin fillet. The folding ventral fin is unchanged. One configuration (possibly the first) had a simple delta wing and retained MiG-23-type intakes with variable intake ramps, while the second introduced leading-edge root extensions of greater sweep and intakes with variable shock-cone centrebodies. Both configurations appeared to retain the MiG-23's ventral cannon pod, and carried outboard underwing fuel tanks and inboard PL-10 air-to-air missiles. Because the aircraft is as yet unbuilt, it probably has not been assigned to a particular factory (eg. Harbin, Xian or Chengdu) and is thus listed under the broad CATIC (China National Aero-Technology Import and Export Corporation).

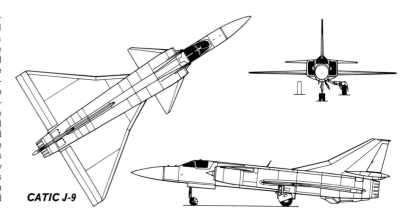

CATIC J-9

Cerva CE.43 Guépard

Cerva no longer exist

The **Cerva CE.43 Guépard** was an all-metal version of the **Wassmer 4/21 Prestige** lightplane, a four/five-seater powered by a 186-kW (250-hp) Lycoming IO-540 engine. The prototype flew on 18 May 1971, production ending in 1976 at 43 aircraft. Wassmer and Société Siren combined to form CERVA (the Consortium Européen de Realisation et de Ventes d'Avions). The French military was a customer, and 19 are still in service, most with the Centre d'Essais en Vol and one with the Aéronavale.

Cessna Model 150/152

Cessna Aircraft Company (Subsidiary of Textron Inc.)
PO Box 7706, Wichita, Kansas
67277-7706, USA

The **Model 150** was flown as a prototype on 15 September 1957, and entered production in the following August, marking Cessna's re-entry in the side-by-side two-seat lightplane market. Powered by a 100-hp (74.6-kW) Continental O-200-A, the Model 150 was built in sub-types A to N, each embodying progressive improvements (eg. the **Models 150D** and **150F** respectively introduced a cut-down rear fuselage and a swept vertical tail). Reims licence-built Models 150F to M in France (as the **F150F** to **F150M**), and a fully aerobatic version of the standard Model 150 with a strengthened airframe, the **Aerobat**. The **Model 152** was the Model 150M with a 110-hp (82-kW) Textron Lycoming O-235 engine. This, too, was licence-built by Reims and produced in an Aerobat version.

Both Models 150 and 152 were adopted by a number of air arms for primary tuition and liaison tasks. Examples of the former (both built by the parent company and Reims) are currently serving with the **Burundi** army aviation (one), the **Haitian air corps** (three), the air component of the **Iranian army** (two), the **Ivory Coast** Air Transport and Liaison Group (two), the

Paraguayan navy (four), the **Somali aeronautical corps** (four, probably grounded), the **Peruvian air force** (two) and navy (one), and the air forces of **Sri Lanka** (two of five delivered) and **Zaïre** (15).

The Model 152 at present serves with the air components of the **Botswana defence force** (two), the **Gabonese air force** (one) and the **Mexican navy** (seven). In Aerobat form it is operated by the air forces of **Bolivia** (12) and **Ecuador** (four).

SPECIFICATION

Cessna Model 150
Wing: span 32 ft 8.5 in (9.97 m); aspect ratio 6.7; area 157.00 sq ft (14.59 m²)
Fuselage and tail: length 23 ft 11 in (7.29 m); height 8 ft 6 in (2.59 m); tailplane span 10 ft 0 in (3.05 m);

wheel track 7 ft 7.75 in (2.32 m); wheel base 4 ft 10 in (1.47 m).
Powerplant: one Teledyne Continental O-200-A rated at 100 hp (74.5 kW)
Weights: empty equipped 1,000 lb (454 kg); maximum take-off 1,600 lb (726 kg)
Fuel and load: internal fuel 26 US gal (98 litres) plus provision for 12 US gal (45.8 litres) of auxiliary fuel; external fuel none; maximum ordnance none
Speed: never-exceed speed 141 kt (162 mph; 261 km/h); maximum level speed 'clean' at sea level 109 kt (125 mph; 201 km/h); maximum cruising speed at 7,000 ft (2135 m) 106 kt (122 mph; 196 km/h); economical cruising speed at 10,000 ft (3050 m) 82.5 kt (95 mph; 153 km/h)
Range: ferry range 735 nm (846 miles; 1361 km); range 420 nm (484 miles; 779 km)
Performance: maximum rate of climb at sea level 670 ft (204 m) per minute; service ceiling 14,000 ft (4265 m); take-off run 735 ft (224 m) at maximum take-off weight; take-off distance to 50 ft (15 m) 1,385 ft (422 m) at maximum take-off weight; landing distance

from 50 ft (15 m) 1,075 ft (328 m) at normal landing weight; landing run 445 ft (136 m) at normal landing weight

Cessna Model 152
generally similar to the Cessna Model 150 except in the following particulars:

Surprisingly few air forces use the Cessna 150, the most popular civilian flying club trainer, in the basic training role. These Sri Lankan 150s are used for liaison.

Powerplant: one Textron Lycoming O-235-L2C rated at 110 hp (82 kW)
Weights: maximum take-off 1,670 lb (757 kg)
Speed: maximum cruising speed at 7,000 ft (2135 m) 107 kt (123 mph; 198 km/h)
Performance: maximum rate of climb at sea level 715 ft (218 m) per minute; take-off run 725 ft (221 m)

Cessna **Model 172/T-41 Mescalero**

Cessna introduced the 150-hp (112-kW) Lycoming O-320-E2D-powered **Model 172** four-seat commercial lightplane in November 1955. A military version was procured off the shelf in July 1964 by the USAF for initial flight screening. Two hundred and four aircraft were purchased and were designated **T-41A Mescalero**. Subsequent versions based on the 210-hp (157-kW) Continental IO-360-D-powered **Model R172** were the US Army's **T-41B** (255 procured), the USAF's **T-41C** (52 procured) and the **T-41D** (238 procured) for supply under the Military Assistance Program. More than 250 T-41s remain in service with the USAF and US Army; T-41Ds, together with similar Model 172s or Reims-built **FR172**s obtained in off-the-shelf purchases, were delivered to the armed services of some 30 countries. Current operators include **Angola, Bolivia, Chile, Colombia, Dominican Republic, Ecuador, El Salvador, Greece, Guatemala, Honduras, Indonesia, Ireland, South Korea, Liberia, Nicaragua, Pakistan, Panama, Peru**, the **Philippines, Saudi Arabia, Thailand, Trinidad and Tobago** and **Turkey**. In Ireland the Cessnas, actually Reims-built **FR172H** and **FR172K Rocket**, are used in a front-line role, flying army co-operation, security

escort and border patrol duties with the Gormanstown-based Army Co-operation Squadron.

SPECIFICATION

Cessna Model 172F (T-41A Mescalero)
Wing: span 35 ft 7.5 in (10.86 m); aspect ratio 7.3; area 174.0 sq ft (16.16 m²)
Fuselage and tail: length 26 ft 11 in (8.20 m); height 8 ft 9.5 in (2.68 m); tailplane span 11 ft 4 in (3.45 m); wheel track 8 ft 3.5 in (2.53 m); wheel base 5 ft 4 in (1.63 m)
Powerplant: one Teledyne Continental O-300-C rated at 145 hp (108 kW)
Weights: operating empty 1,245 lb (565 kg); maximum take-off 2,300 lb (1043 kg)
Fuel and load: internal fuel 42 US gal (159 litres); maximum payload 980 lb (445 kg)
Speed: maximum level speed at sea level 121 kt (139 mph; 224 km/h); maximum cruising speed at 9,000 ft (2745 m) 114 kt (131 mph; 211 km/h)
Range: ferry range 556 nm (640 miles; 1030 km); range 534 nm (615 miles; 990 km)
Performance: maximum rate of climb at sea level 645 ft (196 m) per minute; service ceiling 13,100 ft (3995 m); take-off run 865 ft (264 m) at maximum take-off weight; landing run 520 ft (158 m) at maximum landing weight

Military Cessna 172s are designated T-41. This one serves with the Pakistani air force for liaison duties, though the type is also used for primary training by the air force academy.

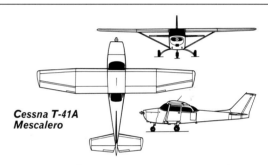

Cessna T-41A Mescalero

Cessna **Model 180/182/U-17**

Utilising the same wing as the Model 172, the Cessna **Model 180** four-seat light cabin monoplane flew as a prototype on 26 May 1952 with a 225-hp (168-kW) Continental O-470-A engine, production deliveries commencing in the following February. Manufactured in progressively improved versions (**Models 180A** to **180G**), it was also modified for the utility role (**Models 180H** to **180K**), in which form it was named **Skywagon**, seven of the **Model 130H** version being ordered under the US MAP as **U-17C**s.

The Model 180 was procured in small quantities for liaison and utility tasks by a number of armed forces. It remains in service with the **Philippine air force** (six), **Guatemala** (two), **Honduras** (one), **Nicaragua** (four), **Mexico** (three), **El Salvador** (three) and **Venezuela** (two).

The **Model 182** was introduced in 1956 and was fundamentally a Model 180 with a fixed tricycle undercarriage and a 230-hp (172-kW) Continental O-470-R engine. The

aircraft, along with the **Model 182A** production version, was named **Skylane**. In line with parent company practice, it was manufactured in progressively refined versions through **Model 182R**. This version offered a turbocharged 230-hp (172-kW) Textron Lycoming O-540-L3C5D engine in place of the Continental O-470; the Model R182 differed only by having a retractable undercarriage. The **Models 182J-L** and **Model 182N** were licence-built in Argentina by DINFIA, and the **Model 182P**, **Model 182Q** and **R182** in France by Reims Aviation as the **F182P, F182Q**, and **FR182**, respectively.

More than 30 Model 182s remain in the inventory of the **Argentine air force**; six are operated by the **Guatemalan air force**; the **Venezuelan** air force and army operate nine and three, respectively; and individual examples are flown by the **Royal Lesotho defence force**, the **Peruvian army**, and the air forces of **El Salvador** and **Uruguay**.

SPECIFICATION

Cessna Model 180 Skywagon
Wing: span 35 ft 10 in (10.92 m); aspect ratio 7.52; area 174.00 sq ft (16.16 m²)
Fuselage and tail: length 25 ft 9 in (7.85 m); height 7 ft 9 in (2.36 m); tailplane span 10 ft 10 in (3.30 m); wheel track 7 ft 8 in (2.33 m)
Powerplant: one Teledyne Continental O-470-R rated at 230 hp (171.5 kW)
Weights: empty equipped 1,560 lb (707 kg); maximum take-off 2,800 lb (1270 kg)
Fuel and load: internal fuel 65 US gal (246 litres) plus provision for 84 US gal (318 litres) of ferry fuel; external fuel none
Speed: maximum level speed 'clean' at sea level 148 kt (170 mph; 274 km/h); maximum cruising speed at 6,500 ft (1980 m) 141 kt (162 mph; 261 km/h); economical cruising speed at 10,000 ft (3050 m) 105 kt (121 mph; 195 km/h)
Range: ferry range 803 nm (925 miles; 1489 km); range 604 nm (695 miles;

1118 km)
Performance: maximum rate of climb at sea level 1,090 ft (332 m) per minute; service ceiling 19,600 ft (5975 m); take-off run 625 ft (190 m) at maximum take-off weight; take-off distance to 50 ft (15 m) 1,205 ft (367 m) at maximum take-off weight; landing distance from 50 ft (15 m) 1,365 ft (416 m) at normal landing weight; landing run 480 ft (146 m) at normal landing weight

Cessna Model 182 Skylane

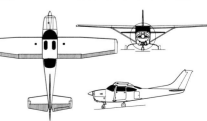

Cessna Model 185/U-17A Skywagon

Basically a strengthened **Model 180C** airframe and intended for the multi-purpose role, the **Model 185 Skywagon** light utility aircraft was first flown in July 1960. Accommodation was provided for up to six persons, and the passenger seats were removable to permit the entire cabin to be utilised for freight transportation. A glass-fibre belly cargo pod was optional, and provision was made for the attachment of skis or floats.

A total of 262 of the **Models 185B, C, D** and **E** (each of which introduced minor changes) was ordered as **U-17A**s for supply to recipients of the Military Assistance Program. These were followed by 205 **Model A185E** and **F Skywagons** with 285-hp (212-kW) Continental IO-520-D engine as **U-17B**s.

Substantial numbers of U-17As and Bs remain in military service, together with small numbers of the essentially similar Model 185 Skywagon. The largest operator is **Turkish army aviation**, with almost 100 U-17s in its inventory. These are used primarily for basic fixed-wing training, but can also be called on for FAC duties. Other army air components utilising the U-17A and/or Model 185 Skywagon are those of **Greece** and **Iran**, both of which have some 20 U-17s on strength, **Peru** with three and **Thailand** with 14. Four serve with the **Panamanian** national air service. Additional users of these Cessna utility aircraft include the air forces of **Bolivia** (12),

Nicaragua, Paraguay (three), **Peru** (three), **Philippines** (15) and **Uruguay** (eight).

SPECIFICATION

Cessna Model 185 Skywagon
generally similar to the Cessna Model 180 Skywagon except in the following particulars:
Powerplant: one Teledyne Continental IO-520-D

The Turkish army's Cessna 185s wear a businesslike olive drab colour scheme, with small patches of red to improve conspicuity. The powerful little taildragger is an excellent training aircraft, especially for pilots destined for similarly configured aircraft like the Cessna Bird Dog. The 185 can also be used in the forward air control role itself, and in the FAC training role.

rated at 300 hp (224 kW)
Weights: empty equipped 1,600 lb (726 kg); maximum take-off 3,350 lb (1519 kg)
Fuel and load: internal fuel 65 US gal (246 litres) plus provision for 19 US gal (72 litres) of auxiliary fuel; external fuel none
Speed: maximum level speed 'clean' at sea level 155 kt (178 mph; 286 km/h); maximum cruising speed at 7,500 ft (2285 m) 147 kt (169 mph; 272 km/h); economical cruising speed at 10,000 ft (3050 m) 112 kt (129 mph; 208 km/h)

Range: ferry range 899 nm (1,035 miles; 1665 km); range 573 nm (660 miles; 1062 km)
Performance: maximum rate of climb at sea level 1,010 ft (308 m) per minute; service ceiling 17,150 ft (5230 m); take-off run 770 ft (235 m) at maximum take-off weight; take-off distance to 50 ft (15 m) 1,365 ft (416 m) at maximum take-off weight; landing distance from 50 ft (15 m) 1,400 ft (427 m) at normal landing weight; landing run 480 ft (146 m) at normal landing weight

Cessna Models 206/207/210 Super Skywagon/Centurion

The Cessna **Models 206, 207** and **210** were the principal representatives of a family of light cabin monoplanes confusingly assigned non-sequential type numbers. The first of these was, in fact, the Model 210, which, flown as a prototype on 25 February 1957, was developed from the **Model 182B** with a 260-hp (194-kW) Continental IO-470-E engine and a retractable undercarriage. Progressively improved versions (**Models 210A** to **210R**) were developed, these being known as the **Centurion** from the **Model 210D**, which introduced the 285-hp (212-kW) Continental IO-520-D engine. With an optional TSIO-520 engine with turbo-supercharger, this was known as the **Turbo Centurion**, and, with cabin pressurisation, as the **Pressurised Centurion** (**P210N** and **P210R**). A few Model 210s remain in military service and are operated by the air forces of **Bolivia** (three), **Dominica** (one) and the **Philippines** (three used for weather reconnaissance).

The **Model 206 Super Skywagon**, introduced in 1964, was evolved from the **Model 205**, which, in turn, was a fixed-undercarriage version of the **Model 210C**. Like the Model 205, the 206 had internal capacity raised from four to up to six seats, power being provided by a 285-hp (212-kW) Continental IO-520-A in place of the preceding model's 260-hp (194-kW) IO-470-S.

TOGW was increased by 300 lb (136 kg) and a double cargo door was provided in the starboard side. Versions of the Super Skywagon with progressively minor changes were the **U206** to **U206E**, while the **U206F** introduced a camber-lift wing and the **U206G** was dubbed **Stationair** when fitted with a turbocharged engine.

Various versions of the Model 206 serve in liaison and utility roles with several military services, the largest operator being the air force of the **Israeli defence force** with more than 20. The **Bolivian air force** and navy possess about 10, the **Paraguayan air force** has three, **Costa Rica**'s public security air section has four, and the **Peruvian** and **Venezuelan** armies have two and four, respectively.

The **Model 207 Skywagon** was a stretched development of the **Model 206D** with an 18-in (46-cm) baggage section ahead of the windshield and a 27-in (68.5-cm) plug aft of the wing to provide for seven seats in four rows. It was initially fitted with a 300-hp (224-kW) IO-520-F engine or turbocharged TSIO-520-G, but in the **Model 207A** the optional turbocharged engine was changed to a 310-hp (231-kW) TSIO-520-M. From 1980, the Model 207A was fitted with eight seats and became the **Stationair 8**. The Model 207 is operated by the **Argentine army** (five), the

One of six Cessna U206Fs used by the French Gendarmerie in the surveillance role. They augment helicopters.

Indonesian air force (four) and army (two), and the **Paraguayan air force** (five).

SPECIFICATION

Cessna Model 206 Stationair
Wing: span 36 ft 7 in (11.15 m); aspect ratio 7.63; area 175.50 sq ft (16.30 m²)
Fuselage and tail: length 28 ft 0 in (8.53 m); height 9 ft 6.75 in (2.92 m); tailplane span 13 ft 0 in (3.96 m); wheel track 8 ft 1.75 in (2.48 m)
Powerplant: one Teledyne Continental IO-520-F rated at 300 hp (224 kW)
Weights: empty 1,710 lb (776 kg); maximum take-off 3,600 lb (1633 kg)
Fuel and load: internal fuel 65 US gal (246 litres) plus provision for 19 US gal (72 litres) of auxiliary fuel;

external fuel none
Speed: maximum level speed 'clean' at sea level 151 kt (174 mph; 280 km/h); maximum cruising speed at 6,500 ft (1980 m) 142 kt (164 mph; 264 km/h); economical cruising speed at 10,000 ft (3050 m) 114 kt (131 mph; 211 km/h)
Range: ferry range 886 nm (1,020 miles; 1641 km) with auxiliary fuel; range 695 nm (800 miles; 1287 km) with standard fuel
Performance: maximum rate of climb at sea level 920 ft (280 m) per minute; service ceiling 14,800 ft (4510 m); take-off run 900 ft (274 m) at maximum take-off weight; take-off distance to 50 ft (15 m) 1,780 ft (543 m) at maximum take-off weight; landing distance from 50 ft (15 m) 1,395 ft (425 m) at normal landing weight; landing run 735 ft (224 m) at normal landing weight

Cessna Models 208/U-27 Caravan I

The largest single-engined aircraft built by Cessna and of wholly new design, albeit retaining the classic high wing and fixed tricycle-gear configuration, the Cessna **Model 208** was the first all-new single-engined general aviation aircraft designed from the outset to be powered by a turboprop. Initially flown in engineering prototype form on 9 December 1982, the Model 208 was conceived for both civil and military roles, the military version, designated **U-27A Caravan I**, appearing in 1986. The U-27A can

accommodate a pilot and up to nine passengers, and is powered by a 600-hp (448-kW) Pratt & Whitney Canada PT6A-114 turboprop.

Intended for a range of missions that include freight delivery, logistic support, paratroop and supply dropping, medevac, electronic surveillance, forward air control, troop transportation, maritime patrol and SAR, the U-27A possesses one centreline and six wing hardpoints. It has been proposed with a 360° FLIR turret and Stinger

AAM self-defence armament to meet a USAF Special Operations Command gunship requirement. Military customers have included the **Liberian army** (one example), the **Brazilian air force** (seven) and the **Thai army** (10).

SPECIFICATION

Cessna Model 208A Caravan I
Wing: span 52 ft 1 in (15.88 m); aspect ratio 9.6; area

279.40 sq ft (25.96 m²)
Fuselage and tail: length 37 ft 7 in (11.46 m); height 14 ft 2 in (4.32 m); tailplane span 20 ft 6 in (6.25 m); wheel track 11 ft 8 in (3.56 m); wheel base 11 ft 7.5 in (3.54 m)
Powerplant: one Pratt & Whitney Canada PT6A-114 flat-rated at 600 shp (447 kW)
Weights: empty 3,800 lb (1724 kg); maximum take-off 7,300 lb (3311 kg)
Fuel and load: internal fuel 2,224 lb (1009 kg); no external fuel; maximum payload 3,000 lb (1361 kg)
Speed: maximum operating speed 175 kt (202 mph;

325 km/h); maximum cruising speed at 10,000 ft (3050 m) 184 kt (212 mph; 341 km/h)
Range: 1,370 nm (1,578 miles; 2539 km)

Performance: maximum rate of climb at sea level 1,050 ft (320 m) per minute; maximum operating altitude 27,600 ft (8410 m); take-off run 970 ft (296 m)

at maximum take-off weight; take-off distance to 50 ft (15 m) 1,665 ft (507 m) at maximum take-off weight; landing distance from 50 ft (15 m) 1,550 ft (472 m) at

normal landing weight; landing run 645 ft (197 m) at normal landing weight
g limits:: -1.52 to +3.8

Cessna **Model 305/L-19/O-1 Bird Dog**

Built as a private venture and first flown in December 1949, the Model 305 was winning contender in an April 1950 US Army competition for a tandem two-seat liaison and observation monoplane. Ordered in June 1950 as the **L-19** and named **Bird Dog**, the aircraft was redesignated **O-1** in 1962. The first production Bird Dog was rolled out in November 1950. Subsequently, a total of 2,499 of the **O-1A** version was built, a further 66 being completed as **O-1B**s for the US Marine Corps, 307 having dual controls as **TO-1D**s and the definitive series model being the **O-1E**, of which 494 were delivered. The last-mentioned variant, introduced in 1957, featured uprated equipment, and served with distinction with the USAF in Vietnam. Fuji in Japan built 14 **L-19E-1**s and eight **L-19E-2** instrument trainers after delivery of 107 ex-US Army

L-19As to the JGSDF in 1954/55, with the local name of **Soyokaze** (Breeze). Despite their age, more than 200 Bird Dogs remain in active military inventories worldwide, the principal operators being the **South Korean air force** (20), and the army air components of **Pakistan** (40), **Thailand** (28) and **Turkey** (50); other operators include **Austria** (five), **France** (two), **Indonesia** (two), **Italy** (three) and **Malta** (five).

SPECIFICATION

Cessna Model 305C (O-1E Bird Dog)
Wing: span 36 ft 0 in (10.97 m); aspect ratio 7.45; area 174.00 sq ft (16.16 m²)
Fuselage and tail: length 25 ft 9 in (7.85 m); height 7 ft 3.5 in (2.22 m)

Austrian Cessna O-1 Bird Dogs continue in the FAC role with Flieger-regiment III, operating in conjunction with Saab 105s.

Powerplant: one Continental O-470-11 rated at 213 hp (159 kW)
Weights: empty 1,614 lb (732 kg); maximum take-off 2,400 lb (1087 kg)
Speed: maximum level speed 'clean' at sea level 131 kt (151 mph; 243 km/h); maximum cruising speed

at 5,000 ft (1525 m) 90 kt (104 mph; 167 km/h)
Range: range 460 nm (530 miles; 853 km)
Performance: maximum rate of climb at sea level 1,150 ft (351 m) per minute; service ceiling 18,500 ft (5640 m)

Cessna **Model 310/320/L-27/U-3 Skyknight**

The first of the post-World War II Cessna light twins, the Cessna **Model 310** five-seater powered by 240-hp (179-kW) Continental O-470-B engines was flown as a prototype on 3 January 1953. It was to remain in production in successive versions (**Models 310** to **310R**) until 1981, a number being acquired by military services for communications and liaison tasks. The **Model 310D** introduced a swept vertical tail and the **Model 310G** featured a six-seat cabin, the latter becoming the **Model 320 Skyknight** with turbocharged TSIO-470-3 engines. Later variants such as the **Model 310P**, **310Q** and **310R** varied in detail changes and introduced more powerful engines.

The USAF contracted for 80 **Model 310A**s off the shelf for communications as the **L-27A** (later **U-3A**), these being followed by 36 **Model 310E**s as **L-27B**s (later **U-3B**s). Many of these were passed to the Army National Guard and Army Reserve, being finally withdrawn in the late 1980s. A few Model 310s remain in military

service, including **France**'s Armée de l'Air (12), the air wing of the **Tanzanian People's Defence Force** (six 310Qs), the **Colombian air force** (two), **Indonesian army** (two 310Ps), **Iranian army** (six 310Ps) and the **Venezuelan navy** (two). Individual examples serve with the air forces of **Madagascar**, **Mexico**, **Paraguay**, the **Philippines**, **Trinidad and Tobago**, and **Uruguay**. The **Ecuadorean navy** and the **Peruvian air force** each possess a single Model 320. The largest operator is the **Zaïrean air force**, with over 10 310Rs.

SPECIFICATION

Cessna Model 310L (U-3A)
Wing: span 36 ft 11 in (11.25 m); aspect ratio 7.61; area 179.0 sq ft (16.63 m²)
Fuselage and tail: length 29 ft 6 in (8.99 m); height 9 ft 11 in (3.02 m); tailplane span 17 ft 0 in (5.18 m); wheel track 12 ft 0 in (3.66 m); wheel base 9 ft 6 in (2.90 m)

Five Cessna 310s are used by Colombia's Escuadron Avanzada 613 for navigation and multi-engine pilot training.

Powerplant: two Teledyne Continental IO-470-VO each rated at 260 hp (194 kW)
Weights: empty 3.125 lb (1418 kg); maximum take-off 5,200 lb (2360 kg)
Fuel and load: internal fuel 51 US gal (193 litres) plus provision for 41 US gal (155 litres) of auxiliary fuel in two wing tanks
Speed: maximum level speed at sea level 206 kt (237 mph; 381 km/h); maximum cruising speed at 6,500 ft (1980 m) 190 kt (219 mph; 352 km/h); economical cruising speed at 10,000 ft (3050 m) 155 kt

(170 mph; 288 km/h)
Range: ferry range 1,680 nm (1,935 miles; 3114 km) with 41 US gal (155 litres) of auxiliary fuel; range 675 nm (777 miles; 1248 km)
Performance: maximum rate of climb at sea level 1.540 ft (470 m) per minute; service ceiling 19,900 ft (6065 m); take-off run ft m) at maximumtake-off weight; take-off distance to 50 ft (15 m) 1,726 ft (523 m) at maximum take-off weight; landing distance from 50 ft (15 m) 1,582 ft (482 m) at max landing weight

Cessna **Model 318B/T-37 Tweet**

The T-37 was developed to meet a 1952 USAF requirement for a jet-powered primary trainer. Two **XT-37** prototypes were ordered, and the first flew on 12 October 1954, powered by 920-lb st (4.1-kN) YJ69-T-9 turbojets (licence-built versions of the French Turboméca Marboré) in the wingroots. The aircraft had side-by-side seating for the crew under a one-piece canopy and behind a one-piece windscreen, with a central strengthening strip. Overall configuration was conventional, although the horizontal tailplane was located midway up the fin to remain clear of the jet exhaust. The manual controls had electric trimmers, while flaps and wide-track undercarriage were hydraulically actuated.

Cessna T-37Bs and T-37Cs are operated by 361 Mira in the training role. This aircraft is one of the T-37Bs acquired secondhand from the Royal Jordanian Air Force.

An initial batch of 10 **T-37A**s was followed by 524 more basic A models. The first one flew on 27 September 1955 but service entry was delayed until 1957 by the need for modifications. During 1959 production switched to the 1,025-lb st (4.56-kN) J69-T-25-engined **T-37B**, which also introduced improved navigation and communications equipment and provision for wingtip fuel tanks. A total of 466 was built, some being exported. Forty-seven were funded by the Luftwaffe but remained in the USA, in USAF markings, for training Luftwaffe pilots. All surviving T-37As were also brought up to T-37B standard through modification. From April 1961, the USAF switched to 'straight-through' jet training on the T-37, as had been planned, but high costs forced the reintroduction of a 30-hour primary phase on the T-41A in 1965. All-through jet training was briefly reintroduced, but today pilots are 'screened' on the T-41.

The T-37 was to have been replaced by the Fairchild T-46A, but this aircraft was cancelled in 1986. A proposed T-37 derivative, the **T-48**, attracted little support, and from 1989 the Sabreliner Corp. began supplying modification kits to the USAF to allow its surviving T-37s to be structurally rebuilt for extended service. Current plans call for the T-37 to be replaced by the winning JPATS contender, which may be a turbo-prop-powered aircraft.

The ultimate Tweet was never used by the USAF, instead being built for export and for Military Assistance Program and Foreign Military Sales. A total of 269 **T-37C**s were built, all incorporating provision for a limited light strike capability with a K14C gunsight, and underwing pylons (one on each wing) which could carry stores of up to 250 lb (113 kg), including a General Electric 0.5-in machine-gun pod. A survey or reconnaissance camera can be carried in the fuselage.

These T-37s wear the markings of Pakistan's 'Sherdils' aerobatic team, flown by pilots from the air academy at Risalpur. Pakistani T-37s will be replaced by a turboprop trainer and by the CNAMC K-8.

Cessna Model 318B (T-37B Tweet)

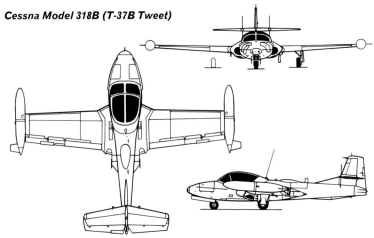

Cessna **Model 318E/A-37 Dragonfly**

A light attack derivative of the T-37 basic trainer, the side-by-side two-seat **A-37 Dragonfly** flew as a prototype (**YAT-37D**) on 22 October 1963, powered by two 2,400-lb st (10.67-kN) General Electric J85-GE-5 turbojets. Thirty-nine T-37Bs were similarly converted (with J85-GE-17A engines derated to 2,400 lb st/10.67 kN) on the assembly line to become **A-37A**s. These aircraft, like the two YAT-37Ds, featured armour protection, an internally-housed 7.62-mm Minigun, eight wing stores stations for ordnance and fuel, wingtip fuel tanks, ground-attack avionics and larger wheels and tyres.

Stressed to 6g rather than 5g, a full-production version was ordered by the USAF as the **A-37B**; this version introduced inflight refuelling capability and J85-GE-17A engines rated at 2,850 lb st (12.67 kN). Deliveries began in May 1968, with a total of 577 examples manufactured, production being completed in 1975. The A-37B could carry up to 5,680 lb (2576 kg) of bombs, rockets and stores dispensers, and at least 130 were retrospectively fitted with avionics optimised for the forward air control role as **OA-37B**s. The last USAF A-37s retired in 1992.

Both A-37B and OA-37B serve extensively with Latin American air arms. **Chile** has operated the A-37B since 1974, and has some 20 serving in operational training and light attack roles with Grupo 12 at Punta Arenas. **Colombia** has a similar number of A-37Bs and OA-37Bs with Grupo Aéreo III at Barranquilla, having flown Dragonflies since 1980. **Ecuador** has operated A-37Bs since 1976, some 10 remaining with Escuadron 2311 'Dragones' at Manta. **Guatemala**, the earliest Latin American Dragonfly operator, received its first A-37Bs in 1971, and seven remain with its

Recent deliveries of ex-USAF A-37Bs to the Fuerza Aérea Colombiana have included at least four FAC-configured OA-37Bs. All aircraft wear an effective camouflage scheme with toned-down national markings, except for a tiny national tricolour in full colour on the trailing edge of the rudder.

Escuadrón de Caza-Bombardeo at La Aurora. **Honduras** has had A-37Bs since 1975 and OA-37Bs since 1984, and has a dozen of these at La Ceiba with its Escuadrilla de Ataque. **Peru** has 16 A-37Bs remaining from 36 supplied 1975-77, these equipping Escuadrones 711 and 712 of Grupo Aéreo 7 at Piura. **Salvador** has six A-37Bs and OA-37Bs remaining from 19 A-37Bs and three OA-37Bs delivered since 1982. **Uruguay** has 15 A-37Bs with Grupo de Aviación 2 at Durazno, these remaining from some 20 received through the 1970s and 1980s.

Other current operators of the A-37B are **South Korea** and **Thailand**. The former has some two dozen ex-South Vietnamese aircraft with its 12th Fighter Wing, these having been received in September-October 1976, and the latter has a dozen A-37Bs (and ex-T-37s converted to a generally similar standard) at Ubon Ratchathani with

Squadron 211 of Wing 21. **Vietnam** holds some A-37Bs in storage, these being ex-South Vietnamese aircraft captured at the end of the Vietnamese conflict (and including some actually used operationally at the end of the war) and since unsuccessfully offered for sale on several occasions.

Thailand gained its A-37Bs in 1975, on the fall of South Vietnam, flown by fleeing pilots. This one wears a new grey scheme.

span 13 ft 11.25 in (4.25 m); wheel track 14 ft 0.5 in (4.28 m); wheel base 7 ft 10 in (2.39 m)
Powerplant: two General Electric J85-GE-17A each rated at 2,850 lb st (12.68 kN) dry
Weights: basic empty 6,211 lb (2817 kg); empty equipped 5,843 lb (2650 kg); maximum take-off 14,000 lb (6350 kg)
Fuel and load: internal fuel 3,307 lb (1500 kg); external fuel up to four 100-US gal (378-litre) drop tanks; maximum ordnance 4,100 lb (1860 kg)
Speed: never-exceed speed 455 kt (524 mph; 843 km/h); maximum level speed at 16,000 ft (4875 m) 440 kt (507 mph; 816 km/h); maximum cruising speed at 25,000 ft (7620 m) 425 kt (489 mph; 787 km/h)

Range: range with maximum internal and external fuel at 25,000 ft (7620 m) 878 nm (1,012 miles; 1628 km); range with maximum warload 399 nm (460 miles; 740 km)
Performance: maximum rate of climb at sea level 6,990 ft (2130 m) per minute; service ceiling 41,765 ft (12730 m); take-off run 1,740 ft (531 m) at maximum take-off weight; take-off distance to 50 ft (15 m) 2,595 ft (791 m) at maximum take-off weight; landing distance from 50 ft (15 m) 6,600 ft (2012 m) at normal landing weight; landing run 4,150 ft (1265 m) at maximum landing weight or 1,710 ft (521 m) at normal landing weight

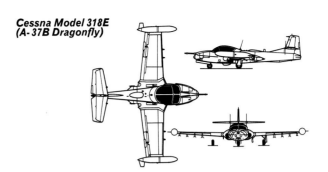
Cessna Model 318E
(A-37B Dragonfly)

Cessna **Model 337/O-2 Super Skymaster**

A development of the distinctive centre-line-thrust **Model 336 Skymaster** six-seat light twin, the **Model 337 Super Skymaster**, flown as a prototype on 30 March 1964, differed in having a retractable undercarriage and uprated 210-hp (157-kW) Continental IO-360-C engines. In December 1966, the Model 337 was ordered by the USAF for forward air control duties as the **O-2A**, with wing hardpoints for marker flares, rockets or gun pods; a total of 501 O-2As was delivered from April 1967. Thirty-one commercial Model 337s ordered off the shelf were adapted for psycho-warfare as **O-2B**s, these each having three loudspeakers and provision for leaflet dispensers.

Turbocharged Skymasters

The **Model 337B** introduced the turbocharged TSIO-360-A engine (**T337B**) as an option, and cabin pressurisation was first made available with the **Model 337G** (**P337G**). A military version developed in France by Reims Aviation (which licence-manufactured successive commercial versions as the **F337E** to **F337H**) was known as the **FTB337G Milirole**. This had four wing hardpoints and the new high-lift flaps (as part of Robertson STOL modifications) introduced with the commercial Model 337G (**F337G**). A further military version,

similarly fitted with four wing hardpoints, was marketed by Summit Aviation as the **Sentry O2-337**, this being an adaptation of the turbocharged T337.

SPECIFICATION

Cessna Model 337M (O-2A)
Wing: span 38 ft 0 in (11.58 m); aspect ratio 7.13; area 202.5 sq ft (18.81 m²)
Fuselage and tail: length 29 ft 9 in (9.07 m); height 9 ft 4 in (2.84 m); tailplane span 10 ft 0.625 in (3.06 m); wheel track 8 ft 2 in (2.49 m); wheel base 7 ft 10 in (2.39 m)
Powerplant: two Teledyne Continental IO-360C/D each rated at 210 hp (157 kW)
Weights: empty 2,848 lb (1292 kg); maximum take-off 5,400 lb (2449 kg)
Fuel and load: internal fuel 82 US gal (348 litres) plus provision for 56 US gal (212 litres) of auxiliary fuel in two wing tanks; external fuel none
Speed: maximum level speed at sea level 173 kt (199 mph; 320 km/h; cruising speed at 10,000 ft (3050 m 125 kt (144 mph; 232 km/h)
Range: typical range 920 nm (1,060 miles; 1706 km)
Performance: maximum rate of climb at sea level 1,180 ft (360 m) per minute; service ceiling 19,800 ft (5885 m); take-off distance to 50 ft (15 m) 1,545 ft (471 m) at maximum take-off weight; landing distance from 50 ft (15 m) 1,650 ft (503 m) at maximum landing weight

Six Cessna 337s, four of which wear this colourful red and white scheme, are flown by the Sri Lankan air force maritime squadron.

OPERATORS

Zimbabwe operates the 16 survivors of 18 Reims-built FTB 337Gs obtained clandestinely in February 1976 by the Rhodesian air force. Named **'Lynx'**, these were fitted with turbocharged engines and were armed with two 7.62-mm (0.303-in) machine-guns above the cabin and 37-mm SNEB rockets, Frantans (frangible plastic-shelled napalm tanks), small bombs and flare dispensers. They undertook light strike, COIN and FAC duties during Rhodesia's long bush war and were fitted with redesigned heat-shielded exhausts as a counter to SA-7 SAMs. Commercial versions are in service with the **Burkina Faso** and **Togo** air forces, each having one Model

337D; the **Sri Lanka** air force (four Model 337FBs and two Skymasters of unidentified sub-type); the navies of **Ecuador** (two T337Fs and one Model 337G); **Mexico** (two Model 337Fs) and **Peru** (one P337G); the **Chilean army** (three Model 337Gs); and the **Jamaica Defence Force**'s Air Wing (one Model 337G). The Reims-built Super Skymaster serves with the **Burkina Faso** and **Togo** air forces, each operating a single F337E. The Summit Sentry 02-337 derivative version is operated by the **Haitian air corps** (four) and **Thai air force** (five). Ex-USAF O-2As remain with the **Costa Rican Public Security air section** (two), the **Dominican air force** (four), the **South Korean air force** (seven) and the **Salvadorean air force** (seven); the last-mentioned service also operates one O-2B.

Cessna **Model 400 Series, Titan and Golden Eagle**

The models in the 400 series are the largest of the propeller-driven Cessna light transport aircraft, examples of most of which have been procured in small numbers by military services. First to appear was the **Model 411**, an eight-seat aircraft powered by two 375-hp (280-kW) Continental GTSIO-520-M engines and flown as a prototype on 18 July 1962. The **Model 411A** was similar apart from a lengthened baggage nose and optional extra engine nacelle fuel tanks. Several remain in service with **France**'s Armée de l'Air from 12 originally acquired for communications tasks, and one Model 411 serves with both the **Mexican navy** and **Thai air force**.

Progressive development led to the **Model 401**, which, flown on 26 August 1965, was a lower-priced alternative to the Model 411. This variant had substantially the same airframe but was powered by 300-hp (224-kW) TSIO-520-E engines set further outboard on the wings and had a six-seat interior. The parallel **Model 402**, similar apart from a reinforced cabin floor and an optional cargo door, was the recipient of several small military orders. The **Models 402A** and **B** introduced minor changes, but the **Model 402C** was characterised by a longer-span wing, bonded wet wing with tip tanks and 325-hp (242-kW) TSIO-520-VB engines.

The Model 402 is operated by the air

forces of **Bolivia** (one for photo survey), Colombia (two in concert with two **Model 404**s), **Malaysia** (10) and **Paraguay** (one). In addition, the aircraft is in the inventory of the **Bolivian navy** (one), **Mexican navy** (two) and the air detachment of the **Venezuelan National Guard** (which operates at least one example).

A stretched version of the Model 402B with a larger vertical tail and 375-hp (280-kW) Continental GTSIO-520-M engines was first flown on 26 February 1975 as the **Model 404 Titan**. The Model 404 has been delivered to several military air arms, including the US Navy (one example operated as the **C-28A**), **Royal Bahamas Defence Force** (one example together with single examples of the **Model 414** and **Model 421**), **Bolivian air force** (one), **Dominican air force** (one Model 404 alongside a single Model 401) and the air wing of the **Tanzanian People's Defence Force** (two).

Pressurised versions

The **Model 414** is a pressurised version of the Model 401B with two 310-hp (231-kW) Continental TSIO-520-N engines, a single example being operated by the **Royal Bahamas Defence Force**. The **Model 421** is essentially a pressurised version of the Model 411A with 375-hp (280-kW) Continental GTSIO-520-D engines. Successive

The RNZAF's three Cessna 421s were sold during late 1990 as an economy measure, but the type is in widespread military use elsewhere. The Cessna 421 is distinguished by its long nose and round windows.

production versions of the latter were the **Model 421A** with detail changes, the **Model 421B** with repositioned GTSIO-520-E engines on longer-span wings, a longer nose and strengthened undercarriage, and the **Model 421C** with a wet wing and GTSIO-520-L engines. Four Model

421s are used by **Turkish army aviation**, and single examples are included in the inventories of the **Ivory Coast**, the **Pakistan army**, and the air forces of **Paraguay** and **Sri Lanka**.

A Cessna 402 of No. 2 Squadron, Royal Malaysian air force, based at Simpang for liaison and staff transport duties. Cessna's versatile twins are popular light transport and liaison aircraft, especially with the world's smaller air forces. More than 1,600 Cessna 402s were built.

SPECIFICATION

Cessna Model 421A
Wing: span 39 ft 10.25 in (12.15 m) with tip tanks; aspect ratio 7.95; area 200.00 sq ft (18.58 m²)
Fuselage and tail: length 33 ft 9 in (10.29 m); height 11 ft 8 in (3.56 m); tailplane span 17 ft 0 in (5.18 m);

wheel track 14 ft 8 in (4.47 m); wheel base 10 ft 5.75 in (3.20 m)
Powerplant: two Teledyne Continental GTSIO-520-D each rated at 375 hp (280 kW)
Weights: empty 4,252 lb (1928 kg); maximum take-off 6,840 lb (3102 kg)
Fuel and load: internal fuel 175 US gal (662 litres) standard or 202 US gal (765 litres) optional; external fuel none

Speed: maximum level speed 'clean' at 16,000 ft (4875 m) 240 kt (276 mph; 444 km/h) and at sea level 207 kt (238 mph; 383 km/h); maximum cruising speed at 22,500 ft (6860 m) 227 kt (261 mph; 420 km/h); economical cruising speed at 25,000 ft (7620 m) 196 kt (226 mph; 364 km/h)
Range: ferry range 1,488 nm (1,713 miles; 2756 km) with optional fuel; range 1,020 nm (1,174 miles; 1889 km) with standard fuel

Performance: maximum rate of climb at sea level 1,680 ft (512 m) per minute; service ceiling 27,000 ft (8230 m); take-off run 2,040 ft (622 m) at maximum take-off weight; take-off distance to 50 ft (15 m) 2,563 ft (781 m) at maximum take-off weight; landing distance from 50 ft (15 m) 2,110 ft (643 m) at normal landing weight; landing run 1,045 ft (319 m) at normal landing weight

Cessna **Model 500/550/560 Citation Series**

Small numbers of several derivative versions of the **Cessna Model 500**, all possessing the generic appellation of **Citation**, have been procured by various military services. An eight-seat business jet powered by two 2,200-lb st (9.78-kN) Pratt & Whitney JT15D-1 turbofans, the Model 500 Citation flew as a prototype on 15 September 1969. From late 1976, the **Model 500 Citation I** superseded the original series version, featuring a higher aspect ratio wing and JT15D-1A engines. One example currently serves in the photo survey role with the **Argentine army**. Operators of this Citation version for liaison and communication tasks are the **Chinese People's Liberation Army Air Force** (three), and the air forces of **Mexico** and **Venezuela** (one each) and the **Ecuadorean navy** (one).

The **Model 550 Citation II** was first flown on 31 January 1977 and introduced a fuselage lengthened by 3 ft 9 in (1.14 m) to raise capacity to 12 seats, increased fuel capacity and 2,500-lb st (11.12-kN) JT15D-4 engines. This variant serves with the **Spanish navy** (three) and the air forces of **Myanmar** (one), **Turkey** (four) and **Venezuela** (two).

The **Model S550 Citation S/II** was first flown on 14 February 1984 and introduced a new aerofoil, wing leading-edge cuffs and JT15D-4B turbofans. A variant of this sub-type was adopted by the US Navy as a radar trainer. With a shorter wing span and 2,900-lb st (12.89-kN) JT15D-5 engines, this became the **Model 552/T-47A**. Fifteen were acquired by the service and were operated from Pensacola, FL, by VT-86 until

replaced by the Rockwell T-39 Sabreliner. The normal crew of the T-47A included a civilian pilot, a US Navy instructor and three students. A further development of the S/II flew as an engineering prototype on 18 August 1987. Designated **Model 560 Citation V**, the type featured JT15D-5A engines and incorporated a 2-ft (0.61-m) fuselage stretch. Deliveries commenced in April 1989. The Citation V is currently operated by the **Moroccan air force** (two), the **Seychelles** defence force (one) and the **Venda Defence Force**.

SPECIFICATION

Cessna Model 552 (T-47A Citation)
Wing: span 46 ft 6 in (14.18 m)
Fuselage and tail: length 47 ft 10.75 in (14.60 m); height 14 ft 9.75 in (4.51 m); tailplane span 19 ft 0 in (5.79 m); wheel track 17 ft 7 in (5.36 m); wheel base

Left: Pilots seconded from the Seychelles Coast Guard Air Wing fly the Presidential/VIP Cessna Citation V. Small numbers of these bizjets are used by air forces and government flights.

Below: This Spanish Cessna 550 Citation II is designated TR.20 locally, and is fitted with a survey camera in a wingroot fairing. It serves with Esc. 403 at Cuatro Vientos.

18 ft 2.5 in (5.55 m)
Powerplant: two Pratt & Whitney Canada JT15D-5 each rated at 2,900 lb st (12.89 kN) dry
Weights: empty equipped 9,035 lb (4098 kg); maximum take-off 15,000 lb (6804 kg)
Fuel and load: internal fuel 5,820 lb (2640 kg); external fuel none

Speed: maximum level speed at 40,000 ft (12190 m) 420 kt (484 mph; 779 km/h); maximum cruising speed 402 kt (463 mph; 745 km/h)
Range: typical range 1,700 nm (1,958 miles; 3151 km)
Performance: maximum rate of climb at sea level about 4,000 ft (1219 m) per minute; service ceiling 43,000 ft (13100 m)

Cessna **Model 526 CitationJet JPATS**

First flown on 21 December 1993, the **Model 525 CitationJet JPATS** was closely based upon the CitationJet business jet, retaining the same Williams International F129 turbofans buried in a new fuselage with a new blown canopy covering tandem cockpits and with a new low-set tailplane. The engines are 'fed' by plain D-section intakes above and ahead of each wingroot. The only twin-engined contender for the USAF/USN JPATS requirement, the aircraft is also the only completely indigenous design in the competition. If successful, the aircraft would be built at the com-

pany's Mid-Continent facility. A second prototype joined the flight test programme during early 1994 for certification and demonstration, prior to the expected award of a contract in December 1994, for the first 151 of an anticipated 766-aircraft order.

The CitationJet JPATS trainer made its maiden flight in primer finish, such was the perceived urgency of getting airborne before the end of 1993. The aircraft is the only all-new, all-American trainer being submitted to meet the JPATS.

Changhe Aircraft Factory **Z-8**

Changhe Aircraft Factory
PO Box 109, Jingdezhen
Jiangxi 333002, PRC

At the same time that China's Aviation of the **People's Liberation Navy** placed orders for 16 Aérospatiale SA 321Ja Super Frelon helicopters, arrangements were begun to establish production of versions of the Super Frelon in China. Design work was begun in 1976 but was suspended from 1979 to mid-1984. Development work at the Changhe Aircraft Factory at Jingdezhen (Jiangxi province) resulted in a prototype first flight on 11 December

1985, with a second flown in October 1987. Domestic type approval was awarded on 8 April 1989. With the designation **Zhishengji-8** (for the eighth vertical take-off aircraft type), the Super Frelon entered production against an initial contract for 10 for the Naval Air Force. The first of these was handed over on 5 August 1989 to the PLA Naval Air Force for service trials.

Although based on the SA 321Ja utility/transport version of the Super Frelon,

the Z-8 is expected to undertake a variety of duties including troop transport, SAR, ASW/ASV, minelaying/sweeping, aerial survey and fire-fighting.

The Z-8 is of wholly indigenous manufacture, although some components are of French origin. The Changzhou (CLXMW) WZ6 turboshafts are derived from the Super Frelon's Turboméca Turmo IIIC engines. Work commenced in 1975, followed by testing in 1980-82 and first flight

on a Z-8 in 1985. Although not quite as powerful as the Turmo IIIC, the WZ6 nevertheless has a power reserve of 20 per cent at sea level.

In addition to the crew of two or three, the Z-8 can accommodate 27 fully armed troops in the cabin, or 39 without equipment; up to 15 stretchers and a medical attendant; or a BL-212 jeep and its crew. Loading is carried out via a hydraulically actuated rear door and a starboard-mounted sliding door at the front of the cabin. SAR equipment can include a 275-kg (606-lb) capacity hydraulic rescue hoist and two five-person liferafts. The Z-8 may also be equipped with sonar, search radar, sonobuoys or other equipment for fire-fighting and geological survey. It may be fitted additionally with depth charges, torpedoes, anti-shipping missiles or mine-laying/mine-sweeping gear.

SPECIFICATION

Changhe Z-8
Rotor system: main rotor diameter 18.90 m (62 ft 0 in); tail rotor diameter 4.00 m (13 ft 1.5 in); main rotor disc area 280.47 m2 (3,019 sq ft); tail rotor disc area 12.57 m2 (135.27 sq ft)

Fuselage and tail: length overall, rotors turning 23.035 m (75 ft 7 in); height overall 6.66 m (21 ft 10.25 in) with rotors turning
Powerplant: three Changzhou (CLXMW) Wozhou-6 each rated at 1156 kW (1,550 shp)
Weights: empty equipped 7550 kg (16,645 lb); normal take-off 10592 kg (23,351 lb); maximum take-off 12074 kg (26,618 lb)
Fuel and load: internal fuel 3900 litres (1,030 US gal) plus provision for 1900 litres (502 US gal) of auxiliary fuel in cabin tanks; external fuel none; maximum payload 5000 kg (11,023 lb)
Speed: never-exceed speed 315 km/h (170 kt; 195 mph); maximum cruising speed at optimum altitude 266 km/h (143 kt; 165 mph); economical cruising speed at optimum altitude 255 km/h (137 kt; 158 mph)
Range: ferry range 1400 km (755 nm; 870 miles) with auxiliary fuel; range 820 km (442 nm; 509 miles) with standard fuel on two engines; endurance 4 hours

The Changhe Z-8 serves with the Chinese navy. This aircraft, still in primer finish, has ASW radar radomes in the fronts of the undercarriage sponsons.

43 minutes with standard fuel
Performance: maximum rate of climb at sea level 690 m (2,263 ft) per minute; service ceiling 6000 m (19,685 ft); hovering ceiling 5500 m (18,045 ft) in

ground effect and 4400 m (14,435 ft) out of ground effect

Chengdu **JJ-5/FT-5**

*Chengdu Aircraft Industrial Corporation
PO Box 800, Chengdu
Sichuan 610092, PRC*

The basic Chinese-built MiG-17F was produced by the Shenyang Aircraft Factory, but later derivatives were developed and constructed by Chengdu. The first such development was the **J-5A**, which was basically a Chinese-built MiG-17PF with AI radar in a larger, longer, forward fuselage. Relatively small numbers were produced, and none are known to have been exported. The prototype made its maiden flight on 11 November 1964.

More successful was the **JJ-5**, a two-seat trainer derivative of the J-5. This had a slightly lengthened fuselage, and the nose intake and jetpipe were refined. Development began in 1965, when it was becoming clear that the MiG-15UTIs then in use lacked performance and had some unacceptable handling characteristics. The cres-

cent wing of the MiG-17, with its reduced sweep on the outer wings, solved many of these problems, including a tendency to pitch up at high angles of attack and unpredictable handling at transonic speeds.

The JJ-5 first flew on 8 May 1966, and 1,061 had been built by 1986, when production ceased. It was powered by a Wopen WP-5D turbojet which remained an obvious copy of the Rolls-Royce Nene. The JJ-5 has been exported (as the **FT-5**) to a number of customers, most notably **Pakistan**, which uses the aircraft as the standard advanced jet trainer. Others have been procured by **Albania**, **Bangladesh**, **Sri Lanka**, **Sudan** and **Zimbabwe**, and perhaps by **North Korea** and **Tanzania**. Interestingly, Mikoyan itself never designed a two-seat MiG-17 variant, since the Soviet air

forces regarded the MiG-15UTI as being adequate for the training of MiG-17 and MiG-19 aircrew.

SPECIFICATION

Chengdu JJ-5
Wing: span 9.628 m (31 ft 7 in); aspect ratio 4.10; area 22.60 m2 (243.27 sq ft)
Fuselage and tail: length 11.50 m (37 ft 9 in); height 3.80 m (12 ft 5.75 in); wheel track 3.85 m (12 ft 7.5 in)
Powerplant: one Xian (XAE) Wopen WP-5D rated at 26.48 kN (5,952 lb st) dry
Weights: empty equipped 4080 kg (8,995 lb); normal take-off 5400 kg (11,905 lb); maximum take-off 6215 kg (13,701 lb)

Fuel and load: internal fuel 1500 litres (396 US gal); external fuel up to two 400-litre (106-US gal) drop tanks
Speed: never-exceed speed at 5000 m (16,405 m) 1048 km/h (565 kt; 651 mph); normal operating speed 'clean' at optimum altitude 775 km/h (418 kt; 482 mph)
Range: ferry range 1230 km (664 nm; 764 miles) with drop tanks; endurance 2 hours 38 minutes with drop tanks
Performance: maximum rate of climb at sea level 1620 m (5,315 ft) per minute; service ceiling 14300 m (46,915 ft); take-off run 760 m (2,493 ft) at maximum take-off weight; landing run 830 m (2,723 ft) at maximum landing weight

Two FT-5s serve with Sri Lanka's only fast-jet unit, No. 5 Squadron, for jet conversion training onto the Chengdu F-7BS.

Today in Pakistani service, the FT-5 serves with No. 1 Fighter Conversion Unit at Mianwali in the advanced tactical training role.

Chengdu **J-7/F-7** 'Fishbed'

China was granted a licence to manufacture the MiG-21F-13 and its Tumanskii R-11F-300 engine in 1961, and a handful of Mikoyan-built aircraft were delivered to serve as patterns. Not all the necessary technical documents had been delivered by the time the two countries severed ties, however, and J-6 (MiG-19) production was accordingly given a higher priority. A MiG-21-based prototype was constructed at Shenyang and first flew on 17 January 1966, powered by the Wopen WP-7, which was claimed to be an improved R-11F-300. Certificated for production in June 1967, despite the enormous upheavals of the Cultural Revolution and January Storm, the initial batch of aircraft was manufactured by the Shenyang Aircraft Factory. Some of these were later delivered to **Albania** and **Tanzania** as **F-7A**s.

Production transferred to Chengdu, where the basic aircraft received the new designation **J-7I**, retaining the F-7A tag for export. Broadly equivalent to the late-series MiG-21F-13, the aircraft had the later medium-chord tailfin but retained two 30-

Early versions of the F-7 had an undernose pitot probe, and were broadly equivalent to the early MiG-21F-13, with a 30-mm cannon in each wingroot but with the later broad-chord tailfin. This PL-5-armed aircraft is a J-7II, identifiable by its separate canopy and windscreen. The J-7II also introduced a more powerful and reliable engine.

Sri Lanka operates four aircraft which it designates F-7BS. These combine Chinese avionics in a J-7II fuselage with the four-pylon wing of the F-7M. They are Sri Lanka's only front-line fast jets.

Right: Full-standard F-7Ms equip Nos 5 and 35 Squadrons of the Bangladesh air force at Dhaka and Chittagong. The aircraft are pooled and wear the markings of both units.

mm cannon under the wingroots, like the earliest 'Fishbed-Cs'.

Early J-7s were not popular with their pilots, not least because of their unusual and failure-prone linked canopy and ejection seat, whereby the canopy worked as a blast shield on ejection. Development of the **J-7II** began in 1975, and the new variant incorporated a new Type II ejection seat under a conventional jettisonable upward/rearward-hinging canopy and separate windscreen. The new seat had a powerful rocket motor for smoother acceleration and a higher trajectory, and gave ground-level ejection capability for the first time (at speeds in excess of 140 kt). The J-7II also had provision for a 720-litre (158.4-Imp gal) centreline fuel tank and a relocated brake chute in a tubular fairing at the base of the fin; the aircraft made its maiden flight on 30 December 1978. To give improved performance the more powerful (13,448-lb st/ 59.8-kN) Wopen WP-7B engine was fitted,

A patch on the nose shows where the short-lived Skybolt name has been overpainted on this AIM-9P Sidewinder-armed F-7P of No. 20 Squadron, one of four Pakistani squadrons operating the type in the air defence role.

which also gave longer time between over-haul figures (these were doubled to 200 hours), better heat shielding and longer life. The later WP-7B(M) was fitted to later air-craft, and featured an APU fuelled by kerosene, rather than petrol.

There are reports that an improved ver-sion of the J-7II, with an air data computer, modern HUD and redesigned wing, first flew in April 1990 under the designation **J-7E**. This has a cranked arrow wing, with new outer panels of increased span and area. Powered by an uprated WP-7F engine, the J-7E has four underwing pylons and is reportedly compatible with the PL-8 AAM. The basic J-7II has been widely exported, in several sub-variants. The **F-7B** is a mini-mum-change variant, apparently with R.550 Magic compatibility. The F-7B has been exported to **Egypt** and **Iraq**, and some Chi-nese sources have stated that a delivery to **Jordan** took place in 1982.

Four F-7Bs with F-7M wings, designated **F-7BS**, have also been delivered to **Sri Lanka** for service with No. 5 Squadron. These aircraft retain Chinese avionics, and have never been photographed with more than two underwing pylons, although pre-

sumably four can be fitted.

The J-7II is also available in an upgraded form, under the designation **F-7M Air-guard**. This has an extra pair of underwing pylons and a strengthened undercarriage, and the pitot probe is relocated above the nose. Internally, the F-7M features a GEC Avionics 956 HUDWAC, a new longer-range ranging radar with improved ECCM charac-teristics, a new air data computer, radar altimeter, IFF and secure communications, all served by an improved electrical system, and an improved Wopen WP-7B(BM) pow-erplant. The aircraft also has a strengthened windscreen and is compatible with the Chi-nese PL-7 AAM. The F-7M has been exported to **Bangladesh**, **Iran** and report-edly **Jordan**. **Zimbabwe**'s aircraft may be F-7Bs or later F-7Ms.

A similar version, the **F-7P Skybolt**, was exported to **Pakistan**. The 'Skybolt' name was quickly dropped, and was over-painted on the noses of Pakistan's first batch of aircraft soon after delivery. The F-7P incorporated 24 modifications to meet Pakistani requirements, but differs little in external appearance. The Mk IV ejection seat is considerably improved with a drogue

gun and enhanced auto-separation, and can be used at ground level at speeds in excess of 75 kt. Only nine pins need to be removed before flight, instead of 11 on the original F-7M seat. The Chinese ejection seat is to be replaced by a Martin-Baker Mk 10L. All four underwing weapons pylons are wired for the carriage of air-to-air missiles, includ-ing the R.550 Magic and AIM-9 Sidewinder. Twenty were delivered before production switched to the further improved **F-7MP**, 60 of which were delivered. In Pakistani ser-vice the F-7MP retains the simple F-7P des-ignation but can be recognised by pairs of tiny forward and rear hemisphere RWR antennas on each side of the fin tip. The F-7P and F-7MP equip four PAF squadrons.

Chengdu has also produced a longer-range all-weather version of the J-7, in asso-ciation with the Guizhou factory which builds two-seat JJ-7/FT-7 trainers. Desig-nated **J-7III**, the aircraft is externally similar to the Soviet MiG-21M, with the same SPS blown flaps, underfuselage 23-mm gun pod, broad-chord tailfin, bulged spine, and blast fences below the auxiliary intakes. Design began in 1981 and yielded a flying prototype on 26 April 1984. The J-7III has a new all-

ARMAMENT
The F-7P can be fitted with up to four underwing pylons (though two is more usual) and these can be used to carry a variety of stores. In Pakistani service, the aircraft can carry AIM-9P Sidewinders (shown here), or MATRA R.550 Magics. The centreline hardpoint is usually used for the carriage of a supersonic fuel tank. Air-to-air missiles are augmented by a pair of NORINCO Type 30-1 belt-fed cannon, with 60 rounds per gun, mounted in the wingroots.

INTAKE
The F-7P uses a simple pitot intake in the nose, with a variable conical centrebody sliding in and out to match intake area to flight conditions and thrust demanded. The centrebody is computer controlled and is fully variable, whereas on the original MiG-21F-13 it had only three positions. It houses the aircraft's primitive ranging radar.

COCKPIT
Whereas the original MiG-21F-13 and J-7I had single-piece forward-hinging canopies with a built-in windscreen, the F-7P has a more conventional canopy with a separate, fixed three-piece windscreen.

weather radar in an enlarged radome, and uses the F-7P's Type IV ejection seat. The aircraft is powered by the 14,550-lb st (64.72-kN) Wopen WP-13, which was developed from the WP-7 but features an improved compressor and bearings, and a host of measures to enhance reliability.

Unbuilt versions of the J-7 include the **Chengdu/Grumman Sabre** or **Super 7**. This was to have been built for Pakistan and was to have featured a Westinghouse APG-66 radar in a solid nosecone, a new wide-angle HUD, and lateral air intakes in the wingroots. The aircraft was to have been re-engined, with either a General Electric F404/RM-12 or a Turbo Union RB.199. Enlarged wings featured computer-controlled leading-edge manoeuvre slats, and an enlarged spine housed extra fuel. Other improvements included provision of an arrester hook, single point pressure refuelling and strengthened undercarriage. The Super 7 pilot surveyed the world from a new F-20-style canopy and frameless wrap-around windscreen, and sat on a new ejection seat. Development was suspended by the US government after the Tienanmen Square massacre, but seems to have been restarted using a mix of Russian and non-US Western technology. One hundred RD-33 engines (which power the MiG-29) have been purchased for the programme, for example.

SPECIFICATION

Chengdu F-7M Airguard
Wing: span 7.154 m (23 ft 5.625 in); aspect ratio 2.2; area 23.00 m² (247.58 sq ft)
Fuselage and tail: length 13.945 m (45 ft 9 in) excluding probe and 14.885 m (48 ft 10 in) including probe; height 4.103 m (13 ft 5.5 in); tailplane span 3.74 m (12 ft 3.25 in); wheel track 2.692 m (8 ft 10 in); wheel base 4.807 m (15 ft 9.25 in)
Powerplant: one Liyang (LMC) Wopen WP-7B(BM) rated at 43.15 kN (9,700 lb st) dry and 59.82 kN (13,448 lb st) with afterburning. This is derived from the Tumanskii R-11F-300
Weights: empty 5275 kg (11,629 lb); normal take-off 7531 kg (16,603 lb)
Fuel and load: internal fuel 2385 litres (630 US gal); external fuel up to 1680 litres (444 US gal) in one 720-litre (190.2-US gal) drop tank and two 500-litre (132-US gal) drop tanks or three 500-litre (132-US gal) drop tanks; maximum ordnance 1000 kg (2,205 lb), usually comprising underwing AAMs (up to four AIM-9 or similar) with a single centreline fuel tank
Speed: maximum level speed 'clean' between 41,000 and 60,700 ft (12500 and 18500 m) 2175 km/h (1,175 kt; 1,350 mph)
Range: ferry range 2230 km (1,203 nm; 1,386 miles) with drop tanks; combat radius 600 km (324 nm; 373 miles) on a hi-lo-hi interdiction mission with two 150-kg (331-lb) bombs and three 500-litre (132-US gal) drop tanks, or 370 km (200 nm; 230 miles) on a lo-lo-lo close air support mission with four rocket launchers, or 650 km (351 nm; 404 miles) on a long-range interception mission with two AAMs and three 500-litre (132-US gal) drop tanks; endurance 45 minutes on a CAP at 36,000 ft (10975 ft) with two AAMs and three 500-litre (132-US gal) drop tanks
Performance: maximum rate of climb at sea level 10800 m (35,433 ft) per minute; service ceiling 59,700 m (18200 m); take-off run 700 to 950 m (2,297 to 3,117 ft) at normal take-off weight; landing run 600 to 900 m (1,969 to 2,953 ft)
g limits: +8

Chengdu Aircraft Corporation F-7P

This Chengdu F-7P serves with No. 20 Squadron at Rafiqi, and was one of the initial batch of 20. Later Pakistani aircraft were officially F-7PMs with a new cockpit layout and some avionics improvements. All Pakistani F-7s use the simple F-7P designation in service, and wear a two-tone air superiority grey colour scheme, sometimes with toned-down national insignia, as seen here.

COLOUR SCHEMES
Chinese and Sri Lankan J-7s and F-7s mostly wear an off-white, pearl grey colour scheme, but other operators have chosen darker greys or desert camouflage.

POWERPLANT
The original J-7I and J-7II were powered by the 12,676-lb (56.4 kN) Wopen WP-7 (Tumanskii R11F-300) turbojet, whereas the F-7M and F-7P use the 13,448-lb (59.82 kN) Wopen WP-7B, and the heavyweight all-weather J-7III uses the 14,550-lb (64.72 kN) Wopen WP-13.

UPGRADED DERIVATIVES
The proposed Super 7, being continued despite the ending of US participation, will incorporate advanced avionics and a real air-intercept radar. Potential powerplants include the Klimov RD-33 used by the MiG-29.

EJECTION SEAT
Many export F-7s, including those operated by Pakistan, are fitted with the Martin-Baker Mk 10 zero-zero rocket-powered ejection seat.

AVIONICS
The F-7P uses predominantly Western avionics and systems, including a GEC Avionics 956 HUDWAC (Head-Up Display and Weapons Aiming Computer).

Christen **Pitts S-2**

Aviat Inc.
Airport Box 1149, Afton
Wyoming 83110

First flown in September 1944, the Pitts **S-1 Special** was a highly successful single-seat aerobatic biplane that gave rise in 1967 to a two-seat derivative, the **S-2A Special**. More than 1,500 Pitts Specials have been built, mostly by amateur constructors. The original Pitts Enterprises was acquired by Christen Industries Inc. in 1981, production of both single- and two-seaters continuing at the Aerotek factory in Afton, WY. Pitts biplanes have been chosen by several air force aerobatic teams, notably the Venezuelan 'Falcons' and Chilean 'Halcones', but neither of these teams currently flies its Pitts. Closely associated with the Royal Jordanian air force, the 'Royal Jordanian Falcons' team flew three S-2As.

Chile's 'Halcones' display team has now transitioned to the Extra 300, which has also replaced those of the 'Royal Jordanian Falcons'. Individual aircraft serve with a variety of military unit's flying clubs.

CNAMC/PAC **K-8 Karakorum**

Nanchang Aircraft Manufacturing Company
PO Box 5001-506, Nanchang
Jiangxi 330024, PRC

Subject of a jointly-financed programme shared between **China** and **Pakistan**, the **K-8 Karakorum** was designed by China Nanchang Aircraft Manufacturing Company (CNAMC), which is also primarily responsible for construction and flight development. Pakistan Aeronautical Complex (PAC) contributes manpower at the Nanchang complex as well as some funding, to give a 25 per cent market share. Responsibility for marketing is undertaken by China National Aero-Technology Import & Export.

The K-8 is a basic jet trainer of conventional straight-wing tandem-seat configuration. PAC is responsible for manufacture of the fin, tailplane and some other components to give a total share of approximately 25 per cent of the airframe. First identified as the **Nanchang L-8**, it is named for the mountain range on the China/Pakistan border. For the benefit of international marketing it features a considerable proportion of Western equipment, including a Garrett TFE731 turbofan, Collins EFIS and Martin-Baker CN10LW lightweight ejection seats. Provision is made for light armament on four wing pylons plus a centreline 23-mm gun pack with self-computing optical gunsight, giving the K-8 a light strike capability

in addition to a weapons training role. Each station can carry up to 250 kg (551 lb) of stores.

Full-scale development was launched in 1987 with construction of three flying and one static trials aircraft. The first of these flew on 21 November 1990; two more prototypes were flown in 1991, with another in 1992. The test programme was set for completion by the first quarter of 1993. A pre-production batch of 15 aircraft was launched, the first of which flew in 1993, and plans were made for evaluation of aircraft from this batch by the air forces of China and Pakistan. The PAF is reported to have a requirement for 75 K-8s; total Chinese procurement is uncertain.

The K-8 Karakorum is a single-engined advanced jet trainer being jointly developed by China and Pakistan.

SPECIFICATION

CNAMC/PAC K-8 Karakorum
Wing: span 9.63 m (31 ft 7.25 in); aspect ratio 5.45; area 17.02 m² (183.2 sq ft)
Fuselage and tail: length (including nose probe) 11.60 m (38 ft 0.75 in); height 4.21 m (13 ft 9.75 in); wheel track 2.43 m (7 ft 11.75 in); wheel base 4.38 m (14 ft 4.5 in)
Powerplant: one 16.01-kN (3,600-lb st) Garrett TFE731-2A-2A turbofan

Weights: empty equipped 2687 kg (5,924 lb); maximum take-off (clean) 3630 kg (8,003 lb); maximum take-off (with external stores) 4330 kg (9,546 lb)
Fuel and load: internal fuel 780 kg (1,720 lb); external fuel (two drop tanks) 390 kg (860 lb); maximum external stores 950 kg (2,094 lb)
Speed: never-exceed speed 950 km/h (512 kt; 590 mph); maximum level speed at sea level 800 km/h (432 kt; 497 mph); approach speed 200 km/h (108 kt; 124 mph)

Range: with maximum internal fuel 1400 km (755 nm; 870 miles); with maximum internal/external fuel 2250 km (1,214 nm; 1,398 miles); endurance (maximum internal fuel) 3 hours; endurance (maximum internal/external fuel) 4 hours 25 minutes
Performance: maximum climb rate at sea level 1620 m (5,315 ft) per minute; service ceiling 13000 m (42,650 ft); take-off run 410 m (1,345ft); landing run 512 m (1,680 m)
g limits: -3 to +7.33

Convair **240/C-131/440**

Convair (itself a product of the 1943 merger of Consolidated and Vultee)
was absorbed by General Dynamics in 1954, as the Convair Division,
losing its separate identity during the early 1960s

By the end of 1993 no more than two examples of the family of Convair twin-engined transports remained in military service. This duo comprised a single, elderly, ex-civilian **Convair 240**, operated by the Grupo Aéreo de Transporte Especiales (GATE) in Paraguay, and one surviving **Convair 440** in service with Transporte Aéreo Militar (TAM), a component of the Bolivian air force. A handful of piston-engined **C-131A Samaritan** and turboprop **VC-131H**s were used through the 1980s by US Air Force and Air National Guard and US Navy Reserve, respectively. The C-131

has since been replaced by the C-9, C-12 and C-26 in USAF/ANG service. VR-48 of the USNR transferred its last C-131H to the US Department of State on 30 August 1990 and relinquished the type in favour of the C-20. Several C-131s remained active with the Department of State in 1994.

Bolivia is the only remaining military user of the Convair 440, while Paraguay still uses the 240. Other Convairs serve with paramilitary agencies, including the US Department of State.

Convair **880**

The **Convair 880** first flew on 27 January 1959, but proved to be too expensive for any major sales success. A number survived for some years with small operators after their initial first-line service was over.

A single aircraft (BuNo. 161572) was acquired in the early 1980s by the US Navy for trials work, under the non-standard designation **UC-880**. Based at Patuxent River, it flew with the Naval Air Test Center (now

the Naval Air Warfare Center/Aircraft Division). A single hose-drum unit was incorporated in the lower rear fuselage for refuelling work, and the aircraft sported a large ventral radome and numerous antennas for equipment test work. It retired in 1994.

The last flying Convair 880 was operated by the US Navy from the NAWC at Patuxent River, fulfilling a variety of test and support roles.

Convair QF-106 Delta Dart

In 1991, the Convair QF-106 began to replace the North American QF-100 as the USAF's principal FSAT (Full-Scale Aerial Target) and is now in full use with the 475th Weapons Evaluation Group at Tyndall AFB, FL, and at Holloman AFB, NM.

The F-106 first flew on 26 December 1956, and occupied an important place in the air defence network of the United States for many years. The Delta Dart retired from service with the New Jersey ANG in 1989. It was chosen as the next-generation FSAT because its speed and manoeuvrability better represented high-performance targets for air-to-air missile engagements. One hundred and ninety-four **QF-106** conversions by Honeywell are planned for the US Air Force, the conversion involving removal of some systems, installation of remote-piloting equipment (although the QF-106 remains 'man-rated'), and fitment of propane burners under wing pylons to provide infra-red sources for heat-seeking missiles. The last fully manned F-106, NASA's vortex flap research F-106B, has now been withdrawn from use.

Convair QF-106s are operated as unmanned target drones, remaining capable of manned flight. They are operated by the 475th Weapons Evaluation Group's 82nd TATS (Tactical Aerial Target Squadron) at Tyndall AFB, Florida. The aircraft are regularly expended in missile trials and missile/gunnery competitions. Underwing pylons carry propane burners to give a stronger IR signature.

SPECIFICATION

Convair F-106A Delta Dart
Wing: span 38 ft 3.5 in (11.67 m): aspect ratio 2.32: area 631.3 sq ft (58.65 m²)
Fuselage and tail: length (including nose probe) 70 ft 8.75 in (21.56 m); height 20 ft 3.3 in (6.18 m); wheel track 15 ft 5.67 in (4.71 m): wheel base 24 ft 1.5 in (7.35 m)
Powerplant: one Pratt & Whitney J75-P-17 turbojet rated at 17,200 lb st (76.51 kN) dry and 24,500 lb st (108.98 kN) with afterburning
Weights: empty 24,155 lb (10957 kg); maximum take-off 41,831 lb (18974 kg)
Fuel and load: internal fuel 9,841 lb (4464 kg); external fuel (two drop tanks) 4,654 lb (2111 kg)
Speed: maximum speed at 40,000 ft (12192 m) 2413 km/h (1302 kt; 1,500 mph); combat speed at 52,000 ft (15850 m) 1090 km/h (588 kt; 676 mph)
Range: on internal fuel 1150 miles (1850 km); combat radius 490 miles (790 km)
Performance: initial climb rate 39,800 ft (12131 m) per minute: service ceiling 58,000 ft (17678 m)

Curtiss C-46 Commando

Curtiss ceased to exist in 1954, the aeroplane division of Curtiss Wright having closed earlier, during 1947

Like the famed Douglas C-47, the nearly contemporary **Curtiss C-46 Commando** demonstrated extraordinary longevity of service, albeit in much smaller quantities. In the two decades following the end of World War II, air arms of a dozen or more nations used ex-USAAF **C-46As** and, as a consequence of such service in **China**, a quantity of these twin-engined transports passed eventually into the inventory of the Chinese People's Liberation Army Air Force. A modification programme introduced the locally-produced 1380-kW (1,850 hp) HS8 radial 14-cylinder engine based on the Shvetsov ASh-82V in the surviving Chinese C-46s, and it is believed that a handful may remain airworthy in China's remoter areas. Elsewhere, the last surviving military C-46A was thought to be in service with the **Haitian air corps**.

Dassault (Breguet/Dassault-Breguet) Atlantic

*Dassault Aviation
9 Rond-Point Champs-Elyseés
75008 Paris*

The **Atlantic 1** originated in a 1957 NATO requirement (NBMR-2) for a long-range maritime reconnaissance aircraft. The winner was the **Breguet Br.1150** (this company being absorbed by Dassault in 1971), fabricated by the SECBAT (Société d'Etudes et de Construction de Breguet Atlantic) consortium, which then included SABCA and SONACA in Belgium, Fokker in Holland, Dornier and MBB in West Germany, Aérospatiale in France and Aeritalia in Italy. Assembled by Breguet, the first of four prototypes was flown at Toulouse on 21 October 1961.

Carrying 12 crew, the Atlantic is equipped with Thomson-CSF search radar in a retractable bin and American ASW avionics similar to those of the Lockheed Neptune. Standard NATO stores can be carried in the 30 ft (9.15 m) unpressurised weapons bay in the lower section of the 'double bubble' fuselage, most of the external skin being light alloy sandwich. The first of 20 for the **West German navy** and 40 for France's **Aéronavale** entered service in December 1965. French aircraft serve with 21F and 22F at Nîmes-Garons and 23F and 24F at Lann-Bihoué. The Aéronavale began retirement of first-generation Atlantics in 1992, although some aircraft will be retained for surveillance tasks, perpetuating the detachments already established at Djibouti, Dakar (Senegambia), Réunion and in the Antilles. German Atlantics of MFG 5, Kiel-Holtenau

(except for five equipped for Elint missions under the Peace Peek programme) have completed an update programme involving new Texas Instruments radar, Emerson Electric sonar and Loral ESM equipment in wingtip pods. In parallel, airframe improvements have doubled flying life to 10,000 hours. By contrast, the six survivors of nine delivered to No. 321 Squadron of the Royal Netherlands navy at Valkenburg in 1969-72 began phasing out in January 1984, replaced by P-3Cs. **Italy**'s 18 Atlantics were supplied between June 1972 and July 1974 to complete production, and are operated by 30° Stormo at Cagliari/Elmas and 41° Stormo at Catania/Sigonella on patrols of the Mediterranean. **Pakistan** obtained three from the French navy in 1975-76; wearing 'navy' titles, these are flown by No. 29 Squadron of the Pakistan air force from Sharea Faisal (Drigh Road).

Six German Atlantics were modified to serve as Elint platforms under the codename Peace Peek. One has since been lost.

Most of the Aéronavale's basic Atlantics have been replaced by the newer Atlantique, and some have been scrapped.

SPECIFICATION

Dassault Aviation (Breguet/Dassault-Breguet) Atlantic 1
Wing: span 36.30 m (119 ft 1 in); aspect ratio 10.95; area 120.34 m² (1,295.37 sq ft)
Fuselage and tail: length 31.75 m (104 ft 2 in); height 11.33 m (37 ft 2 in); tailplane span 12.31 m (40 ft 4.5 in); wheel track 9.00 m (29 ft 6.25 in); wheel base 9.44 m (31 ft 0 in)
Powerplant: two Rolls-Royce Tyne RTy.20 Mk 21 each rated at 6,100 ehp (4549 ekW)
Weights: empty equipped 25000 kg (55,115 lb); maximum take-off 44500 kg (98,104 lb)
Fuel and load: internal fuel 18500 kg (40,785 lb); external fuel none; maximum ordnance 3500 kg (7,716 lb)
Speed: maximum level speed 'clean' at optimum altitude 658 km/h (355 kt; 409 mph); maximum cruising speed at 7200 m (23,620 ft) 556 km/h (300 kt; 345 mph); normal patrol speed at optimum altitude 315 km/h (170 kt; 196 mph)
Range: ferry range 9000 km (4,856 nm; 5,592 miles); endurance 18 hours 0 minutes
Performance: service ceiling 10000 m (32,810 ft); take-off distance to 10.5 m (35 ft) 1500 m (4,921 ft) at maximum take-off weight

Left: Italian Atlantics are due to remain in service for some time and are being upgraded with Atlantique systems, and will also receive a Nimrod acoustics processor.

Right: Pakistan operates three ex-French navy Atlantics. These serve with No. 29 Squadron, at Sharea Faisal.

Dassault **Atlantique 2 (ATL 2)**

Originally called the **ANG (Atlantic Nouvelle Génération)**, the **Dassault Atlantique 2** was intended as a multi-national programme to replace the Atlantic (now called Atlantic 1) with its various users. **France** is currently the sole customer, though that country's requirement for 30 aircraft (originally 42) makes the project viable even if the rate of manufacture is too low for competitive costings.

After very prolonged studies, the Atlantique 2 was designed as a 'minimum-change' aircraft, totally new in avionics, systems and equipment but with these packaged into an airframe differing only in ways to increase service life, reduce costs and minimise maintenance. Structural changes include detail redesign to give a 30,000-hour fatigue life, improved bonding and anti-corrosion protection, and better inter-panel sealing. An Astadyne gas-turbine auxiliary power unit is fitted, and production machines are fitted with Ratier-BAe propellers with larger composite blades.

The Atlantique 2's sensors include the Thomson-CSF Iguane frequency-agile radar with a new interrogator and decoder, an SAT/TRT Tango FLIR in a chin turret, over 100 sonobuoys in the rear fuselage, a new Crouzet MAD receiver in the tailboom, and the Thomson-CSF ARAR 13 ESM installation with frequency analysis at the top of the fin and D/F in the new wingtip nacelles. All processors, data buses and sensor links are of standard digital form, navaids include an inertial system and Navstar satellite receiver, and every part of the avionics and communications has been upgraded. This avionics fit represents a substantial improvement over the first-generation Atlantic 1, and is cost-effective due to the minimal airframe changes incurred. The main weapons bay, housed in the unpressurised lower fuselage, can accommodate all NATO standard bombs, depth charges, two ASMs, up to eight Mk 46 torpedoes or

seven French Murène advanced torpedoes. A typical load consists of one AS37 Martel or one AM39 Exocet ASM and three torpedoes. Additional stores up to 3500 kg (7,716 lb) may be carried on four underwing pylons, including future ASMs, AAMs and equipment pods. The Atlantique has a rarely used secondary transport function, and could also be used in a limited overland electronic reconnaissance role.

The first Atlantique 2 flew in May 1981 and production deliveries began in 1989. Flottille 23F was the first unit to convert, the process being completed in 1991. Flottille 24F, also at Lann-Bihoué, took delivery of its Atlantique 2s in 1992. Flottilles 21F and 22F, based at Nîmes-Garons, began conversion in 1994.

Proposed variants of the Atlantique 2 include a Nimrod replacement for the RAF, with additional turbofans (possibly Garrett TFE731s) in pods under the wing and with either Allison T406s or General Electric T407s replacing the Tynes; an **Atlantique 3** with further improvements; and the **Europatrol**, a derivative aimed at the replacement of NATO's P-3 Orions. A Tyne upgrade has also been proposed for the Atlantique.

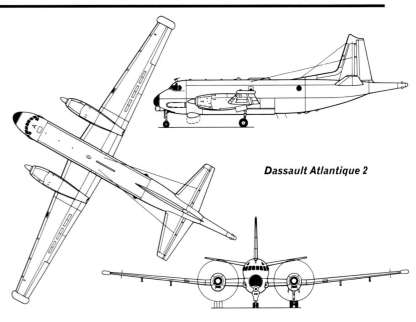

Dassault Atlantique 2

WEAPON OPTIONS

The Atlantique 2 has an internal weapons bay for the carriage of various bombs, up to eight depth charges and torpedoes. The latter can either be a maximum of eight Mk 46 or seven Murène weapons. The bay can also accommodate two anti-ship missiles, currently either AM39 Exocet or AS37 Martel. A typical load comprises one Exocet and three torpedoes. Additional missile armament can be carried on four underwing pylons, comprising ARMAT anti-radiation missiles or Magic 2 self-defence air-to-air missiles. Aft of the weapons bay is a sonobuoy launcher with over 100 buoys. Up to 160 smoke markers and flares are also carried, launched through the lower rear fuselage.

SPECIFICATION

Dassault Aviation Atlantique 2

Wing: span 37.42 m (122 ft 9.25 in) including wingtip ESM pods; aspect ratio 10.9; area 120.34 m² (1,295.37 sq ft)

Fuselage and tail: length 31.62 m (103 ft 9 in); height 10.89 m (35 ft 8.75 in); tailplane span 12.31 m (40 ft 4.5 in); wheel track 9.00 m (29 ft 6.25 in); wheel base 9.40 m (30 ft 10 in)

Powerplant: two Rolls-Royce Tyne RTy.20 Mk 21 each rated at 6,100 ehp (4549 ekW)

Weights: empty equipped 25600 kg (56,437 lb); normal take-off 44200 kg (97,443 lb) for the ASW or ASV roles, or 45000 kg (99,206 lb) for the combined ASW and ASV roles; maximum take-off 46200 kg (101,852 lb)

Fuel and load: internal fuel 18500 kg (40,785 lb); external fuel none; maximum external ordnance

3500 kg (7,716 lb); maximum internal ordnance 2500 kg (5,511 lb)

Speed: never-exceed speed Mach 0.73; maximum level speed 'clean' at optimum altitude 648 km/h (349 kt; 402 mph); maximum cruising speed at 7200 m (23,620 ft) 555 km/h (300 kt; 345 mph); normal patrol speed between sea level and 1525 m (5,000 ft) 315 km/h (170 kt; 196 mph)

Range: ferry range 9075 km (4,897 nm; 5,639 miles); operational radius 3333 km (1,799 nm; 2,071 miles) for a 2-hour patrol in the ASV role with one AM9 Exocet missile, or 1850 km (999 nm; 1,150 miles) for a 5-hour patrol in the ASW role at 1000 m (3,280 ft), or 1110 km (599 nm; 690 miles) for an 8-hour patrol in the ASW role at low altitude; endurance 18 hours

Performance: maximum rate of climb at sea level 884 m (2,900 ft) per minute; service ceiling 9145 m (30,000 ft); take-off distance to 10.5 m (35 ft) 1840 m (6,037 ft) at maximum take-off weight; landing distance from 10.5 m (35 ft) 1500 m (4,921 ft) at normal landing weight

Although superficially externally similar to the Atlantic 1, the Atlantique 2 has a completely revised equipment fit which makes it a far more capable maritime patroller. The most notable differences are the Tango FLIR sensor in a chin-mounted turret, and the revised wingtip/fintip antenna installations for the ESM equipment. The airframe is essentially similar to the earlier variant but has far greater corrosion protection, highly necessary for prolonged flight in the demanding overwater regime. The standard crew comprises two pilots, flight engineer, observer in glazed nose, radio navigator, ESM/ECM/MAD operator, tactical co-ordinator, radar-IFF operator and two acoustic operators. Two additional observers can be carried.

Dassault (Dassault-Breguet) **Etendard IVM/P**

The original **Dassault Etendard** (standard, or national flag) was the company's entry in a 1955 NATO competition for a light strike fighter able to operate from unpaved strips. Dassault developed subsequent versions, which were deemed to be underpowered. As a private venture, Das-

sault installed the much more powerful SNECMA Atar 08 turbojet and this version, which first flew on 24 July 1956, was designated **Etendard IV**. After rejection by the NATO nations in favour of the Fiat G91, the Etendard underwent a protracted modification programme to meet an **Aéronavale**

requirement for a carrier-based attack and reconnaissance aircraft.

Two versions were developed to fulfil these maritime roles. Compared with the original land-based aircraft, both maritime variants are equipped with such standard naval features as long-stroke undercarriage,

arrester hook, catapult attachments and associated strengthening, folding wingtips and a high-lift system which combined leading-edge and trailing-edge flaps, as well as two perforated belly airbrakes.

Initial deployment

The first version was designated **Etendard IVM** and deployed aboard the carriers *Foch* and *Clemenceau* (Flottilles 11F and 17F) along with the training unit 15F.

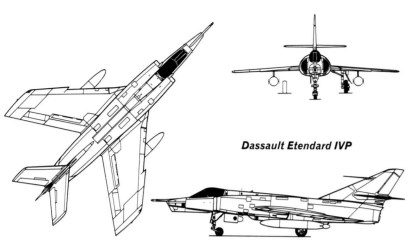

Dassault Etendard IVP

The elderly Etendard IVPs of 16 Flottille are maintained at Landivisiau to provide carrierborne detachments for reconnaissance and buddy tanking. Retirement of the fleet is expected in 1995, the Etendard IVM having retired from the training role in 1991.

The prototype of this variant flew for the first time on 21 May 1958, and was followed by six pre-production aircraft. The first of 69 production Etendard IVMs for the French navy was delivered on 18 January 1962, and production was completed in 1964. The Etendard IVM was equipped with Aïda all-weather fire-control radar and Saab toss-bombing computer. A unique nose-mounted underfin blade fairing contained the guidance aerial for the AS20 radio-command missile (now obsolete). The Etendard

IVM was withdrawn from service in July 1991 and has been replaced by the Super Etendard (described separately).

The seventh Etendard was the prototype of the **Etendard IVP**, a reconnaissance/tanker version, of which 21 were ordered. The first flight was made on 19 November 1960. The primary design changes include nose and ventral stations for three and two OMERA reconnaissance cameras (replacing attack avionics and guns respectively), an independent navigation

system, a fixed nose probe for inflight refuelling, and a 'buddy-pack' hose-reel unit designed by Douglas to allow Etendard-to-Etendard refuelling. The Etendard IVP remains in Aéronavale service with Flottille 16F at Landivisiau with no immediately obvious replacement, although it is scheduled to be retired in 1995. The 10 to 12 survivors are used for carrierborne reconnaissance and as buddy tankers for the Super Etendard, having seen action over Bosnia.

SPECIFICATION

Dassault-Breguet Etendard IVP
Wing: span 9.60 m (31 ft 6 in); aspect ratio 3; area 29 m² (312 sq ft)
Fuselage and tail: length 14.40 m (47 ft 3 in); height 4.30 m (14 ft 1 in)

Powerplant: one SNECMA Atar 8B turbojet rated at 43.16 kN (9,700 lb) thrust
Weights: empty 5900 kg (13,000 lb); normal take-off 8165 kg (18,000 lb); maximum take-off 10200 kg (22,485 lb)
Fuel and load: internal fuel 3300 litres (726 Imp gal); external fuel two 600-litre (132-Imp gal) underwing tanks; maximum external ordnance 1360 kg (3,000 lb)
Speed: maximum level speed 'clean' at optimum altitude Mach 1.08; maximum level speed 'clean' at sea level 1099 km/h (683 mph); landing speed 220 km/h (138 mph)
Range: low-level sortie at sea level 600 km (370 miles); medium-altitude sortie 1600 km (1,000 miles); ferry range 3000 km (1,860 miles)
Performance: maximum rate of climb at sea level 6000 m (19,685 ft) per minute; service ceiling 15500 m (50,850 ft); take-off distance 700 m (2,295 ft); landing distance without tailchute 800 m (2,625 ft); landing distance with tailchute 500 m (1,640 ft)

Dassault (Dassault-Breguet) **Falcon/Mystère 10**

A t the 1969 Paris air show, Dassault-Breguet announced the go-ahead of its **Mystère 10** (later **Falcon 10**), a smaller yet faster cousin to its successful Mystère/Falcon 20. The prototype flew on 1 December 1970 with General Electric CJ610 turbojets, but these were soon changed for Garrett geared turbofans. A very neat machine similar in layout to the Falcon 20 family, it differed in having wings of higher aspect ratio for improved cruise efficiency, with full-span slats and double-slotted flaps, the latter being worked hydraulically like the primary flight controls. By the time production ended in 1990, 226 examples had been delivered, the later production machines having minor changes and being designated **Mystère-Falcon 100**. Components were made by diverse companies in France, Spain and Italy, Dassault-Breguet handling assembly and test.

Small numbers of Falcon 10s were sold to governments as VIP transports and to foreign military customers. In addition, the French **Aéronavale** took delivery of seven specially-equipped **Mystère-Falcon 10MER** aircraft. These fulfil a range of important tasks which include acting as 'silent' (non-emitting) targets to test air-defence systems and interceptors, as conventional night and instrument pilot trainers, for calibration of radars and approach systems (especially on ships), and for transport, casevac and VIP communications. At least one has been fitted with four wing pylons

on which have been seen ESM and RWR receivers, ECM jammer pods, chaff/dispenser pods and various forms of armament. The aircraft fly with Escadrille de Servitude 57S at Landivisiau, at least four aircraft being configured for radar training.

SPECIFICATION

Dassault Aviation Falcon/Mystère 10
Wing: span 13.08 m (42 ft 11 in); aspect ratio 7.1; area 24.10 m² (259.42 sq ft)
Fuselage and tail: length 13.86 m (45 ft 5.75 in); height 4.61 m (15 ft 1.5 in); tailplane span 5.82 m (19 ft 1 in); wheel track 2.86 m (9 ft 5 in); wheel base 5.30 m (17 ft 4.75 in)
Powerplant: two Garrett TFE731-2 each rated at 3,230 lb st (14.37 kN) dry
Weights: empty equipped 4880 kg (10,760 lb); maximum take-off 8500 kg (18,740 lb)
Fuel and load: internal fuel 2680 kg (5,908 lb); external fuel none; maximum payload 1090 kg (2,400 lb) declining to 840 kg (1,852 lb) with maximum fuel
Speed: maximum cruising speed at 7620 m (25,000 ft) 912 km/h (492 kt; 566 mph)
Range: 3560 km (1,920 nm; 2,210 miles) with four passengers
Performance: operational ceiling 13715 m (45,000 ft) with four passengers; balanced take-off field length 960 m (3,150 ft) with four passengers and fuel for a 1850-km (999-nm; 1,150-mile) stage, or 1325 m (4,347 ft) with four passengers and maximum fuel; landing field length 1065 m (3,494 ft) with four passengers

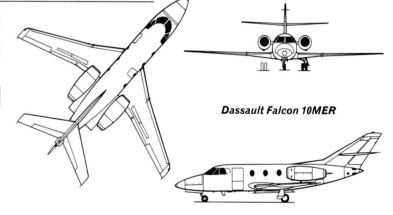

Dassault Falcon 10MER

The Mystère 10MER fulfils a variety of roles for the Aéronavale. Seven aircraft are assigned to Escadrille 57S at Landivisiau, used for transport and liaison, radar systems training and target facilities.

Dassault (Dassault-Breguet) **Falcon/Mystère 20/200/HU-25**

O riginally called the **Mystère 20**, the **Dassault-Breguet Falcon 20** twin-engined business jet first flew on 7 May 1963. From the outset it was developed as a 'top of the range' aircraft, with extensive integral tankage, fully powered controls and General Electric CF700 aft-fan engines flat-rated at 4,200 lb (18.58 kN) thrust each, with target-type reversers. The 69-in

(1.75- m) diameter cabin could be furnished for up to 12 passengers, though corporate versions seated nine or fewer passengers. Initial US sales resulted from a link with PanAm (today's Falcon Jet Corporation is a Dassault subsidiary), and this helped sales of many specially-equipped versions for military purposes. All versions described have conventional metal fail-safe structures, man-

ufacture of which is shared with other companies in France and Spain. The leading-edge slats, slotted flaps, wing-mounted air-brakes, flight controls and twin-wheel landing gear units are all actuated hydraulically. Engine bleed air is used for wing and engine inlet de-icing.

In January 1977 the sale of 41 **Falcon 20G** aircraft to the US Coast Guard (desig-

nated **HU-25A Guardian**) introduced the unique three-spool ATF3 turbofan, which was fitted as standard from 1983 in production **Falcon 200s**. The fuselage has been modified to incorporate two observation windows and a drop hatch for rescue supplies, which typically weigh up to 3,200 lb (1450 kg). The normal crew consists of two pilots, two observers and a sensor systems

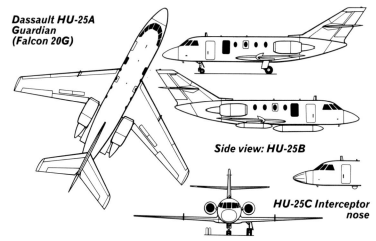

Dassault HU-25A Guardian (Falcon 20G)

Side view: HU-25B

HU-25C Interceptor nose

Pollution monitoring is a role of the seven HU-25Bs serving with the USCG, equipped with SLAR pod and linescan. The HU-25B was deployed to the Gulf region after the 1991 conflict to monitor oil slicks, operating from Bahrain.

operator. The HU-25A was obtained for medium-range, all-weather SAR, maritime surveillance and environmental protection duties. In original configuration, the machines were given a sophisticated array of equipment including an AN/APS-127 radar. Communications equipment includes dual HF, VHF-AM, IFF, single VHF-FM and UHF radios. Navaids include an inertial platform, Omega, dual VOR/ILS/MB, DME, ADF, radio altimeters, R-nav system and TACAN. The HU-25A has four fuselage hardpoints to carry rescue packs and four underwing hardpoints for sensor pods.

Today just over half of the Guardians delivered remain in their original configuration. Seven aircraft have been further modified as **HU-25Bs**. These differ by having a Motorola AN/APS-131 SLAR in a fuselage pod offset slightly to starboard, a Texas Instruments RS-18C linescan unit in another pod under the starboard wing and a laser-illuminated TV under the port wing. The Coast Guard operates these Guardians on surveillance duties with responsibility for detection of maritime pollution. A further nine aircraft have been modified for drug interdiction duties under the designation **HU-25C Interceptor**. Fitted with Westinghouse AN/APG-66 search radar in the

nose, turret-mounted WF-360 FLIR sensor and new secure communications gear, the HU-25C is tasked with the pursuit and identification of suspicious sea and air traffic, and entered service in May 1988.

The **Falcon 20H Gardian** maritime surveillance version is operated by the French Aéronavale in the Pacific by 9 Escadrille de Servitude at Tontouta, New Caledonia, and 12S at Faaa, Tahiti. Two aircraft are tasked with patrol and SAR duties within French territorial economic zones in the Pacific. The Gardian has extremely comprehensive avionics including Thomson-CSF Varan radar and VLF Omega navigation, and is characterised by a an extra-large observation window in the port side of the fuselage.

The **Falcon 200 Gardian 2** was a simplified export version marketed for Exocet attack, ESM/ECM, target designation and target towing, but is now cancelled. The basic Falcon 200 is offered with equipment for every kind of specialised role. Libya and France's Armée de l'Air use the **Falcon 20 SNA** version with Mirage radar and electronics for training in low-level attack, while the UK (Royal Navy) and Norway are among seven users of EW/ECM versions.

Further French Falcons have radar installed for training of Mirage 2000, Mirage IVP and Mirage F1CR crews. Dassault has modified a Falcon 20 to test the Rafale's RBE2 radar. The majority of users, however, fly small numbers of the Falcon 20/200 on VIP and staff transport duties. Dassault ended production in 1988 of all Falcon 20/200 variants, although there are several ongoing update programmes.

France and the US Coast Guard are the major operators of the Falcon/Mystère 20. Other operators are Belgium, Central African Republic, Chile, Djibouti, Egypt, Guinea-Bissau, Iran, Libya, Morocco, Norway, Pakistan, Peru, Portugal, Spain, Sudan, Syria and Venezuela. Virtually all fly the aircraft in a staff/VIP transport function, although Norway uses the type for ECM training. The same role is performed by Falcon 20s of Flight Refuelling Aviation, a UK-based civilian contractor supporting NATO activities.

SPECIFICATION

Dassault Aviation Falcon/Mystère 200

Wing: span 16.32 m (53 ft 6.5 in); aspect ratio 6.5; area 41.00 m² (441.33 sq ft)

France operates many special variants of Falcon 20. The Aéronavale flies the Gardian on maritime patrol duties, characterised by the large observation window. They serve in New Caledonia and Tahiti.

Fuselage and tail: length 17.15 m (56 ft 3 in); height 5.32 m (17 ft 5 in); tailplane span 6.74 m (22 ft 1 in); wheel track 3.34 m (10 ft 11.5 in); wheel base 5.74 m (18 ft 10 in)
Powerplant: two Garrett ATF3-6A-4C each rated at 5,200 lb st (23.13 kN) dry
Weights: empty equipped 8250 kg (18,188 lb); maximum take-off 14515 kg (32,000 lb)
Fuel and load: internal fuel 4845 kg (10,681 lb); external fuel none; maximum payload 1265 kg (2,789 lb) with maximum fuel
Speed: maximum cruising speed at 9150 m (30,020 ft) 870 km/h (470 kt; 541 mph); economical cruising speed at 12500 m (41,010 ft) 780 km/h (421 kt; 485 mph)
Range: range 4650 km (2,509 nm; 2,889 miles) with eight passengers and maximum fuel
Performance: service ceiling 13715 m (45,000 ft); balanced take-off field length 1420 m (4,659 ft) with eight passengers and maximum fuel; landing distance with eight passengers 1130 m (3,707 ft)

Dassault **Falcon/Mystère 50**

Dassault's first new business jet to complement the Falcon 20 was the small Falcon 10. In the mid-1970s the decision was taken to produce an aircraft which, while offering the same cabin cross-section as the Falcon 20, would have much greater range. The immediate objective was a trans-USA capability with a typical corporate payload of two crew and nine passengers, and this requirement was met by the Dassault design. The original prototype **Falcon/**

Mystère 50 was first flown on 7 November 1976 and was followed by the first production aircraft on 2 March 1979.

The Falcon 50 has the same external fuselage cross-section as the Mystère-Falcon 20, but has been extensively redesigned, introducing area ruling (a sharply waisted rear fuselage and engine pod designed by computational fluid dynamics) and an advanced new wing with compound leading-edge sweep and optimised

supercritical section. The innovative decision was taken to fit three engines, the choice falling on an uprated version of the Garrett TFE731 geared turbofan engine used in the Falcon 10 and 100. The third engine duct extends well forward above the rear fuselage, the inlet being faired into a vertical tail less acutely swept than that of previous Falcons. The tailplane has increased span and slight anhedral and is fitted with normal and high-rate emergency incidence controls. The wing is fitted with full-span slats and double-slotted flaps, giving a maximum lift coefficient greater than that of previous Falcons and enabling a similar field length to the Falcon 20/Gardian. The cabin can be furnished for similar groups of passengers; a typical arrangement seats eight or nine, with aft toilet, and forward crew toilet, galley and wardrobe.

A total of 225 Falcon 50s had been sold by 1992. VIP versions, usually for four/five passengers, have been bought by the governments of **Djibouti**, **France**, **Iraq**, **Italy**

(three convertible to air ambulance configuration), **Jordan**, **Morocco**, **Portugal**, **Rwanda**, **Spain** (operated under the designation **T.16**), **Sudan** and **Yugoslavia**.

SPECIFICATION

Dassault Aviation Falcon/Mystère 50

Wing: span 18.86 m (61 ft 10.5 in); aspect ratio 7.6; area 46.83 m² (504.09 sq ft)
Fuselage and tail: length 18.52 m (60 ft 9.25 in); height 6.97 m (22 ft 10.5 in); tailplane span 7.74 m (25 ft 4.75 in); wheel track 3.98 m (13 ft 0.25 in); wheel base 7.24 m (23 ft 9 in)
Powerplant: three Garrett TFE731-3 each rated at 3,700 lb st (16.46 kN) dry
Weights: empty equipped 9150 kg (20,172 lb); maximum take-off 17600 kg (38,801 lb) standard or 18500 kg (40,785 lb) optional
Fuel and load: internal fuel 7040 kg (15,520 lb); external fuel none; maximum payload 1570 kg (3,461 lb) standard or 2170 kg (4,784 lb) optional
Speed: maximum cruising speed at optimum altitude 880 km/h (432 kt; 497 mph)
Range: range 6480 km (3,497 nm; 4,027 miles) with eight passengers
Performance: service ceiling 14935 m (49,000 ft); balanced take-off field length 1365 m (4,478 ft) with eight passengers and maximum fuel; landing run 1080 m (3,543 ft) with eight passengers

Military use of the Falcon 50 is restricted to staff/VIP transport. Portugal is one such user, this aircraft operating with Esquadra 504. The unit is based at Montijo, and also flies the Falcon 20.

Dassault Falcon/Mystère 900

Superficially similar to the Falcon 50, this stretched version of the Falcon tri-jet – known as **Mystère 900** in French service – has a fuselage of greater cross-section, providing an additional 8 cm (3 in) of passenger headroom, uprated engines and slightly modified wings. Intended primarily for civilian use, it first flew on 21 September 1984. The first of two VVIP Mystère 900s was delivered to the **French air force**'s Groupe de Liaisons Aériennes Ministérielles at Villacoublay in November 1987. Similarly-tasked machines have been bought by **Algeria**, **Australia**, **Gabon**, **Malaysia**, **Nigeria** and **Spain**, the latter assigning the local designation **T.18**. Two **Falcon 900**s were delivered to the **Japan ASDF** for long-range maritime surveillance duties.

These aircraft are fitted with US search radar, operations control station, special communications radio, HU-25A Guardian-style observation windows and a drop hatch for sonobuoys, flares and markers.

SPECIFICATION

Dassault Aviation Falcon/Mystère 900
Wing: span 19.33 m (63 ft 5 in); aspect ratio 7.6; area 49.03 m² (527.75 sq ft)
Fuselage and tail: length 20.21 m (66 ft 3.75 in); height 7.55 m (24 ft 9.25 in); tailplane span 7.74 m (25 ft 4.75 in); wheel track 4.45 m (14 ft 7.25 in); wheel base 7.93 m (26 ft 0.25 in)
Powerplant: three Garrett TFE731-5AR-1C each rated at 4,500 lb st (20.02 kN) dry

Weights: empty equipped 10170 kg (22,421 lb); operating empty 10545 kg (23,348 lb); maximum take-off 20640 kg (45,503 lb)
Fuel and load: internal fuel 8690 kg (19,158 lb); external fuel none; maximum payload 1885 kg (4,156 lb)
Speed: maximum cruising speed at 11000 m (36,090 ft) 893 km/h (492 kt; 555 mph)
Range: 7227 km (3,900 nm; 4,491 miles) with eight passengers or 6412 km (3,460 nm; 3,984 miles) with maximum payload
Performance: maximum cruising height 15550 m (51,015 ft); balanced take-off field length 1515 m (4,970 ft) with eight passengers and maximum fuel; balanced landing field length 700 m (2,297 ft) at 12250 kg (27,006 lb)

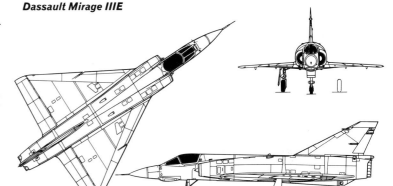

Two Mystère 900s serve with France's Groupe de Liaison Aériennes Ministérielles (GLAM). As its name implies, the unit provides transport for high-ranking government officials.

Dassault Mirage III

One aircraft established the reputation of France as a manufacturer of world-class jet fighters: the **Mirage III**. With just the right blend of speed, sophistication and simplicity, this Mach 2 delta provided the core of French air defence and attack forces during the 1960s and well into the 1970s, while gaining significant overseas sales which were to lead to follow-up orders for later Mirages and other French defence equipment. The prototype flew on 17 December 1956, but the last of 1,422 Mirage IIIs, 5s and 50s (the two last-mentioned described separately) was not completed until 1992. Even then, several air forces had just completed or were in the process of upgrading their Mirage IIIs for further service.

Discounting some designation anomalies, 'Mirage III' covers aircraft equipped with nose radar, the first of which for the Armée de l'Air were 10 **IIIA** pre-series machines and – entering service in July 1961 – 95 interceptor **IIIC**s. These had rocket motors in the rear fuselage to assist the 58.84-kN (13,227-lb st) afterburning SNECMA Atar 9B-3 turbojet when undertaking high-altitude missions, although the facility was little used. The IIIC has been withdrawn, as have most of the **IIIB** two-seat trainers, although a few **IIIB-1** test-beds and **IIIB-RV** refuelling trainers may remain. Single-seat **IIICZ**s exported to South Africa were withdrawn in October 1990, but 19 **IIICJ** veterans of Middle East wars were transferred from Israel to Argentina in 1982 and remain in service.

The second phase of Mirage III development was the **IIIE**, flown on 5 April 1961 and optimised for strike/attack as well as interception. Retaining Thomson-CSF Cyrano II radar and with engine modestly uprated to Atar 09C standard at 60.81 kN

Argentina's Mirage IIIEAs carry the basic interceptor armament of one MATRA R.530 and two R.550 Magics.

(13,669 lb), the IIIE series has a 30-cm (12-in) avionics bay added behind the cockpit, Doppler navigation and slight undercarriage changes to accommodate an AN52 nuclear bomb or large drop-tank on the fuselage centreline. France received 183, plus 20 equivalent **IIIBE** trainers. The IIIE's nuclear tasking was lost to Mirage 2000Ns in 1988 and by 1994 only one French squadron remained in the defence-suppression and conventional attack roles. This will retire in mid-1994. With a camera nose, the IIIE became the Mirage **IIIR**, 70 of which were delivered to the FAF, the last 20 as **IIIRD**s with Doppler. All of these have been supplanted by Mirage F1CRs.

Abroad, Argentina received 17 **IIIEA**s for interception, armed with MATRA R.530 radar-homing and R.550 Magic heat-seeking AAMs. Brazil acquired 16 **IIIEBR**s and, from 1988, six ex-French aircraft upgraded with foreplanes and new avionics, to which standard 10 older aircraft are being raised. In Lebanon, the 10 Mirage **IIIEL**s have long been in storage, while Pakistan is expanding its fleet by rebuilding many of the 50 **IIIO**s bought in 1990 after Australia withdrew its fleet. These will join the survivors of 18 **IIIEP**s and 13 reconnaissance **IIIRP**s bought new by the PAF.

Four more countries have chosen extensive Mirage update programmes, but that for Spain's **Mirage IIIEE**s (locally designated **C.11**) fell victim to funding cuts in 1992 and the aircraft have been withdrawn. South Africa bought 17 **IIIEZ**s, four **RZ**s and four **R2Z**s, the last-mentioned fitted with 70.61-kN (15,873-lb st) Atar 09K50s. Upgrading of the IIIEZs is under way to Atlas Cheetah (described separately) standard, following similar conversion of **IIIDZ** and **IIID2Z** two-seat trainers. Switzerland received 36 Mirage **IIIS** and 18 **IIIRS** aircraft, which are now fitted with new avionics and canards. Since new, the IIIS has been a non-standard Mirage, equipped with a Hughes TARAN 18 radar and navigation

suite for compatibility with Hughes Falcon AAMs. Venezuela bought seven Mirage **IIIEV**s, followed by Mirage 5s, all of which are being uprated to **Mirage 50EV** configuration. All Mirage IIIE operators have small numbers of two-seat **IIID** conversion trainers.

WEAPON OPTIONS

Cannon armament of 30-mm DEFA 552 cannon with 125 rounds per gun. Basic IIIC interceptor version with centreline pylon for one radar-guided missile, initially Nord 5103 or MATRA R.511, subsequently MATRA R.530 (Hughes AIM-26 Falcon on Swiss aircraft). Two wing pylons for infra-red guided missile, either AIM-9B/P Sidewinder or MATRA R.550 Magic (V3 Kukri on South African aircraft). Attack capability in form of JL-100 fuel tank/rocket pod.
Mirage IIIE multi-role aircraft introduced a maximum of five pylons with a maximum weapon load of 4000 kg (8,818 lb) including most free-fall bombs and

Brazil's fleet of Mirage IIIEBRs (illustrated) and IIIDBRs has been reworked by Dassault, complete with the obligatory canard foreplanes.

Dassault Mirage IIIE

rocket pods. Attack missiles include Aérospatiale AS30 and MATRA AS37 Martel. French aircraft wired for AN52 15-kT yield tactical nuclear free-fall bomb.

SPECIFICATION

Dassault Aviation Mirage IIIE
Wing: span 8.22 m (26 ft 11.6 in); aspect ratio 1.94; area 35.00 m² (376.75 sq ft)
Fuselage and tail: length 15.03 m (49 ft 3.5 in); height 4.50 m (14 ft 9 in); wheel track 3.15 m (10 ft 4 in); wheel base 4.87 m (15 ft 11.75 in)
Powerplant: one SNECMA Atar 9C-3 rated at 41.97 kN (9,436 lb st) dry and 60.80 kN (13,668 lb st) with afterburning, and provision for one jettisonable SEPR 844 rocket booster rated at 14.71 kN (3,307 lb st)
Weights: empty 7050 kg (15,542 lb); normal take-off 9600 kg (21,164 lb); maximum take-off 13700 kg (30,203 lb)
Fuel and load: internal fuel 2390 litres (631.4 US gal) increasable by 550 litres (145 US gal) if the rocket pack is not fitted; external fuel up to two 1700-, 1300-, 1100- or 625-litre (449-, 343-, 291- or 165-US gal) drop tanks, or two 500-litre (132-US gal) non-jettisonable supersonic tanks, or two 250-litre (66-US gal) JL-100 combined drop tanks/rocket launchers, or two 1100-litre (291-US gal) fuel/electronic equipment tanks; maximum ordnance 4000 kg (8,818 lb)

There were two basic styles of two-seater, the IIIB with a standard radome (although without radar), and the IIIBE/D with a solid nose. Illustrating the former is a IIIB-2(RV), with dummy refuelling probe for training Mirage IV pilots.

Speed: maximum level speed 'clean' at 12000 m (39,370 ft) 2350 km/h (1,268 kt; 1,460 mph); cruising speed at 11000 m (36,090 ft) 956 km/h (516 kt; 594 mph)
Range: ferry range 4000 km (2,152 nm; 2,486 miles) with three drop tanks; combat radius 1200 km (647 nm; 746 miles) on a hi-hi-hi mission with very small warload
Performance: maximum rate of climb at sea level more than 5000 m (16,405 ft) per minute; climb to 11000 m (36,090 ft) in 3 minutes 0 seconds; service ceiling 17000 m (55,775 ft) or 23000 m (75,460 ft) with rocket pack; take-off run between 700 and 1600 m (2,297 and 5,249 ft) depending on mission-related

maximum weight; landing run 700 m (2,297 ft) with brake chute
g limits: +4.83 in a sustained turn at Mach 0.9 at 5000 m (16,405 ft)

OPERATORS

There is much confusion surrounding the Mirage III/5/50 family, some members being designated as Mirage 5s but bearing all the characteristics (i.e. Cyrano air-to-air radar) of the Mirage IIIE. For simplicity, the operators are presented according to designation. The numbers relate to actual deliveries rather than surviving aircraft:
Argentina: IIIBJ (3), IIICJ (19), IIIDA (4), IIIEA (17) – a large proportion remain in active service
Australia: IIID (16), IIIO(F) (49), IIIO(A) (51) – final flight of Australian Mirage in 1989. Survivors stored pending sale to Pakistan
Brazil: IIIDBR (6), IIIDBR-2 (2), IIIEBR (16), IIIEBR-2 (4) – local designation of F-103D for two-seater and

F-103E for single-seater. 18 believed left in service following upgrade
France: IIIB (27), IIIB-1 (5), IIIB-2(RV) (10), IIIBE (17), IIIC (95), IIIE (183), IIIR (50), IIIRD (20) – Mirage IIIC withdrawn from service, and Mirage IIIE due for retirement in 1995, ending front-line service. A handful of aircraft used by the Centre d'Essais en Vol
Israel: IIIBJ (5), IIICJ (72) – survivors sold to Argentina
Lebanon: IIIBL (2), IIIEL (10) – survivors unserviceable
Pakistan: IIIDP (5), IIIEP (18), IIIRP (13), IIIO (43), IIID (7) – original purchases mostly still in service and being augmented by upgraded ex-RAAF aircraft
South Africa: IIIBZ (3), IIICZ (16), IIIDZ (3), IIID2Z (11), IIIEZ (17), IIIRZ (4), IIIR2Z (4) – early aircraft withdrawn from service, while EZs and D2Zs undergoing Cheetah

The reconnaissance variants of Mirage III feature a revised nose with a fan of cameras underneath the nose, and a forward-facing unit in the chisel-shaped extreme nose. The Swiss Mirage IIIRS fleet has been updated with canards and Dalmo Victor RWR antennas.

upgrade
Spain: IIIDE (6), IIIEE (24) – retired
Switzerland: IIIBS (4), IIICS (1), IIIDS (2), IIIRS (18), IIIS (36) – survivors active after canard upgrade
Venezuela: IIIDV (3), IIIEV (7) – in process of update to 50EV standard

Dassault **Mirage IV**

In 1954 the French government decided to create a national Force de Frappe (nuclear deterrent), one element of which would be a manned bomber. Originally planned as a bigger aircraft with large Pratt & Whitney engines, the **Dassault Mirage IV** was finally scaled down as the **Mirage IVA** with two Atar turbojets, which meant that it could not fly two-way missions to Soviet targets. The prototype flew on 17 June 1959, and following considerable further development a production run of 50 was authorised, later followed by a further 12. The force was completed in March 1968, but since then upgrading of aircraft still in

service has been a continuous process.
Aerodynamically, the Mirage IVA is broadly similar to a scaled-up Mirage III, with side-by-side engines, pilot and navigator in tandem cockpits with upward-hinged canopies, four-wheel bogie main landing gears, tall steerable twin-wheel nose gear and a slender nose terminating in an inflight-refuelling probe. This probe is vital to any mission, because virtually all combat sorties are planned on the basis of one or more refuellings from a Boeing C-135FR tanker or via a buddy pack from an accompanying Mirage IVA. Navigation is by a CSF surveillance radar under the belly, Marconi

Doppler, Dassault computer and SFENA autopilot, more recently upgraded by adding dual inertial systems. OMERA Robot strike cameras are fitted, and the original weapon load comprised a 60-kT nuclear bomb recessed into the rear fuselage, though by removing the large drop tanks it is possible to carry six conventional bombs or four AS37 Martel anti-radar missiles. For many years the force at readiness comprised 36 aircraft (of 51 bomber versions available) assigned to EB 91 and EB 94 and dispersed in small groups around seven bases. In emergency, further dispersal is possible, using chemicals to harden tracts of farmland and six rockets under each wing to blast the aircraft off after a short run. Some were configured for reconnaissance with a semi-recessed camera/SLAR package.

In the late 1980s 19 Mirage IVAs (18 and an attrition replacement) were converted to **Mirage IVP** standard, and this is the only version left in service. Together with updated avionics including a twin inertial platform and Thomson-CSF Serval RWRs, the IVP introduced the ability to carry the Aérospatiale ASMP stand-off nuclear missile on a pylon under the belly. ASMP offers a 300-kT TN81 warhead, and variable delivery profiles dependent on altitude with a maximum range of 155 miles (250 km) at high level, increasing survivability.

A Mirage IVP blasts off from Mont-de-Marsan, using all 12 RATOG bottles. The latter allowed the Mirage IV to react quickly, and to launch from semi-prepared strips.

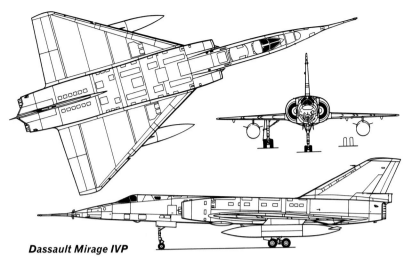

Dassault Mirage IVP

A reduction in the Mirage IV force means that only 14 are operational, serving with two squadrons of Escadre de Bombardement 91, Force Aériennes Stratégiques. Each squadron maintains a detachment, so Mirage IVs are deployed to four bases for security reasons. EB 1/91 'Gascogne' is headquartered at BA118 Mont-de-Marsan, and has its detachment at BA115 Orange/Caritat, while EB 2/91 'Brétagne' is based at Cazaux and detaches to BA125 Istres/Le Tubé. EB 91 has also completely absorbed the Mirage IV training task previously undertaken by CIFAS 328 at Bordeaux.

SPECIFICATION

Dassault Aviation Mirage IVP
Wing: span 11.85 m (38 ft 10.5 in); aspect ratio 1.8; area 78.00 m² (839.61 sq ft)
Fuselage and tail: length 23.50 m (77 ft 1.2 in); height 5.65 m (18 ft 6.4 in)

Powerplant: two SNECMA Atar 9K-50 each rated at 49.03 kN (11,023 lb st) dry and 70.61 kN (15,873 lb st) with afterburning
Weights: empty equipped 14500 kg (31,966 lb); maximum take-off 31600 kg (69,666 lb)
Fuel and load: internal fuel 14000 litres (3,698 US gal); external fuel up to two 2500-litre (660-US gal) drop tanks; maximum ordnance 900 kg (1,984 lb) in missile role or 7200 kg (15,873 lb) in bomber role
Speed: maximum level speed 'clean' at 11000 m (36,090 ft) 2338 km/h (1,262 kt; 1,453 mph) or at sea level about 1349 km/h (728 kt; 838 mph); normal penetration speed at 11000 m (36,090 ft) 1913 km/h (1,172 kt; 1,189 mph)
Range: ferry range 4000 km (2,158 nm; 2,486 miles) with drop tanks; typical combat radius 1240 km

This aircraft was one of two involved in ASMP trials, and shows the position of the missile pylon and the bombing radar. The ASMP is available with either TN80 150-kT yield warhead or TN81 of 30-kT yield. Using terrain avoidance profiles at low level, the ASMP has a range of about 80 km (50 miles). At high altitude this is extended to 250 km (155 miles).

(668 nm; 771 miles)
Performance: climb to 11000 m (36,090 ft) in 4 minutes 15 seconds; service ceiling 20000 m (65,615 ft)

Dassault **Mirage 5/50**

In 1966 the Israeli air force asked Dassault to build a simplified version of the Mirage IIIE optimised for the daytime VFR ground-attack mission. The basic changes in developing this **Mirage 5** were to move the avionics racking from behind the cockpit to the nose, deletion of radar being the main feature. Extra fuel was added in the fuselage, and the nose reprofiled to be much slimmer. Two extra fuselage weapons pylons were added, splayed outwards, so that a maximum of 4000 kg (8,818 lb) of stores could be carried in addition to 1000 litres (220 Imp gal) of fuel, although such a configuration would demand a long runway for take-off. Alternatively the Mirage 5 could be used in the daytime fighter role with infra-red air-to-air missiles, cannon and up to 4700 litres (1,034 Imp gal) of external fuel. The prototype first flew on 19 May 1967.

Using the designation **Mirage 5J**, the Israeli order for 50 was embargoed by President de Gaulle and the stored aircraft were then delivered to the Armée de l'Air as the **Mirage 5F**. The survivors flew with EC 2/13 and EC 3/13, with the former disbanding and the latter receiving Mirage F1CTs.

Following the initial order, the Mirage 5 proved popular with many customers around the world, who wanted a cheap but potent fighter-bomber. Dassault produced a two-seat **Mirage 5D** and reconnaissance-configured **Mirage 5R** to complement the basic model. As the production run of 525 aircraft progressed, the original no-frills aircraft became available with an ever-greater range of avionics options, including reintroduction of the radar. Lightweight radars such as the Cyrano IV, Agave or Aïda II were fitted, or laser rangefinders. Indeed, Dassault could mix and match a wide range of avionics to suit any nation's requirements, and many aircraft have been upgraded during their service lives. Identifying variants of the Mirage deltas is a highly confusing topic, made all the worse by radical upgrade programmes led by both Dassault and IAI, and IAI's own construction/upgrading programme which encompasses the Nesher, Dagger, Kfir and Nammer variants (described under IAI).

Greater thrust

A major programme was the **Mirage 50**, which introduced the Atar 9K-50 engine, as developed for the Mirage F1. The greater thrust endows the aircraft with better runway performance, faster acceleration, larger weapon load and improved manoeuvrability. The prototype Mirage 50 first flew on 15 April 1979, and Chile was the first customer with an order for 16,

although four South African IIIR2Zs had already been delivered with 9K-50 engines. The Mirage 50 package is available as a conversion of both Mirage IIIs and 5s, and the complete range of Mirage III/5 avionics/weapons is available on the Mirage 50, thereby bringing together the two separate development strands of the Dassault deltas, but at the same time creating further confusion concerning designations.

Over half of the Mirage III/5/50 operators have opted for update programmes, pursued either with indigenous systems integrators or with help from Dassault or IAI. Important modifications applied to many of the aircraft concerned include the addition of refuelling probes, improved nav/attack

Egypt's Mirage 5E2s were equipped to a high standard with fin-mounted radar warning receivers and an undernose laser rangefinder.

avionics and the fitment of canard foreplanes to improve manoeuvrability and runway performance. Brief details of these are given with the current Mirage 5/50 user list which follows: Abu Dhabi has **Mirage 5AD** fighters, **5RAD**s for reconnaissance and **5DAD** trainers. No upgrade programme has been announced. Argentina has **Mirage 5P**s in addition to IAI Daggers. These have been updated with laser rangefinder, HUD and refuelling probe. Belgium recently operated **5BA** ground attack

The Mirage 5 stemmed from an Israeli order for a low-cost day fighter, but the order was embargoed. The Mirage 5Js subsequently became 5Fs, and were delivered to the Armée de l'Air. They mainly served with EC 13, which operated the survivors until June 1994 when EC 2/13 disbanded.

Dassault Mirage 5BR

This Mirage 5BR wears the striking colours applied to celebrate 42 Smaldeel/Escadrille's 70th anniversary. Belgium was a major operator of the Mirage 5, and had embarked on an upgrade programme (MIRSIP) to improve 15 of its 5BAs and five 5BRs. In the event, the Mirage 5 was retired in December 1993, despite the MIRSIP programme proceeding.

LOCAL CONSTRUCTION
SABCA assembled all but the first examples of the three Belgian variants, and was also involved in the manufacture of several components, including rear fuselages and nosecones. The Atar engines were also assembled locally, and some of the equipment was indigenous.

RECONNAISSANCE
For its operational role, the Mirage 5BR was equipped with five British-made Vinten cameras arranged to peer obliquely sideways, downwards or forwards through windows in the nose section. A panoramic camera can be mounted in station 2, which has an extended fairing.

POWERPLANT
The Mirage 5BR is based on the airframe/engine combination of the IIIE, and thus has the same stretched forward fuselage (with intake lip behind the rear edge of the canopy) and variable-area petal-type afterburner nozzle. The engine is the Atar 09C-3, which develops 58.8 kN (13,228 lb) thrust with reheat.

FUEL
Two integral tanks in each wing hold 685 litres (181 US gal), pushing total internal capacity to 3330 litres (880 US gal). This is usually augmented by wing tanks holding 1000 litres (264 US gal).

---

aircraft, **5BD** two-seaters and **5BR**s with reconnaissance nose. Of these, 15 **BA**s and five **BD**s were being upgraded with HUD, laser rangefinder and canards to serve with 42 Smaldeel/Escadrille, although all were retired in December 1993 as the MIRSIP programme neared completion. Interest in the aircraft has come from Chile and the Philippines.

Chile operates **Mirage 50C**s and a **50DC** with Grupo 4 of 4 Brigada Aérea at

Although designated Mirage 5DE, this is one of Libya's radar- and Doppler-equipped aircraft – to all intents and purposes a Mirage IIIE.

Punta Arenas. With IAI assistance, ENAER is upgrading them to **50CN Pantera** standard, which involved the fitment of canard foreplanes and Israeli avionics. Colombia operates **5COA**s in the fighter role, **5COR**s for reconnaissance and **5COD** two-seaters with Escuadrón de Combate 212. IAI, which also supplied Kfirs, completed the conversion of the 5CODs with some Kfir avionics and 50 per cent Kfir canards. The remainder of the fleet is being converted with 75 per cent canards in Colombia, being designated **Mirage 50M**.

Egypt has completed a minor update programme on some of its Mirages. These comprise **5SDE/SSE** interceptors, **5SDR**

reconnaissance platforms, **5SDD** trainers and **5E2** attack aircraft. Gabon operates **5G** interceptors, **5G-II** attack aircraft and **5DG** two-seaters. Libya has Mirage **5D**s in the attack role, **5E**s for fighter duties, **5DR**s for reconnaissance and **5DD**s for training. Pakistan has updated its Mirage fleet with new avionics. Aircraft in service include various Mirage III models and **5PA**s and Cyrano- or Agave-equipped **5PA2**s and **5PA3**s for fighter-bomber and anti-shipping work, plus **5DPA** and **5DPA2** for conversion. Peru has upgraded its fleet with refuelling probes and laser rangefinder. The fleet comprises Mirage **5P4**s and **5DP4**s. Venezuela has re-engined both single- and two-seat aircraft with Atar 9K-50s, raising their designation to Mirage **50EV** and **50DV,** respectively.

New 50EVs and a 50DV are in service, augmented by secondhand aircraft upgraded to 50EV standards. Venezuelan aircraft feature canards, refuelling probe, Cyrano IVM3 radar and Exocet capability. Zaïre has not upgraded its aircraft, and operates Mirage **5M**s and a **5DM** trainer.

Information on relevant numbers is presented within the 'Operators' section.

Fully upgraded, the Mirage III/5 is still a highly capable warplane. Representing the pinnacle of Dassault upgrades is this Venezuelan 50EV, with Atar 09K-50 engine, refuelling probe, Serval RWR, canard foreplanes, ULISS 81 INS and Cyrano IV-M3 radar.

Pakistan's 5PA2 and 5PA3 aircraft feature a more rounded nose housing a multi-mode radar. The 5PA2 has the Cyrano IV for air-to-air work and the 5PA3 (illustrated) an Agave unit for anti-ship duties with the Exocet missile.

WEAPON OPTIONS

Similar to those of Mirage III family, although not nuclear-capable. Some aircraft designated Mirage 5 have Cyrano fire-control radar and are in effect Mirage IIIs. These can launch radar-guided air-to-air missiles, but other Mirage 5 family members cannot. Egypt's Mirage 5s employ US weapons, including the Rockeye cluster bomb. Venezuelan and some Pakistani aircraft (5PA3) have Cyrano IVM3 or Agave radar and the ability to launch the AM39 Exocet anti-ship missile.

OPERATORS

Abu Dhabi: 5AD (12), 5DAD (3), 5EAD (14), 5 RAD (3) – 23 single-seat fighters, three reconnaissance aircraft and the three trainers remain in service
Argentina: 5P (10) – nine remain in service
Belgium: 5BA (63), 5BR (27), 5BD (16) – remaining Mirages retired in December 1993
Chile: 50C (6), 50DC (3), 50FC (8) – all single-seaters and one trainer serve with Grupo 4. Aircraft being converted to 50CN Pantera standard
Colombia: 5COA (14), 5COD (2), 5COR (2) – 10 fighters and all reconnaissance/trainers still in service. In the process of update to 50M standard
Egypt: 5SDE (54), 5SDD (6), 5SDR (6), 5E2 (16) – most remain in service
Gabon: 5DG (4), 5G (3), 5G-II (4) – two 5G, three 5G-II and three 5DG remain in service
Libya: 5D (53), 5DD (15), 5DE (32), 5DR (10) – around 35 5Ds, 30 5DEs, eight 5DRs and 10 5DEs are thought to survive, but serviceability is low
Pakistan: 5DPA2 (2), 5PA (28), 5PA2 (28), 5PA3 (12) – most still in service
Peru: 5P (22), 5P3 (10), 5P4 (2), 5DP (4), 5DP3 (2) – current fleet comprises 12 single-seaters upgraded to 5P4 standard and three 5DP4 two-seaters
Venezuela: 5V (6), 5DV (1), 5EV (9) – fleet undergoing upgrade to 50DV/EV standard, including Mirage IIIs
Zaïre: 5M (8), 5DM (3) – serviceability of fleet is low

SPECIFICATION

Dassault Aviation Mirage 5A (Mirage 5F)
Wing: span 8.22 m (26 ft 11.6 in); aspect ratio 1.94; area 35.00 m2 (376.75 sq ft)
Fuselage and tail: length 15.55 m (51 ft 0.2 in); height 4.50 m (14 ft 9 in); wheel track 3.15 m (10 ft 4 in); wheel base 4.87 m (15 ft 11.75 in)
Powerplant: one SNECMA Atar 9C rated at 41.97 kN (9,436 lb st) dry and 60.80 kN (13,668 lb st) with afterburning
Weights: empty equipped 7150 kg (15,763 lb); normal take-off 9900 kg (21,825 lb); maximum take-off 13700 kg (30,203 lb)
Fuel and load: internal fuel 2860 litres (755.5 US gal); external fuel up to two 1700-, 1300-, 1100- or 625-litre (449-, 343-, 291- or 165-US gal) drop tanks, or two 500-litre (132-US gal) non-jettisonable supersonic tanks, or two 250-litre (66-US gal) JL-100 combined drop tanks/rocket launchers, or two 1100-litre (291-US gal) non-jettisonable fuel/electronic equipment tanks; maximum ordnance 4000 kg (8,818 lb)
Speed: maximum level speed 'clean' at 12000 m (39,370 ft) 2350 km/h (1,268 kt; 1,460 mph); cruising speed at 11000 m (36090 ft) 956 km/h (516 kt; 594 mph)
Range: combat radius 1250 km (675 nm; 777 miles) on a hi-lo-hi attack mission at Mach 0.85 with two 400-kg (882-lb) bombs and maximum external fuel, or 685 km (370 nm; 426 miles) on a lo-lo-lo attack mission at Mach 0.6 with two 400-kg (882-lb) bombs and maximum external fuel
Performance: maximum rate of climb at sea level 11160 m (36,614 ft) per minute; service ceiling 18000 m (59,055 ft) or 23000 m (75,460 ft) with rocket pack; take-off run between 915 m (3,002 ft) at normal take-off weight and 1830 m (6,004 ft) at maximum take-off weight; landing run 1830 m (6,004 ft) at maximum landing weight

Dassault Aviation Mirage 50M
Wing: span 8.22 m (26 ft 11.6 in); aspect ratio 1.94; area 35.00 m2 (376.75 sq ft); optional canard foreplane area 1.00 m2 (10.76 sq ft)
Fuselage and tail: length 15.56 m (51 ft 0.6 in); height 4.50 m (14 ft 9 in); wheel track 3.15 m (10 ft 4 in); wheel base 4.87 m (15 ft 11.75 in)
Powerplant: one SNECMA Atar 9K-50 rated at 49.03 kN (11,023 lb st) dry and 70.82 kN (15,873 lb st) with afterburning
Weights: empty equipped 7150 kg (15,763 lb); normal take-off 10000 kg (22,046 lb); maximum take-off 14700 kg (32,407 lb)
Fuel and load: internal fuel 2288 kg (5,044 lb) for

One of many dramatic upgrade programmes, the ENAER Pantera 50CN is based on the Mirage 50 with uprated engine, but also features a Kfir-style nose with Elta EL/M-2001B ranging radar, fin-mounted Caiquen III radar warning receivers, IAI-designed canards and numerous avionics upgrades.

Mirage III conversions or 2710 kg (5,974 lb) for Mirage 5 conversions; external fuel up to two 1700-, 1300-, 1100- or 625-litre (449-, 343-, 291- or 165-US gal) drop tanks, or two 500-litre (132-US gal) non-jettisonable supersonic tanks, or two 250-litre (66-US gal) JL-100 combined drop tanks/rocket launchers, or two 1100-litre (291-US gal) non-jettisonable Bidon Cyclope fuel/electronic equipment tanks; maximum ordnance 4000 kg (8,818 lb)
Speed: maximum level speed 'clean' at 12000 m (39,370 ft) 2338 km/h (1,262 kt; 1,453 mph); cruising speed at 11000 m (36,090 ft) 956 km/h (516 kt; 594 mph)
Range: combat radius 1315 km (710 nm; 817 miles) of a hi-hi-hi interception mission with two AAMs and three drop tanks, or 1260 km (680 nm; 783 miles) on a hi-lo-hi attack mission with two 400-kg (882-lb) bombs and three drop tanks, or 630 km (340 nm; 391 miles) on a lo-lo-lo attack mission with two 400-kg (882-lb) bombs and three drop tanks
Performance: maximum rate of climb at sea level 11160 m (36,614 ft) per minute; climb to 13715 m (45,000 ft) in 4 minutes 42 seconds; service ceiling 18000 m (59,055 ft); take-off run 800 m (2,625 ft) with two Magic AAMs or 1830 m (6,004 ft) at maximum take-off weight; landing run 1830 m (6,004 ft) at normal landing weight

Dassault **Mirage F1A/D/E**

While most export customers for the Mirage F1 interceptor series were content to specify aircraft based on the original Armée de l'Air F1C (described separately), the South African Air Force recognised the advantages of a simplified version for day visual attack missions. This exactly parallels the Mirage 5, which is a similar simplified version of the Mirage III. Like the Mirage 5, the resulting **Dassault-Breguet Mirage F1A** is visually distinguished by having a slender conical nose, resulting from removal of the large Cyrano IVM radar. In its place is the ESD Aïda II ranging radar as fitted to some Mirage 5 versions. Again like the Mirage 5s, the large instrument boom housing the pitot/static heads is attached on the underside of the nose, out of the way of the Aïda II radar set.

The main advantages of the Mirage F1A are its relatively low cost and extra range/payload capability. The main avionics racking is moved from behind the cockpit to the nose, making room for an extra fuselage tank. Other additions are a Doppler radar, and a retractable refuelling probe. The Mirage F1A was bought by Libya (16) and South Africa, which received 32 aircraft designated **Mirage F1AZ** for service with No. 1 Sqn. In addition to Aïda radar, South African F1AZs are fitted with a laser-ranger. A licence to build the Mirage and its Atar engine is held by Armscor, though Atlas Aircraft, the main South African aircraft manufacturer, has never announced more than the manufacture of parts. South African F1AZs were involved in offensives into Angola and anti-guerrilla operations in south-west Africa, utilising MATRA F4 rocket pods in addition to indigenous CFD-200 chaff/flare dispensers and bombs.

On 22 December 1974 Dassault flew a prototype designated **Mirage F1E**, powered by the then-new M53 engine. This aircraft failed to win large orders from four European NATO countries, and the M53-powered version was abandoned. Instead, and repeating the practice established with the Mirage III, the designation was then applied to an upgraded multi-role fighter/attack version for export customers. Outwardly resembling the F1C, the F1E has a SAGEM inertial system, EMD.182 central digital computer, VE.120C head-up display, Crouzet air-data computer and digital arma-

Only South Africa and Libya purchased the F1A. Libyan F1ADs are rarely seen, this example carrying a squadron badge.

ment/navigation controls. Like all F1 versions, the F1E can be fitted with comprehensive radar-warning receivers, chaff/flare dispensers and active ECM jammer pods, the most important of the latter being the Thomson-CSF Remora and Caiman. The **Mirage F1D** is essentially similar to the F1B (described separately) trainer procured by the Armée de l'Air, differing only by being based on the F1E export variant, although they are fitted with SEMMB Mk 10 zero-zero ejection seats with command ejection. These trainers are fully combat capable and have been acquired in small numbers by some F1E operators.

Most export F1D/Es have been fitted

Iraq's first batch of F1EQs were principally fighters, armed with Super 530F and Magic 1 missiles.

The F1D (and essentially similar F1B) is a two-seater conversion/continuation trainer. Qatar operates a pair of F1DDAs.

with bullet antennas for Thomson-CSF BF radar warning receiver and VOR aerials located in the fin. In addition, some aircraft received an HF fillet aerial at the forward joint of the fin. Iraqi F1Es were used extensively in the eight-year war with Iran, and more recently during the Gulf War in 1991. Basic multi-role aircraft (**F1EQ**, **F1EQ-2**) were followed by the **F1EQ-4** with refuelling probe and reconnaissance pod capability, and **F1EQ-5** and **F1EQ-6** with Thomson-CSF Agave radar and Exocet capability.

The F1EQ-6 had SHERLOC RWR from the outset, also retrofitted to the F1EQ-5s.

WEAPON OPTIONS

The attack-optimised F1A features two 30-mm DEFA 553 cannon with 125 rounds per gun. One centreline and two underwing pylons can mount a wide variety of unguided stores up to 4000 kg (8,820 lb), with MATRA Magic air-to-air missiles on the wingtip rails. South African F1AZs carry a variety of Israeli and indigenous weapons, including Armscor 250-kg (550-lb) fragmentation bombs and rocket pods.
The multi-role F1E can carry similar weapons, but is also equipped to fire radar-guided missiles. Iraqi F1EQ-5s and F1EQ-6s carry Exocet anti-ship missiles.

OPERATORS

Mirage F1As were sold to South Africa (32 F1AZs) and Libya (16 **F1AD**s accompanied by six **F1BD** trainers).

The Mirage F1E has achieved some degree of export success and has been acquired by Ecuador (16 **Mirage F1JA**s based on the F1E and two **Mirage F1JE** trainers), Iraq (110 **F1EQ**s ordered, although only 93 have been delivered), Jordan (17 **F1EJ**s), Libya (16 **F1ED**s), Morocco (14 **F1EH**s and six **F1EH-200**s), Qatar (12 **F1EDA**s and two **F1DDA** trainers) and Spain (22 **F1EE-200**s operated under the local designation **C.14B**).

Iraq's later Mirages are fitted with Agave radar and wear a slate-blue colour scheme for the anti-ship role.

SPECIFICATION

Dassault Aviation Mirage F1A/E
generally similar to Mirage F1C (described separately) except in the following particulars:
Fuselage and tail: length 15.30 m (50 ft 2.5 in)
Weights: empty 7600 kg (16,755 lb)
Speed: maximum level speed 'clean' at 11000 m (36,090 ft) 2125 km/h (1,146 kt; 1.320 mph)
Performance: maximum rate of climb at sea level 12000 m (39,370 ft) per minute with afterburning

Dassault Mirage F1AZ

Surviving South African Mirages wear this distinctive camouflage scheme. National and squadron insignia are often oversprayed. The aircraft serves with No. 1 Sqn, based at Hoedspruit, the last SAAF Mirage F1 user following the retirement of the F1CZs.

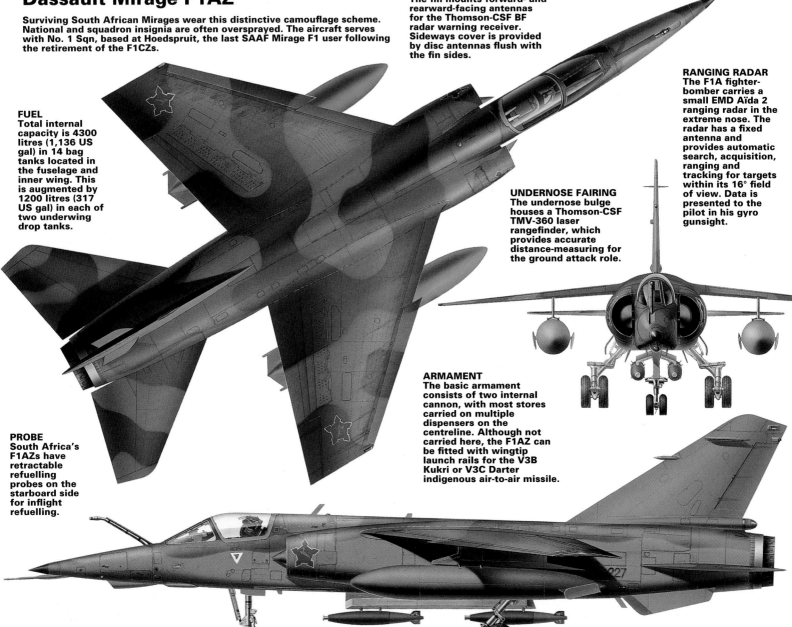

RADAR WARNING
The fin mounts forward- and rearward-facing antennas for the Thomson-CSF BF radar warning receiver. Sideways cover is provided by disc antennas flush with the fin sides.

RANGING RADAR
The F1A fighter-bomber carries a small EMD Aïda 2 ranging radar in the extreme nose. The radar has a fixed antenna and provides automatic search, acquisition, ranging and tracking for targets within its 16° field of view. Data is presented to the pilot in his gyro gunsight.

FUEL
Total internal capacity is 4300 litres (1,136 US gal) in 14 bag tanks located in the fuselage and inner wing. This is augmented by 1200 litres (317 US gal) in each of two underwing drop tanks.

UNDERNOSE FAIRING
The undernose bulge houses a Thomson-CSF TMV-360 laser rangefinder, which provides accurate distance-measuring for the ground attack role.

ARMAMENT
The basic armament consists of two internal cannon, with most stores carried on multiple dispensers on the centreline. Although not carried here, the F1AZ can be fitted with wingtip launch rails for the V3B Kukri or V3C Darter indigenous air-to-air missile.

PROBE
South Africa's F1AZs have retractable refuelling probes on the starboard side for inflight refuelling.

Dassault Mirage F1B/C

Despite its suffix, the **Mirage F1C** was the initial production version of Dassault's successor to the Mirage III/5. Forsaking the delta for a high-mounted wing and conventional tail surfaces, the private venture prototype flew on 23 December 1966 and was officially adopted in May 1967, when three prototypes were ordered. With more power provided by a 70.61-kN (15,873-lb st) SNECMA Atar 09K50 reheated turbojet, the F1 easily out-performs the Mirage III, offering 43 per cent more internal fuel capacity, 2.5 tonnes more on gross weight despite a smaller wing area, 30 per cent shorter take-off run, 25 per cent slower approach speed and improved manoeuvrability at all speeds. Much of this derives from the fact that the F1 is fitted with flaps and leading-edge slats, neither of which is compatible with the Mirage III's delta wing.

To meet the prime requirement for an all-weather interceptor, the F1C is equipped with a Thomson-CSF Cyrano IV monopulse radar operating in I/J band. A later modification to IV-1 standards added limited lookdown capability, but as ground attack is only a secondary role for the F1C there are no ground mapping or continuous target ranging options. Single targets only can be tracked, but radar performance is noticeably degraded by poor weather. F1C production deliveries began in May 1973 and were followed in December of the same year by re-equipment of the first squadron, a component of 30 Wing at Reims, east of Paris. F1Cs were initially restricted in armament to their two internal 30-mm cannon. In 1976, the MATRA R.530 was issued to F1C units, followed a year later by the new heat-seeking MATRA R.550 Magic attached to wingtip rails. One or two R.530FEs were carried, options being between radar-homing and IR versions of the missile. In December 1979, the differently-shaped Super 530F-1 entered service with the F1C force, initially carrying one under each wing.

The Armée de l'Air acquired 83 basic F1Cs, of which the final 13 were fitted with Thomson-CSF BF radar warning receiver 'bullet' antennas on the fin. The first series of F1Cs equipped two squadrons of 30 Wing, followed by two in 5 Wing at Orange and two of 12 Wing at Cambrai. A further 79 machines, delivered between March 1977 and December 1983, have fixed refuelling probes and are designated **F1C-200**. Probe installation requires a minute plug in the forward fuselage, increasing the aircraft's length by 7 cm (3 in). All three wings operated a mixture of F1Cs and F1C-200s, allowing 10 Wing at Creil to equip one squadron and 12 Wing to gain a third component. In 1985, Creil's aircraft became the third squadron of 30 Wing.

The structure of three wings of three squadrons each was completed by the

Above: EC 1/30 was due to relinquish its F1C-200s in 1994. This example carries a Super 530F under the wing, the standard medium-range weapon.

Right: EC 4/30 maintains a 10-12 aircraft deployment in support of the French garrison in Djibouti. The sand and chocolate scheme reflects the arid terrain.

OCU, which was based at Orange. The AA ordered 20 **F1B** tandem-seat trainers, delivered between October 1980 and March 1983 for pilot conversion. Incorporation of a second cockpit adds only 30 cm (12 in) to the standard F1C's length, as remaining space is made by deleting the fuselage fuel tank and both internal cannon. Empty weight increases by 200 kg (441 lb), due partly to the installation of two French-built Martin-Baker Mk 10 zero-zero ejection seats (the F1C having Mk 4 seats with a forward speed limitation). Otherwise, the F1B is combat capable and can compensate for its internal deficiencies by carrying cannon pods and external fuel tanks. Refuelling probes occasionally fitted to the aircraft are, in fact, dummies for training with C-135FR tankers.

Availability of the Mirage 2000C reduced French Mirage F1B/F1C/-200 squadrons to six by 1993, comprising two in 12 Wing and four in 30 Wing, one of which is detached to Djibouti, its aircraft wearing sand and chocolate camouflage in place of blue-grey and regularly carrying ground attack ordnance. Mirage F1Cs displaced by the 2000C are being converted to **F1CT** standard (described separately).

Exports of the F1C have been made to six countries, four of which went on to adopt the multi-role F1E (described separately). South Africa received the first of 16 **F1CZ**s in 1975 for No. 3 Squadron at

Waterkloof. They saw action in the confrontation with Angola until the coming of relative peace resulted in the squadron disbanding in September 1992 and putting its Mirages into storage. Likewise active in African skies, Morocco's 30 **F1CH**s, supplied from 1978, flew from Sidi Slimane and advanced bases in support of missions against guerrilla forces in Western Sahara. Jordan began receiving 17 **F1CJ**s in 1981 for 25 Squadron at Shaheed Mwaffaq as-Salti AB, Azraq, and Kuwait took 18 **F1CK**s (from 1976) and nine **F1CK2**s (from 1984) for 18 and 61 Squadrons at Ali al Salem AB. The CK2 standard, to which all survivors have been upgraded, includes air-to-surface capability, as evidenced by delivery of MATRA ARMAT anti-radar missiles. Kuwaiti F1s fought in defence of their country in August 1990 and during the Operation Desert Storm liberation of January-February 1991. Kuwait was ahead of France in ordering the two-seat version, its first **F1BK** flying on 26 May 1976.

Greece is the sole F1 operator not to obtain a trainer, all its 40 aircraft being **F1CG**s delivered from August 1975. Based at Tanagra, near Athens, they were dispersed on arrival of Mirage 2000s: 342 Squadron to Heraklion and 334 Squadron to

Agrinion. A further NATO country, Spain, bought 45 Mirage **F1CE**s with the local designation **C.14A**, equipping 141 and 142 Squadrons at Los Llanos from 1975. The C.14A's radars have since been upgraded to Cyrano IVM standard, adding air-to-surface modes, and they also have the option of carrying AIM-9P Sidewinder AAMs.

WEAPON OPTIONS

Standard air-to-air configuration of two AIM-9 or Magic IR missiles on wingtip rails, and either one MATRA R.530 on centreline or two Super 530F on wing pylons. DEFA 553 30-mm cannon with 125 rounds per gun standard. Basic ground attack capability available. Other missile alternatives include ARMAT anti-radiation missiles (France and Kuwait) and V3B Kukri/V3C Darter (South Africa).

SPECIFICATION

Dassault Aviation Mirage F1C
Wing: span 8.40 m (27 ft 6.75 in) without tip stores and about 9.32 m (30 ft 6.75 in) with tip-mounted Magic AAMs; aspect ratio 2.82; area 25.00 m² (269.11 sq ft)
Fuselage and tail: length 15.30 m (50 ft 2.5 in); height 4.50 m (14 ft 9 in); wheel track 2.50 m (8 ft 2.5 in); wheel base 5.00 m (16 ft 4.75 in)
Powerplant: one SNECMA Atar 9K-50 rated at 49.03 kN (11,023 lb st) dry and 70.21 kN (15,785 lb st) with afterburning
Weights: empty 7400 kg (16,314 lb); normal take-off 10900 kg (24,030 lb); maximum take-off 16200 kg (35,715 lb)
Fuel and load: internal fuel 4300 litres (1,136 US gal); external fuel up to one 2200-litre (581-US gal) and two 1130-litre (298-US gal) drop tanks; maximum ordnance 6300 kg (13,889 lb)
Speed: maximum level speed 'clean' at 11000 m (36,090 ft) 2338 km/h (1,262 kt; 1,453 mph)
Range: combat radius 425 km (229 nm; 264 miles) on a hi-lo-hi attack mission with 14 250-kg (551-lb) bombs, or 600 km (324 nm; 373 miles) on a lo-lo-lo attack mission with six 250-kg (551lb) bombs and two

Jordan operates both the air defence F1CJ (illustrated), which wears a light grey camouflage, and the multi-role F1EJ which wears tactical three-tone camouflage.

EC 3/30 conducts all Mirage F1 training for the Armée de l'Air, and consequently has a high proportion of F1B two-seaters.

drop tanks, or 1390 km (749 nm; 863 miles) on a hi-lo-hi attack mission with two 250-kg (551-lb) bombs and three drop tanks; endurance 2 hours 15 minutes on a CAP with two Super 530 AAMs and one drop tank

Performance: maximum rate of climb at sea level 12780 m (41,930 ft) per minute with afterburning; service ceiling 20000 m (65,615 ft); take-off run 600 m (1,969 ft) at 11500 kg (25,353 kg); landing run 670 m (2,198 ft) at 8500 kg (18,739 lb)

Dassault Aviation Mirage F1B
generally similar to the Dassault Aviation Mirage F1C except in the following particulars:
Wing: span 8.44 m (27 ft 8.3 in) without tip stores
Fuselage and tail: length 15.55 m (51 ft 0.2 in); height 4.49 m (14 ft 8.8 in)
Weights: operating empty 8200 kg (18,078 lb) including pilots; normal take-off 11200 kg (24,691 lb)
Fuel and load: internal fuel 3850 litres (1,017 US gal); external fuel up to one 2200-litre (581-US gal) and two 1130-litre (298-US gal) drop tanks; maximum ordnance 6300 kg (13,889 lb)
Speed: maximum level speed 'clean' at 11000 m

The F1CK-2 was similar to the F1E, and had a ground attack role. This example carries retarded bombs.

(36,090 ft) 2338 km/h (1,262 kt; 1,453 mph)
Range: normal mission endurance 2 hours 0 minutes for training
Performance: maximum rate of climb at sea level 4200 m (13,780 ft) per minute without afterburning; stabilised supersonic ceiling 16000 m (52,495 ft)

OPERATORS

Delivery totals given:
France: F1B (20), F1C (166) – remaining aircraft serve with EC 3/12, EC 1/30, EC 3/30 and EC 4/30, the latter based in Djibouti
Greece: F1CG (40) – serve with 334 and 342 Mira
Iraq: F1BQ (15) – augment F1EQ single-seat force
Jordan: F1BJ (2), F1CJ (17) – service with No. 25 Sqn in air defence role
Kuwait: F1BK (2), F1BK-2 (4), F1CK (18), F1CK-2 (9) – all single-seaters upgraded to F1CK-2 standard which is multi-role version similar to F1E with ARMAT capability. Fifteen escaped Iraqi invasion to fly 128 combat missions in the Gulf War. All withdrawn from use in 1993 following delivery of Hornets
Morocco: F1CH (30) – used in air defence role
South Africa: F1CZ (16) – used for air defence by No. 3 Sqn, scoring several kills over Angolan MiGs. Unit disbanded September 1993 with remaining aircraft being stored. Two aircraft used by Atlas and one by Leningrad (Klimov) to test re-engining with RD-33 engine. Re-engining of remaining aircraft may follow
Spain: F1BE (6), F1CE (45) – serve on multi-role squadrons alongside F1EEs

Dassault Mirage F1CE

Spain's mixed F1 force is now all concentrated in Ala 14. This unit maintains a detachment on the Canaries to provide air defence for the island group. All Spanish Mirages have an important secondary ground attack tasking.

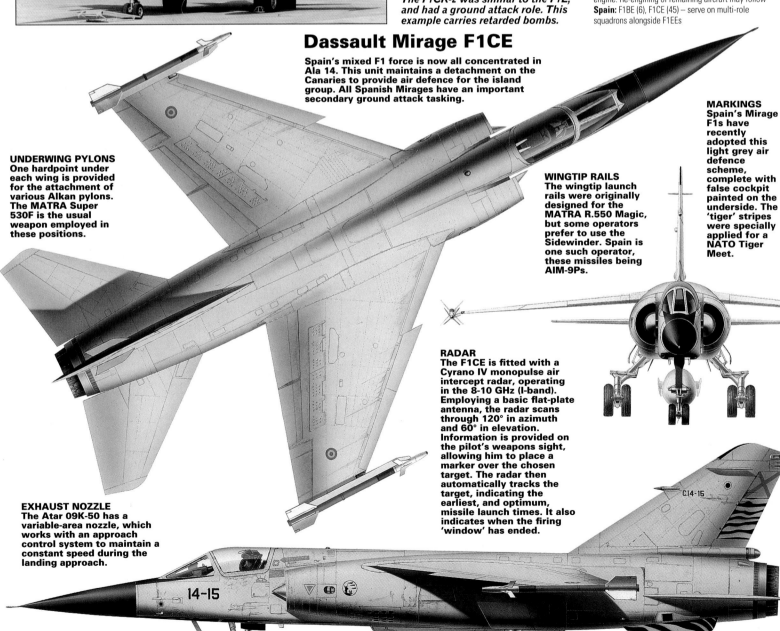

UNDERWING PYLONS
One hardpoint under each wing is provided for the attachment of various Alkan pylons. The MATRA Super 530F is the usual weapon employed in these positions.

WINGTIP RAILS
The wingtip launch rails were originally designed for the MATRA R.550 Magic, but some operators prefer to use the Sidewinder. Spain is one such operator, these missiles being AIM-9Ps.

MARKINGS
Spain's Mirage F1s have recently adopted this light grey air defence scheme, complete with false cockpit painted on the underside. The 'tiger' stripes were specially applied for a NATO Tiger Meet.

RADAR
The F1CE is fitted with a Cyrano IV monopulse air intercept radar, operating in the 8-10 GHz (I-band). Employing a basic flat-plate antenna, the radar scans through 120° in azimuth and 60° in elevation. Information is provided on the pilot's weapons sight, allowing him to place a marker over the chosen target. The radar then automatically tracks the target, indicating the earliest, and optimum, missile launch times. It also indicates when the firing 'window' has ended.

EXHAUST NOZZLE
The Atar 09K-50 has a variable-area nozzle, which works with an approach control system to maintain a constant speed during the landing approach.

Dassault Mirage F1CR

As soon as it was clear that the Mirage F1 would support a major production run, Dassault studied a dedicated reconnaissance version, the major potential customer being the **Armée de l'Air** which would need to replace its Mirage IIIRs. With the escalating price of combat aircraft, a strong case existed for the development of pods that could be carried by non-dedicated aircraft. In fact, some Armée de l'Air Mirage F1s, and those of some export customers, notably Iraq's F1EQs, have been seen with various centreline reconnaissance pods.

Development did continue of a dedicated tactical reconnaissance platform for the Armée de l'Air, designated **Mirage F1CR-200**, the first of which flew on 20 November 1981. For its intended role, the Mirage F1CR carries a wealth of reconnaissance equipment both internally and externally. An SAT SCM2400 Super Cyclope infra-red linescan unit is installed in place of the cannon, and an undernose fairing houses either a 75-mm Thomson-TRT 40 panoramic camera or 150-mm Thomson-TRT 33 vertical camera. Other internal equipment includes a Cyrano IVMR radar with extra ground-mapping, blind let-down, ranging and contour-mapping modes compared to the fighter's radar, and provision of a navigation computer and ULISS 47 INS.

Additional sensors are carried in various centreline pods, these including Thomson-CSF Raphaël TH side-looking airborne radar, HAROLD long-range oblique camera or Thomson-CSF ASTAC electronic intelligence pod. Various combinations of cameras can

During the latter part of the Gulf War ER 33's Mirages flew alongside Jaguars on bombing missions.

also be mounted in a pod. A refuelling probe is on the starboard side of the nose.

Sixty-four F1CRs were ordered, of which 52 remain in service. The first production aircraft flew on 10 November 1982, and the first squadron, Escadron de Reconnaissance 2/33 'Savoie', became operational at BA124 Strasbourg/Entzheim in July 1983. ER 1/33 'Belfort' and ER 3/33 'Moselle' followed, conversion from Mirage IIIRs being completed in 1988. F1CRs were dispatched to Saudi Arabia for participation in Desert Shield/Storm, where they were used for reconnaissance missions before being

grounded due to confusion with Iraqi Mirage F1EQs. When allowed to resume flying, they displayed their little-known secondary ground attack role by being used to drop bombs on Iraqi positions, their radar making them more effective than Jaguars. In 1994, ER 33 will move to Reims.

SPECIFICATION

Dassault Aviation Mirage F1CR-200
generally similar to the Dassault Aviation Mirage F1C except in the following particulars:

Weights: empty about 7900 kg (17,416 lb)
Speed: maximum level speed with a centreline mission pod at 11000 m (36,090 ft) 1915 km/h (1,033 kt; 1,190 mph)
Range: operational radius 1390 km (749 nm; 863 miles) on a hi-lo-hi mission with one mission pod and two drop tanks

An F1CR-200 on patrol over northern Iraq, during the UN effort to protect Kurdish populations. The aircraft carries Raphaël SLAR on the centreline, ECM pod and chaff dispenser and wingtip Magic 2s.

Dassault Mirage F1CT

A logical product of the shortfall in French ground attack capability and a surplus of air defence fighters following Mirage 2000C deliveries, the **Mirage F1CT** derives its designation from being a tactical (*tactique*) air-to-ground version of the F1C interceptor – specifically, the probe-equipped F1C-200. Two prototypes were converted by Dassault at Biarritz (the first flying on 3 May 1991) and 55 more are fol-

lowing from the air force workshops at Clermont-Ferrand/Aulnat by 1995. Deliveries began on 13 February 1992, allowing one squadron of 13 Wing at Colmar to achieve IOC in November of that year.

The F1CT programme upgrades intercep-

The F1CT conversion gives ageing interceptors a new lease of life. The wraparound camouflage is unique to this variant, as is the undernose laser rangefinder. Interception capability is retained.

tors to a similar standard to the tactical recce F1CR. Radar changes from Cyrano IV to IVMR, with additional air-to-ground modes, and is backed by a SAGEM ULISS 47 inertial platform, Dassault Electronique M182XR central computer, Thomson VE120 HUD, Thomson-TRT TMV630A laser rangefinder beneath the nose, Martin-Baker Mk 10 zero-zero ejection seat, improved radar warning receiver, chaff/flare dispensers and secure radio.

Structurally, the cockpit is rebuilt and the wing strengthened and modified for activa-tion of the outboard hardpoints, while the port cannon is removed to make space for the additional equipment and the whole airframe is rewired and fitted with new dielectric panels. Strengthening of the centreline pylon permits carriage of the large, 2200-litre (484-Imp gal) tank originally developed for the Iraqi Mirage F1EQ. Externally, the blue-grey air defence camouflage is exchanged for wrap-around green and grey.

The F1CT carries bombs and rocket pods for its new mission, but retains the ability to launch Super 530 and Magic 2 AAMs as a pure interceptor.

SPECIFICATION

Dassault Aviation Mirage F1CT
generally similar to the Dassault Aviation Mirage F1C

Dassault **Mirage 2000B/C/E/R**

For the third Mirage generation, Dassault returned to the delta configuration, using a negative longitudinal stability and a fly-by-wire flight control system to eliminate many of the shortcomings of a conventionally-controlled delta such as the Mirage III. As such, the Mirage 2000 has its predecessor's big high-lift wing, large internal volume (for fuel and avionics) and low wave drag, but the improved agility, slow speed handling and more docile landing speed available from a computer-controlled, naturally unstable aircraft: the best of all worlds. Conceived in 1972 and originally known as **Delta 1000**, the aircraft remained a low-key project until December 1975, when cancellation of the

Abu Dhabi's Mirage 2000 order included eight 2000RAD reconnaissance aircraft with provision for carrying various centreline pods. These include the COR-2 optical sensor pod shown here.

projected, twin-engined Dassault ACF left the Armée de l'Air without a new interceptor programme. An official specification was written round the aircraft in March 1976 and priority given to development in time for a 1982 service debut.

Now standard equipment of the French fighter arm, the Mirage 2000 has a large wing – and thus low loading – fitted with leading-edge slats which deploy automatically during combat manoeuvring. Two-piece elevons occupy the trailing edge. Whereas a Mirage III raising elevons to rotate for take-off would be forcing itself back onto the runway, an unstable delta has the centre of gravity behind the aerodynamic centre and so lowers elevons (creating lift) to achieve rotation. The take-off run is shorter and greater weapon loads can be carried in comparison to an aerodynamically-stable delta. Engine air intakes of the 2000 are the traditional Mirage type with movable half-cone centrebodies and are fitted with small strakes which create vortices at high angles of attack and so help to minimise yaw. Construction is of traditional metals, but with sparing use of carbon-fibre for some doors and panels.

New-generation engine

SNECMA's M53 reheated turbofan – perhaps more accurately described as a 'leaky turbojet' because of its low bypass ratio of 0.32 – was transferred to the Mirage 2000 after the ACF's demise. On the 83.36 kN (18,839 lb st) of a single M53-2, the first of five prototype Mirage 2000s was airborne at Istres on 10 March 1978 and gave a convincing display of slow-speed manoeuvrability at Farnborough a mere six months later.

India's Mirage 2000Hs were purchased for the air defence role, and can fire the Super 530D missile.

The first 15 Mirage 2000s had black radomes covering the RDM radar. This did not have a target illuminator for the Super 530 missile, despite the weapon being carried by this aircraft.

AIR-TO-AIR WEAPONS
Peru's Mirages are equipped with the standard export RDM radar, and are therefore restricted to the Super 530F missile (as opposed to the RDI/530D combination used by the French which is not approved for export). MATRA Magic 2 infra-red missiles are the short-range armament, augmented by the internal 30-mm DEFA 554 cannon.

ATTACK WEAPONS
Peru's Mirage 2000s have a true multi-role tasking. They regularly carry the ATLIS laser designator pod for use with Aérospatiale AS30L laser-guided missiles, and BGL 1000 LGBs. Alternatively a variety of unguided bombs can be carried, and reconnaissance pods.

Dassault Mirage 2000P

The only South American purchaser of the Mirage 2000, Peru initially ordered 24 2000P single-seaters and two 2000DP two-seaters, but was forced by budgetary considerations to cut the single-seat buy to just 10. These aircraft equip Escuadrón 412, Grupo de Caza 4, based at La Joya.

RADAR
The Thomson-CSF RDM radar is a low PRF Doppler multi-purpose system. It offers four basic modes: air-to-air search and interception, air-to-ground attack, strikemapping and terrain avoidance, and maritime search. In the air-to-air mode the radar offers a 60° cone of coverage with antenna drive rates of 50° or 100° per second.

DEFENCES
The Mirage 2000 is well-protected against missile threats, all equipment being integrally mounted. The Thomson-CSF Serval radar warning receiver has antennas in the fin fairing and outer wings, and provides a threat display in the cockpit. ECM jammers are mounted in the tailcone bullet fairing and fin.

GUNS
The DEFA 554 cannon weighs 80 kg (176 lb) and is 2.01 m (6 ft 7in) long. The weapon is a single-barrel revolving-chamber gas-operated weapon, with two rates of fire available: 1,800 rpm for air-to-air and 1,100 rpm for air-to-ground. The RDM radar provides a 3.5° beamwidth for automatic tracking within the HUD sight.

MAGIC MISSILE
Weighing 90 kg (198 lb) at launch, of which 13 kg (28.6 lb) is the high explosive warhead, the Magic 2 has an effective range of 5 km (3.1 miles). The weapon is detonated by RF fuse.

SUPER 530F MISSILE
The Super 530F has a length of 3.54 m (11 ft 7 in) and a launch weight of 245 kg (540 lb). The effective range is 25 km (15.5 miles).

A fin of broader chord with less complex leading-edge shape and trailing-edge root fairings were introduced during the test programme and fitted to the first production **Mirage 2000C** for its initial flight at Bordeaux on 20 November 1982. As with the 36 machines which followed, power was increased to 88.26 kN (19,842 lb st) through installation of an M53-5. In line with Dassault variant suffix policy, there was no Mirage 2000A, as this would have been a non-radar aircraft.

Mirage 2000C deliveries began in April 1983, allowing the first squadron to achieve IOC in July 1984. Eventually, three squadrons of the 2nd Fighter Wing at Dijon were equipped with early production aircraft having -5 engines and the multi-role Thomson-CSF RDM (Radar Doppler à Modulations). These early aircraft are to be upgraded to 2000-5 standard from 1994-97. From the 38th 2000C onwards, these changed to 64.3-kN (14,462-lb st) M53-P2 powerplants and Thomson-CSF/Dassault Electronique RDI (Radar Doppler à Impulsions) nose radar. RDI, development of which was delayed, has a new slotted flat-plate antenna and is optimised for look-

down/shoot-down intercepts with the MATRA Super 530D semi-active radar-homing AAM. Two Super 530s are normally carried on inboard wing pylons, accompanied by a pair of short-range IR-guided MATRA 550 Magic 2s outboard – plus, of course, the pair of DEFA 554 30-mm cannon. With RDM radar, Mirage 2000Cs carried Super 530F and Magic 1 missiles. RDI/M53-P2 aircraft serve with the 5th Wing at Orange and 12th at Cambrai. Both series can be fitted with a detachable refuelling probe.

A two-seat trainer, the Mirage **2000B** flew in production form on 7 August 1983.

Increased in length by only 19 cm (7½ in), it loses 110 litres (24 Imp gal) of internal fuel and both cannon in order to accommodate the second Martin-Baker Mk 10 zero-zero ejection seat. From the 15th aircraft radar is RDI, although all trainers have M53-5 engines. French 2000Bs and Cs are sometimes, and confusingly, referred to jointly as **Mirage 2000DA**s, for Défense Aérienne (Air Defence). Orders were prematurely terminated in 1991 as an economy measure when 136 Mirage 2000Cs and 32 2000Bs were under contract. French attack versions are discussed separately.

Dassault Mirage 2000B/C/E/R

The Mirage 2000B two-seater sacrifices no combat capability, but has a reduced fuel capacity.

For export, the RDM-equipped, M53-P2-powered variant is designated **Mirage 2000E** (or **2000ED** in trainer guise) and equipped to carry up to 6300 kg (13,890 lb) of ground attack ordnance as an alternative to AAMs. In addition to free-fall weaponry, Mirage 2000Es have been cleared to launch MATRA ARMAT anti-radar missiles and Aérospatiale AS30L laser-guided missiles (accompanied by Thomson-CSF ATLIS designator pods). Egyptian aircraft, delivered in 1986-88, comprise 16 Mirage **2000EM**s and four **2000DM**s. India ordered a total of 42 M53-5-engined **2000H**s and seven **2000TH** trainers which were received between 1985 and 1988 by Nos 1 and 7

Squadrons at Gwalior, wearing air defence camouflage. These have since been re-engined with M53-P2 turbofans and are compatible with Super 530D missiles, perhaps confirming reports that Antilope 5 or RDI radar is fitted. Plans were abandoned for Hindustan Aeronautics to assemble a further 45 kits and build 65 from indigenous parts when alternative MiG-29 'Fulcrums' were bought from the USSR in 1984.

Peru obtained 10 Mirage **2000P**s and two **2000DP**s in 1986-87, employing them mainly on attack duties with 412 Squadron at La Joya. Like their French counterparts, Abu Dhabi's aircraft had their combat debut in the 1991 Gulf War, operating from their peacetime base at Maqatra, but saw no action. ADAF Mirages comprise 22 **2000EAD**s, six **2000DAD** trainers and eight **2000RAD** reconnaissance variants

supplied between 1989 and 1990. The **2000R** has a radar nose and carries its sensors in the form of centreline pods: COR2 multi-camera; SLAR 2000 side-looking airborne radar; or HAROLD long-range optical. All the ADAF Mirages have the MATRA Spirale chaff/flare system and provision for AIM-9P Sidewinder AAMs in addition to Super 530 and Magic. Half also feature improved ECM bought from Elettronica of Italy. Greece took delivery of 36 **2000EG**s and four **2000BG**s in 1988-92. The aircraft are shared by 331 and 332 Squadrons of 114 Wing at Tanagra where they provide the primary air defence for Athens. They have an enhanced version of the Thomson-CSF Serval radar warning receiver fitted to all Mirage 2000B/C/Es. In 1992, Pakistan agreed to buy 44 aircraft – either new Mirage 2000Es or secondhand 2000Cs (RDM/M53-5) from French stocks – but Jordan was forced by financial problems to cancel an order for 12 aircraft in 1991.

WEAPON OPTIONS

Two internal DEFA 554-30-mm cannon with 125 rounds per gun. Five underfuselage and four underwing hardpoints. Maximum weapon load 6300 kg (13,890 lb). Standard air defence load-out is two MATRA Magic 2 infra-red missiles and two Super 530D radar-guided missiles. Early aircraft only equipped to fire Super 530F. In ground attack role up to 18 250-kg bombs or BAP 100 anti-runway bombs, two 900-kg BGL 1000 laser-guided bombs, six Belouga cluster bombs, two AS30L laser-guided missiles, two

ARMAT anti-radiation missiles or two AM39 Exocet anti-ship missiles are options.

SPECIFICATION

Dassault Aviation Mirage 2000C
Wing: span 9.13 m (29 ft 11.5 in); aspect ratio 2.03; area 41.00 m² (441.33 sq ft)
Fuselage and tail: length 14.36 m (47 ft 1.25 in); height 5.20 m (17 ft 0.75 in); wheel track 3.40 m (11 ft 1.75 in); wheel base 5.00 m (16 ft 4.75 in)
Powerplant: one SNECMA M53-P2 rated at 64.33 kN (14,462 lb st) dry and 95.12 kN (21,384 lb st) with afterburning
Weights: empty 7500 kg (16,534 lb); normal take-off 10680 kg (23,545 lb); maximum take-off 17000 kg (37,478 lb)
Fuel and load: internal fuel 3160 kg (6,966 lb); external fuel up to 3720 kg (8,201 lb) in one 1300-litre (343-US gal) and two 1700-litre (449-US gal) drop tanks; maximum ordnance 6300 kg (13,889 lb)
Speed: maximum level speed 'clean' at 11000 m (36,090 ft) more than 2338 km/h (1,262 kt; 1,453 mph)
Range: ferry range 3335 km (1,800 nm; 2,072 miles) with drop tanks; combat range more than 1480 km (800 nm; 920 miles) with four 250-kg (551-lb) bombs, or more than 1850 km (1,000 nm; 1,150 miles) with two drop tanks
Performance: maximum rate of climb at sea level 17060 m (55,971 ft) per minute; service ceiling 18000 m (59,055 ft); climb to 15000 m (49,215 ft) 4 minutes; time to intercept a Mach 3 target at 24400 m (80,050 ft) from brakes-off less than 5 minutes; take-off run about 450 m (1,476 ft) at normal take-off weight
g limits: +9 normal and +13.5 ultimate

OPERATORS

Delivery totals:
Abu Dhabi: 2000EAD (22), 2000DAD (6), 2000RAD (8)
Egypt: 2000EM (16), 2000BM (4)
France: 2000B (32), 2000C (136)
Greece: 2000EG (36), 2000BG (4)
India: 2000H (42), 2000TH (7)
Peru: 2000P (10), 2000DP (2)

The Mirage 2000C is best-known for its fighter role, but it does have a considerable ground attack capability. Shown here is the ARMAT anti-radiation missile, carried by an early production EC 2 aircraft.

Dassault **Mirage 2000-5**

Significant enhancement of the Mirage 2000C/E series was launched in 1986 with a view to improving export prospects. Two trials aircraft tested elements of the new programme: Mirage 2000-3 with a five-screen pilot's display from the Rafale programme replacing the original instrumentation, and Mirage 2000-4 integrating the new MATRA MICA AAM, four of which can be carried in a rectangular pattern beneath the inner wings, augmented by a pair of MATRA Magic 2s outboard. These features, when added to a Thomson-CSF RDY multi-mode radar, a new central processing unit, a holographic HUD, an ICMS Mk 2 countermeasures suite and an additional electrical generator, produced the **2000-5**. A trainer prototype flew on 24 October 1990 and was followed by a single-seat equivalent on 27 April 1991. Options available include MATRA Super 530 or BAe Sky Flash AAMs in place of MICA and (from 1995) an M53-P20 powerplant with an increased thrust rating of 98.06 kN (22,046 lb st).

RDY radar is optimised for air interception and is capable of tracking eight targets while scanning. However, its other modes include land and sea options similar to the RDM of Mirage 2000Es, so that the 2000-5 is also able to launch a pair of Aérospatiale AM39 Exocet anti-ship missiles as well as MATRA ARMAT, Aérospatiale AS30L and laser-guided bombs. The MATRA APACHE stand-off weapons dispenser is to be integrated when it enters service. In 1992, Dassault failed to interest Finland in 67 Mirage 2000-5s but received a commitment from **Taiwan** for 60. This order was confirmed in late 1992 and includes 1,000 Magic 2 and MICA AAMs. The first aircraft is scheduled

Above right: Mirage 2000-04 was the testbed for the Dash 5's MATRA MICA missiles. Under the port wing is the MICA EM active-radar version, while under the starboard is the MICA IR infra-red version, distinguished by its blunt nose. Both versions employ inertial guidance for most of their flight, with mid-course update from the launch aircraft's radar. They then switch to autonomous guidance for the terminal phase. The missile is believed to have a range in the order of 50 km (31 miles).

Right: The first true 2000-5 was this two-seater, demonstrating the carriage of four MICA missiles and two Magics. The Dash 5 has additional RWR aerials on the fin.

for delivery in 1995. The first 17 **Armée de l'Air** Mirage 2000Cs are to be upgraded to this standard from 1994-97, having their RDM radars replaced by RDY, and receiving a new cockpit and new upgraded M53 turbofans.

SPECIFICATION

Dassault Aviation Mirage 2000-5
generally similar to the Dassault Aviation Mirage

2000C except in the following particulars:
Powerplant: one SNECMA M53-P20 rated at 98.07 kN (22,046 lb st) with afterburning
Weights: empty 7500 kg (16,534 lb); normal take-off 9500 kg (20,944 lb); maximum take-off 15000 kg (33,069 lb)

Dassault **Mirage 2000D/N/S**

French requirements for an interdictor to replace the Mirage IVP in carrying an Aérospatiale ASMP stand-off nuclear bomb resulted in Dassault receiving a contract in 1979 for two prototypes of what was then designated **Mirage 2000P (Pénétration)** but soon became the **2000N (Nucléaire)**. Based on the 2000B two-seat trainer, the strike Mirage has a strengthened airframe for low-level flight and con-

siderable differences in avionics. Most significant is a Dassault Electronique/Thomson-CSF Antilope 5 nose radar optimised for terrain following, ground mapping and navigation, but with additional air-to-air and air-to-sea modes. The radar displays information in the pilot's HUD and on a three-colour head-down display with moving-map overlay, and provides automatic terrain following down to 91 m (300 ft) at speeds up

to 600 kt (1112 km/h; 691 mph). In the rear seat, the WSO has twin inertial navigation systems, two altimeters and an additional moving map.

ASMP, carried on the centreline pylon, delivers a 150- or 300-kT warhead up to 80 km (50 miles) from a low-altitude launch point. Outboard the Mirage 2000N carries a pair of large, 2000-litre (528-US gal) drop-tanks and two self-defence MATRA Magic AAMs. Further protection is provided by the Serval radar warning receiver (as 2000C), Dassault Electronique Sabre electronic jammers and a MATRA Spirale chaff/flare sys-

tem. From the 32nd French 2000N onwards, Mirage 2000Ns are equipped to carry alternative loads of conventional ordnance up to a maximum of 6300 kg (13,890 lb). This can include Aérospatiale

The primary role of the 2000N is launch platform for the ASMP nuclear missile. This is the standard configuration, with self-defence Magic 2s and large wing tanks. The initial 2000N batch is tasked only with ASMP carriage, and is designated 2000N-K1.

Left: The second 2000N was used in the development effort for the 2000D. Here it carries a pair of BGL 1000 laser-guided bombs but without the associated ATLIS designator.

Right: The 2000S is the export version of the 2000D, and has similar weapons. Shown are AS30Ls, with Rubis FLIR pod and ATLIS designator.

AS30L and MATRA BGL bombs (both guided by a Thomson-CSF ATLIS laser designation pod), MATRA APACHE stand-off munitions dispensers, Aérospatiale AM39 Exocet anti-ship missiles, MATRA ARMAT for anti-radar attacks, MATRA Durandal anti-runway bombs and other rockets, cluster bombs and area-denial weapons. In service the ASMP-only aircraft are known as **2000N-K1** while the dual-role aircraft are **2000N-K2**s.

Initially flown on 3 February 1983, the 2000N achieved IOC in July 1988 when the first of an eventual three squadrons in 4 Wing at Luxeuil was reformed. Orders for 2000Ns were reduced as a result of lessening tensions in Europe, but delays with the

Rafale programme generated a requirement for more aircraft with only conventional weapons capability. The latter became the **Mirage 2000N' (N Prime)**, a confusing

designation which was amended to **2000D**. When further orders were curtailed in 1991, **France** had ordered 75 Mirage 2000Ns (31 ASMP/K1, 44 ASMP/conventional/K2) and 75 Mirage 2000Ds. The first 2000D flew on 19 February 1991, its differences from earlier standard comprising deletion of the interface between ASMP and the aircraft's navigation equipment, addition of a global positioning system and a redesign of cockpit instrumentation. All versions have provision for a refuelling probe immediately ahead of the windscreen, offset to starboard. Mirage 2000Ds are being delivered from 1993 onwards to 3 Wing at Nancy, although the unit's No. 2 Squadron became operational with interim equipment of 2000N-K2s in September 1991.

Dassault announced in 1989 that an export version of the 2000D would be avail-

able from 1994, known as the **Mirage 2000S (Strike)**. It also has Antilope 5 radar and terrain-following capability. No orders have been received.

WEAPON OPTIONS

Mirage 2000D/N has nine hardpoints: one centreline and two inboard wing hardpoints stressed for 1800 kg (3,970 lb) each, four fuselage hardpoints stressed for 400 kg (880 lb) each and two outer wing hardpoints stressed for 300 kg (660 lb) each; maximum external load 6300 kg (13,890 lb); outer wing pylons usually carry MATRA Magic 2 infra-red air-to-air missiles in all configurations.
Nuclear strike: single 850-kg (1,874-lb) Aérospatiale ASMP stand-off nuclear missile (150-kT or 300-kT yield) on LM-770 centreline pylon, and two underwing fuel tanks.
Precision attack: MATRA BGL laser-guided bombs (250 kg/550 lb, 400 kg/880 lb or 1000 kg/2,200 lb) or

ECM
The 2000N has the Serval RWR system with VCM-65 cockpit display. A Caméléon jammer is carried at the base of the fin. The suite is to be updated to ICMS Mk 1 standard, an integrated system combining Serval, Spirale and new Sabre jammers.

POWERPLANT
The 2000N is powered by the M53-P2, rated at 64.3 kN (14,462 lb) thrust dry and 95.1 kN (21,385 lb) with afterburning. The engine is 5.07 m (16 ft 7.5 in) long and has a diameter of 1.055 m (3 ft 5.5 in). The dry weight is only 1500 kg (3,307 lb).

Dassault Mirage 2000N-K1

Augmenting the Mirage IVP in the nuclear role, the Mirage 2000Ns of 4 Escadre de Chasse are assigned to the Forces Aériennes Stratégiques. The wing operates approximately 45 aircraft in three squadrons, this aircraft wearing the markings of Escadron de Chasse 1/4 'Dauphiné'.

ASMP MISSILE
Designed to provide a more credible penetration capability than Mirage IVs armed with free-fall weapons, the ASMP (Air-Sol Moyenne Portée) missile has a reported range of 80 km (50 miles) from low-altitude launch and 250 km (155 miles) from high altitude. A solid propellant booster accelerates the missile to Mach 2, when a ramjet takes over. Intakes for this motor are mounted on the sides. Guidance is inertial with terrain mapping.

SPIRALE
The 2000N-K1s were not originally fitted with Spirale countermeasures, but these have been retrofitted. The system consists of integral infra-red warning receivers, and an interface with the radar warning receivers. These trigger the launch of chaff (starboard) or flare (port) cartridges from boxes in the wing/fuselage fairings. A missile plume detector is located in each Magic launcher.

RADAR
The Dassault Electronique/Thomson-CSF Antilope V is a J-band attack radar, providing ground mapping and terrain-following functions with additional air-to-air capability. The data is presented on a head-up display and on a colour head-down multi-function display.

NAVIGATION
For accurate navigation the 2000N has a twin ULISS 52P inertial navigation system. The 2000D also has Navstar GPS equipment for INS updates.

The 2000D was declared operational on 29 July 1993, when six aircraft of EC 5/330 (part of the CEAM trials unit) were announced ready for combat. The aircraft are destined for service with EC 3 at Nancy.

two 520-kg (1,145 lb) Aérospatiale AS30L laser-guided missiles on inboard wing pylons, with ATLIS designator pod on starboard forward fuselage station and centreline fuel tank.

Airfield attack: two MATRA APACHE stand-off dispensers with Samanta anti-runway sub-munitions, 12 MATRA Durandal runway-penetrating weapons or 18 Brandt BAP100 runway-cratering munitions.

Defence suppression: two MATRA ARMAT anti-radiation missiles on underwing pylons.

Maritime attack: two Aérospatiale AM39 Exocet anti-ship missiles on underwing pylons.

General attack: two MATRA APACHE stand-off dispensers armed with either Arcadie anti-armour or Mimosa general purpose sub-munitions on underwing pylons, 18 Brandt BAT120 anti-armour munitions, six MATRA Belouga cluster bombs, six Brandt BM 250 or BM 400 modular bombs, four MATRA F4 rocket pods with 18 68-mm rockets each, or two Dassault CC630 gun pods with two 30-mm cannon each.

Reconnaissance/jamming: COR2 multi-sensor reconnaissance, AA-3-38 HAROLD LOROP, NOR real-time reconnaissance, TMV-018 Syrel Elint or TMV-004 Caiman ECM systems pod-mounted on centreline station.

Inflight refuelling: Intertechnique 231-300 'buddy' refuelling pod on centreline pylon.

Additional equipment: Rubis FLIR pod on forward port fuselage station; TMV-002 Remora jammer.

Dassault Aviation Mirage 2000D
generally similar to the Dassault Aviation Mirage

Right: Mixing nuclear with conventional capabilities is the 2000N-K2. This desert scheme can be applied over the standard green and grey camouflage for contingency out-of-area operations or deployments to Red Flag exercises.

2000C except in the following particulars:
Wing: span 9.26 m (3 ft 4.5 in)
Fuselage and tail: length 14.55 m (47 ft 9 in); height 5.15 m (16 ft 10.75 in)
Speed: maximum level speed 'clean' at 11000 m (36,090 ft) 2338 km/h (1,262 kt; 1,453 mph); penetration speed at 60 m (197 ft) 1112 km/h (600 kt; 691 mph)

Dassault **Rafale A**

Dassault's **Avion de Combat Experimentale**, or **ACX**, evolved as an early 1980s technology demonstrator for a national combat aircraft programme even before France's withdrawal from the European Fighter Aircraft project in August 1985.

The withdrawal was prompted ostensibly because the French forces, and especially the navy, wanted a lighter and smaller design weighing just over 8 tonnes (17,637 lb). While emerging with a 9.5-tonne (20,945-lb) basic mass empty, similar to the

The one-off Rafale A was considerably larger than the service aircraft developed from it. Now grounded, it was instrumental in the development of the combat aircraft and its new technology M88 engines.

EAP, the ACX demonstrator, first flown on 4 July 1986, established and proved the basic aerodynamic design, configuration and performance of the planned **Rafale**, or ACT, as well as its fly-by-wire control system and mainly composite structure, although using two 68.6-kN (15,422-lb) GE F404-400 as interim powerplants.

After 460 initial test sorties, including touch-and-go deck-landings on the French carrier *Clemenceau*, Rafale A's port F404 was replaced by one of 15 flight development examples of the ACT's definitive SNECMA M88-2 turbofans, then reheat-rated at 73.5 kN (16,523 lb). With these engines the aircraft resumed flight trials on 27 February 1990, reaching Mach 1.4 in dry thrust and 40,000 ft (12192 m). Continuing ACX development, comprising 197 more flights by 1 July 1992 and many since, allowed cancellation in 1991 of the originally planned second Armée de l'Air prototype, C02, as part of major French defence economies. The Rafale A made its 865th and last flight on 24 January 1994.

Dassault Aviation Rafale A
Wing: span 11.20 m (36 ft 9 in); wing aspect ratio 2.67; wing area 47.00 m² (505.92 sq ft)
Fuselage and tail: length 15.80 m (51 ft 10 in); wheel track 2.675 m (8 ft 9.25 in); wheel base 5.185 m (17 ft 0.25 in)
Powerplant: two SNECMA M88-2 each rated at 48.69 kN (10,946 lb st) dry and 72.96 kN (16,402 lb st) with afterburning
Weights: basic empty 9500 kg (20,944 lb); normal take-off 14000 kg (30,864 lb); maximum take-off 20000 kg (44,092 lb)
Fuel and load: internal fuel more than 4250 kg (9,369 lb); external fuel up to two 2000-litre (528-US gal) drop tanks
Speed: maximum level speed 'clean' at 11000 m (36,090 ft) 2125 km/h (1,147 kt; 1,321 mph)
Performance: take-off run 400 m (1,313 ft) at 14000 kg (30,864 lb) or about 700 m (2,297 ft) at 20000 kg (44,092 lb)
g limits: -3.6 to +9

Dassault **Rafale B/C/D**

Originally known as the **ACT (Avion de Combat Tactique)**, the multi-role Rafale will replace up to half a dozen French air force strike/interceptor and recce types, including the Mirage III and 5, Mirage F1 and Jaguar, and probably the strategic Mirage IVP. While retaining the ACX's main design features, the Armée de l'Air's generic **Rafale D** family (D=*discret*, or stealth) is fractionally smaller and lighter than the demonstrator, with an empty weight below 9 tonnes (19,841 lb). Changes to reduce the radar cross-section include more rounded wingroot fairings, internally gold-coated canopy, radar-absorbing dark grey paint and a reprofiled rear-fuselage/fin

junction. The fin itself is lower and is topped by an ECM fairing to house Rafale's Spectra automated and integrated defensive sub-systems' RWR and lateral IR missile-launch detector windows.

Rafale D's canard mounting fairings have small forward extensions to house Spectra antennas, the all-moving canards themselves – linked with undercarriage extension to tilt 20° upwards to provide extra lift for

The sole Rafale C prototype displays its carefully blended wing/fuselage surfaces and the wingtip carriage for MATRA Magic 2 missiles.

Dassault Rafale B/C/D

Both Armée de l'Air versions in flight: the service has decided to procure the two-seat Rafale B as the predominant combat version, considering the workload to be too high for a single pilot on many key missions. Service entry is now expected in the year 2002, as the navy's need is considered greater than that of the air force.

landing – being bigger than the ACX's, and of superplastic-formed titanium instead of carbon composites. Composites and other new materials comprise over 50 per cent of the definitive Rafale's airframe weight instead of about 30 per cent in the ACX. An aerodynamic addition from the ACX is a small curved strake from the wingroot leading edge to the outer intake wall, above the muzzle port for the 30-mm (1.18-in) GIAT-built DEFA M791B cannon in the starboard fuselage. Rafale armament also comprises 14 (less one fuselage pylon in the navalised ACM) underwing and ventral fuselage weapons stations with an 8-tonne (17,637-lb) total capacity.

Stores options

Five of the stores stations have fuel tank pick-ups, or all may be used for such weapons as up to eight MATRA MICA semi-active radar-guided or IR-homing AAMs, Aérospatiale AS30L laser-guided stand-off ASMs, MATRA Defence Apache stand-off munitions dispenser, the nuclear medium-range ASMP or projected long-range ASLP, and Aérospatiale AM39 Exocet anti-ship missiles. These operate in conjunction with Rafale's Thomson-CSF/Dassault Electronique RBE2 fire-control radar, the first in Europe with two-plane electronic scanning. Based on Thomson-CSF's Radant phased-array beam-steering system, the RBE2 incorporates terrain-following, navigation, ground-attack and interception functions, with instant mode-transfer capability, automatic multi-target tracking and simultaneous targeting with up to eight AAMs.

The first batch of Rafales for the **Armée de l'Air** will not have ASMP capability, and will lack certain other systems of the definitive aircraft such as Spectra, helmet-mounted sight and automatic terrain-following. They will be known as S01 aircraft, this measure having been taken to expedite the programme (first-batch naval aircraft will also be similarly downgraded). Second-batch S02 Rafales will have a high-discretion jam-resistant passive optronic surveil-

lance and imaging system with a laser rangefinder, or Optronique Secteur Frontale (IRST), mounted forward of the cockpit and supplementing the radar for the passive multi-target identification and angular tracking at ranges up to 70-80 km (44-49 miles).

Following operational experience with its Jaguars and Mirage 2000Cs during the Gulf War, which demonstrated the demanding workload involved in current single-pilot combat operations, the French air force reviewed its Rafale D procurement plans to increase the proportion of two-seat operational versions, despite their higher cost. This inevitably resulted in smaller overall totals within specified budget allocations, although such contractions, in any case, accord with French post-Soviet long-term planning economies. These will see the planned turn-of-the-century 450 combat aircraft establishment cut back to around 390, and Rafale D procurement reduced from the original 250, including 25 two-seat operational trainers, to 235. In late 1992, Defence

Minister Joxe said these would be split between only 95 single-seaters and 140 two-seat versions, for service from 2002. From 1996, production Rafales are scheduled to be fitted with uprated M88-3 turbofans developing 93 kN (20,907 lb) of thrust for take-off.

The single-seat **Rafale C** prototype made its first flight on 19 May 1991, and remains the only such prototype of the air force single-seater. A single two-seat **Rafale B** first flew on 30 April 1993, fitted with RBE2 and Spectra system. Originally envisaged as a combat-capable conversion trainer for the single-seater, this is now being developed as the principal Armée de l'Air operational variant.

SPECIFICATION

Dassault Aviation Rafale C
Wing: span 10.90 m (35 ft 9.125 in) with tip-mounted AAMs; wing area 46.00 m² (495.16 sq ft)

Fuselage and tail: length 15.30 m (50 ft 2.375 in)
Powerplant: two SNECMA M88-3 each rated at 86.98 kN (19,555 lb st) with afterburning
Weights: maximum take-off 21500 kg (47,399 lb)
Fuel and load: internal fuel more than 5325 litres (1,407 US gal); external fuel up to one 1700-litre (449-US gal), two 2000-litre (528-US gal) and/or two 1300-litre (343-US gal) drop tanks; maximum ordnance 6000 kg (13,228 lb)
Speed: maximum level speed 'clean' at 11000 m (36,090 ft) 2125 km/h (1,147 kt; 1,321 mph)
Range: combat radius 1093 km (590 nm; 679 miles) on a low-level penetration mission with 12 250-kg (551-lb) bombs, four MICA AAMs and 4300 litres (1,136 US gal) of fuel in three drop tanks, or 1853 km (1,000 nm; 1,152 miles) on a long-range air-to-air mission with eight MICA AAMs and 6600 litres (1,742 US gal) of fuel in four drop tanks
Performance: take-off run 400 m (1,312 ft) at normal take-off weight for an air defense mission or 600 m (1,969 ft) at maximum take-off weight for an attack mission
g limits: -3.6 to +9

Dassault **Rafale M**

Originally known as the **Avion de Combat Marine (ACM)**, the prototype Rafale M01 first flew on 12 December 1991, being followed by M02 on 8 November 1993. Main ACM changes weighing some 1,653 lb (750 kg) concern major reinforcement of the Messier-Bugatti undercarriage, the long-stroke mainwheel legs of which must absorb no-flare landing impacts of up to 21 ft/sec (6.5 m/sec), with decelerations of -4.5g, against only 10 ft/sec (3 m/sec) for land-based Rafales. ACM nose-leg design was also the first in France to require attachment of a take-off catapult bar, plus provision of a 'jump-strut' for automatic unstick rotation, which will work in conjunction with a small 'ski-jump' bow-ramp. For accelerated take-offs, the **Rafale M** nose gear stores catapult loads of about 90 tonnes (198,416 lb) from initial compression following application of full engine power. Off the catapult, after automatic severance of the deck hold-back link, the released shock-strut immediately restores its accumulated energy, its abrupt extension

raising the aircraft's nose to shorten its take-off run. It then automatically reconfigures by reactivation of its metering holes, for optimum shock absorption for landing.

After initial tests on a modified Mirage 2000 at the CEAT aeronautical test centre in Toulouse, the M01 undercarriage underwent its first full-scale trials in mid-1992. Phase 1 of the trials at NAS Lakehurst, NJ, comprised 39 clean aircraft catapult launches at up to 135 kt (155 mph; 250 km/h) which, apart from demonstrating the required jump-strut performance, also confirmed operation of the 360° electro-hydraulic swivelling twin nosewheels. In Phase 2, at the USN Air Test Center, Patuxent River, MD, 68 arrested landings were made on a simulated carrier deck, as well as six inflight arrester-wire engagements. Further simulated deck trials were conducted in January 1993, before Rafale M01 first went to sea, on the carrier *Foch*, from 1 April of that year. Carrier trials with both maritime prototypes are continuing, although the carrier requirements of the

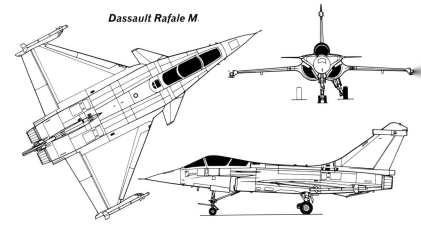

Dassault Rafale M.

Bosnian situation caused severe disruptions. A removable bow ramp is fitted to *Foch* when required for tests, but in the

future a permanent installation will employ a hinged ramp, which can be lowered for the launching of other aircraft types.

Aéronavale's Rafale M requirement remains unchanged at 86 navalised single-seat interceptor/strike versions, the French navy being the first Rafale recipient from planned deliveries of 14 ACMs to reform Flottille 14F in 1998. These will equip the nuclear-powered carrier *Charles de Gaulle*, now due to commission the same year. Funding for a long-planned sister vessel, *Le Richelieu*, was promised in late 1992 by Defence Minister Pierre Joxe in the 1995-97 budget period, for commissioning in 2006, to allow for periodic refits of *Charles de Gaulle*. Like the air force, the navy will receive its first batch of 20 Rafales in reduced-capability S01 form to bring forward operational service. Subsequent aircraft will be to the definitive S02 form with ASMP, OSF, Spectra, helmet-mounted sight and voice command controls.

Rafale M underwent its dummy deck trials at Lakehurst and Patuxent River. The carrier trials were undertaken aboard **Foch.**

Dassault **Super Etendard**

After much political in-fighting, a mid-1970s French naval requirement for 100 new carrier-based strike-fighters, for which procurement of navalised Jaguar Ms was originally proposed, eventually resulted in a 1973 contract to Dassault-Breguet for 60 developments of the Etendard IV. Dassault had already produced 69 Etendard IVM strike-fighters and 21 tactical-recce IVPs for the **Aéronavale**'s new carriers since mid-1962. The upgraded **Super Etendard** was planned with an 11,025-lb st (49-kN) SNECMA Atar 8K-50 instead of the original 9,923-lb (44-kN) Atar 8C, and some 90 per cent airframe commonality. A new wing leading-edge profile and redesigned flaps ensured a mainly unchanged carrier deck performance, despite heavier operating weights.

To widen its anti-ship strike and air-to-air capabilities, the Super Etendard also featured a new SAGEM/Kearfott ETNA nav/attack system, and a Thomson-CSF/Electronique Serge Dassault Agave I-band monopulse radar in place of the Etendard IVM's basic GAMD Aïda 7, a SAGEM-Kearfott SKN602 INS, Crouzet 66 air data computer and associated 97 nav display and armament systems, Thomson-CSF VE-120 HUD, LMT TACAN, and TRT radio altimeter. A retractable air-refuelling probe is fitted forward of the cockpit.

Three Etendard IVM airframes were converted as Super Etendard prototypes, flying from 29 October 1974. Seventy-one production Super Etendards then began replacing Etendard IVs and F-8E(FN) Crusader interceptors in Aéronavale's Flottilles 11F, 14F and 17F from June 1978, the first having initially flown on 24 November 1977.

By the time the Falklands War started in April 1982, the **Argentine navy** (sole Super Etendard export customer) had received the first five of 14 aircraft on order to equip CANA's 2° Escuadrilla at Cdte Espora NAB when not carrier-based, together with five AM39 Exocets. Operating from Rio Gallegos, these made their

Dassault Super Etendard

operational debut sinking HMS *Sheffield* off the Falklands on 4 May 1982, followed by the destruction of the supply ship *Atlantic Conveyor* on 25 May, for no Super Etendard losses. At least three have since been lost by 2° Escuadrilla of 3° Escuadra, which still operates the rest from Cdte Espora. In October 1983 five Aéronavale Super Etendards were leased to the **Iraqi air force** and a substantial number of AM39s were sold for use against Iranian tankers in the Iran/Iraq war, scoring many successes. The four surviving aircraft were returned to France in early 1985 following replacement by Agave-equipped Mirage F1EQs.

A mid-1980s upgrade programme costing some FF2 billion ($400 million) was planned to extend the long-range attack and anti-ship strike capabilities of the Aéronavale's nearly 60 surviving Super Etendards. Some 53 had already been modified at Cuers to launch the 300-kT Aérospatiale ASMP stand-off nuclear weapon. Main changes were avionics modernisation, including new cockpit instrumentation, HOTAS, and a new Electronique Dassault Anemone radar which incorporated track-while-scan, air-to-surface ranging, ground mapping and search functions. New systems include a Thomson-CSF wide-angle (22°) HUD with TV or IR imaging, SHERLOC RWR and a VCN65 ECM display, SAGEM INS and a UAT90 weapons and air data computer with more processing capacity. Provision is also made for night-vision goggles, while airframe changes to ensure a 6,500-hour fatigue life will help extend Super Etendard service to about 2008.

Argentina's first five Super Etendards in formation: these were the aircraft which had been delivered by the start of the Falklands War, and which were reponsible for two sinkings during the conflict.

Left: The nuclear strike role for the Aéronavale is undertaken by the Super Etendard armed with a single ASMP missile. This is balanced by a fuel tank on the opposite wing.

Right: Super Etendards form the bulk of the carrier air wing. Combat deployments included service over Lebanon and Bosnia.

The prototype upgraded Super Etendard first flew from Istres on 5 October 1990, Dassault modifying two more for operational development. Following disbandment of Flottille 14F in July 1991, prior to its eventual re-equipment as Aéronavale's first Rafale M fighter unit, its Super Etendards replaced the last 11 Etendard IVPs equipping Escadrille de Servitude 59S at Hyères for operational conversion of French naval pilots after deck-landing training in Fouga Zéphyrs at the same base. Flottilles 11F and 17F at Landivisiau and Hyères comprise the Aéronavale's remaining front-line Super Etendard squadrons and will operate the aircraft being upgraded by the Cuers naval workshops from 1993 to 1998.

SPECIFICATION

Dassault Aviation Super Etendard
Wing: span 9.60 m (31 ft 6 in); width folded 7.80 m (25 ft 7 in); aspect ratio 3.23; area 28.40 m² (305.71 sq ft)
Fuselage and tail: length 14.31 m (46 ft 11.5 in); height 3.86 m (12 ft 8 in); wheel track 3.50 m (11 ft 6 in); wheel base 4.80 m (15 ft 9 in)
Powerplant: one SNECMA Atar 8K-50 rated at 49.03 kN (11,023 lb st) dry
Weights: empty equipped 6500 kg (14,330 lb); normal

take-off 9450 kg (20,833 lb); maximum take-off 12000 kg (26,455 lb)
Fuel and load: internal fuel 3270 litres (864 US gal); external fuel up to one 600-litre (158-US gal) and two 1100-litre (290-US gal) drop tanks; maximum ordnance 2100 kg (4,630 lb)
Speed: maximum level speed 'clean' at 11000 m (36,090 ft) 1380 km/h (744 kt; 857 mph) and at sea level 1180 km/h (637 kt; 733 mph)
Range: combat radius 850 km (459 nm; 528 miles) on a hi-lo-hi anti-ship mission with one AM39 Exocet missile and two drop tanks
Performance: maximum rate of climb at sea level 6000 m (19,685 ft) per minute; service ceiling more than 13700 m (44,950 ft)

WEAPON OPTIONS

For anti-ship roles, the Super Etendard carries two Aérospatiale AM39 Exocets, or up to 2100 kg (4,630 lb) of other stores on two fuselage and four underwing pylons. In addition to AN52 tactical nuclear bombs or the ASMP stand-off missile, these can also accommodate four 68-mm (2.68-in) rocket pods, laser-guided weapons, up to 27 BAP 100 or 120 concrete-piercing bombs, drop tanks or ECM pods, or MATRA Magic short-range AAMs, supplementing two internal 30-mm (1.18-in) DEFA cannon, with 125 rpg.

Dassault/Dornier **Alpha Jet**

Following 1960's Franco-German studies into future advanced training requirements, national specifications were merged in 1968 and a joint development and production programme agreed in July 1969. This involved 200 aircraft for each country, from national assembly lines, for which the TA501 project submitted by Dassault, Breguet and Dornier was selected in July 1970, after comparative studies of the SNIAS/MBB E.650 Eurotrainer and VFW-Fokker VFT-291. All three projects proposed using two 10.98-kN (2,470-lb) thrust SNECMA/Turboméca Larzac 02 turbofans, the Luftwaffe having rejected further single-engine high-performance aircraft purchases following heavy F-104 losses.

The resultant **Alpha Jet**, derived from the Breguet 126 and Dornier P.375 projects, had shoulder-mounted swept wings and stepped tandem cockpits, Martin-Baker AJRM4 (French) or Stencel S-III-S3 (FRG) ejection seats, and lateral engine nacelle stowage of the short low-pressure mainwheel units. French and German equipment fits vary considerably, the Luftwaffe having

then decided to continue military pilot training in the US, changing its requirements to a light ground-attack replacement for its Fiat G91R/3s. This necessitated advanced nav/attack systems, including a Lear-Siegler twin-gyro INS, Litton Doppler navigation radar, Kaiser/VDO HUD, and a belly-mounted 27-mm (1.06-in) Mauser MK 27 cannon pod. French Alphas can carry a ventral 30-mm (1.18-in) DEFA 553 cannon pod with 150 rounds, both variants having four underwing pylons for up to 2500 kg (5,511 lb) of stores, including bombs, rockets, missiles or drop tanks.

Programme go-ahead

Alpha Jet development was finally approved in February 1972, two prototypes being ordered in each country from newly-combined Dassault-Breguet and Dornier. The first, F-ZJTS, flew at Istres on 26 October 1973, the second (D-9594/F-ZWRU) following at Oberpfaffenhofen on 9 January 1974, and the remaining two by the year's end. During development, Larzac 04-C1 engine output increased to 13.19 kN

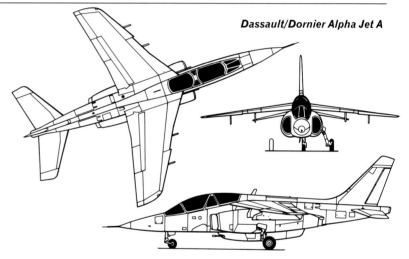

Dassault/Dornier Alpha Jet A

(2,965 lb) in the C6 version, and outer wing leading-edge extensions, plus a change to single-slotted Fowler flaps and hydraulic

servo-powered control surfaces, allowed transonic performance to be combined with approach speeds of only 110 kt (127 mph; 204 km/h). Later the Luftwaffe Alpha Jets were re-engined with the Larzac 04-C20 of 14.12 kN (3,175 lb) thrust.

French production **Alpha Jet E**s (Ecole) began flying from Istres on 4 November 1977, six arriving at CEAM for service trials in 1978. Replacement of Lockheed/Canadair T-33s in Armée de l'Air training units started in May 1979 with GE 314 at Tours, 12 Alphas then equipping the 'Patrouille de France' national aerobatic team in the same year. Other French training units re-equipped by 1985 included the 8e Escadre at Cazaux, replacing the last 30 Mystère IVAs for weapons training from April 1982.

Left: Luftwaffe Alpha Jets were intended for the light attack role, and usually carried an underfuselage cannon pod.

Below: French Alphas are employed on advanced training duties.

German production started with the first **Alpha Jet A** (Appui Tactique) flying on 12 April 1978 at Oberpfaffenhofen. Each country eventually ordered only 175 aircraft.

The last German Alpha Jet delivery, in January 1983, completed re-equipment of JBG 41 at Husum, JBG 43 at Oldenburg and JBG 49 at Furstenfeldbruck, plus 18 for JBG 44 shadow training unit at Beja, in Portugal. These were being withdrawn from late 1992 for planned disposal to France, Portugal and Turkey, apart from 45 to be retained by JBG 49 for lead-in fighter training. By early 1994 only 50 had been delivered to Portugal, the future of the others remaining uncertain. Egypt assembled 26 **Alpha Jet MS1** trainers at Helwan from September 1982 onwards, following receipt of four completed by Dassault.

In 1980 work began on an alternative close support version, which first flew on 9 April 1982. In addition to light attack and anti-helicopter roles, the new version had great potential for the fighter lead-in training role. New avionics included a SAGEM ULISS 81 INS, Thomson-CSF VE 110 CRT HUD and TMV 630 laser rangefinder in a modified nose and TRT AHV 9 radio altimeter, linked through a digital databus. Customers for this variant were Egypt (with designation **MS2**) and Cameroon. As with the MS1, Egypt received the first four MS2s from Dassault, and co-produced the remainder.

The **Alpha Jet NGEA** (Nouvelle Génération Appui/Ecole, later known as **Alpha Jet 2**) programme was launched to further the previous work on the MS2. In addition to the new avionics, the Alpha Jet 2 featured provision for MATRA Magic 2 air-to-air missiles, and uprated Larzac 04-C20 engines.

Dassault has also proposed an MS2-derived **Alpha Jet 3 Advanced Training System**, or **Lancier**, with twin multi-function cockpit displays for mission training with such sensors as AGAVE or Anemone radar, FLIR, laser, video and ECM systems, plus advanced weapons. This has yet to proceed beyond the flying testbed stage. Dassault later proposed a naval trainer version, with strengthened landing gear, to replace the Aéronavale's Zéphyr trainers.

OPERATORS

Delivery numbers given:
Belgium: Alpha Jet E (33)
Cameroon: close support Alpha Jet (7)
Egypt: MS1 (30), MS2 (15)
France: Alpha Jet E (175)
Germany: Alpha Jet A (175)
Ivory Coast: Alpha Jet E (12)

Above: Qatar's Alpha Jets serve with No. 11 Close Support Squadron, and in peacetime undertake weapons training. In wartime they would form a light attack unit, crewed by instructors.

Morocco: Alpha Jet E (24)
Nigeria: Alpha Jet E (24)
Portugal: Alpha Jet A (50)
Qatar: Alpha Jet E (6)
Togo: Alpha Jet E (5)

SPECIFICATION

Dassault Aviation (Dassault-Breguet)/Dornier Alpha Jet E (Alpha Jet Advanced Trainer/Light Attack Version)
Wing: span 9.11 m (29 ft 10.75 in); aspect ratio 4.8; area 17.50 m² (188.37 sq ft)
Fuselage and tail: length 11.75 m (38 ft 6.5 in); height 4.19 m (13 ft 9 in); tailplane span 4.33 m (14 ft 2.5 in); wheel track 2.71 m (8 ft 10.75 in); wheel base 4.72 m (15 ft 5.75 in)
Powerplant: two SNECMA/Turboméca Larzac 04-C6 each rated at 13.24 kN (2,976 lb st) dry
Weights: empty equipped 3345 kg (7,374 lb); normal take-off 5000 kg (11,023 lb); maximum take-off 8000 kg (17,637 lb)
Fuel and load: internal fuel 1520 or 1630 kg (3,351 or

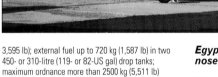

3,595 lb); external fuel up to 720 kg (1,587 lb) in two 450- or 310-litre (119- or 82-US gal) drop tanks; maximum ordnance more than 2500 kg (5,511 lb)
Speed: maximum level speed 'clean' at 10000 m (32,810 ft) 916 km/h (494 kt; 569 mph) and at sea level 1000 km/h (539 kt; 621 mph)
Range: ferry range more than 4000 km (2,159 nm; 2,486 miles) with four drop tanks; operational radius 670 km (361 nm; 416 miles) on a lo-lo-lo training mission with two drop tanks, or 540 km (291 nm; 335 miles) on a lo-lo-lo training mission on internal fuel, or 1450 km (782 nm; 901 miles) on a hi-hi-hi training mission with two drop tanks, or 1230 km

Egypt has 15 Alpha Jet MS2s, with nose-mounted laser rangefinder.

(664 nm; 764 miles) on a hi-hi-hi training mission on internal fuel; endurance more than 3 hours 30 minutes at high altitude on internal fuel or more than 2 hours 30 minutes at low altitude on internal fuel
Performance: maximum rate of climb at sea level 3660 m (12,008 ft) per minute; climb to 9150 m (30,020 ft) in less than 7 minutes; service ceiling 14630 m (48,000 ft); take-off run 370 m (1,215 ft) at normal take-off weight; landing run about 500 m (1,640 ft) at normal landing weight

The Alpha Jet is primarily used as an advanced trainer, and several nations have put its agility and performance to good use for aerobatic displays. Belgium uses the aircraft (left) for solo displays, while the 'Patrouille de France' uses the type (right) for formation displays.

de Havilland **D.H.104 Devon/Dove**

First flown on 25 September 1945 in civil guise, the eight- to 11-seat **de Havilland D.H.104 Dove** proved to be one of the most successful small transports of the immediate post-war era. Production of 544 aircraft included military versions, at first

developed for the **RAF** to Specification C.13/47 as the **Devon C.Mk 1** with 330-hp (246-kW) DH Gipsy Queen 71 or **Devon C.Mk 2** with 400-hp (298.5-kW) Gipsy Queen 175 engines. The **Sea Devon C.Mk 20** variant was operated by the **RN**.

Few Doves remain in service. Sri Lanka has just retired its aircraft to storage after having used them for maritime patrols.

Britain Memorial Flight, and with the MoD(PE) in the UK. Other examples are in **Jordan** and **Sri Lanka** (the latter in flyable storage). Jordan's single surviving Dove was returned to the UK for overhaul at

SPECIFICATION

de Havilland Dove 7 and 8
Wing: span 57 ft 0 in (17.37 m); aspect ratio 9.70; area 335.0 sq ft (31.12 m²)

Gipsy Queen 70-3 inline piston engines
Weights: empty 6,580 lb (2985 kg); maximum take-off 8,950 lb (4060 kg)
Fuel and load: internal fuel capacity 130 Imp gal (591.5 litres); external fuel none; payload 1,868 lb (847 kg)

payload
Performance: climb rate at sea level 750 ft (229 m) per minute; service ceiling 20,000 ft (6100 m); take-off distance to 50 ft (15 m) 2,366 ft (721 m); landing distance from 50 ft (15 m) 2250 ft (686 m)

de Havilland **D.H.106 Comet**

The de Havilland D.H.106 Comet was the world's first jet airliner to enter regular service and first flew on 27 July 1949. **Comet C.Mk 2**s and **C.Mk 4**s served RAF Transport Command until 1967 and 1975, respectively, three other **Mk 2R**s having a specialised Elint role in the RAF. The only other military user was the RCAF, with two **Series 1A** transports. Several ex-civil Comets became important testbeds for systems and equipment in the hands of

MoD(PE) at DRA (formerly RAE) Farnborough and Bedford. Of these, one **Comet 4**, XV814 (ex-BOAC G-APDF) was retired from on radio and avionics trials at Farnborough in early 1993 to provide spares for a **Comet 4C** (XS235 'Canopus') which was still serving with the A & AEE in 1994.

The last flying Comet is XS235, operating as a testbed with the A&AEE at Boscombe Down.

de Havilland **D.H.114 Heron**

Sri Lanka's Herons are in open storage, but remain flyable. This example is a Riley Heron with flat-six engines.

Evolved as a complementary larger version of the D.H.104 Dove, the **D.H.114 Heron** featured a longer fuselage of similar cross-section, and an enlarged wing for four 250-hp (186.5-kW) DH Gipsy Queen 30 Mk 2 engines. Military use included four for the Queen's Flight in Britain (one **C.Mk 3**, three **C.Mk 4**) and five for the RN, all now

out of service. At least nine other nations acquired the Heron in small numbers for military service. **Sri Lanka**'s Herons remain in flyable storage. These include examples with the original Gipsy engines and those which had undergone the **Riley Heron** conversion with flat-six Lycoming engines.

de Havilland Canada **DHC-1 Chipmunk**

de Havilland Inc.
Garrett Boulevard, Downsview,
Ontario, M3K 1Y5, Canada

First aircraft designed by DHC, the **de Havilland Canada DHC-1 Chipmunk** was a primary trainer developed immediately after World War II and first flown on 22 May 1946. Powered initially by a 145-hp (108-kW) DH Gipsy Major 1C, this low-wing monoplane seated the student pilot and instructor in tandem under a single-piece sliding canopy and featured fixed tailwheel landing gear. Of all-metal stressed-skin construction, the Chipmunk was originally only partially aerobatic but was ordered into production in Canada for the RCAF.

After evaluation in the UK, Specification 8/48 was issued by the British Air Ministry and production was undertaken by the parent company in the UK. Designated **Chipmunk T.Mk 10**, 735 examples were delivered to the RAF, equipping almost every primary flying training unit in the service. The fully-aerobatic Chipmunk T.Mk 10 differed from the Canadian-built **Chipmunk T.Mk 1** for the RCAF in having a multipanel sliding canopy and being powered by the Gipsy Major 8. Some of the RAF Chipmunks later had their flying controls removed from the rear cockpit when, in the 1950s, they joined RAF light communications flights in Germany.

Canadian production amounted to 218 aircraft, later versions (from the **DHC-1B-1** onwards) being fully aerobatic, military exports were undertaken to Chile (**DHC-1B-S4**), Egypt (**DHC-1B-S1**) and Thailand (**DHC-1B-S2**); these were all powered by Gipsy Major 10s. With this engine the aircraft served with the RCAF as the **Chipmunk T.Mk 2**.

Two hundred and seventeen Chipmunks were produced in the UK during the 1950s and supplied, as the **Chipmunk T.Mk 20** powered by the Gipsy Major 10 Series 2, to 10 foreign air forces, while civilianised **Chipmunk T.Mk 21** aircraft were

sold to the air forces of Portugal and Ceylon. Licence-production was also undertaken by OGMA in Portugal, which produced 60 aircraft. Canadian export **Chipmunk T.Mk 30** trainers were sold to Colombia, Uruguay and Lebanon.

In the early 1990s military Chipmunks still served as trainers in **Portugal** and **Sri Lanka** (in storage), while 10 surviving **Thai** aircraft had been re-engined with Rolls-Royce Continental IO-360s. In the **RAF** a total of about 70 Chipmunk T.Mk 10s was still flying in the training role in 1993, equipping the Elementary Flying Training School at RAF Swinderby and 12 of the 13 Air Experience Flights. A single example serves with the Battle of Britain Memorial Flight for tailwheel training, and two with the RAF's Berlin Station Flight at RAF Gatow (until mid-1994). The Swinderby Chipmunks were replaced by Slingsby T-67s during 1993. The British Army possessed about 16 Chipmunk T.Mk 20s in its Advanced and Intermediate Fixed-Wing Flights for training purposes.

de Havilland Canada DHC-1 Chipmunk T.Mk 10

SPECIFICATION

de Havilland Canada DHC-1 Chipmunk T.Mk 10
Wing: span 34 ft 4 in (10.45 m); aspect ratio 6.81; area 172.50 sq ft (16.03 m²)
Fuselage and tail: length 25 ft 5 in (7.75 m); height 7 ft 0 in (2.13 m)

Powerplant: one de Havilland Gipsy Major 8 rated at 145 hp (108 kW)
Weights: empty equipped 1,425 lb (646 kg); maximum take-off 2,014 lb (914 kg)
Fuel and load: external fuel none; maximum ordnance none
Speed: maximum level speed 'clean' at sea level 120 kt (138 mph; 222 km/h); cruising speed at optimum altitude 101 kt (116 mph; 187 km/h)

Range: 243 nm (280 miles; 451 km)
Performance: maximum rate of climb at sea level 800 ft (244 m) per minute; climb to 5,000 ft (1525 m) in 7 minutes 18 seconds; service ceiling 15,800 ft (4815 m)

The main use of the RAF Chipmunks is to provide flight experience to air cadets.

Initial training for UK Army Air Corps pilots is provided on Chipmunk T.Mk 10s at Middle Wallop.

de Havilland Canada DHC-2 Beaver

Having first flown in August 1947, the seven-passenger Pratt & Whitney R-985-AN-1-engined **DHC-2 Beaver** STOL utility transport won a 1951 joint US Army/Air Force design contest for a new liaison aircraft. Two Army and four Air Force evaluation **YL-20** Beavers preceded major joint-service contracts in 1952, totalling by late 1960 959 **L-20A**s, including six slightly-modified **L-20B**s. Most went to the US Army, comprising its main fixed-wing inventory, and became popular during the Korean War. As **U-6A**s in the 1962 'utility' redesignations, US Army Beavers were also used on skis in Alaska and elsewhere. Three remain active with the **USN Test Pilot's School**.

Military operators included Argentina (six), Australia (two), Austria (six), Cambodia, Chile (15), Colombia (18), Cuba (three), Dominica (four), Finland (one), Ghana (14), Haiti (two), Indonesia (one), Iran (five), Kenya (10), South Korea, Laos (six), Netherlands (nine), Oman (four), Peru (four), Philippines (six), Thailand (four), Turkey (eight), United Kingdom (42), Uruguay (one), Yugoslavia and Zambia (nine). Few Beavers now remain in military use, probably limited to nine in **Colombia**, two in **Haiti** and one in **Turkey**.

Having built 1,691 Beavers by the early 1960s, DHC switched production to a turbo-prop version, the **DHC-2 Mk III**, powered by a 550-shp (410.30-kW) Pratt & Whitney Canada PT6A-6A. This first flew on 30 December 1963 with a 30-in (76-cm) longer forward fuselage and two more passenger seats, plus a taller square-cut fin and ventral strake. DHC-2 Mk III orders totalled 59 by early 1968, known military customers in the early 1990s including the **Uganda Police Air Wing**.

SPECIFICATION

de Havilland Canada DHC-2 Beaver
Wing: span 48 ft 0 in (14.63 m); aspect ratio 9.22; area 250.00 sq ft (23.225 m2)
Fuselage and tail: length 30 ft 4 in (9.25 m); height 9 ft 0 in (2.74 m); tailplane span 15 ft 10 in (4.83 m); wheel track 10 ft 2 in (3.10 m); wheel base 22 ft 9 in (6.94 m)
Powerplant: one Pratt & Whitney R-985 Wasp Junior rated at 450 hp (336 kW)
Weights: empty 2,850 lb (1293 kg); operating empty 3,000 lb (1361 kg); maximum take-off 5,100 lb (2313 kg)
Fuel and load: internal fuel 95 US gal (359 litres) plus provision for 43.25 US gal (164 litres) of auxiliary fuel in two wing tanks; external fuel none; maximum payload 1,350 lb (613 kg)
Speed: maximum level speed 'clean' at 5,000 ft (1525 m) 139 kt (160 mph; 257 km/h) and at sea level 122 kt (140 mph; 225 km/h); maximum cruising speed at 5,000 ft (1525 m) 124 kt (143 mph; 230 km/h) and at sea level 117 kt (135 mph; 217 km/h); economical cruising speed at 5,000 ft (1525 m) 113 kt (130 mph; 209 km/h) and at sea level 109 kt (125 mph; 201 km/h)
Range: 676 nm (778 miles; 1252 km) with maximum fuel or 419 nm (483 miles; 777 km) with maximum payload

Colombia operates a few Beavers on light transport duties. Original deliveries totalled 18.

Performance: maximum rate of climb at sea level 1,020 ft (311 m) per minute; service ceiling 18,000 ft (5485 m); take-off run 560 ft (170 m) at maximum take-off weight; take-off distance to 50 ft (15 m) 1,015 ft (310 m) at maximum take-off weight; landing distance from 50 ft (15 m) 1,000 ft (305 m) at normal landing weight; landing run 500 ft (152 m) at normal landing weight

---

de Havilland Canada DHC-3 Otter

Scaled up from the successful Beaver, with a bigger (600-hp/447.6-kW) Pratt & Whitney R-1340-S1H1-G radial engine, the 11-passenger STOL **DHC-3 Otter** first flew on 12 December 1951. It was also designed for use on wheels, floats, amphibious floats or skis. Launch orders included 39 for the Royal Canadian Air Force (later increased to 69) and, following demonstrations in 1953, the US Army received its first six **YU-1** versions in March 1955. These preceded further batches of 84, 70 and 29, or 189 **U-1A**s in all, plus 13 US Navy **UC-1**s (later **U-1B**s). Otter production eventually totalled over 460 by 1966.

The RAF acquired a single ski-equipped Otter (XL710) for the 1956 British Trans-Antarctic Expedition. Other military customers included Argentina (three), Australia (two), Bangladesh (four), Burma (nine), Cambodia (one), Chile (seven), Colombia (four), Costa Rica (three), Ethiopia (four), Ghana (12), India (33), Indonesia (10), Nicaragua (four), Nigeria (three), Norway (eight), Panama (five), Paraguay (one) and the Philippines (two), most now being retired. The **US Navy Test Pilot's School** uses a single U-1B, another remains active in **Nicaragua**, and two are in use in **Panama**.

SPECIFICATION

de Havilland Canada DHC-3 Otter
Wing: span 58 ft 0 in (17.68 m); aspect ratio 8.97; area 375.00 sq ft (34.84 m2)
Fuselage and tail: length 41 ft 10 in (12.75 m); height 12 ft 7 in (3.84 m); tailplane span 21 ft 2 in (6.46 m); wheel track 11 ft 2 in (3.42 m); wheel base 27 ft 10 in (8.49 m)
Powerplant: one Pratt & Whitney R-1340-S1H1-G/S3H1-G rated at 600 hp (447 kW)
Weights: empty 4,431 lb (2010 kg); operating empty 5,287 lb (2398 kg); maximum take-off 8,000 lb (3629 kg)
Fuel and load: internal fuel 213.75 US gal (809 litres); external fuel none; maximum payload 3,150 lb (1429 kg)
Speed: maximum level speed 'clean' at 5,000 ft (1525 m) 139 kt (160 mph; 257 km/h) and at sea level 133 kt (153 mph; 246 km/h); maximum cruising speed at 5,000 ft (1525 m) 120 kt (138 mph; 222 km/h) and at sea level 115 kt (132 mph; 212 km/h); economical cruising speed at optimum altitude 105 kt (121 mph; 195 km/h) and at sea level 105 kt (121 mph; 195 km/h)
Range: 1,320 nm (1,520 miles; 2446 km) with

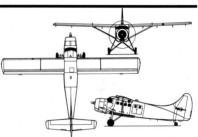

de Havilland Canada DHC-3 Otter

maximum fuel or 760 nm (875 miles; 1408 km) with a 2,100-lb (953-kg) payload; endurance 8 hours 36 minutes
Performance: maximum rate of climb at sea level 850 ft (259 m) per minute; service ceiling 18,800 ft (5730 m) with S1H1-G engine or 17,400 ft (5305 m) with S3H1-G engine; take-off run 630 ft (192 m) at maximum take-off weight; landing distance from 50 ft (15 m) 880 ft (268 m) at normal landing weight; landing run 440 ft (134 m) at normal landing weight

---

de Havilland Canada DHC-4 Caribou

Conceived in an attempt to combine the payload of the Douglas DC-3 with the STOL performance of the DHC-2 and DHC-3, the **de Havilland Canada DHC-4 Caribou** is a shoulder-wing twin-engined aircraft powered by two 1,450-bhp (1081-kW) Pratt & Whitney R-2000-7M2 14-cylinder radials. Accommodation was initially for up to 32 troops or, in an ambulance version, up to 22 litter patients. The high-aspect-ratio wing with full-span double-slotted flaps (the outboard components acting as independent ailerons) incorporates anhedral on the inboard sections to reduce the length of the main landing gear units and allow the cabin floor to be no higher than truck-bed height to facilitate rear loading. The rear ramp can be lowered for inflight paradropping.

The DHC-4 was first flown on 30 July 1958, but already the US Army had ordered five evaluation **YAC-1** aircraft in the previous year. Preliminary US type approval was gained in December 1960 at a gross weight of 26,000 lb (11794 kg), this being applicable to the basic DHC-4 and the **AC-1** (later **CV-2A**) in US Army service. Later the **DHC-4A** obtained type approval at 28,500 lb (12928 kg) gross weight, this version entering US service as the **CV-2B**. Operational use by the US Army encompassed delivery of infantry troops and their light wheeled vehicles (the CV-2B could carry two fully loaded jeeps and their crews) from major airports to forward landing strips from where they could be taken into combat by helicopters. CV-2s saw considerable action in Vietnam but, being the largest aircraft ever operated by the US Army, were transferred to the USAF early in 1967, and the surviving 134 aircraft were redesignated **C-7A**.

Only limited use of the DHC-4A was made by the Canadian Armed Forces and by 1979 all had been retired, most of them being supplied to the air forces of Colombia, Oman and Tanzania. The Caribou, on account of its good STOL qualities, proved very popular among air forces obliged to operate over mountainous and jungle terrain and about 30 continue to provide military transport service in **Australia**, **Cameroon**, **Liberia** and **Malaysia**. Total DHC-4 production was 307 aircraft, with manufacture ending in 1973.

SPECIFICATION

de Havilland Canada DHC-4A Caribou
Wing: span 95 ft 7.5 in (29.15 m); aspect ratio 10.0; area 912.00 sq ft (84.72 m2)
Fuselage and tail: length 72 ft 7 in (22.13 m); height 31 ft 9 in (9.70 m); tailplane span 36 ft 0 in (10.97 m); wheel track 23 ft 1.5 in (7.05 m); wheel base 25 ft 8 in (7.82 m)
Powerplant: two Pratt & Whitney R-2000-7M2 Twin Wasp each rated at 1,450 hp (1081 kW)
Weights: operating empty 18,260 lb (8283 kg) including two crew; normal take-off 28,500 lb (12928 kg); maximum take-off 31,300 lb (14197 kg)
Fuel and load: internal fuel 820 US gal (3137 litres); external fuel none; maximum payload 8,740 lb (3965 kg)
Speed: maximum level speed 'clean' at 6,500 ft (1980 m) 188 kt (216 mph; 347 km/h); maximum cruising speed at 7,500 ft (2285 m) 158 kt (182 mph; 293 km/h); economical cruising speed at 7,500 ft (2285 m) 158 kt (182 mph; 293 km/h)
Range: range 1,135 nm (1,307 miles; 2103 km) with maximum fuel or 210 nm (242 miles; 390 km) with maximum payload
Performance: maximum rate of climb at sea level 1,355 ft (413 m) per minute; service ceiling 24,800 ft (7560 m); take-off distance to 50 ft (15 m) 1,185 ft (361 m) at maximum take-off weight; landing distance from 50 ft (15 m) 1,235 ft (376 m) at normal landing weight; landing run 670 ft (204 m) at normal landing weight

The Royal Malaysian air force flies the DHC-4 on assault transport duties.

de Havilland Canada DHC-5 Buffalo

Despite being evolved largely in concert with (and to meet the requirements of) the US Army, the **de Havilland Canada DHC-5 Buffalo** failed to secure a production contract from that service because of the transfer of the US Army's large fixed-wing aircraft to the USAF in 1967, the latter being adequately equipped with military transports. Designed to accommodate up to 41 combat troops, a Pershing missile, a 105-mm (4.13-in) howitzer or a 3/4-ton truck, the DHC-5 (first flown on 9 April 1964) is a twin-turboprop shoulder-wing monoplane of similar configuration to, but larger than, the Caribou (it was originally termed the **Caribou II**), but without anhedral on the wing centre-section. With maximum STOL payload of 12,000 lb (5443 kg), the current **DHC-5D** requires no more than a 984-ft (300-m) take-off ground run.

The first four aircraft produced in 1964-65 were delivered to the US Army under the designation **YAC-2** (later changed to **CV-7A** and subsequently **C-8A**) but, as already stated, no American production order followed. Instead, 15 **DHC-5As** were delivered to the **Canadian Armed Forces** in 1968 with the designation **CC-115**, and of these six serve today in the SAR role. **Brazil** was the first overseas military customer in 1969, eventually receiving 18 aircraft designated **C-115B** locally, most of which were to serve as transports at Campo Grande. **Peru**'s air force received 16 DHC-5As and these equip a transport squadron at Jorge Chavez.

Without the intended American orders, this level of sale was inadequate to support further production, and manufacture of the DHC-5A ended in 1972. Development was confined to proposed re-engined versions (**DHC-5B** with CT64-P4C and **DHC-5C** with CT64-P4C or Rolls-Royce Dart RDa.12 turboprops), neither of which was built. Instead, the **DHC-5D** with General Electric CT64-820-4 engines attracted sufficient interest overseas and in 1974 this version re-entered production. Ten DHC-5Ds sold to **Egypt** featured LAPES for the paradropping of supplies; in 1985 four of these were converted as navigation trainers by the Swedish company Swedair. The Buffalo is currently operated by the air forces of **Abu Dhabi** (defence force), **Cameroon**, **Ecuador**, **Kenya**, **Mauritania**, **Mexico** (and Mexican navy), **Sudan**, **Tanzania**, **Togo**, **Zaïre** and **Zambia**. Total production of all versions of the DHC-5 reached 123 aircraft, with production ending in December 1986.

SPECIFICATION

de Havilland Canada DHC-5 Buffalo
Wing: span 96 ft 0 in (29.26 m); aspect ratio 9.75; area 945.00 sq ft (87.79 m²)
Fuselage and tail: length 79 ft 0 in (24.08 m); height 28 ft 8 in (8.73 m); tailplane span 32 ft 0 in (9.75 m); wheel track 30 ft 6 in (9.29 m); wheel base 27 ft 11 in (8.50 m)
Powerplant: two General Electric CT64-820-1 each rated at 3,055 ehp (2278 ekW)
Weights: operating empty 23,157 lb (10505 kg) including three crew; maximum take-off 41,000 lb (18598 kg)
Fuel and load: internal fuel 2,087 US gal (7900 litres); external fuel none; maximum payload 13,843 lb (6279 kg)
Speed: maximum level speed 'clean' and maximum cruising speed 'clean' at 10,000 ft (3050 m) 235 kt (271 mph; 435 km/h); economical cruising speed at 10,000 ft (3050 m) 181 kt (208 mph; 335 km/h)
Range: 1,885 nm (2,171 miles; 3493 km) with maximum fuel and a 4,000-lb (1814-kg) payload, or 440 nm (507 miles; 815 km) with maximum payload
Performance: maximum rate of climb at sea level 1,890 ft (576 m) per minute; service ceiling 30,000 ft (9145 m); take-off run 1,040 ft (317 m) at maximum take-off weight on grass; take-off distance to 50 ft (15 m) 1,540 ft (470 m) at maximum take-off weight from grass; landing distance from 50 ft (15 m) 1,020 ft (342 m) at normal landing weight on grass; landing run 610 ft (186 m) at normal landing weight on grass

Canada uses a few Buffalos for rescue tasks in the mountains.

de Havilland Canada DHC-6 Twin Otter

Originally developed in the 1960s and first flown on 20 May 1965, the **de Havilland DHC-6 Twin Otter** was first powered by two 579-ehp (432-kW) PT6A-6 turboprop engines and was intended to extend the transport potential of the popular single-engined DHC-3 Otter while retaining the efficient high-lift wing for STOL performance. The new 13/18-seat transport retained no more than the original basic wing structure with its full-span double-slotted flaps and ailerons, and from the fourth aircraft onwards adopted PT6A-20 engines. Optional conversion from fixed tricycle-wheel landing gear to floats or skis was available.

FAA type approval was gained in 1966 and quickly led to commercial orders, but military interest was slow to materialise.

Nevertheless, eight aircraft were delivered to the **Canadian Armed Forces** as **CC-138** search and rescue aircraft, and after 115 Series 100 aircraft had been completed production switched to the **DHC-6 Series 200** with lengthened nose and increased baggage capacity; 115 examples of this version were produced (few of them for military customers) before DHC embarked on the current **DHC-6 Series 300**. In this version, the more powerful PT6A-27 engines allow capacity to be increased to 20 passengers, and an increase in maximum take-off weight of 1,000 lb (454 kg).

Current military Twin Otter operators are **Argentina**, **Benin**, **Chile**, **Ecuador**, **Ethiopia**, **France**, **Haiti**, **Nepal**, **Norway**, **Panama**, **Paraguay**, **Peru**, **Sudan** and **Uganda**. A total of 10 DHC-6s was supplied to the **USA** as the **V-18 Twin Otter**. Eight survivors are currently operated, comprising two **UV-18Bs** by the USAF Academy and six **UV-18A** aircraft by the Alaska ArNG's 1-207th Aviation Group.

In 1982 DHC offered three dedicated military Twin Otter variants: the **DHC-6-300M** was a 15-troop transport convertible to 20 seats, or with paratroop or ambulance layout; the **DHC-6-300M(COIN)** was a counter-insurgency variant with provision for armour protection, a cabin-mounted machine-gun and underwing ordnance; and the **DHC-6-300MR** was a maritime reconnaissance model with search radar under the nose and underwing searchlight pod. A single DHC-6-300MR has been purchased by the Senegal Department of Fisheries.

SPECIFICATION

de Havilland Canada DHC-6 Twin Otter Series 300
Wing: span 65 ft 0 in (19.81 m); aspect ratio 10.1; area 420.00 sq ft (39.02 m²)
Fuselage and tail: length 51 ft 9 in (15.77 m); height 19 ft 6 in (5.94 m); tailplane span 20 ft 8 in (6.30 m); wheel track 12ft 2 in (3.71 m); wheel base 14 ft 10.5 in (4.53 m)
Powerplant: two Pratt & Whitney Canada PT6A-27 each rated at 620 shp (462 kW)
Weights: operating empty 7,415 lb (3363 kg) including two crew; maximum take-off 12,500 lb (5670 kg)
Fuel and load: internal fuel 2,583 lb (1171 kg); external fuel none; maximum payload 4,280 lb (1941 kg) for 100 nm (115 miles; 185 km)
Speed: maximum cruising speed at 10,000 ft (3050 m) 182 kt (210 mph; 338 km/h)
Range: 700 nm (806 miles; 1297 km) with a 2,500-lb (1134-kg) payload
Performance: maximum rate of climb at sea level 1,600 ft (488 m) per minute; service ceiling 26,700 ft (8140 m); take-off run 700 ft (213 m) at maximum take-off weight for STOL or 860 ft (262 m) at maximum take-off weight for normal operation; take-off distance to 50 ft (15 m) 1,200 ft (366 m) at maximum take-off weight for STOL or 1,500 ft (457 m) at maximum take-off weight for normal operation; landing distance from 50 ft (15 m) 1,050 ft (320 m) at normal landing weight for STOL or 1,940 ft (591 m) at normal landing weight for normal operation; landing run 515 ft (157 m) at normal landing weight for STOL or 950 ft (290 m) at normal landing weight for normal operation

The Twin Otter's 'go-anywhere' ability makes it highly attractive to air arms with difficult terrain to cover. Chile uses its aircraft on airline-style operations in regions with few roads.

de Havilland Canada DHC-7 Dash 7

Representing a courageous attempt to exploit the demand by 'third-level' airlines for medium-capacity accommodation by extending DHC's unsurpassed experience in STOL transports, the **de Havilland Canada DHC-7 Dash 7** was first flown on 27 March 1975, gaining its type approval certificate 25 months later. Four PT6A-50 turboprops drive large-diameter propellers at low speed to achieve low noise-level blade-tip speeds. The high-mounted, high-aspect-ratio wing is equipped with large-area double-slotted flaps and includes a pair of inboard spoilers acting as lift-dumpers on landing and an outboard pair acting differentially in flight to assist aileron control.

Accommodation in the **DHC-7 Series 100** is for up to 50 passengers in a circular-section pressurised fuselage, or mixed freight/seats in the **DHC-7 Series 101**.

The Dash 7 has been sold in small quantities to military users. Two aircraft, designated **CC-132**, were supplied to the Canadian Armed Forces, comprising a VIP 32-seater and a Series 101 with mixed cargo and passenger layout. Both aircraft flown by No. 412 Squadron of the CAF, based at Lahr in West Germany, were replaced by DHC-8s. One DHC-7 is operated by the **Venezuelan navy** on maritime patrol duties, and three serve with the **US Army** under the 'Grizzly Hunter' programme, using advanced sensors in drug interdiction and battlefield surveillance roles.

SPECIFICATION

de Havilland Canada DHC-7 Dash 7 Series 100
Wing: span 93 ft 0 in (28.35 m); aspect ratio 10.00; area 860.0 sq ft (79.90 m²)
Fuselage and tail: length 80 ft 7.7 in (24.58 m); height 26 ft 2.0 in (7.98 m); wheel track 23 ft 6.0 in (7.16 m); wheel base 27 ft 6 in (8.38 m)
Powerplant: four Pratt & Whitney Aircraft of Canada PT6A-50 turboprop engines, each flat rated at 1,120 shp (835 kW)
Weights: basic empty weight 27,000 lb (12247 kg); maximum take-off weight 44,000 lb (19958 kg)
Fuel and load: maximum useable fuel (standard tanks) 9,925 lb (4502 kg); external fuel none; payload (50 passengers or cargo) 11,310 lb (5130 kg)

Speed: maximum cruising speed at 8,000 ft (2440 m) at all-up weight of 41,000 lb (18597 kg) 231 kt (266 mph; 428 km/h)
Range: at 15,000 ft (4,575 m) with 50 passengers and baggage, at long-range cruising speed 690 nm (795 miles; 1279 km); with standard fuel and 6,500-lb (2948-kg) load, long-range cruising speed 1,170 nm (1,347 miles; 2168 km)
Performance: climb rate at sea level 1,220 ft (372 m) per minute; service ceiling 21,000 ft (6400 m); FAR Pt 25 take-off field length at all-up weight of 41,000 lb (18597 kg) and 25° flap 2,260 ft (689 m); FAR Pt 25 STOL landing field length at maximum landing weight and 45° flap 1,950 ft (594 m)

The 'Grizzly Hunter' aircraft of the US Army are used in the large drug interdiction campaign.

de Havilland (Bombardier) DHC-8 Dash 8/E-9

In the same way that companies world-wide have targeted niche areas, market research in the late 1970s by de Havilland Canada brought the conclusion that a 30/40-seat short-haul transport (slotting between the company's 19-seat DHC-6 Twin Otter and 50-seat DHC-7 Dash 7) could prove a profitable venture. Thus, design of the **de Havilland Canada DHC-8** was initiated, followed by the construction of four flying prototypes. The first machine (C-GDNK) recorded the type's maiden flight on 20 June 1983. These four prototypes saw extensive flying in a test programme that led to certification by Canada and the United States before the end of 1984.

The DHC-8, named **Dash 8**, is in many respects a twin-engined reduced-scale version of the DHC-7, but with less emphasis on STOL performance. Its configuration includes a high-set wing (to optimise cabin space) and a T-tail well clear of the slip-stream from the four-bladed constant-speed/reversible propellers, driven in production aircraft by two Pratt & Whitney Canada PW120A turboprops. The landing gear is of retractable tricycle type with twin wheels on each unit, the main units being

housed in the engine nacelles when raised. As configured for commuter use the cabin seats 36, but other options include layouts for up to 40 passengers, or mixed pasenger/cargo traffic, or a 17-seat corporate interior. The production **Dash 8 Series 100** is available in **Commuter** and **Corporate** versions, the latter typically carrying 17 passengers over a range of 1,520 miles (2446 km) with full IFR reserves. Operated by a flight crew of two, plus a cabin attendant, the Dash 8 has a flight deck and cabin which are both air-conditioned and pressurised. The **Series 200** introduced uprated PW123C engines among other improvements, while the **Series 300** is a stretched variant which first flew on 15 May 1987. The **Series 400** programme relates to a further stretch yet to be launched.

The Dash 8 is currently operated in small numbers by three air forces. **Canada** acquired two **CC-142 (DHC-8M-100)** transports for No. 412 Squadron and four **CT-142** navigation trainers with mapping radar in an extended nose. Three standard DHC-8-100s serve with the **Kenyan air force** on transport duties. Two aircraft are operated by the **US Air Force** by the

475th WEG at Tyndall AFB, FL. Designated **E-9A**, the pair is used for range support, and the aircraft are equipped with phased array radar in a large fuselage fairing and telemetry/communications relay equipment.

SPECIFICATION

de Havilland DHC-8 Dash 8M Series 100
Wing: span 85 ft 0 in (25.91 m); aspect ratio 12.4; area 585.00 sq ft (54.35 m²)
Fuselage and tail: length 73 ft 0 in (22.25 m); height 24 ft 7 in (7.49 m); elevator span 26 ft 0 in (7.92 m); wheel track 25 ft 10 in (7.87 m); wheel base 26 ft 1 in (7.95 m)
Powerplant: two Pratt & Whitney Canada PW120A each rated at 2,000 shp (1491 kW)
Weights: operating empty 22,000 lb (9979 kg); maximum take-off 34,500 lb (15649 kg)

Fuel and load: internal fuel 5,678 lb (2576 kg) with option for a maximum of 10,244 lb (4646 kg); external fuel none; maximum payload 9,000 lb (4082 kg) in passenger configuration or 9,849 lb (4467 kg) in freight configuration
Speed: maximum cruising speed at 15,000 ft (4570 m) 267 kt (308 mph; 497 km/h) and at 20,000 ft (6095 m) 265 kt (305 mph; 492 km/h)
Range: 1,190 nm (1,370 miles; 2205 km) with maximum passenger payload or 550 nm (633 miles; 1019 km) with maximum freight payload
Performance: maximum rate of climb at sea level 1,560 ft (475 m) per minute; certificated ceiling 25,000 ft (7620 m); balanced take-off field length 3,150 ft (960 m) at maximum take-off weight; balanced landing field length 2,980 ft (908 m) at normal landing weight

The enlarged nose radar identifies this as a CT-142 navigation trainer.

Dornier Do 27

*Dornier Luftfahrt GmbH
Dornier Airfield, D-8031 Wessling,
Germany*

Marking the post-war re-emergence of the famed Dornier name, the **Do 25** was developed under the direction of Dr Claudius Dornier working in the Oficinas Tecnicas Dornier set up in Madrid. The first of two Do 25 prototypes was flown on 25 June 1954, the aircraft being an all-metal high-wing monoplane with fixed undercarriage and STOL performance. Powered by a 150-hp (112-kW) ENMA Tigre G-4-B piston engine, the four-seat Do 25 evolved into the **Do 27** with a 275-hp (205-kW) Lycoming GO-480-B1A6 engine, production of which was initiated by CASA in Spain (as the **C-127**) to meet a Spanish air force requirement for 50 of these general-purpose light transport and communications aircraft.

The Do 27 prototype was in fact completed by the reconstituted Dornier Werke in Germany, and production was initiated there also, with the first production aircraft flying on 17 October 1956. Production of the Do 27 in Germany totalled 571 examples and was completed in 1966. A large

proportion of this total was for military use, including 177 **Do 27A-1**s with gross weight of 1570 kg (3,460 lb); 88 **Do 27A-3**s with increased gross weight of 1750 kg (3,858 lb); 65 **Do 27A-4**s with wide track undercarriage and gross weight of 1850 kg (4,080 lb); 86 dual-control **Do 27B-1**s and 16 **Do 27B-2**s at the higher gross weight. All of these were for the Luftwaffe, which eventually took 428 into its inventory, including some ex-civil models.

Production of the Do 27 also included 14 of the **H-2** model for the Swiss air force with 340-hp (253-kW) GSO-480-B1B6 engine, three-bladed propeller and enlarged tail unit. Twelve **Do 27J-1**s were delivered to the Belgian army, and the Portuguese air force received 16 **Do 27K-1**s and 24 **K-2**s, slightly differing versions of the Do 27A-4. When the Luftwaffe began to dispose of its Do 27As, Portugal acquired at least a further 76, and others went to Nigeria (20), Israel (20), Sudan (three), Turkey (three) and the Congo (two). Some of the Portuguese air-

craft eventually found their way into the Angolan air force. The Do 27 has been additionally used by the air arms of Burundi, Guinea-Bissau, Belize, Rwanda and Sweden. Small numbers remain in service.

Israel maintains a handful of single-engined Do 27s for light transport and training. These serve alongside the Do 28A/B twin-engined development.

Dornier Do 28

Building on its experience gained with the Do 27, Dornier developed in 1959 a twin-engined derivative as the **Do 28**. First flown on 29 April 1959, the Do 28 used essentially the same fuselage as the Do 27, with a nose fairing replacing the latter's

engine and a transverse beam through the lower fuselage to carry a pair of 180-hp (134-kW) Lycoming O-360-A1A engines. The wing span was extended while the chord remained unchanged. Production totalled 60 each of the **Do 28A-1** and **B-1** versions, the latter with 290-hp (216-kW)

IO-360s and other modifications, and was primarily for civilian use. Several Do 28s were used by the Nigerian and Katangan forces during the conflicts in those African countries. Other military users are the **Turkish army** (three) and the **Israel Defence Force/Air Force**.

Dornier Do 28D/Model 128 Skyservant

Although retaining the same configuration as the Do 28 and displaying an obvious family resemblance, the **Do 28D Skyservant** was almost totally a new design. First flown on 23 February 1966, the Do 28D was a further step in Dornier's evolution of rugged light transports with STOL performance and combined military and civil applications. Powered by 380-hp (284-kW) Lycoming IGSO-540-A1E engines, the Do 28D had a larger, flat-sided fuselage that was readily adaptable for specialised roles, a new tail unit, all-new systems and equipment, and a wing similar to that of the original Do 28.

After Dornier had built the prototype and six production Do 28Ds, the wing span was increased by 50 cm (1 ft 7 in) and gross weight by 150 kg (330 lb). This established the **Do 28D-1** production standard, 54 being built including four as VIP transports for the **Luftwaffe**. The improved **Do 28D-2** version was then selected by the Luftwaffe as its standard light transport/communications aircraft, with an order for 101 supplemented by 20 for the **Bundesmarine**. Numerous detail refinements were made in the Do 28D-2, which had an internal redesign to lengthen the cabin by 15 cm (6 in), increased fuel capacity and gross weight increased first to 3800 kg (8,370 lb) and eventually to 4015 kg (8,844 lb).

Production of the Do 28D-2 totalled 172 and was almost wholly for military or quasi-military users. Other than the German air force and navy, these included **Cameroon** (two), **Ethiopian police** (two), **Israel** (15), **Kenya** (six), **Malawi** (six), **Morocco** (two, for maritime patrol), **Nigeria** (20), **Somalia** police air wing (two), **Thailand**'s border police (three), **Turkey** (nine) and **Zambia** (10). At least six more went to the Turkish army from ex-Luftwaffe stocks, which also provided 12 for **Greece**. One of the Luftwaffe Skyservants was fitted with turbo supercharged TIGO-540 engines and flown by Dornier in March 1980 as the **Do 28D-2T**, and conversion of the entire fleet followed. Two of the Bundesmarine aircraft were fitted with LM Ericsson SLAR, IR/UV scanners and cameras for pollution control duty starting in January 1986, under the designation **Do 28D-2OU**.

During 1980, Dornier replaced the Do 28D-2 in production with the generally similar but updated **Model 128-2** (the 'Do' prefix being dropped at this time). Only a handful of Dornier 128-2s was built, including two for the Transportes Aériens de **Benin** and two for the **Nigerian air force**.

Dornier had also adapted the Skyservant for turboprop power, at first fitting a pair of 400-shp (298-kW) Lycoming LTP101-600 engines in the **Do 28D-5X**, flown on 9 April 1978. This same prototype was then fitted with similarly derated Pratt & Whitney Canada PT6A-110 turboprops and, as the **Do 28D-6X**, flew on 4 March 1980. With the latter engines, the **Turbo-Skyservant** entered limited production as the **Dornier 128-6**, the principal order being for 16 for the Nigerian air force. Three others went to the Cameroon air force for the maritime surveillance role, with MEL Marec radar in a chin installation.

SPECIFICATION

Dornier Do 28D-1 Skyservant
Wing: span 15.50 m (50 ft 10.25 in); aspect ratio 8.4; area 28.60 m² (307.86 sq ft)
Fuselage and tail: length 12.00 m (39 ft 4.5 in); height 3.90 m (12 ft 10 in); tailplane span 6.20 m (20 ft 4 in); wheel track 3.52 m (11 ft 6 in); wheel base 8.50 m (27 ft 10.75 in)
Powerplant: two Textron Lycoming IGSO-540 each rated at 380 hp (283 kW)
Weights: empty 2166 kg (4,775 lb); maximum take-off 3650 kg (8,047 lb)
Fuel and load: internal fuel 822 litres (217 US gal); external fuel none
Speed: maximum level speed 'clean' at 10,500 ft (3200 m) 173 kt (199 mph; 320 km/h); maximum cruising speed at 10,000 ft (3050 m) 155 kt (178 mph; 286 km/h); economical cruising speed at 10,000 ft (3050 m) 124 kt (143 mph; 230 km/h)
Range: 976 nm (1,124 miles; 1810 km)
Performance: maximum rate of climb at sea level 1,180 ft (360 m) per minute; service ceiling 24,280 ft (7400 m); take-off distance to 50 ft (15 m) 1,140 ft (347 m) at maximum take-off weight for STOL or 1,700 ft (518 m) at maximum take-off weight for conventional operation; landing distance from 50 ft (15 m) 1,220 ft (372 m) at normal landing weight for STOL or 1,960 ft (597 m) at normal landing weight for conventional operation

Turkey operates a considerable number of Do 28D-2s, several featuring unidentified radomes.

Dornier Do 228

When Dornier adopted the designation 128-2 and 128-6 for the Skyservant variants previously known as the Do 28D-2 and Do 28D-6, two further derivatives of the basic twin-engined transport were in the project phase as the **Do 28E-1** and **Do 28E-2**. Given a go-ahead in November 1979, these then became the **Dornier 228-100** and **228-200** respectively, differing essentially only in fuselage length and operational weights.

Using the same fuselage cross-section as the Skyservant, the Dornier 228-100 was sized to seat 15 passengers, while the longer 228-200 would seat 19. Prototypes flew, respectively, on 28 March and 9 May 1981, and deliveries began (for airline use) in 1982.

Of just over 200 Dornier 228s built (by 1994), the majority are for commercial use, the major exception being the **Indian Air Force** and the **Indian Coast Guard**. The latter began to operate the first of 36 **Dornier 228-201**s in July 1986, these having MEL Marec II radar, a Swedish IR/UV linescan sensor and other special features. At least 43 Dornier 228-201s are being acquired by the Indian Air Force, and the **Indian Navy** has a requirement for 27, depending like the Coast Guard upon the assembly/licence-production line set up by HAL at Bangalore. After Dornier had delivered three 228-201s to the Indian CG (and five for airline use), HAL flew the first Indian-assembled aircraft on 31 January 1986.

One 228-201 was evaluated by both the **Bundesmarine** and **Luftwaffe**, this later becoming a 'hack' for use by the latter, while the former acquired another fully equipped for maritime pollution control which is now operated by MFG 5. Other military users are **Finland** (multi-sensor aircraft for para-military Frontier Guard), **Malawi** (three 228-201s and a single **228-202**), **Niger** (one -201 delivered in April 1986), **Nigeria** (one -100 transport and two VIP -200s), the Royal **Oman** police air wing (two -100s), and the **Royal Thai navy** (three equipped for maritime reconnaissance with Bendix 1500 radar).

India is the largest military operator of the Do 228, aircraft serving with the Air Force, Navy (illustrated) and Coast Guard. The latter service has aircraft equipped with search radar in a fairing under the forward cabin.

SPECIFICATION

Dornier Do 228 Maritime Patrol Version A
Wing: span 16.97 m (55 ft 8 in); aspect ratio 9.0; area 32.00 m² (344.46 sq ft)
Fuselage and tail: length 15.04 m (49 ft 4.125 in); height 4.86 m (15 ft 11.5 in); tailplane span 6.45 m (21 ft 2 in); wheel track 3.30 m (10 ft 10 in); wheel base 5.53 m (18 ft 1.25 in)
Powerplant: two Garrett TPE331-5-252D each rated at 715 shp (533 kW)
Weights: empty, standard 2960 kg (6,526 lb); operating empty 3935 kg (8,675 lb); maximum take-off 5980 kg (13,183 lb)
Fuel and load: internal fuel 1885 kg (4,155 lb) plus provision for 395 kg (871 lb) of auxiliary fuel; external fuel none; maximum payload 2117 kg (4,667 lb)
Speed: average cruising speed at optimum altitude for maximum range 165 kt (190 mph; 305 km/h), or for maximum endurance 100 kt (115 mph; 185 km/h)
Range: 940 nm (1,982 miles; 1740 km) with standard fuel; search time at maximum-range cruising speed at 2,000 ft (610 m) close to base 7 hours 45 minutes, or at maximum range cruising speed at 2,000 ft (610 m) 400 nm (460 miles; 740 km) from base 3 hours 45 minutes, or at maximum-endurance cruising speed at 2,000 ft (610 m) close to base 9 hours 45 minutes, or at maximum-endurance cruising speed at 2,000 ft (610 m) 400 nm (460 miles; 750 km) from base 4 hours 45 minutes
Performance: maximum rate of climb at sea level 1,910 ft (582 m) per minute; service ceiling 28,000 ft (8535 m); take-off run 1,450 ft (442 m) at maximum take-off weight; take-off distance to 50 ft (15 m) 1,945 ft (592 m) at maximum take-off weight

Douglas DC-3/C-47 Dakota/Turbo Dakota

Of all the types of aircraft serving with military forces worldwide, the **Douglas C-47/DC-3** is perhaps the best-known and probably the longest serving. As the commercial Douglas DST transport, the prototype of this ubiquitous family first flew on 17 December 1935. Production Model DC-3s were in airline service before World War II, and the first military examples entered US Army Air Corps service in October 1938. The definitive military **C-47 Skytrain** began deliveries in February 1942 and by the time production ended in 1946 a total of 10,655 aircraft of basic DC-3 type had been built, all but a few hundred in military guise. Numerous designations were applied to different versions used by the US Army Air Force and Navy, of which the **C-47**, **C-53** and **C-117** variants were the most significant. The name **Dakota** was adopted in Britain and became widely used. The type was also built in the Soviet Union as the **Lisunov Li-2**.

The basic **C-47A Skytrain** was powered by two 1,200-hp (896-kW) Pratt & Whitney R-1830-90D or -92 radials. It had a normal take-off weight of 29,300 lb (13320 kg) and accommodated up to 28 troops or four tons of cargo. Retired from US service from 1945 onwards, thousands of C-47As became available for sale or donation to other air forces (or for adaptation for commercial service). In 1994, relatively small numbers remained operational with the air arms of about three dozen nations, of which the most important, numerically, were the **Republic of China** (Taiwan), **Colombia**, **Greece**, **Israel**, **Salvador**, **South Africa**, **Thailand**, **Turkey** and **Vietnam**. In Colombia, Salvador and Thailand, examples of the **AC-47** gunship are also being used, with three side-firing 7.62-mm machine-guns mounted in the cabin.

Many efforts have been made to enhance the performance of the C-47/DC-3, as well as to prolong its service life and to extend its utility. In particular, a number of turboprop installations have been made, of which the latest and apparently most successful, in military applications, is that developed by Basler Turbo Conversions Inc. The **Basler Turbo-67** introduces two Pratt & Whitney Canada PT6A-67R turboprops with five-bladed Hartzell propellers, and a lengthening of the forward fuselage by 3 ft 4 in (1.02 m) to bring the pilots forward of the plane of the propellers and preserve CG within acceptable limits. Revisions in the cabin layout increase the seating capacity to a maximum of 34 troops or five LD3 cargo containers.

Deliveries of the Turbo-67 began in 1990, recipients including the air forces of Colombia, **Bolivia**, **Guatemala** and Salvador (with an AC-47 gunship conversion as well as a transport). Early in 1992, the South African Air Force began to accept the **C-47TP Super Dakota** conversion by Professional Aviation, similar in almost all respects to the Basler Turbo-67. Production conversion lines set up by the SAAF at the Swartkops and Ysterplaat bases were to convert the entire fleet of over 40 Dakotas to this standard, with the first assigned to No. 35 Squadron at Cape Town in 1992 for SAR duty.

Some of Israel's C-47s are used in an electronic warfare role, and are festooned with antennas.

SPECIFICATION

Douglas C-47 Dakota
Wing: span 95 ft 0 in (28.96 m); aspect ratio 9.15; area 987.00 sq ft (91.69 m²)
Fuselage and tail: length 64 ft 6 in (19.66 m); height 16 ft 11.5 in (5.16 m)
Powerplant: two Pratt & Whitney R-1830-92 Twin Wasp each rated at 1,200 hp (895 kW)
Weights: operating empty 17,720 lb (8038 kg); normal take-off 25,200 lb (11431 kg); maximum take-off 28,000 lb (12701 kg)
Fuel and load: internal fuel 4,820 lb (2186 kg); external fuel none; maximum payload 6,600 lb (2994 kg)

Speed: never-exceed speed 206 kt (237 mph; 381 km/h); maximum level speed 'clean' at optimum altitude 187 kt (215 mph; 346 km/h); maximum cruising speed at 5,000 ft (1525 m) 168 kt (194 mph; 312 km/h); economical cruising speed at 6,000 ft (1830 m) 143 kt (165 mph; 266 km/h)
Range: 1,311 nm (1,510 miles; 2430 km) with maximum fuel or 304 nm (350 miles; 563 km) with maximum payload
Performance: maximum rate of climb at sea level 1,070 ft (326 m) per minute; service ceiling 21,900 ft (6675 m)

Colombia operates two AC-47 gunships, distinguished by the blast deflector around the door and blanked-off rear windows.

Douglas **DC-4/C-54 Skymaster**

The **Douglas DC-4** was conceived as the fourth in the Douglas Commercial series of transport aircraft, and first flew on 26 March 1942 (after an earlier **DC-4E** prototype, in June 1938, proved to be unsuitable for development). Early production of the DC-4 was absorbed by the USAAF under the **C-54** designation, leaving commercial exploitation to follow post-war. Like the DC-3, the DC-4/C-54 found its way into the inventories of many air forces around the world but few currently remain. The final users of the type were the air forces of **Mexico** (two, now grounded), **Niger** (one), the **Republic of Korea** (two remaining from 17 received from US stocks in 1966-67) and **South Africa** (two equipped for Elint duties, all believed grounded). The **Skymaster** was designed to be flown with a crew of five and normally accommodated up to 50 equipped troops or a freight load of 32,000 lb (14515 kg).

SPECIFICATION

Douglas DC-4
Wing: span 117 ft 6 in (35.82 m); aspect ratio 9.44; area 1,462.00 sq ft (135.82 m²)
Fuselage and tail: length 93 ft 10 in (28.60 m); height 27 ft 7 in (8.41 m)
Powerplant: four Pratt & Whitney R-2000-2SD-13G Twin Wasp each rated at 1,450 hp (1081 kW)
Weights: empty equipped 43,300 lb (19641 kg); normal take-off 63,500 lb (28804 kg); maximum take-off 73,000 lb (33113 kg)
Fuel and load: internal fuel 9,500 lb (4309 kg); external fuel none; maximum payload 14,200 lb (6441 kg)

Speed: maximum speed 'clean' at optimum altitude 230 kt (265 mph; 426 km/h); maximum cruising speed at 10,000 ft (3050 m) 180 kt (207 mph; 333 km/h)
Range: 1,893 nm (2,180 miles; 3510 km) with maximum fuel or 999 nm (1,150 miles; 1851 km) with maximum payload

Two of South Africa's DC-4s were used for Elint and EW work.

Douglas **DC-6/C-118 Liftmaster**

Development of the **Douglas DC-6** represented a logical evolution from the DC-4, with which it shared the same configuration, but featured enlarged dimensions, increased power and greater load capacity. First flown on 15 February 1946, the 76-seat DC-6 was produced principally for commercial use, but 167 were built for the USAF and USN with the **C-118A** and **R6D-1** designations. Several foreign air forces acquired ex-commercial **DC-6A**s, **DC-6B**s or, in a few cases, C-118As, and of these about a dozen were still flying in 1994. The final users of the type include the air forces of **Colombia**, **Guatemala**, **Honduras**, **Mexico**, **El Salvador**, **South Korea** and **Taiwan**.

SPECIFICATION

Douglas DC-6B
Wing: span 117 ft 6 in (35.81 m); aspect ratio 9.17; area 1,463.00 sq ft (139.91 m²)
Fuselage and tail: length 105 ft 7 in (32.18 m); height 29 ft 3 in (8.92 m)
Powerplant: four Pratt & Whitney R-2800-CB17 Double Wasp each rated at 2,500 hp (1864 kW)
Weights: operating empty about 62,000 lb (28123 kg); maximum take-off 107,000 lb (48534 kg)
Fuel and load: internal fuel 32,950 lb (14946 kg); external fuel none; maximum payload 24,565 lb (11143 kg)
Speed: never-exceed speed 312 kt (359 mph; 578 km/h); maximum cruising speed at optimum altitude 274 kt (316 mph; 509 km/h); typical cruising speed at 20,000 ft (6095 m) 234 kt (270 mph; 435 km/h)

Range: 2,320 nm (2,672 miles; 4300 km) with maximum fuel or 1,650 nm (1,900 miles; 3058 km) with maximum payload
Performance: maximum rate of climb at sea level 1,120 ft (341 m) per minute; balanced take-off field length 6,150 ft (1875 m) at maximum take-off weight; balanced landing field length 5,000 ft (1525 m)

Taiwan was one of the last military users of the DC-6, this aircraft flying on services to Quemoy. It has recently been replaced by Boeing 727s.

Douglas **DC-8/EC-24A**

First of the Douglas jetliners and launched to compete with the Boeing 707, the **Douglas DC-8** first flew on 30 May 1958. Production ended in May 1972 with 556 built in six major series and numerous sub-variants. Of these, the **Series 10** to **Series 50** were dimensionally similar, with a fuselage length of 150 ft 6 in (45.87 m) and typically about 120 seats; differences concerned engine choice, fuel capacity and operating weights. Two different longer fuselages were offered in the **Series 60** versions, to seat up to 259 or 189 passengers, and the **Series 70** designation identified a retrofit programme for the Series 60 to introduce 22,000-lb (97.86-kN) thrust CFM56 turbofans in place of Pratt & Whitney JT3D turbojets.

The French **Armée de l'Air** was the first of the small number of military users of the DC-8, acquiring one **Series 55CF** new and several others ex-airline. The constitution of the French fleet has varied from time to time, the final disposition comprising a single Series 55 and three **Series 72**s (converted from **Series 62**s) that equip ET 3/60 'Esterel' in the 60ᵉ Groupe de Transport for long-range strategic transport and in the VIP role from Charles de Gaulle, Paris. A fifth DC-8, a **Series 53**, also serves in the ECM/Elint role, flown by the 51 Escadron Electronique 'Aubrac' in CTAA at Evreux.

Two ex-Swissair DC-8 **Series 62CF**s equipping the Escuadrilla Presidencial of the **Fuerza Aérea Peruana** are the only other aircraft of this type remaining in military service in the transport role. More specialised is the single **Series 54F** freighter, ex-United Airlines, flown by the **US Navy** as the **EC-24A** since 1987. This unique aircraft, with an extensive electronic suite, serves with the Fleet Electronic Warfare Support Group (FEWSG) to simulate the C³ threat in fleet exercises.

Two one-off specials are the DC-8 SARIGUE (left) used by the French for electronic reconnaissance, and the EC-24A (right), used by the US Navy for fleet ECM exercises. The latter is operated by Chrysler from Waco.

EH Industries EH.101 Merlin

EH Industries Ltd
500 Chiswick High Road
London W4 5RG, UK

The **EH.101** has its roots in the Westland WG 34 design that was adopted in late 1978 to meet Britain's Naval Staff Requirement 6646 for a Sea King Replacement (SKR). Work on the WG 34 was cancelled before a prototype had been completed, however, opening the way for revision of the design to meet both Royal Navy and Italian navy requirements. Negotiations between Westland and Agusta began in November 1979. This led to the setting up of European Helicopter Industries Ltd, which was given a formal go-ahead in February 1984, when the two governments agreed to fund nine prototypes, and subsequent development.

Although replacing the Sea King was the primary objective, determining the size and weight of the EH.101 design, several other potential roles were planned from the outset, including military and civil transport and utility duties. Some roles can be performed using the same basic fuselage as the naval helicopter but, alternatively, the EH.101 can be fitted with a modified rear fuselage incorporating a ramp. The nine prototypes ordered were assigned specific tasks concerned with the basic dynamics, specific RN and Italian Marina ASW equipment fits, the military tactical/logistic transport, the civil utility version and the commercial **Heliliner**.

The EH.101 is a three-engined helicopter with a single five-bladed composite main rotor, and BERP-derived high-speed tips. Much use is made of composites throughout, although the fuselage itself is mainly of aluminium alloy. Systems and equipment vary with role and customer. For the Royal Navy, which calls the EH.101 the **Merlin HAS.Mk 1**, IBM is the prime contractor in association with Westland and provides equipment as well as overall management and integration; other avionics include GEC

Ferranti Blue Kestrel 360° search radar, GEC Avionics AQS-903 processing and display system, Racal Orange Reaper ESM and Ferranti/Thomson-CSF dipping sonar. Armament on the Merlin comprises four Marconi Sting Ray torpedoes, with two sonobuoy dispensers. Options include the Exocet, Harpoon, Sea Eagle and Marte Mk 2 missiles.

The initial RN requirement for 50 Merlins to operate from Type 23-frigates, 'Invincible'-class aircraft-carriers, RFAs and other ships or land bases has been reduced to 44 for delivery starting in 1996 costing £1.5 billion. These are to be powered by the 2,312-shp (1724-kW) Rolls-Royce Turboméca RTM 322 turboshafts, whereas the Italian navy, which is expected to acquire up to 24 EH.101s (16 orders with eight on option), has specified 1,714-shp (1278-kW) General Electric T700-GE-T6A engines, assembled in Italy. Earlier variants of the GE engine, (the commercial CT7), were used to power the prototypes, the first of which (PP1, ZF641: a non-specific, basic test vehicle) flew at Yeovil on 9 October 1987. A similar Agusta-built basic model (PP2), flew in Italy on 26 November 1987. Next to fly in Italy, on 26 April 1989, was a prototype of the Italian ASW version (PP6), followed in the UK by a basic ASW version (PP4, ZF644) on 15 June and the Merlin prototype (PP5, ZF649) on 24 October in the same year. PP3 and PP8 were both finished to civilian Heliliner standard.

The Italian PP2 was lost in an accident on 21 January 1993, resulting in a suspension of all flight testing until 24 June that year. The RTM 322 engines were first flown (in PP4) in July 1993, and subsequently fitted to PP5.

A prototype with the ramp (Agusta-built PP7) flew on 18 December 1989, representing the military utility variant, which is expected to be ordered by the RAF as its

next medium-lift helicopter. The first customer for the utility variant was to have been Canada, which ordered 15 EH.101s, for SAR duties. Replacing 13 existing CH-113A Labradors (Boeing-Vertol CH-46s), these aircraft were to have been designated **CH-149 Chimo**. Canada also ordered 35 naval versions to meet its New Shipborne Aircraft requirement for a Sea King Replacement, designated **CH-148 Petrel**. Assembled and fitted out by IMP Group Ltd in Canada, these EH.101s were to be powered by 1,920-shp (1432-kW) CT7-6A1 turboshafts. The deal was a hard-fought one, subject to constant scrutiny and not unimportant to the success of the EH.101. Deliveries were scheduled to begin in late 1997 (CH-148)/early 1998 (CH-149). However, an increasingly bitter argument over the costs versus acquisition of less complex aircraft saw the EH.101 become a campaign issue in the Canadian elections of 1993. The pro-EH.101 Conservative government was ousted by Jean Chrétien's Liberal party who, true to their pledge, cancelled the entire programme. This will allegedly cost Canada more in punitive cancellation costs then if the buy had gone ahead, to say nothing for the jobs and industrial offsets lost.

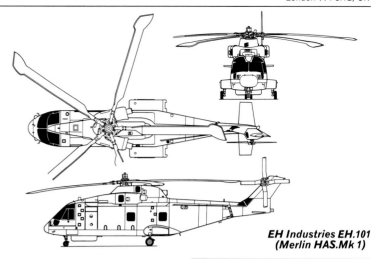

**EH Industries EH.101
(Merlin HAS.Mk 1)**

SPECIFICATION

European Helicopter Industries EH.101 Merlin (naval model)

Rotor system: main rotor diameter 61 ft 0 in (18.59 m); tail rotor diameter 13 ft 2 in (4.01 m); main rotor disc area 2,922.60 sq ft (271.51 m²); tail rotor disc area 136.17 sq ft (12.65 m²)

Fuselage and tail: length overall, rotors turning 74 ft 10 in (22.81 m) and fuselage 74 ft 9.6 in (22.80 m); length with main rotor blades and tail pylon folded 52 ft 6 in (16.00 m); height overall 21 ft 10 in (6.65 m) with rotors turning and with main rotor blades and tail pylon folded 17 ft 1 in (5.21 m)

Powerplant: (British helicopters) three Rolls-Royce/Turboméca RTM322-01 each rated at 2,312 shp (1724 kW) and 2,100 shp (1566 kW) for maximum and intermediate contingencies respectively, or (Italian helicopters) three General Electric T700-GE-T6A each rated at 1,714 shp (1279 kW), 1,682 shp (1254 kW) and 1,437 shp (1071 kW) for maximum contingency, intermediate contingency and continuous running respectively

Weights: (estimated) basic empty 15,700 lb (7121 kg); operating empty 20,500 lb (9298 kg); maximum take-off 29,830 lb (13530 kg)

Fuel and load: internal fuel 7,580 lb (3438 kg) plus provision for 1,896 lb (860 kg) of auxiliary fuel; external fuel none; maximum ordnance 2,116 lb (960 kg)

Speed: never-exceed speed 167 kt (192 mph; 309 km/h); average cruising speed 160 kt (184 mph; 296 km/h); economical cruising speed 140 kt (161 mph; 259 km/h)

Range: ferry range 1,000 nm (1,152 miles; 1853 km) with auxiliary fuel; endurance 5 hours on station with maximum weapon load

Right: HMS Iron Duke, a Type 23 frigate, is typical of the vessels from which the RN's Merlins will operate.

Below: The military utility EH.101 is designed to lift six tons or 30 equipped troops. This is PP9, the final, Italian-built (civil) utility version.

EMBRAER (Neiva) T-25 Universal

Empresa Brasileira de Aeronáutica SA
Caixa Postal 343
12227-901 São José dos Campos, SP, Brazil

The **T-25 Universal** was developed by the Neiva company (acquired by EMBRAER in 1980) to meet a **Brazilian air force** requirement for a basic trainer to replace the T-6 Texan and S-11/S-12 Instructor. The specification called for side-by-side

seating with provision for a third occupant behind the two pilots. Prototype testing began on 29 April 1966 and production deliveries started in the late summer of 1971, against Brazilian air force requirements that eventually totalled 140. About

100 remain in service, for primary and specialised training roles and for general duties. Brazilian student pilots in their second and third years at the Air Force Academy fly 25 and 50 hours respectively on the T-25 before moving on to the Tucano. The sole

export order was for 10 aircraft from the **Chilean army**, five of which were transferred to the air force in 1979. These were subsequently phased out of service in 1983 when five were transferred to the **Fuerza Aérea Paraguaya**, where they still serve.

EMBRAER EMB-110/111 Bandeirante

The aircraft which launched EMBRAER as a force among aerospace manufacturers was first flown on 19 August 1972, in response to a light transport requirement by the **Brazilian air force** and the country's airlines. A nine-seat predecessor powered by the same Pratt & Whitney Canada PT6A engines had been tested in prototype form (as the **YC-95** or **EMB-100**), but the **EMBRAER EMB-110 Bandeirante** (Pioneer) featured a much larger cabin which found favour with civil operators overseas, as well as with the Brazilian military.

The first three of 80 Bandeirantes ordered by the **Brazilian air force** were delivered in February 1973. The type is now the mainstay of the transport force, serving in one squadron of the Rio-based 2° Grupo, seven others allocated to the regional air commands, and also in a transport conversion unit. The 60 **C-95** models were 12-seat versions, and were supplemented by 20 **C-95A** (**EMB-110K1**) freighters with a 0.85-m (2 ft 9½ in) stretch ahead of the wing, uprated PT6A-34 turboprops (replacing -27s) and a 1.80 x 1.42 m (71 x 56 in) freight door. This door incorporates a 1.30 x 0.80-m (51 x35-in) opening to facilitate air dropping or for use as an emergency exit.These were followed by 31 examples of the **C-95B**, a military version of the improved **EMB-110P** civil model, two of which were also bought by **Gabon**.

None of the Brazilian air force Bandeirante units is exclusively equipped with the C-95. In 2o Grupo de Transporte at Galeao they are augmented by a handful of older, larger BAe 748s, while the regional air command units operate their Bandeirantes alongside Piper Senecas. The regional units are 1 ETA at Belem, 2 ETA at Recife, 3 ETA at Galeao, 4 ETA at Cumbica, 5 ETA at Brasilia and 6 ETA at Porto Alegre. The **Uruguayan air force** took delivery of five 15-seat **EMB-110C**s in 1975, and the **Chilean navy** bought three navalised **EMB-110CN**s in the following year.

Four specialised versions have also entered Brazilian military service. The first of these to join the Brazilian air force was the eight-seat **EC-95** for checking and calibration of navigation aids. Four of these (designated **EMB-110A** by the manufacturer) are in service. These aircraft serve with the Grupo Especial de Inspecão e Vigilancia (GEIV – Special Inspection and Checking Group) at Rio de Janeiro, alongside a handful of ageing EC-47 Dakotas.

The EC-95 was followed by six seven-seat **R-95** (**EMB-110B**) photographic survey versions. These have apertures in the cabin floor to accommodate a Zeiss camera and associated equipment. Doppler and inertial navigation systems are also fitted. The R-95s serve with 6° Grupo of the Coastal Command (COMCAS) at Recife and supplement three RC-130E Hercules. One example of the EMB-110B has been acquired by Uruguay. Two previously undelivered EMB-110P1A civilian transports were bought by the **Colombian air force** along with three for the **Peruvian government** the following year.

COMCAS also operates the **P-95** maritime surveillance version which the company designates **EMB-111A**. Twenty-one of these joined the two squadrons of 7° Grupo, which had been inactive since its last Lockheed P-2 Neptunes were retired in 1976. An Eaton-AIL AN/APS-128 Sea Patrol search radar is housed in a large nose radome, and is fully integrated with the aircraft's inertial navigation system. A high-power searchlight, signal cartridge launcher and an ESM system are also carried, and rockets can be launched from four underwing pylons. Wingtip fuel tanks increase the aircraft's endurance to nine hours.

Brazilian P-95s are locally known as the '**Bandeirulha**', a contraction of 'Bandeirante Patrulha'. Brazil later bought a second batch of improved **P-95B** aircraft with upgraded avionics and strengthened airframes. All P-95s have been brought up to this standard. 1 Esquadrao of 7° Grupo de Aviacao is based at Salvador, while 2 Esquadrao flies from Florianopolis. Six **EMB-111AN** aircraft were delivered to the Chilean navy, and a single example to the **Gabonese air force**.The Chilean navy EMB-111ANs were delivered in lieu of four surplus SP-2E Neptunes embargoed by the US government, and are used by VP-3 in the maritime patrol role. The two EMB-111As are also operated by the air forces of **Angola**.

A SAR version is designated **SC-95B**, or **EMB-110P1(K)**. Deliveries began in late

The armed maritime reconnaissance P-95 Bandeirante (EMB-111) has been bought in two batches by the Brazilian navy; 12 P-95s and 10 improved P-95Bs.

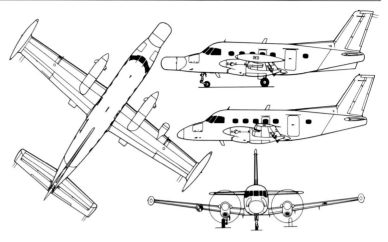

EMBRAER EMB-111A Bandeirante/P-95 (EMB-110/C-95 side view)

1981 of eight to 10° Grupo of COMCAS at Campo Grande. Six stretchers can be accommodated alongside observation and rescue personnel. Two 'bubble' windows are fitted on each side of the fuselage. One was also delivered to **Senegambia**.

SPECIFICATION

EMBRAER EMB-111 (P-95A)
Wing: span 15.95 m (52 ft 4 in) with tip tanks; aspect ratio 8.07; area 29.10 m2 (313.23 sq ft)
Fuselage and tail: length 14.91 m (48 ft 11 in); height 4.91 m (16 ft 1.25 in); tailplane span 7.54 m (24 ft 9 in); wheel track 4.94 m (16 ft 2.5 in); wheel base 4.26 m (13 ft 11.75 in)

Powerplant: two Pratt & Whitney Canada PT6A-34 each rated at 750 shp (559 kW)
Weights: empty equipped 3760 kg (8,289 lb); maximum take-off 7000 kg (15,432 lb)
Fuel and load: internal fuel 2550 litres (674 US gal)
Speed: maximum cruising speed at 10,000 ft (3050 m) 194 kt (223 mph; 360 km/h); economical cruising speed at 1,000 ft (3050 m) 187 kt (2154 mph; 347 km/h)
Range: 1,590 nm (1,830 miles; 2945 km)
Performance: maximum rate of climb at sea level 1,190 ft (362 m) per minute; service ceiling 25,500 ft (7770 m); take-off run 2,135 ft (650 m) at maximum take-off weight; take-off distance to 50 ft (15 m) 3,445 ft (1050 m) at maximum take-off weight; landing distance from 50 ft (15 m) 2,100 ft (640 m) at normal landing weight; landing run 1,475 ft (450 m) at normal landing weight

EMBRAER EMB-120 Brasilia

From the success of the Bandeirante, which established EMBRAER as a major force in the commuter airliner market, the Brazilian firm decided to step up to a much improved, stretched development. From its inception in 1979, the EMB-120 Brasilia progressed towards its maiden flight on 27 July 1983, becoming one of the first of the 1980s 'new generation' of commuter aircraft. The Brasilia was designed for two-crew operations with a load of 30 passengers, and utilised a semi-monocoque fuselage with a low wing and cantilever T-tail. It was certified by the Brazilian CTA in May 1985, powered by a pair of 1,590-shp (1185-kW) Pratt & Whitney Canada PW115 turboprops. The first civilian delivery was made to Atlantic Southeast Airways in the United States on June 1985 and since then over 330 Brasilias have been ordered. The type achieved its 2,000,000th flying hour in January 1993, having carried over 41,000,000 passengers by that time.

The **Brazilian air force** has so far been the only military customer for the EMB-120. Five VIP transport versions designated **VC-97** were delivered between 1987 and 1988, but one was written off in a training acci-

EMBRAER's EMB-120 Brasilia has thus far failed to emulate the military sales of the EMB-110/111 Bandeirante family. The sole customer has been the home air force, taking delivery of five aircraft.

dent in July 1988. The remaining aircraft are operated by 6° ETA of the Comando Aéreo Regional based at the capital, Brasilia. The VC-97 is equivalent to the **EMB-120RT** (Reduced Take-off), the standard production version introduced from the fourth aircraft. This saw a change in powerplant from the original PW115 to the 1,800-shp (1,342-kW) PW118 turboprop, driving four-bladed Hamilton Standard propellers. A hot-and-high version, powered by PW118As, is also available. The next version was the extended-range **EMB-120ER** which offers an increased maximum take-off weight. This entails no major structural changes and so earlier aircraft can be easily brought up to this standard. The longer-legged EMB-120ER formed the baseline for the next version to be offered, the 1992 **EMB-120X** (provisional) **Improved Brasilia**. launched in 1994 as the **EMB-120ER Advanced**,

this aircraft incorporates many detail and style changes along with new avionics and an improved cabin. The EMB-120ER benefits from the work EMBRAER has completed on its new advanced turboprop, the CBA-123, and is available for delivery from August 1994.

Of more interest to military customers are the **EMB-120 Cargo**, an all-cargo version stressed for loads of up to 4,000 kg (8,818 lb), the **EMB-120 Combi**, capable of carrying 19 passengers and 1100-kg (2,425-lb) of freight, and the **EMB-120QC** (Quick Change) which can be transformed from its standard 30-seat layout to a 3500-kg (7,716-lb) capacity freighter in 50 minutes. First commercial deliveries of the EMB-120QC were made in May 1993.

EMBRAER EMB-121 Xingu

Between 1976 and 1987 EMBRAER built 105 examples of the **EMB-121 Xingu**, half of this total being delivered for military use in **Brazil** and **France**. Conceived as a corporate transport derived from the **EMB-120 Bandeirante** commuter, the Xingu offered comfortable seating for six passengers in a pressurised fuselage, combined with a T-tail and a wing/powerplant installation based on that of the Bandeirante. Powered by two PT6A-28 turboprops and with a gross weight of 5200 kg (11,466 lb), the Xingu prototype entered flight test on 10 October 1976, followed by a pre-production aircraft on 20 May 1977 with increased gross weight of 5670 kg (12,500 lb). The last Xingu was delivered on 19 August 1987.

The first six production **Xingu I**s were delivered to the Forca Aérea Brasileira as **VU-9**s to be operated as VIP transports by the 6° Esquadrão de Transporte Aérea; six more were acquired later, as well as two ex-civil examples, with the new designation **EC-9**.

In September 1980 the French defence ministry selected the Xingu to serve in both the Armée de l'Air and Aéronavale as a multi-engine trainer and fast communications aircraft. An order was placed for 41 Xingus: 25 **EMB-121AA** for the Armée de l'Air and 16 **EMB-121AN** for the Aéronavale. Deliveries began in March 1982 and were completed by the end of 1983. In the Armée de l'Air, the Xingu serves primarily with GE 319 at Avord in the training role, with a few detached to the communications squadrons. Naval use is centred on 52S, the training squadron at Lahn-Bihoué, with several Xingus attached to 10S.

SPECIFICATION

EMBRAER EMB-121 Xingu
Wing: span 14.45 m (47 ft 5 in); aspect ratio 7.18; area 27.50 m² (296.00 sq ft)
Fuselage and tail: length 12.25 m (40 ft 2.25 in); height 4.74 m (15 ft 6.5 in); tailplane span 5.58 m (18 ft 3.75 in); wheel track 5.24 m (17 ft 2.25 in); wheel base 2.88 m (9 ft 5.5 in)
Powerplant: two Pratt & Whitney Canada PT6A-28 each rated at 680 shp (507 kW)
Weights: empty equipped 3620 kg (7,984 lb); maximum take-off 5670 kg (12,500 lb)
Fuel and load: internal fuel 1666 litres (440 US gal); external fuel none; maximum payload 860 kg (1,896 lb)
Speed: maximum cruising speed at 11,000 ft (3355 m) 243 kt (280 mph; 450 km/h); economical cruising speed at 20,000 ft (6095 m) 197 kt (227 mph; 365 km/h)
Range: 1,270 nm (1,462 miles; 2353 km) with maximum fuel and a 610-kg (1,345-lb) payload, or 1,225 nm (1,411 miles; 2270 km) with a 780-kg (1,720-lb) payload
Performance: maximum rate of climb at sea level 1,400 ft (426 m) per minute; service ceiling 26,000 ft

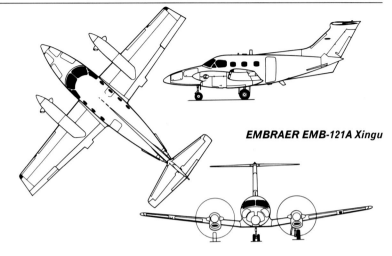

EMBRAER EMB-121A Xingu

(7925 m); take-off distance to 50 ft (15 m) 2,840 ft (866 m) at maximum take-off weight; landing distance from 50 ft (15 m) 2,790 ft (850 m) at maximum landing weight

The chief operators of the EMB-121 are the Armée de l'Air (left) and the Aéronavale (right), which between them accounted for a substantial part of the Xingu's production run. They are used on navigation training exercises and liaison flights.

EMBRAER EMB-312/312H Tucano

Development of the turboprop, high-performance **EMBRAER EMB-312 Tucano** (Toucan) trainer started in 1978 in response to a **Brazilian air force** specification for a Cessna T-37 replacement. First flown on 16 August 1980, the initial **T-27 Tucano** was delivered to the Air Force Academy near São Paulo in September 1983. Most of the 133 aircraft ordered by the FAB (including 10 in 1990 and five in 1993) are operated by this unit, although some will also serve in a conversion unit. An option for 40 more T-27s is held. The Brazilian air force formation aerobatic team, the 'Escuadron de Fumaca' ('Smoke Squadron'), received T-27 Tucanos to replace its ageing North American Harvards, and has displayed extensively throughout the American continent.

Designed from the outset to provide a 'jet-like' flying experience, the Tucano has a single power lever governing both propeller pitch and engine rpm, ejector seats, and a staggered tandem-place cockpit. Four underwing hardpoints can carry up to 1000 kg (2,205 lb) of ordnance for weapons training.

An export order for 134 Tucanos was concluded with **Egypt** in September 1983. All except the first 10 of these were licence-assembled at Helwan. The Egyptian air force operates only 54 locally-assembled Tucanos, about 80 aircraft having been supplied to the **Iraqi** air force. These were followed by deliveries (including current firm orders) to the air forces of **Argentina** (30) **Honduras** (12), **Iran** (25), **Paraguay** (five), **Peru** (30) and **Venezuela** (31). Another major order came into effect in October 1991 (though it was placed in July 1990) when **France** announced its intention to purchase 80 EMBRAER-built **EMB-312F** aircraft for delivery from July 1993. This French version boasts an increased fatigue life, ventral airbrake and French avionics. The first two aircraft had been delivered to the CEV test establishment at Mont-de-Marsan by July 1993. Twenty will be delivered between July 1994 and July 1995, the second batch of 28 between July 1995 and July 1996, and the final 30 in two even batches finishing in May 1998. A further South American customer was the **Colombian** air force, which had received 14 by the end of 1992.

The Tucano's most notable export success came in March 1985, when it won a hotly-contested British order for 131 aircraft to replace the **RAF**'s BAe (Hunting) Jet Provosts. In order to secure the contract, the aircraft's engine was replaced with the considerably more powerful 820-kW (1,100-shp) Garrett TPE331-12B turboprop, and extensive redesign and replacement of systems was undertaken to meet more rigorous RAF criteria, on life span and bird-strike resistance. The Tucano is produced under licence by Shorts in Belfast, which is manufacturing 130 for the RAF and additionally produced aircraft to the same standard for the air forces of **Kenya** (12) and **Kuwait** (16). Total firm orders, including Shorts-built versions, stood at 654 aircraft by early 1994, of which almost 600 exam-

Above: This FAB T-27 wears the badge of 2ª ELO (liaison and observation squadron), Coastal Command, a former T-25 operator.

Below: FAB T-27s are now adopting this two-tone grey scheme, in addition to base codes. Here, 'PV' stands for Porto Velho.

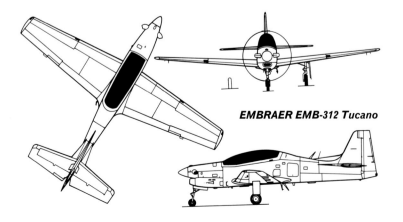

EMBRAER EMB-312 Tucano

ples had been delivered. The Shorts-built **S312** (referred to by the RAF as the **Tucano T.Mk 1**) is described in more detail in a separate entry.

In June 1991, EMBRAER announced the **EMB-312H Super Tucano**, featuring an uprated P&WC PT6A-68/1 engine. Fuselage plugs fore and aft totalling 1.37 m (4 ft 6 in) have been inserted to accommodate the 1193-kW (1,600-shp) turboprop and to maintain stability and CoG. This version is offered in the USAF/USN JPATS competition, in association with Northrop. A converted Tucano (PP-ZTW) toured bases in the US during August 1992, before the first production standard aircraft (PP-ZTV) flew on 15 May 1993. During 1994 it is expected that the Brazilian government will order 50 new, armed aircraft under the designation **EMBRAER ALX** (essentially single-seat Super Tucanos). These will be operated by the air force, but purchased by the planning ministry as part of its anti-narcotics and smuggling operations. By 1996 up to 120 ALXs may be obtained, though this total may comprise a number of standard two-seat Tucanos as well.

This Tucano is an EMBRAER-owned development ship which served as a Garrett-powered testbed for the RAF's Tucano development, before being converted to EMB-321H standard by September 1991. The Super Tucano has been further developed, becoming the armed, single-seat ALX.

SPECIFICATION

EMBRAER EMB-312 Tucano
Wing: span 11.14 m (36 ft 6.5 in); aspect ratio 6.4; area 19.40 m2 (208.82 sq ft)
Fuselage and tail: length 9.86 m (32 ft 4.25 in); height 3.40 m (11 ft 1.75 in); tailplane span 4.66 m (15 ft 3.5 in); wheel track 3.76 m (12 ft 4 in); wheel base 3.16 m (10 ft 4.5 in)
Powerplant: one Pratt & Whitney Canada PT6A-25C rated at 750 shp (559 kW)
Weights: basic empty 1810 kg (3,991 lb); normal take-off 2550 kg (5,622 lb); maximum take-off 3175 kg (7,000 lb)
Fuel and load: internal fuel 529 kg (1,166 lb); external fuel up to two 330 litre (81.2-US gal) ferry tanks; maximum ordnance 1000 kg (2,205 lb)

Speed: never-exceed speed 280 kt (322 mph; 519 km/h); maximum level speed 'clean' at 10,000 ft (3050 m) 242 kt (278 mph; 448 km/h); maximum cruising speed at 10,000 ft (3050 m) 222 kt (255 mph; 411 km/h); economical cruising speed at 10,000 ft (3050 m) 172 kt (198 mph; 319 km/h)
Range: ferry range 1,797 nm (2,069 miles; 3330 km) with two ferry tanks; typical range 995 nm (1,145 miles; 1844 km) with internal fuel; endurance about 5 hours 0 minutes with internal fuel

Performance: maximum rate of climb at sea level 680 m (2,231 ft) per minute; service ceiling 30,000 ft (9145 m); take-off run 1,250 ft (381 m) at normal take-off weight; take-off distance to 50 ft (15 m) 2,330 ft (710 m) at normal take-off weight; landing distance from 50 ft (15 m) 1,985 ft (605 m) at normal landing weight; landing run 1,215 ft (370 m) at normal landing weight
g limits: -3 to + 6 at normal take-off weight or -2.2 to +4.4 at maximum take-off weight

---

EMBRAER **EMB-326 Xavante**

Under licence from Aermacchi, EMBRAER assembled 166 **MB-326GB** basic jet trainer/ground attack aircraft for the **Força Aérea Brasiliera**, operated under the local designation **T-26**. Armed aircraft are designated **AT-26**, all carry the name **Xavante**, a Brazilian Indian tribe.

About 100 Xavantes have remained in Brazilian service, shared between the light attack and training roles. Operating in the former capacity are 1ª Esq in the 4° Grupo de Aviacao de Caca at Fortaleza and 1° Esq and 3° Esq in 10° GAvCa at St Maria. Among the aircraft at the latter base are a number equipped with cameras and flight-refuelling probes, with the designation **RT-26** to indicate the reconnaissance role. Before

joining the AT-26 squadrons, pilots convert on the same type at the training centre at Natal.

Additional aircraft were assembled for export to **Paraguay** (10) and **Togo** (six). Brazil has transferred 11 of its AT-26s to **Argentina**, where Italian-built MB 326s were already in service. The Brazilian-assembled **EMB-326GB**s also remain in service in the light attack/weapons training roles.

SPECIFICATION

EMBRAER EMB-326 Xavante
generally similar to the Aermacchi M.B.326

Deliveries of 166 EMB-326GB Xavantes to the Força Aérea Brasiliera took place between 1971 and 1981. The Xavante has six underwing hardpoints, and for reconnaissance duties the inner station on the port wing can be fitted with a pod housing four 70-mm Vinten cameras.

ENAER **T-35 Pillán**

Empresa Nacional de Aeronáutica de Chile
Avienda José Miguel Carrera 11087
P.36 ½, Santiago, Chile

Beginning in 1980, ENAER assembled 27 Piper PA-28 Dakotas for flying clubs and the **Chilean air force**, the latter sought a similar two-seat fully-aerobatic trainer. Piper responded by developing the PA-28R-300, based on the Saratoga with a new centre-section, an aerobatic wing, and a 300-hp (224-kW) Lycoming engine. Two Piper-built prototypes first flew on 6 March and 31 August 1981, followed by three assembled by ENAER.

Known in Chile as the **T-35 Pillán** (Devil), the aircraft entered production for the Chilean air force as a basic, intermediate and instrument flying trainer. Deliveries began to the Air Academy in August 1985, comprising a total of 60 **T-35A** primary and 20 **T-35B** instrument trainers, both types

serving in the Escuela de Aviación 'Capitan Avalos' at El Bosque, Santiago. A few also serve at Los Cerillos, where Grupo 11 provides support for II Brigada, Ala 2.

ENAER has also produced 41 **T-35C** Pilláns for **Spain**, assembled by CASA, to serve with the air force as the **E.26 Tamiz**. These are used for primary training at the General Air Academy, San Javier; several are also operated by Ala 54 in Mando de Materiel (Personnel Command). The **T-35D** instrument trainer has been procured by the **Panamanian** national air service (10 delivered in 1988-89) and **Paraguay** (15). On 5 March 1988, ENAER flew the prototype **T-35S**, powered by an Allison 250-B17 turboprop for use as an aerobatic trainer and display aircraft.

SPECIFICATION

ENAER T-35A Pillán
Wing: span 29 ft 0 in (8.84 m); aspect ratio 5.7; area 147.34 sq ft (13.69 m2)
Fuselage and tail: length 26 ft 3 in (8.00 m); height 8 ft 8 in (2.64 m); tailplane span 10 ft 0 in (3.05 m); wheel track 9 ft 11 in (3.02 m);
Powerplant: one Textron Lycoming IO-540-K1K5 rated at 300 hp (224 kW)
Weights: empty equipped 2,050 lb (930 kg); normal take-off 2,900 lb (1315 kg) for aerobatics; maximum take-off 2,950 lb (1338 kg)
Fuel and load: internal fuel 462 lb (210 kg); external

fuel none; maximum ordnance 1,100 lb (499 kg)
Speed: never-exceed speed 241 kt (277 mph; 446 km/h); maximum level speed 'clean' at sea level 168 kt (193 mph; 311 km/h); maximum cruising speed at 8,800 ft (2680 m) 144 kt (166 mph; 266 km/h)
Range: 650 nm (748 miles; 1204 km) at 55 per cent power or 590 nm (679 miles; 1093 km) at 75 per cent power; endurance 5 hours 36 minutes at 55 per cent power or 4 hours 24 minutes at 75 per cent power
Performance: maximum rate of climb at sea level 1,525 ft (465 m) per minute; climb to 10,000 ft (3050 m) in 8 minutes 48 seconds; service ceiling 19,160 ft (5840 m); take-off run 940 ft (287 m) at maximum take-off weight; take-off distance to 50 ft (15 m) 1,620 ft (494 m) at maximum take-off weight

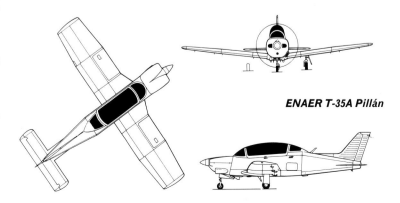

The Pillán is now the Fuerza Aérea de Chile's primary trainer, serving in both T-35A form and the IFR-equipped T-35B. In Spanish hands, as the Tamiz (T-35C), it is also an integral part of the training syllabus.

ENAER T-35A Pillán

ENAER T-35DT Aucán (Turbo Pillán)

Design studies for a **Turbo Pillán** began in 1985, and in 1986 ENAER fitted a Pillán (CC-PZH) with a 420-shp (313-kW) Allison 250-B17D turboprop to produce the **T-35TX Aucán** (Blithe Spirit). After its maiden flight in February of that year, and the first public showing at FIDAE, the Aucán chalked up some 500 flying hours until 1987, when it was returned to ENAER for further modification. It subsequently took to the air, in a revised form, having been modified with a sideways-opening, one-piece canopy. In 1990 ENAER awarded the US Soloy Corporation, of Olympia, Washington, a contract to further develop the Allison 250 installation and produce a modification kit for existing piston-engined T-35 Pilláns. Soloy has forged the market in such piston-to-turbine conversions, having started out

by modifying helicopters such as the Bell Model 47 and Hiller H-12. The first Pillán to receive the Soloy treatment (CC-PZG) flew in March 1991 and ENAER are marketing this version as the **T-35DT Turbo Pillán**.

SPECIFICATION

ENAER T-35DT Turbo Pillán
generally similar to the ENAER T-35A Pillán except in the following particulars:
Fuselage and tail: length 28 ft 2.5 in (8.60 m); wheel base 6 ft 6.75 in (2.00 m)
Powerplant: one Allison 250-B17D rated at 420 shp (313 kW)
Weights: empty equipped 2,080 lb (943 kg)
Fuel and load: internal fuel 73.4 US gal (277.8 litres)
Speed: maximum level speed 'clean' at sea level 176 kt

Bearing the legend 'Allison Turbine Power' on the nose, this is the original Allison 250-powered ENAER T-35TX, Aucán, first flown in February 1986. ENAER have now moved on to the T-35DT.

(203 mph; 326 km/h); maximum cruising speed at 7,600 ft (2315 m) 182 kt (209 mph; 337 km/h)
Range: 300 nm (345 miles; 556 km)
Performance: maximum rate of climb at sea level 1,750 ft (533 m) per minute; service ceiling 24,300 ft (7405 m); take-off run 880 ft (268 m) at maximum take-

off weight; take-off distance to 50 ft (15 m) 1,500 ft (457 m) at maximum take-off weight; landing distance from 50 ft (15 m) 2,150 ft (655 m) at maximum landing weight; landing run 1,057 ft (322 m) at maximum landing weight

---

Enstrom F-28/Model 280/480 (TH-28)

The Enstrom Helicopter Corp.
PO Box 490, 2209 North 22nd St, Twin County Airport
Menominee, San Antonio, TX 78217, USA

The first **Enstrom F-28** light helicopter flew in May 1962, and some 900 examples have been built in successive models. The **F-28F Falcon** is the current basic utility model, certificated in 1981 and fitted with a 225-hp (168-kW) Textron Lycoming HIO-360-FIAD flat-four engine with turbo-supercharger.

Similarly powered, the **Model 280FX** appeared in 1985 featuring a number of refinements such as a redesigned air inlet system, fully-faired skid landing gear, covered tail rotor shaft, tail rotor guard and a new tailplane with endplate fins. Both versions are fitted with a three-bladed main rotor.

The first military sale was not made until 1989 when 15 of the three-seat **Model 280FX** helicopters were supplied to the **Chilean** army for primary training. Subsequently, the **Peruvian** army acquired 10 F-28Fs. In 1994 **Columbia** will receive 12 F-28Fs under the FMS programme.

Below: The Chilean army operates 15 Enstrom 280FXs as primary trainers. This version differs from the Model 280 by having a faired-over rear-rotor drive shaft, and other aerodynamic refinements.

The Model 280FX served as the basis for Enstrom's four-seat **Model 480**, which became its entrant for the US Army's NTH (New Training Helicopter) competition, as the **TH-28**. After a modified Allison 250-powered 280FX was flown in December 1988, the first true 'wide-body' (three-seats) Model 480 took to the air in October 1989. The TH-28 was certified in September 1992 and four aircraft embarked on a 1,500-hour test programme. Intended as a basic trainer and light patrol helicopter, the TH-28 featured military spec systems such as crash-worthy fuel tanks and crew seating, and the cockpit could be configured for VFR or IFR operations. In the event, the TH-28 lost out to the the Bell TH-67 in the NTH competition.

SPECIFICATION

Enstrom Model F-28F Falcon
Rotor system: main rotor diameter 32 ft 0 in (9.75 m); tail rotor diameter 4 ft 8 in (1.42 m); main rotor disc area 804.25 sq ft (74.71 m²); tail rotor disc area 17.10 sq ft (1.59 m²)
Fuselage and tail: length overall, rotors stationary 29 ft 3 in (8.92 m); height overall 9 ft 2 in (2.79 m) to

top of rotor head; skid track 7 ft 3 in (2.21 m)
Powerplant: one Textron Lycoming HIO-360-F1AD rated at 225 hp (168 kW)
Weights: empty equipped 1,570 lb (712 kg); maximum take-off 2,600 lb (1179 kg)
Fuel and load: internal fuel 42 US gal (159 litres) plus provision for 13 US gal (49 litres) of auxiliary fuel in a baggage compartment tank; external fuel none
Speed: never-exceed speed, maximum level speed 'clean' between sea level and 3,000 ft (915 m) and

maximum cruising speed 97 kt (112 mph; 180 km/h); economical cruising speed at optimum altitude 89 kt (102 mph; 165 km/h)
Range: 228 nm (263 miles; 423 km); endurance 3 hours 30 minutes
Performance: maximum rate of climb at sea level 1,450 ft (442 m) per minute; certificated operating ceiling 12,000 ft (3660 m); hovering ceiling 7,700 ft (2345 m) in ground effect at 2,600 lb (1179 kg) and 8,700 ft (2650 m) out of ground effect at 2,050 lb

Above: Peru purchased 10 Enstrom F28Fs, the baseline Enstrom helicopter, to replace the Bell 47 as the Army's basic trainer.

Below: The latest development of the F-28 for the military market is the four-seat TH-28 (480). This is the essentially civilian-spec prototype.

Eurocopter (Aérospatiale) SA 330 Puma

Eurocopter France
PO Box 13
F-13725 Marignane, France

Standard transport helicopter of the French army, to whose specification it was designed, the Puma is in service with many air arms around the globe. The Puma represents the first successful venture in medium helicopter design by France, the earlier products of Sud Aviation – Sikorsky S-58 and SA 321 Super Frelon – relying wholly or partly on US technology. The official requirement called for day or night operation in all weathers and all climates,

although power reserves and a radar installation to meet those demands were not available until the design had been developed over several years. Royal Air Force needs for a Whirlwind and Belvedere replacement resulted in the Puma being included in the 1967 Anglo-French helicopter agreement. As a result, Westland built 292 Gazelles and 48 Pumas, in return for which France bought the grand total of 40 Westland Lynxes.

Eight prototypes of the **SA 330** were ordered in June 1963, the first taking to the air at Marignane on 15 April 1965 and the last going to the UK for evaluation. On 25 November 1970, just over two years after that delivery, the first of an initial batch of 40 **Puma HC.Mk 1**s for the RAF flew at Yeovil. Two Turboméca Turmo turboshafts of 984 kW (1,320 shp) each gave a maximum take-off weight of 6400 kg (14,109 lb) and limiting speed of 151 kt (280 km/h; 174

mph) to the initial production versions. These were **SA 330B** for ALAT (Aviation Légère de l'Armée de Terre), **SA 330C** for military export, **SA 330E** as the RAF's Puma HC.Mk 1, and the civilian **SA 330F**. In 1974, availability of the 1174-kW (1,575-shp) Turmo IVC powerplant better equipped the Puma for hot-and-high operations, increasing its take-off weight to 7400 kg (16,314 lb) and maximum speed to 158 kt (294 km/h; 182 mph). Production in this guise con-

The Puma HC.Mk 1s of No. 1563 Flight are the last RAF aircraft left in Belize, following the departure of the Harriers of No. 1417 Flight. They are based at Belize Intl.

For their deployment to Kuwait and Iraq during the Gulf War, French army Pumas adopted identification stripes, along with a desert paint scheme.

cerned the civilian **SA 330G** and military **SA 330H**, although the French air force, which bought 37, used the misleading designation **SA 330Ba**.

Glass-fibre rotors became available in 1977, uprating the G and H to **SA 330J** and **SA 330L** respectively. The new blades were retrofitted to some early aircraft, including those of the RAF and 40 per cent of ALAT's 132 SA 330Bs. In addition, the French army bought 15 SA 330Ba versions and a few replacements from the Romanian line after Aérospatiale ended production with the 686th Puma. ICA (now IAR) at Brasov, Romania, obtained a licence for the SA 330L in 1977 and had built about 200 by mid-1994, (this version is described separately). While Pumas normally carry 15 fully-equipped troops or 2 tonnes of internal cargo (2.5 tonnes underslung), the Romanian variant has a powerful armament option, typically comprising four underslung rocket pods and four AT-3 'Sagger' ATMs above the outrigger pylons, plus two machine-gun pods scabbed to the forward fuselage. British Army and ALAT Pumas can carry a pintle-mounted machine-gun in the cabin door, some of the latter's machines additionally receiving a prominent nose-mounted OMERA ORB 37 radar. Five of Portugal's 10 Pumas have ORB 31 radar and flotation gear for their SAR task and all were converted locally by OGMA during the late 1980s to **SA 330S** standard with SA 330L systems and rotors, plus Makila power-plants as in the Super Puma. In Indonesia, IPTN assembled 11 SA 330Js (**NSA-330**) from French kits, the last in 1983.

Some Portuguese Pumas, such as this SAR aircraft based in the Azores, carry OMERA ORB-31 Hercules radar and flotation gear.

South Africa, isolated by the UN arms embargo, pursued its own line of Puma development which culminated in the Atlas XH-2/CSH-2 Rooivalk attack helicopter. More recognisable as Pumas were the two **Atlas XTP-1** testbeds (described separately) of the SA 330, which undertook development work for the Rooivalk and led to a possible 'gunship Puma' which underwent SAAF evaluation as a potential alternative to the Rooivalk, when the latter was facing cancellation. Using Rooivalk systems and weapons pylons, the gunship Puma (which has been fitted with a variety of weapons options) has carried Atlas Swift laser-guided ATGMs and Atlas Darter or Viper AAMs. South Africa has undertaken its own Makila re-engining programme, turning Pumas into **Gemsboks**, now **Oryx** (described separately), with the additional power necessary to replace Super Frelons.

RAF Pumas are particularly advanced in terms of operational equipment, having acquired 'polyvalent' air intake filters, an ARI.18228 radar warning receiver, cockpit lighting compatible with night vision goggles and, for the 1991 Gulf War, M.130 chaff/flare dispensers and AN/AAR-47 missile approach warning systems. RAF Pumas in Northern Ireland additionally have an AN/ALQ-144 IR jammer to deflect heat-seeking missiles. Some of these RAF Pumas are believed to be equipped with the Ferranti/Barr and Stroud Type 221 thermal imager for surveillance duties, under the codename Pleasant 3.

One ALAT Puma is testbed for the Orchidée/HORIZON surveillance radar (described in the AS 532 entry). Romania is offering a 'glass cockpit' version called **Puma 2000** (described seperately), with a night vision system and pilot's helmet-mounted display.

Eurocopter France (Aérospatiale) SA 330 Puma

The French Orchidée battlefield surveillance radar programme was shelved in 1990, to be reactivated in the Gulf war. The success there of the development aircraft lead to a new programme, HORIZON.

Eurocopter (Aérospatiale) SA 330 Puma

Royal Air Force Puma HC.Mk 1s (and Wessexes also), such as this No. 230 Sqn aircraft, are adopting a two-tone green wrap-around camouflage scheme in favour of their original green and black finish.

The standard Aviation Légère de l'Armée de Terre (ALAT) camouflage for its SA 330Bs is this smart three-tone green and brown one.

OPERATORS

Abu Dhabi (UAE): SA 330C/F (9)
Argentina: SA 330L (1) – coast guard
Cameroon: SA 330C (2)
Chile: SA 330F/L (15) – army
Ecuador: SA 330L (1) – army
Ethiopia: IAR.330 (1)
France: SA 330B/H (30), SA 330B/H (125) – army
Gabon: SA 330C/H: 2/2
Guinea Republic: IAR.330 (1)
Indonesia: SA 330J/L (14)
Iraq: SA 330 (22)
Ivory Coast: SA 330C (3)
Kuwait: SA 330H (6)
Lebanon: SA 330L (9)
Malawi: SA 330J (1)
Morocco: SA 330C (30)
Nepal: SA 330C/G (1/1)
Nigeria: SA 330L (2)
Pakistan: SA 330J (35) – army
Portugal: SA 330C (10)
Romania: IAR-330 (90)
Senegambia: SA 330F (2)
South Africa: SA 330F/J/L (65), Oryx (25)
Spain: SA 330C/H/J (HT.19) (5)
Togo: SA 330 (1)
United Kingdom: HC.Mk 1 (41)
Zaïre: SA 330C/IAR-330 (9)

SPECIFICATION

Eurocopter France (Aérospatiale) SA 330L Puma
Rotor system: main rotor diameter 15.00 m (49 ft 2.5 in); tail rotor diameter 3.04 m (9 ft 11.5 in); main rotor disc area 176.71 m2 (1,902.20 sq ft); tail rotor disc area 7.26 m2 (78.13 sq ft)
Fuselage and tail: length overall, rotors turning 18.15 m (59 ft 6.5 in) and fuselage 14.06 m (46 ft 1.5 in); height overall 5.14 m (16 ft 10.5 in) and to top of rotor head 4.38 m (14 ft 4.5 in); wheel track 2.38 m (7 ft 10.75 in); wheel base 4.045 m (13 ft 3 in)
Powerplant: two Turboméca Turmo IVC each rated at 1175 kW (1,575 shp)
Weights: empty 3615 kg (7,970 lb); maximum take-off 7500 kg (16,534 lb)
Fuel and load: internal fuel 1544 litres (408 US gal) plus provision for 1900 litres (502 US gal) of auxiliary fuel in four cabin tanks; external fuel up to two 350-litre (92.5-US gal) auxiliary tanks; maximum payload 3200 kg (7,055 lb)
Speed: never exceed speed 204 km/h (158 kt; 182 mph); maximum cruising speed 'clean' at optimum altitude 271 km/h (146 kt; 168 mph)
Range: 572 km (308 nm; 355 miles)
Performance: maximum rate of climb at sea level 552 m (1,810 ft) per minute; service ceiling 6000 m (19,685 ft); hovering ceiling 4400 m (14,435 ft) in ground effect and 4250 m (13,940 ft) out of ground effect

Eurocopter (Aérospatiale) SA 341/342 Gazelle

Successor to the Sud Alouette II, the **Gazelle** originated in a mid-1960s project by Sud Aviation. Despite using many of its predecessor's dynamic systems, the **X.300**, soon renamed **SA 341**, achieved increased speed and manoeuvrability through adoption of a more powerful turboshaft, re-styled cabin, covered tailboom, and advanced rotor technology. Part of the last-mentioned came from a 1964 agreement with MBB for joint development of a rigid main rotor head and glass-fibre blades

– normal today, but both advanced concepts for their time. Simplicity, strength and reduced maintenance demands are achieved by a rigid head, but a compromise was made at the prototype stage, by which the Gazelle's main rotors have flap hinges without drag hinges. Additionally, the revolutionary 'fenestron', or fan-in-fin tail rotor, was designed to be shielded from forward airflow. Plans were for it to be disengaged to save power during cruising, at which time vertical tail surfaces would be able to take

over the task of offsetting torque. Airflow problems around the freewheeling fan resulted in the fenestron being rotated at all times, although it does still allow a power saving of five per cent.

UK requirements to expand its rotary-wing industry resulted in the Anglo-French helicopter agreement of 22 February 1967, by which the Gazelle, Puma and British-designed Lynx came under joint Westland-Sud (Aérospatiale after 1 January 1970) parentage. The **SA 340** prototype flew on

12 April 1968 with conventional rotors and the Alouette II's 268-kW (360-shp) Astazou II powerplant, following abandonment by Turboméca of the proposed 336-kW (450-shp) Oredon. A machine with more representative rotors followed on 12 April 1968, demonstrating control difficulties which resulted in the above-mentioned compromises in the design. Revised as the SA 341, and named Gazelle in July 1969, the pre-production version had a longer cabin with

The Qatar Emiri Air Force's HOT missile-armed SA 342Ls operate in support of the army's French-built AMX-30S main battle tanks.

two rear access doors, larger tail surfaces and a 440-kW (590-shp) Astazou III. Series manufacture began with a civil-registered demonstrator flying on 6 August 1971.

Six versions were launched initially: **SA 341B**, the British Army Gazelle **AH.Mk 1**; **SA 341C**, Royal Navy **HT.Mk 2** trainer; **SA 341D**, Royal Air Force **HT.Mk 3** trainer; **SA 341E**, RAF **HCC.Mk 4** VIP transport (all with Astazou IIIN); **SA 341F**, **French army** (ALAT) with Astazou IIIC; **SA 341G**, civilian; and **SA 341H**, military export. When the Westland line closed in 1984, it had built 294 Gazelles, including 282 for the UK forces, 212 of which were AH.Mk 1s. No HCC.Mk 4s were constructed as such. Generally unarmed, the AH.Mk 1 carried rockets during the 1982 Falklands War, while nearly 70 were fitted during the late 1980s with roof-mounted GEC-Ferranti AF532 magnifying sights for target finding. Of 170 SA 341Fs, ALAT converted 40 to carry four Euromissile HOT anti-tank missiles as **SA 341Ms** and 62 with a GIAT M621 20-mm cannon to starboard and SFOM 80 sight as the **SA 341F/Canon**. Others have acquired a SFIM M334 Athos scouting sight similar to that of the AS 532.

Powered by a 640-kW (858-shp) Astazou XIVH, the **SA 342** flew in prototype form on 11 May 1973, replacing the SA 341 after 628 had been built in France and the UK. Foreign exports began with the civil **SA 342J** and military **SA 342K**, the latter soon replaced by **SA 342L**s with an improved fenestron. The ALAT equivalent is designated **SA 342M** and over 200 have been delivered since 1 February 1980, armed with four HOTs and an M397 sight, the latter to be replaced by the night-capable Viviane during the early 1990s. For the 1991 Gulf War, 30 were converted to **SA 342M/Celtic** with a pair of MATRA Mistral SAMs on the port side and a SFOM 80 sight. The definitive anti-helicopter model, with four Mistrals and a T2000 sight, will be designated **SA 342M/ATAM** on 30 conversions. SA 342Ms have an Astazou XIVM turboshaft with automatic start-up and a maximum take-off weight of 1900 kg (4,188 lb), increased to 2000 kg (4,409 lb) in wartime. Avionics include an autopilot and a Sextant Nadir self-contained navigation system, including Doppler. Upward-facing exhaust diffusers are optional for combat.

Egypt, Iraq, Morocco and Syria, among others, have equivalents to the HOT- and cannon-armed Gazelles, but versions built in Yugoslavia by SOKO at Mostar (Bosnia-Herzegovina) have Russian armament options. Following 132 **SA 341H Partizans**,

French Army Light Aviation (ALAT) fields some 710 helicopters including the survivors of 170 S 341Fs, 200 SA 342Ms and a further 18 SA 342Ls, originally built for China. A mix of HOT-armed SA 342Ms is seen here backed up by unarmed Gazelle/Athos scouts. A Mistral AAM fit is under development.

SOKO was well advanced with 170 SA 342Ls before civil war intervened in 1991. Versions comprise the **SA 341L HERA** scout and **SA 342L GAMA**, the latter armed with four AT-3 'Sagger' ATMs and two SA-7 'Grail' SAMs, plus an M334 sight. The Arab-British Helicopter Company in Egypt assembled 48 SA 342Ls from French kits, deliveries beginning in December 1983. Twelve Egyptian Gazelles have SFIM Osloh I laser designation systems for artillery direction.

OPERATORS

Abu Dhabi (UAE): SA 342 (11)
Angola: SA 342 (13)
Burundi: SA 342L (2)
Cameroon: SA 342L (4)
Cyprus: SA 342L-1 (3) – national guard
Ecuador: SA 342K/L (13) – army
Egypt: SA 342K/L (84), SA 342L (12) – army
France: SA 342M (185), SA 341M/F (100/55)
Gabon: SA 342L (5)
Guinea Republic: SA 342M (1)
Iraq: SA 342L (40)
Ireland: SA 342L (2)
Jordan: SA 342L (2)
Kenya: SA 342K (1)
Kuwait: SA 342K (20)
Lebanon: SA 342L (7)
Libya: SA 342 (40)

Former Yugoslavian Gazelles are now largely in the hands of the Serbian JRV. These have been active in the Balkan fighting since the invasion of Slovenia in June 1991 and can carry an effective armament of four AT-3 'Sagger' ATGMs or two SA-7 'Grail' AAMs on removable pylons.

Eurocopter France (Aérospatiale) SA 342 Gazelle

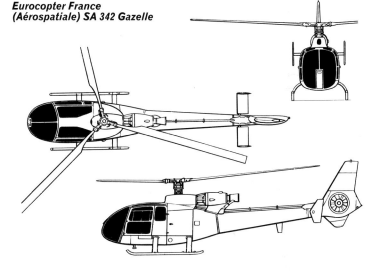

Morocco: SA 342L (24)
Qatar: SA 342L (14), SA 341G (2) – police
Rwanda: SA 342L (6)
Senegal: SA 341H (1)
Serbia (Yugoslavia): SA 341/342L 119
　　　　　　　　　　　SA 341 (1) – navy
Slovenia: SA.341 (1)
Syria: SA 342 (55)
Trinidad and Tobago: SA 341G (2)
Tunisia: SA 342 (2)
United Kingdom: HT.Mk 3/HCC Mk 4 (27/3) – RAF
　　　　　　　　HT.Mk 2/HT.Mk 3 (26) – navy
　　　　　　　　AH.Mk 1 (160) – army

SPECIFICATION

Eurocopter France (Aérospatiale) SA 341F Gazelle
Rotor system: main rotor diameter 10.50 m (34 ft 5.5 in); fenestron diameter 0.695 m (2 ft 3.375 in); main rotor disc area 86.59 m² (932.08 sq ft); fenestron disc area 0.38 m² (4.08 sq ft)

Fuselage and tail: length overall, rotor turning 11.97 m (39 ft 3.2 in) and fuselage 9.53 m (31 ft 3.2 in); height overall 3.18 m (10 ft 5 ¼ in) and to top of rotor head 2.72 m (8 ft 11 in); skid track 2.015 m (6 ft 7.3125 in)
Powerplant: one Turboméca Astazou IIIA rated at 440 kW (590 shp)
Weights: empty 920 kg (2,028 lb); maximum take-off 1800 kg (3,968 lb)
Fuel and load: internal fuel 445 litres (117.5 US gal) plus provision for 290 litres (76.5 US gal) of auxiliary fuel in two tanks; external fuel none; maximum payload 700 kg (1,540 lb)
Speed: never-exceed speed at sea level 310 km/h (168 kt; 193 mph); maximum cruising speed at sea level 264 km/h (142 kt; 164 mph); economical cruising speed at sea level 233 km/h (125 kt; 144 mph)
Range: 670 km (361 nm; 416 miles) with standard fuel
Performance: maximum rate of climb at sea level 540 m (1,770 ft) per minute; service ceiling 5000 m (16,405 ft); hovering ceiling 2850 m (9,350 ft) in ground effect and 2000 m (6,560 ft) out of ground effect

Prospective RAF rotary wing pilots win their spurs on the Gazelle HT.Mk 3s at No. 2 FTS, Shawbury. The unit's second squadron flies the Wessex.

The two Gazelles operated by No. 1 Wing, Irish Air Corps, were advertised for sale in 1993 but have now been firmly retained for basic training.

Eurocopter (Aérospatiale) SA 365 Dauphin

In the early 1970s Aérospatiale (now known as Eurocopter France) began development of a helicopter to supersede the Alouette III. The initial version, known as the **SA 360 Dauphin**, featured a four-bladed main rotor, a 13-bladed fenestron, tailwheel landing gear and standard accommodation for a pilot and up to nine passengers. A 980-shp (731-kW) Turboméca Astazou XVI powered the first prototype, which first flew on 2 June 1972. The 1,050-shp (783-kW) Astazou XVIIIA powered production aircraft and, despite development of a dedicated **SA 361H** military helicopter, it was obvious that the Dauphin's military potential lay with a twin-engined helicopter. One SA 361 was taken on charge by the French army for trials, and is still in use.

Designated **SA 365C Dauphin 2**, the twin-engined version is powered by a pair of 650-shp (485-kW) Turboméca Arriel turboshafts, and flew for the first time on 24 January 1975. Greater success was achieved by the **SA 365N**, which introduced a retractable tricycle undercarriage, greater use of composites in the construction and other improvements. This model first flew on 31 March 1979, and was followed by the **SA 365N1**, which introduced an 11-bladed fenestron and uprated Arriel 1C1 engines. Further improvements resulted in the **SA 365N2** with Arriel 1C2 engines and the option for an EFIS cockpit. In January 1990 the Aérospatiale helicopters were redesignated, the Dauphin 2 becoming the **AS 365N**. Aérospatiale developed three dedicated military variants, the **AS 365F**, **AS 365M** (both described under the **AS 565 Panther** entry) and **SA 366G** (described separately).

In 1980 China's CATIC (Chinese national aero technology import-export corporation) signed a licence-production deal with Aérospatiale, to develop a version of the AS 365N destined for use with the People's Liberation Army. An initial batch of 50 **Harbin (HAMC) Z-9 Haitun**s (Dolphin) was built, the first (French-built, Chinese-

assembled) example flying in 1982. Gradually, more indigenous components were assimilated in the run until the last example was delivered in January 1992. Under the provisions of a further agreement signed in 1988, Harbin is currently building the **Z-9A-100** which is almost wholly Chinese in origin. This version made its maiden flight on 16 January 1992. Chinese type approval was obtained on 30 December 1992. Z-9s were adopted by CAAC, the national airline, and several army units. An anti-tank version armed with the Norinco Red Arrow ATGM flew in late 1988/early 1989, and the navy is also seeking an anti-submarine warfare version.

SPECIFICATION

Eurocopter (Aérospatiale) AS 365N1 Dauphin 2
Rotor system: main rotor diameter 11.94 m (39 ft 2 in); fenestron diameter 1.10 m (3 ft 7.4375 in); main rotor disc area 111.97 m² (1,205.26 sq ft); fenestron disc area 0.95 m² (10.23 sq ft)
Fuselage and tail: length overall, rotor turning 13.88 m (45 ft 6.5 in) and fuselage 11.63 m (38 ft 1.875 in); height overall 3.98 m (13 ft 0.75 in) and to top of rotor head 3.52 m (11 ft 6.5 in); wheel track 1.90 m (6 ft 2.75 in); wheel base 3.61 m (11 ft 10.25 in)
Powerplant: two Turboméca Arriel 1C1 each rated at 540 kW (724 shp) for take-off and 437 kW (586 shp)

for continuous running
Weights: empty equipped 2161 kg (4,764 lb); maximum take-off 4100 kg (9,039 lb)
Fuel and load: internal fuel 1135 litres (300 US gal) plus provision for 180 litres (47.5 US gal) of auxiliary fuel in a baggage compartment tank
Speed: never-exceed speed at sea level 296 km/h (160 kt; 184 mph); maximum cruising speed

level 283 km/h (153 kt; 176 mph); economical cruising speed at sea level 260 km/h (140 kt; 161 mph)
Range: 852 km (460 nm; 530 miles) on standard fuel
Performance: maximum rate of climb at sea level 396 m (1,300 ft) per minute; service ceiling 3600 m (11,810 ft); hovering ceiling 2100 m (6,890 ft) in ground effect and 1100 m (3,610 ft) out of ground effect

Usually a lucrative market for Aérospatiale types, comparatively few Dauphins have found their way into French military service. This single SA 365 is operated by the GLAM (Groupe de Liaison Aériennes Ministérielles), the air force's Villacoublay-based ministerial transport unit. Small numbers also fly with the ALAT (army aviation).

The Z-9 (AS 365N) is in production in China, along with a licensed version of the Super Frelon. Z-9 and Z-9As serve with the AFPLA and navy.

Eurocopter France (Aérospatiale) AS 365N2 Dauphin II

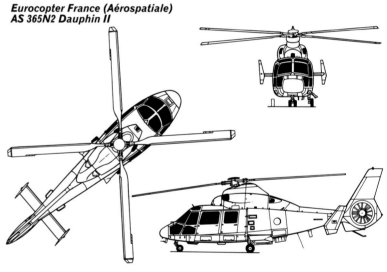

One of the few military operators of the SA 365C is Sri Lanka. Obtained in 1977, its two VIP-configured examples are currently withdrawn from use.

Eurocopter (Aérospatiale) SA 366/HH-65 Dolphin

Under the designation **SA 366G1**, Aérospatiale developed a variant of the Dauphin to answer a **US Coast Guard** requirement to replace its elderly Sikorsky HH-52s. In order to satisfy political requirements, the **Dolphin** featured many US-built components, including a pair of Textron Lycoming LTS101-750A-1 engines, each rated at 680 shp (507 kW). The Dolphin has been criticised for being underpowered, especially in recent times as ever more equipment has been added. A programme to re-engine with Allison/Garrett LHTEC T800s reached prototype trials stage but has progressed no further.

The **HH-65A** is intended to operate the SRR (short-range recovery) mission from both shore bases and Coast Guard vessels. Several design features contribute to improving safety of operations, including the passive failure characteristics of the automatic flight control system, and omnidirec-

tional airspeed system which provides information while the aircraft is hovering. Inflatable flotation bags are provided for waterborne operations up to sea state 5. The communications and navigation equipment was the responsibility of prime contractor Rockwell Collins, and includes comprehensive radio systems and a datalink for transmission of parameters such as aircraft position to ship or shore base. A nose-mounted Northrop See Hawk FLIR sensor aids poor weather rescue operations. The HH-65's all-weather rescue equipment includes a starboard-side rescue hoist and searchlight. The standard crew of three comprises pilot, co-pilot and hoist operator.

The first HH-65A flew in France on 23 July 1980, and was later shipped to an Aérospatiale division in Texas for fitment of US equipment and certification. The first aircraft was delivered to the Coast Guard on 1 February 1987, procurement totalling 96.

Eurocopter France (Aérospatiale) HH-65A Dolphin (AS 366G1)

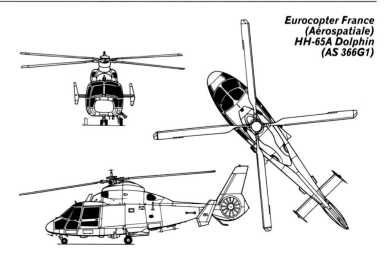

Two of these are loaned to the United States Navy Test Pilots' School at Patuxent River, while the others are distributed to Coast Guard Air Stations at Astoria, Borenquin, Brooklyn, Cape Cod, Cape May, Chicago, Corpus Christi, Detroit, Elizabeth City, Houston, Los Angeles, Miami, Mobile, New Orleans, North Bend, Port Angeles, Sacramento, San Diego and Savannah.

Two United States Coast Guard trials aircraft were purchased by **Israel**, which at one time intended to buy a further 20 for service from its naval patrol boats.

SPECIFICATIONS

Eurocopter (Aérospatiale) HH-65A Dolphin
Rotor system: main rotor diameter 11.94 m (39 ft 2 in); fenestron diameter 1.10 m (3 ft 7¼ in); main rotor disc 111.90 m2 (1,204.5 sq ft); fenestron disc area 0.95 m2 (10.23 sq ft)
Fuselage and tail: length overall, rotors turning 13.88 m (45 ft 6.5 in) and fuselage 11.63 m (38 ft

1¾ in); height overall 3.98 m (13 ft ¾ in) and to top of rotor head 3.52 m (11 ft 6.5 in); wheel track 1.90 m (6 ft 2.75 in); wheel base 3.61 m (11 ft 10.25 in)
Powerplant: two Textron Lycoming LTS101-750A-1 each rated at 680 shp (507 kW)
Weights: empty equipped 2718 kg (5,992 lb); maximum take-off 4050 kg (8,928 lb)
Fuel and load: internal fuel 1135 litres (300 US gal) plus provision for up to 180 litres (47.5 US gal) of auxiliary fuel in one optional baggage compartment tank or 475 litres (125.5 US gal) of ferry fuel in an optional tank replacing the rear seats; external fuel now
Speed: never-exceed speed 175 kt (324 km/h; 201 mph); maximum cruising speed at optimum altitude 139 kt (257 km/h; 160 mph)
Range: 410 nm (472 miles; 760 km) with maximum fuel or 216 nm (400 km; 248 miles) with maximum passenger payload; rescue range 166 nm (307 km; 191 miles); endurance 4 hours 0 minutes
Performance: hovering ceiling 2290 m (7,510 ft) in ground effect and 1627 m (5,340 ft) out of ground effect

The USCG's HH-65A Dolphin fleet has been the subject of controversy regarding its Arriel-derived LTS 101-750B-2 powerplant. Re-engining options with the promise of improved performance have, so far, been discounted.

Eurocopter (Aérospatiale) **AS 532 Cougar (AS 332)**

Logically, if unimaginatively, known as the **AS 332 Super Puma** when first proposed in 1974, the **Cougar** was devised as a successor to the SA 330. Retaining the Puma appearance, including retractable undercarriage, and profiting from glass-fibre rotor technology, the Super Puma is most readily identifiable by its prominent ventral fin and nose radome for optional Bendix/King RDR 1400 or Honeywell Primus 500 weather radar. Primarily aimed at the civil market, the helicopter nevertheless incorporates features of value to military operators, including a gearbox operable for one hour without lubricant and rotors which remain safe for 40 hours after hits by 12.7-mm (0.5-in) small-arms fire. The Puma's Turmo powerplants gave way to a pair of Makila 1As delivering 1327 kW (1,780 shp) and able to wind up from idle to full power in just 1.5 seconds. Certain Super Puma components (including Makila engines and elements of the tail unit) have been incorporated into South Africa's extensive Puma upgrade programme (described under the **Atlas Gemsbok** entry).

First flown on 13 September 1978, the Super Puma entered service in 1981 as the **AS 332B** and civilian **AS 332C**. Both these initial variants retained the Puma's 11.4-m3 (402.6-cu ft) cabin volume, with seating for 21 passengers or 12-15 equipped troops. The following year, deliveries began of the 'stretched' **AS 332M** and civilian **AS 332L**, lengthened by 76 cm (30 in) and with 13.3 m3 (469.7 cu ft) of volume to permit carriage of four extra passengers.

In January 1990, military variants were renamed Cougar, renumbered **AS 532** and

adopted new variant suffixes: **AS 532AC** and **UC** for short fuselage, military armed/unarmed; **AS 532AL** and **UL** for long fuselage, military armed/unarmed; **AS 532MC**, naval SAR and surveillance; and **AS 532SC**, naval, armed anti-submarine/anti-ship. Both maritime models were previously **AS 332F**, there being no long-fuselage maritime model. Civil production has concentrated on the **AS 332L Super Puma**, of which over 70 are in service, mainly in oil exploration support. The current production version is the **AS 332L1** and a further improved version, the **AS332L Tiger**, has been developed for North Sea oil support operator Bristow Helicopters. Later examples of **Cougar Mk I** have Makila 1A1s of 1400 kW (1,877 shp).

A development prototype first flew on 6 February 1987 of the **Cougar Mk II** (**AS 332L2 Super Puma II**), featuring 1569-kW (2,104-shp) Makila 1A2s and a further fuselage stretch to accommodate 28 passengers. Mk IIs entered service in 1992 and will be used as the platform for French army aviation's (ALAT) HORIZON battlefield surveillance radar in the late 1990s. The French army originally requested 20 aircraft equipped with the Orchidée system, trialled on an AS 330B. This proved prohibitively expensive and was cancelled in 1990, only to be resurrected for Operation Desert Storm (Operation Daguet). The experience gained from its 24 operational missions led to the HORIZON (Hélicoptère d'Observation Radar et d'Investigation sur ZONe) project. Eurocopter received a development contract in October 1992 for two aircraft, combining the capabilities of Orchidée with the

endurance of the larger AS 532UL, and the first (fully-equipped) flight took place on 8 December 1992. Delivery of the first aircraft to the ALAT occurred in April 1994 and the army has six **AS 532UL HORIZON**s on order. The French army is also replacing its original AS 330s with AS 532 Cougars, the first 22 aircraft being delivered to the Force d'Action Rapide by the end of 1991.

While armament options for the army Cougar are restricted to gun and rocket pods, the AS 532SC has provision for a pair of Aérospatiale AM39 Exocet anti-ship missiles or homing torpedoes. Operation from ship platforms is also possible, using hauldown gear to permit flying in rough seas.

Large sponsons with inflatable floats are standard naval equipment, and are optional on other models. Having produced standard AS 330 Pumas under licence during the early 1980s, **IPTN (Eurocopter)** in Indonesia moved on to AS 332C and AS 332L Super Puma production (described seperately), rolling out their first aircraft for a civilian customer in April 1983. Four have so far been delivered to the Indonesian navy as transports, along with a VIP version for the ministry of finance, and three AS 332L-1s for the Presidential flight in 1992. Indonesian aircraft are designated **NAS 332**. Other foreign service designations include Brazil (**CH-34**), Spain (**HD.21** – SAR, **HT.21** – VIP) and Sweden (**Hkp 10** – SAR). By early 1994 over 400 Super Pumas/Cougars had been ordered, with half the production dedicated to military orders.

Sweden's long-range SAR capability increased with the delivery of 12 Hkp 10s (AS 332M-1s), replacing older Vertol V-107s. Hkp 10s fly with F15 and F21.

A confirmed Aérospatiale operator, the Swiss air force took a major step forward in 1987 with the acquisition of its first AS 332s in preference to the Sikorsky UH-60.

The AS 532s of the Royal Saudi Naval Force are Exocet-capable. During the Gulf war they flew from their base at Al Jubail on maritime patrol missions.

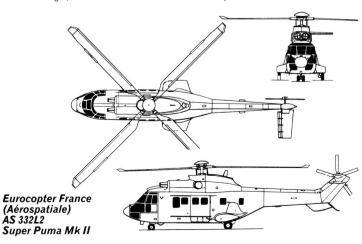

Eurocopter France (Aérospatiale) AS 332L2 Super Puma Mk II

Eurocopter AS 532 Cougar (AS 332)

OPERATORS

Abu Dhabi (UAE): AS 332B/M/M1 (6/2/2)
Argentina: AS 532UC (24) – army
Brazil: AS 332M (10); AS 332F (6) – navy
Cameroon: AS 332L (11)
Chile: AS 532SC (6) – navy; AS 332B (2) – army
China: AS 332 (6)
Ecuador: AS 332B (6) – army
France: AS 332C/L 3/2; AS 332M (30) – army
Gabon: AS 332L (1) – Presidential guard
Indonesia: AS 332 (7); AS 332L (7) – navy
Japan: AS 332L (3) – army
Jordan: AS 332M-1 (12)
Kuwait: AS 532SC (4) – navy
Malaysia: NAS 332M (5)
Mexico: AS 332L (4)
Nepal: AS 332L (1)
Nigeria: AS 332L-1 (2)
Oman: AS 332 (2)
Panama: AS 332L (2)
Qatar: AS 332F (12)
Saudi Arabia: AS 532UC/SC (6/6) – navy
Singapore: AS 332M (28)
South Korea: AS 332L (1)
Spain: AS 332B (11); AS 332 (18) – army
Sweden: AS 332M-1 (12)
Switzerland: AS 332M-1 (15)
Togo: AS 332L (1)
Turkey: AS 532UL (20) – army
Venezuela: AS 332M-1 (8)
Zaïre: AS 332 (1)

SPECIFICATION

Eurocopter (Aérospatiale) AS 532UC Cougar
Rotor system: main rotor diameter 15.60 m
(51 ft 2.25 in); tail rotor diameter 3.05 m (10 ft 0 in); main rotor disc area 191.13 m² (2,057.43 sq ft); tail rotor disc area 7.31 m² (78.64 sq ft)
Fuselage and tail: length overall, rotors turning 18.70 m (61 ft 4.25 in) and fuselage 15.53 m
(50 ft 11.5 in) including tail rotor; height overall 4.92 m (16 ft 1.75 in), with blades and tail pylon folded 4.80 m (15 ft 9 in) and to top of rotor head 4.60 m (15 ft 1 in); wheel track 3.00 m (9 ft 10.25 in)
Powerplant: two Turboméca Makila 1A1 each rated at 1400 kW (1,877 shp)
Weights: empty 4330 kg (9,546 lb); normal take-off 9000 kg (19,841 lb) with an internal load; maximum take-off 9350 kg (20,615 lb) with an external load
Fuel and load: internal fuel 1497 litres (395 US gal) plus provision for 1900 litres (502 US gal) of auxiliary fuel in four cabin tanks; external fuel up to two 325-litre (86-US gal) auxiliary tanks; maximum payload 4500 kg (9,921 lb)
Speed: never-exceed speed 278 km/h (150 kt; 172 mph); maximum cruising speed at sea level 262 km/h (141 kt; 163 mph)
Range: 618 km (334 nm; 384 miles) with standard fuel; endurance 3 hours 20 minutes
Performance: maximum rate of climb at sea level 420 m (1,378 ft) per minute; service ceiling 4100 m (13,450 ft); hovering ceiling 2700 m (8,860 ft) in ground effect and 1600 m (5,250 ft) out of effect

Eurocopter (Aérospatiale) AS 532MC/SC Cougar
generally similar to the Eurocopter (Aérospatiale) AS 532UC Cougar except in the following particulars:
Fuselage and tail: height overall 4.92 m (16 ft 1.75 in) and with main rotor blades and tail rotor folded 4.80 m (15 ft 9 in)
Weights: empty 4500 kg (9,921 lb)
Speed: maximum cruising speed at sea level 240 km/h (130 kt; 149 mph)
Range: 870 km (470 nm; 540 miles) with standard fuel
Performance: maximum rate of climb at sea level 372 m (1,220 ft) per minute

Eurocopter (Aérospatiale) AS 532UL Cougar
generally similar to the Eurocopter (Aérospatiale) AS 532UC Cougar except in the following particulars:
Fuselage and tail: length, fuselage 16.29 m (53 ft 5.5 in) including tail rotor; wheel base 5.28 m (17 ft 4 in)
Weights: empty 4460 kg (9,832 lb)
Fuel and load: internal fuel 2020 litres (533 US gal) plus provision for 1900 litres (502 US gal) of auxiliary fuel in four cabin tanks
Range: 842 km (455 nm; 523 miles) with standard fuel ferry range 1245 km (671 nm; 773 miles) with auxiliary fuel

Eurocopter (Aérospatiale) AS 532U2 Cougar Mk II
Rotor system: main rotor diameter 16.20 m (53 ft 1.75 in); tail rotor diameter 3.15 m (10 ft 4 in); main rotor disc area 206.12 m² (2,218.73 sq ft); tail rotor disc area 7.79 m² (83.88 sq ft)
Fuselage and tail: length overall, rotors turning

19.50 m (63 ft 11 in) and fuselage 16.74 m (54 ft 11 in); height overall 4.97 m (16 ft 4 in) with tail rotor turning and to top of rotor head 4.60 m (15 ft 1 in); stabiliser span 2.17 m (7 ft 1.5 in); wheel track 3.00 m (9 ft 10 in); wheel base 5.28 m (17 ft 4 in)
Powerplant: two 1569-kW (2,014-shp) Turboméca Makila 1A2 each rated at 1373 kW (1,841 shp) for take-off and 1236 kW (1,657 shp) for continuous running
Weights: manufacturer's empty 4760 kg (10,493 lb); normal take-off 9500 kg (20,943 lb); maximum take-off 10000 kg (22,046 lb)
Fuel and load: internal fuel 1596 kg (3,519 lb) in standard tanks or 1516 kg (3,342 lb) in crashworthy tanks plus provision for up to 3949 litres (1,043 US gal) of auxiliary fuel; external fuel none; maximum payload 4500 kg (9,921 lb)
Speed: never exceed speed 327 km/h (177 kt; 203 mph); maximum cruising speed at optimum altitude 273 km/h (147 kt; 170 mph); economical cruising speed at optimum altitude 242 km/h (131 kt; 150 mph)
Range: 796 km (430 nm; 496 miles) with standard fuel; ferry range 1176 km (635 nm; 730 miles) with auxiliary fuel; endurance 4 hours 20 minutes with standard fuel
Performance: maximum rate of climb at sea level 384 m (1.260 ft) per minute; service ceiling 4100 m (13,450 ft); hovering ceiling 2540 m (8,335 ft) in ground effect and 1900 m (6,235 ft) out of ground effect

---

Eurocopter (Aérospatiale) AS 350 (AS 550) Ecureuil/Fennec

First flown on 27 June 1974, the four/five-seat **AS 350 Ecureuil** (squirrel) was developed as a successor for the Alouette as a light multi-purpose helicopter. Featuring a Starflex-type main rotor hub, the prototype was powered by a Textron Lycoming LTS 101 turboshaft, but the second AS 350, flown on 14 February 1975, used a Turboméca Arriel. Intended for commercial use, the **AS 350B** and **AS 350C** entered production with Arriel 1B and LTS 101 engines respectively, the latter being aimed at the US market, and known as the **AStar**.

A fully-armed version of the Ecureuil was developed as the **AS 350L**, with a wide range of weapon options including a 20-mm M621 cannon, twin 7.62-mm gun pods, various rocket pods and the Saab/Emerson Electric Heli-TOW anti-tank system with four Hughes TOW ATGMs. Twelve of the latter ordered by Denmark were redesignated **AS 550C2 Fennec** in 1990 before delivery. Other military versions offered became **AS 550U2** (unarmed, utility), **AS 550A2** (armed, cannon or rockets), **AS 550C2** (armed, anti-tank missiles), **AS 550M2** (unarmed naval utility) and **AS 550S2** (armed naval anti-shipping).

The Ecureuil has been assembled under licence in Brazil by Helibras and is similar to AS 350B standard. Versions are identified as

HB 350B/B1 (unarmed) or **HB 350L1** (armed), with the name **Esquilo**. Deliveries comprised HB 350B/B1s for the Brazilian air force, under the local designations **CH-50** and **TH-50** for communications and training, respectively, and nine for the Brazilian navy's HU-1 general-purpose helicopter squadron (1° Esquadrão de Helicopteros de Emprego Geral), with optional machine-gun and rocket pod armament. The Brazilian army has 16 fully-armed HB 350L1s for its 1st Aviation Battalion at Taubate, São Paulo, using the designation **HA-1** (with 20 more ordered in 1992).

OPERATORS

Abu Dhabi (UAE): AS 350 (1)
Australia: AS 350B (6) – navy; AS 550U (18) – army
Benin: AS 350B (1)
Botsawana: AS 350L (2)
Brazil: HB 350B (30); HB 350B (9) – navy AS 350 (20) – army
Central African Republic: AS 350B (1)
Denmark: AS 550C2 (12) – army
Ecuador: AS 350B (4) – army

Danish AS 550C2s are referred to as Fennecs and equipped with ESCO Heli-TOW systems.

France: AS 350B (22) – navy; AS 350 (1) – army
Gabon: AS 350B (2)
Guinea Republic: AS 350 (1)
Mali: AS 350B (1)
Paraguay: HB 350B (3)
Peru: AS 350B-1 (3)
Singapore: AS 350E (6), AS 550C2/U2 (10/10)
Tunisia: AS 350B (6)

SPECIFICATION

Eurocopter (Aérospatiale) AS 550 Fennec
Rotor system: main rotor diameter 10.69 m (35 ft 0.75 in); tail rotor diameter 1.86 m (6 ft 1.25 in); main rotor disc area 89.75 m² (966.09 sq ft); tail rotor disc area 2.72 m² (29.25 sq ft)

Fuselage and tail: length overall, rotors turning 12.94 m (42 ft 5.5 in) and fuselage 10.93 m (35 ft 10.5 in) including tail rotor; height overall 3.34 m (10 ft 11.5 in); skid track 2.28 m (7 ft 5.75 in)
Powerplant: one Turboméca Arriel 1D1 rated at 546 kW (732 shp)
Weights: empty 1220 kg (2,689 lb); maximum take-off 2250 kg (4,960 lb)
Fuel and load: internal fuel 540 litres (142.6 US gal)
Speed: never-exceed speed at sea level 287 km/h (155 kt; 178 mph); maximum cruising speed at sea level 246 km/h (133 kt; 153 mph)
Range: 666 km (360 nm; 414 miles)
Performance: maximum rate of climb at sea level 534 m (1,750 ft) per minute; service ceiling 4800 m (15,750 ft); hovering ceiling 2550 m (8,350 ft) out of ground effect

In May 1984 HC-723 of the Royal Australian Navy received six AS 350Bs. They have been fitted with a lightweight Doppler nav system.

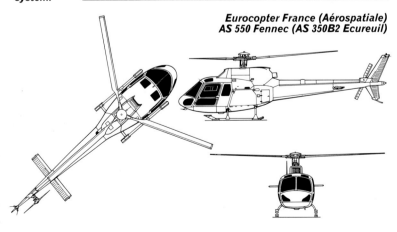

Eurocopter France (Aérospatiale)
AS 550 Fennec (AS 350B2 Ecureuil)

Eurocopter (Aérospatiale) AS 355 Ecureuil 2/AS 555 Fennec

A twin-engined version of the AS 350 Ecureuil was launched by Aérospatiale in mid-1978 and the first of two prototypes flew on 28 September 1979. Many components of the original single-engined design were retained, the major changes being concerned with the powerplant, transmission, fuel system and fuselage structure. The first production version was the **AS 355E** with 313-kW (420-shp) Allison 250-C20F turboshafts, followed by the **AS 355F** with wide-chord rotor blades and other improvements. Known as the **Ecureuil 2** or, in North America, the **Twin Star**, the twin-engined version was designated **AS 355M** for military use, this changing to **AS 555 Fennec** in January 1990.

Principal user of the military version is the French air force, which has ordered a total of 52. Eight **AS 355F1**s serve with the 67e Escadre d'Hélicoptères at Villacoublay and with EHOM 68 in French Guyana, the latter armed with an M621 20-mm cannon on the starboard fuselage side. Delivered from 19 January 1990, the remaining 44 are **AS 555AN** Fennecs, with 340-kW (456-shp) Turboméca Arrius-1M turboshafts, of which 24 are for training use and others used in anti-helicopter role with a centrally-mounted 20-mm cannon and T-100 sight. The French army (ALAT) began to take delivery in February 1992 of 10 **AS 555UN** Fennecs for IFR training. In Brazil, the **AS 355F2** has been assembled by Helibras as the **HB 355F2 Esquilo**, with the Brazilian air force taking 13 for service as armed **CH-55**s (11) with 1° Esq of 8° Grupo de Aviacão at Manaus and as VIP transport **VH-55**s (two) in the Grupo de Transporte Especial at Brasilia. Nine more serve the Brazilian navy as **UH-12B**s, for which the Helibras designation is **HB 355F2**. Aérospatiale has demonstrated an **AS 555SR** naval version of the Fennec carrying a Bendix 1500

radar under the nose, a Crouzet MAD and armament of two homing torpedoes as alternative to the cannon or rocket armament of the **AS 555AR**. Other Fennec variants are the **AS 555UR** utility model and **AS 555MR** naval utility model.

OPERATORS

Benin: AS 355M-2 (2)
Brazil: AS 355F (13); AS 355F-2 (11) – navy
Djibouti: AS 355F/M (2/1)
Fiji: AS 355F-1 (1)
France: AS 355F-1/N (52); AS 555UN (4) – army
Malawi: AS 355 (2)
Sierra Leone: AS 355 (2)

SPECIFICATION

Eurocopter (Aérospatiale) AS 555N Fennec
Rotor system: main rotor diameter 10.69 m (35 ft 0.75 in); tail rotor diameter 1.86 m (6 ft 1.25 in); main rotor disc area 89.75 m2 (966.09 sq ft); tail rotor disc area 2.72 m2 (29.25 sq ft)
Fuselage and tail: length overall, rotors turning 12.94 m (42 ft 5.5 in) and fuselage 10.93 m (35 ft 10.5 in) including tail rotor; height overall 3.34 m (10 ft 11.5 in); skid track 2.28 m (7 ft 5.75 in)
Powerplant: two Turboméca TM 319 Arrius -1M each rated at 340 kW (456 shp) for take-off and 295 kW (395 shp) for continuous running
Weights: empty 1382 kg (3,046 lb); normal take-off 2540 kg (5,600 lb); maximum take-off 2600 kg (5,732 lb)
Fuel and load: internal fuel 730 litres (193 US gal); external fuel none
Speed: never exceed speed at sea level 278 km/h (150 kt; 172 mph); maximum cruising speed at sea level 225 km/h (121 kt; 140 mph)
Range: 722 km (389 nm; 448 miles); operational radius 129 km (70 nm; 80.5 miles) on SAR mission with two survivors; endurance 1 hour with two torpedoes, or 2 hours 20 minutes with one torpedo or one cannon or two rocket launchers, or 1 hour 50

Eurocopter France (Aérospatiale) AS 555UN Fennec

Of 52 AS 555 Fennecs delivered to the Armée de l'Air, 44 are TM 319-powered AS 555ANs, but the first eight were AS 555Fs fitted with Allison 250 turboshafts.

minutes with one cannon and two rocket launchers
Performance: maximum rate of climb at sea level 408 m (1,340 ft) per minute; service ceiling 4000 m

(13,125 ft); hovering ceiling 2600 m (8,530 ft) in ground effect and 1550 m (5,085 ft) out of ground effect

Eurocopter (Aérospatiale) AS 365 Dauphin II/AS 565 Panther

A multi-role military prototype of the twin-engined **Dauphin** was flown on 29 February 1984 as the **AS 365M**, after earlier development of the single-engined **SA 361H** to investigate and demonstrate the potential military application for light assault and anti-tank duties. The AS 365M could carry 10-12 soldiers, or an armament of eight HOT ATGMs or 44 SNEB rockets. A further developed prototype appeared in April 1986 as the **AS 365K**, for which the name **Panther** was adopted. Variants of the Panther now marketed are the basic armed **AS 565AA**, the anti-tank **AS 565CA**, the utility **AS 565UA**, the armed naval **AS 565SA** and the unarmed **AS 565MA** for SAR and other naval tasks. Helibras assembles the AS 565 in Brazil as the **BH 565**, designated **HM-1** by the Brazilian army, which has purchased 36.

One AS 565 was fitted with a pair of LHTEC T800-LHT-800 turboshafts in a joint Aérospatiale/LTV programme to offer the US Army a UH-1H replacement. This prototype first flew as the **Panther 800** in the US on 12 June 1992.

Prior to redesignation of the AS 365 in the Panther series, Saudi Arabia ordered 24 of the navalised **AS 365F**, comprising four in **AS 565SC** configuration for SAR duties with ORB 32 radar and the remainder as **AS 565SA**s with Agrion 15 radar and an armament of four Aérospatiale AS15TT anti-shipping missiles. Three AS 365Fs acquired by the French navy are used for plane guard

duties aboard the *Jeanne d'Arc* by Flottille 35S, with a potential requirement for a further 15 AS 565MAs and perhaps an additional 25. Five **AS 365N2**s ordered by the Republic of China police in 1992 are used for SAR and patrol duties in Taiwan.

Other purchasers of AS 365Fs include Ireland, with two for fishery patrol from the corvette *L. E. Eithne* and three for SAR and transport duties. All Irish aircraft are fitted with Bendix RDR-1500 radar, SFIM 155 autopilot, Sextant ONS 200A and Nadir Mk

The Irish Air Corps operates five AS 365Fs from its main base at Casement Aerodrome, Baldonnel, with a west-coast SAR detachment at Finner Camp, Co. Donegal.

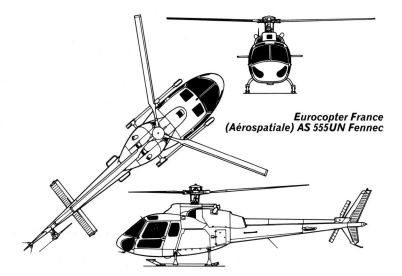

The Brazilian army operates 36 Panthers, under the local designation HM-1. Its final 10 aircraft were assembled by Helibras.

Eurocopter (Aérospatiale) AS 365 Dauphin II/AS 565 Panther

II navigation, Cina B Doppler and auto-stab with a five-screen EFIS cockpit. The two dedicated naval aircraft are fitted with Harpoon deck landing gear. Angola has six cannon-armed **AS 565AA**s for patrol and reconnaissance and 10 **AS 565UA** transports. Chile has ordered four armed AS 565MAs to be equipped with Murène torpedoes or Exocet missiles.

Chinese production of the AS 365 Dauphin began in 1982 at Harbin, with 50 completed by 1992 and work started on second batch of 30. Production includes **Z-9** and **Z-9A** versions (named **Haitun** in Chinese service) equivalent to **AS 365N** and **N1** respectively, with Chinese-built

Arriel 1C and 1C1 engines designated WZ8 and WZ8A. Nine Z-9As have been acquired by the Royal Thai navy.

OPERATORS

Angola: SA 365M (12)
Brazil: SA 565UA (36)
China: Z-9/Z-9A (80)
France: SA 365F (4) – navy
India: SA 365F (5)
Ireland: SA 365F (5)
Saudi Arabia: AS 565MA (4), AS 565SA (20) – navy
Taiwan: SA 365N-2 (5)
Thailand: Z-9A (9) – navy

SPECIFICATION

Eurocopter (Aérospatiale) AS 565UA Panther
Rotor system: main rotor diameter 11.94 m (39 ft 2 in); fenestron diameter 1.10 m (3 ft 7 in); main rotor disc area 111.97 m² (1,205.26 sq ft); fenestron disc area 0.95 m² (10.23 sq ft)
Fuselage and tail: length overall, rotor turning 13.68 m (44 ft 10.6 in) and fuselage 12.11 m (39 ft 8.75 in); height overall 3.99 m (13 ft 1 in) and to top of rotor head 3.52 m (11 ft 6.5 in); wheel track 1.90 m (6 ft 2.75 in); wheel base 3.61 m (11 ft 10.25 in)
Powerplant: two 584-kW (783-shp) Turboméca Arriel 1M1 each rated at 558 kW (749 shp) for take-off and 487 kW (560 kW) for continuous running

Weights: empty 2193 kg (4,835 lb); normal take-off 4100 kg (9,039 lb); maximum take-off 4250 kg (9,369 lb)
Fuel and load: internal fuel 1135 litres (300 US gal) plus provision for 180 litres (47.5 US gal) of auxiliary fuel in a baggage compartment tank; external fuel none; maximum payload 1600 kg (3,527 lb)
Speed: never exceed speed 296 km/h (160 kt; 184 mph); maximum cruising speed at sea level 278 km/h (150 kt; 173 mph)
Range: 875 km (472 nm; 544 miles) with standard fuel
Performance: maximum rate of climb at sea level 420 m (1,378 ft) per minute; hovering ceiling 2600 m (8,530 ft) in ground effect and 1850 m (6,070 ft) out of ground effect

---

Eurocopter (MBB) BO 105

Eurocopter Deutschland
PO Box 9801140, D-8000 Munich 80
Germany

Work on the agile **BO 105** started in 1964, and the first prototype flew on 16 February 1967 under the power of two Allison 250-C18 turboshafts, followed by two more prototypes, one of which featured the MAN-Turbo 6022 engine. For production aircraft the Allison 250-C20 was chosen. The basic **BO 105C** and **BO 105CB** (introduced in 1975) can carry five and one pilot, although the **BO 105CBS** is a slightly stretched version carrying six. Their most important feature is the rigid GRP main rotor with a hingeless (except for the feathering hinge) forged titanium hub. This makes the BO 105 fully aerobatic and agile in its anti-tank/scout roles. In addition to manufacture at Eurocopter Deutschland at Donauwörth, the BO 105 is assembled by CASA in Spain, IPTN in Indonesia and Eurocopter Canada, the latter being wholly responsible for the **BO 105LS** hot-and-high version, which is powered by uprated Allison 250-C28C engines.

By far the most important customer was the German army (Heeresflieger), buying 100 **BO 105M**s for the scout role under the designation **VBH** (Verbindungs und Beobachtungs Hubschrauber), and 212 **BO 105P**s for the anti-armour role under the designation **PAH-1** (Panzerabwehr-Hubschrauber-1). The latter are armed with six Euromissile HOT anti-tank missiles in horizontal, side-by-side tubes, aimed through a roof-mounted stabilised sight. The PAH-1 is the subject of three updating programmes, the first of which is the **PAH-1A1 Phase 1**, which fits new rotor blades, improved cooling and intakes, entering service in 1991. Under consideration is the **PAH-1 Phase 2**, to provide night-fighting capability with infra-red roof-mounted sight and digital HOT 2 missiles on lightweight 'diagonally' staggered pylons. This shelved programme may be revived if the planned buy of PAH-2 Tigers is reduced. Finally, consideration was being given to the conversion of 54 PAH-1s to **BSH** (Begleitschutz Hubschrauber) standard for use as escorts, adding four Stinger air-to-air missiles. The **BO 105/Ophelia** was a trials aircraft for evaluation of mast- and helmet-mounted sighting systems.

BO 105s also achieved substantial export sales, proving able to fulfil a number of role requirements, including short-range SAR, utility and VIP transport, light attack, scouting and anti-armour work. Of the current operators, Iraq is the most important numerically with about 75, followed by Spain which operates over 70 locally-assembled aircraft. The Spanish army operates three variants, comprising 28 anti-armour **BO 105ATH**s (designated **HA.15**) with HOT missiles, 18 armed reconnaissance **BO 105GSH**s (designated **HR.15**) with 20-mm Rheinmetall cannon, and 14 unarmed **BO 105LOH**s (also **HR.15**) for observation duties. The LOHs were subsequently modified with two 7.62-mm

machine-guns to become GSHs.

Since 1977 IPTN in Indonesia manufactured the BO 105 under licence as the **NBO-105**, with rotors and transmission supplied from Germany. Current production version, from aircraft No. 101 onwards, is the stretched **NBO-105S**. Aircraft are currently being completed at a rate of 2½ per month, with deliveries approaching 130, largely for the Indonesian armed forces and government departments. Sweden operates ESCO Helitow-equipped BO 105CBSs, and unarmed SAR aircraft as the **Hkp 9B**.

OPERATORS

Bahrain: BO 105C (3)
Brunei: BO 105CB/CBS (5/1)
Chile: BO 105CB (6)
Ciskei: BO 105 (1)
Colombia: BO 105CB (2) – army
Dubai (UAE): BO 105S (6)
Germany: BO 105P/M (208/96) – army
Indonesia: NBO 105C/CB (12); NBO 105SC (4) – navy; NBO 105C/CB (18) – army
Iraq: BO 105C (75)
Jordan: NBO 105C (3)
Kenya: BO 105S (1)
Lesotho: BO 105CBS (2)
Mexico: BO 105C/CB (6/5) – navy
Netherlands: BO 105C (28)
Peru: BO 105C/L (18/6)
Philippines: BO 105C/SC (4/10) – navy
Sierra Leone: BO 105C (1)
Spain: BO 105 (68)
Sweden: BO 105CB (20)
Trinidad and Tobago: BO 105CBS (1)

SPECIFICATION

Eurocopter (MBB) BO 105CB
Rotor system: main rotor diameter 9.84 m (32 ft 3.5 in); tail rotor diameter 1.90 m (6 ft 2.75 in); main rotor disc area 76.05 m² (818.62 sq ft); tail rotor disc area 2.835 m² (30.52 sq ft)
Fuselage and tail: length overall, rotors turning 11.86 m (38 ft 11 in) and fuselage 8.56 m (28 ft 1 in); height overall 3.00 m (9 ft 10.25 in)
Powerplant: two Allison 250-C20B each rated at 420 shp (313 kW) for take-off and 400 shp (298 kW) for continuous running
Weights: empty 1276 kg (2,813 lb); normal take-off 2400 kg (5,291 lb); maximum take-off 2500 kg (5,511 lb)
Fuel and load: internal fuel 456 kg (1,005 lb) plus provision for 320 kg (705 lb) of auxiliary fuel in a cabin tank; external fuel none
Speed: never-exceed speed at sea level 145 kt (167 mph; 270 km/h); maximum cruising speed 'clean' at sea level 130 kt (150 mph; 242 km/h)
Range: ferry range 600 nm (691 miles; 1112 km) with auxiliary fuel; range 355 nm (409 miles; 658 km) with maximum payload
Performance: maximum rate of climb at sea level 1,575 ft (480 m) per minute; maximum operating altitude 17,000 ft (5180 m); hovering ceiling 8,400 ft (2560 m) in ground effect and 5,300 ft (1615 m) out of ground effect

To the German army the armed BO 105 is the PAH-1 (now upgraded to PAH-1A1 standard). Unarmed scout aircraft are designated VBH.

Sweden's BO 105s (Hkp 9Bs) serve in both armed and unarmed versions. This is one of the latter, a SAR Hkp 9B with emergency flotation gear.

In 1982 the Mexican navy received six BO 105Cs, followed by six Bo 105CBs in 1986. The BO 105s can operate from the navy's 'Halcon'-class corvettes.

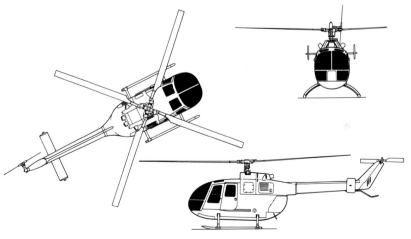

Eurocopter Germany (MBB/Deutsche Aerospace) BO 105

Eurocopter (MBB)/Kawasaki BK 117

Primarily of commercial interest, the **BK 117** emerged as a joint venture between Germany and Japan, with first prototype flight on 13 June 1979 and first production examples flown in Japan on 24 December 1981 and Germany on 23 April 1982. At the 1985 Paris air show, MBB exhibited the **BK 117A-3M**, a dedicated military version with eight HOT-2 missiles, roof-mounted sight, trainable machine-gun turret under the cockpit, ECM and Racal Prophet RWR systems and a CRT cockpit. Utilising the capacious airframe to the full, MBB trialled several weapons fits including pylon-mounted rocket pods and four TOW missiles. A mast-mounted sight was also fitted. By 1988, however, no customers had been found and the BK 117A-3M was abandoned, leaving the military market solely to 'civilian' aircraft.

About two dozen BK 117s have entered military service, from a total production of some 360. They include a batch of 16 **BK 117B-1**s delivered from September 1988 to March 1989 to the **Iraqi** air force for SAR duty. This variant is powered by two 442-kW (592-shp) Textron Lycoming LTS-101-750B-1 turboshafts and accommodates a pilot and up to 10 passengers (more usually seven). A straight-in cargo loading facility is offered through clamshell doors at

the rear of the cabin. IPTN in Indonesia once again signed a licence-production deal with Eurocopter to build **NBK-117**s, but completed only four.

Other military users include the defence forces of all four of the homelands granted nominal independence by the South African government, comprising **Ciskei** (three **BK 117A-1**), **Bophuthatswana** (two **BK 117A-3**), **Transkei** (two A-3) and **Venda** (two A-3). Two are also in use with **Sharjah**, as part of the United Arab Emirates armed forces. Quasi-military users include the **US Customs Service** (flown by the Puerto Rico-based **FURA** organisation) which has three equipped for mission support with FLIR, searchlight and cockpit lighting, and the **Peruvian** ministry of the interior with two for anti-drug surveillance. The Technical Research and Development Institute (formerly Command) of the **Japan Air Self-Defence Force** operates a single aircraft from Gifu as part of its Air Proving Wing.

SPECIFICATION

Eurocopter (MBB)/Kawasaki BK 117B-2
Rotor system: main rotor diameter 11.00 m (36 ft 1 in); tail rotor diameter 1.956 m (6 ft 5 in); main rotor disc

This BK 117 wears the (English) legend of the JASDF's Technical Research and Development Institute. The BK 117 is in auspicious company as part of this, the JASDF's air proving wing, flying alongside various examples of the F-15, F-4, T-33, T-2 and C-1.

area 95.03 m² (1,022.9 sq ft); tail rotor disc area 3.00 m² (32.34 sq ft)
Fuselage and tail: length overall, rotors turning 13.00 m (42 ft 8 in) and fuselage 9.91 m (32 ft 6¼ in)
Powerplant: two Textron Lycoming LTS 101-750B-1 each rated at 528 kW (708 shp) for take-off and 516 kW (692 shp) for maximum continuous
Weights: basic empty 1727 kg (3,807 lb); maximum take-off, with internal and external load 3350 kg (7,385 lb)
Fuel and load: total internal 697 litres (184 US gal)

plus provision for 200 litre (53 US gal) in auxiliary tank
Speed: never-exceed speed 150 kts (278 km/h; 172 mph); maximum cruising speed 135 kts (250 km/h; 155 mph)
Range: at sea level with standard fuel, no reserves 292 nm (541 km/335 miles)
Performance: maximum forward rate of climb , at sea level 660 m (2,165 ft) per minute; maximum operating altitude 4575 m (15,000 ft); hovering ceiling 3565 m (11,700) in ground effect and 2955 m (9700 ft) out of ground effect.

Eurocopter HAC Tigre/PAH-2 Tiger/HAP Gerfaut

The **Eurocopter Tiger** has its origins in Germany's requirement for a second-generation Panzerabwehr-Hubschrauber (**PAH-2**). With the French army seeking an anti-tank helicopter (Hélicoptère Anti-Char, or **HAC**) in a similar category, a Memorandum of Undertaking was signed in 1984 for the joint development of a new aircraft. The programme was halted in mid-1986 to allow a complete reappraisal of requirements and costs, to be resumed in March 1987 in a modified form to cover a common anti-tank version, and an armed escort version (Hélicoptère d'Appui Protection, or **HAP**) for the French army.

To handle the programme, Aérospatiale in France and MBB in Germany set up the jointly-owned Eurocopter GmbH; subsequently, all helicopter activities of the two companies have been merged under the Eurocopter name. A development contract awarded to Eurocopter on 30 November 1989 provided for five aircraft, of which three are unarmed aerodynamic prototypes, one is in full anti-tank configuration representing the **Tiger** (Germany)/**Tigre** (France) and one is the escort **Gerfaut**. As finally configured, the Tiger (the generic name for the helicopter) has a slender low-drag fuselage with two seats in tandem,

stepped and offset to each side of the centreline. The structure makes extensive use of composites, and an advanced four-bladed composite semi-rigid main rotor is fitted. The three-bladed tail rotor is of Aérospatiale's Spheriflex type and a fixed tricycle undercarriage is used, with single wheels. Weapons carriage is on anhedral stub wings with provision for a cannon turret undernose.

Redundant hydraulic, electrical and fuel systems contribute to the Tiger's survivability, and a MIL-STD-1553B databus provides the basis for the avionics system and integration of weapons system with crew-controlled sensors. End-plate fins fitted on the

tailplane for early prototype flights were discarded for a time, and later re-introduced in a more forward position.

In its German **PAH-2 Tiger** configuration, the helicopter was to have carried up to eight HOT 2 or Trigat missiles, or four of these weapons plus four Stinger 2 AAMs for self-defence. Sighting would have been by means of a mast-mounted FLIR for the

The prototype French Gerfaut escort/scout (foreground) formates on the first Tigre anti-tank helicopter. Both are now involved in the flight test programme.

pilot, who has a helmet sight. This variant has been abandoned in favour of a utility (or, more accurately, multi-role) version, since the upgraded MBB BO105 is now felt to be adequate to meet the anti-armour threat, but not the intervention and crisis reaction needs, of the 1990s.

Germany has therefore decided on a new variant, known as **UHU** (Unterstützungs-hubschrauber), of as yet unknown configuration but optimised for multi-role duties, including escort work. This might infer greater air-to-air capability (not least for self-defence), perhaps using the DAV millimetre-wave radar being developed by Dassault Electronique for the Tiger/Tigre.

The French **HAC Tigre** uses similar armament and equipment to the PAH-2 but will use MATRA Mistral AAMs for defence. The **HAP Gerfaut** will have a 30-mm GIAT cannon in an undernose turret and will carry two 22-round 68-mm unguided SNEB 68-mm rocket pods, plus either four Mistral AAMs or two 12-round rocket pods. Roof-mounted TV, FLIR, laser rangefinder and direct optics will be used on the Gerfaut.

As part of the Tiger development programme, an Aérospatiale Panther was used as a testbed for the MTR 390 engines, flying for the first time on 14 February 1991. Three other testbeds – two Pumas and a Dauphin – were used to test the mast-mounted sight, the night-vision sight and the fire control system. On schedule, the first of the Tiger prototypes (PT1) flew at Marignane on 29 April 1991, at first with a mast-mounted sight, but reconfigured a year later with a canopy sight in the Gerfaut configuration. PT2 (a Gerfaut with all essential avionics and systems) was rolled out at

Ottobrunn on on 9 November 1991 and first flew on 22 April 1993. PT3 followed it into the air on 19 November 1993. While both these aircraft will serve, at first, as avionics testbeds, they will be converted to full Gerfaut and Tiger standard respectively, by 1997. The fully-equipped Gerfaut (PT4) and Tiger/Tigre (PT5) are to fly in October 1994 and March 1995. It is likely that the (German) PT5 will be completed to UHU standard.

Estimated requirements, subject to final confirmation, are for 75 HAP and 140 HAC for France and 212 PAH-2/UHU for Germany. The German order has been subject to serious revision and the 1995 budget submission included funds for only 75 aircraft. It now looks as if this will be returned to its original level, which will have beneficial cost implications for a third potential European operator. The British army is also looking for an 'off-the-shelf' battlefield helicopter to be chosen in late 1994. British Aerospace is leading the Eurocopter bid for the 90-helicopter order, and contacts have been made with French and German authorities. The UK has been offered full membership of the Tiger project should the aircraft be selected for the British armed forces, which would improve the terms of its purchase appreciably. Despite the army's original preference for an existing, uncomplicated helicopter, this deal may prove persuasive.

In March 1994 Eurocopter and MTU were forced to make changes to the MTR 390 engine, having suffered three turbine-blade failures. Vibration, due to air flow through the turbine, caused the loss of sections of blade after its shroud failed. The modified engine now has fewer stator

vanes ahead of the the turbine, and a lighter containment shroud. By mid-1994 all 15 engines involved in the test programme, including those flying on a Panther testbed, had been so modified

Early schedules for deliveries have slipped. The French 1995-2000 arms procurement Bill has set back the first Gerfaut delivery to 2001, with the Tigre following within a year. Originally deliveries were scheduled to commence to the army in 1997 and 1998 respectively. The UHU/Tiger should start to reach the German Bundeswehr in 1999.

SPECIFICATION

Eurocopter HAC Tigre and PAH-2 Tiger
Rotor system: main rotor diameter 13.00 m (42 ft 7.75 in); tail rotor diameter 2.70 m (8 ft 10.25 in); main rotor disc area 132.73 m² (1,428.76 sq ft); tail rotor disc area 5.73 m² (61.63 sq ft)
Fuselage and tail: fuselage 14.00 m (45 ft 11.25 in);

height overall 4.32 m (14 ft 2 in) to top of turning tail rotor and 3.81 m (12 ft 6 in) to top of rotor head; wheel track 2.40 m (7 ft 10.5 in); wheel base 7.65 m (25 ft 1 in)
Powerplant: two MTU/Turboméca/Rolls-Royce MTR 390 each rated at 958 kW (1,285 shp) for take-off and 873 kW (1,171 shp) for continuous running
Weights: basic empty 3300 kg (7,275 lb); normal take-off 5800 kg (12,787 lb); maximum overload take-off 6000 kg (13,227 lb)
Fuel and load: internal fuel 1360 litres (359 US gal); external fuel none
Speed: maximum cruising speed at optimum altitude 280 km/h (151 kt; 174 mph); economical cruising speed at optimum altitude 250 km/h (135 kt; 155 mph)
Range: endurance 3 hours 10 minutes
Performance: maximum rate of climb at sea level more than 600 m (1,969 ft) per minute; hovering ceiling over 2000 m (6,560 ft) out of ground effect

French aircraft PT1 in HAP Gerfaut configuration displays its 30-mm Giat AM-30781 cannon, 22-round SNEB pods, Mistral AAMs and mast-mounted STRIX sight.

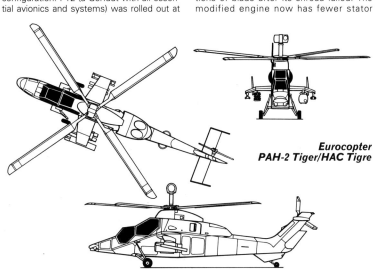

Eurocopter PAH-2 Tiger/HAC Tigre

Eurofighter **European Fighter Aircraft 2000**

Eurofighter Jagdflugzeug GmbH
Arabellastrasse 16 (PO Box 860366)
D-8000 Munich 81, Germany

As a follow-on to the tri-national Tornado programme, the Eurofighter consortium was formed in June 1986 by the same three countries – Britain, Germany and Italy (soon joined by Spain) – to produce an air superiority fighter by the late 1990s. Other European countries, notably France, had been involved in earlier **EFA** discussions, but shunned the final consortium to pursue independent programmes.

Much experience was gained with main EFA concepts, including an unstable aerodynamic configuration with canard foreplanes, active digital fly-by-wire control system, complex avionics, multi-function cockpit displays, carbon-fibre composites and extensive use of aluminium-lithium alloys and titanium and even direct voice input, from BAe's **Experimental Aircraft Programme** (EAP). This was funded (after German withdrawal) jointly by the UK MoD

and industry, with some Italian participation from 1982. First flying on 8 August 1986, the twin-RB.199 EAP amassed invaluable data in 259 test sorties totalling over 195 hours before retirement on 1 May 1991.

Finalised in September 1987, the EFA European Staff Requirement for Development specified a relatively light and sophisticated twin-turbofan single-seat fighter optimised for BVR and close air combat, but capable of secondary air-to-surface roles and operation from short, austere air strips, with a low radar cross-section and high

The EAP demonstrator had excellent high-alpha capability. At high angles of attack the lower lip of the sophisticated vari-cowl chin intake hinged down to ensure a clean, uninterrupted supply of air to the engine in all flight regimes.

supersonic performance, agility and carefree handling. Germany and Italy sought only air-to-air roles, but accepted the common specification of a 9.75-tonne (21,495-lb) basic mass empty, 50 m² (538.2 sq ft) gross wing area, and 90-kN (20,233-lb) reheat thrust per engine. These were new EJ200 twin-spool turbofans from the Eurojet consortium (comprising Rolls-Royce, MTU, Fiat Avio and SENER (now ITP) in Spain) with some 30 per cent fewer parts than the Tornado's RB.199, and with 60 kN (13,488 lb) maximum dry thrust.

A £5.5 billion contract signed on 23 November 1988 covered building and testing until 1999 of eight prototypes, including two two-seat versions, in Britain (three), Germany (two), Italy (two) and Spain (one), funded in proportion to national industrial participation: 33 per cent each by BAe and MBB (now Deutsche Aerospace), 21 per cent by Aeritalia (now Alenia), and 13 per cent by CASA. Eventual purchase was envisaged from 1996 of 765 EFAs; 250 each for the RAF and the Luftwaffe, 165 for the AMI and 100 for the Ejercito del Aire.

After major contention, in May 1990 the new ECR-90 multi-mode pulse-Doppler look-up/look-down fire-control radar with multiple target search and detection was chosen for EFA (over an uprated Hughes APG-65), to be developed and produced by GEC Ferranti, with FIAR in Italy and INISEL in Spain. While optimised for Hughes AIM-120 use, ECR-90 also provides continuous wave illumination for semi-active radar-guided air-to-air missiles. Four AAMs may be carried in semi-recessed low-drag fuselage stations, with nine other stores pylons (three also plumbed for drop tanks), having a 14,330-lb (6500-kg) total capacity. Cannon armament comprises a 27-mm (1.06-in) Mauser Mk 27 in the starboard fuselage.

EFA's radar is supplemented by an infra-red search and tracking system (IRST), with passive multi-target tracking and imaging, for which the Eurofirst group of FIAR (Italy), Thorn-EMI Electronics (UK) plus Eurotronica (Spain) received a development contract in mid-1992. This followed orders for integrated defensive aids sub-systems placed with a Marconi Defence Systems/Elettronica consortium to cover missile approach, laser and radar warning systems, wingtip ESM/ECM pods, chaff/flare dispensers and towed decoys, although Germany and Spain may seek cheaper off-the-shelf equipment.

A production investment decision was originally due by early 1993, but EFA cost studies by incoming German Defence Minister Volker Rühe in April 1992, which challenged the system unit price estimates of DM133.9 million (then $83.7 million) as unaffordable, resulted in major project reviews against threats of a German withdrawal. After considering seven possible EFA revisions, mostly single-engined, the four nations agreed on a slightly simplified and less capable New EFA or Eurofighter 2000 variant in late 1992, with options for cheaper individual equipment fits, reducing system unit costs to a minimum DM90 million. The German aircraft seem likely now to incorporate 'off-the-shelf' avionics (such as the APG-65 radar), lower levels of self protection equipment and other reductions, leading to a 30 per cent cut in overall cost.

While Britain is still nominally committed to its original 250-full standard EFA requirement, with initial deliveries in about 2000, Germany now plans to have only eight squadrons with 12-15 aircraft each, reducing Luftwaffe purchases with reserves to about 138 (potentially as few as 120). Germany is also deferring its EFA production decision until 1995, for service from 2002 or later.

Within days of DA.1's first flight, the British-assembled DA.2 flew from Warton, piloted by BAe's director of flight operations, Chris Yeo.

This would see Germany's workshare fall to 22 per cent, and the UK's rise to 42 per cent. Italy now requires only 130 EFAs to re-equip five squadrons from 2005 (having leased 24 ex-RAF Tornado F.Mk 3s in the interim) and an OCU, while Spain will fund no more than 72 Eurofighters (and has been offered 40 ex-USAF F-16A/Bs, by Lockheed, in the meantime, cutting overall EFA programme totals to less than 600 aircraft.

The first two EFA prototypes, DA.1 (98+29) and DA.2 (ZH588) flew on 27 March and 6 April 1994 from Manching and Warton, for 45 and 50 minutes respectively. Both are fitted with interim RB.199-22 turbofans, and Alenia's DA.3 will be the first with definitive EJ200 engines. DA.3 is due to fly before the end of 1994, but problems in integrating the EJ200's digital engine-control unit (developed by DASA and MTU), may delay this. The British-assembled aircraft was flight ready in advance of DA.1, but BAe was committed to waiting for the 'rival' to fly first. Prior to DA.1's flight DASA introduced revised software to permit high-speed taxiing runs before the March date. This came after the aircraft burst a tyre in similar trials in late January 1994, and was no doubt influenced by the troubled JAS 39 project, in which BAe is also involved.

BAe's DA.4 is the first two-seat EFA and also the ECR-90 development prototype, while MBB will use DA.5 for avionics and weapons integration. CASA will assemble and fly the second two-seat prototype (DA.6) with Alenia building DA.7, now the last development aircraft following the economies, which cut two prototypes.

Having passed the hurdle of its first flight, Eurofighter 2000 now faces a wrangle over workshare, specifically any diminution in German involvement. DA.1 was scheduled for transferral to BAe at Warton after 10 flying hours, but this period has been extended in deference to German objections. BAe and GEC-Marconi are also interested in increasing their managerial input in the flight control system (FCS), which previously has been the sole preserve of DASA. FCS development was central to Eurofighter 2000's three-year delay. Furthermore, DASA is now proposing utilising FCS software developed for the X-31 demonstrator aircraft, flying in the USA for the German MoD/DARPA/US Navy. DASA is keen to incorporate its X-31 experience in the European aircraft, to the extent that it has already proposed a thrust-vectoring mid-life update, for Eurofighter. This 'Kampfwertsteigerung', or combat improvement programme, could see the addition of 'paddles' to the EJ200 powerplant, as X-31 itself is progressing towards tailless flight in late 1995 with just such a system.

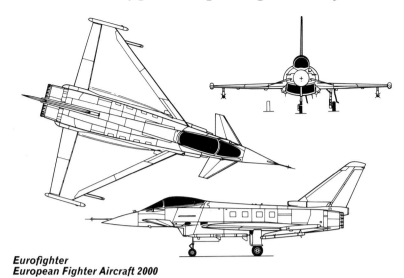

Eurofighter European Fighter Aircraft 2000

SPECIFICATION

Eurofighter European Fighter Aircraft 2000
Wing: span 10.50 m (34 ft 5.5 in); wing aspect ratio 2.205; wing area 50.00 m² (538.21 sq ft); canard foreplane area 2.40 m² (25.83 sq ft)
Fuselage and tail: length 14.50 m (47 ft 7 in); height about 4.00 m (13 ft 1.5 in)
Powerplant: two Eurojet EJ200 each rated at about 60.0 kN (13,490 lb st) dry and 90.0 kN (20,250 lb st) with afterburning
Weights: empty 9750 kg (21,495 lb); maximum take-off 21000 kg (46,297 lb)
Fuel and load: internal fuel 4000 kg (8,818 lb); external fuel up to one 1500-litre (396-US gal) and two 1000-litre (264-US gal) drop tanks; maximum ordnance

Seen during its public unveiling, this aircraft is BAe-assembled DA.4, the first two-seater. DA.1 and 2 are primarily concerned with flight system testing, while DA.3 is the first with EJ200 engines. DA.4 is the primary ECR-90 radar testbed.

6500 kg (14,330 lb)
Speed: maximum level speed 'clean' at 11000 m (36,090 ft) 2125 km/h (1,147 kt; 1,321 mph)
Range: combat radius between 463 and 556 km (250 and 300 nm; 288 and 345 miles)
Performance: take-off run 500 m (1,640 ft) at normal take-off weight; landing run 500 m (1,640 ft) at normal landing weight
g limits: -3 to +9

Excalibur Queenaire 800 (U-8F)

Excalibur Aviation Company
8337 Mission Road, San Antonio
Texas 78214, USA

San Antonio-based Excalibur Aviation Co. specialised for many years in the conversion of Beechcraft Twin Bonanzas and Queen Airs to improve their performance. The Excalibur **Queenaire 800** modification of the Queen Air 65, A65 and 80 has been sold to the **US Army**, and more than 50 Beech U-8Fs (described separately) have been modified to enhance their service life with the Army National Guard. The Queenaire 800 introduces 400-hp (298-kW) Textron Lycoming IO-720-A1B flat-eight

engines with Hartzell three-bladed, constant-speed, fully-feathering propellers, new engine mountings, exhaust system and low-drag nacelles, and fully-enclosed wheel well doors. Similar modifications to Queen Air A80 and B80 are referred to as Excalibur **Queenaire 8800**s. By 1994 approximately 170 had been undertaken, most notably for the US Army but also for a small number of other military customers, such as **Argentina**, **Colombia** and the **Dominican Republic**.

SPECIFICATION

Excalibur Queenaire 800 and 8800
generally similar to the Beech Queen Air Model 65, A65 and 80 except in the following particulars:
Powerplant: two Textron Lycoming IO-720-A1B each rated at 400 hp (298 kW)
Weights: empty equipped (Queenaire 800) 5,400 lb (2,449 kg), (Queenaire 8800) 5,800 lb (2631 kg); maximum take-off, (Queenaire 8000) 8,000 lb (23268 kg), (Queenaire 8800) 8800 lb (3991 kg)

Range: with maximum fuel and reserves, (Queenaire 800) 1,322 nm (2451 km/1,523 miles), (Queenaire 8800) 1,547 nm (2867 km/1,782 miles)
Performance: maximum cruising speed at 8,300 ft (2530 m) 201 kt (372 km/h; 231 mph); maximum rate of climb at sea level, (Queenaire 800) 1,5235 ft (468 m) per minute, (Queenaire 8800) 1,490 ft (454 m) per minute; stalling speed, gear and flaps down, (Queenaire 800), 68 kts (126km/h;78 mph), (Queenaire 8800), 70 kt (129 km/h; 80 mph); service ceiling, (Queenaire 800) 19,700 ft (6005 m), (Queenaire 8800) 18,700 ft (5700 m)

Extra 300

Under the direction of Walter Extra, the German company produced the **Extra 300** tandem two-seat unlimited aerobatic aircraft powered by a Textron Lycoming AEIO-540-L1B5 flat-six engine. The earlier **Extra 230** had a wooden wing, but the Extra 300 uses a composite unit. Only two military customers have purchased the type, these being the **French** and **Chilean** air forces. Six were delivered in 1989-90 to Grupo de Aviación No. 11 at Santiago-Los Cerillos for use by the Escuadrilla de Alta Acróbacia, better known as the Chilean air force's display team 'Los Halcones', which formerly flew the Pitts S-2A/S. The French air force's 'Equipe de Voltige' has purchased an **Extra 300** and an **Extra 300S** for aerobatic use at Salon de Provence. The quasi-military Royal Jordanian 'Falcons' team has also re-equipped with the Extra 300.

SPECIFICATION

Extra 300
Wing: span 8.00 m (26 ft 3 in); aspect ratio 5.98; area 10.70 m2 (115.17 sq ft)
Fuselage and tail: length 7.12 m (23 ft 4.25 in); height 2.62 m (8 ft 7.25 in); tailplane span 3.20 m (10 ft 6 in); wheel base 1.80 m (5 ft 11 in)
Powerplant: one Textron Lycoming AEIO-540-L1B5 rated at 300 hp (224 kW)
Weights: empty 630 kg (1,389 lb); normal take-off 820 kg (1,808 lb) for single-seat aerobatics or 870 kg (1,918 lb) for two seat aerobatics; maximum take-off 950 kg (2,094 lb)
Fuel and load: internal fuel 38 litres (10 US gal); external fuel none; maximum ordnance none
Speed: never-exceed speed 220 kt (253 mph; 407 km/h); maximum level speed 'clean' at optimum altitude 185 kt (213 mph); 343 km/h); maximum manoeuvring speed 158 kt (182 mph; 293 km/h)
Range: 526 nm (605 miles); 974 km)
Performance: maximum rate of climb at sea level 3,300 ft (1006 m) per minute; take-off distance to 50 ft

(15 m) about 248 m (814 ft) at maximum take-off weight; landing distance from 50 ft (15 m) about 548 m (1,798 ft) at normal landing weight
g limits: -10 to +10 single-seat aerobatic, or -8 to +8 two-seat aerobatic, or -3 to +6 at max take-off weight

'Los Halcones' are the Chilean air force aerobatic display teams, and one of several such groups which have traded in their Pitts Specials for the new German-built mounts.

Fairchild A-10/OA-10 Thunderbolt II

Fairchild Aircraft Incorporated
PO Box 790490, San Antonio
Texas 78279-0490, USA

Originally conceived as a counter-insurgency aircraft to help the war effort in South East Asia, the **Fairchild A-10A Thunderbolt II** emerged as a dedicated close air support aircraft, with the primary role of destroying enemy armour. In this role it is in the process of being replaced by the Lockheed F-16, but the 'Warthog' has adopted a new role of forward air control.

Two **YA-10A**s were built in answer to the USAF's AX competition. These were judged the winner on 18 January 1973 after evaluation against the Northrop A-9, and were followed by six pre-production aircraft.

The first of these was subsequently converted into the sole two-seat **YA-10B**, or **N/AW A-10**, intended for night/adverse weather work, with the addition of a weapons system officer. This programme was cancelled, but 707 A-10As followed the eight development machines.

'Warthog' is a name that has stuck with the A-10, largely on account of its awkward looks. The design, however, is central to the ability of the A-10 to operate effectively in a lethal battlefield environment. Until the recent innovation of an autopilot, the A-10 had to be constantly flown hands-on by the

pilot. This has obvious disadvantages for long flights, but bestows outstanding agility on the aircraft, enabling it to jink and weave at very low level. Survivability is the key to the shape of the A-10, the engines being mounted high on the rear fuselage where they are shrouded from ground fire from most angles by either the wings or tailplane. A strong structure and system redundancy ensures the A-10 can stay aloft with large amounts of battle damage, including an engine or fin shot away. Titanium armour 'bathtubs' protect both the pilot and the ammunition tank.

Furthermore, the aircraft was designed for rapid and easy maintenance. In a combat scenario the A-10 would fly a large number of short sorties, spending the minimum amount of time on the ground while refuelling and re-arming. Rapid maintenance and repair can also be accomplished at this time, by virtue of simple systems and ready-access panels.

Gulf veteran 'Hogs' from the New Orleans-based 706th TFS 'Cajuns' break for the camera on their return from Operation Desert Storm.

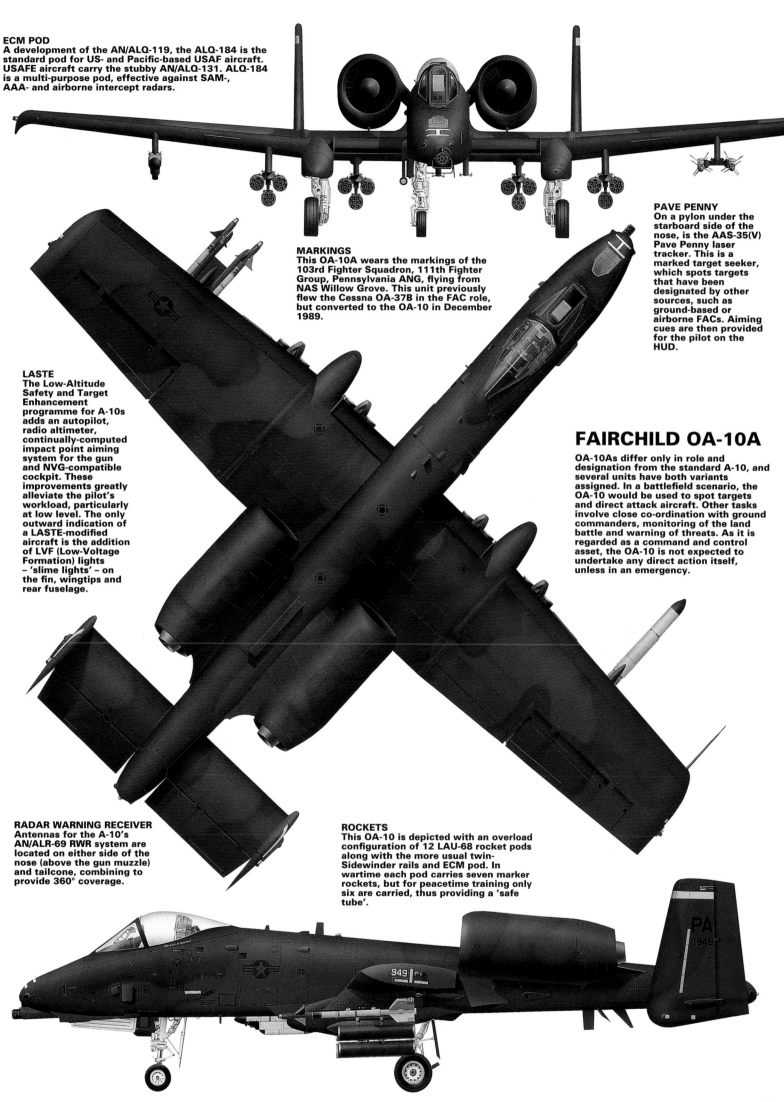

ECM POD
A development of the AN/ALQ-119, the ALQ-184 is the standard pod for US- and Pacific-based USAF aircraft. USAFE aircraft carry the stubby AN/ALQ-131. ALQ-184 is a multi-purpose pod, effective against SAM-, AAA- and airborne intercept radars.

MARKINGS
This OA-10A wears the markings of the 103rd Fighter Squadron, 111th Fighter Group, Pennsylvania ANG, flying from NAS Willow Grove. This unit previously flew the Cessna OA-37B in the FAC role, but converted to the OA-10 in December 1989.

PAVE PENNY
On a pylon under the starboard side of the nose, is the AAS-35(V) Pave Penny laser tracker. This is a marked target seeker, which spots targets that have been designated by other sources, such as ground-based or airborne FACs. Aiming cues are then provided for the pilot on the HUD.

LASTE
The Low-Altitude Safety and Target Enhancement programme for A-10s adds an autopilot, radio altimeter, continually-computed impact point aiming system for the gun and NVG-compatible cockpit. These improvements greatly alleviate the pilot's workload, particularly at low level. The only outward indication of a LASTE-modified aircraft is the addition of LVF (Low-Voltage Formation) lights – 'slime lights' – on the fin, wingtips and rear fuselage.

FAIRCHILD OA-10A

OA-10As differ only in role and designation from the standard A-10, and several units have both variants assigned. In a battlefield scenario, the OA-10 would be used to spot targets and direct attack aircraft. Other tasks involve close co-ordination with ground commanders, monitoring of the land battle and warning of threats. As it is regarded as a command and control asset, the OA-10 is not expected to undertake any direct action itself, unless in an emergency.

RADAR WARNING RECEIVER
Antennas for the A-10's AN/ALR-69 RWR system are located on either side of the nose (above the gun muzzle) and tailcone, combining to provide 360° coverage.

ROCKETS
This OA-10 is depicted with an overload configuration of 12 LAU-68 rocket pods along with the more usual twin-Sidewinder rails and ECM pod. In wartime each pod carries seven marker rockets, but for peacetime training only six are carried, thus providing a 'safe tube'.

Fairchild A-10/OA-10 Thunderbolt II

In terms of ordnance, the A-10 is designed around the enormous GAU-8/A 30-mm seven-barrelled rotary cannon, which is the world's most powerful airborne gun. However, the principal weapon of the A-10 is the AGM-65 Maverick missile, which has either TV- or IR-guidance. This provides good stand-off range for the anti-armour role or against other 'hard' targets. Various cluster and free-fall bombs can also be carried, although use of these would force an overflight of the target, which is likely to be in the thick of a heavily-gunned battlefield, and so are rarely employed.

Avionics of the A-10 remained very basic for most of the aircraft's career. A HUD was provided, and a screen for displaying images from Mavericks. A Pave Penny seeker on a pylon under the forward fuselage spotted targets designated by laser. No laser designator or rangefinder is fitted. Most current aircraft have received the LASTE modification, which finally adds an autopilot to relieve the arduous task of keeping the A-10 straight and level throughout the flight. LASTE also improves gun accuracy considerably, while the most visible feature is the addition of formation lights.

Entering service at Davis-Monthan AFB, AZ, the A-10 was first flown by the 355th

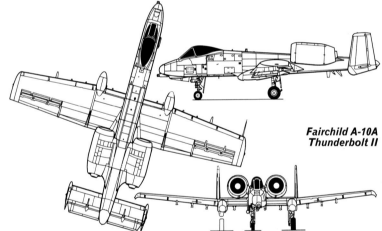

Fairchild A-10A Thunderbolt II

TFTW, and was later issued to the 23rd TFW, 354th TFW and various Reserve/ANG units in the CONUS, and units in Korea and Alaska. By far its most important theatre was Europe, where the 81st TFW flew six squadrons from the twin bases at Woodbridge and Bentwaters in England.

Debates raged as to the vulnerability of the A-10, and it was finally decided to gradually withdraw the type in favour of the F-16. At the same time, redundant A-10s became available to replace the ancient OV-10 in the forward air control role. Without any change to the aircraft, these were redesignated **OA-10A** and distributed to tactical air support squadrons. For the FAC role the A-10s are armed with AIM-9s for self-defence and rocket pods for marking targets.

While the A-10 force was put into decline, both as a result of USAF policy and of more general force cutbacks resulting from the 'peace dividend', the 'Warthog' suddenly found itself at war. Under the auspices of the 354th TFW (Provisional), 144 A-10s from the US and UK flew many Desert Storm missions, involving anti-armour work, air defence suppression and 'Scud' hunting. Throughout the conflict, the A-10 performed admirably, resulting in the destruction of huge numbers of tanks, artillery pieces and vehicles. A pilot from the 10th TFW at Alconbury and another from the 706th TFS at New Orleans were both credited with shooting down Iraqi helicopters. On 25 February 1991 two aircraft from the 76th TSFS/23rd TFW claimed 23 tanks destroyed in one day, under the direction of an OA-10 FAC. The highest mission

total worn by any aircraft was 86, by 'The Fortune Teller' (78-0593/MB) from the 353rd TFS/354th TFW which operated along with all deployed A-10s, from King Fahd Airport, Saudi Arabia.

WEAPON OPTIONS

The A-10 is built around the General Electric GAU-8/A Avenger 30-mm, seven-barrelled cannon. It is spun up to its full firing rate of 4,200 rounds per minute in 0.55 seconds, and has a maximum capacity of 1,350 30-mm rounds in a linkless feed system. The rounds are fed from the drum onto a continuous belt to the gun, while spent cartridges and unfired rounds are returned via the belt to the drum. The ammunition is held in a drum that is 6 ft 1 in (1.85 m) long and 2 ft 9 in (0.85 m) in diameter. The gun and feed system is over 13 ft (4 m) long, of which 7 ft 6 in (2.30 m) is barrel. Three types of ammunition are provided for the GAU-8/A. The PGU-13/B is an HEI (High Explosive, Incendiary) round, suitable for use against soft targets, or lightly armoured vehicles. It has a fragmenting jacket filled with standard explosives. The PGU-14/B is the API (Armour-Piercing, Incendiary) round and is of greatest use against armour. A lightweight, aluminium body surrounds a depleted uranium core, which is of very substantial mass, and penetrates armour through kinetic effect alone. While the round is (supposedly) minimally radioactive, uranium is highly flammable and combusts with the heat of the impact once inside a tank. Finally, the PGU-15/B is a TP (Training Practice) round, with no explosive filling. It matches the ballistics of the HEI round for aerial marksmanship. For normal combat sortie, the HEI and API are carried in a ratio of 1:5 (Combat Mix). Despite the manifest ability of the gun, the AGM-65 Maverick is the weapon of choice for the A-10's primary anti-armour mission. Two versions of the 8-ft 2-in (2.49-m) missile are in general use: the AGM-65B with TV scene magnification guidance, and the AGM-65D with an imaging infra-red (IIR) seeker. Both versions have a 125-lb (57-kg) shaped-charge, high explosive warhead, though the AGM-65D is heavier than the AGM-65B. A third version can also be found in use with the A-10, the AGM-65G. This is an IIR weapon with an improved seeker enabling the pilot to designate a specific point within a larger heat source. For use against larger, fixed targets (such as SAM or radar sites), it carries a 300-lb (136-kg) blast penetration warhead. On the port outboard pylon a twin-rail AIM-9L Sidewinder launcher is now a standard fitting, while an ECM pod balances it on the opposite wing. Four pylons are located under each wing (two inboard of undercarriage) along with three under the fuselage. The centreline pylon and its two flanking hardpoints cannot be used simultaneously. Maximum external load is 16,000 lb (7257 kg). The A-10 can carry a potential maximum load of 10 AGM-65 or 28 Mk 82 500-lb LDGP bombs, or 16 Mk 84 1,000-lb bombs, or eight CBU-87 cluster munitions, or 16 CBU-52/71 cluster munitions, two SUU-23/25/30/65 dispensers, practice bombs, assorted ECM pods, travel pods and up to three drop tanks (one centreline). The A-10 has been cleared for, but seldom carries, GBU-10/12 LGBs, BLU-52 tear-gas canisters, M117 LDGP bombs, and the UK's BL755 cluster bomb. A typical general-purpose load for the A-10 during Desert Storm comprised single Mavericks on each main wing pylon, and six SUU-30/64/65 cluster bombs on the unoccupied pylon. Standard ordnance for the OA-10, along with the GAU-8A, is the LAU-68 rocket pod, with a maximum of seven rounds carried. The rockets are Mk 66 motors, usually with white phosphorus warheads.

Capt. Bob Swain piloted 'Chopper Popper', which gained the A-10's first air-to-air kill (type unsure, but probably an MBB BO 105), on 6 February 1991, using its GAU-8. A second A-10 gun kill was chalked up against an Mi-8 nine days later.

OPERATORS

Despite the outstanding results gained by the A-10 in the war with Iraq, the draw-down process continued. In 1994 the A/OA-10 was serving with the 23rd Fighter Wing at Pope AFB, NC, 57th Wing at Nellis AFB (A-10 Weapons School and 422nd TES), the 355th FW at Davis-Monthan AFB and the 20th FW at Shaw AFB within Air Combat Command. One squadron (354th FS) of the 355th Wing is based at McChord AFB, Washington, to support local Army ground units. In other CONUS commands, the A-10 still serves with the 442nd FW (Richards-Gebaur AFB, MO), 917th FW (Barksdale AFB, LA) and 930th Fighter Group (Grissom AFB, Indiana) of the Air Force Reserve, the 103rd FG (Bradley IAP, CT), 104th FG at Barnes Airfield, Massachusetts, the 110th FG (A-10 and OA-10 at Battle Creek, MI), 111th FG (OA-10 at Willow Grove, PA), and 175th FG (A-10 and OA-10 at Baltimore, MD) within the Air National Guard structure and a handful of test/evaluation units.

Outside the CONUS structure two squadrons of OA-10s fly with the 51st Wing at Osan AB, Korea (19th TASS) and the 354th Wing at Eielson AFB, AK (11th TASS). Once the bastion of A-10 power, USAF Europe is left with only the 510th Fighter Squadron (renumbering as the 81st FS) at Spangdahlem, Germany. The parent unit is the 52nd FW.

No export sales were made of the A-10, although in 1994 50 aircraft were being readied at Davis-Monthan AFB for delivery to the Turkish air force (announced in June 1993), and potentially to be based at Eskisehir. Subsequently, this deal has been suspended owing to US reluctance to fund a Turkish buy, which effectively costs the US Government $2 million per aircraft. More deliveries of surplus US aircraft may be made in the future. Greece was also touted as a prospective recipient of surplus aircraft, but this now looks unlikely.

This ALQ-184-equipped OA-10A is based at Eielson AFB, Alaska, with the 354th Wing (formerly the 343rd).

SPECIFICATION

Fairchild Republic A-10A Thunderbolt II
Wing: span 57 ft 6 in (17.53 m); aspect ratio 6.54; area 506.00 sq ft (47.01 m²)
Fuselage and tail: length 53 ft 4 in (16.26 m); height 14 ft 8 in (4.47 m); tailplane span 18 ft 10 in (5.74 m); wheel track 17 ft 2.5 in (5.25 m)
Powerplant: two General Electric TF34-GE-100 each rated at 9,065 lb st (40.32 kN) dry
Weights: basic empty 21,541 lb (9771 kg); operating empty 24,959 lb (11321 kg); forward airstrip armed 32,771 lb (14865 kg); max take-off 50,000 lb (22680 kg)
Fuel and load: internal fuel 10,700 lb (4853 kg); external fuel up to three 600-US gal (2271-litre) drop tanks; maximum ordnance 16,000 lb (7,258 kg) or, with full internal fuel, 14,341 lb (6505 kg)

Speed: never-exceed speed 450 kt (518 mph; 834 km/h); maximum level speed 'clean' at sea level 381 kt (439 mph; 706 km/h)
Range: ferry range 2,131 nm (2,454 miles; 3949 km) with drop tanks; combat radius 540 nm (620 miles; 1000 km) on a deep strike mission or 250 nm (288 miles; 463 km) on a close air support mission with

a 1.7-hour loiter
Performance: maximum rate of climb at sea level 6,000 ft (1828 m) per minute; take-off run 4,000 ft (1220 m) at maximum take-off weight or 442 ft (1,450 ft) at forward strip weight; landing run 2,000 ft (610 m) at max weight or 1,300 ft (396 m) at forward strip weight

---

Fairchild **AU-23A Peacemaker**

After acquiring, in 1966, a licence to produce the Pilatus PC-6 Turbo Porter light transport, Fairchild developed an armed version for the USAF-managed Credible Chase programme. This was intended to produce a 'mini-gunship' for the South Vietnamese air force, armed with a side-firing 20-mm cannon and a range of other weapons and sensors. Fifteen **Fairchild AU-23A Peacemaker**s were purchased by the USAF for evaluation (against the Helio AU-24A) but procurement for the VNAF did not proceed. All the AU-23As were allocated to the Royal Thai air force in 1973 through the Pave Coin programme, and the RTAF ordered 20 more two years later after transferring five to the air police.

Based at Lop Buri under the control of No. 2 Wing, the AU-23A Peacemakers serve with No. 202 Squadron in the COIN and armed utility role. The primary armament of one XM-197 cannon, firing 700 rpm, is supplemented by two side-firing or underwing pod-mounted 7.62-mm SUU-11A/A Miniguns firing at 2,000 or 4,000 rpm. Four wing hardpoints supplement a 500-lb (227-kg)

fuselage centreline position to give a maximum external load of 2,000 lb (908 kg), which can include SUU-40 flare launchers, 0.50-in (12.7-mm) machine-gun pods, 2.75-in and 5-in Zuni unguided rocket pods, fragmentation, napalm or general-purpose high-explosive bombs, assorted smoke or chemical dispensers, camera pods, loud hailers or leaflet dispensers.

SPECIFICATION

Fairchild AU-23A Peacemaker
Wing: span 49 ft 8 in (15.14 m); aspect ratio 7.96; area 310.01 sq ft (28.80 m²)
Fuselage and tail: length 36 ft 10 in (11.23 m);

height 12 ft 3 in (3.73 m); elevator span 16 ft 9.5 in (5.12 m); wheel track 9 ft 10 in (3.00 m); wheel base 25 ft 10 in (7.87 m)
Powerplant: one Garrett TPE331-1-101F rated at 650 shp (485 kW)
Weights: maximum take-off 6,100 lb (2767 kg)
Fuel and load: internal fuel 127 US gal (480 litres); external fuel none; maximum ordnance 700 lb (318 kg)
Speed: maximum level speed 'clean' at optimum altitude 151 kt (174 mph; 280 km/h); cruising speed at optimum altitude 142 kt (163 mph; 262 km/h)
Range: typical range 485 nm (558 miles; 898 km)
Performance: maximum rate of climb at sea level 1,500 ft (457 m) per minute; service ceiling 22,800 ft (6950 m); take-off run 510 ft (155 m) at maximum take-off weight; landing run 295 ft (90 m) at normal landing weight

---

Fairchild **C-119 Flying Boxcar**

More than 1,000 C-119s were built after its first flight in November 1947. Derived from the wartime C-82 Packet, the **Fairchild C-119 Flying Boxcar** became the tactical transport workhorse of the USAF, replacing both the C-82 and C-47, and was built also for the USN, USMC, India, Italy and Belgium. Other air forces acquired fleets of C-119s retired from USAF service, among them the **Republic of China** air force, which received 120 of the **C-119G** model in 1969. About half of these remain in service with Nos 102 and 103 Squadrons in the 6th Troop Carrier and Anti-Submarine Combined Wing at Pingtung and are expected to continue into the 21st century as the only surviving military C-119s.

The C-119G was Fairchild's final production variant, featuring an increased gross weight and first introducing Aeroproducts propellers. Typically, 62 fully-equipped troops can be carried, and there are paradrop doors in each side of the split clamshell-type rear cargo-loading doors to permit simultaneous departures from each side of the aircraft.

SPECIFICATION

Fairchild Hiller C-119G Flying Boxcar
Wing: span 109 ft 3 in (33.30 m); aspect ratio 8.53; area 1,400.00 sq ft (130.06 m²)
Fuselage and tail: length 86 ft 6 in (26.36 m);

The Fairchild C-119 is still largely the backbone of the Republic of China Air Force transport effort, equipping two units. A small number of C-130s are in use also.

height 26 ft 4 in (8.03 m)
Powerplant: two Wright R-3350-89W Cyclone each rated at 3,400 hp (2535 kW)
Weights: empty 39,982 lb (18136 kg); maximum take-off 74,400 lb (33748 kg)
Speed: maximum level speed 'clean' at 17,000 ft

(5180 m) 257 kt (296 mph; 476 km/h); maximum cruising speed at optimum altitude 174 kt (200 mph; 322 km/h)
Range: 1,890 nm (2,280 miles; 3669 km)
Performance: maximum rate of climb at sea level 750 ft (229 m) per minute

Fairchild C-123 Provider

No military transport had a more unusual origin than the **Fairchild C-123 Provider**, the evolution of which can be traced back to design of an all-metal troop and cargo glider, the Chase XG-20. After a prototype XG-20 had been fitted with two R-2800 Double Wasp piston engines, the USAF bought 302 production examples of the **C-123B** from Fairchild, including 24 intended from the start for Venezuela and Saudi Arabia. In the transport role, the Provider can carry 60 equipped troops or 50 stretchers. A post-production modification programme added a pair of underwing jet pods to boost performance in the **C-123K** version.

As well as serving as tactical transports and in several specialised roles in Vietnam, C-123Bs and C-123Ks were added to the inventories of several Asian air forces comprising the Philippines, South Korea, South Vietnam, Taiwan and **Thailand**, which remains the largest user, with 10 Providers serving in No. 602 Squadron of Wing 6 at Don Muang. They are soon due to be retired in favour of G222s, along with a similar number of long-in-the-tooth C-123s flying with the Air Transport Wing of the **Republic of Korea** air force at Pusan. A pair of C-123Ks is believed to be still in service with the **Fuerza Aérea El Salvador**.

Amazingly, a large share of the Royal Thai Air Force's transport taskings fall on the old but broad shoulders of the Fairchild C-123K Provider. These veterans still serve with 602 Sqn, as part of No. 6 Wing at Bangkok (Don Muang). This is a C-123K with a single podded J85 turbojet under each wing for extra thrust.

SPECIFICATION

Fairchild Hiller C-123K Provider
Wing: span 110 ft 0 in (33.53 m); aspect ratio 9.89; area 1,223.00 sq ft (113.62 m²)
Fuselage and tail: length 76 ft 3 in (23.92 m); height 34 ft 1 in (10.39 m)
Powerplant: two Pratt & Whitney R-2800-99W Double Wasp each rated at 2,500 hp (1865 kW) and two General Electric J85-GE-17 each rated 2,850 lb st (12.69 kN) dry
Weights: empty 35,366 lb (16042 kg); operating empty 36,576 lb (16591 kg); maximum take-off 60,000 lb (18288 kg)
Fuel and load: maximum payload 15,000 lb (6804 kg)
Speed: maximum level speed 'clean' at 10,000 ft (3050 m) 198 kt (228 mph; 367 km/h); max cruising speed at 10,000 ft (3050 m) 150 kt (173 mph; 278 km/h)
Range: ferry range 2,848 nm (3,280 miles; 5279 km); range 899 nm (1,035 miles; 1666 km) with maximum payload
Performance: take-off run 1,167 ft (356 m) at maximum take-off weight; take-off distance to 50 ft (15 m) 1,809 ft (551 m) at maximum take-off weight; landing distance from 50 ft (15 m) 1,800 ft (549 m) at normal landing weight

---

Fairchild (Swearingen) C-26/Metro III/Merlin IV/MMSA (SMA)

In March 1988, the USAF selected the **Fairchild Metro III** transport to replace the Convair C-131s used by the **ANG**, and commenced deliveries in March 1989 of 13 under the designation **C-26A**. These serve in the Air National Guard Operational Support Aircraft (ANGOSA) role, with quick-change interiors for passengers, stretchers or cargo. A further contract awarded in January 1991 provided for up to 53 **C-26Bs** with delivery starting January 1992; these are fitted with TCAS II, GPS and microwave landing systems, the first US military aircraft to be so equipped. A single **UC-26C** serves with the Texas ANG on anti-drug missions, fitted with APG-66 radar and a FLIR to intercept low-flying aircraft.

Fairchild has also marketed the Metro as a **Special Mission Aircraft** (SMA), with various configurations for maritime patrol, submarine detection, flight inspection, photo reconnaissance, AEW and Elint roles. The **Swedish air force** acquired a **Merlin IVC** (Metro III equivalent) for use as a VIP transport, designated **Tp 88**, and took delivery in 1987 of a second splinter-camouflaged Tp 88 for development of an AEW version. This aircraft has been fitted with a large dorsal planar radar antenna housing for Ericsson PS-890 Erieye E/F band radar, with which it first flew (with operational radar) in May 1991. The Swedish air force has a requirement for about a dozen similar AEW aircraft but has elected to use the Saab 340 as its AEW platform.

Fairchild has now flown and exhibited its Metro 23-derived **Multi-Mission Surveillance Aircraft** (MMSA). This is a rapidly configurable airframe, capable of undertaking survey, surveillance, Elint and conventional reconnaissance duties while retaining its transport/VIP/air ambulance capability. Along with Lockheed Fort Worth (formerly General Dynamics), Fairchild has developed a centreline systems pod for the MMSA, along with C3I consoles in the cabin, a dedicated surveillance radar fit and accompanying cockpit systems. The pod can house a Loral FLIR and infra-red line scan, electro-optical cameras, LOROP (LOng Range OPtical) gear, air-to-air and sea surveillance radar. Fitting of the GEC-Marconi Seaspray 2000 radar is under investigation. Aircraft will be built, and fitted out, on demand. A Mitsubishi FLIR can also be provided for the pilot.

Fairchild have delivered small numbers of VIP transport Metro III/Merlin IVs to other military customers including **Argentina** (Merlin IVA – three), and **Thailand** (Merlin IVA – two). The MMSA was under evaluation by Turkey, Poland and Hungary in 1993/94 but Turkey, at least, opted for the Britten-Norman Islander-based MSSA.

Right: Sweden flies the Metro III/Tp 88 as a VIP transport, along with Beech 200s.

Below: the MMSA is the current 'special mission' Metro.

SPECIFICATION

Fairchild C-26A/B
Wing: span 57 ft 0 in (17.37 m); aspect ratio 10.5; area 309.0 sq ft (28.71 m²)
Fuselage and tail: length 59 ft 4.25 in (18.09 m); height 16 ft 8 in (5.08 m); tailplane span 15 ft 11.5 in (4.86 m); wheel track 15 ft 0 in (4.57 m); wheel base 19 ft 1.5 in (5.83 m)
Powerplant: two Garrett TPE331-121UAR each rated at 1,119 shp (834 kW)
Weights: operating empty 9,180 lb (4164 kg); maximum take-off 14,500 lb (6577 kg) standard or 16,000 lb (7257 kg) optional
Fuel and load: internal fuel 4,342 lb (1969 kg); external fuel none; maximum payload 5,000 lb (2268 kg)
Speed: maximum cruising speed at 15,000 ft (4570 m) at 12,500 lb (5670 kg) 279 kt (321 mph; 517 km/h); economical cruising speed at 25,000 ft (7620 m) 252 kt (290 mph; 467 km/h)
Range: at optional maximum take-off weight 1,063 nm (1,224 miles; 1,970 km) or at standard maximum take-off weight 384 nm (442 miles; 711 km)
Performance: maximum rate of climb at sea level 2,370 ft (722 m) per minute; service ceiling 27,500 ft (8380 m); take-off distance to 50 ft (15 m) 3,340 ft (1018 m) at standard maximum take-off weight; landing distance from 50 ft (15 m) 2,450 ft (747 m) at normal landing weight

---

FAMA/FMA IA-50 Guaraní II

Developed from the Huanquero and Guaraní I, the **IA-50 Guaraní II** was developed for the **Argentine air force** as a transport and utility aircraft. The first Guaraní II flew on 23 April 1963. The type features a low-set wing with two Turboméca Bastan VI turboprops, a cabin for up to 15, and a large, sharply-swept tail. One was fitted with ski undercarriage for Antarctic operations. Forty-one were built, including prototypes, and all served in Argentina.

A handful remains in service with II Brigada Aérea at Base Aérea General Urquiza at Parana. Four were configured for photo-survey, and three fly navaid and landing system calibration flights. All survivors are to be replaced by surplus US C-12 Hurons during 1994.

SPECIFICATION

FAMA/FMA IA-50 Guaraní II
Wing: span 19.59 m (64 ft 3.25 in) without tip tanks; aspect ratio 9.18; area 41.81 m² (450.05 sq ft)
Fuselage and tail: length 15.30 m (50 ft 2.5 in); height 5.61 m (18 ft 5 in); tailplane span 6.50 m (21 ft 4 in)
Powerplant: two Turboméca Bastan VIA each rated at 930 shp (693 kW)
Weights: empty equipped 3924 kg (8,650 lb); maximum take-off 7200 kg (15,873 lb) without tip tanks and 7750 kg (17,085 lb) with tip tanks
Fuel and load: internal fuel 1910 litres (505 US gal) plus 144 litres (38 US gal) in two non-jettisonable tip tanks; maximum payload 1500 kg (3,307 lb)
Speed: maximum level speed 'clean' at optimum altitude 270 kt (311 mph; 500 km/h); maximum cruising speed 265 kt (305 mph; 491 km/h)
Range: 2575 km (1,389 nm; 1,600 miles) with maximum fuel or 1995 km (1,077 nm; 1,240 mile) with maximum payload
Performance: maximum rate of climb at sea level 805 m (2,640 ft) per minute; service ceiling 41,000 ft (12500 m); take-off run 420 m (1,380 ft) at maximum take-off weight

FAMA/FMA IA-58 Pucará

Fábrica Militar de Aviones SA
Avienda Fuerza Aérea Argentina Km 5½
5103 Guarnicíon Aérea Córdoba, Argentina

Meeting a **Fuerza Aérea Argentina** (**FAA**) requirement for a close air support, reconnaissance and counter-insurgency aircraft, the **Pucará** was an indifferent performer in the 1982 Falklands War with the United Kingdom and consequently suffered a loss of support for its *modus operandi*. The Pucará concept originated in the early 1960s, when anti-guerrilla and counter-insurgency were the types of warfare anticipated by Argentina. Fabrica Militar de Aviones (FMA) was then a component of the FAA's Support Command and produced the **IA-58** design with twin turboprops and all-metal construction. The prototype flew on 20 August 1969, powered by a pair of 674-kW (904-ehp) Garrett TPE331-U-303 powerplants, but the production version utilised 671-kW (1,022-ehp) Turboméca Astazou XVIGs, which powered the second aircraft for its maiden flight on 6 September 1970.

Named for the stone forts built by the indigenous South American people, the Pucará is a manoeuvrable and rugged aircraft able to operate from short, rough airstrips – 80 m (262 ft) is enough when helped by three JATO bottles. A tall, retractable tricycle undercarriage provides ample space for weapons and the generous propeller ground clearance necessary for flights from uneven land. Crew are provided with Martin-Baker Mk 6 zero/zero ejection seats, the rear occupant having full dual controls and a cockpit floor raised 25 cm (10 in). The forward windscreen is armoured, as is the cabin floor. In practice, a second crew member is rarely necessary for COIN missions and the aircraft is usually flown with the rear seat empty.

Weapons, which are aimed with a SFOM 83A-3 sight, include fixed armament of two 20-mm Hispano cannon under the nose and four 7.62-mm Browning machine-guns abreast of the cockpit. With these and full fuel load, an additional 1500 kg (3,307 lb) of external stores can be carried in the form of bombs, rockets, cannon pods, napalm drop tanks or reconnaissance pods.

The first production **IA-58A** flew on 8 November 1974 and deliveries began to the FAA in 1976 for three squadrons of Grupo 3 at Reconquista and one squadron of 9 Grupo at Comodoro Rivadavia. Early action was seen late in 1976 against rebel forces

in north-west Argentina. An initial order for 60 was augmented by a follow-on batch of 48, but the last 22 of these were not accepted by the FAA and offered for sale. Furthermore, a total of 40 surplus aircraft were made available for export in 1986, as soon as production had ended. All 24 aircraft deployed to the Falkland Islands in 1982 were lost to sabotage, ground fire and bombing, or were captured by British forces, one of these latter later flying in British military markings for evaluation. Another was lost operating from Comodoro Rivadavia, although a Pucará shot down a Westland Scout helicopter. Prior to the conflict, in October 1981, the first of six aircraft diverted from FAA orders had been delivered to **Uruguay** for Grupo de Aviación 2 of Brigada Aérea II at Durazno. **Colombia** was presented with three for drugs interdiction operations in late 1989, these flown by Escuadrón 212 of Grupo II at Apiay. Argentina now has only 40 aircraft with two remaining squadrons of Grupo 3. Some have the rear cockpit deleted in favour of additional fuel. Work on installation of a new navigation and attack system (SINT) began in the late 1980s, but was soon terminated due to financial problems.

More ambitious upgrades also failed to gain acceptance. **IA-58B** was the designation for a single prototype, flown 15 May 1979, with cannon uprated to two 30-mm DEFA 553s, deeper forward fuselage and improved avionics. The planned 40 aircraft emerged as IA-58As. Taking aboard lessons of the Falklands War, the **IA-58C** 'Pucará Charlie' was a proposed rebuild of IA-58As with two DEFA 553s in addition to the six 20-mm and 7.62-mm weapons, the front cockpit faired over, rear cockpit enlarged and protected by further armour, and weapon options expanded with Martin Pescador (Kingfisher) ASMs and MATRA Magic self-defence AAMs. Additional avionics were added in the form of a radar warning receiver, Omega/VLF navigation and radar altimeter, while the engines gained self-start capability and modified exhausts to reduce infra-red emissions. Only one prototype was produced, and flew on 30 December 1985. It has been suggested that the FAA is considering retrofitting its surviving Pucarás to IA-58C standard, but no progress has been made.

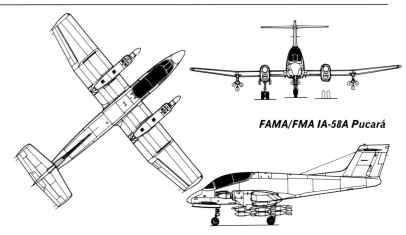

FAMA/FMA IA-58A Pucará

IA-66 was the designation of a sixth prototype Pucará which flew in 1980, powered by 746-kW (1,000-ehp) Garrett TPE331-11-601W engines driving Dowty Rotol propellers. The latter were replaced by McCaulley units in 1983, but no production aircraft were ordered. Several reported contracts for IA-58As have failed to materialise, such as 50 for **Egypt** and 12 for the **Central African Republic**, although one of six aircraft for **Mauritania** was actually painted before the 1978 order was cancelled. **Iraq** requested 20 in 1985, but was turned down by the Argentine government. In 1992 four IA-58As were supplied to **Sri Lanka**.

SPECIFICATION

FAMA/FMA IA-58A Pucará
Wing: span 14.50 m (47 ft 6.8 in); aspect ratio 6.94; area 30.30 m² (326.16 sq ft)
Fuselage and tail: length 14.253 m (46 ft 9 in); height 5.362 m (17 ft 7 in); tailplane span 4.70 m (15 ft 5 in); wheel track 4.20 m (13 ft 9.25 in); wheel base 3.885 m (12 ft 9 in)
Powerplant: two Turboméca Astazou XVIG each rated at 729 kW (978 shp)
Weights: empty equipped 4020 kg (8,862 lb); normal take-off 5300 kg (11,684 lb); maximum take-off 6800 kg (14,991 lb)
Fuel and load: internal fuel 1000 kg (2,205 lb); external fuel up to 1359 kg (2,997 lb) in one 1100- or

318-litre (290- or 84-US gal) and two 318-litre (84-US gal) drop tanks; maximum ordnance 1500 kg (3,307 lb)
Speed: never exceed speed 405 kt (466 mph; 750 km/h); maximum level speed 'clean' at 9,845 ft (3000 m) 270 kt (311 mph; 500 km/h); maximum cruising speed at 19,685 ft (6000 m) 259 kt (298 mph; 480 km/h); economical cruising speed at optimum altitude 232 kt (267 mph; 430 km/h)
Range: ferry range 3710 km (2,002 nm; 2,305 miles) with three drop tanks; combat radius 225 km (121 nm; 140 miles) on a lo-lo-lo attack mission with a 1500-kg (3,307-lb) warload, or 325 km (175 nm; 202 miles) on a lo-lo-hi attack mission with a 1500-kg (3,307-lb) warload, or 350 km (189 nm; 217 miles) on a hi-lo-hi attack mission with a 1500-kg (3,307-lb) warload, or 400 km (216 nm; 248 miles) on a lo-lo-lo attack mission with a 1000-kg (2,205-lb) warload, or 575 km (310 nm; 357 miles) on a lo-lo-hi attack mission with a 1000-kg (2,205-lb) warload, or 650 km (350 nm; 404 miles) on a hi-lo-hi attack mission with a 1000-kg (2,205-lb) warload
Performance: maximum rate of climb at sea level 1080 m (3,543 ft) per minute; service ceiling 32,800 ft (10000 m); take-off run 300 m (984 ft) at 5500 kg (12,125 lb); take-off distance to 50 ft (15 m) 705 m (2,313 ft) at 5500 kg (12,125 lb); landing distance from 50 ft (15 m) 603 m (1,978 ft) at 5100 kg (11,243 lb); landing run 200 m (656 ft) at 5100 kg (11,243 lb)
g limits: +3 to -6

In December 1989 Colombia received three IA-58As for 'anti-narcotics' operations, alongside AC-47s.

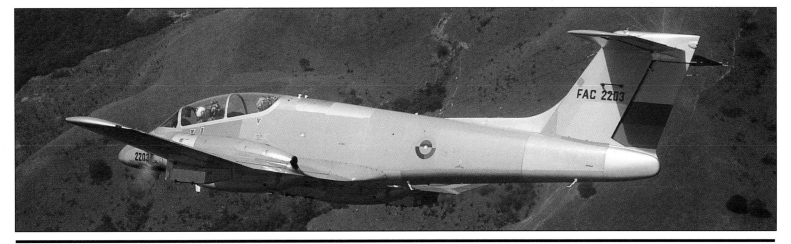

FAMA/FMA IA-63 Pampa

Argentina's Fabrica Militar de Aviones SA (FMA, or Military Aircraft Factory), which is operated by the Argentine air force, started **IA-63** development in 1979 to replace the FAA's ageing licence-built four-seat FMA Morane-Saulnier MS.760 Paris II light jets used since 1958 as armed trainers, from 48 originally procured. FMA

received technical assistance with design of the Pampa from Dornier, based on its Alpha Jet advanced trainer experience, and the Pampa was selected after the evaluation of seven joint project studies. It retained an Alpha Jet-type configuration, although with unswept wings and tailplane in a lighter airframe powered by a single 3,500-lb (15.57-kN)

Garrett TFE731-2-2N turbofan. Other design features include dual-system hydraulic servo primary controls with three-axis electro-mechanical trim and an emergency ram-air turbine. Hydraulic power is also used for operation of the tricycle landing gear, single-slotted Fowler-type flaps, and the twin air brakes above the rear fuselage.

Student and instructor are accommodated in stepped tandem UPC (Stencil) S-III-S31A63 lightweight zero-zero ejection seats in the pressurised cockpit. Dornier

also built the wings and tailplanes of the three flying and two static test prototypes, the first of which (EX-01) made its initial flight on 6 October 1984, and is continuing to assist FMA with Pampa marketing. Plans did not materialise for a fourth prototype, powered by a 2,900-lb (12.9-kN) Pratt & Whitney JT15D-5 turbofan.

The first of 18 IA-63s, comprising three pre-series and 15 initial production Pampas from a planned batch of 64, were delivered to II Squadron of the 4 Brigada Aerea, also

FAMA/FMA IA 63 Pampa

known as the Escuela de Caza (Fighter School), at El Plumerillo from March 1988 to provide advanced training and weapons instruction. In the latter role and for light attack duties, for which most FAA Pampas are being upgraded, the IA-63 has four underwing and one fuselage weapons pylons, with a maximum capacity of 3,417 lb (1550 kg). This could include a ventral 30-mm DEFA cannon pod with 145 rounds, and up to six Mk 81 250-lb (114-kg) bombs or two each of Mk 81s and 500-lb Mk 82 (227-kg) bombs.

FAA plans for Pampa procurement included a requirement for 36 more aircraft for front-line units, increasing total purchases to 100 aircraft, but severe funding problems have delayed further production deliveries. Similar problems have been encountered with a deck-training version in which the Argentine navy was interested for its carrier 25 de Mayo.

A version of the IA-63, known as the **Pampa 2000**, is being offered for the US JPATS programme by FMA in conjunction with the Vought Aircraft Company, plus Loral for ground-based training, UNC for aircraft logistics support and Allied Signal as suppliers of the engine, avionics and environmental control system. The second prototype (EX-02) and two production aircraft were sent to the US for modification to Pampa 2000 standard. If selected, **Vought** would build the aircraft in Dallas using 90 per cent US components. The programme suffered a blow with the loss of EX-02 in the UK on 31 August 1992, prior to its debut at that year's Farnborough show. In September 1993 the Pampa 200 began a two-month tour of USAF and USN bases, beginning at Andrews AFB, Maryland.

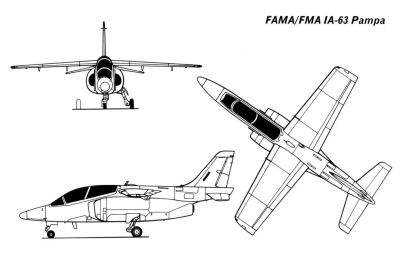

FAMA/FMA IA-63 Pampa

SPECIFICATION

FAMA/FMA IA-63 Pampa
Wing: span 9.686 m (31 ft 9.25 in); aspect ratio 6.0; area 15.633 m² (168.27 sq ft)
Fuselage and tail: length 10.93 m (35 ft 10.25 in) excluding probe; height 4.29 m (14 ft 1 in); tailplane span 4.576 m (15 ft 0.33 in); wheel track 2.663 m (8 ft 8.75 in); wheel base 4.418 m (14 ft 6 in)
Powerplant: one Garrett TFE731-2-2N rated at 3,500 lb st (15.57 kN) dry
Weights: empty equipped 2821 kg (6,219 lb); normal take-off 3800 kg (8,377 lb); maximum take-off 5000 kg (11,023 lb)
Fuel and load: internal fuel 1118 kg (2,465 lb) including 415 litres (109 US gal) of auxiliary fuel in outer-wing tanks; external fuel none; maximum ordnance 1160 kg (2,557 lb)
Speed: maximum level speed 'clean' at 7000 m (22,965 ft) 442 kt (509 mph; 819 km/h) or at sea level 405 kt (466 mph; 750 km/h); cruising speed at 4000 m (13,125 ft) 403 kt (464 mph; 747 km/h)
Range: ferry range 1853 km (1,000 nm; 1,151 miles) with auxiliary fuel; range 1500 km (809 nm; 932 miles); mission radius 440 km (237 nm; 273 miles) on a hi-hi-hi

air-to-air gunnery mission with a 250-kg (551-lb) warload, or 360 km (194 nm; 223 miles) on a hi-lo-hi air-to-ground mission with a 1000-kg (2,205-lb) warload; endurance 3 hours 48 minutes
Performance: maximum rate of climb at sea level 1560 m (5,118 ft) per minute; service ceiling 12900 m

(42,325 ft); take-off run 424 m (1,390 ft) at 3700 kg (8,157 lb); take-off distance to 15 m (50 ft) 700 m (2,297 ft) at 3700 kg (8,157 lb); landing distance from 15 m (50 ft) 850 m (2,789 ft) at 3500 kg (7,716 lb); landing run 461 m (1,512 ft) at 3500 kg (7,716 lb)
g limits: -3 to +6 (+4.5 sustained)

Below: The Pampa is now operational with the Fuerza Aérea Argentina. Aircraft serials are carried only inside the nosewheel door.

Right: The second IA 63 served as the prototype for the Pampa 2000, but crashed during a display practice at Bournemouth in 1992.

FFA AS 202 Bravo

FFA Flugzeugwerke Altenrhein AG
CH-9423 Altenrhein
Switzerland

Designed as the **S.202** by SIAI-Marchetti in Italy, the **Bravo** two/three-seat trainer was launched as a joint project between that company and Flug und Fahrzeugwerke AG in Switzerland. Prototypes were flown on 7 March and 7 May 1969, respectively in Switzerland and Italy. FFA took full control in 1973, with subsidiary Repair AG responsible for marketing. Production was primarily for military flying schools, and was concentrated on the 180-hp (134-kW) **AS 202/18A** variant, although it included 34 of the 115-hp (86-kW) **AS 202/15** variant. FFA also built prototypes with a 260-hp (194-kW) Lycoming (**AS 202/26A**) and with a 320-shp (239-kW) Allison 250-B17 turboprop (**AS 202/32**).

Production of the AS 202/18A has included four sub-variants. The **A1** has an aerobatic gross weight of 950 kg (2,094 lb) and was supplied to **Morocco** (18, used at the flying school at Menara-Marrakesh) and to **Uganda** (eight for the central flying school). The **A2** has a gross weight of 980 kg (2,160 lb), electric trim and an extended canopy. **Iraq** received 48 of this model for its IrAF College at Tihret; between 10 and 12 were reported to have been transferred to the **Royal Jordan Air Force**. The **A3** had mechanical trim and a 24-volt electrical system. **Indonesia** acquired 40, to serve in No. 101 Squadron (Skwadron Latih Mulah) at the flying school (Sekolah Penerbang) at Adisutjipto. Finally, the **Royal Flight of Oman** acquired four A4s, with weight increased to 1,010 kg (2,226 lb) and CAA-approved special instrumentation. Production halted in 1989, with 180 delivered, though the line remains open for orders.

SPECIFICATION

FFA AS 202/18A Bravo
Wing: span 9.75 m (31 ft 11.75 in); aspect ratio 6.5; area 13.86 m² (149.19 sq ft)
Fuselage and tail: length 7.50 m (24 ft 7.25 in); height 2.81 m (9 ft 2.75 in); tailplane span 3.67 m (12 ft 0.5 in); wheel track 2.25 m (7 ft 4.5 in); wheel base 1.78 m (5 ft 10 in)
Powerplant: one Textron Lycoming AEIO-360-B1F rated at 180 hp (134 kW)
Weights: empty equipped 710 kg (1.565 lb); normal take-off 980 kg (2,160 lb) for aerobatics; maximum take-off 1080 kg (2,381 lb)
Fuel and load: internal fuel 170 litres (44.9 US gal); external fuel none; maximum ordnance none
Speed: never exceed speed 173 kt (199 mph; 320 km/h);

maximum level speed 'clean' at sea level 130 kt (150 mph; 241 km/h); maximum cruising speed at 8,000 ft (2440 m) 122 kt (141 mph; 226 km/h); economical cruising speed at 10,000 ft (3050 m) 109 kt (126 mph; 203 km/h)
Range: with maximum fuel and no reserves 615 nm (1140 km; 707 miles)
Performance: maximum rate of climb at sea level 800 ft (244 m) per minute; service ceiling 17,000 ft (5180 m); take-off run 215 m (705 ft) at maximum take-off weight; take-off distance to 50 ft (15 m) 415 m (1,360 ft) at maximum take-off weight; landing distance from 50 ft (15 m) 465 m (1,525 ft) at normal landing weight
g limits: -3 to +6

Indonesia is the major user of the Bravo, having received 40 AS 202A3s as primary trainers.

FLS (Lovaux) Optica/Scoutmaster

FLS Aerospace (Lovaux) Ltd
Bournemouth International Airport
Christchurch, Dorset BH23 6NW, UK

Designed primarily for use as a specialised observation aircraft by civil and quasi-military agencies, the **OA7-300 Optica** has applications for coastal patrol, visual reconnaissance and liaison duty. An electronic surveillance version has also been proposed as the **Scoutmaster**, equipped with search radar and FLIR. The private-venture Optica, designed by Edgley, was first flown on 14 December 1979. Subsequent small-scale production by Brooklands Aerospace ended after a factory fire destroyed nine aircraft before delivery, and the Lovaux subsidiary of FLS Aerospace acquired the design in 1990, transferring production to its Bournemouth factory. Production resumed in 1992 after UK certification in December 1991. Small numbers of Opticas have been delivered to civilian and police customers, but no military orders have yet been received.

SPECIFICATION

FLS Aerospace (Lovaux) Optica OA7-300
Wing: span 39 ft 4 in (11.99 m); aspect ratio 9.1; area 170.50 sq ft (15.84 m2)
Fuselage and tail: length 26 ft 9 in (8.15 m); height 7 ft 7 in (2.31 m) over tailplane and 6 ft 6 in (1.98 m) over shroud excluding antenna; tail unit span 11 ft 2 in (3.40 m) to centreline of booms; wheel track 11 ft 2 in (3.40 m); wheel base 9 ft 0 in (2.73 m)
Powerplant: one Textron Lycoming IO-540-V4A5D rated at 260 hp (194 kW)
Weights: empty equipped 2,090 lb (948 kg); maximum take-off 2,900 lb (1315 kg)
Fuel and load: internal fuel 250 litres (66 US gal); external fuel none
Speed: never-exceed speed 140 kt (161 mph; 259 km/h); maximum level speed 'clean' at optimum altitude 115 kt (132 mph; 213 km/h); maximum cruising speed at optimum altitude 103 kt (109 mph; 191 km/h);

FLS was concerned solely with civil airliner maintenance until it acquired the assets of Brooklands Aerospace in 1990. Part of this deal included rights to the Brooklands (formerly Edgley) Optica.

economical cruising speed at optimum altitude 86 kt (99 mph; 159 km/h)
Range: 570 nm (656 miles; 1056 km) at 70 kt (81 mph; 130 km/h) or 370 nm (426 miles; 685 km) at 110 kt (127 mph; 204 km/h); endurance 8 hours at 70 kt (81 mph; 130 km/h) or 2 hours 45 minutes at 110 kt (127 mph; 204 km/h)

Performance: maximum rate of climb at sea level 810 ft (247 m) per minute; service ceiling 14,000 ft (4275 m); take-off run 1,082 ft (330 m) at maximum take-off weight; take-off distance to 50 ft (15 m) 1,548 ft (472 m) at maximum take-off weight; landing distance from 50 ft (15 m) 1,820 ft (555 m) at normal landing weight

FLS (Trago Mills) SAH-1 Sprint

The **SAH-1** has the potential to be an excellent military basic and primary trainer. It has impeccable handling characteristics, sensible, robust, no-frills engineering, a roomy side-by-side cockpit and superb all-round vision. The brainchild of a Cornish supermarket magnate (the Trago Mills chain of shops), the prototype was constructed under the Trago Mills name and bore as its designation the initials of its designer, Sidney Arthur Holloway. The aircraft first flew on 23 August 1983 and received rave reviews, and was borrowed by the ETPS at Boscombe Down, whose commandant, Air Vice Marshal Geoff Cairns, later became test pilot.

The prototype was powered by a 120-hp (89.52-kW) Textron Lycoming O-235-L2A engine driving a fixed-pitch propeller, but production aircraft will be fitted with a 160-hp (119.36-kW) AEIO-320-DB. Plans for a line in Hungary fell through, but the company was bought out by Orca Aircraft in 1988, which collapsed one year later. The **SAH-1** itself was too good to be lost, however, and all rights were sold to FLS (Lovaux) in October 1991. The first production example flew on 16 December 1993.

In the hands of FLS, the Sprint finally gained its UK CofA on 17 July 1994. The fully aerobatic production aircraft is now a serious contender in the military market.

Fokker F27 Friendship

Apart from the Antonov An-24/26 family, the **Fokker F27 Friendship** is the world's best-selling airliner in the 50-seat class. Originally planned as a 32-seat passenger aircraft, its efficiency led to stretching into the 50- and even 60-seat class and, as the **F-27J** and **FH-227**, 205 were made under licence by **Fairchild** in the USA. All versions have a high-mounted high-aspect wing with slotted flaps and integral tanks, a pressurised fuselage with a 2.49-m (98-in) wide cabin and 1.93-m (76-in) high, pneumatically-operated undercarriage and pneumatic de-icers on all leading edges.

By 1960 Fokker was offering the **F27 Mk 300 Combiplane**, with large forward cargo doors, strong floor and quick-change passenger/cargo interior. With further minor modifications this became the **F27 Mk 300M Troopship**, nine of which were sold to the **KLu** (Royal Netherlands air force) to follow three Series 100s. The name Troopship was subsequently dropped, and for many years the standard military model was the **F27 Mk 400M**, first flown in 1965. This was fitted with 1700-ekW (2,280-ehp) Dart Mk 536 turboprops, replaced from 1984 by the more efficient Mk 552 model. Normal accommodation is 46 paratroops in folding canvas seats, dispatched through doors on each side at the rear. Alternatively, 6025 kg (13,283 lb) of cargo or 24 USAF-type stretchers and nine seats may be carried. A cartographic version is also available with inertial navigation system, two super-wide-angle cameras and a navigation sight and optional target-tow gear. Fokker also built the **F27 Mk 500**, with a fuselage lengthened to 25.06 m (82 ft 2.5 in) for up to 60 seats.

In addition to the Netherlands, the F27 is currently operated in the transport role by **Algeria** (three), **Argentina** (13), **Bolivia** (five), **Côte d'Ivoire** (one), **Finland** (three), **Ghana** (four), **Guatemala** (three), **Iceland** (coast guard), **India** (two for the coast guard), **Indonesia** (seven), **Iran** (18), **Mexico** (seven), **Myanmar** (four), **New Zealand** (three, stored), **Pakistan** (three), **Peru** (one), **Philippines** (nine), **Senegambia** (six), **Sudan** (one), **Thailand** (two) and **Uruguay** (three) and the **US Army** (two, designated **C-31A**). The C-31As were used by the US Army's 'Golden Knights' display team.

In 1975 Fokker completed definition of a specialised maritime patrol version of the F27 as the **Fokker F27 Maritime**. Intended for all forms of coastal surveillance, SAR and environmental control missions, the Maritime has a crew of up to six and can mount 12-hour patrols. It is equipped with Litton APS-504 search radar in a belly blister, nose-mounted Bendix weather radar, and a fully comprehensive navigation system, as well as a fully equipped tactical compartment, crew rest areas and bulged observation windows to the flight deck and rear of the cabin. This version was subsequently sold to **Angola** and **Peru** (where it is no longer operated) and is currently in use in the **Netherlands** (two), **Nigeria** (two), **Pakistan** (four), **Philippines** (three), **Spain** (three) and **Thailand** (three).

Thailand's aircraft are armed, but otherwise not to **Maritime Enforcer** standard. This variant is tasked for armed surveillance, ASW, anti-ship attack and other combat roles, and is equipped with a LAPADS processor system for active and passive sonobuoys, MAD and comprehensive ESM and IR detection systems, plus optional underwing searchlight. The **Maritime Enforcer 2** is based on the next-generation **Fokker 50** (described separately), with PW 124 engines, six-bladed propellers and completely new systems.

SPECIFICATION

Fokker F27 Mk 400M Troopship
Wing: span 29.00 m (95 ft 2 in); aspect ratio 12.0; area 70.00 m2 (753.50 sq ft)
Fuselage and tail: length 23.56 m (77 ft 3.5 in); height 8.50 m (27 ft 11 in); tailplane span 9.75 m (32 ft 0 in); wheel track 7.20 m (23 ft 7.5 in); wheel base 8.74 m (28 ft 8 in)
Powerplant: two Rolls-Royce Dart RDa.7 Mk 532-7 each rated at 2,050 shp (1528.5 kW) plus 525 lb st (2.34 kN) dry
Weights: manufacturer's empty 24,720 lb (11213 kg); operating empty 25,307 lb (11479 kg) in freight configuration, or 26,240 lb (11902 kg) in medevac configuration, or 26,696 lb (11655 kg) in paratroop configuration; maximum take-off 45,000 lb (20412 kg)
Fuel and load: internal fuel 5140 litres (1,358 US gal); external fuel none; maximum payload 12,863 lb (5834 kg) in freight configuration, or 11,991 lb (5439 kg) in medevac configuration, or 12,425 lb (5635 kg) in paratroop configuration
Speed: normal cruising speed at 20,000 ft (6095 m) 259 kt (298 mph; 480 km/h)
Range: 670 nm (771 miles; 1241 km) with maximum space-limited payload, or 540 nm (622 miles; 1001 km) with maximum payload, or 975 nm (1,123 miles; 1807 km) with maximum fuel and an 8,842-lb (3961-kg) payload
Performance: maximum rate of climb at sea level 1,620 ft (494 m) per minute; service ceiling 30,000 ft (9145 m); take-off run 3,900 ft (1189 m) at 42,000 lb (19051 kg)

Left: The Philippines air force operates eight F27s as transports and one as a Presidential aircraft.

Right: The Pakistan navy obtained four F27s, and both were then converted by Fokker to full F27MPA standard from 1985, supplanting Breguet Atlantics.

Fokker F28 Fellowship

NV Koninklijke Nederlandse Vliegtuigfabreik Fokker
PO Box 12222, NL-1100 AE, Amsterdam-Zuidoost
The Netherlands

Prototype development of the **Fokker F28 Fellowship** twin-jet airliner began with a first flight on 9 May 1967. Production of 241 F28s between 1968 and 1986 included about 20 for military or quasi-military use, the type being particularly successful as a Presidential transport in several smaller nations, most notably in South America and Africa, where its rough-field capability is most appreciated. The most widely used versions were the original 65-seater **Mk 1000** (with fewer seats in VIP configuration), and the **Mk 1000-C** with side-loading freight door and mixed passenger/cargo interior. With the same fuselage, the **Mk 3000** featured increased wing span and uprated engines, while the **Mk 4000** had a longer fuselage accommodating 79 seats.

Examples of the Mk 1000 are flown for Presidential and VIP transportation by **Argentina** (two, air force), **Colombia** (one, air force), **Gabon** (one, operated in civilian marks for the government), **Netherlands** (Dutch Royal Flight, civil registered), **Indonesia** (one, air force), **Ivory Coast** (one, operated in civilian marks for the government), **Peru** (one, air force) and **Togo** (one, operated in civilian marks for the government), while a similar role is performed

by a Mk 3000 in **Ghana** (one, air force) and **Tanzania** (one, operated in civil marks for the government). The **Argentine navy** also operates three F 28 Mk 3000s, and one was deployed to Saudia Arabia in support of coalition operations during Desert Storm. A Mk 4000 can be found in service with the **Ivory Coast** (one, operated in civilian marks for the government). Also, in Colombia, is a single Mk 3000C used by the military airline **SATENA** (based at Bogota), while a similar role is performed by one Mk 4000 of Esc 1111 in **Ecuador**, this being the designation of the military airline **TAME** (based at Quito). This aircraft is civil registered but has been allocated a military serial. In Argentina, the airline **LADE** has the use of four Mk 1000-Cs, in its military role as II Escuadron de Transporte in I Transport Wing. While these aircraft undertake scheduled services to remote (uneconomic) destinations, they wear military colours. **Malaysia** – another early operator of the F28 Mk 1000 – has retired the last of two.

SPECIFICATION

Fokker F28 Mk 3000 Fellowship
Wing: span 25.07 m (82 ft 3 in); aspect ratio 7.96;

area 79.00 m² (850.38 sq ft)
Fuselage and tail: length 27.40 m (89 ft 10.75 in); height 8.47 m (27 ft 9.5 in); tailplane span 8.64 m (28 ft 4.25 in); wheel track 5.04 m (16 ft 6.5 in); wheel base 8.90 m (29 ft 2.5 in)
Powerplant: two Rolls-Royce Spey RB.183-2 Mk 555-15P each rated at 9,900 lb st (44.04 kN) dry
Weights: operating empty 36,997 lb (16781 kg); maximum take-off 73,000 lb (33113 kg)
Fuel and load: internal fuel 17,240 lb (7820 kg) standard or 23,080 lb (10469 kg) optional with centre section tankage; external fuel none; maximum payload

19,000 lb (8618 kg)
Speed: maximum cruising speed at 22,965 ft (7000 m) 454 kt (523 mph; 843 km/h); economical cruising speed at 30,000 ft (9145 m) 466 kt (421 mph; 678 km/h)
Range: 1,710 nm (1,969 miles; 3169 km) with maximum fuel and 65 passengers
Performance: maximum cruising altitude 35,000 ft (10670 m); balanced take-off field length 5,200 ft (1585 m) at maximum take-off weight; balanced landing field length 3,495 ft (1065 m) at normal landing weight

The photograph caption:
Fokker's F28 has proved a popular choice for VIP units in South America. Since 1971 the FAC (Colombian air force) has flown this one example as part of its Presidential flight.

Fokker 50/Enforcer 2/Kingbird/60 Utility

The **Republic of China** air force is the first customer for the **Fokker 50** in its basic transport configuration, with three acquired in 1992. The F50 is a lengthened, re-engined derivative of the F27, first flown on 28 December 1985 and intended primarily for the airline market. In this guise, it can carry 46 to 68 passengers, with combi and all-cargo versions also available.

A range of special-purpose variants is available, based for the most part on equipment fits originally proposed with the F27. These variants include the **Black Crow 2** comm/Elint version, fitted with an ARCO Systems AR-7000 Sigint system; the unarmed **Maritime Mk 2**, fitted with Texas Instruments AN/APS-134 search radar; the armed **Maritime Enforcer Mk 2**

The Enforcer Mk 2 has provision for four torpedoes (Mk 44, 46, Stingray or similar), or depth charges, along with Exocet, Harpoon, Sea Eagle or Sea Skua anti-ship missiles.

for maritime patrol; the **Kingbird Mk 2** for AEW with phased array radar; the **Sentinel Mk 2** with AN/APS-134(V)7 synthetic aperture radar, AN/APS-135(V) SLAR, and podded EO imaging system for surveillance and reconnaissance; and the **Troopship Mk 3** stretched to incorporate a forward cargo door to starboard and capable of carrying 50 troops with paradrop facility. The prototype Enforcer made its maiden flight on 27 January 1993, the only version yet to fly.

In early 1994 deliveries began of four F50s for the **Singapore** air force, as Skyvan replacements with No. 121 Sqn, at Changi. Singapore has options on three further transport versions and is the launch customer for the Maritime Enforcer with five aircraft on order. The latter will be fitted with a 360° radar (Texas Instruments APS-134), a GEC VOO-1069 FLIR, a CAE ASQ-504(V) internal MAD and a CDC UYS-503 sonobuoy processing suite.

An order in 1994 from the **Royal Netherlands Air Force** launched

Fokker's latest military turboprop development, the **Fokker 60 Utility**. Based on the Fokker 50 Utility/Troopship, the F60 is stretched by a further 1.62 m (5 ft 4 in) to accommodate a cargo door measuring 3.05 x 1.78 m (10 ft x 5 ft 10 in), which enables the aircraft to carry an F100 engine for an F-16. Fokker is also developing and integrating a dedicated infra-red suppression and RWR fit for the Dutch air force. The cost of this will be covered through a royalty agreement between Fokker and the air force for the first 12 export aircraft fitted with similar equipment.

SPECIFICATION

Fokker 50 Maritime Enforcer Mk 2
Wing: span 29.00 m (95 ft 1.75 in); aspect ratio 12.0; area 70.00 m² (753.50 sq ft)
Fuselage and tail: length 25.247 m (82 ft 10 in); height 8.317 m (27 ft 3.5 in); tailplane span 9.746 m (31 ft 11.75 in); wheel track 7.20 m (23 ft 7.5 in);

wheel base 9.70 m (31 ft 10 in)
Powerplant: two Pratt & Whitney Canada PW125B each flat-rated at 2,500 shp (1864 kW)
Weights: operating empty 29,352 lb (13314 kg); normal take-off 45,900 lb (20820 kg); maximum take-off 47,500 lb (21545 kg); maximum emergency take-off 50,000 lb (22680 kg)
Fuel and load: maximum fuel 16,000 lb (7257 kg) including two 938-litre (248US gal) underwing auxiliary tanks
Speed: normal cruising speed at optimum altitude 259 kt (298 mph; 480 km/h); typical patrol speed at 2,000 ft (610 m) 149 kt (172 mph; 277 km/h)
Range: ferry range 3,680 nm (4,237 miles; 6820 km); operational radius 1,200 nm (1,382 miles; 2224 km) with a 4,000-lb (1814-kg) mission load
Performance: service ceiling 25,000 ft (7620 m); take-off run 5,000 ft (1524 m) at 47,000 lb (21320 kg); landing run 2,500 ft (762 m) at normal landing weight

The second Fokker 50 served as the the Enforcer 2 prototype, and performed the initial systems and avionics integration.

Fokker 100

First flown on 30 November 1986, the **Fokker 100** is an extensively modernised, upgraded and lengthened derivative of the F28, offering airlines a 107-seat twin-turbofan short/medium-range airliner. Some 250 have been ordered, with more than 100 on option, and production proceeds at a rate exceeding five a month. Among customers to date only one is of quasi-military nature, involving a single air-

craft leased as a Presidential transport in the **Ivory Coast**. A VIP version with an appropriate cabin layout and optional belly fuel tanks is designated **Fokker Executive Jet 100**. There is also a quick-change cargo version, the **Fokker 100QC**.

SPECIFICATION

Fokker 100
Wing: span 28.08 m (92 ft 1.5 in); aspect ratio 8.4; area 93.50 m² (1,006.46 sq ft)
Fuselage and tail: length 35.53 m (116 ft 6.75 in);

height 8.50 m (27 ft 10.5 in); tailplane span 10.04 m (32 ft 11.25 in); wheel track 5.04 m (16 ft 6.5 in); wheel base 14.01 m (45 ft 11.5 in)
Powerplant: two Rolls-Royce Tay Mk 620-15 each rated at 13,850 lb st (61.61 kN) dry, or two Rolls-Royce Tay Mk 650-15 each rated at 15,100 lb st (67.17 kN) dry
Weights: typical operating empty 24355 kg (53,693 lb); maximum take-off 43090 kg (94,996 lb) standard or 44450 kg (97,993 lb) optional
Fuel and load: internal fuel 13040 litres (3,445 US gal) standard or 14590 litres (3,854 US gal) optional; external fuel none; maximum payload 12385 kg (27,304 lb)

Speed: maximum operating speed 'clean' at 24,200 ft (7375 m) 452 kt (520 mph; 837 km/h)
Range: 1,340 nm (1,543 miles; 2,483 km) at standard maximum take-off weight with 107 passengers and Tay Mk 650-15 engines, or 1,525 nm (1,756 miles; 2826 km) at optional maximum take-off weight with 107 passengers and Tay Mk 650-15 engines
Performance: service ceiling 35,000 ft (10670 m); balanced take-off field length 6,070 ft (1850 m) at maximum take-off weight with Tay Mk 620-15 engines or 5,512 ft (1680 m) at maximum take-off weight with Tay Mk 650-15 engines; balanced landing field length 4,594 ft (1400 m) at maximum landing weight

Fuji-Bell **HU-1H and Advanced 205B**

Fuji Heavy Industries Ltd
Subaru Building, 7-2, 1-chome
Nishi-shinjuku Shinjuku-ku, Tokyo 160, Japan

The sole production source of the Bell Model 205 helicopter is now Fuji in Japan, which manufactures the Bell UH-1H under sub-licence from Bell's Japanese licensee, Mitsui and Co. An earlier production programme involved the construction of 34 Bell 204Bs and 22 Bell 204B-2s. The standard production model for the **JGSDF** is designated **HU-1H** and utilises the same airframe as the Bell UH-1H, but introduces composite rotor blades and a two-bladed tractor tail rotor. The first Fuji-built example flew in July 1973. Over 130 Fuji-built Bell UH-1B/Hs have been delivered to the JGSDF, 40 of which have been converted

for mine-laying duties. A total of 149 HU-1Hs had been ordered by the end of 1993.

A joint Fuji-Bell upgrade of the Model 205 first flew in Texas on 23 April 1988. Initially designated the **Advanced Model 205A-1**, this version introduces UH-1N-type tapered rotor blades, a Textron Lycoming T53-L-703 engine, and Model 212-type transmission rated at 962 kW (1,290 shp) with LIVE (Liquid Inertial Vibration Eliminator). It has now been redesignated the **Advanced 205B**. The upgraded variant was demonstrated to the US Army and undertook a sales tour of the Far East in 1989, but has so far failed to secure any orders.

SPECIFICATION

Fuji-Bell UH-1H
Rotor system: main rotor diameter 48 ft 0 in (14.63 m); tail rotor diameter 8 ft 6 in (2.59 m); main rotor disc area 1,809.56 sq ft (168.11 m2); tail rotor disc area 56.74 sq ft (5.27 m2)
Fuselage and tail: length overall, tail rotor turning 44 ft 10 in (13.67 m) and fuselage 40 ft 7 in (12.37 m); height overall 14 ft 6 in (4.42 m) with tail rotor turning and 13 ft 0.75 in (3.98 m) to top of rotor head; stabiliser span 9 ft 4 in (2.84 m); skid track 8 ft 6.5 in (2.60 m)
Powerplant: one Kawasaki (Textron Lycoming)

T53-K-13B rated at 1,400 shp (1044 kW)
Weights: empty 5,270 lb (2390 kg); maximum take-off 9,500 lb (4309 kg)
Fuel and load: internal fuel 223 US gal (844 litres) plus provision for 300 US gal (1136 litres) of auxiliary fuel in two tanks; external fuel none; maximum payload 3,880 lb (1759 kg)
Speed: maximum level and cruising speed at optimum altitude 110 kt (127 mph; 204 km/h)
Range: at sea level 252 nm (290 miles; 467 km)
Performance: maximum rate of climb at sea level 1,600 ft (488 m) per minute; service ceiling 12,600 ft (3840 m); hovering ceiling 13,600 ft (4145 m) in ground effect and 1,100 ft (335 m) out of ground effect

Fuji **KM-2/T-3**

After building 124 examples of the Beech T-34A under licence, Fuji developed an improved **KM-2** version to serve the **JMSDF** as a primary trainer. The first flew in July 1962 and was delivered in late September. Sixty-two were procured with the name **Kornadori** (robin), although this name is no longer used. The KM-2 was powered by a 340-hp (254-kW) Lycoming IGSO-480-A1C6 engine and supplied primarily to the 201st Kyoiku Kokutai (air training squadron) at Ozuki, where about 20 remained in 1994. Two **TL-1**s delivered to **JGSDF** in 1981 are army equivalents of the KM-2 and remain in service as trainers at the Koku Gakko (air training school). Equivalent to the KM-2 for the **JASDF**, the **T-3** first flew on 17 January 1978, production of 50 being spread over the next 14 years for service with the 11th and 12th Hiko Kyoikudans (flying training wings). Based at Shizuhama and Hofu respectively, the T-3s provide the first 75 hours of primary pilot training in the JASDF.

SPECIFICATION

Fuji KM-2B
Wing: span 10.04 m (32 ft 11.25 in); aspect ratio 6.11; area 16.50 m2 (177.61 sq ft)

Fuselage and tail: length 8.036 m (26 ft 4.25 in); height 3.023 m (9 ft 11 in); elevator span 3.712 m (12 ft 2.25 in); wheel track 2.924 m (9 ft 7 in); wheel base 2.266 m (7 ft 5.25 in)
Powerplant: one Textron Lycoming IGSO-480-A1A6 rated at 340 hp (254 kW)
Weights: empty 1120 kg (2,469 lb); maximum take-off 1510 kg (3,329 lb)
Fuel and load: internal fuel 70 US gal (265 litres); external fuel none; maximum ordnance none
Speed: never-exceed speed 223 kt (257 mph; 413 km/h);

Though it bears the hallmarks of the Beech design, Fuji's T-3 is intended as a successor to the T-34 Mentor. JASDF pilots who have completed their 75-hour course in the T-3 graduate to the newly-arrived Kawasaki T-4.

maximum level speed 'clean' at 16,000 ft (4875 m) 203 kt (234 mph; 377 km/h); maximum cruising speed at 8,000 ft (2440 m) 177 kt (204 mph; 328 km/h); economical cruising speed at 8,000 ft (2440 m) 137 kt (158 mph; 254 km/h)
Range: 521 nm (600 miles; 965 km)
Performance: maximum rate of climb at sea level

1,520 ft (463 m) per minute; service ceiling 26,800 ft (8170 m); take-off run 870 ft (265 m) at maximum take-off weight; take-off distance to 50 ft (15 m) 1,650 ft (503 m); landing distance from 50 ft (15 m) 1,430 ft (436 m) at normal landing weight; landing run 780 ft (238 m) at normal landing weight

Fuji **T-1**

Japan's first indigenous jet aircraft design to enter production, the **Fuji T-1** evolved as a basic trainer for the **JASDF**. It featured modestly swept wings and tandem seating beneath a long canopy. The definitive version was to be powered by the 2,645-lb st (11.8-kN) Ishikawajima-Harima J3-IHI-3 engine, and was designated Fuji **T1F1**. However, a Bristol Orpheus 805 engine was used in the initial production batch of 44 **T-1A**s (Fuji **T1F2**s) ordered by the JASDF after testing two prototypes, the first of which flew on 19 January 1958. These were followed by 20 **T-1B**s with the J3 engine, initially flown in the converted first prototype on 17 May 1960. The designation **T-1C** (**T1F3**) referred to aircraft retrofitted with an uprated 3,085-lb st (13.8-kN) J3-IHI-7 engine, first flown in April 1965. The T-1 was named **Hatsutaka** (Young Hawk) in 1964 but the name is no longer used.

Delivery of T-1As began in 1959, deliveries of the T-1B ending in 1963. Most aircraft went into service with the 13th Hiko Kyoikudan (Air Training Wing) at Ashiya, for the second phase of pilot training. The type remains in service, but from 1988 has been phased out in favour of the Kawasaki T-4.

Few Fuji T-1s remain in service. Those that do are largely in the hands of the APW and 13th ATW.

SPECIFICATION

Fuji T-1A
Wing: span 10.49 m (34 ft 5 in); aspect ratio 4.95; area 22.22 m2 (239.18 sq ft)
Fuselage and tail: length 12.12 m (39 ft 9.2 in); height 4.08 m (13 ft 4.6 in); tailplane span 4.40 m (14 ft 5 in); wheel track 3.20 m (10 ft 6 in); wheel base 3.86 m (12 ft 8 in)

Powerplant: one Rolls-Royce (Bristol Siddeley) Orpheus Mk 805 rated at 4,000 lb st (17.79 kN) dry
Weights: empty equipped 2420 kg (5,335 lb); normal take-off 4150 kg (9,149 lb); maximum take-off 5000 kg (11,023 lb)
Fuel and load: internal fuel 370 US gal (1401 litres); external fuel up to two 120-US gal (454-litre) drop tanks; maximum ordnance 680 kg (1,500 lb)
Speed: maximum level speed 'clean' at 36,000 ft (10975 m) 499 kt (575 mph; 925 km/h) but limited in

practice to 464 kt (534 mph; 859 km/h); cruising speed at 30,000 ft (9145 m) 334 kt (385 mph; 620 km/h)
Range: ferry range 1,004 nm (1,156 miles; 1860 km) with drop tanks; range 702 nm (808 miles; 1300 km) with standard fuel
Performance: maximum rate of climb at sea level 6,500 ft (1981 m) per minute; service ceiling 47,245 ft (14400 m); take-off run 1,300 ft (396 m) at normal take-off weight; take-off distance to 50 ft (15 m) 2,000 ft (610 m) at normal take-off weight

Fuji T-5

Fuji developed a turboprop version of the KM-2 in 1984 as the **KM-2D**, the prototype making its first flight on 28 June that year. Certification in Japanese aerobatic and utility categories was obtained on 14 February 1985. With an emerging requirement to update its fleet of KM-2 trainers, the **JMSDF** contracted Fuji in March 1987 for the development of a further improved turboprop variant, the **KM-2Kai**, featuring a modernised cockpit with side-by-side seating and a sliding canopy in place of the original KM-2's side doors and the KM-2B's tandem seats. There is room in the cockpit for a further two seats. Designated **T-5** in Japan's joint services system, the first production KM-2Kai flew on 27 April 1988, and orders have been placed to date for 29 T-5 conversions of KM-2s. Service use is concentrated in 201 Kokutai of the Ozuki Kyoiku Kokuyun, alongside the remaining KM-2Bs.

This is the first production Fuji T-5 (KM-2Kai) delivered to the JASDF. Procurement is proceeding at a modest pace whenever yearly funding is released.

SPECIFICATION

Fuji KM-2Kai (T-5)
Wing: span 10.04 m (32 ft 11.25 in); aspect ratio 6.11; area 16.50 m² (177.61 sq ft)
Fuselage and tail: length 8.44 m (27 ft 8.25 in); height 2.96 m (9 ft 8.5 in); elevator span 3.712 m (12 ft 2.25 in); wheel track 2.924 m (9 ft 7 in); wheel base 2.266 m (7 ft 5.25 in)
Powerplant: one Allison 250-B17D flat-rated at 350 shp (261 kW)
Weights: empty 1082 kg (2,385 lb); normal take-off 1585 kg (3,494 lb); maximum take-off 1805 kg (3,979 lb)
Fuel and load: internal fuel 644 kg (1,420 lb)

Speed: never exceed speed 223 kt (256 mph; 413 km/h); maximum level speed 'clean' at 8,000 ft (2440 m) 193 kt (222 mph; 357 km/h); economical cruising speed at 8,000 ft (2440 m) 155 kt (178 mph; 287 km/h)
Range: 510 nm (587 miles; 945 km)
Performance: maximum rate of climb at sea level 1,700 ft (518 m) per minute; service ceiling 25,000 ft (7620 m); take-off run 990 ft (302 m) at maximum take-off weight; take-off distance to 50 ft (15 m) 1,410 m (430 m); landing distance from 50 ft (15 m) 1,690 ft (515 m) at normal landing weight; landing run 570 ft (174 m) at normal landing weight

General Dynamics F-111A/D/E/G, R/F-111C and FB-111A

Developed to meet a **US** joint service requirement for a long-range interceptor (Navy) and deep-strike interdictor (Air Force), the **General Dynamics F-111** had a long and troubled development, and it was not until late in its career that it achieved its true potential. The **F-111B** Navy fighter was cancelled in 1968 after having proved considerably overweight, creating a vacuum that was eventually filled by the F-14 Tomcat. The Air Force variants were more successful, but the 'Aardvark' suffered many setbacks before emerging as arguably the world's best long-range interdictor platform.

Among the many innovations introduced by the F-111, the most notable was the variable-geometry wing – the first on a combat aircraft. The wing sweeps from 16° to 72.5°, conferring the ability to take off with a heavy load of fuel and weapons yet achieve supersonic speed at low level and up to Mach 2.5 at altitude. A 'clean' F-111 has the ability to 'supercruise' (fly supersonically without afterburner), a feature made much of with the ATF requirement of the 1990s. Power is provided by a pair of fuel-efficient TF30s, but in the early versions the thrust was considered insufficient. Although there is a weapons bay, most ordnance is carried on the wing pylons. The side-by-side crew occupy a cockpit escape capsule, which ejects in one piece – another novelty of the type.

The F-111 first flew on 21 December 1964, and the first of 141 **F-111A**s entered service in 1967. This variant saw service in South East Asia in 1968 and 1972-75. The second production variant was the **F-111E**, which differed from the A model by having slightly upgraded avionics. These aircraft served for most of their career at Upper Heyford in England. Following was the **F-111D**, which had more powerful engines and radically updated avionics system. When it worked, the system was by far the most capable fitted to any 'Aardvark', but it was maintenance-intensive and ultimately proved over-ambitious. The F-111D served with the 27th TFW at Cannon AFB, NM, until final retirement in late 1992.

Strategic Air Command purchased the **FB-111A** model, which was equipped for strategic nuclear missions. This featured longer-span wings for additional range. When these were retired, some were reworked for the 27th TFW as **F-111G**s, and these served in a training role until 1993. Currently the only early-generation aircraft left in USAF service are 25 F-111Es which were transferred to Cannon in 1993 to fulfil a type conversion role with the 428th Fighter Squadron, 27th Fighter Wing. All these aircraft have received the AMP avionics upgrade.

Export sales were limited to **Australia**, although the Royal Air Force ordered (and subsequently cancelled) the type. Australia's aircraft were delivered in 1973 after a prolonged wrangle over technical difficulties. Featuring the long-span wings of the FB-111A but the low-powered engines and avionics of the F-111A, the **F-111C** was purchased for service with No. 82 Wing at RAAF Amberley, Queensland, which received 24. Four ex-USAF F-111As were purchased as attrition replacements and modified to F-111C standard, and in the early 1990s the RAAF purchased 15 F-111Gs (FB-111As). Originally these were to be held in storage for when the current F-111C fleet reached the end of its fatigue life, but the first examples have already entered service. All RAAF F-111C/Gs have entered an Avionics Upgrade Program.

No. 82 Wing has two squadrons. No. 1 Squadron is the main strike unit, flying 12 aircraft. These can be equipped with the Pave Tack acquisition/designation pod, laser-guided bombs and GBU-15 EO-guided bombs (although the associated datalink pod was not supplied, limiting GBU-15 attacks to line-of-sight only) and a complete range of free-fall weapons, including the indigenous Karinga cluster bomb. A maritime attack capability is conferred by the ability to launch up to four AGM-84 Harpoon anti-ship missiles; AGM-88 HARM is also integrated with the F-111C.

In addition to strike duties, No. 6 Squadron is tasked with type conversion and with reconnaissance. For the latter role it operates four **RF-111C** aircraft. These were modified from F-111Cs with a multi-sensor reconnaissance pallet mounted in the former bomb bay. The pallet mounts panoramic and vertical cameras, TV monitors and infra-red linescan. A single F-111 is assigned for test duties to the ARDU (Aircraft Research and Development Unit) at RAAF Edinburgh, New South Wales.

Above: No. 6 Sqn, with its blue lightning flash, is the RAAF's de facto F-111 OCU, but is also tasked with a reconnaissance role. This is undertaken by four RF-111Cs, one of which is seen here.

Below: Operating outside the dedicated F-111 world of No. 82 Wing is the Aircraft Research and Development Unit (ARDU), based at RAAF Edinburgh. It is assigned this F-111C, largely for weapons trials.

SPECIFICATION

General Dynamics F-111A and F-111E
generally similar to the General Dynamics F-111F except in the following particulars:
Powerplant: two Pratt & Whitney TF30-P-3 each rated at 18,500 lb st (82.29 kN) with afterburning
Weights: operating empty 46,172 lb (20943 kg); maximum take-off 91,300 lb (41414 kg)
Fuel and load: internal fuel 5,033 US gal (19052 litres

SPECIAL FEATURES
Australian F-111Cs have been heavily modified since their introduction, becoming almost as capable as USAF F-111Fs. All are compatible with the AVQ-26 Pave Tack laser designator and can carry the GBU-15 electro-optical, glide bomb. Unique among the F-111 community is their AGM-84 Harpoon, and AGM-88 HARM capability.

WING STRUCTURE
The F-111C has inherited the long-span wings of the FB-111, which span 70 ft (21.34 m) at minimum angle, compared to 63 ft (19.20 m) for USAF F-111s. At maximum sweep this decreases to 33 ft 11 in (10.34 m) for the F-111C as opposed to 31 ft 11½ in (9.74 m) for USAF aircraft. The wings move between 16° and 72.5°, feature a NACA 63 aerofoil section throughout and are built around five spars. The skin is made from sculpted panels, each machined in one piece running from root to tip.

AUP
Rockwell has developed an Avionics Update Program (AUP) similar to the Pacer Strike modification for F-111Fs. The most important element of this is the substitution for 256K weapons computers of the 64K units now carried. Other USAF improvements, such as the very high-speed integrated-circuit computer complex (VCC), will most likely be added in time.

ARMAMENT
In the precision strike role, RAAF F-111s are equipped with 2,000-lb GBU-10 (illustrated) and 500-lb GBU-12 Paveway II LGBs. Ten Pave Tack laser designators are available to provide guidance for these weapons. A self-defence fit of two AIM-9P Sidewinders can be carried on shoulder pylons. An important new addition to the F-111's armoury is the AGM-84 Harpoon anti-ship missile, which significantly increases Australia's ability to protect its sea lanes.

MARKINGS
The Australian 'Aardvarks' were delivered in the standard three-tone 'South East Asia' scheme of the USAF, with black undersides, and thus most have remained. However, the first AUP aircraft was repainted in the US in an overall grey scheme and this is likely to be adopted fleetwide. The fin is adorned with the squadron marking, in this case No. 6 Sqn's blue lightning bolt. No. 1 Sqn once wore a similar yellow flash, but this has now given way to a swept numeral '1' (still in yellow) with a kookaburra superimposed. All aircraft retain the national flag on the fintip, in front of the rudder.

General Dynamics F-111C

Finally acquired in 1973 after a 10-year procurement nightmare, the F-111Cs have provided the RAAF with its prime strike aircraft ever since. They have also been developed into a long-range reconnaissance platform, and adapted for increasingly important maritime strike duties. Currently undergoing the AUP upgrade in the USA, F-111s will remain in RAAF service for many years yet. To this end, 15 ex-USAF F-111Gs (converted FB-111As) have been acquired to augment the F-111Cs.

General Dynamics F-111F

Last of the F-111's production variants, the **F-111F** is also the last in operational service with the **US Air Force**, flying with the 522nd, 523rd and 524th Fighter Squadrons of the 27th Fighter Wing at Cannon AFB, NM.

Production of the F-111F totalled 106, initial deliveries going to Mountain Home AFB, ID, from 1972. In 1977 the force was deployed to Lakenheath in England with the 48th TFW. In 1992, the force returned to the United States after replacement by the F-15E Eagle.

Although not as capable in avionics terms as the F-111D, the F-111F nevertheless proved much easier to maintain. Mk IIB avionics, as developed for the FB-111A, were combined with the Weapons Control

Panel from the F-111E. The main attack radar is the AN/APQ-161, allied to the AN/APQ-171 terrain-following radar.

By far the most important improvement introduced by the F-111F was the uprated powerplant, the TF30-P-100, which raised thrust:weight ratio from 0.39 in the early variants to 0.53. Thus, the F was the only version not considered to be underpowered.

F-111Fs were built (like all 'Aardvarks' except for the FB-111A/F-111G) with provision for a 20-mm Vulcan cannon in the weapons bay, but in practice this has never been used. For self-defence the F-111F routinely carries the AIM-9P-3 Sidewinder – later versions of this missile have larger fins and there is insufficient clearance for their use. On the F model, the weapons bay is

now used primarily for the carriage of the AN/AVQ-26 Pave Tack pod, which incorporates a FLIR sensor and bore-sighted laser rangefinder/designator. This allows the aircraft to autonomously deliver laser-guided bombs.

Primary weapons of the F-111F are the 500-lb GBU-12 Paveway II, 2,000-lb GBU-10 Paveway II and 2,000-lb GBU-24 Paveway III laser-guided bombs. The latter allows a low-level delivery profile with great accuracy, or delivery at medium altitude from a greater stand-off range. Both 2,000-lb weapons are available with either a standard Mk 84 warhead or a BLU-109 penetration warhead for use against hardened targets such as bunkers or aircraft shelters. The GBU-28 'Deep Throat' is a 4,800-lb Paveway III

weapon hastily developed during Desert Storm to penetrate and destroy very deep bunkers. Only two were delivered, on the last night of the conflict.

Additionally, the F-111F routinely carries a wide range of 'dumb' ordnance, including iron bombs, cluster weapons and BLU-107 Durandal runway-cratering munitions. The capability remains for the carriage of free-fall nuclear weapons, principally the B61 tactical weapon. An F-111F speciality is the GBU-15 2,000-lb EO-guided bomb. This has either a Mk 84 or BLU-109 warhead, and has either a TV- or IR-seeker adapted from those fitted to Maverick missiles. For stand-off launch, the AXQ-14 or ZWS-1 datalink pod is fitted to guide the GBU-15s.

F-111Fs have seen considerably more action than other variants. Aircraft from the 48th TFW at Lakenheath were chosen to attack targets around Tripoli during the April 1986 Operation El Dorado Canyon raid. In August 1990 the wing began to deploy 'Aardvarks' to Taif in Saudi Arabia, and during the ensuing Gulf War 66 F-111Fs were in-theatre. Using a wide range of weapons, but specialising in LGB attacks, the F-111Fs proved to be the real workhorses of the air war, accounting for the greatest proportion of targets destroyed in Iraq and Kuwait. Apart from the 'bunker-busting' GBU-28 attacks, notable exploits were the GBU-15 attack on an oil pumping station to halt an environmentally disastrous flow of oil into the Gulf, 'tank-plinking' anti-armour missions with GBU-12s, the leading role in the

Left: A fully armed F-111F of the 492nd TFS 'Bowlers'/48th TFW (Provisional) displays its warload of GBU-24 Paveway III LGBs and AIM-9P-3 Sidewinders for defence.

Left: This is the 2,000-lb GBU-28 'Deep Throat' penetration bomb dropped on the Al Taji command bunker on the last night of the Gulf War. The GBU-28 was specially developed using spare naval gun barrels as strong casings.

Below: The USAF's F-111 (and EF-111) fleet is now centralised at Cannon AFB. They are scheduled to remain in service until 2015 at the earliest.

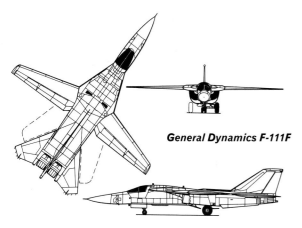

General Dynamics F-111F

shelter and bridge take-down campaign, and a direct hit on an ammunition store which caused the largest man-made non-nuclear explosion ever recorded by seismologists.

Since the end of the Gulf War, a detachment of F-111Fs (with a number of F-15Es) remains in Turkey as part of Operation Provide Comfort. The 84 surviving F-111Fs are undergoing the Pacer Strike update, managed by Rockwell. This replaces analog systems with digital avionics, and will keep the F-111Fs current up to their planned retirement date in 2010. Despite the considerable capabilities of the F-111F in the low-

level, night/adverse weather precision attack regime (unmatched by any other current type), the force is a prime candidate for early retirement. All USAF F-111 airframes, including EF-111s (described separately), are now concentrated in a six-squadron wing at Cannon AFB.

SPECIFICATION

General Dynamics F-111F
Wing: span 63 ft 0 in (19.20 m) spread and 31 ft 11.4 in (9.74 m) swept; aspect ratio 7.56 spread and 1.55

swept; area 525.00 sq ft (48.77 m²) spread and 657.07 sq ft (61.07 m²) spread
Fuselage and tail: length 73 ft 6 in (22.40 m); height 17 ft 1.4 in (5.22 m)
Powerplant: two Pratt & Whitney TF30-P-100 each rated at 25,100 lb st (111.65 kN) with afterburning
Weights: operating empty 47,481 lb (21537 kg); maximum take-off 100,000 lb (45360 kg)
Fuel and load: internal fuel 5,025 US gal (19021 litres); external fuel up to four 600-US gal (2271-litre) drop tanks; maximum ordnance 31,500 lb (14228 kg)
Speed: maximum level speed 'clean' at 36,000 ft (10975 m) 1,433 kt (1,650 mph; 2655 km/h); cruising speed at high altitude 496 kt (571 mph; 919 km/h)

Four F-111F loaded with GBU-24A/Bs prepare to taxi out from their shelters at Taif, Saudi Arabia, during Operation Desert Storm. The first F-111s arrived in Saudi on 25 August 1990, but had to wait until the night of 16 January 1991 for action.

Range: more than 2,540 nm (2,925 miles; 4707 km) with internal fuel
Performance: service ceiling 60,000 ft (18290 m); take-off distance to 50 ft (15 m) 3,120 ft (951 m); landing run less than 3,000 ft (915 m) at normal landing weight

Gloster **Meteor**

Britain's first jet fighter to achieve production, the Meteor has now all but disappeared after lengthy service in several versions. In the UK, one **D.Mk 16** target drone continues to serve at DRA Llanbedr (with one in storage); this version is a derivative of the original **F.Mk 8** single-seat fighter. For trials of its ejection seats, Mar-

tin-Baker has long made use of specially-modified **T.Mk 7 (Mod)** two-seaters (often referred to as **T.Mk 7½**), and has four airframes at Chalgrove, of which two are used to provide spares for the airworthy pair.

The last Meteors can be found with ejection-seat manufacturer Martin-Baker (above, named 'Asterix') and the DRA, with a Meteor D.Mk 16 drone.

Grob **G 103 Viking** and **G 109 Vigilant**

Burkhart Grob Luft- und Raumfahrtb GMBH & Co KG
Am Flugplatz, D-8939 Mattsies
Germany

The German sailplane producer Grob has specialised in the development of glass-fibre airframes. To replace a long-serving fleet of wooden gliders used by the Volunteer Gliding Schools of the ATC, the British Defence Ministry selected in 1984 the **Grob G 103 Twin II Acro** tandem two-seat sailplane. An order for 100 was placed and the designation **Viking T.Mk 1** assigned to these aircraft, delivery of which began in September 1984. The Viking T.Mk 1 now equips those Air Cadet Volunteer Gliding Schools that provide winch-launched training, with the **Vigilant T.Mk 1 (Grob G 109)** at the self-launching schools.

The **G 109B** powered sailplane was first flown in March 1983 as a version of the G 109 with increased wing span. Production ended in 1986 but was resumed in 1990 to meet an RAF order for 53. As the **Vigilant**

T.Mk 1, the G 109B entered service in March 1990 and serves at the Volunteer Gliding Schools of the ATC and CCF, and at the Air Cadets Central Gliding School. The Vigilant is powered by a Limbach engine, while the G 109B is usually fitted with a 90-hp (67-kW) Grob 2500 engine. This variant is used by the quasi-military **Royal Thai Aero Club** at Don Muang.

SPECIFICATION

Grob G 109
Wing: span 16.60 m (54 ft 5.5 in); aspect ratio 13.5; area 20.40 m² (219.59 sq ft)
Fuselage and tail: length 7.80 m (25 ft 7 in); height 1.80 m (5 ft 10.75 in)
Powerplant: one Limbach L 2000 EB 1A rated at 80 hp (59 kW)

Weights: empty 580 kg (1,278 lb); maximum take-off 825 kg (1,818 lb)
Fuel and load: internal fuel 80 litres (21.1 US gal); external fuel none
Speed: maximum level speed 'clean' at optimum

altitude 129 kt (149 mph; 240 km/h) in smooth air or 100 kt (115 mph; 185 km/h) in rough air
Performance: best glide ratio 30 at 65 kt (75 mph; 120 km/h); minimum sinking speed 3.77 ft (1.15 m) per second at 51 kt (59 mph; 95 km/h)

To the RAF's Volunteer Gliding Schools the Grob G 109 is known as the Vigilant T.Mk 1. The type has replaced Slingsby Ventures at the 12 VGS sites.

Grob/E-Systems/Garrett Egrett/Strato 1

A 'poor-man's U-2R', the Egrett originated to meet a **Luftwaffe** requirement for a long-duration high-altitude surveillance aircraft, after plans to acquire a squadron of Lockheed TR-1s had been abandoned. A three-company group collaborated to initiate the project, comprising Grob in Germany, and E-Systems and Garrett in the US, from which the name **Egrett** was derived. Grob was primarily responsible for design of the essentially glass-fibre airframe, Garrett contributed the powerplant, and E-Systems, as programme leader, was responsible for systems integration.

The Egrett concept makes use of a single-seat fuselage providing adequate space for a variety of interchangeable mission packages (including electronics, electro-optical or IR surveillance, long-range radar). Long-span wings of very high aspect ratio demonstrate sailplane design influence and underline the Egrett's high-altitude role and, combined with the efficient TPE331 turboprop, allow the aircraft to fly for long periods at high altitude.

A proof-of-concept vehicle, the **D-450 Egrett I**, flew on 24 June 1987 in Germany, and in September 1988 this set a class-altitude record of 53,787 ft (16394 m). The D-450 had a span of 28.00 m (91 ft 10 in) and, unlike the definitive version, was fitted with a fixed main landing gear. It was followed on 20 April 1989 by the first **D-500 Egrett II**, with a second similar D-500 flying on 9 September 1990 and two more completed in 1991. Egrett II has a 33.00-m (108-ft 3-in) wingspan and retractable main gear, stowage for which is provided in wing fairings. The fourth aircraft (**Prisma**) introduced detachable winglets while the fifth, equipped especially for civilian communications relay, was named **Strato 1**.

Funded by the Luftwaffe since 1987, the Egrett-2 met the so-called 'EASysluft' requirement for a data-gathering and evaluation system, which it is the Luftwaffe's responsibility to provide on behalf of all three services. Late in 1992 official approval was given for production of 10 more D-500s, of which one was to be a two-seater, with deliveries from 1997 to 2001. Despite plans being drawn up to base 16 operational Egretts at Pferdsfeld, the Luftwaffe programme was subsequently cancelled in February 1993 in the light of the lack of threat posed by eastern Europe. Construction of the **G-520T** two-seater continued, however, and this aircraft flew on 21 April 1993. This has obtained German

and US certification, but a launch customer has yet to be found.

SPECIFICATION

Grob/E-Systems/Garrett Egrett II
Wing: span 31.40 m (103 ft 0.25 in)
Fuselage and tail: length 12.20 m (40 ft 0.25 in); height 5.80 m (19 ft 0.25 in); wheel track about 4.80 m (15 ft 9 in); wheel base about 3.66 m (12 ft 0 in)
Powerplant: one Garrett TPE331-14F rated at about 800 shp (596.5 kW)
Weights: maximum take-off 4700 kg (10,362 lb)
Fuel and load: internal fuel 1075 kg (2,370 kg); external fuel none; maximum payload 1000 kg (2,205 lb)
Speed: maximum level speed 'clean' at optimum

The model in which the Luftwaffe was interested was the D-500 Egrett II. Various sensors could be housed in the lower fuselage, a direction-finding antenna being shown here.

altitude 240 kt (276 mph; 445 km/h); maximum cruising speed at optimum altitude 190 kt (219 mph; 352 km/h)
Range: endurance limited to between 10 and 12 hours by pilot fatigue
Performance: maximum rate of climb at sea level more than 1,500 ft (457 m) per minute; climb to 40,000 ft (12190 m) in 35 minutes 0 seconds; service ceiling more than 45,000 ft (13715 m); take-off run 2,000 ft (656 m) at maximum take-off weight
g limits: -3 to +5 in gust conditions

Grob Strato 2C

Designed for stratospheric and climatic research, the **Grob Strato 2C** also has potential for development in the military

surveillance role. Construction of a prototype is financed by the German Ministry for Research and Development, with first flight

set for November 1994. Using experience gained with the Egrett-1 programme, Grob adopted all-composite construction and two 400-hp (300-kW) Teledyne Continental GT-550 piston engines driving five-bladed propellers. The crew of two will have a pres-

surised cockpit with galley and toilet, as the Strato 2C has a planned endurance of 48 hours and a maximum range of 25,300 nm (29,130 miles/18100 km) at altitudes up to 85,300 ft (26000 m).

Grumman A-6/KA-6 Intruder

Grumman Corporation
1111 Stewart Avenue, Bethpage
NY 11714, USA

During the Korean War the US services flew more attack missions than any other, in the case of the **US Navy** and **US Marine Corps** primarily with elderly piston-engined aircraft. What they learned during this conflict convinced them of the need for a specially-designed jet attack aircraft that could operate effectively in the worst weather. In 1957 eight companies submitted 11 designs in a US Navy competition for a new long-range, low-level tactical strike aircraft. Grumman's **G-128** design,

selected on the last day of the year, was to fulfil that requirement admirably, becoming a major combat type in the later war in South East Asia, and leading to a family of later versions.

Eight development **A-6A**s (originally designated **A2F-1**) were ordered in March 1959, a full-scale mock-up was completed and accepted some six months later, and the first flight was made on 19 April 1960. The jet pipes of its two 8,500-lb (37.81-kN) static thrust Pratt & Whitney J52-P-6

engines were designed to swivel downwards, to provide an additional component of lift during take-off. This feature was omitted from production aircraft, which instead have jet pipes with a permanent slight downward deflection. The first production A-6As were delivered to US Navy Attack Squadron VA-42 in February 1963, and by the end of the following year deliveries had reached 83, to VA-65, VA-75 and VA-85 of the US Navy and VMA(AW)-242 of the US Marine Corps.

The first unit to fly on combat duties in Vietnam was VA-75, whose A-6As began operating from USS *Independence* in March 1965, and from then Intruders of various models became heavily involved in fighting in South East Asia. Their DIANE (Digital Integrated Attack Navigation Equipment) gave them a first-class operating ability and efficiency in the worst of the humid, stormy weather offered by the local climate, and with a maximum ordnance load of more than 17,000 lb (7711 kg) they were a potent addition to the US arsenal in South East Asia.

An A-6E practises dive attacks with dummy Mk 83 bombs. The Intruder forms the backbone of the US Navy's heavy attack capability, capable of launching most of the stores in the inventory.

Production of the basic A-6A ran until December 1969 and totalled 482 aircraft, plus another 21 built as **EA-6A**s (described separately), retaining a partial strike capability but developed primarily to provide ECM support for the A-6As in Vietnam and to act as Elint gatherers. The first EA-6A was flown in 1963, and six A-6As were also converted to EA-6A configuration. A more sophisticated electronic warfare version, the EA-6B, is described separately.

A-6A conversions

The following variants of the Intruder were also produced by the conversion of existing A-6As. First of these (19 converted) was the **A-6B**, issued to one USN squadron and differing from the initial model primarily in its ability to carry the US Navy's AGM-78 Standard ARM instead of the AGM-12B Bullpup. For identifying and acquiring targets not discernible by the aircraft's standard radar, Grumman then modified 12 other A-6As to **A-6C** standard, giving them an improved capability for night attack by installing FLIR and low-light-level TV equipment in a turret under the fuselage. A prototype conversion of an A-6A to **KA-6D** inflight-refuelling tanker was flown on 23 May 1966, and production contracts for the tanker version were placed. These were subsequently cancelled, but 78 A-6As were instead converted to KA-6D configuration,

Grumman A-6E Intruder

Now in the twilight of its career with the US Marine Corps, the A-6 has given sterling service in supporting ground/amphibious forces, notably in Desert Storm. The final three USMC squadrons are eventually to trade their A-6Es for two-seat F/A-18D Night Attack Hornets, which lack the range and load-carrying ability of the elderly A-6s, but which have far more modern systems.

MARKINGS
This A-6E wears the standard two-tone grey camouflage. The squadron badge of VMA(AW)-533 has been modified to show a laser-guided bomb.

equipped with TACAN instrumentation and mounting a hose-reel unit in the rear fuselage to refuel other A-6s under the 'buddy' system. The KA-6D may be operated as a day-bomber or as an air/sea rescue control aircraft and, since the withdrawal of the EKA-3B from sea-going duty, has been the standard carrier-based tanker aircraft.

Definitive version

On 27 February 1970, Grumman flew the first example of the **A-6E**, an advanced, upgraded development of the the A-6A, which the A-6E succeeded in production. Procurement of 445 of this version was undertaken for the USN and USMC squadrons, of which some 240 are newly built and about 205 are converted from A-6A/B/Cs. The basis of the A-6E, which retains upgraded forms of the airframe and powerplant of the earlier models, is a new avionics fit, founded on the addition of a Norden AN/APQ-148 multi-mode navigation/attack radar, and IBM/Fairchild

TRAM TURRET
Developed by Hughes, the AN/AAS-33 Target Recognition and Attack, Multi-sensor turret contains a laser receiver, laser designator and forward-looking infra-red. The turret interfaces with the aircraft's radar to allow the system to perform high-precision night attack. The fully articulated turret provides near-hemispherical coverage beneath the aircraft.

POWERPLANT
Power is provided by two Pratt & Whitney J52-P-408 turbojets, rated at 9,300 lb (41.4 kN) thrust each. Fitment of the uprated J52-P-409 is under consideration.

RADAR
Housed in the large upward-hinging radome, the Norden AN/APQ-148/156 multi-mode radar is the principal sensor of the avionics suite. It combines the functions of the APQ-92 and APQ-112 of earlier Intruders in one radar, providing search, ground-mapping, tracking and ranging of both fixed and moving targets, terrain avoidance/following and beacon detection/tracking. The APQ-156 designation covers radars upgraded to interface with the TRAM turret. Data is presented on two cockpit displays, the bombardier/navigator having a large DVRI (direct-view radar indicator) screen while the pilot has a smaller vertical display for terrain avoidance/following modes.

FUEL
Maximum internal fuel capacity is 2,344 US gal (8873 litres), to which can be added up to five tanks of 300-US gal (1135-litre) or 400-US gal (1514-litre) size. A fixed probe is fitted for inflight refuelling.

WING SURFACES
The complex wing of the Intruder incorporates spoilers for primary roll control, augmented at low speeds by flaperons. The latter are nearly full-span Fowler units, providing considerable extra lift to reduce approach/take-off speeds in conjunction with leading-edge slats. At the wingtips are split trailing-edge airbrakes.

DOPPLER
The bulge under the rear fuselage houses the APN-153 Doppler navigation radar, which provides updates for the INS.

CONFIGURATION
This A-6E carries a typical weapon load for general-purpose bombing. A total of 18 low-drag bombs is carried on three MERs (multiple ejector racks), with fuel tanks on the outboard pylons.

DEFENCES
The bulged fairing near the top of the fin houses antennas for the self-protection system. ALQ-126 deception ECM and ALR-67 threat warning receiver are mounted here. Other antennas are located in the wingroot leading edge.

The A-6 was heavily committed to Desert Storm with both the Navy and Marine Corps. These aircraft are from Saratoga's VA-35, each armed with 12 Mk 82 retarded iron bombs. The double yellow band on the bombs signifies the Navy's version, which has a special fire-protective coating.

AN/ASQ-133 computerised navigation/attack system, Conrac armament control unit, and an RCA video-tape recorder for assessing damage caused during a strike mission. The Norden APQ-148/156 radar, which replaces the two older radars of the A-6A, provides ground mapping, terrain avoidance/clearance, and target identification/tracking/ rangefinding modes, with cockpit displays for both the pilot and navigator/bombardier, who sit side-by-side in the well-forward cockpit. Nine A-6Es were additionally converted to tanker configuration.

Following the first flight of a test aircraft on 22 March 1974, all US Navy and US Marine Corps Intruders were progressively updated still further under a programme known as **TRAM** (Target Recognition Attack, Multisensor). To the A-6E-standard Intruder, this adds a Hughes turreted electro-optical package of FLIR and laser detection equipment integrated with the Norden radar; adds CAINS (carrier airborne inertial navigation system); provides the capability for automatic carrier landings; and incorporates provision for the carriage and delivery of automatic-homing and laser-guided air-to-surface weapons. The first US Navy squadron to be equipped with the **A-6E TRAM** version was VA-165, which was deployed aboard USS *Constellation* in 1977.

Grumman developments

Further development of the design resulted in the **A-6F**, a revised A-6E airframe with new radar, digitised avionics and F404 turbofans. Three prototypes were flown, the first on 26 August 1987, but the variant was cancelled when the Navy began the pursuit of the 'stealthy' A-12. Grumman for a time continued development of the **A-6G**, basically the F model but retaining the ageing J52 engines. When the A-12 itself was cancelled, the US Navy was left without a major tactical aircraft programme, and the A-6 was faced with continued fleet service with no immediate replacement.

Consequently, the A-6E has been the subject of continuing upgrades. Rewinging with composite units was considered a necessity to keep the fleet airworthy, while

in 1990/91 the US Navy began receiving its first **SWIP** aircraft, which introduced various stand-off weapons capability including AGM-65 Maverick, AGM-84 Harpoon Block 1C, AGM-84E SLAM and AGM-88 HARM. Already the A-6E TRAM had 'smart' weapon capability in the form of laser-guided bombs and AGM-123 Skipper laser-guided missile. Further updating was implemented in late 1992 with the first flight of the Block 1-A upgrade machine, this standard introducing a HUD for the pilot, revised wing fillets and extra fuel.

In service, the A-6 has proved to be a durable and highly versatile warplane. After its baptism of fire in Vietnam, the type has seen action in Lebanon, Libya and the Gulf. As its career has progressed, the weapons repertoire has blossomed, and the latest standard of upgrade can carry virtually every item of ordnance in the US Navy inventory.

Currently the A-6E serves with 13 active-duty US Navy squadrons (VA-34, 35, 36, 52, 65, 75, 85, 95, 115, 145, 155, 165 and 196), two fleet replenishment squadrons (VA-42 and 128), two Reserve units (VA-205 and 304), various trials organisations, and three remaining US Marine Corps units (VMA(AW)-224, 332 and 533). The latter are due to relinquish their aircraft in favour of the two-seat F/A-18D Hornet in the mid-1990s. Two US Navy A-6 units are to disband during each fiscal year, bringing forward the retirement date and ending the rewinging and update programmes.

WEAPON OPTIONS

The A-6 carries its stores on one centreline and four wing pylons, each stressed for a maximum of 3,600 lb (1633 kg). Total weapon load is 18,000 lb (8165 kg). Virtually all of the US Navy/Marine Corps inventory of stores can be carried.

General purpose: up to 22 500-lb (227-kg) Mk 82s or 10 1,000-lb (454-kg) Mk 83s can be carried, although lesser numbers are more common. Bombs available in both low-drag and air-inflatable retard configuration. Alternatively Mk 77 fire bombs or Mk 7/20 cluster bombs (with varying sub-munitions) can be carried

Anti-ship: two AGM-84 Harpoon missiles can be carried on wing pylons, often backed up with iron bombs

Defence suppression: four AGM-88 HARMs carried on wing pylons or up to 26 ADM-141 decoy drones (for saturating air defences with spurious signals)

Precision attack: two AGM-84E SLAM (Stand-off Land Attack Missile) on wing pylons, up to four GBU-10, 12 or 16 laser-guided bombs, two AGM-62 Walleye TV-guided bombs, or two AGM-123 Skipper laser-guided missiles (GBU-16 1,000-lb (454-kg) LGB with rocket motor attached)

Nuclear attack: up to three B57 or B61 free-fall weapons on centreline and two inboard wing pylons
Refuelling: one D-704 buddy-buddy refuelling pod on centreline
Miscellaneous: various naval mines and destructors, ECM jamming pods, AIM-9 Sidewinders (for self-defence) can be carried

SPECIFICATION

Grumman A-6E Intruder
Wing: span 53 ft 0 in (16.15 m); width folded 25 ft 4 in (7.72 m); aspect ratio 5.31; area 528.90 sq ft (49.13 m2)
Fuselage and tail: length 54 ft 9 in (16.69 m); height 16 ft 2 in (4.93 m); tailplane span 20 ft 4.5 in (6.21 m); wheel track 10 ft 10.5 in (3.32 m); wheel base 17 ft 2.25 in (5.24 m)
Powerplant: two Pratt & Whitney J52-P-8B each rated at 9,300 lb st (41.37 kN) dry
Weights: empty 27,613 lb (12525 kg); maximum take-off 58,600 lb (26580 kg) for catapult launch or 60,400 lb (27397 kg) for field take-off
Fuel and load: internal fuel 15,939 lb (7230 kg); external fuel up to 10,050 lb (4558 kg) in five 400-US gal (1514-litre) drop tanks; maximum ordnance 18,000 lb (8165 kg)
Speed: never-exceed speed 700 kt (806 mph; 1297

km/h); maximum level speed 'clean' at sea level 560 kt (644 mph; 1037 km/h); cruising speed at optimum altitude 412 kt (474 mph; 763 km/h)
Range: ferry range 2,818 nm (3,245 miles; 5222 km) with empty tanks dropped or 2,380 nm (2,740 miles; 4410 km) with empty tanks retained; range with maximum military load 878 nm (1,011 miles; 1627 km)
Performance: maximum rate of climb at sea level 7,620 ft (2323 m) per minute; service ceiling 42,400 ft (12925 m); minimum take-off run 3,890 ft (1186 m); take-off distance to 50 ft (15 m) 4,560 ft (1390 m) at maximum take-off weight; landing distance from 50 ft (15 m) 2,540 ft (774 m) at normal landing weight; minimum landing run 1,710 ft (521 m)

The hose-drogue unit projecting from under the rear fuselage identifies the dedicated KA-6D tanker. The aircraft lacks TRAM turret and bombing radar, and the right-hand seat is devoid of all offensive equipment. Three or four KA-6Ds are usually assigned to an Intruder squadron.

Augmenting the KA-6D in the tanker role, the standard A-6E can carry a D-704 refuelling pod on the centreline pylon.

Grumman **EA-6A Intruder**

Based on the original A-6A variant of the Intruder, the **Grumman EA-6A** was conceived in response to a Marine Corps requirement for an EF-10B Skyknight replacement and entered service with three composite reconnaissance/electronic warfare squadrons in the mid-1960s. Production totalled just 27 airframes, of which a dozen were essentially conversions of existing A-6As, and most were retired from front-line service in the late 1970s when the Marines received EA-6B Prowlers.

Externally, the most visible difference between the EA-6A and its attack-dedicated A-6A counterpart was the bulbous fin-top fairing which housed antennas associated with the electronic warfare equipment. This included a Bunker-Ramo AN/ALQ-86 signals surveillance system and AN/ALH-6 signals recording system as well as AN/ALQ-31 and AN/ALQ-76 noise jammers, with the latter being housed in distinctive slab-sided under-wing pods. Although mainly employed for electronic warfare, the EA-6A evidently retained a limited attack capability, although it appears this was seldom used, especially in Vietnam, where it saw extensive service in support of strike aircraft and as a gatherer of intelligence relating to the North's electronic order of battle.

By late 1993, a handful of EA-6As were still in service, operating with VAQ-33 from

The EA-6A was used by the USMC in the EW role. Following replacement by the EA-6B, a few continued in Navy service as EW aggressors.

Key West, FL, under the overall direction of the Fleet Electronic Warfare Support Group. Their principal task was to act as electronic aggressors in the training of **US Navy** air- and sea-borne forces but are now believed to have been withdrawn.

Grumman **EA-6B Prowler**

Production of the US Navy's standard carrierborne electronic warfare aircraft terminated in July 1991 with 170 aircraft built, but efforts at improving the already impressive potential of the **Grumman EA-6B Prowler** are continuing and should lead to the ADVCAP (Advanced Capability) or Block 91 derivative. Development of upgraded receiver and processor equipment associated with the AN/ALQ-99 TJS (Tactical Jamming System) was launched by Litton Industries in 1983, with flight trials getting under way in 1990. Assuming that test objectives are satisfactorily met, deployment of Block 91-configured Prowlers is expected to occur in the second half of the 1990s, with current planning anticipating that these will result from a CILOP remanufacture programme.

Fundamentally a four-seater variation on the well-proven Intruder, the EA-6B entered service during 1971 as a replacement for the EKA-3B Skywarrior. Key equipment includes the TJS, which is capable of operation in fully-automatic, semi-automatic and manual modes and which employs 'noise' jamming originating from a maximum of five external transmitter pods.

Progressive update initiatives have resulted in the appearance of ever more capable versions. Excluding three prototype conversions of A-6As and five development airframes, the first 23 production aircraft were to 'Basic' standard, using ALQ-99 TJS and ALQ-92 with an EW potential that was limited to four specific frequency bands. They were followed in 1973 by the first of 25 **EXCAP** (Expanded Capability) airframes with improved equipment and the ability to cover threats across eight bands using ALQ-99A TJS.

The next version to appear was **ICAP** (Improved Capability), which made its debut in 1976 and which incorporated new display and reduced reaction times, along with AN/ALQ-126 multiple-band defensive breakers, updated radar deception gear and the automatic carrier landing system. In addition to 45 new-build machines, 17 surviving Basic and EXCAP airframes were brought to

the full Improved Capability standard.

Software and display improvements were among the changes made on the **ICAP-II** version, which flew for the first time in June 1980, with all 55 surviving ICAPs being upgraded. ICAP-II is the current service model and is able to handle groups of weapons systems, embodying such refinements as power management and improved identification of hostile emitters, while simultaneously being more reliable and more easily maintained than its predecessors. The external jammer pods were upgraded to be able to generate signals within seven bands (instead of one) and to jam in two bands simultaneously. As with the original ICAP, it has a crew of four and it has also recently acquired the ability to use more direct methods in countering the threat posed by enemy SAM sites, for it is now able to function as a 'shooter' with the AGM-88A HARM defence suppression missile. The **ICAP-II/Block 86** can be distinguished by three new sweptback antennas on the spine and under the nose, associated with HARM capability.

New-build and conversions

Procurement of ICAP-II also followed a twin-track approach, the Navy and Marine Corps receiving a mixture of remanufactured and new-build aircraft to this standard. These presently equip about a dozen deployable Navy squadrons which are mostly concentrated at NAS Whidbey Island, WA, from where they routinely embark aboard aircraft-carriers of both major fleet organisations. Non-deployable and second-line elements comprise a permanently shore-based training unit, a Reserve Force squadron and a specialist EW-dedicated aggressor training squadron at Whidbey Island, plus a second Reserve squadron at NAF Washington/Andrews AFB, MD.

Most recently, EA-6Bs have been upgraded to two **ADVCAP** configurations. The basic ADVCAP has new jammer transmission and passive detection capabilities and an expanded AN/ALE-39 chaff dis-

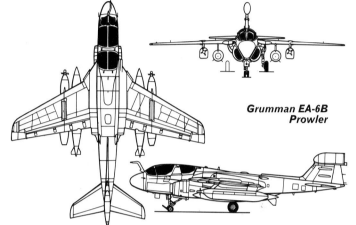

Grumman EA-6B Prowler

penser fit. The aircraft is also fitted with GPS, and has provision for AN/ALQ-165 ASPJ and a new disk-based recorder/programme loader. The prototype first flew on 29 October 1990.

An Avionics Improvement Program will lead to a remanufactured ADVCAP/Block 91 EA-6B with new displays, radar improvements, an improved tactical support jamming suite, AN/ALQ-149 communications jamming system and a digital autopilot. Aerodynamic improvements were developed under the **VEP** (Vehicle Enhancement Program) project and comprise the addition

After rationalisation of their EA-6B assets, the USMC now has four active-duty squadrons.

of fuselage strakes, modified flaps, slats, speed brakes and a fin extension. The VEP prototype first flew on 15 June 1992 and featured uprated powerplants and two additional dedicated HARM pylons.

Marine Corps usage of the Prowler is more limited, comprising four front-line squadrons at MCAS Cherry Point, NC, which operate detachments to the Far East on rotation.

Left: Block 86 EA-6Bs made extensive use of their HARM firing capability during Desert Storm.

Above: This VAQ-137 EA-6B carries a standard load of three ALQ-99 jamming pods and two AGM-88 HARMs.

TAIL FAIRING
Known as the 'football', the large fin-tip fairing houses the principal array of System Integration Receivers (SIRs). These detect hostile transmissions and relay data to the central computer. The fin-top SIRs cover bands 4-9, while the bulged fairings lower down the fin cover bands 1-3.

HARM MISSILE
With a range of approximately 15 miles (25 km), the AGM-88 has a length of 13 ft 8 in (4.17 m) and launch weight of 796 lb (361 kg), of which 145 lb (66 kg) is a high-explosive fragmentation warhead. The seeker is a passive radar head which can be pre-programmed or launched in an opportunist manner. Fusing is by active laser.

CREW STATIONS
The four-man crew consists of pilot (front port) and three ECM Officers. ECMO 1 occupies the front starboard seat, operating the navigation, radar and communications jamming systems. ECMO 2 and 3 sit in the rear cabin, operating the tactical jamming system.

ALQ-99 SYSTEM
The AIL Systems Inc. ALQ-99F is the EA-6B's jamming system, consisting of the SIR receivers, central processing computer and up to five (normally three) pods. These can operate in full auto (detection and automatic assignment of jamming power), semi-auto (ECM operators assign power) and manual (ECM operators manually search spectrum and assign jamming) modes.

FUSELAGE
In order to accommodate the two extra crew stations, the basic A-6 fuselage was lengthened by 4 ft 6 in (1.37 m).

RADAR
The search and navigation radar is the Norden APS-130. This is a downgraded version of the A-6E's APQ-156, with attack functions deleted. The radar provides accurate ground mapping.

SPECIFICATION

Grumman EA-6B Prowler

Wing: span 53 ft 0 in (16.15 m); width folded 25 ft 10 in (7.87 m); aspect ratio 5.31; area 528.90 sq ft (49.13 m²)
Fuselage and tail: length 59 ft 10 in (18.24 m); height 16 ft 3 in (4.95 m); tailplane span 20 ft 4.5 in (6.21 m); wheel track 10 ft 10.5 in (3.32 m); wheel base 17 ft 2 in (5.23 m)
Powerplant: two Pratt & Whitney J52-P-408 each rated at 11,200 lb st (49.8 kN) dry
Weights: empty 31,572 lb (14321 kg); normal take-off from a carrier in stand-off jamming configuration with five jammer pods 54,461 lb (24703 kg) or from

land with maximum internal and external fuel 60,610 lb (27493 kg); maximum take-off 65,000 lb (29484 kg)
Fuel and load: internal fuel 15,422 lb (6995 kg); external fuel up to 10,025 lb (4547 kg) in five 400-US gal (1514-litre) drop tanks
Speed: never-exceed speed 710 kt (817 mph; 1315 km/h); maximum level speed 'clean' at sea level 566 kt (651 mph; 1048 km/h) or with five jammer pods 530 kt (610 mph; 982 km/h); cruising speed at optimum altitude 418 kt (481 mph; 774 km/h)
Range: ferry range 2,085 nm (2,399 miles; 3861 km) with empty tanks dropped or 1,756 nm (2,022 miles; 3254 km) with empty tanks retained; range 955 nm (1,099 miles; 1769 km) with maximum external load
Performance: maximum rate of climb 'clean' at sea level 12,900 ft (3932 m) per minute or with five jammer pods 10,030 ft (3057 m) per minute; service ceiling 'clean' 41,200 ft (12550 m) or with five jammer pods 38,000 ft (11580 m); take-off run 2,670 ft (814 m) with five jammer pods; take-off distance to 50 ft (15 m) 2,850 ft (869 m) 'clean' or 3,495 ft (1065 m) with five jammer pods; landing distance from 50 ft (15 m) 2,700ft (823 m) at maximum landing weight; landing run 1,900 ft (579 m) 'clean' or 2,150 ft (655 m) with five jammer pods

Grumman EA-6B ICAP-II Prowler

The ICAP-II is the current service standard of EA-6B, in its Block 86 version capable of launching the HARM missile. This adds a considerable lethal SEAD capability to the basic jamming function. The ICAP-II vastly increased jamming capability. Previously, each ALQ-99 pod could jam in only one frequency band, but with ICAP-II this increased to any one of seven bands. The pod can also jam in two different bands simultaneously. Improved software and a new AYK-14 central computer further enhanced capability.

DECM
Self-protection for the EA-6B is provided by a deception jamming suite. The forward antenna is at the base of the refuelling probe.

BEERCAN FAIRING
On the trailing edge of the 'football' is the 'beercan' fairing for the aft-facing ALQ-126 DECM system.

163031
VMAQ-2
MARINES

TJS POD
In the ALQ-99F system each Tactical Jamming System pod contains two high-powered noise jammers and a tracking receiver. Electrical power for the pod is provided by an external turbine generator on the front, which spins in the slipstream.

Grumman C-2 Greyhound

As had happened earlier with the S-2 Tracker, the turbine-engined E-2 Hawkeye provided the basis for a COD transport for service with the **US Navy** in the vital role of transferring urgently required personnel and material from shore bases to aircraft-carriers operating at sea, and *vice versa.*

Although its origins in the E-2 Hawkeye are readily apparent, the resulting **Grumman C-2A Greyhound** is significantly different. Perhaps the most notable change related to the fuselage, which is of much greater cross-section, incorporating an upswept aft fuselage section complete with cargo door and an integral loading ramp permitting bulky items such as turbojet engines to be manhandled with relative ease.

Less apparent, but no less important, is the fact that the horizontal and vertical tail surfaces were redesigned, the absence of the Hawkeye's distinctive 'pancake' radome smoothing out airflow patterns in this area and eliminating the requirement for dihedral and inwardly-canted fins and rudders. Of the other changes, perhaps the most notable involved strengthening the nose wheel unit to permit operation at higher gross weights. Fuel capacity was also increased.

As far as payload is concerned, the Greyhound can accommodate up to 39 passengers or 20 stretchers and four attendants or, alternatively, approximately 18,000 lb (8165 kg) of palletised cargo.

Flying for the first time as the **YC-2A** on 18 November 1964, the Greyhound was initially built in only modest numbers, just 19 aircraft being accepted for service with the Navy between 1965 and 1968. Plans to acquire 12 more at this time fell victim to cancellation and, by the early 1970s, attrition had reduced the quantity in service to just a dozen, these operating alongside even older C-1A Traders from Navy installations both in the Pacific and Mediterranean theatres.

Faced with the question of replacing the vintage C-1A, and in view of the attrition of the Greyhound fleet, the Navy opted to reinstate the C-2A in production during 1982. The first examples of 39 additional Greyhounds were delivered to VR-24 at Sigonella, Sicily, shortly before the end of 1985. Under the terms of the $678 million multi-year contract, procurement continued until 1989. Today the C-2A serves with VRC-30 at North Island, VRC-40 at Norfolk and VRC-50 at NAS Cubi Point, Philippines, VR-24 at Sigonella having disbanded in 1993. Additionally, the two Hawkeye training units, VAW-110 at Miramar and VAW-120 at Norfolk, operate small numbers of Greyhounds to train crews for the COD units.

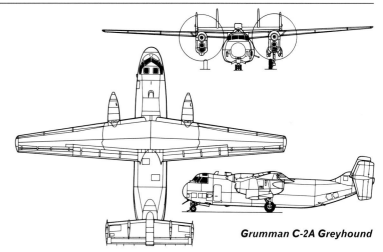

Grumman C-2A Greyhound

SPECIFICATION

Grumman C-2A Greyhound
Wing: span 80 ft 7 in (24.56 m); width folded 29 ft 4 in (8.94 m); aspect ratio 9.28; area 700.00 sq ft (65.03 m2)
Fuselage and tail: length 56 ft 10 in (17.32 m); height 15 ft 10.5 in (4.84 m); tailplane span 26 ft 2.5 in (7.99 m); wheel track 19 ft 5.75 in (5.93 m); wheel base 23 ft 2 in (7.06 m)
Powerplant: two Allison T56-A-425 each rated at 4,912 ehp (3663 ekW)
Weights: empty 36,346 lb (16486 kg); maximum take-off 57,500 lb (26081 kg)
Fuel and load: internal fuel 12,400 lb (5625 kg); external fuel none; maximum payload 10,000 lb (4536 kg) for carrier operation or 15,000 lb (6804 kg) for land operation
Speed: maximum level speed at optimum altitude 310 kt (357 mph; 574 km/h); maximum cruising speed at optimum altitude 260 kt (299 mph; 482 km/h)

Range: ferry range 1,560 nm (1,796 miles; 2891 km); range with a 10,000-lb (4536-kg) payload more than 1,040 nm (1,200 miles; 1930 km)
Performance: maximum rate of climb at sea level 2,610 ft (796 m) per minute; service ceiling 33,500 ft (10210 m) on a ferry mission or 28,800 ft (8780 m) with maximum payload; minimum take-off run 2,180 ft (664 m); take-off distance to 50 ft (15 m) 3,060 ft

The Greyhound is dedicated to supporting carriers at sea, transporting supplies and personnel.

(932 m) at maximum take-off weight; landing distance from 50 ft (15 m) 2,666 ft (691 m) at maximum landing weight or 1,735 ft (529 m) at maximum arrested landing weight; minimum landing run 1,428 ft (435 m)

Grumman E-2 Hawkeye

Initially designated **W2F**, the **E-2 Hawkeye** has been the **US Navy**'s airborne early warning platform since entering service in 1964, in time to perform with distinction during the Vietnam War. The early **E-2A** and **E-2B** versions are no longer in service, today's Hawkeyes being to **E-2C** standard, the first example of which flew on 20 January 1971. Identified by a cooling intake behind the cockpit, the E-2C introduced a new APS-125 radar and far better signal processing compared to its predecessors. The basic E-2C has been the subject of continual updating over the years.

Radar units have changed to APS-138, and from 1989 the APS-139. Now the APS-145 is being fitted to new aircraft and is being retrofitted to earlier aircraft. This radar offers better resistance to jamming and is more capable in an overland role. Other upgrades in the offing concern the IFF (identification, friend or foe) system and the installation of JTIDS (Joint Tactical Information Distribution System). Low-rate production is almost at an end with the delivery of the 139th aircraft for the US Navy, plus export examples.

Great care has to be taken during the approach, as the E-2's large wing span leaves little room for manoeuvre on a crowded deck.

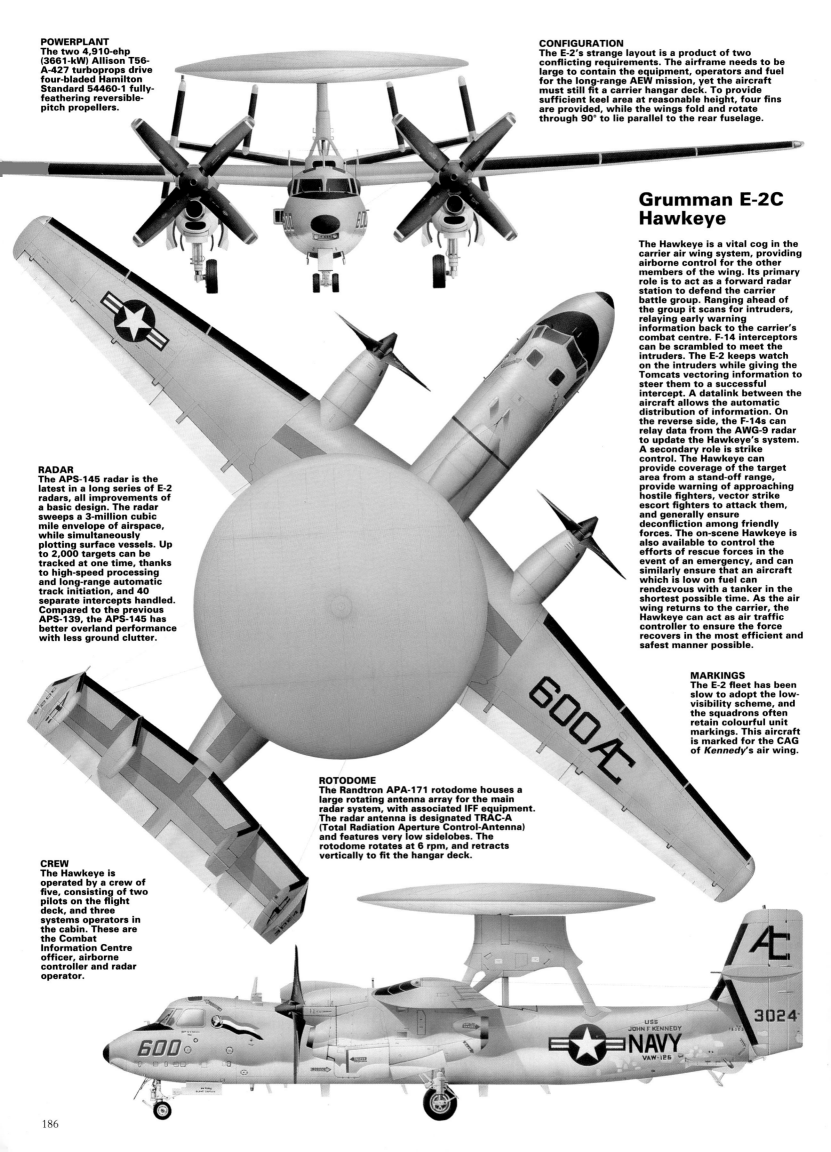

POWERPLANT
The two 4,910-ehp (3661-kW) Allison T56-A-427 turboprops drive four-bladed Hamilton Standard 54460-1 fully-feathering reversible-pitch propellers.

CONFIGURATION
The E-2's strange layout is a product of two conflicting requirements. The airframe needs to be large to contain the equipment, operators and fuel for the long-range AEW mission, yet the aircraft must still fit a carrier hangar deck. To provide sufficient keel area at reasonable height, four fins are provided, while the wings fold and rotate through 90° to lie parallel to the rear fuselage.

Grumman E-2C Hawkeye

The Hawkeye is a vital cog in the carrier air wing system, providing airborne control for the other members of the wing. Its primary role is to act as a forward radar station to defend the carrier battle group. Ranging ahead of the group it scans for intruders, relaying early warning information back to the carrier's combat centre. F-14 interceptors can be scrambled to meet the intruders. The E-2 keeps watch on the intruders while giving the Tomcats vectoring information to steer them to a successful intercept. A datalink between the aircraft allows the automatic distribution of information. On the reverse side, the F-14s can relay data from the AWG-9 radar to update the Hawkeye's system. A secondary role is strike control. The Hawkeye can provide coverage of the target area from a stand-off range, provide warning of approaching hostile fighters, vector strike escort fighters to attack them, and generally ensure deconfliction among friendly forces. The on-scene Hawkeye is also available to control the efforts of rescue forces in the event of an emergency, and can similarly ensure that an aircraft which is low on fuel can rendezvous with a tanker in the shortest possible time. As the air wing returns to the carrier, the Hawkeye can act as air traffic controller to ensure the force recovers in the most efficient and safest manner possible.

RADAR
The APS-145 radar is the latest in a long series of E-2 radars, all improvements of a basic design. The radar sweeps a 3-million cubic mile envelope of airspace, while simultaneously plotting surface vessels. Up to 2,000 targets can be tracked at one time, thanks to high-speed processing and long-range automatic track initiation, and 40 separate intercepts handled. Compared to the previous APS-139, the APS-145 has better overland performance with less ground clutter.

MARKINGS
The E-2 fleet has been slow to adopt the low-visibility scheme, and the squadrons often retain colourful unit markings. This aircraft is marked for the CAG of *Kennedy*'s air wing.

ROTODOME
The Randtron APA-171 rotodome houses a large rotating antenna array for the main radar system, with associated IFF equipment. The radar antenna is designated TRAC-A (Total Radiation Aperture Control-Antenna) and features very low sidelobes. The rotodome rotates at 6 rpm, and retracts vertically to fit the hangar deck.

CREW
The Hawkeye is operated by a crew of five, consisting of two pilots on the flight deck, and three systems operators in the cabin. These are the Combat Information Centre officer, airborne controller and radar operator.

Grumman E-2 Hawkeye

Grumman E-2C Hawkeye

Although best-known as a carrierborne aircraft, the Hawkeye is flown in a land-based role by the export customers. Japan has a large force based at Misawa with 601 Hikotai.

Designed for maximum endurance in a unique role, the Hawkeye has several unusual design features, the most obvious of which is the rotodome, which houses antennas for the main radar and IFF systems. This is raised on jacks before flight, but lowered on deck to fit the hangar. The two T56 turboprops provide sufficient power for carrier operations, yet, combined with the high aspect ratio wing and good internal fuel capacity, provide long patrol endurance. The strange tail arrangement is a compromise between providing enough keel area for aerodynamic purposes and restricting the height to that of the carrier's hangar deck. The wings fold backwards after swivelling through 90°. The large wing span causes some difficulties when landing, requiring a precise approach on the part of the pilots as wingtip clearance on the deck is minimal.

The Hawkeye carries a crew of five, consisting of pilot, co-pilot, CIC (combat information centre) officer, air control officer and radar operator. E-2s usually launch ahead of other carrier aircraft so as to be on station from the beginning of operations. The 'double-cycle' method is often used so that the 'Hummer', as the E-2 is colloquially known,

is airborne throughout two sets of launches and recoveries of tactical aircraft. Flying at an altitude of about 30,000 ft (9145 m), the Hawkeye in the AEW role extends the detection range of the battle group by about 300 miles (480 km) for aircraft and 160 miles (258 km) for cruise missiles. Surface vessels can also be located. Constant communication is maintained with the carrier's CIC by means of a secure datalink.

Datalinks can also be maintained with F-14 Tomcats in the fighter control tasking. The Tomcats themselves can also supply data to the Hawkeye's system. During attacks by tactical aircraft, the Hawkeye can act as an airborne control and command post, supplying directions to attack aircraft and escorting fighters to deconflict them, in addition to providing warnings of hostile aircraft. Air traffic control uses include vectoring aircraft on to tankers, diverting them to alternative landing sites should the carrier be unable to recover them or controlling a traffic stacking pattern in the event of a large-scale recovery process.

In US Navy service, the E-2C flies with active-duty units at NAS Miramar, CA (VAW-112, 113, 114, 116 and 117), NAS Atsugi, Japan (VAW-115), and NAS Norfolk, VA (VAW-121, 122, 123, 124, 125 and 126). Two training units fly the type as fleet replenishment squadrons (VAW-110 at Miramar and VAW-120 at Norfolk), while two USN Reserve squadrons also fly the type (VAW-78 at Norfolk and VAW-88 at Miramar). Until recently the US Coast Guard

operated the type on anti-drug patrols, but these are back with the Navy following the delivery of the Coast Guard's EC-130V radar platform. The **TE-2C** specialist trainer version used by the Navy is no longer believed to be in service.

Foreign interest in the Hawkeye has brought several orders. **Israel** received four in 1978, these aircraft being put to good use in the 1982 war over the Bekaa valley, when IDF/AF fighters destroyed over 80 Syrian MiGs. The **Japanese Air Self-Defence Force** took a batch of four in 1982 and a similar number in 1984, these flying from Misawa with 601 Hikotai and upgraded with APS-145 radar in 1991. Five more were ordered for 1993 delivery. **Egypt** took five from October 1987, and ordered a sixth in 1989. **Singapore** acquired four in 1987, with a further requirement for two. **Taiwan** has bought four aircraft, originally built as E-2Bs but reworked to modern standards as the **E-2T**. The first conversion was completed by Grumman for a 1993 delivery: the remainder are being updated in Taiwan. **Thailand** has a requirement for four aircraft and, finally, **France** is also to acquire four, having a requirement for AEW aircraft to operate from its new nuclear-powered carrier, the *Charles de Gaulle.*

SPECIFICATION

Grumman E-2C Hawkeye

Wing: span 80 ft 7 in (24.56 m); folded width 29 ft 4 in (8.94 m); aspect ratio 9.3; area 700.00 sq ft (65.03 m2)

Fuselage and tail: length 57 ft 6.75 in (17.54 m); height 18 ft 3.75 in (5.58 m); tailplane span 26 ft 2.5 in (7.99 m); wheel track 19 ft 5.75 in (5.93 m); wheel base 23 ft 2 in (7.06 m)

Powerplant: two Allison T56-A-425 each rated at 4,910 ehp (3661 kW)

Weights: empty 38,063 lb (17265 kg); maximum take-off 51,933 lb (23556 kg)

Fuel and load: internal fuel 12,400 lb (5624 kg); external fuel none; maximum ordnance none

Speed: maximum level speed 323 kt (372 mph; 598 km/h); maximum cruising speed at optimum altitude 311 kt (358 mph; 576 km/h); ferry cruising speed at optimum altitude 268 kt (308 mph; 496 km/h)

Range: ferry range 1,394 nm (1,605 miles; 2583 km); operational radius 175 nm (200 miles; 320 km) for a patrol of 3 to 4 hours; endurance with maximum fuel 6 hours 6 minutes

Performance: maximum rate of climb at sea level 2,515 ft (767 m) per minute; service ceiling 30,800 ft (9390 m); minimum take-off run 2,000 ft (610 m); take-off distance to 50 ft (15 m) 2,600 ft (793 m) at maximum take-off weight; landing run 1,440 ft (439 m)

Grumman **F-14A Tomcat**

Designed as a successor to the F-4 in the fleet air defence role for the **US Navy**, the Tomcat was originally conceived to engage and destroy targets at extreme range, before they could pose a threat to the carrier battle group. The **Grumman**

For the tactical reconnaissance role, the F-14A carries the multi-sensor TARPS pod between the engine fairings.

F-14A Tomcat remains a formidable warplane, even though the original F-14A has been in service for more than 20 years. Production of the F-14A for the Navy eventually totalled 556 examples, while 80 broadly similar machines were purchased by **Iran** before the downfall of the Shah. Of the latter, only 79 were actually delivered (one being diverted to the US Navy). The F-14A continues to be the Navy's primary air defence aircraft despite the introduction of

the improved **F-14B** and **F-14D** (described separately) which have been built and deployed in modest numbers.

The key to the F-14's effectiveness lies in its advanced avionics suite, the Hughes AWG-9 fire control system representing the most capable long-range interceptor radar in service, with the ability to detect, track and engage targets at ranges in excess of 100 miles (160 km). Early aircraft also had an IRST system, replacing this during production (and by retrofit) with a long-range video camera known as TCS. The armament options allow the aircraft to engage targets over a huge range from close up to extreme

BVR (beyond visual range).

Although never tested in combat, the Hughes AIM-54 Phoenix remains the longest-ranged air-to-air missile in service today and has demonstrated the ability to detect and kill targets at unparalleled distances. In the medium-range arena, Tomcat has the option of either the AIM-7 Sparrow or the AIM-120 AMRAAM, while for short-range, close-in engagements, the F-14 car-

The Sparrow is the Tomcat's medium-range weapon, filling the gap between the Phoenix and Sidewinder.

Grumman F-14A Tomcat

RADAR
The Hughes AWG-9 radar system is immensely powerful. It can track 24 targets simultaneously, and attack six, while still continuing in the search mode.

NAV/COMM EQUIPMENT
The two blade aerials on the spine serve the UHF/TACAN (front) and datalink/IFF (rear). Radio and navigation equipment includes APX-72 IFF transponder, APX-76 IFF interrogator, ARC-51 and ARC-159 UHF radios, ARR-69 auxiliary receiver, KY-28 cryptographic system, ASN-92 INS, APN-154 beacon augmentor, APN-194 radar altimeter, ARN-84 TACAN and ARA-50 automatic direction-finder.

Grumman F-14A Tomcat

Typical of the 500-plus aircraft delivered to the US Navy before the introduction of the F-14B and F-14D models, this 'Turkey' wears the smart and historic markings of VF-31 'Tomcatters', during the time the squadron was assigned to USS *Forrestal*'s Air Wing Six. The aircraft is configured with a TARPS pod, with Sparrows and Sidewinders for self-defence.

TARPS POD
The Tactical Air Reconnaissance Pod System is carried on the starboard side of the underfuselage. In the nose of the pod is a CAI KS-87B frame camera peering obliquely forwards through a slanted flat-pane window. Further back is a bar window for a Fairchild KA-99 panoramic camera, which gives almost horizon-to-horizon coverage. Finally there is a Honeywell AAD-5 infra-red linescan for night-time and bad weather reconnaissance.

FUEL
The Tomcat is blessed with considerable internal tankage. Integral tanks in the outer wing sections hold 295 US gal (1117 litres) each. Two fuselage fuel tanks either side of the wing carry-through hold 648 US gal (2453 litres) and 691 US gal (2616 litres). Two further feeder tanks raise total internal capacity to 2,385 US gal (9029 litres). Under-intake tanks, as fitted here, each hold 267 US gal (1011 litres).

SPARROW MISSILE
The standard medium-range missile is the AIM-7M/P Sparrow. The M introduced an inverse monopulse seeker, improved ECCM, new warhead and many other features, while the P has further improvements, including a command link to the missile to improve its capabilities against sea-skimming cruise missiles. The missile is 12 ft (3.66 m) long with a body diameter of 8 in (20.3 cm). The central wings have a span of 3 ft 4 in (1.02 m). Launch weight is 507 lb (230 kg), of which 86 lb (39 kg) is a high-explosive blast fragmentation warhead (replacing the continuous rod warhead of earlier variants). This is fused by active radar. The solid propellant motor gives a range of about 28 miles (45 km).

CONTROL SURFACES
The main control surfaces are grouped at the rear. The twin fins each have powerful rudders for yaw control, while the tailplanes are all-moving control surfaces, providing both roll and pitch control. Roll control at low speeds is augmented by overwing spoilers. To keep approach speeds down, the Tomcat has powerful high-lift flaps and slats on the moving portion of the wing, both running nearly full span.

UNDERCARRIAGE
The landing gear is immensely strong to absorb the high sink rate and deceleration on landing. The mainwheels retract forwards, rotating through 90° to lie flat in the wing gloves. The nosewheel has excellent steerability for tight manoeuvring on deck.

Grumman F-14A Tomcat

ries the well-proven AIM-9 Sidewinder. Finally there is a single Vulcan M61A1 20-mm Gatling-type rotary cannon in the lower port fuselage with 675 rounds of ammunition.

Development was initiated in the late 1960s, following on the cancellation of the ill-fated F-111B, leaving the Navy in the unenviable position of having no new fighter in prospect. Grumman had already invested a considerable amount of effort in the navalised F-111B, and used this experience in designing a new variable-geometry fighter (the Model G-303) which was duly selected by the Navy in January 1969. Grumman's use of a variable-geometry wing allowed excellent high-speed performance to be combined with docile low-speed handling characteristics and a high degree of agility. Even today, the F-14A is a superb dogfighter, except when compared with the latest optimised air superiority fighters. A dozen development aircraft were ordered, with the first making its maiden flight on 21 December 1970.

Tomcat into service

The programme made reasonably swift progress, culminating in deliveries to the Navy from October 1972, with the first operational cruise in 1974. Production continued into the 1980s and a total of 26 front-line and four second-line squadrons was eventually equipped with the F-14A.

The introduction of updated F-14B and F-14D versions has reduced the number of

Above: Two Tomcats from VF-2 in the landing pattern, with arrester hooks deployed. The pair shows the differences between the old-style colours and the new low-visibility markings.

Right: The F-14A has always had a limited air-to-ground capability, but until recently this was not exercised. The use of the 'Bombcat' is now more prevalent as the US Navy looks for more multi-role flexibility.

squadrons equipped with the original production model. The total number of squadrons has been further reduced, to 17, including four Reserve squadrons, by the reconfiguration of the carrier air wing to include a larger number of multi-role F/A-18 Hornets, several air wings having already transitioned to a one F-14/three F/A-18 squadron mix. Since plans to rework a substantial number of F-14As to F-14B or F-14D standard have been abandoned, it is nevertheless likely to continue in use for some considerable time, albeit in reducing numbers.

The F-14 has suffered many difficulties since entering fleet service. Many were engine-related, the Pratt & Whitney TF30 turbofan proving something of an Achilles heel. Fan blade losses caused several crashes before improved quality control and steel containment cases alleviated the

worst consequences of engine failure. In addition, the engine was prone to compressor stall, especially during air combat manoeuvring training, and the aircraft's vicious departure characteristics (especially with one engine out) resulted in many further losses. Many problems were solved when the revised TF30-P-414A version of the powerplant was adopted as standard.

In addition to fleet air defence tasks, F-14As are also used for reconnaissance missions, using the Tactical Air Reconnais-

sance Pod System (TARPS), and it is usual for three TARPS-capable aircraft to be assigned to one of each carrier air wing's F-14 units. More recently, the F-14A has also acquired a secondary air-to-ground role, capitalising on a modest attack capability that was built in from the outset, but never utilised. Today the training syllabus includes some emphasis on strike missions, although these would only normally be undertaken in a permissive combat environment. The 'Bombcat' carries only con-

WING
At the heart of the Tomcat's structure is the 22-ft (6.7-m) span wing carry-through, which has dihedral to reduce the cross-sectional area of the fuselage. At each end is the pivot point for the moving wing panel. The wings sweep from 20° to 68° in flight, controlled automatically by a computer which takes air and attitude data and then programmes the wings for optimum performance. In order to reduce the amount of room the Tomcat takes up on the carrier deck, the wings can be swept to a 75° ground oversweep position for parking.

WEAPON OPTIONS

Standard armament consists of an internal M61A1 Vulcan 20-mm six-barrelled cannon, and an AIM-9M Sidewinder on the shoulder launch rail of each pylon under the wing glove. Lower launch rail of each glove pylon can accommodate either an AIM-7M Sparrow or an AIM-54C Phoenix. Four further AIM-7M or AIM-54C can be carried under the fuselage between the engine trunks. AIM-7Ms carried in semi-recessed bays, while AIM-54C mounted on pallets which fit into Sparrow bays. Normal load-out comprises two or four Phoenix under fuselage and two Sparrows on the pylon which, combined with the AIM-9M and cannon, gives a superb all-round mix for the fighter mission. Fuel tanks are often carried on hardpoints under the intakes. In the tactical reconnaissance role the TARPS multi-sensor pod is carried under the rear fuselage, with an ALQ-167 jamming pod on the front starboard Phoenix pallet a common option. Phoenix pallets can also mount bomb racks for 1,000-lb Mk 83 or 2,000-lb Mk 84 GP bombs or other free-fall weaponry.

SPECIFICATION

Grumman F-14A Tomcat

Wing: span 64 ft 1.5 in (19.54 m) spread, 38 ft 2.5 in (11.65 m) swept and 33 ft 3.5 in (10.15 m) overswept; aspect ratio 7.28; area 565.00 sq ft (52.49 m2)

Fuselage and tail: length 62 ft 8 in (19.10 m); height 16 ft 0 in (4.88 m); tailplane span 32 ft 8.5 in (9.97 m); wheel track 16 ft 5 in (5.00 m); wheel base 23 ft 0.5 in (7.02 m)

Powerplant: two Pratt & Whitney TF30-P-412A/414A turbofans each rated at 20,900 lb st (92.97 kN) with afterburning

Weights: empty 40,104 lb (18191 kg) with -414A engines; normal take-off 'clean' 58,715 lb (26632 kg); maximum take-off 59,714 lb (27086 kg) with four Sparrows or 70,764 lb (32098 kg) with six Phoenix; overload take-off 74,349 lb (33724 kg)

Fuel and load: internal fuel 16,200 lb (7348 kg); external fuel up to 3,800 lb (1724 kg) in two 267-US gal (1011-litre) drop tanks; maximum ordnance 14,500 lb (6577 kg)

Speed: maximum level speed 'clean' at high altitude 1,342 kt (1,544 mph; 2485 km/h) and at low altitude 792 kt (912 mph; 1468 km/h); cruising speed at optimum altitude between 400 and 550 kt (460 and 633 mph; 741 and 1019 km/h)

Range: maximum range with internal and external fuel about 1,735 nm (2,000 miles; 3220 km); radius on a combat air patrol with six AIM-7 Sparrows and four AIM-9 Sidewinders 665 nm (766 miles; 1,233 km)

Performance: maximum rate of climb at sea level more than 30,000 ft (9145 m) per minute; service ceiling more than 50,000 ft (15240 m); minimum take-off run 1,400 ft (427 m); minimum landing run 2,900 ft (884 m)

The Tomcat works closely with the E-2C Hawkeye. The two aircraft systems exchange information by datalink.

ventional 'iron' bombs, and has no PGM (precision-guided munition) capability except when operating in conjunction with a separate designator aircraft.

Only a handful of F-14s from the 79 delivered are believed to remain operational with the Islamic Republic of Iran Air Force. These are considered high-value assets, and are used as mini-AWACS aircraft, directing other less capable fighters. At least one was shot down by an Iraqi Mirage F1.

Grumman **F-14B/D** Tomcat

Problems with the Pratt & Whitney TF-30 turbofan engine of the F-14A were a key factor in the development of re-engined and upgraded variants of the Tomcat. One of the original prototype airframes was fitted with two F401-PW-400s and employed for an abbreviated test programme as the **F-14B** as early as 1973-74. Technical problems and financial difficulties forced the abandonment of the programme, and the

aircraft was placed into storage, re-emerging as the F-14B Super Tomcat with F101DFE engines. This engine was developed into the General Electric F100-GE-400 turbofan, which was selected to power production improved Tomcat variants. It was decided to produce two distinct new Tomcats, one designated **F-14A(Plus)** (primarily by conversion of existing F-14As) with the new engine, and another, designated

F-14D, with the new engine and improved digital avionics. The F-14A(Plus) was originally regarded as an interim type, all examples of which would eventually be converted to full F-14D standards.

Subsequently, the F-14A(Plus) was formally redesignated as the F-14B, 38 new-build examples being joined by 32 F-14A rebuilds in equipping half-a-dozen deployable squadrons starting in 1988. These incorporated some avionics changes, including a modernised fire control system, new radios, upgraded RWRs, and various cockpit changes. F-14Bs were the first re-engined

Tomcats to enter fleet service. F-14Bs have equipped six squadrons, VF-24, VF-74, VF-103, VF-142, VF-143 and VF-211, of which VF-24 and VF-211 subsequently transitioned back to the F-14A to leave the F-14B as an Atlantic Fleet-only aeroplane.

Two modified F-14As flew as F-14D prototypes and the first F-14D to be built as

The F-14B and D (illustrated) are quickly distinguished by the revised jetpipes for the new engines. The D model has a twin sensor installation under the nose.

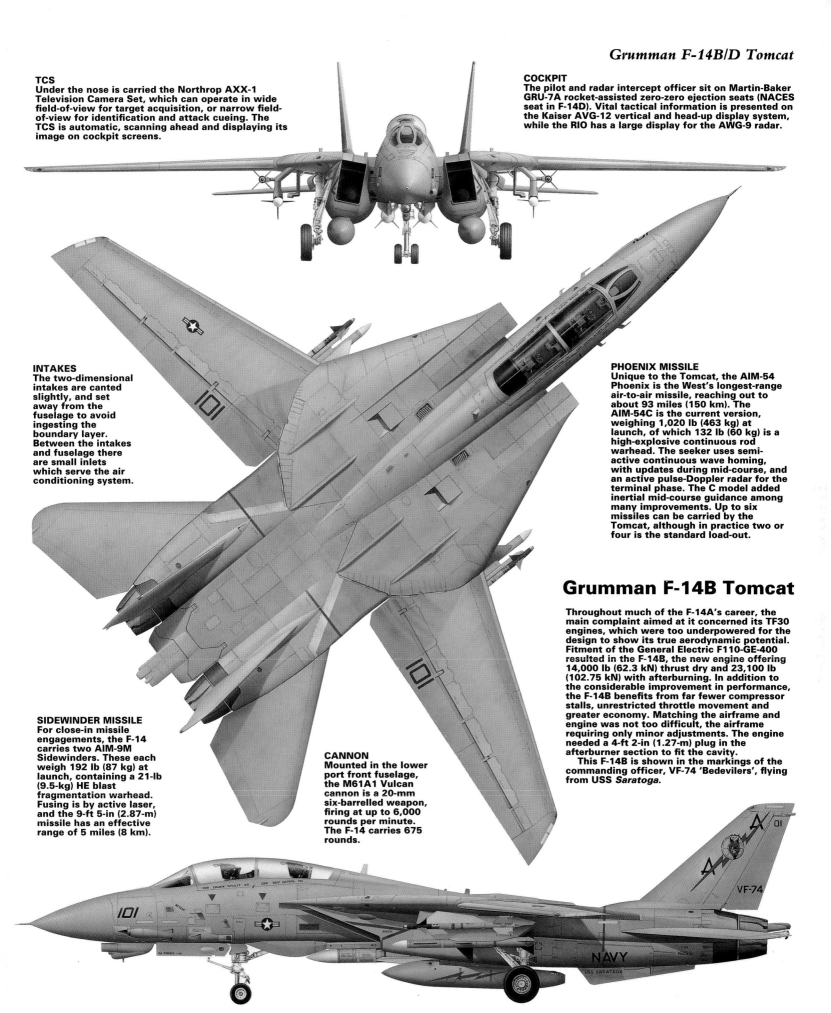

TCS
Under the nose is carried the Northrop AXX-1 Television Camera Set, which can operate in wide field-of-view for target acquisition, or narrow field-of-view for identification and attack cueing. The TCS is automatic, scanning ahead and displaying its image on cockpit screens.

COCKPIT
The pilot and radar intercept officer sit on Martin-Baker GRU-7A rocket-assisted zero-zero ejection seats (NACES seat in F-14D). Vital tactical information is presented on the Kaiser AVG-12 vertical and head-up display system, while the RIO has a large display for the AWG-9 radar.

INTAKES
The two-dimensional intakes are canted slightly, and set away from the fuselage to avoid ingesting the boundary layer. Between the intakes and fuselage there are small inlets which serve the air conditioning system.

PHOENIX MISSILE
Unique to the Tomcat, the AIM-54 Phoenix is the West's longest-range air-to-air missile, reaching out to about 93 miles (150 km). The AIM-54C is the current version, weighing 1,020 lb (463 kg) at launch, of which 132 lb (60 kg) is a high-explosive continuous rod warhead. The seeker uses semi-active continuous wave homing, with updates during mid-course, and an active pulse-Doppler radar for the terminal phase. The C model added inertial mid-course guidance among many improvements. Up to six missiles can be carried by the Tomcat, although in practice two or four is the standard load-out.

Gruman F-14B Tomcat

Throughout much of the F-14A's career, the main complaint aimed at it concerned its TF30 engines, which were too underpowered for the design to show its true aerodynamic potential. Fitment of the General Electric F110-GE-400 resulted in the F-14B, the new engine offering 14,000 lb (62.3 kN) thrust dry and 23,100 lb (102.75 kN) with afterburning. In addition to the considerable improvement in performance, the F-14B benefits from far fewer compressor stalls, unrestricted throttle movement and greater economy. Matching the airframe and engine was not too difficult, the airframe requiring only minor adjustments. The engine needed a 4-ft 2-in (1.27-m) plug in the afterburner section to fit the cavity.

This F-14B is shown in the markings of the commanding officer, VF-74 'Bedevilers', flying from USS *Saratoga*.

SIDEWINDER MISSILE
For close-in missile engagements, the F-14 carries two AIM-9M Sidewinders. These each weigh 192 lb (87 kg) at launch, containing a 21-lb (9.5-kg) HE blast fragmentation warhead. Fusing is by active laser, and the 9-ft 5-in (2.87-m) missile has an effective range of 5 miles (8 km).

CANNON
Mounted in the lower port front fuselage, the M61A1 Vulcan cannon is a 20-mm six-barrelled weapon, firing at up to 6,000 rounds per minute. The F-14 carries 675 rounds.

---

such made its maiden flight on 9 February 1990. The F-14D added digital avionics, with digital radar processing and displays (adding these to standard AWG-9 hardware under the redesignation APG-71), and a side-by-side undernose TCS/IRST sensor pod. Other improvements introduced by the F-14D include OBOGS (on-board oxygen-generating system), NACES ejection seats, and AN/ALR-67 radar warning receiver equipment. Like the F-14A, the F-14D has a limited ground attack capability. The US Department of Defense's decision to cease funding the **F-14D** has effectively halted the Navy's drive to upgrade its force of Tomcats. In consequence, the service has received only 37 new-build examples of the F-14D, while plans to upgrade approximately 400 existing F-14As to a similar standard have also been severely curtailed and only 18 have been updated, ending in March 1993.

Deliveries to the Navy began in November 1990, when training squadron VF-124

Left: An underview of an F-14B shows the Tomcat's hardpoints to advantage. The recesses under the fuselage house Sparrows or mount pallets for Phoenix missiles, bombs, ECM pods or the TARPS pod. Under the forward portion of each intake trunk is an attachment for fuel tanks, while the wing glove section has a pylon for further missiles, including a shoulder rail for a Sidewinder.

Above: The F-14D model was first assigned to VF-124 at NAS Miramar, California. This unit acts as the training unit for the West Coast/Pacific Fleet Tomcat community. The East Coast equivalent, VF-101 at NAS Oceana, received the F-14B model. The Navy has recently announced that all Tomcat training is to be consolidated at Oceana, where VF-101 will operate all three Tomcat variants.

accepted its first F-14D at Miramar. Initially, it appeared that VF-51 and VF-111 would be the first deployable units to convert. However, a subsequent realignment of fleet fighter resources saw VF-11 and VF-31 move from Oceana to Miramar and receive the F-14Ds previously earmarked for VF-51 and VF-111. Since then VF-2 and VF-14 have re-equipped with the F-14D.

SPECIFICATION

Grumman F-14D Tomcat
generally similar to the Grumman F-14A Tomcat except in the following particulars:
Powerplant: two General Electric F110-GE-400 turbofans each rated at 14,000 lb st (62.27 kN) dry and

23,100 lb st (102.75 kN) with afterburning
Range: combat radius on a combat air patrol with six AIM-7 Sparrows and four AIM-9 Sidewinders 1,075 nm (1,239 miles; 1994 km)
Weights: empty 41,780 lb (18951 kg); normal take-off 64,093 lb (29072 kg) for a fighter/escort mission or 73,098 lb (33157 kg) on a fleet air defence mission; maximum take-off 74,349 lb (33724 kg) lb
Speed: maximum level speed 'clean' at high altitude

1,078 kt (1,241 mph; 1997 km/h); cruising speed at optimum altitude 413 kt (475 mph; 764 km/h)
Range: maximum range with internal and external fuel about 1,600 nm (1,842 miles; 2965 km)
Performance: maximum rate of climb at sea level more than 30,000 ft (9145 m) per minute; service ceiling more than 53,000 ft (16150 m); take-off run 2,500 ft (762 m) from land at maximum take-off weight; landing run 2,400 ft (732 m) on land

Grumman F-14 Super Tomcat 21

In recent times, Grumman has devoted a considerable amount of effort to designing advanced Tomcat variants in the hope of securing orders for continued work in either new or rebuild form, partly to fill the gap left by cancellation of the A-12 Avenger and partly as an alternative to the proposed NATF (Navy Advanced Tactical Fighter) project. Most of these projects aimed to enhance the air-to-ground capability of the Tomcat.

The **Quickstrike F-14** was a minimum

change aircraft, with FLIR and expanded radar modes, an NVG-compatible cockpit and extra hardpoints. The Super Tomcat 21 was a more ambitious aircraft, taking the Quickstrike as a starting point and intended as a multi-role alternative to NATF, offering 90 per cent capability at 60 per cent cost.

Two basic versions were envisaged, with the **Super Tomcat 21** being optimised for air-to-air tasks but also being capable of undertaking air-to-ground strike missions. Revamping of aerodynamic aspects centred

around adoption of an enlarged wing glove area as well as a bigger tailplane assembly and revised slat and flap surfaces. Between them, these would bestow extra fuel capacity, giving greatly increased duration, while handling qualities would be improved with a reduced approach speed and the ability to undertake zero-wind launch. Weapons system improvement would include helmet-mounted sighting devices, radar and FLIR pods for attack tasks.

The second version was the **Attack**

Super Tomcat 21. This would be a dedicated strike/attack model, with superior air-to-ground potential. Improvements listed for the baseline Super Tomcat 21 would be augmented by adoption of a new radar, and Grumman's proposal did specifically mention the unit that was under development for the A-12 before it was abandoned. At the present time, it seems unlikely that either proposal will reach fruition, nor will the **ASF-14**, a proposed version using ATF systems and powerplants.

Grumman G-164 Ag-Cat

Since 1968, the **Greek air force** has had responsibility for crop-spraying on behalf of the ministry of works, forming for this purpose Mira 359 Aeroplikis Exipiretisis Dimosion Ypresion (MAEDY, or Air Force Squadron No. 359 for crop-spraying for ministry of works). This led to the unusual appearance of a fleet of Grumman Ag-Cat biplanes in full air force insignia. The **G-164 Ag-Cat** had first flown on 22 May 1957 as Grumman's only venture into agricultural air-

craft, production being handled from the outset by the Schweizer company, which acquired full rights to the design in 1981. Greece acquired 23 Ag-Cats with 450-hp (336-kW) Pratt & Whitney R-985 engines and enclosed cockpits.

A pair of Greek air force Ag-Cats rests between crop-spraying duties. The air force undertakes such work for the government.

Grumman OV-1/RV-1 Mohawk

The **Grumman OV-1/RV-1 Mohawk** is nearing the end of a 35-year service life as the **US Army**'s principal fixed-wing battlefield surveillance and intelligence-gathering aircraft. Though not fast enough to operate at the front in a high-density con-

flict, the Mohawk enjoys unique capabilities for combat support from rough forward airstrips in Third World conflicts.

The crew of two, pilot and observer, sit side-by-side on Martin-Baker J5 ejection seats beneath a bubble-like braced canopy

which offers excellent visibility. All Mohawk variants are equipped with cameras and upward-firing flares for the nocturnal photo-reconnaissance mission. The current OV-1D is dual-role capable, being convertible to either IR or SLAR monitoring missions.

The prototype **YOV-1A** (originally, **YAO-1A**) first flew on 14 April 1959, the only version with dual flight controls and the first turbine-powered aircraft accepted for US Army-wide use. Thirteen service-test and 64 production models were built. The **OV-1B (AO-1B)**, delivered in April 1961, carried AN/APS-94 SLAR in a long pod beneath the right side of the fuselage and introduced a 6-ft (1.83-m) increase in span.

The **OV-1C (AO-1C)**, first delivered in October 1961, introduced the UAS-4 infra-red mapping sensor mounted in the central fuselage and was retrofitted with T53-L-15s used on all subsequent variants. **Israel** received four OV-1Cs (the only overseas purchaser, although the Mohawk was evaluated by France, Germany, Pakistan and the Philippines), subsequently upgraded to OV-1D standard and retrofitted with indigenous sensors.

The definitive Mohawk for battlefield surveillance and target-acquisition duties was the **OV-1D/RV-1D**. Thirty-seven were built new, and 111 earlier Mohawks were upgraded to this standard. The OV-1D's sensors include AN/APD-7 radar surveillance system, AN/AAS-24 infra-red scanners, and KS-60 cameras. Most are now in Army National Guard service. Two GOV-1D ground trainers are based at Fort Eustis, VA.

Some 36 RV-1Ds were converted from earlier airframes under the Quick Look II programme for Elint duties, apparently equipped with AN/ALQ-33 tactical Elint system, AN/ASN-86 inertial navigation system, and real-time data processing and transmission equipment. One example is reported to have been shot down over Central America in 1984.

The US Army does not acknowledge the existence of the **EV-1E Quick Look III** tactical Elint variant used to collect and relay hostile emissions while patrolling a border. Israel reportedly modified one of its airframes as the testbed for this US Army version, which served in Korea and Germany.

One Mohawk was used by NASA for engine-noise monitoring tests with a wing-mounted 2,200-lb (9.78-kN) thrust Pratt & Whitney Canada JT15D-1 turbofan engine. Total production was 380 Mohawks, with production ending in December 1970 and

upgrade work completed in July 1987. OV-1/RV-1 Mohawks are approaching fatigue life limits and have become expensive to operate. By 1996, all will be replaced by RC-12K/N aircraft employing the Guardrail Common Sensor system. Twenty OV-1s were transferred to **Argentina** from US Army stocks, while some US OV-1Ds previously deployed to **South Korea** were handed over to the host nation.

SPECIFICATION

Grumman OV-1D Mohawk
Wing: span 48 ft 0 in (14.63 m); aspect ratio 6.4; area 360.00 sq ft (33.45 m²)

Fuselage and tail: length 41 ft 0 in (12.50 m); height 12 ft 8 in (3.86 m); tailplane span 15 ft 11 in (4.85 m); wheel track 9 ft 2 in (2.79 m); wheel base 11 ft 8.25 in (3.56 m)
Powerplant: two Textron Lycoming T53-L-15 each rated at 1,100 shp (820 kW)
Weights: empty equipped 11,067 lb (5020 kg); normal take-off 13,650 lb (6197 kg); maximum take-off 19,230 lb (8722 kg)
Fuel and load: internal fuel 297 US gal (1125 litres); external fuel up to two 150-US gal (567-litre) drop tanks; maximum ordnance 2,700 lb (1225 kg)
Speed: maximum level speed 'clean' at 5,000 ft (1525 m) 258 kt (297 mph; 478 km/h); maximum cruising speed at optimum altitude 239 kt (275 mph; 443 km/h)
Range: ferry range 1,068 nm (1,250 miles; 1980 km) with drop tanks

The Mohawk is slowly being retired from US Army service, its role having passed to the Beech RC-12, but some surplus aircraft have been supplied to Argentina. The OV-1D can be reconfigured for either infra-red or radar reconnaissance, with interchangeable sensors and cockpit displays.

Performance: maximum rate of climb at sea level 2,350 ft (716 m) per minute; service ceiling 30,300 ft (9235 m); minimum take-off run 580 ft (177 m); take-off distance to 50 ft (15 m) 880 ft (268 m) at maximum take-off weight; landing distance from 50 ft (15 m) 866 ft (264 m) at maximum landing weight; typical landing run 540 ft (165 m)

Grumman **S-2 Tracker**

Grumman S-2E Tracker

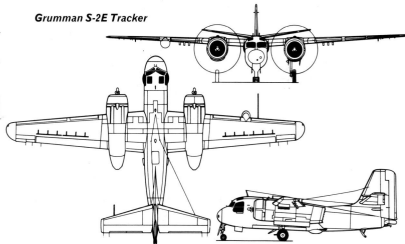

The **Grumman S-2 Tracker** is still used by several nations, some of which have only recently updated their fleets through acquisition of surplus USN S-2s taken from storage at Davis-Monthan AFB, near Tucson in Arizona.

One of the most successful ASW aircraft yet conceived, the Tracker first flew in December 1952 and entered service with the US Navy in 1954. It was continuously updated, while many of the earlier machines found work as utility and training aircraft, as the **US-2A/B** and **TS-2A**, respectively. Some TS-2As remained active as multi-engine pilot trainers until replaced by the Beech T-44A in 1980. Most Trackers currently active are late-production **S-2E**s and **S-2G**s, the latter being an S-2E with updated electronics.

Some operators have opted to convert their aircraft to **Turbo-Tracker** standard, fitting Garrett TPE331-15AW or Pratt & Whitney Canada PT6A-67CF turboprops in conversions offered by IMP (Canada), Bedek (Israel), and Grumman and Marsh in the US.

Remaining Trackers are still active with **Argentina** (six **S-2E(UP) Turbo**s converted by Bedek and three S-2As), **Brazil** (eight S-2As and five S-2Es being converted with IMP kits), **Peru** (seven S-2E and four S-2G), **South Korea** (nine S-2As and 15 S-2Es), **Taiwan** (32 S-2E and S-2Fs in the

process of conversion to Turbo standard), **Thailand** (six S-2F/US-2Cs, likely to have been withdrawn), **Turkey** (33 S-2A/Es) and **Uruguay** (three S-2As and three S-2Gs).

SPECIFICATION

Grumman S-2E Tracker
Wing: span 72 ft 7 in (22.13 m); width folded 27 ft 4 in (8.33 m); aspect ratio 10.63; area 496.00 sq ft (46.08 m²)
Fuselage and tail: length 43 ft 6 in (13.26 m); height 16 ft 7 in (5.06 m); wheel track 18 ft 6 in (5.64 m)
Powerplant: two Wright R-1820-82WA Cyclone each rated at 1,525 hp (1137 kW)
Weights: empty 18,750 lb (8505 kg); normal take-off 24,413 lb (11074 kg); maximum take-off 29,150 lb (13222 kg)

Taiwan retains the Tracker for anti-submarine work. It is one of the nations updating its aircraft with turboprop engines to increase the performance, economy and mission capability. The aircraft fly with the 439th Wing at Pingtung, operated by 33 and 34 Squadrons.

Grumman S-2 Tracker

Fuel and load: internal fuel 4,368 lb (1981 kg);
external fuel none; maximum ordnance 4,810 lb (2182 kg)
Speed: maximum level speed 'clean' at sea level
more than 230 kt (265 mph; 426 km/h); cruising speed
at optimum altitude 180 kt (207 mph; 333 km/h);
patrol speed at 1,500 ft (457 m) 130 kt (150 mph;
241 km/h)
Range: ferry range 1,130 nm (1,301 miles; 2094 km);
range 1,000 nm (1,152 miles; 1853 km); endurance
9 hours
Performance: maximum rate of climb at sea level
1,390 ft (425 m) per minute; service ceiling 21,000 ft
(6400 m); take-off run 1,300 ft (396 m) at maximum
take-off weight; take-off distance to 50 ft (15 m)
1,875 ft (572 m) at maximum take-off weight

*Several companies offer turbine
conversions of Tracker aircraft. IAI
has won a contract to re-engine
Argentina's six aircraft with the
Garrett TPE331-15 turboprop
(installed by Marsh Aviation) and
hopes to gain more orders, despite
other competitors in the S-2 re-
engining market. IAI also offers
avionics upgrading for the S-2,
greatly enhancing its effectiveness.*

Grumman **U-16 Albatross**

The air force of **Greece** is the last of
more than a dozen military air arms that
have operated the **Grumman HU-16
Albatross** SAR and maritime reconnaissance amphibian. Since the first flight of the
Albatross on 24 October 1947, Grumman
built 418, primarily for US Navy and Air
Force, as well as export to foreign countries
through MAP. Powered by two 1,425-hp
(1063-kW) Wright R-1820-76A piston radial
engines, the Albatross was built in two principal versions, initially (**HU-16A**) with a
wing span of 80 ft 0 in (24.38 m) and later
(**HU-16B**) with a span of 96 ft 8 in (29.46 m).

For anti-submarine warfare, a version
with nose-mounted search radar was supplied to Norway. Twelve of these aircraft
were later transferred to Greece, where the
survivors continue in service with 353 Mira
in the 112a Pterix Mahis (Combat Wing) at
Elefsis. In Indonesia four HU-16s were
flown until recently as part of the equipment of No. 5 Skwadron at Semarang
alongside helicopters, flying in the
SAR/transport role.

*Now reaching the end of its long
military career, the Albatross
remains in service only with the
Greek air force's 353 Mira at Elefsina.
The unit is appropriately nicknamed
'Albatros'. The HU-16Bs provide SAR
and coastal patrol cover.*

SPECIFICATION

Grumman HU-16B Albatross
Wing: span 96 ft 8 in (29.46 m); aspect ratio 9.03;
area 1,035.00 sq ft (96.15 m²)
Fuselage and tail: length 62 ft 10 in (19.15 m);
height 25 ft 10 in (7.87 m); tailplane span 31 ft 0 in
(9.45 m)
Powerplant: two Wright R-1820-76A Cyclone each
rated at 1,425 hp (1062 kW)
Weights: empty 22,883 lb (10380 kg); normal take-off
30,353 lb (13768 kg); maximum take-off 34,000 lb
(15422 kg) on water and 37,500 lb (17010 kg) on land
Fuel and load: internal fuel 1,088 US gal (4119

litres); external fuel up to two 295-US gal (1117-litre)
drop tanks; maximum ordnance none
Speed: maximum level speed 'clean' at sea level
205 kt (236 mph; 380 km/h); cruising speed at
optimum altitude 149 kt (172 mph; 277 km/h)
Range: ferry range 3,010 nm (3,466 miles; 5578 km);
range 1,490 nm (1,716 miles; 2761 km)
Performance: maximum rate of climb at sea level
1,170 ft (357 m) per minute; ceiling 23,500 ft
(7165 m)

Grumman/General Dynamics **EF-111 Raven**

Based on the original F-111A production
variant of the General Dynamics swing-
wing strike fighter, the **EF-111A Raven**
evolved as a specialised electronic warfare
platform capable of undertaking stand-off
and penetration escort missions. Responsibility for development was entrusted to
Grumman, which already had considerable
expertise in the EW field, having produced
the EA-6A version of the Intruder for the
Marine Corps and the even more capable
EA-6B Prowler for both the USN and
USMC.

*All EF-111As now serve with the 27th
FW. The two operating units are the
429th and 430th (illustrated)
Electronic Combat Squadrons.*

Indeed, the TJS that forms the core of
the EF-111A's impressive capability is fundamentally a variation of the AN/ALQ-99
TJS as fitted to the EA-6B. The Raven introduces a much improved equipment package, however, with certain key items being
housed internally rather than in underwing
pods as on the EA-6B. It also embodies a
greater degree of automation so as to allow
it to be fully and effectively managed by just

one EWO, rather than three as in the
Prowler. As in all versions of the F-111
family, the Raven pilot and EWO occupy
side-by-side seating in an escape capsule.

Receiving antennas associated with the
TJS are located in the distinctive bulbous
fin-cap fairing, while the jamming transmitters are contained in space previously occupied by the F-111A's internal weapons bay.

CONVERSION PROGRAMME

Grumman was awarded the contract to develop the EF-111 on 26 December 1974. An aerodynamic prototype flew on 15 December 1975, and the first 'full-up' aircraft on 10 March 1977. A total of 42 F-111As was modified, retaining the bomber's TF30-P-3 engines and Triple Plow I intakes. The conversion involved reworking the weapons bay to accommodate the jammers, adding the fin antennas and removing all offensive equipment. The right side of the cockpit was revised to incorporate EW displays and controls, with some navigation equipment being relocated to the pilot's position.

MISSION

The EF-111 operates in three principal roles: stand-off, strike escort and close air support. In the stand-off role the EF-111 supplies jamming from safe airspace. It can either blanket a hostile air defence or, with the aid of lethal SEAD assets, punch a hole through a heavily defended border to provide a corridor through which strike aircraft can flow. In the strike escort role it accompanies the strike force throughout the penetration mission, while in the close support role it neutralises radars in the battlefield while attack aircraft take on armour formations. The EF-111 operates closely with the F-4G Wild Weasel (lethal SEAD) and EC-130H Compass Call (command, control and communications jamming) to present a powerful counter to any air defence system.

JAMMERS

The main jamming equipment is housed in the former weapons bay, with the transmitters housed in the 16-ft (4.9-m) ventral canoe fairing. There are 10 transmitters, five exciters and six digitally-tuned receivers. The equipment covers seven frequency bands. At the rear of the bay are two air-water heat exchangers which cool the system.

SELF-DEFENCE MISSILES

One set of wing pylons is retained to allow the EF-111 to carry AIM-9 Sidewinders for self-defence. The aircraft's performance and onboard jammers are its primary means of defence.

Grumman/General Dynamics EF-111A Raven

Widely known as the 'Spark Vark', the EF-111A provides the US Air Force with its non-lethal SEAD (suppression of enemy air defences) assets. The jamming system is based on that of the EA-6B Prowler, but features greater automation to enable only one electronic warfare officer to operate it. Compared to the Prowler, the EF-111 has far better performance, which allows it to operate more effectively in the strike escort role, especially when supporting high-performance jets such as the F-111 or F-15E. However, it does not have HARM-firing capability, which restricts it to non-lethal SEAD, whereas the Block 86 EA-6Bs can launch the AGM-88.

An underview emphasises the ghostly qualities of the EF-111. All of the jammers are housed in the canoe fairing. As all of the Ravens were converted from F-111As, they inherited the Triple Plow I intakes with large splitter plates.

The canoe fairing hinges open to allow rapid access to the jammers for maintenance.

RECEIVER ANTENNAS

Hostile radar emissions are detected by antennas in the SIR (System Integrated Receiver) pod mounted at the top of the fin (otherwise known as the 'football'). These face forwards, sideways and rearwards, and are augmented by further receivers lower down on the fin and blade antennas on the sides of the engine intake trunks. Receivers provide information to the central computer, which processes the data, analyses and prioritises the threats for display in the cockpit and automatic operation of the jamming system.

and the speed at which those countermeasures could be implemented, but it appears that cuts in defence spending may well curtail the extent of the improvement effort. However, even though updating may not be quite as ambitious as first hoped, there appears to be little likelihood of early or premature retirement, since the EF-111A is still the only dedicated jamming platform in the USAF inventory and is likely to remain unique in that capacity for the foreseeable future.

Reductions in the size of USAFE following the demise of the Warsaw Pact alliance included the withdrawal of the EF-111A squadron from Upper Heyford during 1992. The Raven force is now concentrated in the US under the control of Air Combat Command with the 27th Fighter Wing at Cannon AFB, NM, which now operates all the surviving F-111 variants.

On account of its jamming systems, the EF-111A is well-protected against missile attack. However, its best defence remains the sheer speed and acceleration available at all altitudes.

Protruding beneath the aircraft, these are covered by a 'canoe' radome that measures approximately 16 ft (5 m) in length. Other items of equipment associated with EW role include active and passive ECM systems, and the EF-111 also features an AN/ALR-23 infra-red warning system.

Unarmed warrior

Unlike other variants of the F-111 family, the EF-111A has no armament capability and is therefore forced to rely purely on performance and evasion in the event of running into hostile fighters. The EF-111A was committed to combat during Operation

Desert Storm when it operated from bases at Taif, Saudi Arabia, with the 48th Tactical Fighter Wing (Provisional) and Incirlik, Turkey, with the 7440th Wing (Provisional). Employed mainly in a supporting role by disrupting hostile radars with its jamming, it did manage to emerge victorious in an aerial engagement with an Iraqi Mirage F1 on the first night of the air campaign, when skilful manoeuvring by a Raven pilot caused his pursuer to fly into the ground. This was, in fact, one of the first Iraqi warplanes to be destroyed during the war, although it appears that it was never officially accredited as a 'kill'.

Development of the EF-111A was initiated in 1972, but it was not until 1975 that Grumman received an $89.5 million contract covering the conversion of two prototypes, both of which flew for the first time in 1977. After lengthy and extensive testing of the sophisticated system, production-config-

ured conversions eventually entered service with TAC's 366th TFW at Mountain Home AFB, ID, and others were subsequently assigned to USAFE's 42nd Electronic Combat Squadron at Upper Heyford, England.

Conversion total

A total of 42 aircraft was eventually brought to EF-111A Raven standard by Grumman and most of these are still operational, although one was lost during the Gulf War and at least one other is known to have been destroyed in a crash while assigned to the 42nd ECS in England. Survivors were earmarked for an extensive Service Improvement Program (SIP) which was intended to upgrade existing capability and enhance reliability to counter progressively more sophisticated radar threats.

Part of this work was intended to increase the number of hostile emitters that could be countered by the AN/ALQ-99E TJS

SPECIFICATION

Grumman/General Dynamics EF-111A Raven
generally similar to the General Dynamics F-111A except in the following particulars
Fuselage and tail: length 76 ft 0 in (23.16 m); height 20 ft 0 in (6.10 m)
Powerplant: two Pratt & Whitney TF30-P-3 each rated at 18,500 lb st (82.29 kN) with afterburning
Weights: operating empty 55,275 lb (25072 kg); normal take-off 70,000 lb (31752 kg); maximum take-off 88,948 lb (40347 kg)
Fuel and load: internal fuel 32,493 lb (14739 kg)
Speed: maximum speed at high altitude 1,226 kt (1,412 mph; 2272 km/h); maximum combat speed 1,196 kt (1,377 mph; 2216 km/h); average speed in combat area 507 kt (584 mph; 940 km/h)
Range: combat radius 807 nm (929 miles; 1495 km); unrefuelled endurance more than 4 hours 0 minutes
Performance: maximum rate of climb at sea level 3,300 ft (1006 m) per minute; service ceiling 45,000 ft (13715 m)

Guizhou (GAIC) JJ-7/FT-7

*Guizhou Aviation Industry Corporation
PO Box 38, Anshun,
Guizhou 561000, China*

Developed by the Guizhou Aviation Industry Corporation (GAIC) as a combat-capable two-seat fighter-trainer derivative of the Chengdu J-7 II single-seat fighter (which was, in turn, the result of incremental redesign of the licence-built MiG-21F-13), the **JJ-7**, or **Jianjiao-7**, was first flown on 5 July 1985. Closely resembling the tandem-seat MiG-21U, the JJ-7 has starboard-opening twin cockpit canopies, the aft cockpit being fitted with a retractable periscope and provision being made for a removable saddleback fuel tank. Powered by a 43.15-kN (9,700-lb st) dry and 59.8-kN

(13,448-lb st) afterburning Chengdu WP-7B turbojet, the JJ-7 can carry a centreline ventral twin-barrelled 23-mm cannon pack plus two PL-2B AAMs, two 18-round 57-mm rocket pods or two 250-kg (551-lb) bombs.

The JJ-7 entered production for the **People's Republic of China** air force in 1987, simultaneously being offered with a GEC-supplied avionics suite for export as the **FT-7**. One of the first customers for the export model was the **Pakistan** air force, which procured 15 (as **FT-7Ps**). **Bangladesh** has also bought the type to supplement its two F-7 squadrons.

SPECIFICATION

Guizhou JJ-7/FT-7
Wing: span 7.154 m (23 ft 5.375 in); aspect ratio 2.2; area 23.00 m² (247.58 sq ft)
Fuselage and tail: length 14.874 m (48 ft 9.5 in) including probe; height 4.103 m (13 ft 5.5 in); tailplane span 3.74 m (12 ft 3.25 in); wheel track 2.692 m (8 ft 10 in); wheel base 4.807 m (15 ft 9.25 in)
Powerplant: one Liyang (LMC) Wopen-7B turbojet rated at 43.15 kN (9,700 lb st) dry and 59.82 kN (13,448 lb st) with afterburning
Weights: empty equipped 5330 kg (11,750 lb); normal take-off 7590 kg (16,733 lb); maximum take-off

8600 kg (18,959 lb)
Fuel and load: internal fuel 1891 kg (4,169 lb); external fuel up to one 800- or 400-litre (211- or 127-US gal) drop tank; maximum ordnance 500 kg (1,102 lb)
Speed: maximum level speed 'clean' at 12500 m (41,010 ft) 2175 km/h (1,172 kt; 1,350 mph)
Range: ferry range 1300 km (701 nm; 808 miles) with drop tank; range 1010 km (545 nm; 627 miles) with internal fuel
Performance: maximum rate of climb at sea level about 9000 m (29,530 ft) per minute; service ceiling 17300 m (56,760 ft); take-off run 900 m (2,953 ft) at normal take-off weight increasing to 1100 m (3,609 ft) at maximum take-off weight; landing run 1100 m

Most JJ-7/FT-7s have been produced for the Chinese air arms, but also for Pakistan and Bangladesh. The Pakistani aircraft (right) serves with No. 20 Squadron, while the Bangladeshi aircraft (left) wears the markings of Nos 5 'Supersonics' and 35 'Thundercats' Sqns.

Gulfstream Aerospace (Grumman)
Gulfstream I/TC-4A Academe

*Gulfstream Aerospace Corporation
PO Box 2206, Savannah International Airport,
Savannah, GA 31402, USA*

The **US Navy** adopted a version of the **Grumman Gulfstream I** twin-turboprop executive aircraft in December 1966, for use to train Intruder bombardier/naviga-

tors in the use of the DIANE nav/attack weapon systems of the A-6. A simulated A-6 cockpit was located in the rear of the cabin, together with four identical radar/

navigation training consoles. Since entering service with VA-42 and VA-128, and with the USMC's VMAT-202, nine **TC-4Cs** have been extensively updated to match latest

A-6E avionic standards. A single **VC-4A** is used by the **US Coast Guard** as an executive transport, a role in which single 'G1s' are flown by **Greece** and **Venezuela**.

Left: The TC-4C is used as a trainer for A-6E bombardiers, and has an Intruder weapons system.

SPECIFICATION

Gulfstream Aerospace TC-4C Academe
Wing: span 78 ft 4 in (23.88 m); aspect ratio 10.05; area 610.30 sq ft (56.70 m2)
Fuselage and tail: length 67 ft 10.75 in (20.69 m); height 23 ft 4 in (7.11 m); tailplane span 25 ft 6 in (7.77 m); wheel track 24 ft 2 in (7.37 m); wheel base 19 ft 9.5 in (6.03 m)
Powerplant: two Rolls-Royce Dart RDa.7/2 Mk 529-8X turboprops each rated at 2,210 ehp (1648 ekW)
Weights: empty 24,575 lb (11114 kg); maximum take-off 36,000 lb (16330 kg)

Fuel and load: internal fuel 1,550 US gal (5867 litres); external fuel none; maximum payload 4,270 lb (1937 kg)
Speed: maximum speed at 15,000 ft (4570 m) 317 kt (365 mph; 587 km/h); maximum cruising speed at 25,000 ft (7620 m) 302 kt (348 mph; 560 km/h); economical cruising speed at 25,000 ft (7620 m) 259 kt (298 mph; 480 km/h)
Range: typical range at 30,000 ft (9145 m) 1720 nm (1,980 miles; 3186 km) or at 5,000 ft (1525 m) 995 nm (1,145 miles; 1843 km)
Performance: maximum rate of climb at sea level 1,900 ft (579 m) per minute; service ceiling 33,600 ft (10240 m); take-off distance to 35 ft (10.7 m) 3,000 ft

(914 m) at maximum take-off weight; landing distance from 50 ft (15 m) 2,100 ft (664 m) at maximum landing weight

This single Gulfstream I flies with the Greek air force's 356 'Iraklis' Mira on VIP/staff transport duties. It is based at Elefsina.

Gulfstream Aerospace (Grumman) Gulfstream II/VC-11A

The **Gulfstream II** long-range executive jet was built successively by Grumman, Grumman American and Gulfstream American between October 1966 and March 1980. Only one example, of 258 built, was sold as new for other than civil use. This was an example acquired as a VIP/staff transport by the **US Coast Guard** and designated **VC-11A**, becoming the first pure jet aircraft operated by the CG when delivered in July 1968. A few used Gulf-

stream IIs have been acquired by other military operators for communications and VIP transport duties, including the **US Army** (two VC-11As) and the air forces of **Morocco**, **Oman** and **Venezuela**.

SPECIFICATION

Gulfstream Aerospace Gulfstream II
Wing: span 68 ft 10 in (20.98 m); aspect ratio 5.97;

area 793.50 sq ft (73.72 m2)
Fuselage and tail: length 79 ft 11 in (24.36 m); height 24 ft 6 in (7.47 m); tailplane span 27 ft 0 in (8.23 m); wheel track 13 ft 8 in (4.16 m); wheel base 33 ft 4 in (10.16 m)
Powerplant: two Rolls-Royce Spey RB.168 Mk 511-8 turbofans each rated at 11,400 lb st (50.71 kN) dry
Weights: maximum take-off 57,500 lb (26081 kg)
Fuel and load: internal fuel 22,500 lb (10206 kg); external fuel none
Speed: maximum level speed 'clean' at 25,000 ft

(7620 m) 508 kt (585 mph; 941 km/h); maximum cruising speed at optimum altitude 491 kt (565 mph; 909 km/h)
Range: range 3,005 nm (3,460 miles; 5568 km)
Performance: maximum rate of climb at sea level 5,050 ft (1539 m) per minute; service ceiling 43,000 ft (13105 m); take-off balanced field length 4,070 ft (1241 m) at maximum take-off weight; landing balanced field length 3,080 ft (939 m) at normal landing weight

Gulfstream Aerospace (Grumman) Gulfstream III/C-20/SRA-1

Of similar configuration to the Gulfstream II, the **Gulfstream III** was launched by Grumman American in 1976, its development and production becoming the responsibility of Gulfstream American in 1978 after Grumman sold its interest. The 19-seat Gulfstream III, which first flew on 2 December 1979, features a 24-in (61-cm) stretch and an improved wing with winglets. The **USAF** operates three Gulfstream IIIs as **C-20A**s, and eight **C-20B/C-20C**s (with basic AC instead of DC electrical systems) used by the 89th AW at Andrews AFB for VIP use. Generally similar transport versions are two **C-20D** 14-seat staff transports used by the **US Navy** and two **C-20E**s serving the **US Army**. Gulfstream IIIs are also used in VIP or Presidential transport role by the air forces of **Gabon** (Presidential Guard), **Italy**, **Ivory Coast**, **Mexico**, **Morocco**, **Oman**, **Saudi Arabia** and **Venezuela**.

Three special mission aircraft, designated **SMA-3**, were supplied to the **Royal Danish air force** in 1981/82, and equipped with quickly-convertible interiors to allow their use in a variety of roles including, in particular, fishery patrols. The three are operated by No. 721 Squadron, which also

flies Hercules from its base at at Vaerløse, near Copenhagen. One aircraft is usually detached to Greenland for fishery patrols and SAR support. Equipped as a surveillance and reconnaissance aircraft, a **Gulfstream SRA-1** demonstrator was flown on 14 August 1984 and two aircraft to this standard are operated by **India**, apparently on clandestine Elint missions.

SPECIFICATION

Gulfstream Aerospace Gulfstream III
Wing: span 77 ft 10 in (23.72 m); aspect ratio 6.48; area 934.60 sq ft (86.83 m2)
Fuselage and tail: length 83 ft 1 in (25.32 m); height 24 ft 4.5 in (7.43 m); tailplane span 27 ft 0 in (8.23 m); wheel track 13 ft 10 in (4.22 m); wheel base 35 ft 2 in (10.72 m)
Powerplant: two Rolls-Royce Spey RB.168 Mk 511-8 turbofans each rated at 11,400 lb st (50.71 kN)
Weights: manufacturer's empty 32,300 lb (14651 kg); typical operating empty 38,000 lb (17236 kg); maximum take-off 68,200 lb (30936 kg)
Fuel and load: internal fuel 28,300 lb (12836 kg);

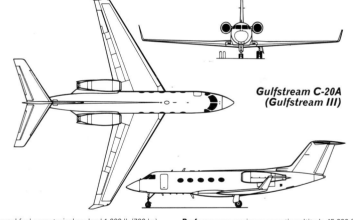

Gulfstream C-20A (Gulfstream III)

external fuel none; typical payload 1,600 lb (726 kg)
Speed: maximum cruising speed at 30,000 ft (9145 m) 501 kt (577 mph; 929 km/h); economical cruising speed at 30,000 ft (9145 m) 453 kt (522 mph; 840 km/h)
Range: 3,647 nm (4,200 miles; 6760 km)

Performance: maximum operating altitude 45,000 ft (13715 m); take-off balanced field length 5,700 ft (1737 m) at maximum take-off weight; landing run 3,400 ft (1036 m) at normal landing weight

Below: All four US services use the C-20 for staff transport duties.

Right: Denmark's G III force is used for SAR and fishery patrols in addition to transport.

Gulfstream Aerospace Gulfstream IV/C-20/SRA-4

First flown on 19 September 1985, the Gulfstream IV was developed from the G III, from which it differed primarily in having a 54-in (1.37-m) fuselage stretch, Rolls-Royce Tay in place of Spey engines, structural improvements, increased fuel capacity and a modernised cockpit. Like the G III, the G IV finds application as a VIP transport for military use, examples to date including a **C-20F** for the **US Army**, five **C-20G**s for the **US Navy** (two for active-duty, two for the Reserve and one for the **USMC**), and a single **C-20H** for the **USAF**. The C-20Gs delivered in 1994 are equipped with cargo doors and convertible passenger/cargo interiors. The US Navy C-20Gs serve with VR-48 at Andrews AFB, where the single C-20H will join earlier USAF C-20 models serving in the 89th MAW. One civil-registered Gulfstream IV serves in the quasi-military VIP transport squadron of the **Egyptian air force** at Cairo East, and another is used for high-altitude navaid checking by the Japanese ministry of transport. The Gulfstream IV is used additionally by the **Botswana** defence force (one), the **Irish Air Corps** (one), the

Turkish air force (three operated by 224 Filo for VIP transportation) and the **Swedish air force** (one for transport/ training and two for Elint duty). The designation **SRA-4** refers to a proposed special-mission version of the Gulfstream IV, for such roles as EW support, electronic surveillance/reconnaissance, maritime patrol, ASW, medevac and priority cargo transport. A prototype/demonstrator was flown in 1988. The designation **EC-20F** referred to a proposed version for the US Navy FEWSG missions.

SPECIFICATION

Gulfstream Aerospace Gulfstream SRA-4
Wing: span 77 ft 10 in (23.72 m) over winglets; aspect ratio 6.0; area 950.39 sq ft (88.29 m2)
Fuselage and tail: length 88 ft 4 in (26.92 m); height 24 ft 10 in (7.57 m); tailplane span 32 ft 0 in (9.75 m); wheel track 13 ft 8 in (4.17 m); wheel base 38 ft 1.25 in (11.61 m)
Powerplant: two Rolls-Royce Tay Mk 611-8 turbofans rated at 13,850 lb st (61.61 kN)
Weights: manufacturer's empty 35,500 lb (16102 kg);

maximum take-off 73,200 lb (33203 kg)
Fuel and load: internal fuel 29,500 lb (13381 kg); external fuel none; maximum payload 6,198 lb (2811 kg) including 600 lb (272 kg) of expendables
Speed: never-exceed speed Mach 0.88; maximum cruising speed at 31,000 ft (9450 m) 509 kt (586 mph; 943 km/h); economical cruising speed at 41,000 ft (12500 m) 454 kt (523 mph; 841 km/h)
Range: operational radius typically 600 nm (691 miles; 1112 km) for a 6-hour patrol with a 6,198-lb (2811-kg) mission payload, or 1,000 nm (1,152 miles; 1853 km) for a 4.3-hour patrol with a 5,518-lb

In Swedish service the G IV is known as the Tp 102, three serving with F16M. This is the single transport version on strength.

(2503-kg) mission payload including six crew and one anti-ship missile
Performance: maximum rate of climb at sea level 4,000 ft (1219 m) per minute; service ceiling 45,000 ft (13715 m); take-off balanced field length 5,250 ft (1600 m); landing distance from 50 ft (15 m) 3,366 ft (1026 m) at normal landing weight

---

HFB (MBB) 320 Hansa

A product of the Hamburger Flugzeugbau before its merger into MBB (itself now a part of DASA), the **HFB 320 Hansa** is notable for its configuration, with a wing of moderate forward sweep. First flown on 21 April 1964 and intended for the corporate market, the seven- to 12-seat Hansa sold only in small numbers, and 16 of the 47 built were delivered to the **Luftwaffe**. Of these, eight used as transports were withdrawn in 1988; the other eight were converted to serve as ECM trainers or for airways calibration. At first flown by FVST 61, they are now operated by No. 323 Staffel in the mainly Tornado-equipped Jagdbomber-Geschwader 32 at Lechfeld.

SPECIFICATION

Hamburger Flugzeugbau HFB 320 Hansa
Wing: span 47 ft 4 in (14.46 m) over tiptanks; area 324.4 sq ft (30.14 m2)
Fuselage and tail: length 54 ft 6 in (16.61 m); height 15 ft 7.5 in (4.76 m); tailplane span 18 ft 2 in (5.55 m); wheel track 7 ft 9 in (2.36 m); wheel base 22 ft 1.5 in (6.74 m)
Powerplant: two General Electric CJ610-1 turbojets rated at 2,850 lb st (12.68 kN)
Weights: empty equipped 10,670 lb (4840 kg); maximum take-off 18,740 lb (8500 kg)
Fuel and load: internal fuel 7,341 lb (3330 kg);

Easily identified by its additional radomes and antennas, and Dayglo panels for high conspicuity, this is one of the HFB 320ECMs used by the Luftwaffe for EW training.

maximum payload 2,650 lb (1200 kg)
Speed: never-exceed speed Mach 0.83; maximum level speed at 26,250 ft (8000 m) 509 mph (819 km/h); economical cruising speed at 39,400 ft (12000 m) 449 mph (723 km/h)
Range: with maximum fuel, 760 lb (345 kg) payload at 39,400 ft (12000 m) and sufficient for diversion and reserves 1,450 miles (2335 km); with maximum

payload and sufficient for diversion and reserves 825 miles (1330 km)
Performance: maximum rate of climb at sea level 4,080 ft (1242 m) per minute; service ceiling 38,000 ft (11600 m); take-off run at 17,640 lb (8000 kg) 3,190 ft (970 m); take-off run to 35 ft (10.5 m) 3,190 ft (970 m); landing distance at 13,230 lb (6000 kg) 1,300 ft (395 m)

Harbin (HAMC) SH-5

*Harbin Aircraft Manufacturing Corporation
PO Box 201, Harbin,
Heilongjiang 150066, China*

The **SH-5**, or **Shuihong-5**, amphibious flying-boat was conceived in the mid-1960s as a maritime patrol and anti-submarine aircraft. Detail design was not completed, however, until February 1970, and the first flying prototype did not enter flight test until 3 April 1976. Some limited production of the SH-5 followed for the air component of the **People's Republic of China** navy, but the first four series aircraft were not handed over until a decade later, on 3 September 1986. These have since been operated from the Tuandao naval air base, Qingdao.

Powered by four Dongan (DEMC) WJ5A turboprops each rated at 3,150 ehp (2349 kW), the SH-5 has a flight crew of five plus three systems/equipment operators. Defensive armament consists of a twin-gun, remotely-controlled dorsal barbette, offensive weaponry including up to 6000 kg (13,228 lb) of depth charges, mines or bombs internally, plus external loads. The

latter may include up to four anti-shipping missiles suspended from wing hardpoints, each outer hardpoint being capable of lifting up to three lightweight torpedoes. SAR and water-bomber versions of the SH-5 have been evaluated, and a bulk cargo variant has been proposed. The Chinese were reportedly seeking an ASW avionics upgrade for the SH-5 in the early 1990s.

SPECIFICATION

Harbin SH-5
Wing: span 36.00 m (118 ft 1.25 in); aspect ratio 9.0; area 144.00 m2 (1550.05 sq ft)
Fuselage and tail: length 38.90 m (127 ft 7.5 in); height 9.802 m (32 ft 2 in); tailplane span 10.50 m (34 ft 5.5 in) over fins; wheel track 3.754 m (12 ft 3.75 in); wheel base 10.50 m (34 ft 5.5 in)
Powerplant: four Dongan (DEMC) Wojiang-5A1 turboprops each rated at 3,150 ehp (2349 ekW)
Weights: empty equipped less than 25000 kg

(55,115 lb) for the SAR and transport roles, or 26500 kg (58,422 lb) for the ASW role; normal take-off 36000 kg (79,365 lb); maximum take-off 45000 kg (99,206 lb)
Fuel and load: internal fuel 13417 kg (29,579 lb); external fuel none; maximum ordnance 6000 kg (13,228 lb) carried internally or maximum payload 10000 kg (22,046 lb)
Speed: maximum level speed 'clean' at optimum altitude 555 km/h (300 kt; 345 mph); maximum cruising speed at optimum altitude 450 km/h (243 kt; 280 mph); minimum patrol speed at optimum altitude 230 km/h (124 kt; 143 mph)
Range: 4750 km (2,563 nm; 2,951 miles); endurance between 12 hours and 15 hours on two engines

The impressive SH-5 undertakes many maritime roles, including ASV, ASW, SAR, fire fighting and minelaying.

Performance: service ceiling 10250 m (33,630 ft); take-off run 548 m (1,798 ft) on water at maximum take-off weight; landing run 653 m (2,143 ft) on water at normal landing weight

---

Harbin Y-11/Y-12

The **Harbin Y-11** was developed as a general utility aircraft to replace **China**'s Antonov An-2/Harbin Y-5. The initial aircraft were powered by two indigenous Quzhou Huosai-6A 213-kW (285-hp) nine-cylinder radial piston engines based on the Ivchenko AI-14RF. These allowed the

aircraft to carry a payload of 940 kg (2,072 lb), which was raised to 1250 kg (2,755 lb) when HS6D engines were fitted. Eight passengers could be carried in addition to two crew.

In order to give better single-engine performance the **Y-11B** was developed, with

350-hp (261-kW) Continental TSIO-550-B flat six engines. The prototype first flew on 25 December 1990 and deliveries began in 1992. The **Y-11BI** is similar, with further upgraded avionics.

The **Y-12I** shares the same configuration as the Y-11, but is of larger overall size, with a bigger fuselage cross-section and a fuselage 'plug' ahead of the wings. The new cabin accommodated up to 17 passengers. It was originally to have been designated

Y-11T1, but the Y-12 designation was adopted before the first flight. The new aircraft was originally to have been powered by a pair of 400-shp (298-kW) Allison 250-B17B turboprops but these were displaced by 500-shp (373-kW) Pratt & Whitney PT6A-11 turboprops. This led to the adoption of the name **'Turbo Panda'** for overseas marketing. Payload/range capability is dramatically improved by comparison with the Y-11. The prototype made its maiden flight on 14 July 1982 and was followed by about 30 production aircraft, most of which were used for geological survey and mineral exploration.

The Y-12I was replaced on the production line by the **Y-12II**, built to international airworthiness standards, powered by 507-kW (680-shp) PT6A-27 engines, and with leading-edge slats deleted. Military customers (all for the Y-12II) include **Sri Lanka** (nine, delivered from 1987), **Iran**, **Paraguay** (at least seven) and **Peru** (six).

SPECIFICATION

Harbin Y-12 II
Wing: span 17.235 m (56 ft 6.5 in); aspect ratio 8.7; area 34.27 m² (368.88 sq ft)
Fuselage and tail: length 14.86 m (48 ft 9 in); height 5.575 m (18 ft 3.5 in); elevator span 5.365 m (17 ft 7.27 in); wheel track 3.60 m (11 ft 9.75 in); wheel base 4.698 m (15 ft 5 in)
Powerplant: two Pratt & Whitney PT6A-27 turboprops each flat-rated at 680 shp (507 kW)
Weights: empty equipped 2840 kg (6,261 lb); operating empty 3000 kg (6,614 lb); normal take-off 4500 kg (9,921 lb) for agricultural use; maximum take-off 5300 kg (11,684 lb)
Fuel and load: internal fuel 1233 kg (2,718 lb); external fuel none; maximum payload 1700 kg (3,748 lb)
Speed: never-exceed speed at 3000 m (9,845 ft) 328 km/h (177 kt; 204 mph); maximum cruising speed at 3000 m (9,845 ft) 292 km/h (157 kt; 181 mph); economical cruising speed 3000 m (9,845 ft) 250 km/h (125 kt; 155 mph)
Range: 1340 km (723 nm; 832 miles)

Performance: maximum rate of climb at sea level 504 m (1,655 ft) per minute; service ceiling 7000 m (22,960 ft); take-off run 340 m (1,115 ft) at maximum take-off weight; take-off distance to 50 ft (15 m) 425 m (1,395 ft) at maximum take-off weight; landing distance from 50 ft (15 m) 500 m (1,640 ft) with

Sri Lanka's No. 2 Transport Wing operates six Y-12s from the base at Ratmalana.

propeller reversal at maximum landing weight; landing run 200 m (656 ft)

Harbin **Z-5/Z-6**

At the same time that the MiG-19 was selected by **China** for licence-production by Shenyang, production of the Mil Mi-4 'Hound' was entrusted to Harbin. Drawings arrived in 1958 and the prototype made its maiden flight on 14 December 1959, with certification following later in the same month. Like the J-6, the **Z-5** suffered

catastrophic quality control problems during the Great Leap Forward, and none was delivered.

Updated drawings were delivered in 1961, and the production tooling was completely rebuilt. The first 'acceptable' Z-5 made its maiden flight on 20 August 1963. The rotor blades of Chinese-built Mi-4s

The Harbin Z-5 forms the backbone of China's rotary-wing fleet, and is used for a wide variety of tasks. This example is seen sowing mines, fitted with chutes to slow their fall.

were originally made from dragon spruce instead of pine, but metal rotor blades were soon developed. The first metal-rotored Z-5 made its maiden flight on 22 June 1966.

The Z-5 was built in several different versions, for which local designations remain unknown. The basic military transport usually had an underfuselage gondola containing a fixed, forward-firing machine-gun, which is missing from others, and from the square-windowed passenger transport. A version delivered to the PLA Navy may have had an undernose radome and other ASW sensors.

At least one Z-5 was re-engined with a Pratt & Whitney PT6T-6 Turbo Twin-Pac and flew for the first time in 1979. The **Z-6** was an unrelated single turboshaft helicopter, whose relationship to the Z-5 (if any) is uncertain. A total of 545 Z-5s had been built by the time production ceased in 1979, including 86 passenger carriers, seven agricultural aircraft, 13 SAR aircraft and two dedicated survey platforms.

SPECIFICATION

Harbin Z-5
Rotor system: main rotor diameter 21.00 m (68 ft 11 in); main rotor disc area 346.36 m² (3,728.31 sq ft)
Fuselage and tail: length overall, rotors turning 25.02 m (82 ft 1 in) and fuselage 16.80 m (55 ft 1 in); height overall 4.40 m (14 ft 5.25 in)
Powerplant: one Harbin (HEF) Huosai-5A radial piston engine rated at 1,700 hp (1268 kW)
Weights: empty 5270 kg (11,618 lb); normal take-off 7200 kg (15,873 lb); maximum take-off 7800 kg (17,196 lb)
Fuel and load: internal fuel 1000 litres (264 US gal) plus provision for 500 litres (132 US gal) of auxiliary fuel in a cabin tank; external fuel none; maximum payload 1600 kg (3,527 lb)
Speed: maximum level speed at 1500 m (4,920 ft) 210 km/h (113 kt; 130 mph); maximum cruising speed at optimum altitude 160 km/h (86 kt; 99 mph)
Range: range 250 km (135 nm; 155 miles) with 11 passengers
Performance: service ceiling 5000 m (16,405 ft); hovering ceiling 700 m (2,295 ft) out of ground effect

Harbin **Z-9**

With the local name **Z-9 Haitun**, the Eurocopter AS 365N (described separately) is built under licence by Harbin for

both civil users and all three air arms. The first batch of agreed production covered 50 aircraft, the later ones to AS 365N1 stan-

dard. The current version is the **Z-9A-100**, of which an anti-tank version (with 'Red Arrow 8' missiles) has been reported.

Hawker Siddeley (de Havilland) **Trident**

Developed for British European Airways, the Trident (initially de Havilland D.H.121) was a stalwart of the British air-

line's fleet for many years, and achieved some small export success. By far the most important sales were to **China**, which

bought four **Trident 1E**s, 33 **Trident 2E**s and two **Trident 3B**s. Some survive in Chinese air force service, most with the com-

mercial division which operates under the China United Airlines title. Serving with this branch are a single 1E, seven 2Es and two 3Bs. Others may serve on VIP and staff transport duties with the regular air force.

Helio **H-395 Super Courier/U-10**

Noted for its excellent take-off and landing capabilities, the Helio range of light transport/utility aircraft originated with the **H-391 Courier** in 1953. More than 100 acquired by the USAF were more powerful four-seat **H-395 Super Courier** versions, designated **U-10A**, **U-10B** and **U-10D**; most were supplied through MAP to other nations or used in South East Asia. A handful remain in use, in the **Royal Thai air force** and the **Peruvian army,** where they are used for liaison duties. Five Super Couriers delivered to the Peruvian air force were fitted with interchangeable float and wheel landing gear.

SPECIFICATION

Helio H-295 Super Courier
Wing: span 39 ft 0 in (11.89 m); aspect ratio 6.5; area

231.00 sq ft (21.46 m²)
Fuselage and tail: length 30 ft 0 in (9.14 m); height 8 ft 10 in (2.69 m); tailplane span 15 ft 0 in (4.57 m); wheel track 9 ft 0 in (2.74 m); wheel base 23 ft 5 in (7.14 m)
Powerplant: one Textron Lycoming GO-480-G1D6 rated at 295 hp (220 kW)
Weights: empty 2,037 lb (924 kg); normal take-off 3,400 lb (1542 kg); maximum take-off 4,420 lb (2005 kg)
Fuel and load: internal fuel 60 US gal (227 litres) standard or 120 US gal (454 litres) optional plus provision for 150 US gal (568 litres) of auxiliary fuel; external fuel none
Speed: maximum level speed 'clean' at sea level 145 kt (167 mph; 269 km/h); maximum cruising speed at 8,500 ft (2590 m) 143 kt (165 mph; 265 km/h); economical cruising speed at optimum altitude 130 kt (150 mph; 241 km/h)
Range: ferry range 2,518 nm (2,900 miles; 4667 km); range 1,198 nm (1,380 miles; 2221 km) with optional

fuel or 573 nm (660 miles; 1062 km) with standard fuel
Performance: maximum rate of climb at sea level 1,150 ft (351 m) per minute; service ceiling 20,500 ft (6250 m); take-off run 335 ft (102 m) at maximum take-off weight for STOL or 700 ft (213 m) at maximum take-off weight for conventional use; take-off distance to 50 ft (15 m) 610 ft (196 m) at maximum take-off weight for STOL or 1,180 ft (360 m) at maximum take-off weight for conventional use; landing distance from 50 ft (15 m) 520 ft (158 m) at normal landing

weight for STOL or 665 ft (203 m) at normal landing weight for conventional use; landing run 270 ft (82 m) at normal landing weight for STOL or 355 ft (107 m) at normal landing weight for conventional use

Thailand's U-10 Couriers are a hang-over from the Vietnam era. Although obsolete, the sturdy airframe is still highly regarded for work in the jungle and operations from primitive airstrips.

Heliopolis **Gomhouria**

Heliopolis has been absorbed by the nationalised aviation industry, headquartered at the aircraft factory at Helwan. Kader and SAKR factories are still located at Heliopolis

The prototype Bücker Bü 181 Bestmann first flew in early 1939, and the type was produced in thousands as an advanced trainer for the Luftwaffe. Post-war production was undertaken in Czechoslovakia as the Zlin 281/381/C.6/C.106, and in Egypt as the **Heliopolis Gomhouria**, where several variants were developed for use as trainers by the Egyptian air force and other Arab air arms.

A simple, side-by-side, two-seat low-wing trainer with non-retractable tailwheel undercarriage, the Gomhouria was powered by the 105-hp (78.3-kW) Walter Minor engine (**Gomhouria Mks 1** and **5**), the 145-hp (109.2-kW) Continental C145 (**Gomhouria Mks 2**, **3** and **4**) or the similarly-powered Continental O-300 (**Gomhouria Mk 6**). Other differences concerned the amount of internal fuel tank-

age and the provision of a 'bubble' canopy. About 300 were built in Egypt, and of these at least 100 are thought to still serve in the training role with the Egyptian air force.

SPECIFICATION

Heliopolis Gomhouria Mk 6
Wing: span 10.60 m (34 ft 9.3 in); aspect ratio 8.32; area 13.50 m2 (145.32 sq ft)
Fuselage and tail: length 7.85 m (25 ft 9 in); height 2.05 m (6 ft 8.7 in); tailplane span 3.00 m (9 ft 10 in); wheel track 1.83 m (6 ft 0 in)
Powerplant: one Teledyne Continental O-300-A rated at 145 hp (108 kW)
Weights: empty equipped 520 kg (1,146 lb); maximum take-off 800 kg (1,764 lb)
Fuel and load: internal fuel 125 litres (33 US gal); external fuel none; maximum ordnance none

A typical Egyptian Heliopolis Gomhouria Mk 6, with bubble canopy and other refinements.

Speed: maximum level speed 'clean' at sea level 225 km/h (122 kt; 140 mph); cruising speed at 2000 m (6,560 ft) 205 km/h (110 kt; 127 mph)
Range: 780 km (421 nm; 485 miles)

Performance: maximum rate of climb at sea level 300 m (984 ft) per minute; service ceiling 6000 m (19,685 ft); take-off distance to 15 m (50 ft) 350 m (1,149 ft) at maximum take-off weight

Hiller **UH-12/H-23 Raven**

Hiller is now part of Rogerson Hiller

Based on an original design by Stanley Hiller in 1948, the **Hiller UH-12E** has been restored to production (under new ownership), having meanwhile passed through many stages of development and production. Well over 2,000 examples have been built for civil use or as **H-23 Ravens** for the US armed forces. Principal military users are the **Argentine army**, which has eight three-seat **UH-12ET**s powered by the Allison 250-C20B turboshaft for liaison duties, and the **Egyptian air force**, with

18 piston-engined UH-12E trainers. Current Hiller designs such as the **RH-1100** and new-model UH-12E are described more fully under a separate Rogerson-Hiller entry.

SPECIFICATION

Hiller UH-12E
Rotor system: main rotor diameter 35 ft 5 in (10.80 m); tail rotor diameter 5 ft 6 in (1.68 m); main rotor disc area 985.16 sq ft (91.52 m2); tail rotor disc area

23.76 sq ft (2.21 m2)
Fuselage and tail: length overall, rotors turning 40 ft 8.5 in (12.41 m) and fuselage 28 ft 6 in (8.69 m); height to top of rotor head 10 ft 1.25 in (3.08 m); skid track 7 ft 6 in (2.29 m)
Powerplant: one 340-hp (253.5-kW) Textron Lycoming VO-540 six-cylinder air-cooled piston engine derated to 305 hp (227.5 kW)
Weights: empty 1,759 lb (798 kg); maximum take-off 2,800 lb (1270 kg)
Fuel and load: internal fuel 46 US gal (174 litres) plus provision for 40 US gal (151.5 litres) of auxiliary

fuel in two fuselage tanks; external fuel none
Speed: never-exceed and maximum level speed at optimum altitude 83 kt (96 mph; 154 km/h); maximum cruising speed at optimum altitude 78 kt (90 mph; 145 km/h)
Range: ferry range 365 nm (420 miles; 676 km) with auxiliary fuel; range 187 nm (215 miles; 346 km) with standard fuel
Performance: maximum rate of climb at sea level 1,290 ft (393 m) per minute; service ceiling 16,200 ft (4940 m); hovering ceiling 10,800 ft (3290 m) in ground effect and 7,200 ft (2195 m) out of ground effect

Hindustan (HAL) **HT-2**

Hindustan Aeronautics Ltd, PO Box 5150 15/1 Cubbon Rd Bangalore 560 001, India

The first powered aircraft designed and built by HAL (Hindustan Aeronautics Limited), the **HT-2** first flew on 5 August 1951 and subsequently entered production to serve the **Indian Air Force** as its primary trainer. Such use ended in 1981, but 22 aircraft were retained at the IAF Elementary Flying School at Bidar for the 30-hour initial training course for army helicopter pilots, and these may remain in use. A conversion programme started in 1983 fitted Lycoming engines in place of the original Cirrus Majors.

SPECIFICATION

HAL HT-2
Wing: span 10.72 m (35 ft 2 in); aspect ratio 7.18; area 16.00 m2 (172.23 sq ft)
Fuselage and tail: length 7.53 m (24 ft 8.5 in);

height 2.72 m (8 ft 11 in)
Powerplant: one Textron Lycoming O-320-H flat-four piston engine rated at 160 hp (119 kW)
Weights: empty equipped 1,540 lb (699 kg); maximum take-off 2,240 lb (1016 kg)
Fuel and load: external fuel none; maximum ordnance none
Speed: maximum level speed 'clean' at sea level 113 kt (130 mph; 209 km/h); cruising speed at sea level 100 kt (115 mph; 185 km/h)
Range: 278 nm (320 miles; 515 km); endurance 3 hours 30 minutes
Performance: maximum rate of climb at sea level 800 ft (244 m) per minute; service ceiling 16,500 ft (5030 m)

This Lycoming-engined Hindustan HT-2 was displayed at India's inaugural aerospace trade show at Yelahanka during December 1993. A handful reportedly remains in use.

Hindustan (HAL) **HJT-16 Kiran I/II**

The **HAL Kiran** (ray of light) was designed to meet an **Indian Air Force** requirement for a trainer similar to the RAF's Hunting Jet Provost. Design of HAL's first jet aircraft began in December 1959, and after subsequent development the prototype made its first flight on 4 September 1964. Intended as a replacement for the DH Vampire, the Kiran shared some of the features of the Jet Provost, including all-metal construction, side-by-side seating, a low wing and the 2,500-lb (11.1-kN) thrust Rolls-Royce Bristol Viper Mk 11 turbojet. In some respects it was more advanced, having a pressurised cockpit and ejection seats specified from the outset (Martin-Baker H4HA seats with zero-altitude capability were fitted).

After completion of a second prototype in August 1965 a pre-production batch of 24

aircraft was launched, the first of these being delivered in March 1968. These and the first series of full production aircraft were unarmed **Kiran Mk I**s, but provision was made in the **Kiran Mk IA** for the carriage of bombs or rocket pods on two wing points stressed to carry 500 lb (227 kg) each. A total of 118 Mk Is was built, of which seven went to the **Indian Navy** and the others to the IAF, primarily to serve at the Air Force Academy at Dundigal, Hyderabad. There, Kiran Is are now used for the first 95 hours of an all-through jet training course, followed by 120 hours of applied training on Mk IAs. Production of the Mk IA totalled 72, with at least four later transferred to the navy. Some interest from abroad was shown in the Kiran Mk 1, notably from Malaysia, but no orders ensued.

In September 1972 a go-ahead was given for an improved version, known as the **Kiran II**, to provide for more complete weapons and tactical training. Two Mk I airframes served as prototypes, and following

a protracted development period the first flew on 30 July 1976. The Kiran II introduced a pair of 7.62-mm machine-guns with 150 rounds each in the nose, a strengthened wing to accept four hardpoints, updated avionics, an improved hydraulic system and a more powerful Rolls-Royce Orpheus engine to replace the Viper II used in the Mks I and IA. Each hardpoint had a

A line-up of Kiran Is of India's Air Force Academy, at Dundigal. Pilots move to the Kiran after primary training/selection on the HPT-32 at Bamrauli or Allahabad. After 75 hours, cadets move on to the Kiran II or the Iskra, depending on whether they are to be streamed to fly a Western type or MiGs.

Left: *Undernose blade antennas and blue tails identify these as Kiran IIs from the Air Academy's Bidar airfield.*

Right: *A line-up of Indian Navy Kirans at INS Hansa. These are used by the 'Phantoms' aerobatic team.*

550-lb (250-kg) capacity and could carry a 50-Imp gal (227-litre) drop tank as an alternative to bombs or rocket pods. Installation of the Orpheus engine resulted in improved speed, climb rate and manoeuvrability. However, radius of action and night flying qualities were found to be unacceptable, and the type was not accepted by the IAF. A second prototype flew in February 1979, but it was not until March 1983 that development was officially completed, allowing deliveries to the IAF to begin in April 1985.

The last Kiran Mk II was delivered in March 1989, production eventually totalling 61 aircraft. Other than six for the Indian Navy, all went to the IAF, and are now used for a six-month course at Bidar prior to new pilots joining an Operational Fighter Training Unit. The Kirans diverted to the Navy serve with No. 551 Squadron (INAS 551), the Sea Harrier training unit.

SPECIFICATION

HAL HJT-16 Kiran Mk II
Wing: span 10.70 m (35 ft 1.25 in); aspect ratio 6.03; area 19.00 m² (204.52 sq ft)

Fuselage and tail: length 10.60 m (34 ft 9.5 in); height 3.635 m (11 ft 11 in); tailplane span 3.90 m (12 ft 9.5 in); wheel track 2.42 m (7 ft 11 in); wheel base 3.50 m (11 ft 6 in)
Powerplant: one HAL-built Rolls-Royce (Bristol Siddeley) Orpheus Mk 701-01 turbojet rated at 4,200 lb st (18.68 kN)
Weights: empty equipped 2995 kg (6,603 lb); normal take-off 4250 kg (9,369 lb); maximum take-off 5000 kg (11,023 lb)
Fuel and load: internal fuel 1775 kg (3,913 lb); external fuel up to two 227 litre (60-US gal) drop tanks; maximum ordnance 1000 kg (2,205 lb)
Speed: never-exceed speed 421 kt (484 mph; 780 km/h);

maximum level speed 'clean' at sea level 363 kt (418 mph; 672 km/h); maximum cruising speed at 15,000 ft (4570 m) 335 kt (386 mph; 621 km/h); economical cruising speed at 15,000 ft (4570 m) 225 kt (259 mph; 417 km/h)
Range: 397 nm (457 miles; 735 km) with standard fuel
Performance: maximum rate of climb at sea level 5,250 ft (1600 m) per minute; service ceiling 39,375 ft (12000 m); take-off run 540 m (1,772 ft) at maximum take-off weight; take-off distance to 50 ft (15 m) 730 m (2,395 ft) at maximum take-off weight; landing distance from 50 ft (15 m) 1440 m (4,725 ft) at normal landing weight

Hindustan (HAL) **HPT-32 Deepak**

Designed as the replacement for the HT-2 as the standard *ab initio* trainer used by the **Indian Air Force**, the **HAL HPT-32** switched from the former's tandem seating to the officially preferred side-by-side arrangement. Space was also provided at the rear of the cabin for an optional third seat, thus giving a limited secondary role for communications. In addition to its normal training functions of instrument flying, navigation exercises, night flying and formation work, the fully-aerobatic HPT-32 was also to be capable of fulfilling a wide range of tasks including observation, liaison, sport flying, SAR, supply dropping, target towing, etc., but protracted development limited its usefulness. Production of an initial batch of 88 is to be followed by a further 32, delivery of which was to begin in 1993. The first prototype flew on 6 January 1977, followed by a second over two years later. These proved unable to meet the specification, and it was not until several design changes (notably aerodynamic improvement

and a stringent programme of weight reduction) had been made that the aircraft was accepted for production. The definitive configuration was achieved with the third aircraft, flown on 31 July 1981.

Production deliveries began in March 1984 but the first official acceptance was delayed until 1985, when deliveries commenced to the Elementary Flying School at Bidar with the formal handing over of 12 aircraft. It was not until the beginning of 1988 that the first student course on the HPT-32 was introduced at the Air Force Academy, using its auxiliary Elementary Flying School at Bamrauli. From initial production, the Indian Navy has taken eight HPT-32s, used by INAS 550 at Cochin.

SPECIFICATION

HAL HPT-32 Deepak
Wing: span 9.50 m (31 ft 2 in); aspect ratio 6.01; area 15.01 m² (161.57 sq ft)

Fuselage and tail: length 7.72 m (25 ft 4 in); height 2.88 m (9 ft 5.5 in); tailplane span 3.60 m (11 ft 9.75 in); wheel track 3.45 m (11 ft 4 in); wheel base 2.10 m (6 ft 10.75 in)
Powerplant: one Textron Lycoming AEIO-540-D4B5 piston engine rated at 260 hp (194 kW)
Weights: basic empty 890 kg (1,962 lb); maximum take-off 1250 kg (2,756 lb)
Fuel and load: internal fuel 229 litres (60.5 US gal); external fuel none; maximum ordnance none
Speed: never exceed speed 240 kt (276 mph; 445 km/h); maximum level speed 'clean' at sea level 143 kt (164 mph; 265 km/h); maximum cruising speed at 10,000 m (3050 m) 115 kt (132 mph; 213 km/h); economical cruising speed at optimum altitude 95 kt (109 mph; 176 km/h)
Range: 401 nm (462 miles; 744 km)
Performance: maximum rate of climb at sea level 335 m (1,100 ft) per minute; service ceiling 5500 m (18,045 ft); take-off run 345 m (1,132 ft) at maximum

Three piston-engined HPT-32 Deepaks in flight. The different colour schemes indicate that these aircraft serve with a test establishment, although the nearest is in Training Command trim.

take-off weight; take-off distance to 15 m (50 ft) 545 m (1,788 ft) at maximum take-off weight; landing distance from 15 m (50 ft) 487 m (1,598 ft) at normal landing weight; landing run 220 m (720 ft) at normal landing weight
g limits: -3 to +6

Hindustan (HAL) **HTT-34**

As a private venture, HAL fitted a 420-hp (313-kW) Allison 250-B17D turboprop in the third HPT-32 to provide an alternative to the piston-engined trainer. As the **HAL HTT-34**, the re-engined prototype flew on 17 June 1984 and a pre-production model with further modifications appeared in 1989. The HTT-34 is 0.35 m (1 ft 1.75 in) longer than the HPT-32 and has a smaller tail surface area. The lighter, but considerably more powerful, engine improves performance, increasing maximum level speed and service ceiling. A reduction in landing run to 200 m (656 ft) may be achieved by selecting reverse pitch on the three-bladed propeller. No orders were placed for the HTT-34 and production now appears unlikely, particularly in view of the develop-

ment of the HTT-35. Production standard aircraft were to have retractable gear.

SPECIFICATION

HAL HTT-34
Wing: span 9.50 m (31 ft 2 in); aspect ratio 6.01; area 15.01 m² (161.57 sq ft)
Fuselage and tail: length 8.07 m (26 ft 5.75 in); height 2.88 m (9 ft 5.5 in); tailplane span 3.60 m (11 ft 9.75 in); wheel track 3.45 m (11 ft 4 in); wheel base 2.10 m (6 ft 10.75 in)
Powerplant: one Allison 250-B17D turboprop rated at 420 shp (313 kW)
Weights: empty 1,909 lb (866 kg); maximum take-off 2,689 lb (1220 kg)
Fuel and load: internal fuel 229 litres (60.5 US gal);

One of the turboprop HTT-34 prototypes. Several of these are on charge with the ASTE (Aircraft and Systems Testing Establishment) at Bangalore.

external fuel none; maximum ordnance none
Speed: maximum level speed 'clean' at sea level 167 kt (192 mph; 310 km/h) and at 9,845 ft (3000 m) 143 kt (165 mph; 266 km/h)
Range: 332 nm (382 miles; 615 km); endurance 3 hours 8 minutes
Performance: maximum rate of climb at sea level

2,132 ft (650 m) per minute; service ceiling 25,000 ft (7620 m); take-off distance to 50 ft (15 m) 870 m (265 m) at maximum take-off weight; landing distance from 50 ft (15 m) 1,526 ft (465 m) at maximum landing weight without propeller reversal or 656 ft (200 m) at maximum landing weight with propeller reversal
g limits: -3 to +6

Hindustan (HAL) **HTT-35**

Although the HTT-34 seems to have been dropped, Hindustan Aeronautics Ltd have not abandoned their attempts to produce a new turboprop-powered trainer for the Indian Air Force, to meet the IAF Air Staff Target 208. This details a replacement for both the HPT-32 and the HJT-16, inferring a requirement for more than 150 air-

craft. Unveiled in mock-up form at Avia India '93 in December 1993, the **HTT-35** is a conventional looking tandem-seat low-wing monoplane, with a distinctively hump-backed appearance and stepped cockpits covered by separate upward-hinging canopies. The retractable tricycle undercarriage retracts inwards (main units) and rear-

wards (nose gear). The pilots will sit on lightweight ejection seats. HAL hope to use either the 1150-shp Garrett TPE-331-12D (flat-rated to 1100 shp/819 kW) or the 1150-shp Pratt and Whitney Canada PT6A-62 (flat rated to 950 shp/707 kW) to power the new aircraft. HAL claim a maximum level speed of 290 mph (470 km/h) at sea level,

to 50 ft (15 m) is 850 ft (260 m), and landing distance from (50 ft) 15m is (1900 ft) 580 m. Sea level rate of climb is calculated as 4000 ft (1220 m) per minute, and service ceiling as 29,500 ft (9000 m). The HTT-35 will be fully aerobatic, with a normal operating load factor of +6 to -3 and a fatigue life of 7,000 flying hours. Integral wing and fuselage tanks will carry 990 lb (450 kg) of fuel, with an inverted system allowing up to 30 seconds inverted flight. This gives a range of 790 miles (1270 km), and allows two high-density aerobatic/spinning sorties to be flown on a single load of fuel. Underwing hard-

gun or rocket pods for weapons training or counter-insurgency. Full-scale development awaits a government go-ahead, which HAL hopes to receive by mid-1994, leading to a first flight 24 months later.

The HTT-35 mock-up, displayed in December 1993, showed the indigenous trainer to have a conventional low-wing and stepped cockpit configuration, reminiscent of the Tucano and PC-9. In service it would replace both the HPT-32 and the HJT-16.

Hoffman **H 36 Dimona**

Wolf Hoffman Flugzeugbau KG, Sportflugplatz
D-8870 Günzberg/Ulm
Germany

First flying on 9 October 1980, at Königsdorf near Munich, the **H 36 Dimona** is a side-by-side two-seat motor glider built in Germany. Power comes from a 59.7-kW (80-hp) Limbach L 2000 EB1C engine, dri-

ving a Hoffman propeller. Low-vibration mountings are employed. The Dimona has a low-set wing, a T-tail and fixed sprung undercarriage, the wheels housed in spats. The wings can be folded back, to lay along

the sides of the fuselage. The cockpit is covered by an upward-hinging canopy, and has a baggage compartment and an 17.5-Imp gal (80-litre) fuel tank behind. This gives a range of about 620 miles (1000 km), with

a fuel consumption of 12 litres per hour at 75 per cent power (180 km/h). Top speed is 130 mph (210 km/h). Fourteen aircraft were purchased by the **Royal Thai air force** for training purposes.

IAI **1124 Westwind/SeaScan**

Israel Aircraft Industries Ltd
Ben Gurion International Airport, Tel Aviv
Israel 70100

After purchasing the design and production facilities for the **Model 1121 Jet Commander** from Rockwell in 1967, IAI further developed the executive twin jet into the **Models 1123** and **1124 Westwind**. Powered respectively by 3,100-lb st (13.7-kN) General Electric CJ610-9 turbojets and 3,700-lb st (16.4-kN) Garrett TFE731-3 turbofans, these two versions were produced almost entirely for civil use. One of each later entered service with the **Honduran air force**, and two Model 1124s serve in the **Chilean navy**, all in the VIP transport role. One was similarly used by President Idi Amin in Uganda and, in response to Uganda air force interest, IAI fitted machine-guns in place of tip tanks on one Model 1123, but these were removed when the deal fell through and the aircraft passed into service with the **Israeli Defence Force/Air Force**.

The IDF/AF also operates three **Model 1124N SeaScan** versions on behalf of the navy for maritime search and patrol mis-

sions. The Seascan carries a nose radar and has provision for a variety of other sensors, as well as two load-carrying pylons on the fuselage sides for torpedoes, missiles or other stores. A Litton AN/APS-504 provides 360° coverage. Four Model 1124s were operated by Rhein-Flugzeugbau until 1990 as target-tugs for the military services in Germany.

SPECIFICATION

IAI 1124N Sea Scan
Wing: span 43 ft 2 in (13.16 m) without tip tanks and 44 ft 9.5 in (13.65 m) with tip tanks; aspect ratio 6.51; area 308.26 sq ft (28.64 m²)
Fuselage and tail: length 52 ft 3 in (15.93 m); height 15 ft 9.5 in (4.81 m); tailplane span 21 ft 0 in (6.40 m); wheel track 11 ft 0 in (3.35 m); wheel base 25 ft 6.75 in (7.79 m)
Powerplant: two Garrett TFE731-3-1G each rated at 3,700 lb st (16.46 kN) dry
Weights: empty equipped 12,300 lb (5578 kg);

maximum take-off 23,500 lb (10660 kg)
Fuel and load: internal fuel 1,300 US gal (4920 litres); external fuel none
Speed: maximum level and maximum cruising speed 'clean' between sea level and 19,355 ft (5900 m) 470 kt (542 mph; 872 km/h); economical cruising speed at 41,000 ft (12500 m) 400 kt (460 mph; 741 km/h)
Range: ferry range 2,900 nm (3,339 miles; 5373 km); operational radius 1,380 nm (1,588 miles; 2555 km) for a 6.5-hour patrol at low altitude, or 2,500 nm (2,878 miles; 4633 km) for an 8-hour patrol at high altitude

This civil-registered Westwind was used for target facilities on behalf of the Luftwaffe, operating from Lübeck.

Performance: maximum rate of climb at sea level 5,000 ft (1524 m) per minute; service ceiling 45,000 ft (13715 m); balanced take-off field length 4,900 ft (1495 m) at maximum take-off weight; landing distance from 50 ft (15 m) 1,700 ft (518 m) at normal landing weight with thrust reversal

IAI **1125 Astra/Astra SP**

Based on the 1124 Westwind, the **IAI 1125 Astra** business jet introduces a low-mounted swept wing with more extensive use of composites materials. The revised wing-mounting arrangement allows for an improved cabin layout with increased headroom. The 2-in (5-cm) wider fuselage has a deeper profile and incorporates a stretch of nearly 2 ft (0.61 m). Only the Westwind's tail unit and Garrett TFE731-3A

powerplant have been retained. A prototype Astra flew on 19 March 1984 and deliveries began two years later. An **Astra SP** (with new avionics and aerodynamics) serves with the government of **Eritrea**.

SPECIFICATION

IAI 1125 Astra

Wing: span 52 ft 8 in (16.05 m); aspect ratio 8.8; area 316.60 sq ft (29.40 m²)
Fuselage and tail: length 55 ft 7 in (16.94 m); height 18 ft 2 in (5.54 m); tailplane span 21 ft 0 in (6.40 m); wheel track 9 ft 1 in (2.77 m); wheel base 24 ft 1 in (7.34 m)
Powerplant: two Garrett TFE731-3A-200G each rated at 3,650 lb st (16.24 kN) dry
Weights: operating empty 12,670 lb (5747 kg) with standard tankage or 12,790 lb (5801 kg) with optional tankage; maximum take-off 23500 lb (10659 kg)
Fuel and load: internal fuel 8,692 lb (3942 kg) plus provision for 673 lb (305 kg) of optional fuel in a 100-US gal (378.5-litre) tank in the forward part of the

baggage compartment; external fuel none; maximum payload 3,330 lb (1510 kg) declining to 3,230 lb (1465 kg) with auxiliary fuel tank installed
Speed: maximum cruising speed at 35,000 ft (10670 m) 465 kt (535 mph; 862 km/h)
Range: 3,110 nm (3,581 miles; 5763 km) with optional fuel and four passengers
Performance: maximum rate of climb at sea level 3,650 ft (1112 m) per minute; certificated ceiling 45,000 ft (13715 m); take-off balanced field length 4,980 ft (1518 m) at 22,700 lb (10296 kg); landing balanced field length 2,645 ft (806 m) at maximum landing weight

IAI **Arava**

The first wholly IAI-designed aircraft to reach production, the **Arava** was originally conceived in 1966 as a 20-seat multi-mission light twin-turboprop STOL aircraft, for both civilian and military customers. The compact design features a high-mounted wing with twin-tail booms and a simple fixed nosewheel landing gear, with single wheels on each unit. Flown in prototype form on 27 November 1969, the Arava was subsequently produced in civil (**Series 101**, **102**) and military (**Series 201**, **202**)

applications; almost all of about 100 built between 1972 and 1988 were for military users. Although intended as a replacement for the **Israeli air force**'s venerable Douglas C-47s, the Arava was not introduced in this capacity until the late 1970s (three leased 201s were operated during the 1973 Arab-Israeli war, however) when Series 201s were delivered. The type's ruggedness, capacious cabin, performance and ability to operate from rough strips make it extremely versatile, and usable for use in a variety of roles.

These aircraft were equipped for a variety of tasks (other than as troop transports) including maritime surveillance (equipped

with search/weather radar), and EW duties in a number of different configurations with pallet-mounted Elint and ESM packages, radomes, and tailcone-mounted rear scanner. Another EW version features a large number of blade antennas on tail booms, fuselage roof and wings. Active jamming is carried out when the aircraft is equipped with the Elta/EL-7010 jammer, for which an auxiliary generator is also installed. Primary IDF/AF Arava operator is No. 126 Squadron at Lod, Israel's main transport and special duties base. The **Royal Thai air force** similarly flies three for the surveillance/ECM mission with 404 Squadron at Takhli.

As the final stage in Arava development,

IAI developed the Series 202 variant in 1977. This introduced an extended fuselage accommodating 30 fully-equipped troops, increased weights, a 'wet' wing and winglets. Initial deliveries began to the Israeli and other air forces in 1984-85. The Series 202 became a retrofit option for Aravas already in service. Both versions of the Arava may be armed with a pair of forward-firing, fuselage-mounted 12.7-mm (0.5-in) machine-guns and up to 12 82-mm (3.23-in) rockets carried on fuselage pylons.

Most of the 16 national air arms that acquired Aravas selected the Series 201 model for use as personnel and/or supply transports. Examples remain in service in

this primary tactical and utility transport role in **Colombia**, **Ecuador** (army and navy air arms), **Guatemala**, **Honduras**, **Mexico**, **El Salvador**, **Swaziland** and **Venezuela** (army). At least one continues to serve in **Bolivia** for anti-drug patrols, and an ex-civil **Series 101B** in **Cameroon** is operated as a military/government VIP transport.

SPECIFICATION

IAI 201 Arava
Wing: span 68 ft 9 in (20.96 m); aspect ratio 10.06; area 470.18 sq ft (43.68 m²)
Fuselage and tail: length 42 ft 9 in (13.03 m); height 17 ft 1 in (5.21 m); tailplane span 17 ft 0.75 in (5.20 m); wheel track 13 ft 2 in (4.01 m); wheel base 15 ft 2 in (4.62 m)
Powerplant: two Pratt & Whitney Canada PT6A-34 each rated at 750 shp (559 kW)

Weights: basic empty 8,816 lb (3999 kg); maximum take-off 15,000 lb (6804 kg)
Fuel and load: internal fuel 440 US gal (1665 litres) plus provision for 540 US gal (2044 litres) of auxiliary fuel in two ferry tanks in the cabin; external fuel none; maximum payload 5,100 lb (2313 kg)
Speed: never-exceed speed 215 kt (247 mph; 397 km/h); maximum level speed 'clean' at 10,000 ft (3050 m) 176 kt (203 mph; 326 km/h); maximum cruising speed at 10,000 ft (3050 m) 172 kt (198 mph; 319 km/h); economical cruising speed at 10,000 ft (3050 m) 168 kt (193 mph; 311 km/h)
Range: 540 nm (622 miles; 1001 km) with a 3,500-lb (1587-kg) payload declining to 140 nm (161 miles; 259 km) with maximum payload
Performance: maximum rate of climb at sea level 1,290 ft (393 m) per minute; service ceiling 25,000 ft (7620 m); take-off run 960 ft (293 m) at maximum take-off weight; take-off distance to 50 ft (15 m) 1,520 ft (463 m) at maximum take-off weight; landing distance from 50 ft (15 m) 1,540 ft (469 m) at normal landing weight; landing run 820 ft (250 m)

Right: A camouflaged IAI Arava 201 of Colombia's Escuadron 712.

Right: Another operator of Arava 201s is the Papua New Guinea Defence Force. Three Arava 201s were grounded and withdrawn in 1989.

IAI **Dagger (Nesher)**

Until the 1967 Six Day War, Israel had come to depend upon the US and France for provision of combat aircraft. Following that war, however, the supply of Dassault Mirage 5Js was halted by an embargo. Faced with the continuing threat of conflict with its Arab neighbours, Israel set about producing its own combat aircraft.

As an interim expedient Israel Aircraft Industries (IAI) started production of an unlicensed copy of the Dassault Mirage 5, complete with its French-built Atar 09C turbojet, of which large stocks existed in the country. The task of building the Mirage without French co-operation was eased by espionage. Production drawings for the Atar were stolen from the Swiss factory which was licence-building the engine for Swiss-built Mirages, and many airframe production drawings were stolen in France.

The new product was termed the **IAI Nesher** (eagle), and from the outset it was capable of mounting a pair of the indigenous Rafael Shafrir short-range air-to-air missiles (externally similar to the American AIM-9 Sidewinder but in fact a wholly new

The revised nose profile of a recently modified Argentine air force 'Finger' standard IAI Dagger.

An Argentine IAI Dagger in its original configuration, with the early (solid) nose shape painted semi-gloss black to simulate a large radome for a Mirage IIIE type radar.

Israel design). The gun armament of two 30-mm DEFA cannon was also retained. The new variant incorporated some indigenous avionics systems, and was fitted with a Martin-Baker Mk 6 ejection seat.

First flown in September 1969, the Nesher entered service with the **Heyl Ha'Avir** in time for the Yom Kippur War of October 1973, when some 40 aircraft saw action and Shafrir missiles achieved a success rate of more than 50 per cent.

The French imposed an arms embargo in the wake of the 1973 war, and this led directly to Project Black Curtain, which resulted in the IAI Kfir (described separately). This also led to the termination of the Nesher programme, after an estimated 51 **Nesher S** single-seaters and 10 **Nesher T** trainers had been completed. These aircraft were frequently used operationally in the long, undeclared war which raged on Israel's borders during the 1970s, but Kfir deliveries rendered them surplus to IDF/AF requirements by 1977.

Argentina, forced to shelve plans to acquire 80 Mirage IIIs (from an order totalling 94) for economic reasons, purchased 26 of the Neshers in 1978 under the export designation **Dagger** (including two two-seaters). These were joined by the rest of the surviving Neshers by 1982, bringing Argentine procurement to 39 **Dagger A** and four **Dagger B**s. They equipped II and III Squadrons (since redesignated I and II Squadrons) of 6° Grupo, VI Brigada Aérea, replacing ageing North American F-86 Sabres. Seventeen were lost during the 1982 Falklands War, during which they operated primarily in the fighter-bomber and

anti-shipping roles, pressing home their attacks with astonishing ferocity and a high degree of precision, although the effectiveness of their attacks was greatly reduced by poorly fused bombs, which often hit British ships without exploding. The survivors have since undergone a three-stage modification programme, which has provided Kfir-type avionics in a recontoured nose, with vortex generators, under the codenames 'Finger-I', '-II' and '-III'.

Argentina continues to operate about 20 IAI Daggers in the fighter-bomber and CAS roles.

IAI **Kfir**

Israel was the first export customer for the Dassault Mirage III, and used the type to great effect during the 1967 and 1973 wars with its Arab neighbours and during the lower intensity of hostilities. Despite its success, **Israel** was aware of the shortcomings of the Mirage, which included very fast take-off and landing speeds and consequently long take-off and landing run, lack of thrust, and primitive avionics. This obvious need for improvement, coupled with arms embargoes, forced Israel first to upgrade its Mirages and then to build its own improved Mirage derivatives.

This process resulted first in Project Salvo, under which Israel's Mirage IIICJs were rebuilt and upgraded, and then in the IAI Nesher, an unlicensed Mirage 5 copy (see separate entry), and eventually in the **IAI Kfir** (lion cub). The development of the Kfir was made possible by Israel's purchase of the F-4 Phantom and its General Electric J79 engine. The first J79-engined Mirage

was a French-built two-seater, and this made its maiden flight on 19 October 1970, joined by a re-engined Nesher in September 1971.

The J79's 11 per cent greater mass flow and higher operating temperature necessitated the provision of enlarged air intakes and extensive heat shielding of the rear fuselage. A large air scoop was added to

IAI Kfir

The first Kfirs were not equipped with canards, and some had a round-tipped radome for their ranging radar. They were essentially little more than J79-engined Mirage 5s, equipped with Israeli avionics and built without a licence.

the leading edge of the tailfin for afterburner cooling. Other airframe changes included a strengthened undercarriage with longer stroke oleos.

There have been persistent reports that some Mirage IIICJs were re-engined with the J79, receiving the local name **Barak** (lightning), but such conversions seem unlikely and have never been photographed. A similar rumour concerned the production of a radar-nosed Kfir, this being caused by photographs of an early aircraft which had its forward fuselage painted black as though it were a radome. The more observant immediately noticed that the nose contours were unchanged, and the pitot position remained the same. The basic Kfir was produced in small numbers (27) and most were later upgraded to **Kfir C1** configuration, with small narrow-span fixed canards on the intakes and rectangular strakes behind the ranging radar, on the sides of the nose. Twenty-five survivors were later lent to the US Navy and US Marines for adversary training (between 1985 and 1989) as **F-21A**s.

The **Kfir C2** was the first full-standard variant, equipped with nose strakes and

A fully-armed Israeli Kfir C7, carrying bombs on the under-intake hardpoints which distinguish this variant. Kfirs remain in service with two IDF/AF front-line squadrons and an OCU, including No. 111 at Ovda and No. 144 at Hatzor.

large fixed canard foreplanes from the outset. The new variant also had a dogtooth wing leading edge. Canards and strakes were first flown on the J79-powered Mirage IIIB which had served as the Kfir prototype, during July 1974. These aerodynamic alterations improved turn and take-off performance along with controllability.

The Kfir C2 also introduced new avionics, including an ELTA M-2001B ranging radar. Other equipment includes an MBT twin-computer flight control system, angle of attack sensor vane on the port side of the forward fuselage (retrofitted to early aircraft), Elbit S-8600 multi-mode navigation and weapons delivery system (alternatively Elbit/IAI WDNS-141), Taman central air data computer and Israel Electro-Optics HUD. One hundred and eighty-five C2s and **TC2** trainers were built, and about 120 of these remain in service with four squadrons, and others are held in flyable storage.

After long delays in gaining US approval to re-export the J79 powerplant, 12 Kfir C2s were sold to **Ecuador** in 1982, and another 11 went to **Colombia** in 1988-89. Both export customers also took delivery of a pair of Kfir TC2s. Virtually all surviving Israeli Kfir C2s and TC2s were upgraded to Kfir **C7** and **TC7** standards, but it is uncertain as to whether any were built as new.

The C7 designation is applied to upgraded aircraft delivered from 1983 onwards. These incorporate a number of avionics improvements, and have what is effectively a HOTAS cockpit. Equipment improvements involve a WDNS-391 weapons delivery and navigation system, an Elbit 82 stores management system, armament control display panel, video subsystems and the ability to release 'smart' weapons. Aerial refuelling provision with either probe or receptacle is optional. Most C2s in IDF/AF service have been upgraded

to C7 standard, and the potential is present to replace ranging radar by an Elta EL/M-2021 I/J-band multi-mode radar as installed in Israel's F-16s. Not all C2s had RWRs – at least initially – but late-production machines have an Elisra SPS-200 comprising two hemispherical sensors under the lower forward fuselage and two on the fin, immediately above the rudder. Jamming pods such as the Elta E/L-8202 can be fitted on the port inboard wing pylon.

The only external difference is the provision of an extra pair of hardpoints under the engine intakes, bringing the total to nine and increasing warload to a maximum of 13,415 lb (6085 kg). An engine overspeed provision, referred to as 'combat plus', can be used to boost thrust to 18,750 lb st (83.41 kN) for brief periods.

During 1993, Israel began seeking export customers for its surplus Kfir C2/C7s, and to this end IAI proposed a further upgrade as the **Kfir C10**. Features of this version, benefitting from Lavi technology, include a new cockpit fit, new radar in an enlarged radome, more external fuel and provision for an IFR probe.

SPECIFICATION

IAI Kfir-C7

Wing: span 8.22 m (26 ft 11.6 in); canard foreplane span 3.73 m (12 ft 3 in); wing aspect ratio 1.94; wing area 34.80 m² (374.60 sq ft); canard foreplane area 1.66 m² (17.87 sq ft)

Fuselage and tail: length 15.65 m (51 ft 4.25 in) including probe; height 4.55 m (14 ft 11.25 in); wheel track 3.20 m (10 ft 6 in); wheel base 4.87 m (15 ft 11.7 in)

Powerplant: one IAI Bedek Division-built General Electric J79-J1E rated at 11,890 lb st (52.89 kN) dry and 18,75b st (83.40 kN) with afterburning

Weights: empty about 7285 kg (16,060 lb); normal take-off 10415 kg (22,961 lb); maximum take-off

Some early Kfir 1s were fitted with vestigial canards under the designation Kfir C1. Some of these were later lent to the US Navy and Marines as F-21As, and were used for dedicated adversary dissimilar air combat training. The US Navy aircraft and some USMC aircraft wore a two-tone grey scheme, while others retained Israeli camouflage.

16500 kg (36,376 lb)

Fuel and load: internal fuel 2572 kg (5,670 lb); external fuel up to 3727 kg (8,216 lb) in three 1700-, 1300-, 825-, 600- and 500-litre (449-, 343-, 218-, 159- or 132-US gal) drop tanks; maximum ordnance 6085 kg (13,415 lb)

Speed: maximum level speed 'clean' at 36,000 ft (10975 m) more than 1,317 kt (1,516 mph; 2440 km/h) or at sea level 750 kt (863 mph; 1389 km/h)

Range: ferry range 1,744 nm (2,000 miles; 3232 km) with one 1300-litre (343US gal) and two 1700-litre (449-US gal) drop tanks; combat radius 419 nm (482 miles; 776 km) on a hi-hi-hi interception mission with two Shafrir AAMs, one 825-litre (218-US gal) and two 1300-litre (343-US gal) drop tanks, or 476 nm (548 miles; 882 km) on a 1-hour CAP with two Shafrir AAMs, one 1700-litre (449-US gal) and two 1300-litre (343-US gal) drop tanks, or 640 nm (737 miles; 1186 km) on a hi-lo-hi attack mission with two 363-kg (800-lb and two 181-kg (400-lb) bombs, two Shafrir AAMs, and one 1300-litre (343-US gal) and two 1700-litre (449-US gal) drop tanks

Performance: maximum rate of climb at sea level 14000 m (45,930 ft) per minute; climb to 50,000 ft (15240 m) in 5 minutes 10 seconds with full internal fuel and two Shafrir AAMs; zoom climb ceiling 75,000 ft (22860 m); stabilised supersonic ceiling 58,000 ft (17680 m); take-off run 1450 m (4,757 ft) at maximum take-off weight; landing distance from 50 ft (15 m) 1555 m (5,102 ft) at 25,500 lb (11566 kg; landing run 1280 m (4,200 ft) at 25,500 lb (11566 kg)

g limits: +7.5

A Fuerza Aérea Colombiana Kfir C2, carrying Rafael Python AAMs underwing. The Colombian aircraft have been upgraded to virtually full C7 standards.

NOSE CONTOURS
All Kfirs, and many IAI-inspired Mirage upgrades, feature a long, slender nose packed with avionics and tipped by a small Elta EL/M-2001B ranging radar. The pitot is underslung, and small strakes are fitted to the sides of the nose. These improve controllability at high angles of attack by generating powerful vortices.

ARMAMENT
Ecuador's Kfirs are used primarily in the air defence and intercept role, although as part of a multi-role wing they do undertake training in the fighter-bomber role. The aircraft are normally armed with a pair of Rafael Shafrir IR-homing air-to-air missiles, the newer, more effective Python not having been supplied. Like all Kfirs and Dagger/Neshers, they have a pair of Rafael-built DEFA 553 30-mm cannon in the wingroots, each with 125 rounds of ammunition. In the ground attack role the aircraft can carry a variety of US, Israeli or French free-fall bombs, but do not have the extra under-intake hardpoints associated with the Kfir C7. The squadron is not believed to practise the use of PGMs or rockets.

CONFIGURATION
The Kfir retains the basic delta-winged configuration of the Mirage III/5/50, with canard foreplanes and small aerodynamic refinements to improve agility and take-off performance.

CANARD FOREPLANES
Ecuadorian Kfirs are fitted with the full-size fixed foreplanes associated with the Kfir C2 and C7. These reduce the take-off run by some 1,500 ft (457 m) and have a similarly dramatic effect on turn performance, reducing longitudinal stability by generating lift ahead of the centre of gravity.

WING
The Kfir's wing lacks the sawcut leading-edge slots of the Mirage and, instead, has extended outboard leading edges, giving a pronounced saw-tooth leading edge discontinuity.

IAI Kfir C2

Like Colombia's Kfirs, Ecuadorian aircraft are nominally Kfir C2s, but with many of the advanced avionics systems of the Kfir C7. Ecuador's Kfir unit is Escuadrón de Combate 2113, part of Grupo 211 at Taura, and its aircraft wear a triangular Kfir badge on the port side of the fin and the starboard side of the nose. The Grupo's other units fly the Jaguar and the Mirage F1. Escuadron 2113 equipped with Kfirs during 1982, and became operational in 1984. The squadron helped Colombian pilots convert to the Kfir during 1989.

CAMOUFLAGE
Ecuador's Kfirs wear a smart two-tone disruptive camouflage scheme, with light grey undersides. National insignia is applied above the port and below the starboard wing.

POWERPLANT
A single General Electric J79-J1E augmented turbojet, the most powerful production variant of the J79, powers the Kfir. Because it has a greater mass flow than the original Mirage's Atar engine, installation of the J79 necessitates bigger intakes, and increased operating temperatures require provision of a dorsal airscoop.

IAI Lavi TD

The **IAI Lavi** (young lion) was launched in February 1980 as a multi-role combat aircraft, and full-scale development began towards the end of 1982. With a prospective IDF/AF requirement for up to 300 aircraft, the FSD phase was to involve six prototypes, of which four would be two-seaters. After the first two of these (both two-seaters with their rear cockpits occupied by test equipment) had flown, on 31 December 1986 and 30 March 1987, respectively, the programme was cancelled, in the teeth of US opposition, budgetary problems and the availability of cut price F-16s. A third airframe was completed, as a true two-seater and using parts of the others, to serve as a technology demonstrator (TD) for advanced cockpit systems and as an equipment testbed. In this form, the **Lavi TD** first flew on 25 September 1989. This aircraft is still flying test sorties, and has been the force behind IAI's highly successful fighter upgrades.

The Lavi TD, completed as a genuine two-seater, was rolled out after cancellation of the programme and was intended as a demonstrator for IAI's advanced fighter technologies, which the company is applying by retrofit to a number of earlier aircraft types, and as an equipment testbed.

SPECIFICATION

IAI Lavi
Wing: span 8.78 m (28 ft 9.67 in); aspect ratio 1.83; area 33.05 m² (355.76 sq ft)
Fuselage and tail: length 14.57 m (47 ft 9.67 in); height 4.78 m (15 ft 8.25 in); wheel track 2.31 m (7 ft 7 in); wheel base 3.86 m (12 ft 8 in)
Powerplant: one Pratt & Whitney PW1120 rated at 13,550 lb st (60.27 kN) intermediate and 20,620 lb st (91.72 kN) with afterburning
Weights: empty about 15,500 lb (7031 kg); normal take-off 22,025 lb (9991 kg); maximum take-off 42,500 lb (19277 kg)
Fuel and load: internal fuel 6,000 lb (2722 kg); external fuel up to 9,180 lb (4164 kg) in drop tanks; maximum external load 16,0000 lb (7257 kg) including 6,000 lb (2722 kg) of ordnance excluding AAMs
Speed: maximum level speed 'clean' above 36,000 ft (10975 m) 1,061 kt (1,222 mph; 1965 km/h); low-level penetration speed 538 kt (610 mph; 997 km/h) with two AAMs and eight 750-lb (340-kg) bombs
Range: combat radius 1,150 nm (1.324 miles; 2131 km) on a hi-lo-hi attack mission with two 1,000-lb (454-kg) or six 250 kg (113-kg) bombs, or 1,000 nm (1,151 miles; 1853 km) on a combat air patrol, or 600 nm (691 miles; 1112 km) on a lo-lo-lo attack mission
Performance: take-off run about 1,000 ft (305 m) at maximum take-off weight

Below: The second prototype Lavi, equipped with a bolt-on retractable inflight-refuelling probe, refuels from an A-4 Skyhawk tanker. The rear cockpit is full of test equipment.

IAI Tzukit

The name **Tzukit** (thrush) has been given by the **IDF/AF** to the **Fouga Magister** trainers and light strike aircraft, about 80 of which remain in service, primarily at the Hatzerim flying school. Original purchases of the Magister were 52 from France and 36 from the Bedek Division of IAI, with subsequent purchases from other

Magister users to maintain the inventory.
Starting in 1981, the **Advanced Multi-Mission Improved Trainer** (**AMIT**) programme resulted in approximately 80 Tzukits undergoing service life extension and modernisation at Bedek. The AMIT programme embraced some 250 modifications to extend service life by 5,000 hours and to improve systems throughout the airframe. Two prototypes were tested in 1981 before production conversions began. The Tzukit is powered by 4.7-kN (1,058-lb st) Turboméca

The Tzukit is an upgraded and modernised conversion of the basic Magister, and is operated by the IDF/AF's flying training school at Hatzerim.

Marboré VIC turbojets; its dimensions and performance are similar to those for the

Fouga CM 170-3 Super Magister (described separately).

IAI Phantom 2000 (Kurnass 2000)

The designation **Phantom 2000 (Kurnass 2000)** is used in **Israel** for an upgrade programme embracing surviving examples of the McDonnell Douglas F-4E Phantom (more than 100), of which 204 were supplied from 1969 to 1976. First flown on 11 August 1987, the Phantom 2000 is structurally strengthened to extend the service life, systems are updated and a MIL STD 1553B dual redundant digital databus is fitted. Cockpit layout is improved and HOTAS installed. An advanced new avionics suite includes Norden/UTC MMRS multi-mode radar, a Kaiser wide-angle HUD and other items. The upgrade programme is handled by the Shaham Division of Bedek Aviation and redelivery to the IDF/AF began on 9 April 1989. A proposed re-engining programme with Pratt & Whitney PW1120 turbofans has been abandoned.

The Kurnass 2000 prototype seen here featured some features not funded for the upgraded aircraft delivered to the IDF/AF. The prototype flew with a Pratt & Whitney PW1120 engine in its starboard nacelle, and then with two of these advanced turbofans, appearing in this configuration at the 1987 Paris Air Salon. The funded upgrade includes an advanced Norden synthetic aperture radar, new avionics and structural modifications. Plans are afoot to retrofit a wrap-around frameless windscreen to upgraded Kurnass 2000s. Kurnass translates as 'heavy hammer'.

IAI/Elta Phalcon

Israel Aircraft Industries is no stranger to the Boeing 707. Over the last 20 years the company has maintained the type for the **IDF/AF**, and also been involved in many conversions for special purposes. These have included tankers with both hose/drogue and boom refuelling systems, signals intelligence platforms, command posts and other electronic specialists. For the last four years, IAI and its electronics

subsidiary, Elta, have been developing an airborne early warning version, named **IAI/Elta Phalcon**.

The name Phalcon relates to the AEW system, rather than the carrier aircraft, which could be virtually any large aircraft such as a 747 or C-130. Within the Phalcon system there are many options to suit customer requirements, including additional ESM, communications and reconnaissance equipment.

At the heart of the system is the Elta EL/2075 phased-array radar. For full coverage there are four antenna arrays – two each side of the forward fuselage housed in giant cheek fairings, one in the nose in a bulbous radome, and one under the rear fuselage. The radomes do add considerable drag, eroding speed performance, but the main concern is for long endurance, which is not dramatically affected. The nose radome has a flattened underside for ground clearance, and its fitment has necessitated the re-siting of the two pitot probes

above the flight deck.

Each EL/2075 array consists of hundreds of fixed antennas, each with an individual transmit/receive module in the forward fuselage. They are electronically steered and scanned, and mounted on a floating bed so that flexing in the aircraft's structure does not affect their alignment. The radar works in L-band, and the electronic steering and power management computer allows it to be very flexible. Detection range is reported to be in the order of 400 km (250 miles) for fighter-sized targets, and around 100 such targets can be processed by the Phalcon at any one time.

Fast scanning is possible, so that area coverage can be maintained while concentrating on an important target. To increase the detection range all power can be assigned in a specific direction. A sharp beam mode keeps track of a fast or manoeuvring target, and scan area can be limited to just the battle area, thereby increasing the scan rate in this region. Track initiation is in the region of two to four seconds, which is roughly a tenth that of rotodome-equipped platforms. Augmenting the radar are IFF, ESM/Elint and Comint suites, processed by a central battle management system for distribution to the 13 or so operator consoles in the main cabin. A command post option has a separate commander's cabin with a huge situation display.

It is likely that the **Israeli air force** operates some of its 707s in Phalcon configuration, and **South Africa**'s No. 60 Squadron is believed to operate two 707s equipped with a partial Phalcon system,

with just the side fairings and no nose radome. **Chile** is the first confirmed customer, specifiying a 260°-coverage system with side fairings and nose radome.

The prototype Phalcon, probably destined for Chile, appeared at the 1993 Paris air show. It is configured with three antenna arrays; a fourth can reportedly be added below the tail. Wingtip antennas serve the aircraft's extensive Elint/ESM system.

IAR (Sud/Aérospatiale) IAR-316B Alouette III

IAROM SA, c/o Technoimportexport SA
2 Doamnei St (PO Box 110)
Bucharest, Romania

Romania's state-owned Aeronautical Construction Enterprise (ICA) began production under licence of the **Aérospatiale SA 316B Alouette III** (described separately) in 1971. Built at Brasov, the **IAR-316B** conformed entirely to the French standard and was powered by the imported 870-shp (649-kW) Turboméca Artouste IIIB turboshaft. Production peaked at 24 Alouettes a year, and a total of about 230 was built. Of these, at least 45 were delivered to the **Aviatiei Militare Romane**, entering service with squadrons at Giarmata, Sibiu and Boboc, where they are used for anti-tank and liaison duties. In armed configuration, the helicopter could be fitted with stub wings carrying six AT-3

'Saggers' above and four 12-round rocket pods below. Machine-guns, normally 7.62-mm weapons, are fitted below the belly and in the starboard cabin door, and a roof-mounted sight can be fitted. The aircraft is also operated by the **Romanian navy**, which received at least six examples for liaison duties. The Alouette III provided the basis for development in Romania of the **IAR-317 Airfox**, described below.

A Romanian-built Alouette III. Romanian production has included large numbers of military versions, some of them armed with guns, rocket launchers and even 9M14 AT-3 'Sagger' ATGMs.

IAR IAR-317 Airfox

To provide a light anti-armour and military training helicopter for the Romanian air force and possible export, the ICA developed a new fuselage to combine with the basic Alouette III transmission and dynamics. As the **IAR-317 Airfox**, the first of three prototypes flew in April 1984, with a new slimline fuselage ahead of the main rotor mast seating a crew of two in tandem. Although the tailboom of the aircraft closely resembled that of the original Alouette III, the structure was completely new. The rear cockpit was raised to provide the pilot with a clear view over the gunner's head, and armour protection was fitted, as well as

toughened glass. A pair of 7.62-mm machine-guns was fitted to the lower front fuselage sides, and a load-carrying beam aft of the rear cockpit provided two or three attachment points each side for up to 750 kg (1,653 lb) of rocket pods, bombs, anti-armour missiles and AAMs. Testing of the Airfox prototypes did not lead to production orders and the project was not revived by the post-Ceausescu administration.

The IAR-317 Airfox is an Alouette III derivative with a low cross-section fuselage, optimised for the light anti-armour role.

IAR (Aérospatiale/Eurocopter) IAR-330L Puma

Under licence agreements with Aérospatiale, IAR in Romania established a production line for the **SA 330L Puma** in 1977 and by mid-1991 had completed 165 helicopters, with production continuing for civil and military customers. Exports have reportedly included some for the **South African Air Force**. The majority of IAR production was for the **Romanian air force**, and included an armed variant developed locally. This carries two 20-mm cannon in cheek pods on the lower front fuse-

lage sides, with ammunition in 540-round boxed belts in the cabin, and with steel tube mountings on each side of the main cabin (behind the entry doors) capable of carrying four rocket pods with eight 120-mm or 16 57-mm rockets, as well as four wire-guided AT-3 'Sagger' anti-armour missiles. Alternatively, up to four 7.62-mm GMP-2 machine-gun pods or four 100-kg (220-lb) bombs can be carried. In addition, pintle mountings are fitted for one machine-gun in each cabin doorway. Some aircraft have been seen

Some Romanian-built armed Pumas feature scabbed-on cannon on the sides of the forward fuselage, but this aircraft merely has outrigger pylons for rocket pods and AT-3 'Sagger' ATGMs.

IAR (Aérospatiale/Eurocopter) IAR-330L Puma

with a roof-mounted sight. A chin turret has also been designed as an option, either for a gun or for a TV/FLIR.

The **IAR-330L Puma** is powered by Turbomecanica (Romania) Turmo IVC turboshafts of 1,575 shp (1175 kW) each, but IAR is now working on the final development of the **Puma 2000**, featuring more powerful engines and a range of advanced equipment as standard or optional fit. First exhibited as a mock-up at the 1992 Farnborough show, the standard Puma 2000 has hands-off cyclic and stick (HOCS), helmet-mounted HUD, EFIS and MIL STD 1553 technology. The aircraft has an NVG compatible cockpit. Options include TV/FLIR for the surveillance role, a laser designator for target acquisition and a wide range of

weapons for anti-armour or infantry fire support missions. Israel's Elbit is primary avionics sub-contractor. The Puma 2000 will be offered as a new-build aircraft or as an upgrade based on the 330J or 330L.

Wearing Coast Guard colours and a striking bird-of-prey insignia, this IAR-330L demonstrator is unarmed, but is equipped with flotation gear and comprehensive navaids. Romanian licence-production of the Aérospatiale Puma began in 1977, primarily for the Romanian air force. A number of armed variants have been produced, and IAR actively markets the aircraft to military and civilian customers.

IAR IAR-823

After many years of producing foreign types under licence, most notably the **Yak-52** (produced only in Romania, and described under Aerostar) IAR began studies for an indigenous military training aircraft during the late 1960s. Although capable of seating five as a touring aircraft, the resulting **IAR-823** is more usually regarded as a two-seater in its role as a primary trainer for the **Romanian air force**. First flown in July 1973, the IAR-823 is powered by a 290-hp (216-kW) Textron Lycoming IO-540-G1D5 flat-six piston engine and is an entirely conventional low-wing monoplane with side-by-side seating for the instructor and trainee pilot (and an optional bench seat for three behind). Production deliveries began in 1974 and approximately 100 were in service by 1985, principally at the 'Aurel Vlaicu' Officer's Military School at Boboc. The IAR-823 is fully aerobatic and has provision for light practice weapons or drop tanks on two wing hardpoints.

The IAR-823 served as the basis for two more advanced trainer aircraft, neither of which reached production status. The first of these was the **IAR-825TP Triumf**, which combined the wing of the IAR-823 (strengthened for stores, but interchangeable with a standard IAR-823 wing) with a

new fuselage, tail unit and landing gear, and using a 680-shp (506-kW) Pratt and Whitney Canada PT6A-15AG turboprop, although the production version was to have used a more powerful 750-shp (558-kW) PT6A-25C. The new tandem cockpits were covered by a large rearward-sliding bubble canopy, giving a good all-round view. The prototype made its maiden flight on 12 June 1982. The **IAR-831 Pelican**, which made its public debut at the 1983 Paris Air Salon, was similar, but combined the airframe of the IAR-825TP with the original 290-hp Textron Lycoming IO-540-G1D5 piston engine of the IAR-823.

The IAR-831 Pelican combined the airframe of the turboprop-powered IAR-825TP with the original Lycoming piston engine of the IAR-823. It did not attain production status.

Above left: The basic IAR-823 is a five-seat tourer, used by the Romanian air force as a two-seat primary trainer.

Above: The turboprop-powered, tandem-seat IAR-825TP Triumf was based on the IAR-823 but did not enter production.

IAR IAR-99 Soim/-109 Swift

The **IAR-99 Soim** (hawk) was designed in the early 1980s in the Institutul de Aviatie at Bucharest and was put into production at Craiova by Intreprinderea de Avioane (IAv). In the reorganisation of the state aircraft industry following the collapse of the Ceausescu regime, the Craiova factory became a part of the Avioane subsidiary of the IAROM holding company.

A conventional design for a straight-wing single-jet aircraft, the Soim was conceived as a basic/advanced trainer with secondary ground attack/close support capability. Tandem seating in zero-zero ejection seats was arranged in a pressurised cockpit with the rear seat raised for improved forward view. For the armed role, provision was made for a removable ventral gun pod containing a 23-mm GSh-23 cannon with 200 rounds. Four wing hardpoints were each stressed for 250-kg (551-lb) loads, comprising bombs, rocket pods, machine-gun pods, AAMs, fuel tanks or similar ordnance.

Following the first flight on 21 December 1985, the IAR-99 entered service with the **Romanian Air Force** (AMR) in 1988 when an initial batch of 20 aircraft became operational at the Bacau flying school, replacing Aero L-29 Delfins, although the latter remain in service for weapons training.

The first IAR-99 Soim prototype, wears non-standard company livery. About 50 camouflaged IAR-99s now serve in the training role at Boboc.

Production of the Soim had reached about 50 by 1994, all for the AMR.

While production of the IAR-99 continues at a very low rate at Craiova following cuts in the military budget, consideration has been given to a modified version with the 4,870-lb st (21.7-kN) Viper 680 replacing the usual Viper 632, which is built in Romania. Jaffe Aircraft in the USA has sought to market an upgraded version outside of Romania. First announced in 1991, it was planned to incorporate major systems and completely updated avionics of Western origin, including a HUD and modern gunsight, with possible modification of the Viper engine to increase thrust. A further upgraded version was discussed with Israel Aircraft Industries in 1992. Designated **IAR-109 Swift**, planned modifications were primarily based on avionics improvements. After a gestation period of two years IAR publicly displayed the Swift for the first time at the Paris Air Show in 1993. This aircraft was originally built as an IAR-99.

SPECIFICATION

IAR-99 Soim (standard version for Romanian air force)
Wing: span 9.85 m (32 ft 3.75 in); aspect ratio 5.19; area 18.71 m² (201.4 sq ft)
Fuselage and tail: length 11.01 m (36 ft 1.5 in); height 3.90 m (12 ft 9.5 in); wheel track 2.69 m (8 ft 10 in); wheel base 4.38 m (14 ft 4.5 in)
Powerplant: one Turbomecanica Romanian-built Rolls-Royce Viper Mk 632-41M turbojet rated at

17.79 kN (4,000 lb st)
Weights: empty, equipped 3200 kg (7,055 lb); maximum take-off weight 4400 kg (9,700 lb)
Fuel and load: maximum usable fuel (internal) 1100 kg (2,425 lb); external fuel 350 kg (772 lb); payload 1000 kg (2,204 lb)
Speed: maximum Mach number 0.76; maximum level speed at sea level 865 km/h (467 kt; 537 mph)
Range: maximum range with internal fuel 683 miles (593 nm; 1100 km); lo-lo-hi 217 miles (189 nm; 350 km)
Performance: maximum climb rate at sea level 6,890 ft (2100 m) per minute; service ceiling 42,325 ft (12,900 m)

Ilyushin **Il-14 'Crate'**

Aviation Complex named after S.V. Ilyushin
125319 Moscow
Russia

Now thoroughly obsolete, the **Il-14** is the Eastern Bloc equivalent of the DC-3/C-47, and has enjoyed a similar success. Like the Dakota, it remains in service in small numbers with a number of air forces. Developed from the similar Il-12 'Coach', the Il-14 also has a tricycle undercarriage, giving the advantage of a level cabin on the ground, but has a stretched fuselage with accommodation for up to 28 passengers. First flown in 1952, the Il-14 entered service in 1954 and some 3,500 were built in the USSR, with further aircraft being licence-built in East Germany and as the **Avia 14** in Czechoslovakia.

A number of variants were produced, most military operators using the **Il-14P** with strengthened cabin floors, twin freight loading doors, provision for a parachute static line and observation blisters aft of the flight deck for a drop controller. The stretched **Il-14M** offered greater accommodation, and the **Il-14T** was a dedicated freighter (often being produced by conversion). In 1979 an ECM platform, reportedly

allocated the codename **'Crate-C'**, was identified, but details of its service use are unavailable. A handful operated in the survey role, and some Czech machines had a stretched glazed nose for survey and mapping duties and were designated **Avia 14FG**. One of the latter survived until 1993 with the Czech air force. Other Il-14 survivors serve in **Albania**, **North Korea**, and **Poland** (including a survey aircraft),

SPECIFICATION

Ilyushin Il-14M 'Crate'
Wing: span 31.70 m (104 ft 0 in); aspect ratio 10.05; area 100.00 m² (1,076.43 sq ft)
Fuselage and tail: length 22.31 m (73 ft 2.25 in); height 7.90 m (25 ft 11 in)
Powerplant: two Shvetsov ASh-82T air-cooled radial piston engines each rated at 1,875 hp (1397 kW)
Weights: empty 12700 kg (27,998 lb); normal take-off weight 17700 kg (39,020 lb); maximum take-off 18500 kg (40,785 lb)
Fuel and load: internal fuel 6500 litres

(1,717 US gal); external fuel none; maximum payload 3300 kg (7,275 lb)
Speed: maximum level speed 'clean' at 2400 m (7,875 ft) 430 km/h (232 kt; 267 mph) and at sea level 400 km/h (217 kt; 248 mph); cruising speed at 3000 m (9,845 ft) 350 km/h (188 kt; 217 mph)
Range: 1500 km (809 nm; 932 miles) with 26 passengers or 400 km (216 kt; 249 miles) with maximum payload
Performance: climb to 5000 m (16,405 ft) in 8

minutes 30 seconds; service ceiling 6500 m (21,325 ft); take-off run 1020 m (3,346 ft); landing run 800 m (2,625 ft)

One of two Il-14s in service with 13th PLT at Krakow-Balice. Two further examples have been withdrawn. The surviving Polish Il-14s are configured for transport and photo-survey respectively.

Ilyushin **Il-18 'Coot'**

Designed as a sophisticated turboprop airliner for Aeroflot's domestic and shorter international routes, the **Il-18**, which first flew in July 1957, remains in service with a variety of civil and military operators worldwide. The initial production version accommodated 75 passengers, and could be powered until the 21st aircraft by Kuznetsov NK-4 or Ivchenko AI-20 turboprops, the latter engine subsequently being adopted as standard. The **Il-18B** introduced the AI-20K engine, with increased maximum take-off weight and accommodating 84 passengers. The **Il-18V** seated 89-100 passengers, and the **Il-18I** (later redesignated **Il-18D**) of 1964 seated 110-122 passengers, this being made possible by extending the pressurised cabin aft by deleting the former cargo hold in the tail. This variant also introduced more powerful AI-20M turboprops and increased fuel tankage in the centre-section. The contemporary **Il-18Ye** was identical, apart from lacking the extra fuel tankage.

Examples of most of these Il-18 variants

have been supplied to a number of military operators for transport and VIP transport duties, but few remain in service today. Current military operators include **China**, **Congo**, **North Korea**, **Romania**, **Syria**, and **Vietnam**. A large number of nominally civilian Il-18s serve as equipment and avionics testbeds, and in the experimental role, and the Gromov Flight Test Centre at Zhukhovskii has large numbers on charge. Some Aeroflot Il-18s seem to be used for military tasks, often being fitted with unusual antennas or equipment fairings, and at least one served as a meteorological research aircraft until replaced by an An-12.

SPECIFICATION

Ilyushin Il-18D 'Coot'
Wing: span 37.42 m (122 ft 9.25 in); aspect ratio 10.0; area 140.00 m² (1,507.00 sq ft)
Fuselage and tail: length 35.90 m (117 ft 9 in); height 10.17 m (33 ft 4 in); tailplane span 11.80 m (38 ft 8.5 in); wheel track 9.00 m (29 ft 6 in); wheel base

12.78 m (41 ft 10 in)
Powerplant: four ZMDB Progress (Ivchenko) AI-20M turboprops each rated at 3169 ekW (4,250 ehp)
Weights: empty equipped 35000 kg (77,160 lb); maximum take-off 64000 kg (141,093 lb)
Fuel and load: internal fuel 30000 litres (7,965 US gal); external fuel none; maximum payload 13500 kg (29,762 lb)
Speed: maximum cruising speed at 8500 m (27,890 ft) 675 km/h (364 kt; 419 mph); economical cruising speed at optimum altitude 625 km/h (337 kt; 388 mph)

The North Korean air force continues to operate the Il-18 as a freighter. North Korean transports are more often seen in 'airline' markings.

Range: 6500 km (3,508 nm; 4,039 miles) with maximum fuel or 3700 km (1,997 nm; 2,299 miles) with maximum payload
Performance: service ceiling 10000 m (32,810 ft); take-off run 1300 m (4,265 ft)

Ilyushin **Il-20/22 'Coot'**

The replacement of the basic Il-18 'Coot' on most Aeroflot routes resulted in a pool of redundant airframes suitable for conversion to military roles. The first such conversion to receive a separate NATO reporting name (**'Coot-A'**) is the **Il-20**, which is a dedicated Elint/radar reconnaissance aircraft seemingly based on the basic Il-18D airframe. Below the fuselage, projecting forward from a point just behind the wing leading edge, the aircraft carries a large, cylindrical underfuselage pod, about 10.25 m (33 ft 7 in) long and 1.15 m (3 ft 9 in) in diameter. The underside of the pod (apart from its streamlined nose and tail sections), through an arc of about 270°, consists of a single dielectric panel and is assumed to house some kind of SLAR. Smaller, more square-section pods, about 4.4 m (14 ft 5 in) long, are mounted on the forward fuselage just below the line of the cabin windows. These seem to have a small door towards the forward end, which can open to allow a camera or some other optical sensor to be used. Two large, very broad-chord trapezoidal blade antennas are mounted above the forward fuselage (some reports suggest these are associated with a satellite communications system), and other antennas

include three large blister fairings (the first teardrop-shaped, the next two more hemispherical) below the centre fuselage; on the centreline. Smaller antenna fairings are carried on the centreline further aft, and there are a number of dielectric panels flush with the fuselage and on the wingtips.

The Ilyushin **Il-22 'Coot-B'** is believed to be an airborne command post or communications relay variant of the Il-18. The aircraft can be identified by a cylindrical pod on the tailfin, and by an array of antennas (mostly blade) above and below the fuselage. The aircraft may also have a long cylindrical or canoe fairing under the belly, considerably smaller than those fitted to the 'Coot-A'. Such modified 'Coots' have been sighted at Zhukhovskii and Pushkin (the latter seems to be a location where former airliners are converted to this standard). Interestingly, most Il-22s retain Aeroflot markings although these are freshly re-applied after conversion. One serves in Ukrainian air force colours.

Unconfirmed reports suggest that the reporting name **'Coot-C'** has been allocated to a third Il-18 derivative, and that examples of this type have been intercepted by NATO interceptors.

Above: The Il-20 'Coot-A' is an Elint/radar recce derivative of the Il-18D, with a massive cylindrical SLAR under the belly.

Below: An Il-22 'Coot-B' at Pushkin, an airfield which is believed to specialise in the conversion of aircraft for Elint and EW roles.

Ilyushin **Il-28 'Beagle'/Il-28U 'Mascot'/**Harbin **H-5**

The **Il-28** was a jet-powered medium bomber which was built in enormous numbers and became Russia's equivalent to the British Canberra, being adapted to fulfil a variety of roles and serving with a large number of export customers. The final Il-28s were retired from Soviet service relatively recently, having ended their days as target tugs and ECM platforms. Some remain in surprisingly good condition on the dumps of vacated Soviet airfields in the former East Germany.

A handful of obsolete Il-28s may remain in use for second-line duties with a small number of air forces. Afghanistan, Hungary, Iraq, North Korea, Poland and Yemen are understood to have retired the aircraft in recent years, leaving **China** and **Romania** as the most likely users (in 1992, a handful of Romanian Il-28s were certainly still operational). Although China builds the Il-28 itself as the **Harbin H-5** it may also still have some Soviet-built aircraft on charge, and may have refurbished the ex-Albanian aircraft it swapped for a Harbin H-5 in the late 1970s.

In 1963, the Chinese aircraft industry initiated a programme under which the Ilyushin Il-28 light tactical bomber was to be manufactured without benefit of a licence from the Soviet Union. The People's Republic of China Air Force had received a number of Il-28 bombers from the Soviet Union, a factory at Harbin being assigned the task of repairing these and manufacturing some replacement parts. The programme of 'reverse-engineering' to copy the bomber was also assigned to Harbin. A prototype of the Chinese Il-28 flew as the H-5, or **Hongzhaji-5**, on 25 September 1966.

H-5 production was launched in April 1967, and continued into the early 1980s, almost 2,000 allegedly having been built by the time that the programme terminated. This total included 186 examples of the **HJ-5** crew trainer, and variants included a tactical reconnaissance version, the **H-5R** (or **HZ-5**), and dedicated torpedo-bombing and target-towing models. Exports included 18 H-5Rs to Romania, some 50 H-5s, H-5Rs and HJ-5s to North Korea, and one H-5 to Albania.

The H-5 remains in service in **Albania**, and in substantial numbers with China's Air Force and with the air component of the **People's Republic of China Navy**. The latter service also operates a number of H-5s adapted to carry Rushton low-level towed targets to simulate sea-skimming anti-shipping missiles. Data for the H-5 is essentially similar to that for the Ilyushin Il-28.

SPECIFICATION

Ilyushin Il-28 'Beagle'
Wing: span 21.45 m (70 ft 4.5 in) without tip tanks; aspect ratio 7.55; area 60.80 m² (654.47 sq ft)
Fuselage and tail: length, fuselage 17.65 m (57 ft 11 in) excluding tail cannon; height 6.70 m (21 ft 11.75 in); tailplane span 7.10 m (23 ft 3.5 in); wheel track 7.40 m (24 ft 3.5 in); wheel base about 8.10 m (26 ft 7 in)
Powerplant: two Klimov VK-1A each rated at 26.48 kN (5,952 lb st) dry
Weights: empty equipped 11890 kg (28,417 lb); normal take-off 18400 kg (40,564 lb); maximum take-off 21200 kg (46,738 lb)
Fuel and load: internal fuel 6600 kg (14,550 lb) including 200 kg (441 lb) in optional tip tanks; external fuel none; maximum ordnance 3000 kg (6,614 lb)
Speed: maximum level speed 'clean' at 4500 m (14,765 ft) 902 km/h (486 kt; 560 mph) or at sea level 800 km/h (432 kt; 497 mph); typical cruising speed at

A single H-5 remains operational with the Albanian air force, and Il-28s remain in use with the Romanian air force.

optimum altitude 876 km/h (472 kt; 544 mph)
Range: 2400 km (1,295 nm; 1,491 miles) at 10000 m (32,810 ft) declining to 1135 km (612 nm; 705 miles) at 1000 m (3,280 ft)
Performance: maximum rate of climb at sea level 900 m (2,952 ft) per minute; climb to 10000 m (32,810 ft) in 18 minutes 0 seconds; service ceiling 12300 m (40,350 ft); take-off run 875 m (2,871 ft) at normal take-off weight or 1150 m (3,773 ft) at maximum take-off weight; landing run 1170 m (3,839 ft) at 14690 kg (32,385 lb)

Ilyushin **Il-38 'May'**

Although the **Il-38** is clearly derived from the Il-18 airliner, the extent of the changes to the new aircraft make it virtually certain that it is a new-build aeroplane, and not a conversion, with the same relationship to its airliner progenitor as the Orion has with the Electra and the Nimrod with the Comet. Certain components may be recovered from surplus Aeroflot Il-18s for re-use, such as wheels, and possibly even the aircraft's Ivchenko AI-20M turboprops and their propellers.

The basic Il-18 fuselage has been lengthened by about 4 m (13 ft 1.5 in), and the wings have been moved forward to compensate for the effect on aircraft centre of gravity of the new role equipment. Most of the original cabin windows have been removed, and the remainder have mostly been reduced in size. The Il-18's original passenger entry doors have all been removed, replaced by a new door on the starboard side at the rear of the cabin, where the Il-18's service door used to be. The flight deck and main cabin are separated by a pressure bulkhead. Other structural alterations include the provision of a MAD stinger projecting aft from the tailcone, and a pair of internal weapons/stores bays fore and aft of the wing structure.

The Il-38 has a standard weather radar in the nose, with its large search radar (NATO reporting name 'Wet Eye') in a distinctive, bulged radome below the forward fuselage, immediately aft of the nosewheel bay. The otherwise smooth skin is disrupted by a handful of antennas, heat exchanger outlets, and by large heat exchanger inlet pods and cable ducts just ahead of the wing.

The bulk of former Soviet Il-38s remain in use with the **AV-MF** (naval air arm). Some aircraft may actually be under **VVS** command however, in a similar fashion to maritime reconnaissance 'Bear-Ds', The only export customer is the **Indian Navy**, whose No. 315 Squadron operates five from INS Hansa at Dabolim, Goa. Il-38s encountered over the Mediterranean in Egyptian markings during the early 1970s were Soviet aircraft operating from Egyptian bases and wearing a 'flag of convenience'. The status of the Il-38 is uncertain, but continuing production of the Tu-142 'Bear-F' may indicate that the latter is Russia's preferred maritime patrol and ASW platform.

Based on the Il-18, but with a redesigned fuselage accommodating tandem weapons bays, radar and sonar, and a tail-mounted MAD, the Il-38 is Russia's most numerous ASW platform, augmented by a smaller number of Tu-142 'Bear-Fs'.

SPECIFICATION

Ilyushin Il-38 'May'
Wing: span 37.42 m (122 ft 9.25 in); aspect ratio 10.0; area 140.00 m² (1,507.00 sq ft)
Fuselage and tail: length 39.60 m (129 ft 10 in); height 10.16 m (33 ft 4 in); tailplane span 11.80 m (38 ft 8.5 in); wheel track 9.00 m (29 ft 6 in); wheel base 12.78 m (41 ft 10 in)
Powerplant: four ZMDB Progress (Ivchenko) AI-20M each rated at 3169 kW (4,250 shp)
Weights: empty equipped 36000 kg (79,365 lb); maximum take-off 63500 kg (139,991 lb)
Fuel and load: internal fuel 30000 litres (7,925 US gal); external fuel none
Speed: maximum level speed 'clean' at 6400 m (21,000 ft) 722 km/h (389 kt; 448 mph); maximum cruising speed at 8230 m (27,000 ft) 611 km/h (330 kt; 380 mph); patrol speed at 600 m (1,985 ft) 400 km/h (215 kt; 248 mph)
Range: ferry range 7200 km (3,885 nm; 4,474 miles); patrol endurance 12 hours 0 minutes
Performance: take-off run 1300 m (4,265 ft) at maximum take-off weight; landing run 850 m (2,789 ft) at normal landing weight with propeller reversal

Ilyushin **Il-62 'Classic'**

With a T-tail, rear-engine configuration closely resembling that of the Vickers/BAC VC-10, the **Il-62** was the first Soviet long-range, four-engined jet airliner to enter service. Developed as a replacement for the turboprop-engined Tu-114 on Aeroflot's most prestigious international routes, the Il-62 made its maiden flight in January 1963, powered by Lyul'ka AL-7 turbojets, pending availability of the Kuznetsov NK8-4 engines used by production aircraft. The improved longer-range **Il-62M** is powered by Soloviev D-30KU turbofans, and with the previous cascade-type thrust reversers replaced by clamshell-type units. These were still only fitted to the outboard engines. The more powerful engines allowed operation at higher gross weights, and an extra fuel tank was installed in the fin. An internal redesign allowed up to 198 passengers to be accommodated.

Although the Il-62 frequently served as a Presidential aircraft in the **USSR**, the aircraft involved retained Aeroflot markings and were operated by civilian crews. They were specially modified for the role, however, with a long dorsal avionics fairing and satellite communications equipment. Recently, these aircraft have relinquished Aeroflot titles, and have been painted in a quasi-government colour scheme, with massive Rossiya (Russia) titles on the fuselage sides. There are no known red-starred Il-62s. The only known truly military Il-62s were three former Interflug aircraft (**Il-62M**s and **MK**s) taken over by the **Luftwaffe** after reunification and operated by TG44 at Marxwalde, which became LTG65; the airfield was renamed Neuhardenburg. These aircraft were withdrawn from military use and sold, leaving only the Russian VIP transports. Marketing of the Il-62 continues (particularly second-hand examples), and further military or government customers may yet emerge.

SPECIFICATION

Ilyushin Il-62M 'Classic'
Wing: span 43.20 m (141 ft 9 in); aspect ratio 6.68; area 279.55 m² (3,009.15 sq ft)
Fuselage and tail: length 53.12 m (174 ft 3.5 in); height 12.35 m (40 ft 6.25 in); tailplane span 12.23 m (40 ft 1.5 in); wheel track 6.80 m (22 ft 3.5 in); wheel base 24.49 m (80 ft 4.5 in)
Powerplant: four PNPP 'Aviadvigatel' (Soloviev) D-30KU each rated at 107.87 kN (24,250 lb st) dry
Weights: operating empty 71600 kg (157,848 lb); maximum take-off 165000 kg (363,757 lb)
Fuel and load: internal fuel 105300 litres (27,817 US gal); external fuel none; maximum payload 23000 kg (50,705 lb)
Speed: normal cruising speed at between 10000 and

The Luftwaffe's former Interflug Il-62s were recently withdrawn and sold. They were replaced by three Airbus A310s (also obtained from Interflug), in the transport role .

12000 m (32,810 and 39,370 ft) between 820 and 900 km/h (442 and 486 kt; 509 and 560 mph)
Range: 7800 km (4,210 nm; 4,848 miles) with a 5100-kg (11,243-lb) payload
Performance: take-off balanced field length 3300 m (10,827 ft) at maximum take-off weight; landing run 2500 m (8,202 ft) at normal landing weight

Ilyushin Il-76 'Candid'

The Il-76 was developed as a successor to the An-12 for both Aeroflot and the **Soviet air force**. Just as the USAF purchased the jet-engined C-141 to augment its propeller-driven Hercules transports, so the Soviet air force turned to a jet aircraft to augment (and eventually supersede) its An-12s. Like the USAF, the Soviets found that for certain tasks the turboprop transport was superior and the Il-76 has still not entirely supplanted the An-12, which will finally be replaced by the An-70T, another turboprop. Larger, heavier and more powerful than the C-141, the Il-76 uses extensive high lift devices, thrust reversers and a high flotation undercarriage to achieve much better short- and rough-field performance, at the expense of only slightly inferior payload and range.

The Ilyushin Il-76 displays several other examples of Soviet design philosophy, with most military versions having a gun turret (with two twin-barrelled 23-mm cannon) in the tail, and with all transport versions having a glazed navigator/drop master position in the lower part of the nose. The cargo hold is fully pressurised and has a titanium floor, with fold-down roller conveyors, and can be quickly reconfigured by using interchangeable passenger, freight or air ambulance modules. Three such modules (each 6.1 m/20 ft long and 2.44 m/8 ft wide) can be fitted, the passenger modules containing 30 passengers in four abreast seats.

Loading is accomplished using two internal overhead winches, each of which can use two 3000-kg (6,615-lb) or four 2500-kg (5,511-lb) hoists. The ramp itself can be used as a lift, with a capacity of up to 30000 kg (66,150 lb). The hold is compatible with international standard containers and pallets.

The first prototype (SSSR-86712) made its maiden flight on 25 March 1971, and by 1974 a development squadron was in service flying Il-76s equipped with tail gun turrets. Series production began in 1975 at Tashkent. More than 750 had been built by the beginning of 1993, and production continues at a rate of about 50 per year. The initial production version was the **Il-76**, which received the NATO reporting name **'Candid-A'**. The codename was retained for the developed **Il-76T** featuring additional fuel tankage in the wing centre-section. The final 'Candid-A' variant is the **Il-76TD** with uprated Soloviev D-30KP-1 engines, which maintain full power at higher outside air temperatures and give improved 'hot-and-high' take-off performance. One soundproofed and specially equipped Il-76TD is used as the support aircraft for Soviet Antarctic expeditions, flying via

Based on an Il-76MD airframe, this aircraft is one of two Il-76 command posts based at Zhukhovskii's LII Flight Research Centre. The aircraft differs from standard in having a large number of extra blade aerials, strakes, antenna pods and an enormous radome fairing above the cockpit.

An Il-76MD in full Soviet air force markings during a rare visit to Britain. The Il-76 largely replaced the An-12, and is in use in huge numbers. The military fleet can be augmented by Aeroflot aircraft.

Maputo in Mozambique. Some military export Il-76 customers, including Iraq, use 'Candid-As', often in addition to 'Candid-Bs'.

Other 'Candid-A' sub-types include four **Il-76LL** engine testbeds, which have tested a number of engines, including the D-236 propfan, the NK-86, the PS-90A and the D-18T turbofans, and the **Il-76DMP**, a one-off fire-bomber conversion carrying up to 44 tonnes of retardant in two cylindrical tanks in the hold, and with special aiming devices for accurate retardant delivery. The equipment can be installed or removed in four hours, and the tanks take about 12 minutes to fill. The tanks can be discharged simultaneously or in series in just over six seconds. The aircraft can also carry up to 384 meteorological cartridges (cloud-seeders) for 'weather modification', or 40 fire-fighting parachutists. Military or pseudo-military users of the 'Candid-A' include **Cuba** and **North Korea**.

Finally, the Moscow Aeroshow at Zhukhovskii in August 1992 revealed two new variants of the basic 'civil' Il-76. With no known Soviet designation two of the aircraft were clearly equipped for some kind of military airborne command post or range control role, despite their Aeroflot colour scheme. They had prominent dorsal canoe radomes above the forward fuselage, a trailing aerial fitting (like that fitted to the EC-130Q, and the 'Bear-J') projecting from the ramp area, and various blade antennas. Small aerial pods, similar to those fitted to the Boeing E-6A Mercury, were carried under the outer wing panels. There were also several examples of an aircraft which appeared to be similar to the A-50 'Mainstay', with a very similar rotodome above

the fuselage. All wore Aeroflot markings and are described in greater detail under the Ilyushin A-50 'Mainstay' heading.

The NATO reporting name **'Candid-B'** is used to identify dedicated military versions of the Il-76, which can be externally identified by the gun turret in the tailcone. Many military 'Candids' also have small ECM fairings between the centre windows at the front of the navigator's compartment, and on each side of the forward and rear fuselage. Packs containing 96 50-mm IRCM flares or chaff cartridges can also be scabbed onto the landing gear fairings and/or the sides of the rear fuselage. The first dedicated military variant was the **Il-76M**, which was equivalent to the civil Il-76T; with uprated D-30KP-1 engines, the designation **Il-76MD** is used. Twenty-four Il-76MDs delivered to **India** to equip one flight of No. 25 Squadron at Chandigarh and No. 44 Squadron at Agra bear the local name **Gajaraj** (King Elephant). Other foreign users are **Iraq**, **Libya** and **Syria**.

SPECIFICATION

Ilyushin Il-76M 'Candid-B'
Wing: span 50.50 m (165 ft 8 in); aspect ratio 8.5; area 300.00 m² (3,229.28 sq ft)
Fuselage and tail: length 46.59 m (152 ft 10.25 in); height 14.76 m (48 ft 5 in)
Powerplant: four PNPP 'Aviadvigatel' (Soloviev) D-30KP each rated at 117.68 kN (26,455 lb st) dry
Weights: maximum take-off 170000 kg (374,780 lb)
Fuel and load: internal fuel about 81830 litres (21,617 US gal); external fuel none; maximum payload 40000 kg (88,183 lb)
Speed: maximum level speed 'clean' at optimum altitude 850 km/h (459 kt; 528 mph); cruising speed between 9000 and 12000 m (29,530 and 39,370 ft) between 750 and 800 km/h (405 and 432 kt; 466 and 497 mph)
Range: ferry range 6700 km (3,617 nm; 4,163 miles); range 5000 km (2,698 nm; 3,107 miles) with maximum payload
Performance: absolute ceiling about 15500 m (50,855 ft); take-off run 850 m (2,790 ft) at maximum take-off weight; landing run 450 m (1,475 ft) at normal landing weight

Ilyushin Il-76MD 'Candid-B'
generally similar to the Ilyushin Il-76M 'Candid-B' except in the following particulars:
Powerplant: four PNPP 'Aviadvigatel' (Soloviev) D-30KP-1 each rated at 117.68 kN (26,455 lb st) dry
Weights: maximum take-off 190000 kg (418,871 lb)
Fuel and load: external fuel none; maximum payload 48000 kg (105,820 lb)

Ilyushin Il-78M 'Midas'

The introduction of inflight-refuelling probes on some Soviet tactical aircraft (notably the Su-24M and MiG-31, but also the Su-27IB, MiG-29K and Su-27P/PU) and the age of Russia's handful of Myasishchev M-4 'Bison' and Tu-16N 'Badger' tankers, led to the need for a new inflight-refuelling aircraft. Conversion of retired bombers was considered but, in the end, a tanker based on the Il-76 'Candid' (which was available in large numbers) was felt to be a better option.

The **Il-78M 'Midas'** is a three-point

tanker based on (or even converted from) the airframe of the Il-76MD military freighter. The aircraft is fitted with three Severin/UPAZ PAE external refuelling units, one under each wing and one mounted on the port side of the rear fuselage. The two underwing pods are reportedly sometimes removed on missions involving only a single

An Il-78 'Midas', unusually in full military markings, trails three hoses in front of its customer, a Tu-142MS 'Bear-H'.

Ilyushin Il-78M 'Midas'

receiver aircraft. Pods are also carried by some tactical aircraft (usually Su-24s) operating in the 'buddy-buddy' role and consist of pylon-mounted square-section self-powered HDUs with a conical front which retracts to open an annular ram air intake, which in turn drives the turbine which powers the refuelling hose winch and fuel pump. The three HDUs can operate at a maximum rate of 2500 litres (550 Imp gal)

per minute (total 7500 litres/1,650 Imp gal per minute), which is a higher rate than Western HDUs can handle, and allows very fast refuelling of formations of tactical aircraft. Red and yellow lights are mounted on the back of each HDU and on the former tail turret, to allow radio-silent contacts.

Internally the Il-78M has a pair of enormous cylindrical tanks pallet-mounted in the hold. Together these contain 35 tonnes (of

the aircraft's 100-tonne total) and since they are distinct from the aircraft's own fuel system represent the total transferable fuel load. The observer sits in the former tail gunner's turret, but has no controls, communicating via radio link with the flight engineer who operates the refuelling controls. Receiver/tanker rendezvous is facilitated by a simple homing radar housed behind a broad flat aft-facing radome ahead of the

standard rear-loading ramp.

The former Soviet Union's only operational Il-78M regiment was based in the **Ukraine** and was retained by that country's air arm after it declared independence, leaving only a handful in Russian hands. Although most Il-78Ms have been noted in Aeroflot colours, at least one has been photographed in full **CIS** air force colours, with a two-digit regimental code.

Ilyushin **Il-86 'Camber'**

Although no military customers have been found for the basic **Il-86** wide-bodied 'Airbus', there is some evidence that a handful of these aircraft is operational in a military or quasi-military role. At least four have been seen at Zhukhovskii wearing full Aeroflot colours, but clearly modified for some kind of command post, missile tracking or avionics test role. Fitted with a huge dorsal canoe antenna above the forward fuselage, the aircraft also have a plethora of

blade aerials above and below the fuselage. Large pods (with dielectric antennas and cooling air intakes) are also carried under the wingroots.

This Il-86, despite its Aeroflot colours, is an airborne command post or range control aircraft. Cabin windows are faired over, and the aircraft carries underwing antenna pods and a massive dorsal radome.

Ilyushin **Il-102**

The **Ilyushin Il-102**, which made its first appearance at the 1992 Moscow Aeroshow, was developed as a competitor to the Su-25 'Frogfoot' and is still being marketed despite its rejection by the Soviet air force and its anachronistic design. It is powered by a pair of non-afterburning RD-33I turbofans based on those used by the MiG-29. During 1992 Ilyushin even went so far as to issue a slim brochure on what they called the 'Il-102 Armoured Close Air Support Aircraft'.

The aircraft has its roots in the **Il-40 'Brawny'**, developed as a dedicated ground attack/close air support aircraft during the late 1940s, as an alternative to simply using obsolete jet fighters. Powered by a pair of RD-9F turbojets (as used in the MiG-19 and later, ironically, by the prototype

Su-25), the Il-40 was a heavily-armoured two-seater, the second seat being in a separate cockpit located adjacent to the trailing edge of the wing and occupied by a rearward-facing gunner, who controlled a remote gun turret in the tailcone. With its mixture of six underwing pylons and six inboard internal weapons bays inside the wing, the aircraft has obvious similarities with 1940s-vintage *shturmovik* ground attack aircraft. An NR-23 23-mm cannon (traversible to near vertical) was fitted for strafing ground targets. The prototype made its maiden flight on 7 March 1955, but flight tests revealed gun-gas ingestion problems which were cured by extending the intakes forward to meet, side-by-side, at the nose. State acceptance tests were passed in January 1955, but the project was cancelled, and the five completed pre-production aircraft were scrapped, on Kruschchev's orders, later that year, in the belief that a dedicated jet *shturmovik* was unnecessary.

A single prototype may have survived.

The design was resurrected in the aftermath of the 1967 Six Day War, during which Israeli fighters armed with 30-mm cannon proved devastatingly effective as tank-killers, This led directly to the requirement which resulted in the Su-25, Sukhoi following the US approach of using a single-seat attack aircraft while Ilyushin opted for a two-seater. Under the designation **Il-42**, Ilyushin revised the original Il-40, only to have their design rejected summarily by the air force. The aircraft was redesignated Il-102, to disassociate it from the Il-40, and a prototype was constructed using company funds and borrowed equipment.

The new aircraft was externally very similar to the Il-40 of 1953, albeit with the tailplanes lowered and given dihedral, with wing fences removed, and with the previously bifurcated engine intakes cut back from the nose to a point level with the cockpit. Whether the Il-102 began life as an Il-40,

or used parts from an uncompleted Il-40, remains unknown. Orders to terminate the project were ignored, the OKB pressing on using the new designation 'Experimental Aircraft No.1' and the pretence that it was a pure research platform. The prototype made its maiden flight on 25 September 1982, and made 250 flights before it was grounded in 1984 when engine life expired (no funding being available for replacement or overhaul). The aircraft was represented to the air force in 1986 as a potential Su-25 replacement, the Su-25T being selected instead, and was shown at the 1992 Moscow Aeroshow, perhaps in an effort to remind the world of Ilyushin's long history as a military aircraft producer.

The sole Il-102 prototype. The aircraft is still being marketed by Ilyushin as a cheap ground attack platform, and to keep the OKB in the military aircraft business.

Ilyushin A-50 'Mainstay'/Il-976

The **'Mainstay'** was developed as a replacement for the Tupolev Tu-126 'Moss', the USSR's first AEW and AWACS platform. Like many early Western AEW aircraft, the 'Moss' was virtually ineffective over land, but was efficient enough to demonstrate the usefulness of an airborne radar station for providing early warning of enemy attack and for controlling defending fighters. Remarkably, development of what the Russians call SDRLO (Systyem Dalnovo Radiolocacio-mnovo Obnarushenya, or Long-Range Radio Location and Detection System) was actually terminated during the 1960s as an economy measure and was then restarted in the face of Western development of the E-3 Sentry.

The **A-50** has a rotodome (influenced more by that carried by the E-3 than that of the Tu-126) above the fuselage, with the nose glazing and tail turret removed and replaced by further radomes, and with a small dorsal canoe radome projecting forward from the leading edge of the wing centre-section. Large horizontal flat plates of unknown purpose are fitted to the rear of each undercarriage fairing.

The 'Mainstay' reportedly entered service during 1984, and after some teething troubles has proved successful and popular. The system's designers admit inferior radar range and multiple target tracking capability by comparison with the E-3, but claim better discrimination of objects and targets on the ground or of low-flying targets against ground 'clutter'. A particular bugbear for crews (used to the luxuriously-appointed 'Moss', which was a converted Tu-114 airliner) is the inferior conditions in which they must work. Noise levels are high, and toilet and galley facilities barely adequate. Rest bunks are not provided at all. Morale problems have been worsened by the move from the Baltic to Pechora in the polar region, where accommodation and facilities are poor even by Soviet standards. The move was made to allow the aircraft to meet threats from what one senior air force commander described as "the most dangerous direction."

Because the Soviet electronics industry lags behind that of the West and has no domestic market for home computers and computer games, equipment tends to be bigger and heavier, and achieving similar equipment performance has been an amazing leap, achieved only at the expense of lightness and simplicity. The separate command and control systems of the separate branches of the armed forces necessitates the installation of duplicate systems for

The Aeroflot colour scheme, glazed nose and wingtip pods identify this aircraft as an Il-976, a rotodome-equipped range control aircraft similar to the full standard A-50 'Mainstay'.

exchanging data, decoding IFF signals, etc. All decoding and interfacing is carried out on board, whereas much of the latter is done on the ground for the E-3 Sentry.

The weight of all the equipment is greater than had been anticipated, and landing gear limitations prevent the aircraft from taking off with a full fuel load, which reduces endurance by about half an hour. This problem is exacerbated by the fact that disturbed airflow from the rotodome makes it very difficult to use the nose-mounted inflight-refuelling probe, and only the most experienced pilots are cleared for the practice.

Inside the cabin a single large screen is used for controlling fighters, with smaller screens monitoring the tactical situation on the ground and in the air, and showing number and type of friendly and enemy aircraft, with details of course, speed, altitude, armament and fuel state. All the screens are fully-digitised colour CRTs, and show friendly forces in red and enemy in blue.

The aircraft's mission computer allows automatic communication of data to and from fighters and ground stations directly, and via satellite using datalinks. When connected to the aircraft's autopilot it can fly the aircraft through pre-programmed search patterns over programmed points on the ground. A-50s typically fly a figure-eight racetrack pattern at about 10000 m (33,000 ft) with 100 km (62 miles) between the centres of the two circles. During exercises the A-50s have demonstrated an ability to control MiG-31 interceptors, directing them onto incoming cruise missiles, while simultaneously supplying submarines with tactical information and controlling Tu-22M-3 'Backfire' bombers and other fighters.

During the Gulf War, two A-50s were deployed to a Black Sea airfield, where they maintained a single-aircraft, round-the-clock

watch over the war zone, able to see every take-off and cruise missile firing in Turkey and over most of Iraq. Further aircraft maintained a standing patrol over the Caspian Sea. Refuelling difficulties were surmounted and the aircraft were supported by 3MS-2 (Myasishchev M-4 'Bison') tankers.

A second rotodome-equipped version of the Il-76 is the **Il-976**, described by some sources as a one-off AEW testbed but in fact already available in considerable numbers, and also described as a range control and missile tracking platform. It may also be a forerunner of the A-50, used for AEW trials and for systems development. At least five aircraft, all wearing Aeroflot markings and civil registration numbers, were present at Zhukhovskii during the 1992 Moscow Aeroshow. The Il-976 differs from the A-50 in retaining the glazed nose of the Il-76, and the glazed tail turret, although the guns are replaced by a bulbous radome. The aircraft also lacks an inflight-refuelling probe and many of the A-50's minor antennas, but is fitted with fat cylindrical wingtip pods.

The A-50 is fitted with a rotodome above the trailing edge of the wing centre-section, and a dorsal canoe.

It has been reported that Beriev is responsible for converting Il-76s to AEW configuration, using equipment supplied by the Ministry of the Radio Equipment Industry, but it is not known whether this refers to the A-50 or the Il-976, or both. Iraq has developed similar AEW versions of the Il-76, which are described separately.

SPECIFICATION

Ilyushin A-50 'Mainstay'
generally similar to the Ilyushin Il-76M 'Candid-A' except in the following particulars:
Fuselage and tail: height 14.76 m (48 ft 5 in)

The definitive production A-50 has a horizontal winglet/blade antenna mounted on the rear part of the landing gear fairing.

IPTN (Eurocopter/MBB) NBO 105

Industri Pesawat Terbang Nusantara (Nusantara Aircraft Industries Ltd)
PO Box 1562, Jalan Pajajaran 154
Bandung 40174, Indonesia

Nusantara Aircraft Industries Ltd (IPTN) in Bandung, Indonesia, produces the **Eurocopter BO 105** helicopter (described separately) under licence from Eurocopter Germany (previously MBB), for both military and commercial users. Between 1976 and 1987, IPTN built 100 **NBO 105**s, then changed to the **NBO 105S** model with a 25-cm (10-in) fuselage stretch and with provision for nose-mounted search or weather radar.

IPTN has developed a multi-purpose delivery system for the NBO 105, comprising fuselage-mounted provision for such armament as unguided rocket pods and machine-gun pods, or reconnaissance sensors includlng FLIR pods. Rocket-armed NBO 105s are included in the 16-strong inventory of this type flown by the Indonesian army (**TNI-AD**). Other military customers for the NBO 105 are the air force (**TNI-AU**) and navy (**TNI-AL**), although the latter's No. 200 Squadron found the type unsuitable for shipboard operation. The type is also used by the Indonesian **Polisi** and the **Royal Jordanian Air Force**.

A rocket-armed NBO-105 of the Indonesian army. The type also serves with the the air force, navy, Polisi and with the Royal Jordanian Air Force.

IPTN (CASA) NC.212 Aviocar

IPTN in Indonesia has been building the **CASA C.212 Aviocar** (described separately) under licence since 1976, primarily to satisfy the domestic demand for both military and civil versions. The first 29 aircraft from the Bandung production line were equivalent to the Spanish **C.212 Series 100** model, with production subsequently changing to the Series 200 model, identified locally as the **NC.212-200**. The **Indonesian air force (TNI-AU)** received two Series 100s and eight Series 200s. These aircraft are used principally by No. 2 Squadron at Kemayoran in the transport role, and for communications duties by No. 4 Squadron at Malany. Both the army and the navy (**TNI-AD** and **TNI-AL**) received four NC.212-200s for routine transport operations; other possible roles include LAPES, SAR, airdropping, maritime patrol, medevac and photographic survey.

An Indonesian-built NC.212A-4 Aviocar in full air force camouflage. The type is used by the Indonesian air force, navy and army.

IPTN (Eurocopter) AS 330 Puma/NAS 332 Super Puma

IPTN assembled 11 **Aérospatiale AS 330J** Pumas in 1981/83 using components from French production, and subsequently delivered 10 to the Indonesian air force (**TNI-AU**), including two in VIP configuration. A batch of 18 Super Pumas then followed, equivalent to the AS 332C, and from this batch the Indonesian navy (**TNI-AL**) received four **NAS 332B** utility models for operation from support vessels used in amphibious operations. One VIP-configured NAS 332 was supplied to the Malaysian government. With the 19th Super Puma, production switched to the equivalent of the **AS 332L**, the version with cabin lengthened by 76.5 cm (30 in). The TNI-AU is among reported customers for this version, with at least one VIP transport on order.

Above left: An Indonesian-built AS 330J in service with the TNI-AU, one of 10 IPTN-built Pumas in use.

Above: Indonesian-built NAS 332F Super Pumas can carry Exocet ASMs and have a chin-mounted radar.

Iraqi Air Force Baghdad 1 and Adnan

Iraqi Air Force, Ministry of Defence
Bab Al Muadam
Baghdad, Iraq

While Soviet conversions of the Ilyushin Il-76 'Candid' for the AEW role are described under the Ilyushin A-50 'Mainstay' heading, two Iraqi AEW conversions deserve separate treatment. The first AEW modification was named **Baghdad 1**, and was an Il-76MD (without tail turret) with the antenna of a Thomson-CSF Tigre surveillance radar mounted inverted behind a blister radome in place of the clamshell and upward-opening rear doors. The Tigre radar is licence-built in Iraq (usually truck-mounted) and signal processing was modified to deal with ground clutter for its new application. The radar is manned by four operators, gives a 180° sweep, and can detect, track and identify targets out to 190 nm (350 km; 218 miles). Unspecified problems with the Baghdad 1 led to the development of a second AEW aircraft, this one having a more conventional 9 m (29 ft 6 in) diameter rotodome atop the fuselage, but no tail turret. Details of this conversion, known as the **Adnan**, remain sketchy. At least three were produced by conversion and one was destroyed during a coalition air attack on Al Taqqaddum on 23 January 1991, the other two then fleeing to Iran, where they may remain.

The radome of one of the two Baghdad 1 Il-76 conversions, with a huge dielectric radome for the Thomson-CSF Tigre surveillance radar mounted in place of the rear loading doors. The aircraft proved unsuccessful, and Iraq instead developed a 'Mainstay' clone.

IRGC Fajr

Intended as a primary trainer, the **Fajr** (Dawn) was built by the Air Industries Division of the Islamic Revolutionary Guard Corps. Flown on 22 February 1988, the prototype (the first aircraft built in Iran since the Islamic revolution) was built based upon **Neico Lancair 235** plans. This was a kit-built US sport aircraft which flew in 1984.

SPECIFICATION

IRGC Fajr (Neico Lancair 235)
Wing: span 23 ft 6 in (7.16 m); area 76.00 sq ft (7.06 m²)

Fuselage and tail: length 19 ft 8 in (5.99 m); height 6 ft 1 in (1.85 m)
Powerplant: one Textron Lycoming O-235 four-cylinder horizontally opposed piston engine rated at 118 hp (88 kW)
Weights: basic empty 650 lb (295 kg); maximum take-off 1,275 lb (578 kg)

Speed: maximum level speed 'clean' at sea level 185 kt (213 mph, 343 km/h)
Range: 868 nm (1,000 miles; 1609 km)
Performance: maximum rate of climb at sea level 1,500 ft (457 m) per minute; take-off run 600 ft (183 m) at maximum take-off weight; landing run 600 ft (183 m) at maximum landing weight

Jodel (SAN) D.140 Mousquetaire/Abeille

Société des Avions Jodel is currently inactive

The title Jodel is a contraction of the names of the type's test pilot, Eduard Joly, and its designer, Jean Delmontez. The Jodel company acted as a design bureau and provider of plans, licensing other companies and individuals to build its designs. The **Jodel D.140 Mousquetaire** was based on the **Jodel D.117** and this was licensed from Jean Delmontez by SAN (Société Aéronautique Normande), who developed the larger, four/five-seater D.140 family with a 180-hp (134 kW) Lycoming engine, revised tail surfaces and other improvements. The prototype was first

flown in July 1958. Production of the **D.140E Mousquetaire IV**, with enlarged tail surfaces, an all-flying tail and modified ailerons, included 18 for the **French air force**, which went on to acquire 14 **D.140R Abeilles**. This has a cut-down rear fuselage with all-round vision canopy and glider-towing hook. Both types remain in use with the Armée de l'Air for recreation flying and (the D.140Rs) for glider-towing with GI 4/312 at Salon and the Ecole de Pupille de l'Air 349 at Grenoble. The D.140s are powered by 180-hp (134-kW) Lycoming O-360 four-cylinder piston engines.

This is one of the D.140R Abeille glider tugs operated by the Armée de l'Air at Salon and Grenoble. The similar D.140 is used for sport flying.

Kaman SH-2F Seasprite

*Kaman Aerospace Corporation
Old Windsor Rd, PO Box No.2
Bloomfield, Connecticut 06002, USA*

Originally designated **K-20** by Kaman, the **Seasprite** was conceived in response to a 1956 **USN** requirement for a high-speed, all-weather, long-range SAR, liaison and utility helicopter. The original **HU2K-1** made its maiden flight on 2 July 1959, and the type was redesignated **UH-2A** in 1962. Successive variants of the aircraft were progressively improved and updated, gaining a second engine (for greater safety margin on ship-based operations), dual mainwheels, and a four-bladed tail rotor, but retained their liaison, utility, SAR and combat rescue roles. All early variants have now been retired or, more often, converted to later standards. Production stopped after the delivery of the last **UH-2B**, bringing production to a total of 190 (all originally single-engined). These comprised four **YUH-2A** prototypes 84 UH-2As and 102 UH-2Bs. At least two were evaluated by the US Army. Further variants were all converted from existing airframes.

The helicopter was first used in the ASW role in October 1970, when the Navy selected the **SH-2D** as an interim LAMPS (Light Airborne Multi-Purpose System) platform. Externally, the SH-2D introduced an undernose radome housing a Litton LN 66 search radar, with an ASQ-81 MAD on the starboard fuselage pylon and a removable sonobuoy rack in the fuselage port side for 15 SSQ-47 active or SSQ-41 passive sonobuoys. Twenty were converted from **HH-2D**s, entering service in 1972.

Deliveries of the definitive **SH-2F**, which also bears the **LAMPS I** designation, commenced in May 1973. Its primary role is concerned with extending the area of protection provided by the outer defensive screen of a carrier battle group. The SH-2F introduced uprated General Electric T58-GE-8F engines, Kaman's advanced '101' rotor which gave a longer life (3,000 hours), improved performance, reliability and maintainability and a strengthened landing gear. A notable external difference concerned the tailwheel, which was relocated forwards, shortening the wheelbase by nearly 6 ft (1.83 m) for greater deck-edge clearance when operating from smaller warships. These modifications allowed the SH-2F to operate at higher all-up weights than the SH-2D. The SH-2F also featured an improved Marconi LN 66HP surface search radar, AN/ASQ-81(V)2 towed MAD bird on a starboard pylon and a tactical nav/comms system, necessitating a sensor operator in addition to the normal crew of two pilots. Offensive capability comprised two Mk 46 torpedoes to engage sub-surface threats. Eighty-eight aircraft were converted from earlier variants (using up virtually every surviving airframe), and 16 surviving SH-2Ds were also brought up to the same standard in a programme completed in 1982.

In March 1972 Kaman completed two **YSH-2E**s as testbeds for the Navy's LAMPS II programme with a new Texas Instruments APS-115 radar in a reconfigured nose. The programme was cancelled

later the same year. Kaman proposed a derivative of the SH-2, known as the **Sealamp**, as a contender for the LAMPS III requirement that was eventually fulfilled by the SH-60B. The aircraft remained unbuilt, although several SH-2s were used to test LAMPS III systems and equipment.

Despite its failure to be selected as the LAMPS III platform, the Seasprite was retained for service aboard US Navy 'Knox'- and 'Kidd'-class frigates, the 'Truxton'-class cruisers and the first two 'Ticonderoga'-class cruisers. All but the first 'Belknap'-class cruisers carry SH-2Fs, as do the first and the third through to the 25th 'Oliver Hazard Perry'-class ASW frigates. Accordingly, the aircraft was reinstated in production during 1981, when the US Navy placed an order for the first batch of an eventual 60 new-build SH-2Fs, the last six being delivered as upgraded **SH-2G**s (described separately). Many of these aircraft, and some earlier SH-2Fs, received AN/ALR-66A(V)1 RWRs and AN/ALE-39 chaff/flare dispensers. In 1992 the SH-2F was operated by eight front-line and three Reserve HSL squadrons, but by the end of April 1994 post-Cold War defence cuts had reduced the force to two Reserve units, the last fleet squadron having been HSL-33. These units transitioned to SH-2Gs during 1994.

From 1987, 16 SH-2Fs received a package of modifications to allow them to operate in the Gulf. This included the provision of an AN/AAQ-16 FLIR under the nose, an AN/ALQ-144 IR jammer, AN/AAR-47 and AN/DLQ-3 missile warning and jamming equipment, and new radios. During the Gulf War of 1991, SH-2Fs tested the ML-30 Magic Lantern laser sub-surface mine

This SH-2F of HSL-34 wears the high-visibility colour scheme associated with the SH-2F until very recently. No active-duty squadrons now fly the SH-2F, which has become a rare bird in US skies.

detector. Two essentially similar ML-90 sets are also to be tested on SH-2s.

The SH-2F has been ordered by **Pakistan** (six aircraft, whose delivery has been halted by embargo), and has been offered to Egypt, Greece, South Korea, Portugal, Taiwan and Thailand. In Portugal and Korea the aircraft lost out to Westland's Super Lynx while Greece and Taiwan already have orders for the SH-60. Orders may still materialise from the other countries. The US Navy has already discovered the versatility and adaptability of the Seasprite airframe, and retired SH-2Fs, especially if brought up to SH-2G standards, would represent an excellent buy for many customers. The aircraft combines compact external dimensions, a rugged, dependable airframe and good handling characteristics.

SPECIFICATION

Kaman SH-2F Seasprite
generally similar to the SH-2G Super Seasprite (see following page) except in the following particulars:

Rotor system: main rotor diameter 44 ft 0 in (13.41 m); tail rotor diameter 8 ft 2 in (2.49 m); main rotor disc area 1,520.53 sq ft (141.26 m2); tail rotor disc area 52.38 sq ft (4.87 m2)

Fuselage and tail: length overall, rotors turning 52 ft 7 in (16.03 m); height overall, rotors turning 15 ft 6 in (4.72 m) and to top of rotor head 13 ft 5 in (4.09 m); wheel base 16 ft 9 in (5.11 m)

Powerplant: two General Electric T58-GE-8F turboshafts each rated at 1,350 shp (1007 kW)

Weights: empty 7,040 lb (3193 kg); maximum normal take-off 12,800 lb (5805 kg); maximum overload take-off 13,300 lb (6033 kg)

Fuel and load: external fuel up to two 60-US gal (227-litre) auxiliary tanks; maximum ordnance 1,200 lb (544 kg)

Speed: maximum level speed 'clean' at sea level 143 kt (165 mph; 265 km/h); normal cruising speed 130 kt (150 mph; 241 km/h)

Range: maximum range 366 nm (422 miles; 679 km)

Performance: maximum rate of climb at sea level 2,440 ft (774 m) per minute; service ceiling 22,500 ft (6860 m); hovering ceiling 18,600 ft (5670 m) in ground effect and 15,400 ft (4695 m) out of ground effect

Many, but by no means all, SH-2Fs received an overall light grey tactical colour scheme in recent years. The SH-2F has already been ordered by Pakistan (whose aircraft are now embargoed) and may attract orders from other countries. In US service, the SH-2F is rapidly giving way to the re-engined and updated SH-2G. The original shape engine pods are clearly evident.

Kaman **SH-2G Seasprite**

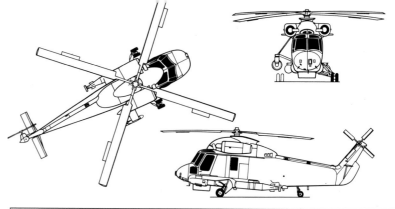

Continued development of Kaman's versatile **Seasprite** helicopter resulted in the appearance of the **SH-2G**. The prototype **YSH-2G**, which first flew on 2 April 1985, was simply a conversion of an **SH-2F** and served as a T700 engine testbed. This was the main modification from SH-2F standard, the SH-2G adopting a pair of General Electric T700-GE-701 turboshaft engines in lieu of the SH-2F's original T58-GE-8Fs. These deliver approximately 10 per cent more power, with commensurate performance benefits and 20 per cent lower fuel burn (allowing increased range), as well as improved reliability and maintainability. In addition, new composite main rotor blades with a service life of 10,000 hours are fitted.

Avionics improvements include MIL-STD 1553 digital databus, AN/UYS-503 onboard acoustic processor, AN/ASN-150 tactical management system and multi-function displays. The SH-2G is expected to retain the package of avionics modifications applied to 16 SH-2Fs for operations in the Gulf, including AN/ALQ-144 IR jammers, AN/AAR-47 missile warning equipment, AN/AAQ-16 FLIR, secure UHF/VHF radios and Magic Lantern laser equipment for sub-surface mine detection.

The SH-2G is also qualified for dipping sonar operations, ASM firing, FLIR sensors, rockets, guns (a 7.62-mm machine-gun may be pintle-mounted in each cabin doorway) and countermeasures. The Mk 50 lightweight aerial torpedo is expected to supersede the Mk 46 weapon currently in service. Two torpedoes may be carried, but a single example is more common. Mk 25 marine smoke markers are also carried in a compartment under the nose and are used to give crew members visual reference when prosecuting a sub-surface contact.

The first flight with full avionics occurred on 28 December 1989 and was followed by deliveries of six new-build examples ordered in FY 1987. The first production

SH-2G was flown in March 1990. No further new production is planned and it is envisaged to retrospectively modernise more than 90 existing SH-2Fs to SH-2G standard, with 24 conversion kits ordered by January 1992. These will now serve with two **US Navy Reserve** light anti-submarine warfare helicopter squadrons, HSL-84 at North Island and HSL-94 at Willow Grove, the Seasprite having been prematurely retired from active-duty use in early 1994 as a result of defence cuts. The Seasprite's long term future is uncertain, since reductions in the HSL community may free up sufficient SH-60B airframes to re-equip the two units.

SPECIFICATION

Kaman SH-2G Super Seasprite
Rotor system: main rotor diameter 44 ft 4 in (13.51 m); tail rotor diameter 8 ft 1 in (2.46 m); main rotor disc area 1,543.66 sq ft (143.41 m²); tail rotor disc area 51.32 sq ft (4.77 m²)
Fuselage and tail: length overall, rotors turning 52 ft 9 in (16.08 m), fuselage excluding tail rotor 40 ft 0 in (12.19 m), and with nose and blades folded 38 ft 4 in (11.68 m); height overall, rotors turning 15 ft 0.5 in (4.58 m), and with blades folded 13 ft 7 in (4.14 m); stabiliser span 9 ft 9 in (2.97 m); wheel track 10 ft 10 in (3.30 m); wheel base 16 ft 10 in (5.13 m)
Powerplant: two General Electric T700-GE-401/401C turboshafts each rated at 1,723 shp (1285 kW)
Weights: empty 7,680 lb (3483 kg); maximum take-off 13,500 lb (6123 kg)
Fuel and load: internal fuel 276 US gal (1045 litres); external fuel up to two 100-US gal (379-litre) auxiliary tanks; maximum payload 4,000 lb (1814 kg)
Speed: maximum level speed 'clean' at sea level 138 kt (159 mph; 256 km/h); normal cruising speed 120 kt (138 mph; 222 km/h)
Range: maximum range 478 nm (500 miles; 885 km) with two auxiliary tanks; operational radius 35 nm (40 miles; 65 km) for a patrol of 2 hours 10 minutes with one torpedo or of 1 hour 30 minutes with two torpedoes; endurance 5 hours with two auxiliary tanks

Performance: maximum rate of climb at sea level 2,500 ft (762 m) per minute; service ceiling 23,900 ft (7285 m); hovering ceiling 20,800 ft (6340 m) in ground effect and 18,000 ft (5485 m) out of ground effect

The SH-2G is immediately recognisable by its redesigned engine nacelles, housing T700 turboshafts.

Kaman **K-MAX (MMIRA)**

Kaman's **K-MAX** was developed as a private venture for military and civil applications. The K-MAX was initially dubbed **Multi-Mission Intermeshing Rotor Aircraft** (MMIRA) and was designed primarily for the logging role and other external medium/heavylift missions, replacing Kaman's previous H-43 Huskie. First flown on 23 December 1991, it retains the classic Kaman configuration with two intermeshing 'teetering' rotors with Kaman's patented aerodynamic servo-flap

rotor control. The transmission is based on the proven design from the H-43, although production gearboxes are taken from the higher power transmission of Kaman's SH-2 naval helicopter due to the K-MAX's greater power on/off cycles. Optimised for single-pilot operations, the prototype K-MAX is powered by a derated Textron Lycoming T53 turboshaft and can lift a 6,000-lb (2722-kg) external load out of ground effect at 8,000 ft (2438 m). Possible military missions include surveillance, communications,

resupply and ordnance delivery, and the design is optimised for unpiloted drone operation and to be readily 'scaleable' for larger or smaller size.

SPECIFICATION

Kaman K-Max (MMIRA)
Rotor system: rotor diameter, each 47 ft 0 in (14.32 m); rotor disc area, total 3,469.89 sq ft (322.35 m²)
Fuselage and tail: length overall, rotors turning 50 ft 6 in (15.39 m); wheel track 11 ft 4 in (3.44 m)
Powerplant: one 1,800-shp (1343-kW) Textron Lycoming T5317A turboshaft flat-rated at 1,500 shp (1119 kW) for take-off and 1,340 shp (1007 kW) for

continuous running
Weights: operating empty 4,100 lb (1859 kg); normal take-off 6,000 lb (2722 kg) without jettisonable load; maximum take-off 10,500 lb (4762 kg) with jettisonable load
Fuel and load: internal fuel 1,541 lb (699 kg); external fuel none; maximum payload 6,000 lb (2722 kg)
Performance: target hovering ceiling 8,000 ft (2440 m) out of ground effect with a 5,000-lb (2268-kg) slung load and fuel for 1 hour 30 minutes

The K-Max is suitable for a range of military roles, and can be flown as a manned helicopter or as a drone. Note the intermeshing rotors.

Kamov Ka-25 'Hormone'

Helicopter Scientific and Technology Complex named after N.I. Kamov
March 8th St
Lubertsy 14007, Moscow, Russia

The Ka-25 family of shipborne helicopters was the aircraft which put Nikolai Kamov's contra-rotating co-axial rotor configuration 'on the map'. The lack of an anti-torque tail rotor brought benefits of lightness and simplicity, and the co-axial rotors made possible a smaller overall rotor diameter. Designed to meet a 1957 **Soviet navy** requirement for a new shipborne ASW helicopter, the first member of the family was the Ka-20 'Harp', which initially flew during 1960 and which formed the basis of the operational 'Hormone'. The production **Ka-25BSh 'Hormone-A'** was of almost identical size and appearance, but was fitted with operational equipment and uprated 900-shp (671-kW) GTD-3F engines (from 1973 replaced by 990-shp/736-kW GTD-3Ms). It entered service in 1967.

Although the lower part of the fuselage is sealed and watertight, the Ka-25 is not intended for amphibious operations, and flotation bags are often fitted to the under-carriage for use in the event of an emergency landing on the water. The cabin is adequate for the job, but is not tall enough to allow the crew to stand upright. Progressive additions of new equipment have made the interior more cluttered. Primary sensors for the ASW mission are the I/J-band radar (NATO 'Big Bulge'), OKA-2 dipping sonar, a downward-looking 'Tie Rod' electro-optical sensor in the tailboom, and a MAD sensor, either in a recess in the rear part of the cabin or in a fairing sometimes fitted below the central of the three tailfins. A box-like sonobuoy launcher can also be scabbed on to the starboard side of the rear fuselage. Dye-markers or smoke floats can also be carried externally. Comprehensive avionics, defensive and navigation systems are fitted.

Armament is not normally carried, although the helicopter can be fitted with a long 'coffin-like' weapons bay which runs

A 'Hormone-B' with wheels retracted out of the way of the radar scan pattern. The round-bottomed radome is a distinctive recognition feature.

along the belly from the radome back to the tailboom, and small bombs or depth charges can be carried on tiny pylons just aft of the nosewheels. The underfuselage weapons bay can carry a variety of weapons, including nuclear depth charges. When wire-guided torpedoes are carried, a wire reel is mounted on the port side of the forward fuselage.

It has been estimated that some 260 of the 450 or so Ka-25s produced were 'Hormone-As', but only a handful remains, fulfilling secondary roles. Although the Ka-25BSh has been withdrawn from front-line use by the navies of the former USSR, small numbers were exported to **India**, **Syria**, **Vietnam** and former **Yugoslavia**, and most of these aircraft remain in use.

The second Ka-25 variant identified in the West was given the NATO reporting name **'Hormone-B'**, but its Soviet designation remains unknown. This variant is externally identifiable by its bulbous (instead of flat-bottomed) undernose radome and small (datalink?) radome under the rear fuselage. This is believed to have been used for acquiring targets and providing mid-course missile guidance, for ship- and submarine-launched SS-N-3 'Shaddock' and SS-N-12 'Sandbox' missiles. It may also allow the 'Hormone-B' to fulfil a secondary AEW role. On the 'Hormone-B' only, the four under-carriage units are retractable and can be lifted out of the scanning pattern of the radar. Today, modern missiles do not usually require mid-course guidance and targeting is usually achieved from greater stand-off ranges, often using long-range fixed-wing aircraft. The 'Hormone-B' thus has no direct replacement, and has been withdrawn from use in its primary role.

The final version of the Ka-25 is the **Ka-25PS**, allocated the NATO reporting name **'Hormone-C'**. Almost certainly converted from redundant 'Hormone-A' airframes, the Ka-25PS is best known as a search and rescue aircraft, although some sources suggest that it initially had a missile guidance role, operating in conjunction with 'Hormone-Bs'. Stripped of ASW systems, the Ka-25PS can carry a practical load of

A Ka-25BSh 'Hormone-A' stripped of ASW equipment and flotation gear for the COD role, carrying 12 passengers.

freight or up to 12 passengers, making it a useful ship-to-ship or ship-to-shore transport and vertrep platform. A quadruple Yagi antenna (NATO 'Home Guard') fitted to many aircraft is reportedly used for homing onto the personal locator beacons carried by aircrew. Most Ka-25PSs also have searchlights, and a 300-kg (660-lb) capacity rescue winch. The Ka-25PS has largely been replaced by SAR versions of the Ka-27 'Helix'.

SPECIFICATION

Kamov Ka-25BSh 'Hormone-A'
Rotor system: rotor diameter, each 15.74 m (52 ft 7.75 in); rotor disc area, total 389.15 m² (4,188.93 sq ft)
Fuselage and tail: length of fuselage 9.75 m (32 ft 0 in); height overall 5.37 m (17 ft 7.5 in); stabiliser span 3.76 m (12 ft 4 in) including endplate surfaces; wheel track 1.41 m (4 ft 7.5 in) for the front unit and 3.52 m (11 ft 6.5 in) for the rear unit
Powerplant: two OMKB 'Mars' (Glushenkov) GTD-3F

turboshafts each rated at 671 kW (898 shp) in early helicopters, or two OMKB 'Mars' (Glushenkov) GTD-3BM each rated at 738 kW (900 shp) in late helicopters
Weights: empty 4765 kg (10,505 lb); maximum take-off 7500 kg (16,534 lb)
Fuel and load: maximum payload 1300 kg (2,866 lb)
Speed: maximum level speed 'clean' at optimum altitude 209 km/h (113 kt; 130 mph); normal cruising speed at optimum altitude 193 km/h (104 kt; 120 mph)
Range: ferry range 650 km (351 nm; 404 miles) with auxiliary fuel; range 400 km (216 nm; 249 miles) with standard fuel

A Ka-25PS 'Hormone-C' search and rescue helicopter. The ventral pannier can be extended downwards by the addition of a bulged stores bay. Smoke floats and searchlights can be fitted.

Kamov Ka-26 'Hoodlum'

The **Ka-26 'Hoodlum-A'** was designed primarily as a multi-role civilian helicopter, and has been adapted for agricultural, firefighting, medevac, survey and light SAR duties. This versatility is largely a result of the helicopter's unusual configuration. The fully enclosed two-seat cabin is attached to a shallow upper fuselage which carries the rotor mast and two very short stub wings (or, perhaps more accurately, pylons) which carry the two Vedeneyev M14V-26 radial engines. Two slender tailbooms extend aft from this, carrying the tailplane and two massive endplate tailfins

and rudders. The resulting space below the rotor mast, between the engines and aft of the cockpit, can carry a variety of pods for passengers, stretchers or cargo, or a hopper for agricultural spraying, or a rescue hoist.

About 850 Ka-26s have been built, plus turbine-engined **Ka-126**s (described separately) built by IAR in Romania, but only a small handful have been procured by military customers, mainly for use in the liaison or border patrol roles. The type may be in service in **Benin**, **Bulgaria** and the **CIS**.

One of Hungary's Ka-26s. The type is still in military service in Bulgaria, and perhaps also in Benin and the CIS. Hungary is understood to have recently retired the last of its 'Hoodlums'.

Kamov Ka-26 'Hoodlum-A'
Rotor system: rotor diameter, each 13.00 m (42 ft 8 in); rotor disc area, total 265.5 m² (2,857.5 sq ft)
Fuselage and tail: length of fuselage 7.75 m (25 ft 5 in); height overall 4.05 m (13 ft 3.5 in) to top of rotor head; stabiliser span 4.60 m (15 ft 1 in); wheel track

11.5 in) for rear unit; wheel base 3.48 m (11 ft 5 in)
Powerplant: two VMKB (Vedeneyev) M-14V-26 air-cooled radial piston engines each rated at 242.5 kW (325 hp)
Weights: operating empty 1950 kg (4,299 lb) stripped, or 2085 kg (4,597 lb) for the freight role with cargo platform, or 2050 kg (4,519 lb) for the freight role with cargo sling, or 2100 kg (4,630 lb) for the

the transport role; maximum take-off 3250 kg (7,165 lb)
Fuel and load: internal fuel 100 kg (220 lb) plus provision for 260 kg (573 lb) of auxiliary fuel; external fuel none; maximum payload 1100 kg (2,425 lb)
Speed: maximum level speed at optimum altitude 170 km/h (91 kt; 105 mph); maximum cruising speed at optimum altitude 150 km/h (81 kt; 93 mph); economical cruising speed at optimum altitude

mph) depending on role
Range: ferry range 1200 km (648 nm; 746 miles) with auxiliary fuel; range 400 km (215 nm; 248 miles) with standard fuel and seven passengers; endurance 3 hours 42 minutes
Performance: service ceiling 3000 m (9,845 ft); hovering ceiling 1300 m (4,265 ft) in ground effect and 800 m (2,625 ft) out of ground effect

Kamov **Ka-27/Ka-28/Ka-32 'Helix'**

Work on the Ka-27 family began in 1969, with Sergei Mikheyev taking over as chief designer after the death of Nikolai Kamov. A totally new design, the Ka-27 retains Kamov's proven coaxial contra-rotating rotor configuration, and has similar overall dimensions to the Ka-25. The availability of a new engine, Isotov's 2,000-shp (1486-kW) TV3, allowed the rotor to absorb double the power output without increasing the diameter or number of blades, but using new methods of construction, a new blade profile and greater blade area. This produced a much larger, more capable helicopter which uses the same amount of deck space as its predecessor, and which can use the same hangars, deck lifts, etc.

The first production variant was the **Ka-27PL 'Helix-A'**, which is the basic ASW version, designed as a replacement for the Ka-25BSh. The prototype made its maiden flight during December 1974, and operational evaluation began in late 1981. The aircraft has a larger fuselage than that of the Ka-25, and incorporates more composite materials and advanced alloys. The lower part of the fuselage is again sealed for buoyancy, and extra flotation equipment can be fitted in boxes on the lower part of the centre fuselage.

The aircraft usually carries a crew of three, with a pilot, navigator and observer or hoist operator behind. The Ka-27 is extremely stable and easy to fly, and automatic height hold, auto transition to and from the hover and autohover are possible in all wind conditions. The Ka-27PL has all the usual ASW and ESM equipment, including dipping sonar and sonobuoys (now carried inside the cabin) and with a new undernose radome housing a shallow rectangular scanner.

The civilian **Ka-32S** is basically similar, using its radar for SAR and ice reconnaissance duties. The borderline between military and civilian variants is not very clear, and some nominally civilian 'Aeroflot' aircraft have been seen operating from Soviet navy warships, while some obviously military aircraft have been exhibited wearing Ka-32 titles.

Export versions of the basic Ka-27PL are designated **Ka-28** and have been sold to **India** and **Yugoslavia**. Further military variants of the Ka-27 are optimised for the search and rescue role and include what appears to be a military version of the simplified civil **Ka-32T 'Helix-C'**, similarly lacking undernose radome but with flotation gear, external fuel tanks and a rescue winch.

The main SAR variant is the radar-equipped **Ka-27PS 'Helix-D'**. This almost inevitably carries external fuel tanks and flotation gear (seldom seen on Soviet 'Helix-As', but sometimes fitted to Ka-28s). A hydraulically-operated 300-kg (660-lb) capacity rescue winch is fitted above the cabin door, with associated downward-pointing floodlights under the port side of the nose and rear cabin. Directional ESM and IFF is

The Ka-28 is a downgraded export version of the Ka-27PL 'Helix-A' used by India, and also delivered to Yugoslavia (seen here).

A Ka-27PL seen without auxiliary tanks and flotation gear. It lacks the bulged pilot's window of late-production and export Ka-28s.

retained, but other operational equipment is deleted. An unidentified box-like fairing, with two protruding spherical objects, is carried below the end of the tailboom, aft of the gyro magnetic heads and Doppler box.

Kamov Ka-27PL 'Helix-A'
Rotor system: rotor diameter, each 15.90 m (52 ft 2 in); rotor disc area, total 397.11 m² (4,274.63 sq ft)
Fuselage and tail: length of fuselage 11.30 m (37 ft 0.9 in) and with rotors folded 12.25 m (40 ft 2.25 in); height overall 5.40 m (17 ft 8.6 in) to top of rotor head; wheel track 1.40 m (4 ft 7 in) for the front unit and 3.50 m (11 ft 5.75 in) for the rear unit; wheel base 3.02 m (9 ft 11 in)
Powerplant: two Klimov (Isotov) TV3-117V turboshafts each rated at 1645 kW (2,205 shp)
Weights: basic empty 6100 kg (13,338 lb); operating empty 6500 kg (14,330 lb); normal take-off 11000 kg (24,251 lb); maximum take-off 12600 kg (27,778 lb)
Fuel and load: maximum payload 5000 kg (11,023 lb)
Speed: maximum level speed 'clean' at optimum altitude 250 km/h (135 kt; 155 mph); maximum cruising speed at optimum altitude 230 km/h (124 kt; 143 mph)
Range: ferry range 800 km (432 nm; 497 miles) with auxiliary fuel; endurance 4 hours 30 minutes
Performance: service ceiling 5000 m (16,405 ft); hovering ceiling 3500 m (11,485 ft) out of ground effect

Right: The Ka-27PS 'Helix-D' is a dedicated naval SAR aircraft.

Kamov **Ka-29TB 'Helix-B'/Ka-29RLD**

The **Ka-29TB** (Transportno Boyevoya) is a dedicated assault transport derivative of the Ka-27/Ka-32 family, intended especially for the support of **Russian navy** amphibious operations and featuring a substantially changed airframe. The first example was seen on the assault ship *Ivan Rogov* in 1987 and was initially assumed to be designated Ka-27B. The NATO reporting name **'Helix-B'** was allocated. Many of the new variants went unnoticed, and it was initially thought to be a minimum-change non-radar version of the basic Ka-27PL.

In fact, the Ka-29TB features an entirely new, much widened forward fuselage, with a flight deck seating three crew side-by-side, one of these acting as a gunner to aim the various rockets carried on the aircraft's braced pylons, and the four-barrelled 7.62-mm cannon hidden behind an articulated door on the starboard side of the nose. The location of the braced pylons precludes the fitting of external fuel tanks or flotation gear. The two-piece curved windscreen of the Ka-27 has given way to a five-piece unit, with three main flat plates at the front and two smaller, slightly blown quarterlights.

A long, braced, air data boom projects forward from the port side of the nose, which is painted black, and which may one day become some kind of radome. Under the nose the Ka-29TB has an electro-optical sensor to starboard and a missile guidance/illuminating radar pod to port, both being similar to devices seen on the Mil Mi-24 'Hind'. The EO sensor is probably a combined FLIR and low-light TV, and the radome is probably associated with the AT-6 'Spiral' missile. An ammunition link ejection chute is located under the nose farther to starboard. Another similarity with the Mil Mi-24 is the replacement of the original sliding cabin door with a horizontally-divided, outward-hinging two-piece door, and the provision of an IRCM jammer on the top of the fuselage/engine fairing.

The basic Ka-29TB airframe also serves as the basis for the **Ka-29RLD**, first seen during carrier trials aboard the *Kuznetsov*, for which a NATO reporting name has not yet been allocated. The two aircraft seen both wore Aeroflot titles, though one of them sported a two-tone grey camouflage scheme. The wider cabin section extends further back (to the rear undercarriage oleo) and ends more abruptly.

Both aircraft are fitted with a huge ventral pannier, which begins just aft of the black-painted nosecone and extends aft along the full length of the cabin, across virtually the full width of the fuselage. The APU seems to be relocated above the engine fairing, with an intake forward and an intake (pointing to starboard) aft. Both aircraft have a new narrow cabin door on the starboard side, just aft of the flight deck. This is horizontally divided and the lower section incorporates a built-in airstair. A square-shaped fairing replaces the window on the upper half.

Large rectangular panniers, of about the same cross-section as the standard flotation gear boxes but extending farther forward (past the nose gear) and aft to the main undercarriage, are fitted to the lower part of the cabin sides. One aircraft had further panniers mounted slightly higher aft of the main undercarriage. Finally, the aircraft has unidentified equipment within a tubular box-like structure mounted on the rear face of the cabin underside.

Despite their Aeroflot markings, these aircraft almost certainly represent the prototypes or development aircraft of a new shipboard AEW platform with planar array radar antennas in the ventral fairing. They are unlikely to retain the armament of the Ka-29TB.

Above: This Ka-29TB is armed with rocket pods and the unusual retractable nose cannon. A missile guidance pod is visible undernose.

Below: The Ka-29RLD has panniers on each side of the fuselage and below the cabin, perhaps containing a planar array radar antenna.

SPECIFICATION

Kamov Ka-29TB 'Helix-B'
generally similar to the Ka-27PL 'Helix-A' except in the following particulars:
Fuselage and tail: wheel base 3.00 m (9 ft 10 in)
Powerplant: two Klimov (Isotov) TV3-117VK turboshafts each rated at 1660 kW (2,226 shp)
Weights: basic empty 5520 kg (12,170 lb)
Speed: maximum level speed 'clean' at sea level 265 km/h (143 kt; 165 mph)
Range: 520 km (280 nm; 322 miles)

Kamov **Ka-50 'Hokum'**

Design of the **Ka-50 'Hokum'** began in 1977 under the direction of Sergei Mikheyev, designer general since 1974. The aircraft was developed as a rival to the Mil Mi-28 in the competition to provide a battlefield attack helicopter for the **Soviet armed forces**. This competition was provoked by the emergence of a new generation of Western battlefield helicopters and represented Kamov's second attempt to produce a land-based attack helicopter, the Ka-25F of 1966 having lost out to the Mil Mi-24. While Mil decided to follow the same overall philosophy as the McDonnell Douglas AH-64 Apache, Kamov worked out its own concept.

Realising that it would be difficult to achieve AH-64 levels of performance with Soviet heavyweight technology and equipment, and believing that Hughes (later McDonnell Douglas Helicopters) had got it wrong in some important respects, Kamov followed an individualistic course. Although the coaxial contra-rotating rotor had become something of a Kamov trademark, the design bureau explored other configurations but quickly came to the conclusion that the advantages of the layout outweighed any disadvantages. Much better agility, reduced vulnerability, compact airframe, benign handling characteristics, a lack of rpm limitations, the ability to take off and land regardless of wind speed and direction, and lower power losses were the crucial factors, while the disadvantages of difficult design problems could be solved by the bureau's considerable experience with the configuration (and probably by no other helicopter company). The conventional single rotor and anti-torque tail rotor configuration was not considered by Kamov, who felt it to be unacceptably vulnerable.

Kamov anticipated problems in keeping weight down, since heavier armour, more powerful armament and advanced sensors would all be required. As a strategic imperative, Kamov decided to work towards meeting the requirement with a single-seat helicopter, using their experience of automated systems on their naval helicopters, which had sophisticated autoland, autohover and even automatic formation flying equipment, together with datalinks for exchanging tactical information between aircraft and ships. Similar systems would clearly be useful in allowing a single-seat battlefield helicopter to operate successfully.

The single-pilot cockpit was successfully demonstrated on the testbench, and in a modified Ka-29TB. Early links with the Sukhoi OKB led to much interchange of ideas, especially concerning the Su-25 ground attack aircraft. At one stage the idea of adapting the Su-25 cockpit for the new helicopter was seriously considered, but eventually rejected. The first prototype made its maiden flight on 27 July 1982, before its rival, under the designation **V.80**. The competitive evaluation ended in October 1986 and the Ka-50 was selected in preference to the Mil Mi-28 due to its better agility, longer missile range, greater ammunition load, heavier armour and more accurate weapons delivery.

Mil's political influence, coupled with widespread lack of faith in the single-pilot concept, led to a three-phase competition that the Ka-50 won at every stage, although in late 1992 Mil still expected an army order of some sort for their helicopter. The first photographs of the Ka-50 were not released officially until early 1992, although the existence of the aircraft had been known since 1984, and Western analysts had produced some surprisingly accurate artist's impressions. The aircraft made a flypast at the

The unarmed third prototype (in silver finish) Ka-50 is seen in company with the much later Werewolf demonstrator, painted black for its role in a feature film.

August 1992 Moscow Aeroshow, but the first opportunity to study the aircraft was not afforded until September, when a Ka-50 was displayed statically at Farnborough.

The tube-launched, laser-beam-riding Vikhr (NATO AT-9 'Whirlwind') missile has a shaped-charge fragmentation warhead and both proximity and contact fuses, and is capable of penetrating reactive armour up to 900 mm (35 inches) thick. Its range exceeds that of most anti-aircraft systems, and it has proved extremely effective in trials. Sixteen can be carried and the proximity fuse and fragmentation jacket make it suit-

able as a last-resort air-to-air weapon, although dedicated AAMs can also be carried. The missiles can be augmented by AS-12 'Kegler' guided missiles or by up to 80 unguided S-8 80-mm rockets in four B-8 pods, by a variety of bombs and by the built-in 30-mm 2A42 cannon. Developed for the BMP AFV, the gun has variable rates of fire and selective feed from two 250-round ammunition boxes (which can be separately loaded with armour-piercing and explosive rounds, allowing the pilot to select the type of ammunition he wishes to fire simply by selecting the correct box) and is extremely resistant to jamming, even in the dusty conditions encountered by armoured personnel carriers, let alone low-flying helicopters.

The gun is installed on the starboard side

of the fuselage, below the wingroot, this location being as close as possible to the helicopter's centre of gravity, and in the strongest and most rigid location to minimise the effect of recoil and to give the greatest possible accuracy. The gun is electro-hydraulically driven and can be traversed through 30° in elevation, and can also move 15° in azimuth.

Combat survivability is enhanced by infrared suppressors in the exhausts, heavily armoured pressurised cockpit, foam-filled, self-sealing fuel tanks, and by the small size and compactness of the transmission and control systems by comparison with conventional helicopters, and by detailed features like the wide-diameter control rods, two-contour rotor blade spars and a high

degree of systems redundancy. Wingtip pods house Vympel UV-26 chaff/flare dispensers. In the event of a catastrophic hit, the pilot can use his Severin/Zvezda K-37 ejection seat. The ejection sequence begins with automatic rotor blade separation, then the doors blow off and a rocket pack extracts the seat.

SPECIFICATION

Kamov Ka-50 Werewolf 'Hokum'
Rotor system: rotor diameter, each 14.50 m (45 ft 6.9 in); rotor disc area, total 330.26 m² (3,555.00 sq ft)
Fuselage and tail: length overall, with rotors turning 16.00 m (52 ft 5.9 in), and fuselage excluding probe and gun 13.50 m (44 ft 3.5 in); height 5.40 m (17 ft 8.6 in)

The normal Russian land forces camouflage, as worn by Mi-8s and Mi-24s, is also applied to several of the Ka-50 prototypes. The coaxial rotors allow the aircraft to dispense with a tail rotor.

Powerplant: two Klimov (Isotov) TV3-117VK turboshafts each rated at 1660 kW (2,226 shp)
Weights: maximum take-off 7500 kg (16,534 lb)
Speed: maximum level speed 'clean' at optimum altitude 350 km/h (188 kt; 217 mph)
Range: combat radius about 250 km (135 nm; 155 miles)
Performance: maximum vertical rate of climb at 2500 m (8,200 ft) 600 m (1,969 ft) per minute; hovering ceiling 4000 m (13,125 ft) out of ground effect

Kamov (IAR) **Ka-126 'Hoodlum-B'**

A multi-role light helicopter with both military and civil applications, the **Kamov Ka-126 'Hoodlum-B'** is a turbine-powered derivative of the **Kamov Ka-26** (described separately). A prototype was flown in the Soviet Union in 1986, followed by the first of a four-aircraft pre-production batch in October 1988. Production was assigned to the IAR factory at Brasov, Romania, where one of the pre-production aircraft was assembled and first flew on 31 December 1988. Orders for 1,000 were expected from the USSR, but only 12 were contracted before the collapse of the Soviet Union, and some unresolved problems with engine vibrations effectively brought the programme to an end. The first production aircraft flew in Romania on 14 February

1989. Seven Ka-126s had been delivered by IAR to Kamov by June 1992, with a few others then under construction at Brasov. Military use is uncertain.

SPECIFICATION

Kamov (IAR) Ka-126 'Hoodlum-B'
generally similar to the Kamov Ka-26 'Hoodlum-A' except in the following particulars:
Fuselage and tail: length of fuselage 7.775 m (25 ft 5.25 in); height overall 4.155 m (13 ft 7.5 in) to top of rotor head; stabiliser span 3.224 m (10 ft 7 in); wheel track 2.56 m (8 ft 4.75 in) for rear unit; wheel base 3.479 m (11 ft 5 in)
Powerplant: one OMKB 'Mars' (Glushenkov) TVD-100 turboshaft rated at 537 kW (720 shp)

A Ka-126 in Aeroflot colours. Military use of this IAR-built helicopter is uncertain, though the type clearly has potential to fulfil some more martial roles.

Weights: maximum take-off 3250 kg (7,165 lb)
Fuel and load: internal fuel 800 litres (211 US gal); external fuel none; maximum payload 1000 kg (2,205 lb)
Speed: maximum level speed at optimum altitude 180 km/h (97 kt; 112 mph); maximum cruising speed at

optimum altitude 160 km/h (86 kt; 99 mph)
Range: range 650 km (351 nm; 404 miles) with standard fuel; endurance 4 hours 30 minutes
Performance: service ceiling 3800 m (12,470 ft); hovering ceiling 1000 m (3,280 ft) out of ground effect

Kawasaki **C-1**

Kawasaki Heavy Industries Ltd
1-18 Nakamachi-Dori, 2-chome, Chuo-Ku
Kobe, Japan

With a requirement to replace Curtiss C-46 Commando transport aircraft then in service, the **Japan Air Self-Defence Force** drew up its C-X specification for an indigenous replacement for a medium-sized troop and freight transport in the early 1970s. Nihon Aeroplane Manufacturing Company began its design in 1966, and even before approval of the full-size mock-up the company was contracted to build two **XC-1** flying prototypes plus a static test airframe. The first of the prototypes, assembled by Kawasaki, made its maiden flight on 12 November 1970, and the flight test programme of both prototypes was

completed by the Japan Defence Agency in March 1973. Following construction of two pre-production aircraft, a first contract was placed for 11 production **Kawasaki C-1** transports.

The C-1 is of conventional modern military transport design, featuring a high-wing monoplane configuration to maximise cabin volume, a fuselage with pressurised and air-conditioned flight deck and cabin/cargo hold, and a rear-loading ramp door which can be opened in flight. The landing gear is of retractable tricycle type, and the aircraft's two turbofan engines are pylon-mounted beneath the wings. The C-1 is operated by a

flight crew of five, and typical loads include 60 fully-equipped troops or 45 paratroops, up to 36 stretchers with attendants, and a variety of equipment or palletised cargo.

A collaborative project, the C-1 was built by Fuji (outer wings), Mitsubishi (centre/aft fuselage/tail surfaces), and Nihon (control surfaces/engine pods), with Kawasaki responsible for forward fuselage, wing centre-section, final assembly and testing. Production of the C-1 totalled 31 examples, including the four prototype/pre-production aircraft, with the last delivery on 21 October 1981. Although built to JASDF requirements, the C-1's maximum payload of

11900 kg (26,266 lb) limited its value and plans for variants did not materialise. The C-1 currently equips two squadrons (*hikotai*) of Support Command, JASDF, comprising the 402nd at Iruma and 403rd at Miho.

A C-1 airframe has been used by the JDA as a flying testbed for the MITI/NAL FJR-710 and Ishikawajima-Harima XF3 turbofan engines, the latter powering the T-4 trainer. More recently, Kawasaki has modfied one as a **C-1Kai** ECM trainer, giving it a flat bulbous nose and tail radomes, an indigenous ALQ-5 ECM system and antennas beneath the fuselage. This serves alongside YS-11Es with the 501st Hikotai of the Electronic

Warfare Training Unit at Iruma. Proposed variants for inflight refuelling, electronic warfare, weather reconnaissance and mine-laying remained stillborn, as did a larger-capacity transport with a stretched fuselage. One aircraft served as the basis for the **NAL Asuka** (described separately), a dedicated quiet STOL testbed which flew with overwing engines and blown flaps.

SPECIFICATION

Kawasaki C-1

Wing: span 30.60 m (100 ft 4.75 in); aspect ratio 7.8; area 120.50 m² (1,297.09 sq ft)

Fuselage and tail: length 29.00 m (95 ft 1.75 in); height 9.99 m (32 ft 9.25 in); tailplane span 11.30 m (37 ft 1 in); wheel track 4.40 m (14 ft 5.25 in); wheel base 9.33 m (30 ft 7.75 in)

Powerplant: two Mitsubishi-built Pratt & Whitney JT8D-M-9 turbofans each rated at 14,500 lb st (64.50 kN) and fitted with thrust reversers

Weights: empty equipped 24300 kg (53,571 lb); normal take-off 38700 kg (85,317 lb); maximum take-off 45000 kg (99,206 lb)

Fuel and load: internal fuel 15200 litres (4,015 US gal); external fuel none; maximum payload 11900 kg (26,235 lb)

Speed: maximum level speed 'clean' at 25,000 ft (7620 m) 435 kt (501 mph; 806 km/h); maximum cruising speed at 35,000 ft (10670 m) 380 kt (438 mph; 704 km/h); economical cruising speed at 35,000 ft (10670 m) 355 kt (409 mph; 658 km/h)

Range: 1,810 nm (2,084 miles; 3353 km) with maximum fuel and a 2200-kg (4,850-lb) payload, or 700 nm (806 miles; 1297 km) with a 7900-kg (17,416-lb) payload

Performance: maximum rate of climb at sea level 3,495 ft (1065 m) per minute; service ceiling 38,000 ft (11580 m); take-off run 2,100 ft (640 m) at maximum take-off weight; take-off distance to 50 ft (15 m) 3,000 ft (914 m) at maximum take-off weight; landing distance from 50 ft (15 m) 2,700 ft (823 m) at 36860 kg (81,261 lb); landing run 1,500 ft (457 m) at 36860 kg (81,261 lb)

Above: A single Kawasaki C-1 was converted for the electronic warfare training role, with the indigenous TRDI/Mitsubishi XJ/ALQ-5 ECM system. The aircraft has several massive dielectric fairings and radomes.

Right: One of the standard transport C-1s serving with 403 Hikotai at Miho, part of Support Command. C-1 transports also fly with 402 Hikotai at Iruma, each unit having a mix of C-1s and NAMC YS-11s on charge. Squadron markings are carried on the tailfins of the C-1s.

Kawasaki **T-4**

With a similar high-winged configuration to the Dassault-Dornier Alpha Jet, the **Kawasaki T-4** was developed as an intermediate jet trainer (with a secondary liaison role) to replace the **JASDF**'s Lockheed T-33 and indigenous Fuji T-1A/B. Design studies were completed in 1982 and four prototypes (designated **XT-4**) were funded in 1984, the first of these making the type's maiden flight on 29 July 1985.

The T-4 is of entirely conventional design, featuring high subsonic manoeuvrability and docile handling characteristics. The tandem

The first and third T-4 prototypes in flight. The T-4 has now begun to replace the Fuji T-1 and Lockheed T-33 in the training role and as a liaison/hack aircraft.

stepped cockpits are fitted with standard dual controls and UPC (Stencel) SHIS-3J ejection seats. Visibility for instructor and pupil is excellent, with a wrap-around windscreen and a one-piece starboard-opening canopy. For the liaison role, a baggage compartment is fitted in the centre fuselage.

The T-4 is a collaborative venture, in which Fuji builds the rear fuselage, supercritical-section wings and tail unit, and Mitsubishi the centre fuselage and air intakes. Kawasaki builds only the forward fuselage, but is responsible for assembly and flight test. Virtually all components are indigenously built, and most are locally designed, including the 3,680-lb st (16.37-kN) Ishikawa-jima-Harima F3-IHI-30 turbofans. Single underwing pylons can carry a 450-litre (99-Imp gal) drop tank, and a centreline pylon can accommodate a target winch, air sampling pod, ECM pod or chaff dispenser.

Production deliveries began in September 1988 and by mid-1992 126 had been

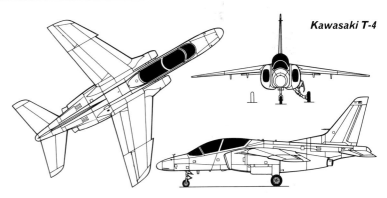

Kawasaki T-4

ordered, and examples were in service with Nos 31 and 32 Squadrons at Hamamatsu and with some operational squadrons and wings as hacks, sometimes wearing a camouflage colour scheme.

Below: This Kawasaki T-4 wears the black panther badge of F-1-equipped 8 Hikotai, with which it serves as a hack, having replaced T-33s with F-1, F-4 and F-15 units.

Kawasaki (Boeing Vertol) KV-107

The **Boeing Vertol Model 107** tandem-rotor helicopter proved attractive for civil use in Japan, and in 1962 Kawasaki secured a manufacturing licence for the type. The first **Kawasaki (Boeing Vertol) KV-107** to be built under this arrangement was flown in May 1962, and in 1965 (following further negotiations) the Japanese company acquired from Boeing Vertol worldwide sales rights.

Since then Kawasaki has built several KV-107 versions, the **KV-107/II** range being powered by 1,250-shp (932-kW) General Electric CT58-110-1 turboshaft engines or licence-built Ishikawajima-Harima CT58-IHI-110-1 engines of similar output. The range includes the **KV-107/II-2** standard 25-passenger airline helicopter and the six/11-seat **KV-107/II-7** VIP transport. The first of the military variants was the **KV-107/II-3**, a mine countermeasures version for the **JMSDF** (two built). The **KV-107/II-4** tactical cargo/troop carrier for the **JGSDF** was more extensively produced (42 built including one fitted out as a VIP transport). This version has a strengthened floor and can accommodate 26 equipped troops on foldable seats or, alternatively, 15 casualties on stretchers. For the **JASDF** Kawasaki developed the **KV-107/II-5** long-range search and rescue helicopter (14 built) with external auxiliary fuel tanks (one each side), a domed observation window, four searchlights, a rescue hoist and an extensive nav/com system. During 1972-74 Kawasaki supplied eight aircraft to the **Swedish navy**; these are designated **Hkp 4C** and have Rolls-Royce Gnome H.1200 powerplants and Decca navigation systems installed in Sweden.

Current **KV-107/IIA** production has more powerful turboshafts for improved performance in 'hot-and-high' or VTOL oper-ations. The range includes seven **KV-107/IIA-3**, 18 **KV-107/IIA-4** (four of them with external auxiliary fuel tanks), and 22 **KV-107/IIA-5** helicopters, these three versions being comparable respectively to the KV-107/II-3, -4 and -5. For **Saudi Arabia** Kawasaki has built one **KV-170/IIA-17** long-range passenger/cargo transport, seven **KV-107/IIA-SM-1** firefighters, four **KV-107/IIA-SM-2** aero-medical/rescue helicopters, two **KV-107/IIA-SM-3** transports, and three examples of the **KV-107/IIA-SM-4** air ambulance.

The Saudi aircraft still serve with the RSAF, and the Hkp 4Cs are retained by the Swedish navy's 11 Helikopterdivisionen at Berga, 12 Hkpdiv at Ronneby and 13 Hkpdiv at Säve, alongside Boeing Vertol-built aircraft. In the home country, KV-107s serve with the JASDF's Air Rescue Wing at Iruma

This KV-107 wears the yellow and white scheme applied to JASDF aircraft, JGSDF KV-107s having dark blue undersides, yellow fuselage sides and white tops, and JMSDF aircraft being painted in dark blue and white. KV-107s also serve with the Swedish and Saudi armed forces.

(with detachments), 11 Kokutai at Shimofusa (JMSDF), and with the JGSDF's Western Air Command at Takayubaru, 101 Hikotai (Naha), and 1 Helicopter Brigade (Kisarazu). These units are in the process of being replaced by other types, notably the Kawasaki-built CH-47J.

SPECIFICATION

Kawasaki KV-107IIA-4
Rotor system: rotor diameter, each 50 ft 0 in (15.24 m); rotor disc area, total 3,926.99 sq ft (364.82 m²)
Fuselage and tail: length overall, rotors turning 83 ft 4 in (25.40 m) and fuselage 44 ft 7 in (13.59 m); height to top of rear rotor head 16 ft 10 in (5.13 m); wheel track 12 ft 11 in (3.94 m); wheel base 24 ft 11in (7.59 m)
Powerplant: two 1,400-shp (1044-kW) General Electric CT58-140-1 or Ishikawajima-Harima (General Electric) CT58-IHI-140-1 turboshafts each rated at 1,250 shp (932 kW) for continuous running
Weights: empty equipped 11,575 lb (5250 kg); normal take-off 19,000 lb (8618 kg); maximum take-off 21,400 lb (9706 kg)
Fuel and load: internal fuel 2,275 lb (1032 kg) plus provision for 7,835 lb (3554 kg) of auxiliary fuel in one 1,087-lb (493-kg) auxiliary and one 6,748-lb (3061-kg) extended-range tank; external fuel none; maximum payload 6,993 lb (3172 kg) at normal take-off weight
Speed: never-exceed speed 146 kt (168 mph; 270 km/h); maximum level speed at sea level 137 kt (158 mph; 254 km/h); maximum cruising speed at 5,000 ft (1525 m) 130 kt (150 mph; 241 km/h)
Range: 592 nm (682 miles; 1097 km) with auxiliary fuel; range 193 nm (222 miles; 357 km) internal fuel
Performance: maximum rate of climb at sea level 2,050 ft (625 m) per minute; service ceiling 17,000 ft (5180 m); hovering ceiling 11,700 ft (3565 m) in ground effect and 8,800 lb (2680 m) out of ground effect

Kawasaki-Boeing Vertol CH-47J Chinook

The **Kawasaki CH-47J** is Japan's licence-built version of the Boeing Vertol CH-47 Chinook (described separately). Two **Boeing CH-47C**s were delivered in 1986 to Japan, followed by a third in component form for assembly by Kawasaki. Two of these were delivered to the **JGSDF**, and one for the **JASDF**. The first CH-47J, which is essentially similar to the advanced CH-47D standard, was subsequently delivered in late 1986.

The CH-47J filled Japan's mid-1980s HH-X requirement, which was drafted to find a replacement for the large numbers of Kawasaki-Vertol KV-107/II-5 helicopters in service with the JGSDF. An eventual requirement exists for up to 42 JGSDF Chinooks (36 ordered to date) for transport

duties and for 16 for the JASDF (all funded and ordered). Initial deliveries were made to the JGSDF's No.1 Helicopter Division (1 Heli Group) at Kisarazu and to the Air Training School's support squadron at Akeno. Twenty-three of the JGSDF aircraft had been delivered by the beginning of 1994. The Japanese Air Self-Defence Force has already received 15 CH-47Js for SAR duties and for the logistics support of remote radar sites. They serve with the Air Rescue unit at Iruma (with detachments elsewhere).

SPECIFICATION

Kawasaki (Boeing Vertol) CH-47J
generally similar to the Boeing (Boeing Vertol) CH-47D

Chinook except in the following particulars:
Powerplant: two Kawasaki (Textron Lycoming) T55-K-712 turboshafts each rated at 4,378 shp (3264 kW)

for take-off and 3,137 shp (2339 kW) for continuous running, in both cases driving a transmission rated at 7,500 shp (5593 kW) on two engines and 4,600 shp (3430 kW) on one engine

This is one of the first CH-47Js delivered to the JGSDF.

Kawasaki-Lockheed P-2J Neptune

After it had built 48 **P2V-7 Owashi** (Giant eagle) aircraft, equivalent to the **Lockheed P-2H Neptune**, for the JMSDF, Kawasaki developed the improved **P2V-7 Kai** with Ishikawajima-Harima-built T64-IHI-10 turboprops replacing the original Wright R-3350 piston engines, and with an all-new avionics suite giving much greater

operational capability. Additional power was provided by licence-built IHI-J3 auxiliary underwing turbojets. First flown on 21 July 1966, the P2V-7 Kai entered production as the **P-2J** and 82 were built by 1979. The aircraft had a 1.3-m (4-ft 2-in) fuselage stretch ahead of the wing, allowing seven operators to be carried in the forward compartment,

with three more aft of the wing spar. Rudder chord was increased by reducing taper, compensating for the extra length forward. They have finally been replaced in the ASW and maritime reconnaissance roles by P-3C Orions, the last squadron converting in late 1993, but a few special-purpose variants remain in **JMSDF** service. These include

the survivors from two **EP-2J**s equipped for Elint duties with HLR-105 and HLR-106 sensors, and four **UP-2J** support aircraft. The EP-2Js had their transparent nosecones replaced with solid radomes, and had a variety of underfuselage antennas too. The UP-2Js, first delivered in December 1979, are equipped to launch Firebee target drones and to tow targets, and carry missile seeker head simulators and jamming gear. Like the EP-2Js, they are operated by the

81st Kokutai at Iwakuni. Others may serve with the 51st Kokutai, the JMSDF's dedicated test and trials unit at Atsugi.

The JMSDF retired its last front-line Neptunes from the 7th Kokutai in late 1993, but special-purpose versions and test aircraft remain active.

SPECIFICATION

Kawasaki-Lockheed P-2J
Wing: span 97 ft 8.5 in (29.78 m) without tip tanks and 101 ft 3.5 in (30.87 m) with tip tanks; aspect ratio 10.0; area 1,000.00 sq ft (92.90 m²)
Fuselage and tail: length 95 ft 10.75 in (29.23 m); height 29 ft 3.5 in (8.93 m); tailplane span 34 ft 0 in (10.36 m); wheel track 25 ft 0 in (7.62 m); wheel base 29 ft 0 in (8.84 m)
Powerplant: two Ishikawajima-Harima (General

Electric) T64-IHI-10E turboprops each rated at 3,060 ehp (2282 ekW) and two Ishikawajima-Harima J3-IHI-7C turbojets rated at 3,085 lb st (13.72 kN)
Weights: empty 42,500 lb (19277 kg); maximum take-off 75,000 lb (34019 kg)
Fuel and load: internal fuel 3,420 US gal (12946 litres) plus provision for 700 US gal (2650

litres) of auxiliary fuel in a weapon-bay tank; external fuel none
Speed: never-exceed speed 350 kt (403 mph; 649 km/h); maximum cruising speed at optimum altitude 217 kt (250 mph; 402 km/h); economical cruising speed at 10,000 ft (3050 m) 200 kt (230 mph; 370 km/h)

Range: 2,400 nm (2,764 miles; 4448 km)
Performance: maximum rate of climb at sea level 1,805 ft (550 m) per minute; service ceiling 30,000 ft (9145 m); take-off distance to 50 ft (15 m) 3,610 ft (1100 m) at maximum take-off weight; landing distance from 50 ft (15 m) 2,885 ft (880 m) at normal landing weight

Kawasaki-Lockheed **P-3 Orion**

Kawasaki is prime contractor for the production under licence and assembly of the **Lockheed P-3C Orion** (described separately) for the **JMSDF**, which has a requirement for 110. Initial aircraft were to the US Navy's Update II standard, with Update III introduced subsequently and the more extensive 1993-Update IV revision using Japanese-made equipment. Lockheed built the first three JMSDF P-3Cs at Burbank, where the first aircraft was accepted on 29 April 1981, with subsequent delivery to Atsugi on 25 December.

Using Lockheed-supplied components for the next four aircraft, Kawasaki flew the first P-3C assembled in Japan on 17 March

1982, with delivery on 26 May for operational testing by the 51st Kokutai. Equipment of the first squadron, 6th Kokutai, began at Atsugi on 30 March 1983, followed by the 3rd Kokutai at the same base. Further P-3C squadrons are the 2nd and 4th at Hachinoe and the 1st and 7th at Kanoya, with a further squadron planned at Iwakuni. The 206th Kokutai at Shimofusa is responsible for conversion training. Orions have now entirely supplanted Neptunes in the ASW role.

Kawasaki has completed three Orions as **EP-3Cs** to operate in the electronic surveillance role, as the first in a planned total of nine required for operation by 81st Kokutai

Large black dorsal and ventral radomes identify this aircraft as one of three EP-3C Elint aircraft. These all serve with the 81st Kokutai.

at Iwakuni. The low- and high- frequency detector systems for these aircraft are produced by NEC and Mitsubishi Electric in Japan. Further variants procured by the JMSDF are two **UP-3C** ECM trainers. A single dedicated **NP-3C** for navaid flight

checking was cancelled, and provision for the role was incorporated into the two UP-3Cs. The P-3Cs built by Kawasaki are powered by 4,910-ehp (3661-kW) Allison T56-IHI-14 turboprops produced in Japan by Ishikawajima-Harima.

Kawasaki (MDH) **OH-6D and OH-6J**

After the Hughes OH-6 had been adopted by the **JGSDF** as its standard observation helicopter and principal rotary wing type, a licence was acquired for its production in Japan by Kawasaki. The initial phase of the programme comprised the acquisition of 117 **OH-6J**s, commencing on 10 March 1969 and completed in 1979. Phase Two marked a switch from the

OH-6J, which was based on the US Army's **OH-6A Cayuse** light observation helicopter, to the **OH-6D**, which was based on the civil **Hughes Model 500D** and was distinguished by its 'T' tailplane with small endplates replacing the OH-6J's V-tail. McDonnell-built helicopters are described separately.

Kawasaki flew its first OH-6D on 2

December 1977 and production has been primarily for JGSDF, which ordered 153 for delivery by the mid-1990s. Both D and J models are widely distributed through the JGSDF, which has 13 squadrons (1 to 13 Hikotai inclusive) flying the helicopter in its intended observation role, as well as for training and other miscellaneous duties. OH-6s are also used in the scout role, oper-

ating in conjunction with the JGSDF's anti-tank AH-1s. These aircraft serve with No. 1 and No. 2 Anti Tank Squadrons. No. 1 Helicopter Brigade includes two KV-107/OH-6/CH-47-equipped units. In addition, the **JMSDF** acquired three OH-6Js in 1973/74 for the 211th Kyoiku Kokutai (Air Training Squadron) at Kanoya, and followed these with OH-6Ds for the same role.

Korean Air **Model 500/520**

Production of the **Hughes Model 500D** helicopter was the first major aircraft programme undertaken by the Aerospace Division of Korean Air, set up at Kim Hae in 1976. More than 300 have been built, in the basic Model 500D and armed **Model 500MD** versions, some 200 for the **Republic of Korea army** and **navy**. Fifty 500MDs for the army were equipped with Hughes BGM-71A TOW anti-tank missiles, while more than 100 Model 500Ds for the

observation/liaison role can carry a 40-mm grenade launcher. Replacement of the Model 500s is planned with the **Model 520MK Black Tiger**, based on the **McDonnell Douglas MD 520N** variant.

One of Korean Air's TOW-armed 500MDs of the Republic of Korea army in flight. The missile sight is mounted in the nose, and exhaust suppressors are also fitted.

Korean government-sponsored programmes

The Korean aircraft industry is involved in a number of ongoing government-sponsored programmes, with **Daewoo Heavy Industries, Korean Air** and **Samsung Aerospace** the key players. Straight licence manufacture and component making are still the most important activities, but the development of indigenous types, and of indigenous derivatives of other people's aircraft, is becoming of increasing importance. Daewoo is working as prime contractor on Korea's indigenous primary trainer, actually the nation's first indigenously designed military aircraft, created by a government agency. Under the designa-

tion **KTX-1**, the first of five prototypes, made its maiden flight in December 1991. The 750-shp (559 kW) Pratt & Whitney Canada PT-6A-25C engined second prototype, with increased dorsal fin area, a two-piece blown canopy and lightweight ejection seats, flew during 1992. Production aircraft may be re-engined with a 1,000-shp (746kW) Pratt & Whitney Canada PT6A-62 or a similarly rated Garrett TPE331. The requirement is for some 100 aircraft.

Daewoo's other activities include production of centre fuselage sections for Korean **F-16**s, **Dornier 328** fuselage shells, **Lynx** helicopter airframes, wing components for

Hawks and **Orion**s and rotor hubs for **Bell 212**s and **412**s. Daewoo is also the prime contractor for the proposed light scout helicopter, which should be a licence-built **Agusta A109CM** or **MBB BO 105CB**. The Agricultural Remote Control Helicopter requirement has been expanded to include some military surveillance roles, and may be met by a Daewoo-built derivative of the **Kamov Ka-37** drone. Another Daewoo helicopter project is the **MK-30**, a proposed licence-built derivative of the Mil Mi-17 with a refined airframe and recontoured Mi-26 type nose.

Korean Air, previously responsible for

F-5E production, maintenance and modifications of various military types, manufactures the Sikorsky S-70 under licence as the **UH-60P**, as well as the MD 520 discussed above. The company will also build centre and rear fuselages for the KTX-1 trainer. Samsung, which produces parts and subassemblies for a number of US-designed civil aircraft, is the prime contractor for the Korean Fighter Programme under which 120 F-16Cs and Ds are being bought off-the-shelf (12), licence-assembled (36), and manufactured (72). The company is also developing the **KTX-2** indigenous jet trainer to replace ROKAF T-33s and T-37s.

6: Robbie Shaw, Alenia. **7:** Aermacchi (two), Greg Meggs. **8:** Aermacchi, Aldo Ciarini, Peter Steinemann. **9:** Carlo Marcora, Robbie Shaw. **10:** Aermacchi, Lockheed, R. Mateboer. **11:** Hendrik J. van Broekhuizen, Frank Rozendaal. **12:** Jon Lake, Vaclav Simecek, Robert Hewson. **13:** Paul Jackson (two), Antoine J. Givaudon, Siegfried Wache. **14:** Antoine J. Givaudon, Peter Steinemann. **15:** Jelle Sjoerdsma, Paul Jackson, Peter Steinemann, Yves Debay. **16:** Aérospatiale. **17:** Jelle Sjoerdsma, Tieme Festner, Aérospatiale. **18:** Peter Steinemann, Aerotec. **19:** Bob A. Munro, Jon Lake. **20:** Agusta (two), Paul Jackson, David Donald. **21:** Peter Steinemann, Georg Mader. **22:** Hans Nijhuis. **23:** Agusta (two), Paul Jackson. **24:** Mario Carneiro, Hans Nijhuis (two). **25:** Robbie Shaw, Peter Steinemann, AIDC. **27:** Airbus Industrie, Michel Fournier, Paul Jackson. **28:** Peter R. Foster, Alenia, Robbie Shaw. **29:** John Gourley, AAC, AMX. **30:** AMX. **31:** AMX (two). **32:** Dragisa Brasnovic, Peter Steinemann. **33:** Dennis Thomsen, Peter Steinemann. **34:** Robert Hewson, Jonny Bonny. **35:** Martin Baumann, Georg Mader, Frank Rozendaal. **36:** Peter Steinemann (two). **37:** Robert Hewson. **38:** Dennis Thomsen. **39:** Antonov, TASS, Jon Lake. **40:** David Donald, Peter Steinemann, Craig P. Justo, Atlas. **41:** Atlas (two). **42:** Atlas, L.J. Vosloo, Herman Potgieter. **43:** via Jon Lake, Herman Potgieter. **44:** Ayres, Beech. **45:** Paul Jackson, Peter Steinemann. **46:** Robert L. Lawson, Peter Steinemann (two). **47:** Hendrik J. van Broekhuizen. **48:** Pat Martin, Peter Gunti, Beech. **49:** Beech (two), Hans Nijhuis. **50:** Randy Jolly, Peter Steinemann. **51:** Paul Jackson, Herman J. Sixma, Peter Steinemann. **52:** Bell (two), Peter Steinemann. **53:** Andrew H. Cline, Peter Steinemann. **54:** US Navy, Peter Steinemann, Israeli Aviation and Space Magazine. **55:** Peter Steinemann (two), M.P. Hopper. **57:** US Navy, Peter Steinemann (two). **58:** Peter Steinemann, Bell. **59:** Bell (three). **60:** Bell (three). **61:** Robert F. Dorr. **62:** Patrick Allen, Bell. **64:** Bell (two), Peter Steinemann. **66:** Randy Jolly. **67:** Randy Jolly (two), David Donald, Ted Carlson/Fotodynamics. **69:** Jim Benson, Joe Bruch. **70:** USAF, David Donald. **71:** Jim Benson, Randy Jolly. **72:** Graham Robson (two), Joe Bruch, David Donald. **73:** Joe Bruch (two), Richard Westcott, Ted Carlson/Fotodynamics. **74:** Robert S. Hopkins III, Boeing, Jeff Rankin-Lowe. **76:** USAF, Paul Carter, Graham Robson, Bob Archer. **77:** USAF, Boeing. **78:** Boeing, IAI, David Donald. **79:** A.B. Ward, Mark Attrill, Robbie Shaw (two). **80:** Stuart Lewis, Boeing, R.E.F. Jones, Philippe Ferretti. **81:** Boeing, Andrew H. Cline. **82:** Randy Jolly, Graham Robson, Boeing. **83:** Chris Schmidt, Boeing. **84:** Boeing (two), Paul Carter. **85:** Grumman. **86:** Paul Jackson (two), BAe. **87:** Robbie Shaw, Peter Steinemann (two). **88:** Peter Steinemann. **89:** Jon Lake, Paul Jackson, Wg Cdr A.P. Mote via Pushpindar Singh. **90:** Paul Jackson, Jon Lake. **91:** Paul Jackson, Peter Gunti. **92:** Ian Black, Bob Archer. **93:** BAe, Peter Steinemann. **94:** Peter Gunti, via Roger Lindsay. **95:** Paul Jackson (two). **96:** via David Donald, Paul Jackson. **97:** Northrop, BAe. **99:** Tony Holmes, Dylan Eklund. **100:** via John Gourley, Peter Steinemann. **101:** David Donald, Tony Paxton. **102:** David Donald, Jeff Puzzullo, Richard Gennis. **103:** BAe (three). **104:** BAe (two). **105:** Robbie Shaw, Fermin Gallego Serra, Sgt Rick Brewell/RAF. **106:** Mike Reyno, Peter J. Cooper. **107:** Peter R. Foster, Canadair. **108:** Canadair, Robbie Shaw. **109:** Robbie Shaw. **110:** Richard Gennis. **111:** Peter Steinemann (two). **112:** Peter Steinemann, Michel Fournier. **113:** Paul Jackson, Peter Steinemann, Hans Nijhuis. **114:** Peter Steinemann (two), Chris Pocock. **115:** Peter Steinemann (two), RNZAF via Jeff Rankin-Lowe. **116:** Jane Price, Bob Archer, Cessna. **117:** Peter Steinemann (two). **118:** Peter Steinemann (three). **120:** Peter Steinemann, Gerry Manning, US Navy. **121:** 475th WEG/USAF, Paul Jackson, Dassault, Peter R. Foster, Peter Steinemann. **122:** Dassault (two). **123:** John Blackman, Tieme Festner. **124:** USCG, Paul Jackson, Peter J. Bish. **125:** David Donald, Peter Steinemann, Mario Carneiro. **126:** Jean-Jacques Petit, Robbie Shaw, Peter R. Foster. **127:** Dassault, via Paul Jackson, via Mark Styling. **128:** Paul Jackson, Peter R. Foster. **129:** Peter Steinemann, Jean-Jacques Petit (two). **130:** Peter Steinemann, Jean-Jacques Petit. **131:** Ray Sumner, Antoine J. Givaudon, Peter Steinemann. **132:** Ben J. Ullings, W.J. Mondy. **133:** Dassault, B. Colin via René J. Francillon. **134:** via Paul Jackson, USAF, Peter Steinemann. **135:** Dassault. **136:** Jean-Jaques Petit, Paul Jackson (two). **137:** via Paul Jackson (three). **138:** Chris Brooks, David Donald. **139:** via Paul Jackson, René J. Francillon, Michel Fournier, Dassault. **140:** Dassault. **141:** Dassault (two). **142:** Paul Jackson (four). **143:** Peter Steinemann (two), Antoine Roels, David Donald. **144:** David Donald, Peter Steinemann (three). **145:** Peter Steinemann (two). **146:** Mike Reyno, Peter Steinemann. **147:** R.E.F. Jones, Andrew H. Cline, Peter Steinemann, via Pushpindar Singh, Alan Key. **149:** Peter Steinemann, Richard Gennis, Robbie Shaw, Paul Jackson, Stephen J. Brennan. **150:** Westland (two). **151:** EMBRAER (two), Paul Jackson (two), Mario Carneiro (two). **153:** EMBRAER (two), ENAER. **154:** ENAER, Enstrom (three). **155:** Jon Lake, Paul Jackson (two), Peter Steinemann. **156:** Paul Jackson, David Donald, Peter Steinemann. **157:** Yves Debay, Paul Jackson (two). **158:** Paul Jackson, Peter Steinemann. **159:** Allison, Peter R. Foster, Peter Gunti, Yves Debay. **160:** Jan Jorgensen, Peter Steinemann. **161:** Michel Fournier, Robert Hewson, Eurocopter. **162:** Paul Jackson, Robbie Shaw, Eurocopter. **163:** Peter Steinemann, Eurocopter. **164:** Eurocopter, Jon Lake. **165:** Eurofighter (two). **166:** David Donald, Randy Jolly. **168:** USAF, Ted Carlson/Fotodynamics. **169:** Randy Jolly, David Donald, Peter Steinemann. **170:** Peter Steinemann, Peter R. Foster, Fairchild. **171:** Peter Steinemann. **172:** FMA (two), FFA. **173:** Robert Hewson (two), Peter Steinemann (two). **174:** Peter Steinemann, Fokker (two). **175:** Peter Steinemann (two). **176:** Fuji, Joe Cupido, Peter Steinemann. **178:** USAF, via Jim Rotramel, Paul Ragusa. **179:** USAF, Jon Lake, Tony Paxton, Paul Jackson. **180:** Grob, Robert L. Lawson. **182:** via Peter B. Mersky, Jim Rotramel, Robert L. Lawson. **183:** Robbie Shaw, Susuau Suzuki via Peter B. Mersky, Rick Morgan via Robert L. Lawson, Robert L. Lawson. **185:** Peter B. Mersky, Grumman. **187:** Robbie Shaw, Michael M. Anselmo, via Peter B. Mersky. **189:** Dave Baranek, Joe Cupido. **190:** Robert L. Lawson, Grumman (two). **192:** Shirley Rankin-Lowe, Peter B. Mersky. **193:** Chris A. Neill, Peter Steinemann. **194:** Paul Jackson, Hans Nijhuis, Craig Kaslon. **195:** USAF, Richard Gennis. **196:** Randy Jolly, Peter Steinemann (two). **197:** Robbie Shaw, Hans Nijhuis, US Navy via Peter B. Mersky, Royal Danish air force. **198:** Peter R. Foster (two). **199:** Peter Steinemann (two). **200:** Paul Jackson, Peter Steinemann. **201:** Peter Steinemann (three), Pushpindar Singh. **202:** Pushpindar Singh, Marcus Fulber. **203:** Peter Steinemann (two), Jelle Sjoerdsma, Salvador Mafé Huertas (two). **204:** Jeff Puzzullo, IAI. **205:** Peter Steinemann. **206:** Alan Key, IAI (two). **207:** David Donald. **208:** Robert Hewson, IAR. **209:** Robert Hewson, Chris Ryan, US Navy. **210:** Achille Vigna, US Navy. **211:** W.G. Turner, Lindsay Peacock. **212:** W.G. Turner, Jon Lake. **213:** Jon Lake, AviaData (two). **214:** Robbie Shaw, Chris Pocock. **215:** Paul Jackson, Jeff Wilson, Yves Debay. **216:** Kaman (two). **217:** Lindsay Peacock. **219:** AviaData (two). **220:** AviaData. **221:** Peter Steinemann, Robbie Shaw, Kawasaki, Randy Jolly. **222:** Peter Steinemann, Kawasaki. **223:** Peter Steinemann, Korean Air.